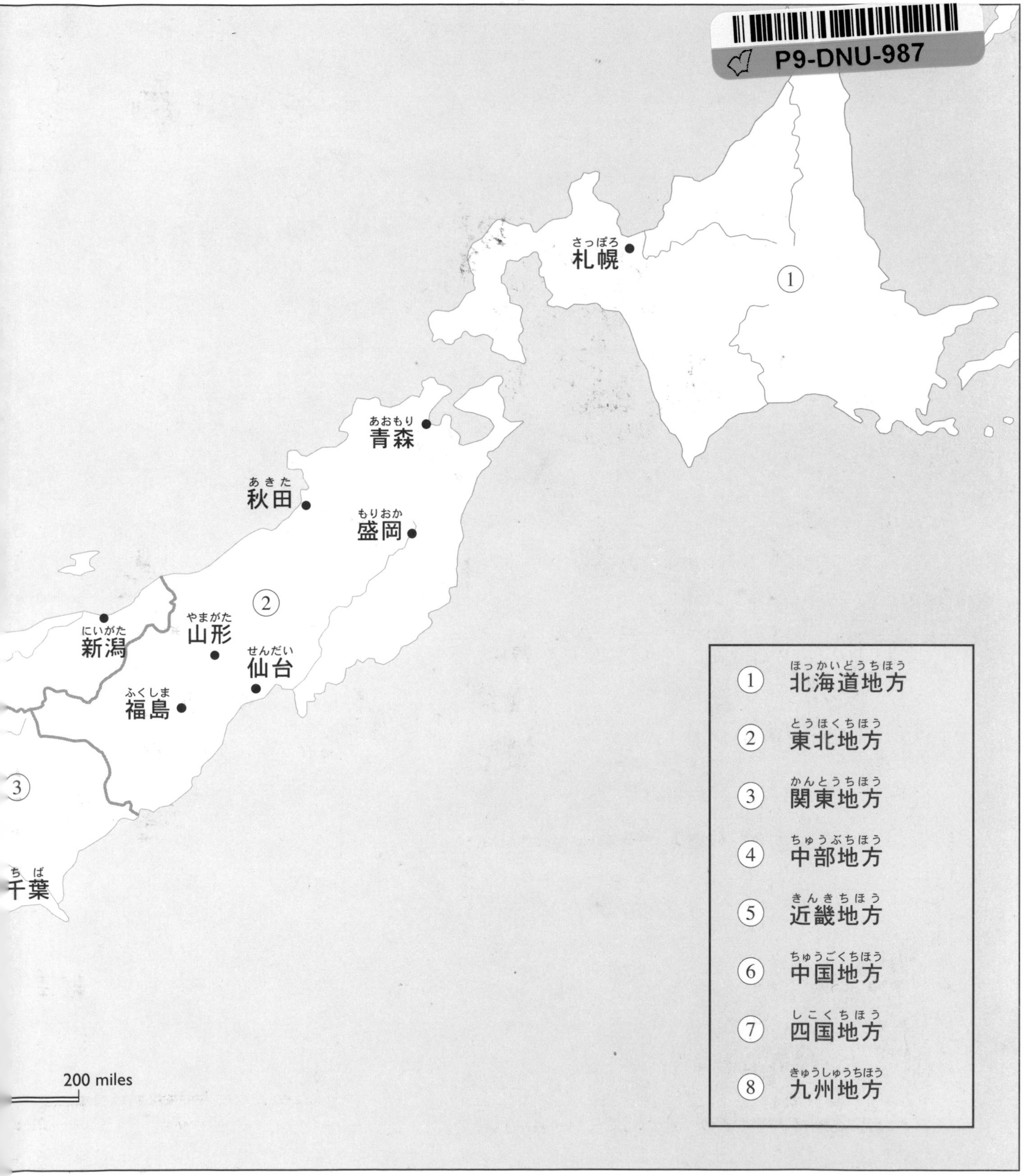
さっぽろ
札幌
1
あおもり
青森
あきた
秋田
もりおか
盛岡
2
にいがた
新潟
やまがた
山形
せんだい
仙台
ふくしま
福島
3
ちば
千葉
200 miles
1 ほっかいどうちほう 北海道地方
2 とうほくちほう 東北地方
3 かんとうちほう 関東地方
4 ちゅうぶちほう 中部地方
5 きんきちほう 近畿地方
6 ちゅうごくちほう 中国地方
7 しこくちほう 四国地方
8 きゅうしゅうちほう 九州地方

Director, Modern Language Programs: E. Kristina Baer
Development Manager: Beth Kramer
Development Editor: Michael Kelsey
Editorial Associate: Lydia Mehegan
Packaging Services Supervisor: Charline Lake
Senior Manufacturing Coordinator: Marie Barnes
Associate Marketing Manager: Tina Crowley Desprez

Cover design by Harold Burch Designs, NYC

Illustration by Steven Snyder

Photo credits

Photographs unless otherwise noted by Andy Boone, International Visual Communications

Page 1: Courtesy Ministry of Foreign Affairs, Consulate General of Japan
Page 176: From PRACTICAL JAPANESE COOKING: EASY AND ELEGANT by Shizuo Tsuji and Koichiro Hata. Photographs by Yoshikatsu Saeki. Copyright © 1986 by Kodansha International, Ltd.
Page 233: Courtesy Aichi Prefectural University, Nagoya, Japan
Page 241: Courtesy Takasagoden Shrine, Nagoya, Japan
Page 379: Courtesy Nagoya University of Foreign Studies, Department of Job Placement
Page 482: Courtesy John Lenihan

Printed in the U.S.A.

Library of Congress Catalog Card Number: 97-72518

ISBN: 0-669-28504-8

3456789-VH-03 02 01

NAKAMA 2

JAPANESE COMMUNICATION, CULTURE, CONTEXT

Yukiko Abe Hatasa
University of Iowa

Kazumi Hatasa
Purdue University

Seiichi Makino
Princeton University

Houghton Mifflin Company
Boston New York

ABOUT THE AUTHORS

Professor Yukiko Abe Hatasa received her Ph.D. in linguistics in 1992 from the University of Illinois at Urbana-Champaign. She is known nationwide, particularly among young Japanese professors and coordinators, as one of the premier Japanese methodologists in the United States and as an experienced coordinator of large teacher training programs. She is currently the coordinator of the Japanese language program at the University of Iowa.

Professor Kazumi Hatasa received his Ph.D. in education in 1989 from the University of Illinois at Urbana-Champaign. He is currently an associate professor at Purdue University. He is recognized internationally for his work in software development for the Japanese language and distributes most of his work as freeware over the Internet. This book is accompanied by his software.

Professor Seiichi Makino received his Ph.D. in linguistics in 1968 from the University of Illinois at Urbana-Champaign. He is an internationally prominent Japanese linguist and scholar who is recognized throughout the world for his scholarship and for his many publications. Before beginning his tenure at Princeton University in 1991, he taught Japanese language, linguistics and culture at the University of Illinois while training lower division language coordinators. He is an experienced ACTFL oral proficiency trainer in Japanese and frequently trains Japanese instructors internationally in proficiency-oriented instruction and in the administration of the Oral Proficiency Interview.

CONTENTS

To the Instructor *xiv*
To the Student *xxiii*
Acknowledgments *xxvii*

PRELIMINARY CHAPTER

REVIEW AND CASUAL SPEECH

Chapter 1 Greetings and Useful Expressions *2*
Casual speech: Omitting verbal endings *2*
Chapter 2 あいさつとしょうかい (Greetings and Introductions) *4*
Casual speech: Using うん for はい／で and いや／ううん for いいえ *5*
Chapter 3 日本の家 (Japanese Houses) *6*
Casual speech: Using ある and いる with よ and ね *9*
Chapter 4 日本のまちと大学 (Japanese Towns and Universities) *9*
Casual speech: Omitting particles は, を, and に; Using the plain forms of adjectives and the copula verb *12*
Chapter 5 毎日の生活１ (Daily Routine 1) *13*
Casual speech: Using the plain form of verbs *16*
Chapter 6 毎日の生活２ (Daily Routine 2) *17*
Casual speech: Omitting or not omitting particles *20*
Chapter 7 好きなことと好きなもの (Activities and Hobbies) *21*
Casual speech: Casual form of ～んです *22*
Chapter 8 かいもの 買物 (Shopping) *23*
Casual speech: Making a request *26*
Chapter 9 レストランとしょうたい (Restaurants and Invitations) *26*
Casual speech: Extending an invitation *28*
Chapter 10 私の家族 (My Family) *29*
Casual speech: Using the contracted from of ～ている *31*
Chapter 11 おもい出 (Memories) *32*
Casual speech: Using the sentence final particle わ with verbs *34*
Chapter 12 けんこう 健康 (Health) *35*
Kanji Review for Volume 1 *37*

CHAPTER 1	New Vocabulary	Culture
天気(てんき)と気候(きこう) (WEATHER AND CLIMATE) Dialogue 寒(さむ)いですね。(It's cold.) *45*	Weather forecasts *40* Climate *41* Temperature *42* Compass directions *43*	Japan's climate *47*
	Integration *82*	

CHAPTER 2	New Vocabulary	Culture
旅行(りょこう) (TRAVEL) Dialogue 今度の休み (This vacation) *90*	Useful verbal expressions related to travel *86* Travel *87* How long is your stay? *88* Conjunctions *89*	Traveling in Japan *93*
	Integration *135*	

CHAPTER 3	New Vocabulary	Culture
お願いとやり方(かた) (ASKING FOR FAVORS AND HOW TO DO SOMETHING) Dialogue コピーきの使(つか)い方(かた) (How to use a copying machine) *148*	Favors *141* How to do something *143* Machines and modern technology *144* Ingredients for cooking *145* Cooking *146*	Vending machines and telephones *150*
	Integration *181*	

Language	Skills
I. Expressing on-going actions and repeated actions, using the て-form of verbs + いる; Describing the characteristics of places, objects, and time, using ～は～が 48 II. Expressing manner of action or outcome of changes, using the adverbial forms of adjectives and noun + に 54 III. Making inferences based on direct observations, using the stem of verbs and adjectives + そうだ 58 IV. Expressing uncertainty, using ～でしょう、～かもしれない and ～かしら／かな 61 V. Expressing reasons, using the plain form + ので 67	Writing Kanji: Component shapes of kanji 1—Introduction 71 Reading Getting used to vertical writing 75 Listening Understanding the organization of prepared speech 79 Dict-a-Conversation 81 Communication Expressing agreement and solidarity using ね and も 81

Language	Skills
I. Expressing intention and plans, using the volitional form of the verb + と思(おも)う, or the plain present form of the verb + つもり or 予定(よてい) 94 II. Expressing direction, using the particle へ; Expressing time limits, using the particle までに 101 III. Reporting speech, using と言(い)う 110 IV. Expressing opinions about things, events, and actions, using the plain form + と思(おも)う 112 V. Expressing chronological order, using 前(まえ) and 後(あと); Expressing occasion, using 時 115	Writing Kanji: Component shapes of kanji 2—Side components 123 Reading Using transition devices 127 Listening Using transition devices, and the difference between そ-series and あ-series words 130 Dict-a-Conversation 133 Communication Introducing a new topic 134

Language	Skills
I. Expressing degrees of politeness in requests, using the て-form of verbs + くださる／くれる／いただく 151 II. Making a negative request using ～ないで下さい; Expressing without doing ~; Using the plain negative form of the verb + で 154 III. Expressing willingness, using verb stem + ましょうか／ましょう 157 IV. Expressing conditions and sequence, using the plain past form + ら 160 V. Trying something, using the て-form of verbs + みる; Expressing movement away from or toward the speaker through space and time, using the て-form of the verb + いく／くる 164	Writing Kanji: Component shapes of kanji 3—Top and bottom components 170 Reading Understanding the characteristics of written instructions 174 Listening Understanding transitive devices used in instructions 178 Dict-a-Conversation 180 Communication Making and declining requests or invitations 180

	New Vocabulary	Culture
CHAPTER 4 きそく (RULES) Dialogue ゆうびんきょく 郵便局と銀行 (POST OFFICES AND BANKS) *191*	Postal and parcel delivery service *186* Banks *187* Schools *188* Things you should or should not do *189*	Postal service and delivery services 193 Banks *194*
	Integration *228*	
CHAPTER 5 私の将来、じゅんび (MY FUTURE, MAKING PREPARATIONS) Dialogue 本田先生の研究室で (At Professor Honda's office) *238*	Thinking about the future *234* Making preparations *235* Transitive and intransitive verbs *236*	Changes in family structure *241* Japanese economy and employment practices *242*
	Integration *277*	
CHAPTER 6 道の聞き方と教え方 (ASKING AND GIVING DIRECTIONS) Dialogue ヒルトンホテルの行き方 (Directions to the Hilton Hotel) *290*	Words used when giving directions *283* Directions *284* Verbs and adjectives used in giving directions *286* Transportation and stations *287*	Streets in Japanese cities *293* The Japanese train system *294*
	Integration *326*	

	Language	Skills
	I. Expressing unacceptable actions or situations, using the て-form + はいけない／だめ *195* II. Expressing obligations and social expectations, the negative stem + ければ／なくてはならない／いけない; Expressing the lack of obligation or social expectations, using なくてもいい *199* III. Expressing the performance of the two actions simultaneously, using the ます-stem of verbs + ながら *205* IV. Listing actions and states, using the plain format し; Implying a reason, using the plain form + し *207* V. Expressing conditions originated by others, using (の)なら *212*	Writing Kanji: Component shapes Part 4—enclosing shapes *216* Reading Bank accounts *220* Privacy *224* Listening Living with host families *226* Dict-a-Conversation *227* Communication Changing the subject *227*

	Language	Skills
	I. Using もう and まだ *243* II. Expressing purpose and reason, using the plain form + ため; Expressing preparation, using the て-form of verbs + おく *247* III. Using transitive and intransitive verbs; Expressing results of intentional actions, using the て-form of verbs + ある *252* IV. Using the particle か (either ～ or ～); Making indirect questions, using ～か(どうか) *257* V. Using question word + も～ negative and question word + でも～ affirmative *260*	Writing Kanji: Types of kanji 5—historical perspective *263* Reading The Japanese and marriage *268* Listening Future plans *272* Dict-a-Conversation *274* Communication Making confirmations and checking comprehension *274*

	Language	Skills
	I. Expressing a route, using the particle を; Expressing a point of departure, using the particle を; Expressing scope or limit, using the particle で *296* II. Expressing chronology, using the て-form of the verb + から; Expressing conditions leading to set consequences, using the plain form + と *298* III. Expressing possibility, using the dictionary form of the verb + ことが出来る *303* IV. Expressing limited degree, using だけ～ affirmative or しか～ negative *305* V. Expressing presuppositions, using the plain form + はず *308*	Writing Kanji: Okurigana *312* Reading Getting to the University of Tokyo *316* Listening Asking for directions *320* Announcements at stations and in trains *321* Dict-a-Conversation *323* Communication How to ask for directions and how to give them *324*

CHAPTER 7 おく 贈り物 (GIFTS) Dialogue たんじょうび アリスさんの誕生日 (Alice's birthday) *337*	New Vocabulary	Culture	
	Gifts *332* Gift-giving related vocabulary *333* Gift-giving occations and purposes *334* Nouns derived from い-adjectives *336*	Gift exchanges *339*	
	Integration *375*		

CHAPTER 8 しゅうしょくそうだん 就職相談 (TALKING ABOUT EMPLOYMENT) Dialogue しゅうしょくそうだん リーさんの就職相談 (Lee-san talks about employment) *384*	New Vocabulary	Culture	
	Honorific and humble expressions *380* Polite expressions *381* Words used at work *383*	Getting a job in Japan *387* Employment of women *388* Hiring of non-Japanese *388*	
	Integration *425*		

Language	Skills
I. Using verbs of giving and receiving 341 II. Expressing desire, using ほしい and the て-form of the verb + ほしい 349 III. Expressing the fact something is easy or hard to do, using the stem of the verb +やすい／にくい 352 IV. Expressing excessiveness, using the stem of the verb or adjective +すぎる 354 V. Expressing an open hypothetical condition, using the ば conditional form 356	Writing Kanji: Statistical facts about kanji and learning tips 363 Reading The etiqette of giving and receiving gifts 368 Listening Christmas 371 Dict-a-Conversation 372 Communication Phrases used when giving or receiving gifts 373

Language	Skills
I. Doing and asking favors, using the て-form of the verb + あげる／くれる／もらう 389 II. Using honorific expressions to show respect 396 III. Using humble expressions to show respect 402 IV. Making or letting someone do something, using the causative form; Requesting permission to do something, using the causative form +て下さい 405 V. Expressing completion, regret, and realization that a mistake was made, using 〜てしまう 409	Writing Kanji: The structure of kanji compounds 412 Reading Job hunting 417 Listening Job interviews 422 Dict-a-Conversation 423 Communication Responding to compliments and expressing politeness and modesty in formal situations 423

CHAPTER 9	New Vocabulary	Culture
もんく 文句 (COMPLAINTS) Dialogue 静かにするように言って下さい。(Please tell him to hold down the noise.) 435	Relationships among people 430 Things you don't want others to do 431 Things you don't want to be forced to do 432 Expressing complaints and annoyance 433 Nouns derived from verbs 434	Neighborhood relations 438
	Integration 470	

CHAPTER 10	New Vocabulary	Culture
かんきょう しゃかい 環境と社会 (THE ENVIRONMENT AND SOCIETY) Dialogue この川で泳げるでしょうか。 (Can I swim in this river?) 480	Disasters 475 Animals 476 Environmental issues 476 A livable society 478	Earthquakes 482 Environmental concerns 482 Crimes 483
	Integration 518	

APPENDIXES

A ENGLISH TRANSLATIONS OF DIALOGUES 523
B ADJECTIVE AND COPULA VERB CONJUGATION 527
C VERB CONJUGATION 528
D LIST OF PARTICLES 530
E KANJI LIST FOR VOLUMES 1 AND 2 535

Japanese-English Glossary 545
English-Japanese Glossary 561
Index 577

Language	Skills
I. Expressing problems and things that have taken place, using the passive form *439* II. Expressing complaints, using the causative-passive form *445* III. Expressing large and small quantities and frequencies, using a quantity expression + も *448* IV. Expressing or requesting efforts to change behavior or to act in a certain way, using the plain present form of the verb + ようにする; Describing what efforts are being made to attain a specific goal, using the plain present form of the verb + よう *451* V. Using the plain form + のに to mean *despite* 〜; *although* 〜 *454*	Writing Kanji: The importance of the sound components of kanji *458* Reading Bullying *463* Listening Annoying things *466* Dict-a-Conversation *468* Communication Expressing complaints or anger, and making apologies *468*

Language	Skills
I. Using the pronoun の and the noun こと *484* II. Forming noun phrases with the nominalizers の or こと *488* III. Expressing a change of state, using 〜ようになる *493* IV. Expressing opinions indirectly, using 〜んじゃない（かと思う） *496* V. Expressing conjecture based on indirect evidence, using 〜らしい; Expressing conjecture based on direct evidence, using 〜ようだ／みたいだ *499*	Writing Kanji: Using a kanji dictionary *504* Reading Expressions used in writing *510* Global warming *510* Listening Problems in my town *514* Dict-a-Conversation *515* Communication Expressing opinions, agreements, and disagreements *516*

TO THE INSTRUCTOR

OBJECTIVES OF THE PROGRAM

Nakama 2 is a complete, flexible intermediate program designed to reinforce the fundamentals of the Japanese language introduced in *Nakama 1* or other introductory-level Japanese language textbooks for college students. It also aims at developing the functional ability to communicate in Japanese beyond the survival level.

Nakama 2 focuses on proficiency-based foreign language learning. It is concerned with the learner's level of proficiency in using Japanese for realistic, communicative purposes. At the end of *Nakama 2*, the successful learner's proficiency level should reach a basic communicative level that corresponds roughly to the Intermediate-to-Mid level of the proficiency guidelines formulated by the American Council on the Teaching of Foreign Languages.

The originality of *Nakama 2* is that it strikes a balance between curricula focused only on speaking and listening over the first two years of instruction and curricula that emphasize equally all four skills from the very beginning. In the first of these curricula, the sudden change from speaking and listening to reading and writing at the third-year level (intermediate) is difficult for students. Students do not have enough time to develop reading proficiency before graduation from a four-year college system. On the other hand, in the second approach, equal emphasis on all four skills from the beginning is overwhelming for most students of Japanese.

Speaking and listening are the foundation of language development in *Nakama 1*. The number of **kanji** and grammar items introduced is limited to promote initial vocabulary development crucial for communicative fluency at the introductory level. Listening and reading strategies are also actively introduced from the beginning, because the ability to obtain useful language input in a meaningful way is crucial for language acquisition.

In *Nakama 2*, the focus gradually shifts to reading and writing at the same time skills in oral communication are being expanded at a discourse level. Approximately 300 **kanji** are introduced along with information about character components, word formation, and dictionary use. Reading activities encourage students not only to use macro-level reading strategies introduced in *Nakama 1* but also to develop micro-level reading skills. Grammar explanations are more detailed than those in *Nakama 1*. Students at this level become more interested not only in how to form grammatical utterances, but also in how to use the language appropriately in various conversational contexts. Therefore, unlike beginning-level students, they are more appreciative of detailed information concerning language use and are less likely to be overwhelmed by the amount of information provided. In addition, *Nakama 2* incorporates both casual and formal speech styles throughout so that students can become more comfortable with daily conversational styles of Japanese. The number of vocabulary items is decreased slightly in *Nakama 2* to compensate for the increased number of **kanji**.

Following are specific descriptions of how the four language skills, **kanji,** and culture are treated in *Nakama 2*.

Speaking

At the beginning of each chapter, students learn new vocabulary by immediate interactive use through extensive exercises. Additionally, these sections provide reviews of related vocabulary items that were previously introduced. A chapter dialogue following the new vocabulary section provides a model conversation with a variety of exercises and motivates students in advance for the active role-playing activities at the end of the chapter that incorporate the language structures and functions introduced in the chapter. Grammar explanations provide information about use so that students may focus on speaking and using the language in the appropriate context. Students apply new language structures and communication strategies through pair-work and group activities.

Listening

Students practice their listening skills by using the Student Audio CD and by doing collaborative work in class. Each chapter dialogue, recorded on the Student Audio CD, is part of a lively story line and can be used independently to familiarize students with the chapter theme. After the language section, the dialogue can be used again for listening comprehension and speaking activities. The listening section encourages students to use strategies introduced in *Nakama 1* and *2* through pre-listening activities. This is followed by more listening activities, post-listening activities, and Dict-a-Conversations, also recorded on the Student Audio CD, which focus on detailed listening skills.

Culture

Special care has been devoted in *Nakama 2* to providing practical insights into Japanese culture. The culture notes specifically discuss those realistic aspects of life in Japan that are crucial to using the language in the target culture. The topics discussed include Japan's climate, traveling in Japan, vending machines, public telephones, postal and parcel delivery services, changes in family structure, transportation, Japanese towns and streets, the metric system, gift exchanges, the Japanese economy, employment practices, job hunting, common problems in the workplace, neighborhood relations, earthquakes, environmental concerns, crime, and a sketch of Japanese history, religions, and related customs.

Writing

Nakama 2 introduces the Japanese writing system in an interactive, highly communicative manner. One of Nakama's key features is to train students to write long texts using transition devices and complex sentences. The pace of this introduction is carefully monitored so as not to overburden students. In Chapter 2, we introduce students to a variety of transition devices and time adverbial clauses, which are reinforced in subsequent chapters. Starting with Chapter 4, various types of conditional clauses and verbal connective forms are introduced. Chapters 9 and 10 introduce expository writing styles to prepare students for advanced-level reading materials.

Kanji

After practicing new **kanji**, students are given a text where they can recognize the **kanji** they have learned. Because the texts include words they do not yet know, students are required to make good use of the reading strategies provided before the readings in each chapter. To familiarize students with authentic Japanese texts, the reading texts in *Nakama 2* do not contain any word boundaries and are written in a combination of **kanji** and **kana**. **Hiragana** superscripts are provided for words containing **kanji** that were not introduced in the current or previous chapters. In the rest of the chapter, unknown words are written in **kana** except for the following two cases:

Words containing **kanji** introduced in any given chapter are written in **kanji** and superscripted up to the reading section for that chapter.

Words containing both **kanji** that have been introduced and **kanji** that have not been introduced are superscripted throughout the chapter. For example, 車 is introduced in Chapter 2. Therefore, the noun **kuruma** *(car)* is written as 車(くるま) before the reading section of this chapter. The word **jitensha** *(bicycle)*, which has the **kanji** 車 and is introduced in Chapter 3, is written as 自転車(じてんしゃ), because the **kanji** 自 and 転 have not yet been introduced. This method was adopted to avoid using inauthentic writing, such as じてん車, and to provide a maximum exposure to newly introduced **kanji** without burdening students.

Reading

The reading sections of *Nakama 2* are preceded by extensive pre-reading activities to reinforce the use of reading strategies introduced in *Nakama 1* and in the first three chapters of *Nakama 2*. Also, the reading activities focus not only on top-down reading strategies, such as skimming and the use of real-world knowledge, but also on reading for details and analyzing discourse organization. Post-reading activities help students to relate textual information to their own language use through writing and discussions.

FEATURES OF *NAKAMA 2*

An extensive review of *Nakama 1* prepares students for *Nakama 2* and helps students who have studied elementary Japanese with a different textbook to make a smooth transition from that book to *Nakama 2*.

- Extensive vocabulary exercises help students to learn new vocabulary and review vocabulary items.
- Chapter dialogues present a lively story line that illustrates typical daily events in Japanese life and provide a realistic context in which to learn the chapter vocabulary and grammatical structures. They introduce both formal and casual speech styles. Dialogue translations appear in Appendix A to encourage guessing meaning from context. Specially created **manga** accompany each chapter dialogue.
- The listening activities are preceded by pre-listening activities to help students understand better the natural flow of Japanese. They are followed by post-listening activities, which encourage students to focus on detailed comprehension and application of information for other communicative purposes. The Dict-a-Conversation, a unique feature of *Nakama,* further reinforces the development of detailed listening comprehension and the formation of conversational discourse.
- Grammar is presented functionally in the form of sample sentences in a clear, easy-to-comprehend boxed format, followed by language notes that provide detailed explanations and focus on direct application in the 話してみましょう sections.
- Exercises progress from structured practice to a wide range of open-ended communicative activities that emphasize pair and group work.
- Culture notes in English explore aspects of contemporary life in Japan that are an essential component of communication.
- *Nakama 2* presents 300 **kanji** in Chapters 1 through 10. A **kanji** section in each chapter starts with useful information about the composition of **kanji,** word formation, the use of dictionaries, and on-line resources. Each **kanji** is presented

with its stroke order, which helps students master correct stroke orders when writing in Japanese and prepares students for the reading section.

- Each chapter reading is accompanied by pre- and post-reading activities to help learners use reading strategies, comprehend text and textual organization, and read texts purposefully. All readings feature **hiragana** superscripts to assist students with character reading.
- Communication sections in each chapter provide practical strategies to develop students' oral proficiency. They are accompanied by audio exercises and models to promote active production.
- Vocabulary is listed at the end of each chapter and organized into essential and passive groups for easy review. Essential vocabulary consists of the words introduced in the New Vocabulary, Language, and Communication sections for students' recognition and production. Passive vocabulary occurs throughout the chapter, but students are not expected to retain it. In *Nakama 2*, supplementary vocabulary is included in the vocabulary index the Workbook.
- Free text-linked web activities may be downloaded from our Modern Language web site at http://www.hmco.com/college.

PROGRAM COMPONENTS

- Student Text with Student Audio CD (0-669-46137-7)
- Workbook/Laboratory Manual (0-669-28507-2)
- Audio CD Program (0-669-28508-0)
- Free text-linked web activities at http://www.hmco.com/college.
- Instructor's Resource Manual (0-669-28505-6)

MATERIALS FOR THE STUDENT

- Student Text: *Nakama 2* has 10 chapters containing new material and one review chapter and is the main component of the program. You will find a description of the student text on pages xxiii–xxv of the To the Student section.
- Student Audio CD: The audio CD is designed to maximize learners' exposure to the sounds of natural spoken Japanese and improve their pronunciation. Included are dialogues, listening sections, Dict-a-Conversations, and Communication sections identified in the student text by a headphone icon. This audio CD comes shrink-wrapped with the student text.
- Workbook/Laboratory Manual: An integral part of *Nakama 2*, the Workbook/Laboratory Manual is designed to reinforce the association of

sound, syntax, and meaning needed for effective communication in Japanese as well as the grammar and vocabulary presented in the textbook. Students who use the Workbook/Laboratory Manual consistently will find this component of great assistance in developing their listening, speaking, reading, and writing skills and in targeting the specific lesson features that require extra review. Each chapter of the Workbook/Laboratory Manual is correlated to the corresponding chapter in the textbook. The activities include sentence completion, dialogue completion, fill-in-the blank exercises, personal questions, sentence combination exercises, **kanji** exercises, and compositions, among others.

The workbook section provides a variety of practice to help students develop their reading and writing skills using the various grammatical patterns learned in each chapter. Occasionally, structured exercises are provided to strengthen students' accuracy with grammar points. Each chapter of the workbook features two communicative activities for each of the five grammar points introduced in the Language section of the textbook, followed by one integration exercise.

The laboratory manual exercises can be done at the language lab and are essential for developing pronunciation, language accuracy, and listening skills. The Pronunciation section practices the words listed in the Essential Vocabulary at the end of each chapter in the textbook. The listening and language accuracy section of each chapter of the laboratory manual features one to three activities for each language point introduced in the corresponding chapter of the textbook.

- Audio CD Program: The Audio CD Program accompanying *Nakama 2* corresponds to the Essential Vocabulary section in the textbook and to the activities in the laboratory manual. The Audio CD Program provides approximately six hours of taped exercises recorded by native speakers.
- Free text-linked web activities may be downloaded from our Modern Language web site at http://www.hmco.com/college.

SUPPLEMENTARY MATERIALS FOR THE INSTRUCTOR

- Instructor's Resource Manual: The Instructor's Resource Manual is made up of four sections. The first section, the Instructor's Guide, is written in both Japanese and English and provides a detailed description of the *Nakama 2* program with concrete suggestions and ideas for the effective implementation of chapter segments and supplementary activities. For example, Chapter 2 contains suggestions on how to teach word attack skills and to increase word recognition speed. The Instructor's Guide also features various games and additional reading and writing activities to expand your teaching options. The second section, entitled Reproducible Materials, contains transparency masters, activity cards, and additional reading materials for the many activity suggestions in the Instructor's Guide.

The Student Audio CD script and the Audio CD Program script make up the third section of the Instructor's Resource Manual, which we have provided for your convenience.

The Answer Keys to textbook, workbook, and laboratory manual activities are provided in the last section of the Instructor's Resource Manual and may be photocopied and distributed to students.

The pages of the Instructor's Resource Manual are perforated for your convenience.

COURSE PLANNING

The following 150-hour semester syllabus reflects how *Nakama 2* can be used over two semesters of 15 weeks with classes meeting five times a week. Chapters 1 through 5 are taught the first semester and Chapters 6 through 10 the second semester. Two to three weeks have been set aside in each semester for review and testing. Instructors may want to complete the Preliminary Chapter (the review of *Nakama 1*) in one week instead of two, depending on their curriculum.

Semester Syllabus 1 (150 hours or more)

	First Semester	Second Semester
Weeks 1–2	Preliminary Chapter and Testing	Chapter 6
Week 3	Chapter 1	Chapter 6
Week 4	Chapter 1	Chapter 7
Weeks 5–6	Chapter 2	Chapter 7
Weeks 7–8	Chapter 3	Chapter 8
Week 9	Review and Testing	Chapter 8, Review and Testing
Weeks 10–11	Chapter 4	Chapter 9
Week 12	Chapter 4 and Chapter 5	Chapter 9 and Chapter 10
Weeks 13–14	Chapter 5	Chapter 10
Week 15	Review and Final Exams	Review and Final Exams

Instructors may want to teach at a slower speed because of the complexity of grammar and the number of **kanji**. Nakama 2 is designed to cover most of the skills and knowledge which should be taught at this level in the first nine chapters, so it is possible to cover the Preliminary Chapter through Chapter 4 in the first semester, and Chapters 5 through 9 in the second semester.

Semester Syllabus 2 (150 hours or less)

	First Semester	Second Semester
Weeks 1–3	Preliminary Chapter and Testing	Chapter 5
Weeks 4–6	Chapter 1	Chapter 6
Weeks 7–8	Chapter 2	Chapter 7
Week 9	Chapter 2, Review and Testing	Chapter 7, Review and Testing
Weeks 10–11	Chapter 3	Chapter 8
Weeks 12	Chapter 3 and Chapter 4	Chapter 8 and Chapter 9
Weeks 13–14	Chapter 4	Chapter 9
Week 15	Review and Final Exams	Review and Final Exams

The following 150-hour quarter syllabus reflects how *Nakama 2* can be used over three 10-week quarters with classes meeting five times a week. The Preliminary Chapter 1 through Chapter 3 are taught in the first quarter, Chapters 4 through 7 in the second quarter, and Chapters 8 through 10 in the third quarter. One to two weeks have been set aside in each quarter for review and testing.

Quarter Syllabus 1 (150 hours or more)

	First Quarter	Second Quarter	Third Quarter
Week 1	Preliminary Chapter	Review and Chapter 4	Review and Chapter 8
Week 2	Preliminary Chapter and Testing	Chapter 4	Chapter 8
Week 3	Chapter 1	Chapter 5	Chapter 8
Week 4	Chapter 1	Chapter 5	Chapter 9
Week 5	Chapter 2	Chapter 5, Review and Testing	Chapter 9
Week 6	Chapter 2	Chapter 6	Chapter 9, Review and Testing
Week 7	Chapter 2, Review and Testing	Chapter 6	Chapter 10
Week 8	Chapter 3	Chapter 7	Chapter 10
Week 9	Chapter 3	Chapter 7	Chapter 10
Week 10	Review and Final Exams	Review and Final Exams	Review and Final Exams

Instructors who wish to teach at a slower speed can cover the Preliminary Chapter through Chapter 3 in the first quarter, Chapters 4 through 6 in the second quarter, and Chapters 7 through 9 in the third quarter.

Quarter Syllabus 2 (150 hours or fewer)

	First Quarter	Second Quarter	Third Quarter
Week 1	Preliminary Chapter	Review and Chapter 4	Review and Chapter 7
Week 2	Preliminary Chapter and Testing	Chapter 4	Chapter 7
Week 3	Chapter 1	Chapter 4	Chapter 7
Week 4	Chapter 1	Chapter 5	Chapter 8
Week 5	Chapter 2	Chapter 5	Chapter 8
Week 6	Chapter 2	Chapter 5, Review and Testing	Chapter 8, Review and Testing
Week 7	Chapter 2, Review and Testing	Chapter 6	Chapter 9
Week 8	Chapter 3	Chapter 6	Chapter 9
Week 9	Chapter 3	Chapter 6	Chapter 9
Week 10	Review and Final Exams	Review and Final Exams	Review and Final Exams

Instructors who are teaching in programs with fewer hours available in the year may want to cover fewer chapters or less material within the chapters. A suggested strategy is not to cover all the chapters as indicated above. Also, instructors may want to cut down on the reading sections if their programs focus on speaking and listening. Instructors may want to eliminate or simplify some grammatical items from each chapter, or they may wish to pick and choose from among the grammatical activities. Instructors should not, however, reduce the vocabulary or **kanji**, which are essential and were carefully selected.

TO THE STUDENT

Nakama 2 is based on the principles that learning a foreign language means learning skills, not just facts and information, and that we learn by doing. Therefore, *Nakama 2* systematically involves you in many activities putting to use the language skills of listening, speaking, reading, and writing. We believe that culture is an integral component of language, too. To help you familiarize yourselves with Japanese culture, we have provided a lively story line of an American student in Japan, culture notes, and communication strategies.

ORGANIZATION OF THE TEXTBOOK

Nakama 2 consists of 11 chapters. In the Preliminary Chapter, you will review basic Japanese grammar, communicative functions, vocabulary, and the 90 **kanji** introduced in *Nakama 1* to prepare you for more advanced study of the Japanese language. You will also learn casual speech styles. At the end of this chapter, as with every chapter in *Nakama 2*, a list of essential and passive vocabulary is provided. Each of the following 10 chapters focuses on a common communicative situation and contains the features listed below.

- Chapter Opener: Each chapter opens with a photograph that sets the scene for the chapter and a list of chapter contents. The language functions introduced in the chapter are listed at the top of the chapter contents. Keeping in mind the functions while you go through the chapter will help you focus on results.
- New Vocabulary: The vocabulary is presented in thematic groups with a variety of communicative activities and activities in context.
- Dialogue: The dialogues feature a lively story line: Alice Arisaka, an American student, spends two years studying in Japan. You will get to know a series of characters and follow them through typical

events in their lives. First, you will look at the **manga** (a cartoon strip) and listen to the recorded dialogue on the Student Audio CD. Then you will match the dialogue frames with the frames of the **manga**. After that you will work on a series of activities to help you understand the contents of the dialogue, the discourse organization, and the use of formal and casual speech styles.

- Culture: Culture notes in English explore historical, economic, and social aspects of Japanese life that are essential to communication.
- Language: Grammar explanations are given in the form of sample sentences in a clear, easy-to-comprehend boxed format followed by examples and language notes that help you understand how to use the grammar appropriately. Class activities that you can do in pairs or in groups put the language structures into practice immediately. Grammar accuracy, however, should not be overlooked. There is a high correlation between successful communication and grammar accuracy.
- Kanji: A total of 300 **kanji** is introduced in Chapters 1 through 10. The **kanji** section in each chapter starts with useful information about the composition of **kanji**, word formation, and use of dictionaries. Each **kanji** is presented with a stroke order to help you master correct stroke orders when writing in Japanese and prepare you for the reading section.
- Reading: The reading texts are accompanied by pre- and post-reading activities designed to help you become a successful reader of Japanese and understand Japanese fully. The reading of unintroduced **kanji** throughout the textbook is given with **hiragana** superscripts. The readings include a small number of unknown words so that you can develop strategies to cope with authentic texts.
- Listening: Listening activities consist of pre-listening activities, listening practice, post-listening activities, and a Dict-a-Conversation. The pre-listening activities help you to apply listening strategies to listening practice for general comprehension. The post-listening activities help you to work on detailed comprehension and to apply the information obtained through listening to other communicative purposes. The next activity is a Dict-a-Conversation recorded on the Student Audio CD packaged with the textbook. After listening to the CD, you write down what you hear, which becomes your partner's lines. Then you create your end of the dialogue.
- Communication: This segment will provide you with knowledge and practice of basic strategies that will facilitate your communication in Japanese. Some of the exercises are recorded to give you oral practice.
- Integration: You will be asked to mobilize all the skills you have learned up to the current point through discussion, interview, and role-play formats.

- Vocabulary List: Vocabulary is listed at the end of each chapter and organized into essential and passive groups for easy review. Essential Vocabulary consists of the words that are introduced in the New Vocabulary, Language, and Communication sections for your recognition and production. Passive vocabulary occurs throughout the chapter, but you are not expected to retain it. In *Nakama 2*, supplementary vocabulary is included in the vocabulary index and in the Workbook.
- Appendices A–E: In the appendices, you will find translations of the chapter dialogues, an adjective conjugation chart, a verb conjugation chart, a list of particles for *Nakama 1* and *2*, and a list of **kanji** from both *Nakama 1*and *Nakama 2*.
- Glossaries and Index: At the end of your textbook, you will find Japanese-English and English-Japanese glossaries and an index.

MATERIALS AND TIPS FOR THE STUDENT

- Student Text with Student Audio CD: *Nakama 2* has 11 chapters with new material and one review chapter, and is the main component of the program.
- Student Audio CD: Free audio CD containing recordings of the dialogues, the Dict-a-Conversation, and other listening activities are packaged with your textbook. This audio CD is designed to maximize your exposure to the sounds of natural spoken Japanese and to help you practice pronunciation.
- Workbook/Laboratory Manual: The workbook section provides a variety of practice to help you develop your reading and writing skills using the various grammatical patterns learned in each chapter. Here are some tips to follow in using the workbook:

  1. Before doing the activities, review the corresponding vocabulary and grammar sections in the textbook.
  2. Do the activities with your textbook closed.
  3. When you write, be creative without overstepping your linguistic boundaries.
  4. Try to use the dictionary sparingly.

  The laboratory manual exercises are essential for developing your pronunciation and listening skills. The pronunciation section practices the words listed in the Essential Vocabulary at the end of each chapter in your textbook. The listening and accuracy section of each chapter of the laboratory manual features activities for each of the five language points introduced in the corresponding chapter of your textbook. Here are some tips to follow when using the laboratory manual:

1. While doing the pronunciation exercises, listen carefully and try to imitate the speakers' pronunciation and intonation accurately.
2. Read the directions and exercise items before doing the listening comprehension activities.
3. Do not be concerned with understanding every word when listening to a long dialogue; your goal should be to do the task that is asked of you in the activity.

Through conscientious use of the Workbook/Laboratory Manual, you should make good progress in your study of the Japanese language.

- Audio CD Program: The Audio CD Program accompanying *Nakama 2* corresponds to the Essential Vocabulary section in your textbook and to the activities in the laboratory manual. It provides approximately six hours of taped exercises recorded by native speakers and is available for student purchase as well as for use in the language lab.
- Free text-linked web activities may be downloaded from our Modern Language web site at http://www.hmco.com/college.

We would like to hear your comments and reactions to *Nakama 2*. Reports on your experience using this program would be of great interest and value to us. Please write us, care of Houghton Mifflin Company, College Division, Modern Languages, 222 Berkeley Street, Boston, MA 02116.

ACKNOWLEDGMENTS

The authors and publisher thank the following people for their recommendations regarding the content of *Nakama 2*. Their comments and suggestions were invaluable during the development of this publication.

Yukie Aida, *University of Texas at Austin, Austin, TX*
Hiroko Kataoka, *University of Oregon, Portland, OR*
Midori Kunitsugu, *Highline Community College*
Tomiko Kuwahira, *Columbia University, New York, NY*
William McClure, *Queens College, CUNY, New York, NY*
Takiko Morimoto, *El Camino College*
Zenryu Shirakawa, *Boston University, Boston, MA*
Yasuko Ito Watt, *Indiana University, Bloomington, IN*
Kikuko Yamashita, *Brown University, Providence, RI*

The authors and publisher also thank the following people for field-testing *Nakama 2*. Their comments contributed greatly to the accuracy of this publication.

Junko Hino, *Princeton University, Princeton, NJ*
Satoru Ishikawa, *Princeton University, Princeton, NJ*
Yoshiko Jo, *Princeton University, Princeton, NJ*
Sayuri Kubota, *University of Iowa, Iowa City, IA*
Yasumi Kuriya, *University of Iowa, Iowa City, IA*
Hideo Makihara, *University of Washington, Seattle, WA*
Kumiko Makihara, *University of Washington, Seattle, WA*
Junko Mori, *University of Iowa, Iowa City , IA*
Fumiko Nazikian, *Princeton University, Princeton, NJ*
Mayumi Oka, *Princeton University, Princeton, NJ*
Amy Snyder Ohta, *University of Washington, Seattle, WA*
Kaoru Ohta, *University of Washington, Seattle, WA*
Junko Saito, *University of Texas at Austin, Austin, TX*
Mayumi Steinmetz, *Shoreline Community College, Seattle, WA*
Keiko Yamaguchi, *North Seattle Community, College and Shoreline Community College, Seattle, WA*

The authors are especially grateful to Dr. Yasuko Makino, Gest Library, Princeton University, Princeton, NJ, for proofreading

Nakama 2. They are also grateful to the following people for their valuable assistance during the development of this project: Kristina Baer, Director, Modern Language Programs; Beth Kramer, Development Manager; Charline Lake, Packaging Services Supervisor; Patricia Foss; Marketing Manager; Tina Crowley Desprez; Senior Marketing Coordinator; Lydia Mehegan, Editorial Assistant; Michael Kelsey, Development Editor and Project Manager; Tomoko Graham for her help with Workbook/Laboratory material; and Nao Hatasa for the handwritten characters in *Nakama 2*.

PRELIMINARY CHAPTER

序章

A library review session

復習(ふくしゅう)とカジュアルスピーチ

REVIEW AND CASUAL SPEECH

Chapter Reviews	*Nakama 1*, Chapters 1 through 12
Casual Speech	Omitting verbal endings
	Using うん for はい and いや / ううん for いいえ
	Using ある and いる with よ and ね
	Omitting particles は, を, and に; Using the plain forms of adjectives and the copula verb
	Using the plain form of verbs
	Omitting or not omitting particles
	Casual form of ～んです
	Making a request
	Extending an invitation
	Using the contracted form of ～ている
	Using the sentence final particle わ with verbs
Kanji Review	**Kanji** review for *Nakama 1*

第一課(だい) Greetings and useful expressions

Review

A. Work with a partner. Role-play the following situations.

1. It is a cold morning. You meet your teacher on your way to school.
2. Your class is over. Say good-bye to your teacher and classmates.
3. You are going out in the evening. You meet a neighbor.
4. Your neighbor gives you some fruit. Thank him or her and ask the name of the fruit in Japanese.
5. Your neighbor tells you that he or she has just bought a デジカメ. You don't know what that is. Ask your neighbor what デジカメ means.
6. You are attending an orientation for international students at Joto University in Tokyo. You don't know anyone sitting around you and would like to get to know the others there.
7. It is a sunny Sunday afternoon. You are walking in a park and meet your friend's mother.
8. You are in a teacher's office and are about to leave.

B. What kinds of requests would you make in the following situations?

1. You didn't understand what your teacher just said.
2. You are talking with a salesperson on the phone, but you can't hear him well.
3. You are talking with a friend on the phone who speaks too fast.
4. You want to know how your name is written in かな.
5. You are about to make an announcement to your class, so you need everybody's attention.
6. You want to know the reading of an unknown かんじ.
7. You want to know the meaning of an unknown かんじ.
8. You want your teacher to check the way you have written a かんじ.
9. You want to know the Japanese word for *numbers*.

Casual speech: Omitting verbal endings

When you ask questions or make requests to your friends, rather than to your teachers, you can use the casual form of speech. Here are some examples of the casual form.

Example

〜て下さい becomes 〜て or 〜てくれる with a rising intonation:
パーティに来て。↗ パーティに来てくれる。↗

何(なん)といいますか becomes 何(なに) with a rising intonation:

"Government" は日本語で何(なに)。↗

何(なん)ですか also becomes 何(なに) with a rising intonation:

あのたてものは何(なに)。↗

A. Now restate the following polite expressions in their casual forms.

1. あれは日本語で何といいますか。
2. ゆっくり話して下さい。
3. このかんじのいみは何ですか。
4. このかんじを読んで下さい。
5. もう一度言って下さい。
6. "Library" は日本語で何と言いますか。
7. このしゃしんを見て下さい。
8. 「らくご」って何ですか。

B. You are talking with a friend in the situations described in sentences 1-5 in Exercise A on page 3, instead of the person specified in the exercise. Change what you would say accordingly.

C. Read the display type in the following ads and figure out what the ads say. Ask your teacher or a friend about any unfamiliar words or かんじ. Ask questions in both polite and casual forms.

第二課(だい)　あいさつとじこしょうかい

Review

A. You are at a party and are trying to get to know the other people there. First create an identification card by selecting one word from each of the following categories.

なまえ：　スミス　キム　ブラウン　シュー

大学：　ニューヨーク大学　シカゴ大学　シドニー大学　東京(とうきょう)大学

学年(がくねん)：　大学院　一年　二年　三年　四年

せんこう：　アジアけんきゅう　けいざい学　けいえい学　こう学

くに：　アメリカ　日本　かんこく　中国(ちゅうごく)　オーストラリア　カナダ

B. Using the identity you have just created in Exercise A, greet and talk with as many people as you can. Remember them because you will be asked to introduce the people you have met to one another.

Example

A:　はじめまして。私はスミスです。どうぞよろしく。
B:　はじめまして。シューです。どうぞよろしく。
A:　シューさんのせんこうは何ですか。
B:　けいざい学です。

C. Using the names in Exercise A, ask about the other people at the party. Find out their names, what they study, where they are from, and so on. Assume that you are at a distance from them.

Example

A:　あの男の人はだれですか。

B:　ああ、あの人はキムさんですよ。

A:　キムさんはどの大学の学生ですか。

B:　東京(とうきょう)大学の学生です。

A:　そうですか。キムさんはどこから来ましたか。

B:　カナダから来ました。

D. You have just joined the Japan Student Association. Introduce yourself, providing the appropriate information for the categories below.

なまえ：________________

～年生：________________

大学のなまえ：________________

せんこう：________________

くに：________________

しゅみ：________________

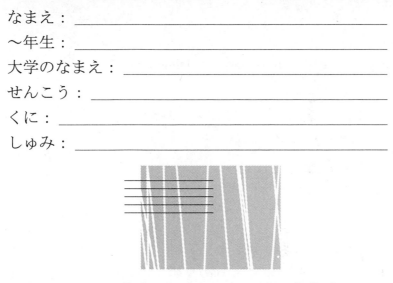

Casual speech: Using うん for はい and いや / ううん for いいえ

In casual conversation, うん is often used instead of はい or ええ, and いや or ううん can be used for いいえ.

Change the following dialogues into casual speech.

Example

Formal: 岩田(いわた)： あの人は山田さんですか。

鈴木(すずき)：はい／ええ、そうです。or いいえ、そうじゃありません。

Casual: 恵子(けいこ)： あの人（は）山田さん？

まもる： うん、そう。or いや／ううん、そうじゃない（よ）。

1. A: ゆっくり話して下さい。
   B: はい。
2. A: 山田さんは大学生ですか。
   B: いいえ、そうじゃありません。
3. A: せんこうはアジアけんきゅうですか。
   B: はい、そうです。
4. A: 一年生ですか。
   B: いいえ、そうじゃありません。

第(だい)三課　日本の家

Review

A. Which of the following items might you find in the rooms or buildings listed in 1–6 below?

ベッド	いす	つくえ	本だな	電話(でんわ)	テレビ	ステレオ	
ふとん	たんす	おしいれ	まど	ドア	いぬ	ねこ	ソファ
テーブル	スタンド	時計(とけい)	とだな	え			

Example

A:　りょうのへやにはどんなものがありますか。
B:　そうですね。ベッドがあります。つくえもあります。

1. りょうのへや ~ dorm
2. きょうしつ
3. 日本の家
4. リビングルーム
5. 子供(こども)のへや
6. キッチン

B. Make questions for which the following phrases could be the answers.

Example

B:　しずかな所です。
A:　大学の図書館(としょかん)はどんな所ですか。

1. しずかな所
2. きれいな人
3. ひろい所
4. りっぱな家
5. ゆうめいなたてもの
6. あたらしいたてもの
7. すてきな人
8. せまい所

C. Work with a partner. You are at Location A and your partner is at Location B. Choose one of the pictures and describe objects pictured around you and your partner. Your partner should deduce which picture was selected. Use location words こそあど and ～に～があります／います。

1

2

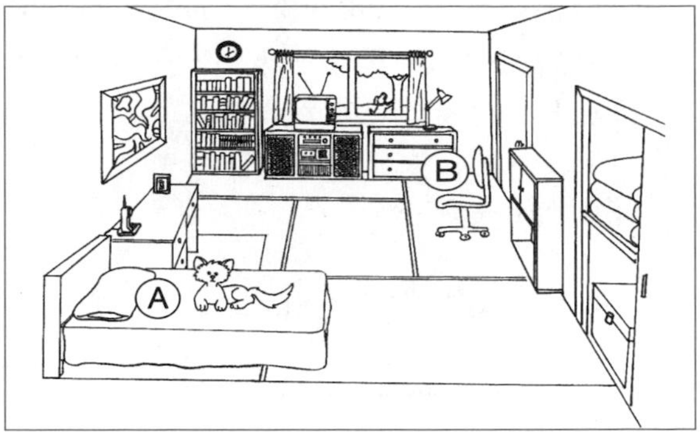

3

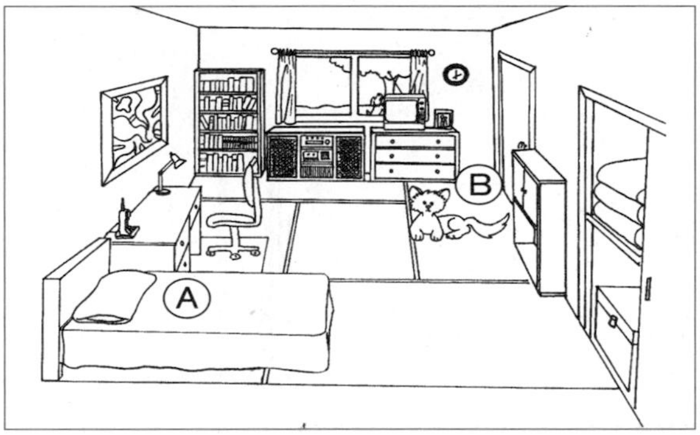

4

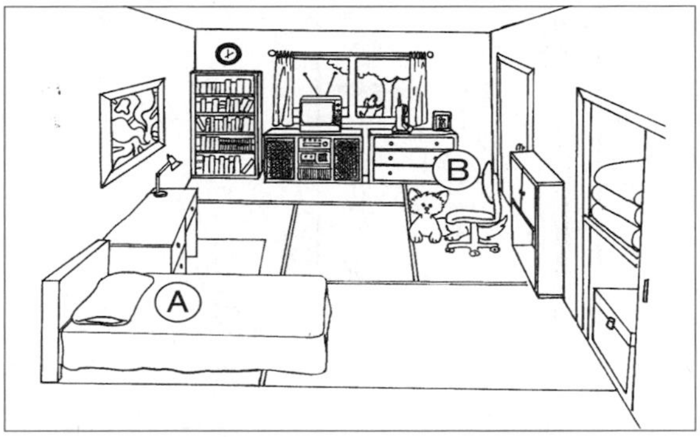

5

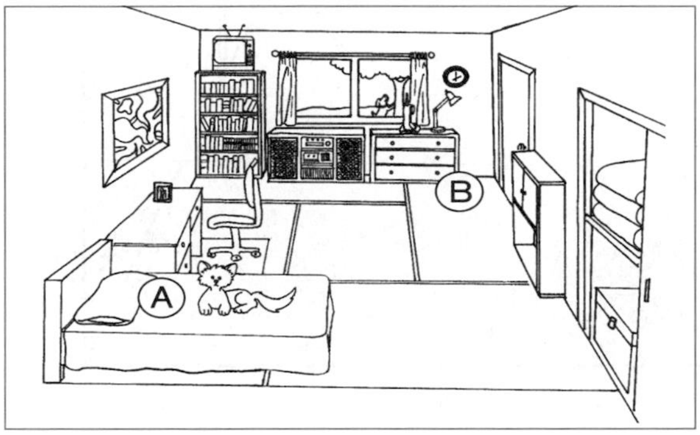

6

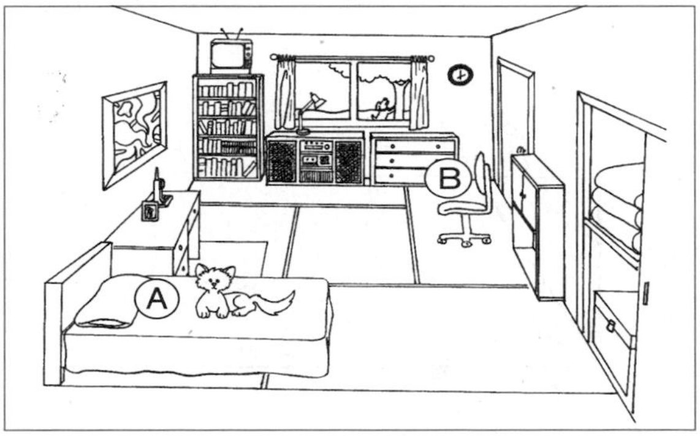

D. Work with a partner. You are moving into a new room with your belongings, and your partner is helping you move in. Draw in where you want to put your belongings in the empty room below. Then tell your partner where to put them in the room. Use the format "locationにobjectをおいて下さい。" Your partner will draw the objects in his or her own picture as you tell him or her where to put them. Compare your picture with the one made by your partner to see if they are identical.

ベッド　つくえ　ランプ　ソファ　テレビ　たんす　本だな

Example

大きいまどのまえにつくえをおいて下さい。

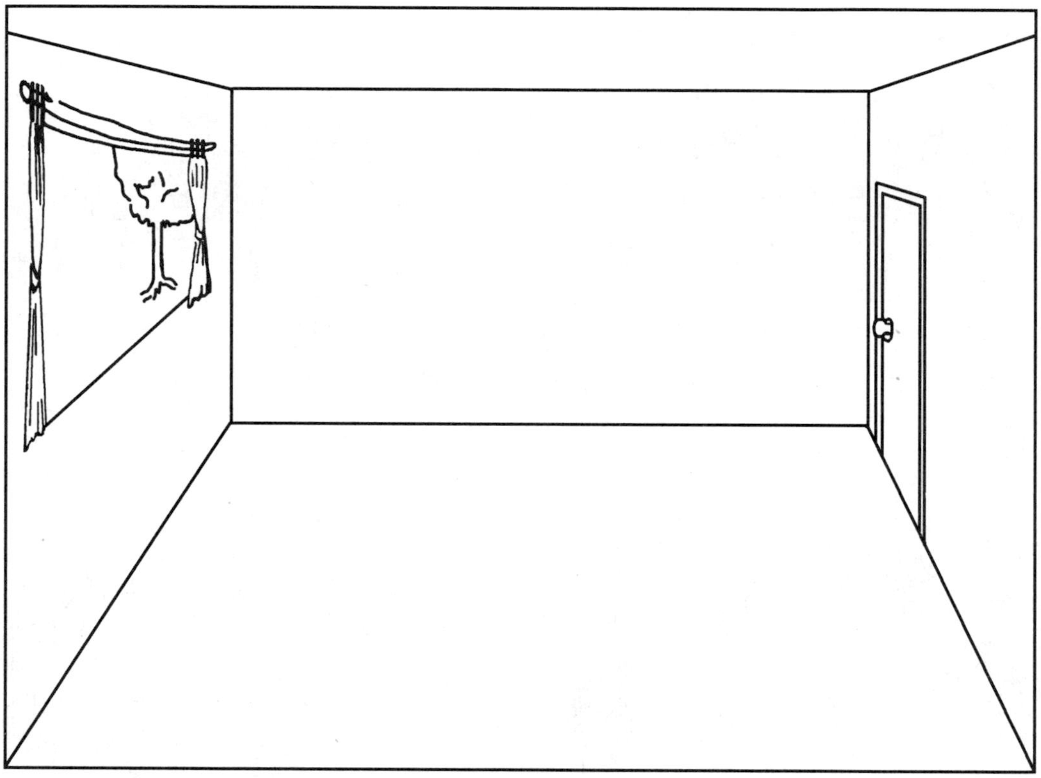

E. Role-play the following situations.

1. You live with a host family in Japan. You have just gotten home.
2. Your Japanese friend takes you to his house and you are at the door. Greet his mother.
3. Your friend's mother tells you to come in. Respond to her.
4. You have a new roommate in your apartment, and he or she is Japanese. Tell him or her where various rooms are located.

Casual speech: Using ある and いる with よ and ね

In casual speech, the verb あります／います becomes ある／いる. This ある／いる is often followed by the particles よ or ね in statements. The question marker か is either omitted or replaced by の in questions. Questions take a rising intonation. The following pair of short exchanges illustrates these differences.

Formal: 岩田(いわた)：　あそこにだれがいますか。
鈴木(すずき)：　山田さんがいます。
Casual: 恵子(けいこ)：　あそこにだれがいる／いるの。
まもる：　山田さんがいるよ。

Change the following dialogues or statements into casual speech.

1. A:　このへやのとなりに何がありますか。
   B:　お手洗(てあら)いがあります。
2. A:　つくえの下に何がいますか。
   B:　ねこがいます。
3. あそこにかいだんがありますね。かいだんの上に電話(でんわ)があります。
4. A:　そこにだれがいますか。
   B:　スミスさんがいます。
5. あ、あそこにきれいなとり (bird) がいますよ。

第(だい)四課　日本のまちと大学

Review

A. Fill in the blanks with appropriate words for buildings and places.

1. コーヒーを飲みに行く所は＿＿＿＿＿＿＿＿＿＿です。
2. 手紙(てがみ)を出しに行く所は＿＿＿＿＿＿＿＿＿＿です。
3. お金がたくさんある所は＿＿＿＿＿＿＿＿＿＿です。
4. 日本のえきのちかくにある小さいたてものは＿＿＿＿＿＿です。
5. 本やざっしを買う所は＿＿＿＿＿＿＿＿＿＿です。
6. 本やざっしや新聞(しんぶん)がたくさんある大きいたてものは＿＿＿＿＿＿＿＿＿＿です。

B. Define the following words in Japanese, using the types of descriptive phrases that were used in Exercise A.

Example

きっさてん：きっさてんはコーヒーを飲みに行く所です。

1. こうえん：＿＿＿＿＿＿＿＿＿＿＿＿＿＿＿＿
2. デパート：＿＿＿＿＿＿＿＿＿＿＿＿＿＿＿＿
3. えき：＿＿＿＿＿＿＿＿＿＿＿＿＿＿＿＿
4. 体育館(たいいくかん)：＿＿＿＿＿＿＿＿＿＿＿＿＿＿＿＿
5. 食堂(しょくどう)：＿＿＿＿＿＿＿＿＿＿＿＿＿＿＿＿
6. きょうしつ：＿＿＿＿＿＿＿＿＿＿＿＿＿＿＿＿
7. 学生会館(かいかん)：＿＿＿＿＿＿＿＿＿＿＿＿＿＿＿＿

C. Work with a partner. Think of kinds of food or other items found in schools or houses that can be described in terms of their type, color, shape, or size. Your partner will ask questions about the type, color, shapes, etc., and will try to deduce what you are thinking about. Try to use the words in the box.

あかい	きいろい	あおい	ちゃいろい	しろい	くろい	みどりの
大きい	小さい	まるい	しかくい	ながい	ほそながい	

Example

A: それは食べ物(もの)ですか。
B: ええ、そうです。
A: それはみどりですか。
B: いいえ、そうじゃないです。
A: じゃあ、あかいですか。
B: ええ、あかいです。
A: 大きいですか。
B: いいえ、大きくありません。
A: トマトですか。
B: はい、そうです。

D. Work as a class. Ask at least three of your classmates where they live. Fill in the following table.

Example

A: ～さんはどんな所に住んでいますか。
B: 私はアパートに住んでいます。
A: そうですか。私もアパートに住んでいます。
B: ああ、そうですか。～さんのアパートはどんな所にありますか。
A: そうですね。私のアパートはこうえんのちかくにあります。
B: そうですか。いいですね。
A: ～さんのアパートの近くにはどんなものがありますか。
B: がっこうがあります。

なまえ	住んでいる所 アパート、うち、りょう	ちかくにあるもの

E. Work as a class. See what you can find out about the characteristics of the places where your classmates are living.

Example

A: ～さんのアパートはどうですか。
B: そうですね。やすいですが、あまりきれいじゃありませんね。
～さんのアパートはどうですか。

Casual speech: Omitting particles は, を, and に; Using the plain forms of adjectives and the copula verb

Particles such as は (topic), を (direct object), and に (direction when used with いく and くる) are often omitted in casual speech, and sentences end with the plain form. The copula verb です is usually omitted in questions, with a rising intonation used instead. In male speech, です is replaced by だ. In female speech, the particle わ often follows a plain form. The particle わ is primarily used by females, and indicates they are making a statement or expressing a feeling or opinion. It can be used together with the particles ね and よ, as in ～わね and ～わよ. The examples below are cases where the topic marker は has been eliminated. Other particle omissions will be discussed later.

Formal	Casual	
	male	female
noun + copula statement 山田さんは学生ですよ。 山田さんは学生じゃありませんよ。 question 山田さんは学生ですか。	山田さん、学生だよ。 山田さん、学生じゃないよ。 山田さん、学生。↗	山田さん、学生よ。 山田さん、学生じゃないわよ。 山田さん、学生。↗
な -adjective + copula statement ここはしずかですね。 ここはしずかじゃありませんね。 question そこはしずかですね。	ここ、しずかだね。 ここ、しずかじゃないね。 そこ、しずか。↗	ここ、しずかね。 ここ、しずかじゃないわね。 そこ、しずか。↗
い -adjective statement それはあたらしいですね。 それはあたらしくありませんね。 question それはあたらしいですね。	それ、あたらしいね。 それ、あたらしくないね。 それ、あたらしい。↗	それ、あたらしいわね。 それ、あたらしくないわね。 それ、あたらしい。↗

A. Work with a partner. Change the following dialogues into casual speech. First, assume both A and B are male. Next, assume both of them are female.

Example

A: あのたてものはりっぱですね。
B: そうですね。
Male A: あのたてもの、りっぱだね。
Male B: そうだね。
Female A: あのたてもの、りっぱね。
Female B: そうね。

1. A: あれ、山田さんはどこですか。
   B: 山田さんですか。今ゆうびんきょくです。
   A: そうですか。ゆうびんきょくはどこですか。
   B: えきのまえに大きいビルがありますね。
   A: ええ。
   B: その中です。
   A: ああ、そうですか。
2. A: 木村(きむら)さんのへやはどうですか。
   B: とてもいいですよ。それにとてもしずかです。山田さんのはどうですか。
   A: せまいですけど、あかるくてきれいですね。
   B: そうですか。

B. Work with a partner. Role-play the following situations using casual speech.

1. You are looking for an apartment. First, fill out the types of features you want for your apartment. Your friend (partner) knows a person who wants to sublease his or her apartment. Ask your partner about the apartment.

   Number of rooms__________ Surrounding area____________

   Size of apartment __________ Types of rooms______________

   Old or new apartment___________

2. You are visiting your friend's college. Ask him or her about various facilities and their locations.

第(だい)五課　毎日の生活 1

Review

A. Work as a class. First, write the number of items you have in the chart. Then ask four classmates which and how many of the items they have with them today, and complete the chart.

Example

A: えんぴつをもっていますか。
B: ええ、もっています。
A: 何本ありますか。
A: 三本あります。

	私	________さん	________さん	________さん	________さん
えんぴつ					
ボールペン					
けしごむ					
ノート					
辞書（じしょ）					
教科書（きょうかしょ）					
かばん					
デーパック					

B. Answer the following questions.

1. 毎朝（まいあさ）何時ごろおきますか。
2. 毎日何時ごろねますか。
3. あさごはんに何を食べますか。
4. おひるごはんによく何を食べますか。
5. たいてい何時ごろじゅぎょうがおわりますか。
6. 毎日何時間ぐらいじゅぎょうがありますか。
7. 毎日何時間ぐらい日本語のべんきょうをしますか。
8. アルバイトをしますか。
9. よくおんがくを聞きますか。
10. おふろに入りますか。シャワーをあびますか。
11. 週末（しゅうまつ）何をしますか。
12. 日本語のじゅぎょうは何曜日にありますか。

C. Ask your classmates the questions in Exercise B, and find out what the most common answers are for each question.

D. Form groups of four. Find out what the members do each day of the week—what classes do they have, do they do some kind of part-time work, etc.? Who has the most classes in a single day? What do your classmates do over the weekend?

Example

A: ～さんは月曜日に何をしますか。

B: 私は九時と十時と三時にじゅぎょうがあります。

A: そうですか。大変(たいへん)ですねえ。

C: 私はじゅぎょうはありませんよ。

D: いいですね。じゃあ、月曜日には何をしますか。

C: アルバイトをします。

なまえ	月曜日	火曜日	水曜日	木曜日	金曜日	土曜日	日曜日
私							

E. Form groups of four. Write a number (between 1 and 99) without showing it to the others. The rest of the people in your group will ask questions using ～は～より大きいですか / 小さいですか。 The person who figures out the correct number wins.

Example

A: 10より大きいですか。小さいですか。

B: 大きいです。

C: じゃあ、60より大きいですか。小さいですか。

B: 小さいです。

～

D: 27ですか。

B: はい、そうです。

F. Look at the train schedule and tell when the following trains depart from Shin-Osaka and arrive at Tokyo.。

	ひかり 200	のぞみ 300	ひかり 126	こだま 404	ひかり 228	こだま 408	ひかり 032	ひかり 232	のぞみ 006	ひかり 034	ひかり 086	のぞみ 010
新大阪（しんおおさか）	6:00	6:12	6:43	9:00	9:57	10:00	10:17	10:39	10:54	11:17	11:26	11:54
京都（きょうと）	6:17	6:27	7:00	9:16	10:17	10:17	10:41	10:56	11:10	11:34	11:44	12:10
名古屋（なごや）	7:07	7:05	7:57	10:15	10:58	11:15	11:18	11:53	11:48	12:18	12:28	12:48
新横浜（しんよこはま）			9:34	12:53		13:53	12:56	13:28		13:56		
東京（とうきょう）	8:56	8:42	9:52	13:10	12:52	14:10	13:14	13:45	13:24	14:14	14:38	14:24

Example

ひかり 200 ごうは六時に大阪(おおさか)を出て、八時五十六分にとうきょうにつきます。

1. のぞみ 300
2. こだま 404
3. ひかり 126
4. のぞみ 006
5. ひかり 086
6. ひかり 232

Casual speech: Using the plain form of verbs

Casual speech utilizes the plain forms of verbs instead of the polite forms. The question marker か is omitted from questions, except for some male speech. The topic marker は and the direct object marker を are also frequently omitted. Similarly, the particle に can be omitted when it is easily inferred from the sentence, such as in the ～にいく／くる／かえる／はいる form.

	Formal	**Casual**
Sentence:	山田さんはごはんを食べます。	山田さん、ごはん、食べる。
	山田さんはごはんを食べません。	山田さん、ごはん、食べない。
Question:	山田さんごはんを食べますか。	山田さん、ごはん、食べる。↗

A. Change the following into casual speech.

Example

A: 今何をしますか。
B: <u>ごはんを食べます。</u>
A: 今、何する。
B: <u>ごはん食べる。</u>

1. A: よくおふろに入りますか。
   B: いいえ、あまり入りません。
2. A: あさごはんを食べますか。
   B: いいえ、食べません。
3. A: 何を飲みますか。
   B: コーヒーを飲みます。
4. A: 今晩(こんばん)何をしますか。
   B: そうですね。テレビを見ます。
5. A: どこに行きますか。
   B: 図書館(としょかん)に行きます。

B. Work with a partner. Role-play the following situations.
   1. You run into a friend you have not seen for a while. Greet him or her and ask what he or she is doing these days.
   2. A Japanese student who has recently arrived in your country wants to know what college life is like. Explain what college students in the United States typically do in a day.

第(だい)六課　毎日の生活２

Review

A. Circle the things you did last weekend. Then ask your partner what he or she did last weekend.

Example

A: 週末(しゅうまつ)ごはんをつくりましたか。
B: ええ、つくりました。

1. ごはんをつくる
2. せんたくをする
3. そうじをする
4. レポートを書く
5. ざっしを買う
6. うんどうをする
7. 手紙(てがみ)を書く
8. 買い物(もの)に行く
9. りょうしんに電話(でんわ)をする

B. Work with a partner. Use the chart below to interview your partner about what he or she has been doing lately and find out how stressful his or her life is.

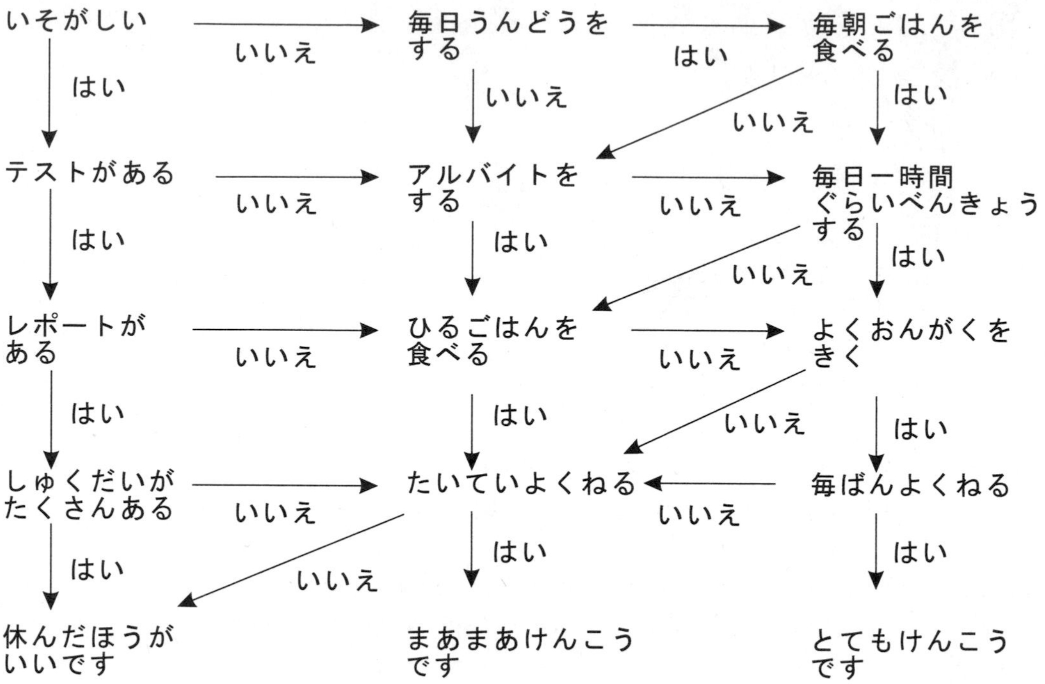

C. Work with a group of four. Make guesses about how often or how long Japanese students do the following activities in Japan, then tell your group what you have guessed. Check with your instructor to find out who made the best guess. Use plain form ～とおもいます *(I think that ～)*.

Example

A: 日本の高校生は一日に何時間ぐらいテレビを見るとおもいますか。
B: 一時間ぐらい見るとおもいます。
C: 私は二時間ぐらい見るとおもいます。
D: 三時間ぐらい見るとおもいます。

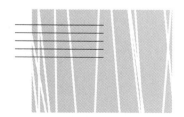

	Your guess	____さん	____さん	____さん
テレビを見る／一日／時間				
べんきょうする／一日／時間				
ねる／一日／時間				
アルバイトをする／一週間／日				
本を読む／一か月／さつ				
えいがを見る／一か月／度				

D. Work with a partner. Using the expressions given below, ask your partner about his or her childhood classes and teachers. Find out why your partner thought these classes or teachers were or were not good (interesting, difficult).

Example

A: どのじゅぎょうがおもしろかったですか。／おもしろくなかったですか。
B: アメリカのれきしのじゅぎょうがおもしろかったです。
A: どうしてですか。
A: 先生がおもしろかったからです。

			どうして
おもしろい／じゅぎょう	はい いいえ		
いい／先生	はい いいえ		
たいへん／クラス	はい いいえ		

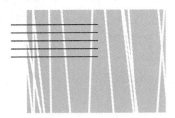

Casual speech: Omitting or not omitting particles

In casual speech, particles are often omitted if they can be understood from verbs, structures, or context. As mentioned earlier, the particles most likely to be omitted are は and を. The particle に can be omitted as well, but because it has many meanings, its omission can be confusing and thus it is not omitted as frequently as are は or を. The particle が is often omitted, especially when it does not follow a question word or the corresponding answer. In contrast, other particles such as から, まで, で, and は(contrast) are not omitted.

A. Work with a partner and change the style of the following exchanges into casual speech.

Example

九時から十時までじゅぎょうがあります。
九時から十時までじゅぎょう、ある（よ）。

1. A: 昨日(きのう)どこに行きましたか。
   B: ともだちとデパートに行きました。
2. A: テストはどうでしたか。
   B: とてもむずかしかったですよ。
3. A: だれが来ましたか。
   B: 田中さんが来ました。
4. A: えきまで何で行きますか。
   B: くるまで行きます。
5. A: 高校の時はよくうんどうをしました。
   B: 今はどうですか。
   A: 今はあまりしませんね。
6. A: あ、あそこに鈴木(すずき)さんがいますよ。
   B: そうですね。山田さんもいますね。
7. A: 病院までバスで行きましたか。
   B: いいえ、バスでは行きませんでした。

B. Work with a partner. Ask your partner about his or her most memorable trip (good or bad). Use the following questions to learn what your partner did on the trip and whether he or she enjoyed the activities. Use casual speech.

1. When, where, and with whom did you go?
2. What did you do?
3. How was the trip (why it was good/bad)?

第七課　好きなことと好きなもの

(だい)

Review

A. Work with a partner. First, write as many words as you can that belong to and/or are associated with each category. Then ask your partner what he or she has written and circle the items that both you and your partner have written down. Write down any word that your partner wrote but you did not.

Example

A:　どんなやさいのなまえを書きましたか。
B:　私はレタスとにんじんを書きました。
A:　私もレタスとにんじんを書きました。そして、トマトも書きました。

1. やさい ________________________________
2. にく ________________________________
3. くだもの ________________________________
4. 飲み物(もの) ________________________________
5. スポーツ ________________________________
6. おんがく ________________________________
7. レジャー ________________________________

B. Work as a class. Ask your classmates what kind of food and drinks they like or dislike. Determine which foods and drinks are the most and least popular in your class.

Example

A:　どんな食べ物(もの)が好きですか。
B:　〜が好きです。
A:　〜はどうですか。
B:　そうですね。〜はあまり好きじゃありません。

C. Work with a partner. Ask your partner what kind of sports or music he or she likes or dislikes and why. Use the casual style.

Example

A: どんなスポーツが好き？
B: ～が好きだよ。(male) ／～が好き。(female)
A: どうして。
B: ～だから。

D. A very rich person wants to give away a large cash prize, but only to the person who best matches his ideal. Select one person to be the donor and ask him or her about his or her favorite things, then interview your classmates, and select the person who best matches the ideal.

Example

A: ～さんはどんなスポーツが好きですか。
B: やきゅうが好きです。
A: そうですか。テニスはどうですか。
B: テニスも好きですよ。でも、へたです。
A: そうですか。じゃあ、おんがくは何が好きですか。

E. Work with a partner. Ask your partner what he or she likes best and least among items in each of the following categories and rank them.

やさい　にく　くだもの　飲み物(もの)　スポーツ　おんがく レジャー

Example

A: やさいの中で何が一番(いちばん)好きですか。
B: トマトが一番(いちばん)好きですね。
A: じゃあ、にんじんとレタスとどちらのほうが好きですか。
B: レタスのほうが好きです。

Casual speech: Casual form of ～んです

In male casual speech, ～んです becomes ～んだ, and in female casual speech it becomes の. The use of の with a rising intonation is common to both males and females when forming questions.

Example

恵子（けいこ）：　どこ、行くの。↗ (male or female)
広子（ひろこ）：　家に帰るの。(female)
まもる：家に帰るんだ。(male)

Work as a class. Ask five classmates what activities they don't like and why. Use casual speech.

Example

A: どんなことをするのがきらいなの。
B: そうじをするのがきらいなんだ。(male) ／きらいなの。(female)
A: どうしてそうじがきらいなの。
B: おもしろくないんだ。(male) ／おもしろくないの。(female)

なまえ	きらいなこと	りゆう (reason)

第八課（だい）　買物（かいもの）

Review

A. Select five classmates and fill in the table with the types of clothing and accessories they are wearing.

なまえ	ふく、アクセサリー

B. Work with a partner. First, write the appropriate counter for each of the following objects. Then your partner should write a number (not larger than 100) and call out one of the objects on the list. Say the correct number-counter expression for that number of that item. You get one point for each correct answer.

Example

Your partner writes 24 and says "Tシャツ." You say "にじゅうよんまい."

セーター	________	ベルト	________	えんぴつ	________
ビール	________	かばん	________	さかな	________
いぬ	________	本	________	ざっし	________
ノート	________	ねこ	________	パンツ	________
バナナ	________	Tシャツ	________	りんご	________

C. Work in groups of four. First, guess how much the following items might cost in Japan (in yen). Then ask the other group members for their guesses. Use the expression 〜とおもいます *(I think that 〜)*. Your instructor will provide actual prices. The person who makes the best guesses is the winner.

Example

A: たまごはいくらだとおもいますか。
B: 100円だとおもいます。〜さんはいくらだとおもいますか。
A: 200円だとおもいます。

	私			
たまご（いつつ）				
テレビ（25インチ）				
ガソリン (gas) 1リッター				
おんがくCD				
ジーンズ				

D. Work with a partner. Playing the role of 先生, make five requests to your partner, who will be the 学生. (You may create unreasonable ones, too. Be imaginative.) Your partner should write the request in English and respond accordingly. Repeat the activity using requests from a customer (きゃく) to a store clerk (てんいん). A list of verbs is provided to assist you.

行く　帰る　飲む　入る　読む　書く　聞く　買う　つくる
話す　あそぶ　うたう　およぐ　とる　出す　つつむ
あびる　おきる　食べる　ねる　見る　かける　出かける
入れる　見せる　くる

Example

先生：～さん、ちょっと。
学生：はい、何でしょうか。
先生：そこでうたをうたって下さい。
学生：それは、ちょっと。

きゃく：　あのう、すみません。
てんいん：はい、何でしょうか。
きゃく：　あのりんごを見せて下さい。

E. Work with a partner. Role-play the following situations.

1. You are at a department store. You want to know which floor houses the kimono department. Ask the person at the information desk.
2. You are at an accessory department and want to see a scarf in the case. Get the attention of a store clerk and ask him or her to take it out for you.
3. You are in a women's clothing department. You want to buy a present for your mother but cannot decide what to get. Your budget is 10,000 yen. Get the attention of a store clerk and explain what you need help with. Respond to questions about size, color preference, etc. Have the clerk show you some items.
4. A store clerk has shown you a sweater. Ask the clerk how much it is. If it is too expensive, ask for a more affordable one. Ask for ones with different colors. Ask for a bigger (or smaller) size.
5. Select the items that you want. Ask the store clerk to put them in a box and put a ribbon on the box.

Casual speech: Making a request

When you make requests to close friends, family members, or children, you don't need to use 〜て下さい. Instead, you only need to use 〜て.

Work with a partner. You are very close friends. Make requests using 〜て. Your partner will act out the situation.

Example

まもる：　その本、とって。
みち子：　はい、どうぞ。(Your partner picks up a book and hands it to you.)

第(だい)九課　レストランとしょうたい

Review

A. しつもんにこたえて下さい。

1. 「和食(わしょく)」って何ですか。
2. 和食(わしょく)にはどんな食べ物(もの)がありますか。
3. ラーメンはどこのくにの食べ物(もの)ですか。そのくにの食べ物(もの)を何といいますか。
   そのくににはほかに (other) どんな食べ物(もの)がありますか。
4. アメリカにはどんなりょうりがありますか。
5. メキシコりょうりにはどんなものがありますか。
6. アメリカにはどんな飲み物(もの)がありますか。日本にはどんな飲み物(もの)がありますか。

B. Work with a group of four. You are at a family-style restaurant. Ask each other what you would like to have and fill out the chart. Use both formal and casual speech.

A:　〜さんは何にしますか。
B:　私は〜にします。
A:　〜さん、何にする。
B:　えっと、〜にする。

なまえ	飲み物と食べ物

C. Work with a partner who was not in your group during Exercise B. You are still in the restaurant and your partner is the server. Using the information from Exercise B, order for your group.

Example

Server: ごちゅうもんは。
A: ビールを三本おねがいします。
Server: はい、ビールを三本ですね。
A: それから、〜。

D. Work as a class. Look at the event calendar below. Choose three things you would like to see or do and invite your classmates to go with you.

Example

A: 〜さん、来週の水曜日に大学のスタジアムでコンサートがあるんですが、いっしょに行きませんか。
B: 水曜日ですか。いいですね。

月曜日	ジャズコンサート（Jay's Cafe, 10 時）
火曜日	「Cats」ミュージカル（大学のコンサートホール、7 時半）
水曜日	ロックコンサート（大学のスタジアム、8 時）
木曜日	バスケットボールのゲーム（大学のスタジアム、8 時）
金曜日	クラシックのコンサート（大学のコンサートホール、8 時）
土曜日	ブックセール（まちのとしょかん、12 時） 日本のえいが（スミスホール、5時と7時）
日曜日	バザー (Bazaar)（キャンパス、1時 〜 5時）

E. Work with a partner. Role-play the following situations, inviting your partner to join you, then discover the details of what you will do with your partner. Use question wordか〜ませんか／〜ましょうか／〜ましょう.

Example

You are with your partner and you are thirsty.

A: 〜さん、何か飲みませんか。

B: ええ、いいですよ。じゃあ、きっさてんに入りましょうか。

A: ああ、いいですね。あそこのきっさてんはどうですか。

B: いいですね。あそこにしましょう。

1. You and your friend are walking on the street. You feel hungry.
2. You are free this weekend and want to go somewhere for fun.
3. You are at your friend's house. You think you would like to see a movie. Check the newspaper to see what is playing, and discuss which movie you would like to see and when with your partner.

Casual speech: Extending an invitation

The casual version of an invitation expressed by 〜ませんか is 〜ない, used with a rising intonation. The plain volitional form 〜う／〜よう is used instead of 〜ましょう. The formation of the plain volitional form will be discussed in Chapter 2.

Work with a partner. Role-play the situations in Exercise E in casual style. Ask your instructor for the plain volitional form of the verbs you need. (For example,「行きましょう」の plain form は何ですか。)

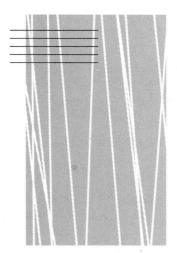

第十課　私の家族

(だい)

Review

A. Look at the following figures. You are クリス. Identify each person using an appropriate kinship term and ordinal number.

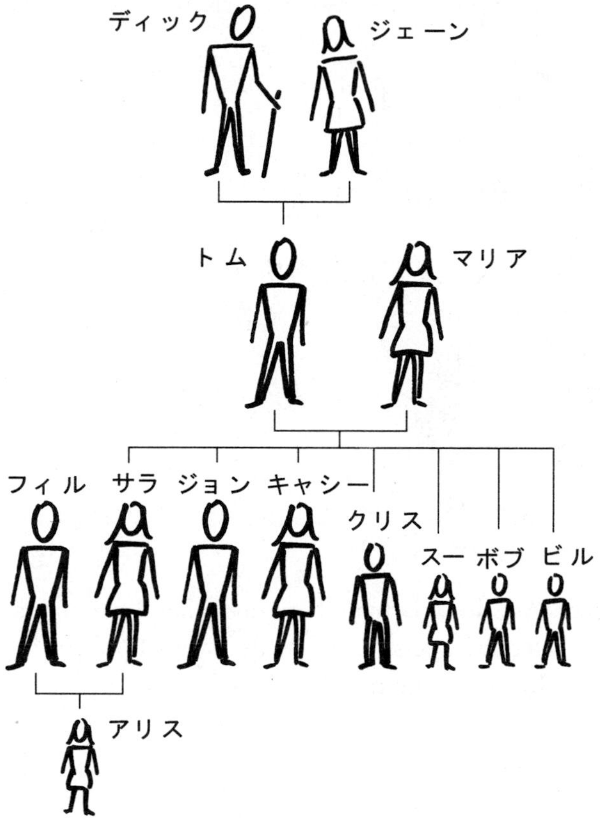

Example

キャシーは私の姉です。上から二番目(ばんめ)の兄弟です。

B. しつもんにこたえて下さい。

1. ～さんのクラスには学生が何人いますか。
2. ～さんの大学には学生が何人ぐらいいますか。先生は何人ぐらいいますか。
3. 日本語の学生は何人いますか。

4. このクラスで一番年(いちばんとし) (age) が上の人は何さいですか。一番(いちばん)年(とし) (age) が下の人は何さいですか。

5. 〜さんは兄弟がいますか。〜さんの家族は何人家族ですか。

6. 〜さんは何さいですか。〜さんは上から何番目(ばんめ)ですか。下から何番目(ばんめ)ですか。

C. Work with a partner. Ask your partner about his or her family members (their physical characteristics, occupations, residence, etc.). Use 〜ている and 〜は〜が .

Example

A: 〜さんのご家族は何人家族ですか。
B: 五人です。
A: そうですか。お父さんはどんな方ですか。
B: そうですね。父は目が大きくて、せが高いです。
A: めがねをかけていますか。
B: ええ、かけています。
A: どんなしごとをしていますか。
B: 大学の先生です。
A: どこに住んでいますか。
B: ロサンゼルスに住んでいます。

D. Work with a new partner. Ask your partner about his or her dream partner in terms of physical characteristics, personality, skills, occupation, etc. Take notes. Use 〜ている, 〜は〜が, and the て-form of verbs.

Example

A: 〜さんはどんな人が好きですか。
B: そうですね。せが高くて、やせている人が好きです。
A: そうですか。かおはどんなかおがいいですか。
B: 目が大きくて、はなが高い人がいいです。
A: じゃあ、せいかく (personality) はどうですか。
B: そうですね。あかるくて、やさしい人がいいですね。
A: どんなことが出来る人がいいですか。
B: うたをうたうのが上手な人がいいですね。

E. Work in groups of three. Describe what type of person your partner in Exercise D liked and choose the best match for him or her from this group.

Example

A: 〜さんはせが高くて、やせていて、目が大きい人が好きです。せいかくはあかるくてやさしい人が好きです。それから、うたをうたうのが上手な人がいいんです。

B: じゃあ、〜さんはどうでしょうか。

A: でも、〜さんより〜さんのほうがせが高いです。

B: そうですね。じゃ、〜さんがいいですね。

Casual speech: Using the contracted form of 〜ている

In casual speech, 〜ている is often shortened to 〜てる.

A. Restate the following exchanges in casual speech, using this type of contraction.

Example

A: あの人はいつもきれいなふくをきていますね。
B: あの人はモデルですよ。

A: あの人、いつもきれいなふくきてるね。
B: あの人モデルだよ。(male) ／ B: あの人モデルよ。(female)

1. A: お父さんはどこに住んでいるんですか。
   B: ニューヨークに住んでいますよ。
2. A: あの人はとてもやせていますね。
   B: ええ、それにとても足がながいですね。
3. A: 田中さんはどの人ですか。
   B: めがねをかけている人ですよ。
4. A: あそこでスミスさんと話している人はだれですか。
   B: ああ、あれは私の妹です。

B. Work with a partner. Your partner will select a celebrity. Quiz your partner about physical characteristics, residence, clothing, and so on to figure out who the celebrity is. Use casual speech.

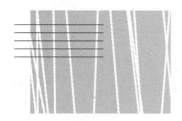

Example

A: その人、かみながい？
B: いいえ、ぜんぜん。
A: じゃあ、何をするのが上手。
B: バスケットボール。
A: どこに住んでるの。
B: シカゴに住んでるよ。
A: マイケルジョーダン？
B: うん、そう。

第(だい)十一課　思(おも)い出

Review

A. しつもんにこたえて下さい。

1. なつ休みは何月何日から何月何日までありますか。冬休(ふゆや)みはどうですか。春休(はるや)みは。
2. 今学期(こんがっき)は何月何日にはじまって、何月何日におわりますか。来学期(らいがっき)はどうですか。
3. 今日(きょう)は何月何日ですか。昨日(きのう)は何月何日でしたか。おとといは何月何日でしたか。
4. 明日(あした)は何月何日ですか。あさっては何月何日ですか。
5. お母さんの誕生日(たんじょうび)は何月何日ですか。
6. 一か月まえは何月何日でしたか。半年まえは何月何日でしたか。
7. 一学期(がっき)は何か月ありますか。夏休(なつや)みは何か月ありますか。

B. Work as a class. First, check off the experiences you have had in the past, and write your approximate age at the time you experienced them. Then ask your classmates whether they have had these experiences. If so, ask when.

Example

A: こうつうじこにあったことがありますか。
B: ええ、あります。
A: そうですか。いつでしたか。
B: 高校三年の時です。／二か月まえです。

	私	いつ	________さん	いつ
こうつうじこにあう				
つりをする				
きものをきる				
たばこをすう				
うみにおよぎに行く				
日本に行く				
日本のえいがを見る				
高い山にのぼる				
和食(わしょく)を食べる				

C. Work in groups of three. One member should choose a place from the box below, and define it using the 〜たり〜たりする form. The other members should try to figure out which place was selected. The person who correctly guesses gets a point. Take turns.

高校　こうえん　きっさてん　ゆうえんち　銀行(ぎんこう)
はくぶつかん　どうぶつえん　スーパー　デパート
体育館(たいいくかん)　図書館(としょかん)　教会(きょうかい)　山　川　病院　ゆうびんきょく
えき　レストラン　食堂(しょくどう)

Example

A: ともだちとべんきょうしたり、あそんだりするところです。
B: としょかんですか。
A: いいえ。

D. Work with a partner. Ask your partner what he or she did or didn't do as a child, and why, using the 〜んです and 〜からです forms.

Example

A: 子どもの時どんなものをよく食べましたか。
B: アイスクリームをよく食べました。
A: どうしてアイスクリームをよく食べたんですか。
B: とてもおいしかったんです。／おいしかったからです。

	________さん	どうして
子どもの時よく食べたもの		
子どもの時あまり食べなかったもの		
子どもの時よくしたこと		
子どもの時あまりしなかったこと		
子どもの時よくあそんだ人		

E. Work with another partner. Report what your partner in Exercise D did or didn't do, using the plain form + そうです (hearsay). Also, use noun modification.

Example

～さんが子どもの時よく食べたものはアイスクリームだそうです。
アイスクリームはやすくておいしかったから、よく食べたんだそうです。

Casual speech: Using the sentence final particle わ with verbs

On page 12, the particle わ is used with adjectives and copula verbs, but it can also be used with other types of verbs as well.

Change B's speech in the following exchanges into female speech.

Example

まもる：　高校の時、よくあそんだの。
ジョン：　うん、あそんだよ。(male)
スー：　ええ、あそんだわよ。(female)

1. A: どうしてつりに行かなかったの。
   B: さむかったんだ。
2. A: たばこすったことある。
   B: ないよ。でも、おさけは飲んだことあるよ。
3. A: 昨日(きのう)は何してたの。
   B: テレビを見たり、本を読んだりしていたんだ。

4. B: 山本（やまもと）さん高校の時、ふじ山（さん）にのぼったことがあるそうだよ。
   A: へえ、木村（きむら）さんは。
   B: ぼくはのぼったことはないんだ。
5. A: あの、スミスさんの誕生日（たんじょうび）はいつ。
   B: 三月五日だよ。何かするの。
   A: パーティするんだ。
   B: それはいいアイデアだね。

第（だい）十二課　健康（けんこう）

Review

A. Describe the symptoms associated with the following physical conditions.

Example

ちゅうじえん (ear infection)

耳がいたくて、気分（きぶん）がわるいです。

1. かぜ
2. かふんしょう (hay fever)
3. ヘルニア (hernia)
4. 食中毒（しょくちゅうどく） (food poisoning)
5. かろう (stress, excessive fatigue)

B. Work with a partner. You are afflicted with one of the health problems listed in the box below, and thus cannot do certain things. Describe what you cannot do, using the て-form and the potential form. Then, ask your partner for suggestions.

Example

A: どうしたんですか。
B: のどがいたくて、みずが飲めないんです。どうしたらいいでしょうか。
A: のどにくすりをつけたらどうですか。

ゆびをきる	足にひどいけがをする
つかれている	はがいたい
からだがかゆい	おなかがいたい
アレルギーがある	こしがいたい
体がよわい	ねつがある

C. Work as a class. First, list three things you would like to do but cannot, and the reasons you cannot do them. Explain your situation to your classmates, and ask for their suggestions. Use casual speech.

Example

A: 旅行(りょこう)に行きたいけど、行けないんだ。
B: どうして。
A: お金がぜんぜんないんだよ。(male) ／お金がぜんぜんないのよ。(female) どうしたらいい？
B: じゃ、アルバイトをしたらどう。

したいけど、出来ないこと	どうして	したらいいこと

D. Work with a partner. Each of you should write a place name on a piece of paper, then put the paper face down. One person asks whether he or she can do certain things at the place his or her partner has written down and tries to guess what the place is on the basis of the answers. If he or she can figure out the place correctly in three tries or fewer, he or she is the winner. Questions must be はい / いいえ questions.

Example

A: ここで本を読んでもいいですか。

B: はい。

A: じゃあ、エアロビクスをしてもいいですか。

B: はい。

A: バスケットボールをしてもいいですか。

B: はい。

A: 体育館(たいいくかん)ですか。

B: はい、そうです。

E. Role-play the following situations.

1. You have a high fever, feel very sick, and don't want to go to school today. Talk with your roommate, explain your physical condition, and ask him or her to turn in your Japanese homework to your teacher for you. Use casual speech.
2. You have a severe stomachache and you cannot eat anything. You also feel tired and may have a fever. Call a nurse, explain your physical symptons to the doctor and ask what you should do.
3. You are at the doctor's office. You recently had a traffic accident and broke your leg. You feel that because the pain is almost gone, you want to participate in sports. Explain your physical condition to the doctor and ask whether you can participate in sports.
4. You want to do something for a friend who helped you when you were hospitalized. Ask another friend who knows him or her very well about what he or she appears to want or want to do and make a decision.

Kanji Review for Volume 1

A. Read the following words.

山田　川口　木の上　木の下　一か月　来月　今月　日本語

病院の中　学生　大学院　日本人　二人　何本　一万円

千人　九月　月曜日　火曜日　八年間　先週　男の子　下さい

目が大きい　手が小さい　耳がいたい　元気　休み　家族

兄弟　十分　四時半　水曜日　薬を飲む　入院　毎年　今年

一日に三度　住所　来週　足がつかれる　体が大きい　今日

住んでいる所　家に帰る　百円　七月　新聞(しんぶん)を読む

銀(ぎん)行に行く　土曜日に学校に来る　おんがくを聞く

好きなもの　母　食堂(どう)で食べる　テレビを見る　電話で話す

手紙(がみ)を書く　本を五さつ買う　会社(しゃ)を出る　六回　毎週

今度　何分ですか　姉と妹　私の父　高い薬　高校の時

女の子に会う　金曜日にしゅくだいを出す

B. Circle the かんじ that does not belong in the group.

1.	山	川	木	水	上	6.	行	出	読	来	帰
2.	五	八	円	千	百	7.	休	手	目	足	耳
3.	父	男	弟	母	妹	8.	上	金	月	土	火
4.	曜	週	年	分	何	9.	入	住	度	聞	書
5.	買	体	話	食	見						

C. How are the かんじ in each pair different?

1.	体	休	6.	上	土
2.	男	田	7.	三	川
3.	読	話	8.	姉	妹
4.	耳	目	9.	母	毎
5.	入	八	10.	回	ロ

単語 (ESSENTIAL VOCABULARY)

Final sentence particles

わ　female speech marker
の　explanation and emotional emphasis marker used by females and children (casual)

Interjections

いや　no (casual)
うん　yes (casual)
ううん　no (casual)

CHAPTER 1

第一課

FINAL
3 dialogues
Family, health, weather
Grammar + Vocab
Ch. 1 + 10-12
Reading - All chps.
Writing ch. 1

Umbrellas are everywhere during the rainy season.

天気(てんき)と気候(きこう)

Weather and Climate

Functions	Describing the weather
New Vocabulary	Weather forecasts; Climate; Air temperature; Compass directions
Dialogue	寒(さむ)いですね。(It's cold.)
Culture	Japan's climate
Language	I. Expressing ongoing actions and repeated actions, using the て-form of verbs + いる; Describing the characteristics of places, objects, and time, using ～は～が
	II. Expressing manner of action or outcome of changes, using the adverbial forms of adjectives and noun + に
	III. Making inferences based on direct observations, using the stem of verbs or adjectives + そうだ
	IV. Expressing uncertainty, using ～でしょう, ～かもしれない, and ～かしら／かな
	V. Expressing reasons, using the plain form + ので
Kanji	Component shapes of **kanji** 1: Introduction
Reading	Getting used to vertical writing
Listening	Understanding the organization of prepared speech
Communication	Expressing agreement and solidarity using ね and も

新(あたら)しい言葉(ことば)

天気予報(てんきよほう) (Weather forecasts)

晴(はれ) sunny 

くもり cloudy 

雨(あめ) rain, rainy 

雪(ゆき) snow, snowy 

晴(はれ)のちくもり sunny and then cloudy 

くもり時々雨(ときどきあめ) cloudy with occasional rain 

くもる to become cloudy

晴(は)れる to become sunny

雨(あめ)がふる to rain

雪(ゆき)がふる to snow

A. 下のひょう (chart) のえのよこに天気(てんき)を書いて下さい。(Write the appropriate weather forecast next to the symbols in the following chart.)

B. しつもんに日本語でこたえて下さい。

1. 今日(きょう)のお天気(てんき)はどうですか。
2. 昨日(きのう)のお天気(てんき)はどうでしたか。
3. 先週の週末(しゅうまつ)はよく晴(は)れていましたか。

気候(きこう) (Climate)

気候(きこう)がいい　the climate is nice

気候(きこう)がわるい　the climate is bad

雨が多(おお)い　a lot of rain, it rains a lot

雨が少(すく)ない　not much rain, it doesn't rain much

風(かぜ)が強(つよ)い　the wind is strong

風(かぜ)が弱(よわ)い　the wind is weak

風(かぜ)がつめたい　the wind is cold

風(かぜ)がふく　the wind blows

台風(たいふう)が来る　a typhoon is coming, will come

気温(きおん)が下(さ)がる　the air temperature falls

気温(きおん)が上(あ)がる　the air temperature rises

むし暑(あつ)い　humid

木(こ)のはがあかくなる　leaves turn red

はながさく　a flower blooms

そらがあおい　the sky is blue

下の言葉(ことば)を おぼえていますか。(Do you remember these words?)

～月(がつ)　季節(きせつ)　暑(あつ)い　寒(さむ)い　涼(すず)しい　暖(あたた)かい　春(はる)　夏(なつ)　秋(あき)　冬(ふゆ)

While 寒(さむ)い and つめたい both mean *cold*, 寒(さむ)い refers to the air temperature being low (e.g., 今日は寒(さむ)い). The word つめたい, on the other hand, refers to something being cold to the touch (e.g., 水がつめたい).

C. Complete the following chart by writing expressions that describe each of the four seasons in your area.

春(はる)	
夏(なつ)	
秋(あき)	
冬(ふゆ)	

D. しつもんに日本語でこたえて下さい。

Note that when the word あなた is used in the following questions, it refers to a second person, *you*. This word is often used in surveys when the identity of the second person is indefinite or is not specific. If you are referring to a specific person, use his or her personal name. The usage of あなた for a specific individual is generally avoided because it can imply that the speaker is female or that there is unusual intimacy or distance in the relationship between the speaker and listener, depending on the context.

1. 今住んでいる所の気候(きこう)はどうですか。
2. よく雪(ゆき)がふりますか。雪(ゆき)は多(おお)いですか。少(すく)ないですか。
3. 今年は雨(あめ)が多(おお)いですか。少(すく)ないですか。
4. あなたが住んでいるまちは夏(なつ)、むし暑(あつ)いですか。むし暑(あつ)くないですか。
5. 秋(あき)にはどんなはながさきますか。春(はる)はどうですか。
6. 台風(たいふう)の時の天気(てんき)はどんな天気(てんき)ですか。
7. 天気(てんき)がいい日のそらはどんなそらですか。
8. あなたが住んでいるまちでは、春(はる)と秋(あき)とどちらのほうが風(かぜ)が強(つよ)いですか。
9. 何時ごろ一番気温(ばんきおん)が下(さ)がりますか。
10. 何時ごろ一番気温(ばんきおん)が上(あ)がりますか。

気温(きおん) (Air temperature)

0度	れいど	1度	いちど	2度	にど
3度	さんど	4度	よんど	5度	ごど
6度	ろくど	7度	ななど / しちど	8度	はちど
9度	きゅうど / くど	10度	じゅうど	-1度	マイナスいちど

Japan uses the Celsius scale to measure temperature. The following table shows equivalent temperatures for Celsius and Fahrenheit.

Celsius →	Fahrenheit
0°C	32°F
10°C	50°F
20°C	68°F
30°C	86°F
40°C	104°F

Fahrenheit →	Celsius
0°F	-17.7°C
20°F	-6.7°C
40°F	4.4°C
70°F	21°C
90°F	32.2°C

日本語でしつもんにこたえて下さい

1. 今何度ぐらいですか。
2. 昨日(きのう)は何度ぐらいでしたか。
3. 寒(さむ)い日は何度ぐらいですか。
4. 涼(すず)しい日は何度ぐらいですか。
5. 暑(あつ)い日は何度ぐらいですか。

方角(ほうがく) (Compass directions)

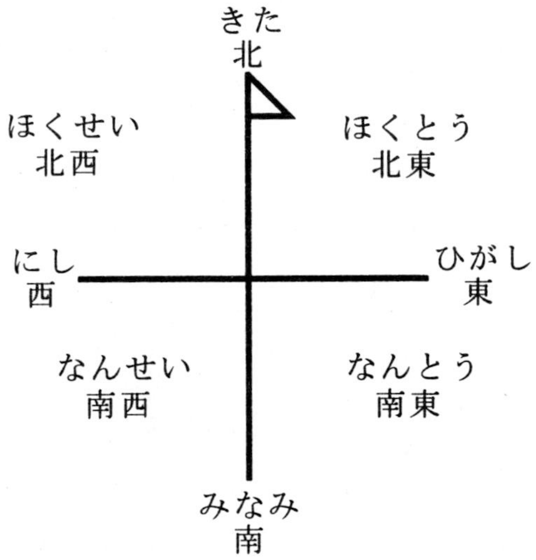

〜の方(ほう) = toward 〜　　北(きた)の方(ほう)　to the north

E. 方角(ほうがく)を書いて下さい。

1. オーストラリアは日本の__________にあります。
2. カナダはアメリカの__________にあります。
3. 日本はかんこくの__________にあります。

4. メキシコはアメリカの＿＿＿＿＿にあります。

5. フランスはスペインの＿＿＿＿＿にあって、ドイツの＿＿＿＿＿にあります。

F. 下のちず (map) を見て、しつもんにこたえて下さい。

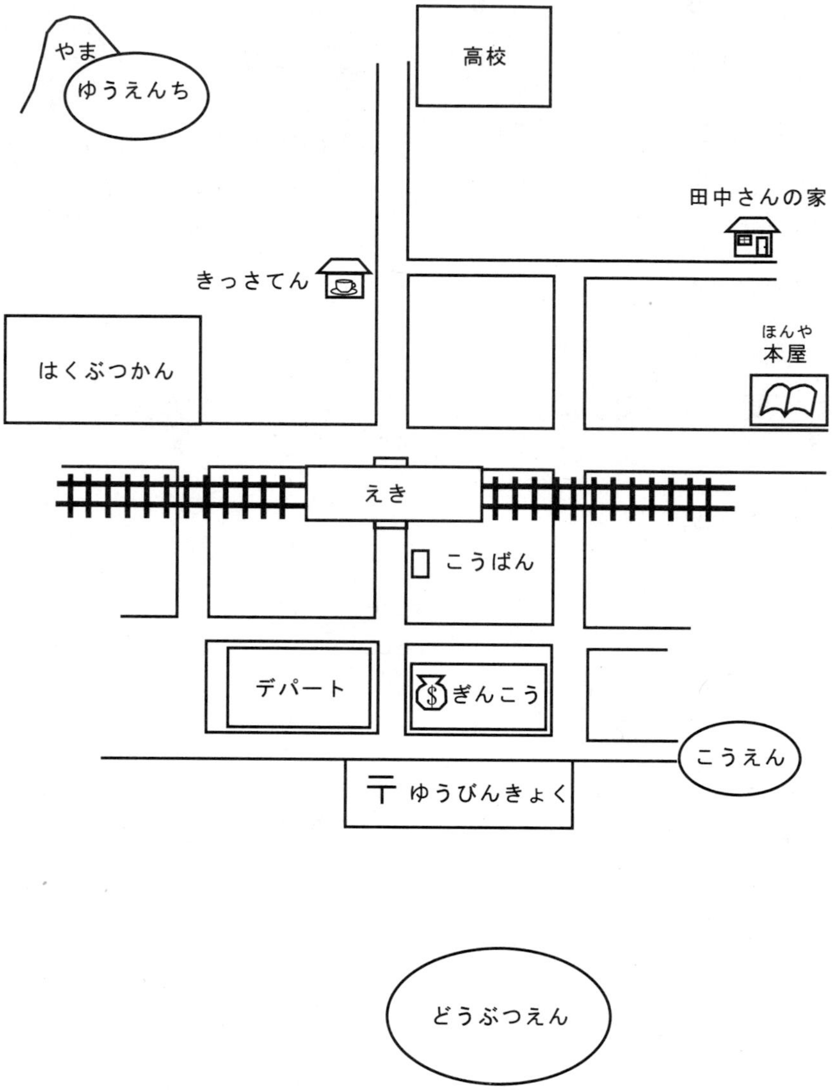

1. えきの北(きた)の方(ほう)に何がありますか。南(みなみ)の方(ほう)に何がありますか。
2. えきの東(ひがし)のほうに何がありますか。西(にし)の方(ほう)に何がありますか。
3. 山はどこにありますか。

4. こうえんはどこにありますか。
5. どうぶつえんはどこにありますか。
6. 田中さんの家はどこにありますか。

ダイアローグ

はじめる前に

日本語でしつもんにこたえて下さい。

1. 今日のお天気(てんき)はどうですか。
2. あなたのまちでは何月ごろ寒(さむ)くなりますか。
3. 冬(ふゆ)の寒(さむ)い日の気温(きおん)は何度ぐらいですか。
4. 冬(ふゆ)の暖(あたた)かい日の気温(きおん)は何度ぐらいですか。
5. あなたのまちでは何月ごろ暑(あつ)くなりますか。

STUDENT

寒(さむ)いですね。(It's cold.)

The following **manga** frames are scrambled, so they are not in the order described by the dialogue. Read the dialogue and unscramble the frames by writing the correct number in the box in the upper right corner of each frame.

道子(みちこ)さんは石田(いしだ)さんにきょうしつで会いました。

道子(みちこ)：　あ、石田(いしだ)さん。おはよう。
石田(いしだ)：　あ。道子(みちこ)さん。今日(きょう)は風(かぜ)がつめたいね。
道子(みちこ)：　ええ、今日(きょう)はちょっと寒(さむ)いわ。
石田(いしだ)：　今晩(こんばん)は雪(ゆき)がふるかもしれないよ。
道子(みちこ)：　そうね。くもってるから、ふるかもしれないわね。
石田(いしだ)：　でも、まだ十一月だよ。
道子(みちこ)：　そうね。今年は冬(ふゆ)がはやく来そうね。ざんねんだけど。
石田(いしだ)：　いやだなあ。寒(さむ)いのは。

先生がきょうしつにいらっしゃいました。(The professor comes into the classroom.)

道子(みちこ)：　あ、先生。おはようございます。
先生：　あ、鈴木(すずき)さん、石田(いしだ)くん。おはよう。寒(さむ)いね。
石田(いしだ)：　本当(ほんとう)に寒(さむ)いですね。気温(きおん)が下(さ)がっていますから、雪(ゆき)がふるかもしれませんね。
先生：　でも、天気予報(てんきよほう)によると雪(ゆき)はふらないそうだよ。

道子(みちこ)さんはまどのそとを見ました。雪(ゆき)がふっています。

道子(みちこ)：　あら、雪(ゆき)がふっているわよ。
石田(いしだ)：　あ。本当(ほんとう)だ。今日(きょう)は寒(さむ)くなりそうだね。

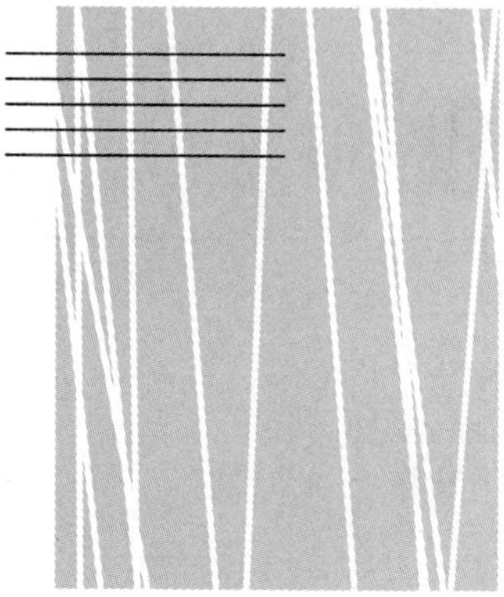

分かりましたか

A. 日本語でしつもんにこたえて下さい。

1. 今、何月ですか。時間はいつごろですか。
2. 今どんな天気(てんき)ですか。
3. 天気予報(てんきよほう)によると今日(きょう)の天気(てんき)はどうですか。
4. 石田(いしだ)さんは冬(ふゆ)が好きでしょうか。

B. Rewrite the above dialogue by changing the Ishida and/or Michiko roles to the following:

1. Michiko becomes Ishida-san's male friend, Katoo Michio.
2. Ishida-san becomes Katoo Michio's female friend, Ishida Noriko.
3. Michiko becomes Katoo Michio, and Ishida is Ishida Noriko.

日本の文化

Japan's climate. How is the climate in your area? How does the climate vary in your country?

Japan lies in the temperate zone and has four distinct seasons. Since the country extends so far from north to south, its climate ranges from subarctic to subtropical. The northernmost island—ほっかいどう—has short springs and summers and is cool with little rain throughout the year. Winters are severe there, with snow, from November through April. On the other hand, the southern islands—おきなわ and いしがきじま—are known for high temperatures and rain throughout the year.

Southeast winds blow across Japan from the Pacific Ocean in the summer, bringing humidity to the Pacific side of the country (たいへいようがわ). In contrast, northwest winds blow across from the Asian continent in the winter. Winters are generally sunny and dry on the Pacific side of Japan, while the Japan Sea side (日本海側(かいがわ)) receives a large amount of snow. There is a period of predominantly rainy weather between spring and summer known as 梅雨(つゆ). It usually begins in June and continues for about a month in all parts of Japan except ほっかいどう. Typhoons (台風(たいふう)) occur most frequently from August through October. They form in the Pacific tropics and move northward.

LANGUAGE

I. Expressing ongoing actions and repeated actions, using the て-form of verbs + いる; Describing the characteristics of places, objects, and time, using ～は～が

A. Ongoing actions

Subject			
Noun	Particle	Verb (て-form) + いる	
風（かぜ）	が	ふいて	いる。

The wind is blowing.

かおり： 何、しているの。
What are you doing?

まさお： しゅくだい、してるんだ。
I'm doing homework.

健一（けんいち）： 行ってきます。
See you later.

お母さん： 強（つよ）い風（かぜ）がふいているから、気をつけてね。
Watch out for the wind; it's blowing hard.

雨（あめ）がふっているんですが、かさがないんですよ。
It's raining, but I don't have an umbrella.

- The verb て-form +いる introduced in Volume 1, Chapter 9, indicates resultant state. This chapter introduces ている to express an ongoing action.

- The verb て-form +いる expresses an ongoing action when used with many action verbs. However, if the verb indicates an instantaneous change of state or transfer (e.g., 行く、けっこんする), then the verb て-form + いる will express a resultant state.

石田（いしだ）さんはおすしを<u>食べている</u>。	Ishida-san <u>is eating</u> sushi. (ongoing action)
石田（いしだ）さんは日本語を<u>話している</u>。	Ishida-san <u>is speaking</u> Japanese. (ongoing action)
鈴木（すずき）さんは<u>けっこんしている</u>。	Suzuki-san is married. (resultant state)

アリスさんは日本に行っている。 Alice has gone to Japan, and she is there. (resultant state)

石田(いしだ)さんはここに来ている。 Ishida-san has come here and is here now. (resultant state)

- The verb て-form + いる is often contracted to the verb て-form + る in conversation (in both formal and casual styles).

ごはんを食べて~~い~~る。 → ごはんを食べてる。
しゅくだいをして~~い~~ます。 → しゅくだいをしてます。
何、して~~い~~るの。 → 何、してるの。

A-1. Repeated actions

Subject		Time	Object		
Noun	Particle		Noun	Particle	Verb て + いる
私	は	毎日	日本語	を	べんきょうしています。

I study Japanese every day.

毎週土曜日にテニスをしています。
I play tennis every Saturday.

けんいち： ブラウンさんはよくサングラスかけてるけど、どうして。
Brown-san often wears sunglasses. Why?

道子(みちこ)： 目が弱(よわ)いからよ。
Because she has weak eyes.

- The use of the verb て-form + いる with many verbs, action verbs, or change-of-state verbs expresses habitual action.

石田(いしだ)さんは毎日おすしを食べている。 Ishida-san eats sushi every day.

アリスさんは時々(ときどき)バスで学校に行っている。 Alice-san sometimes goes to school by bus.

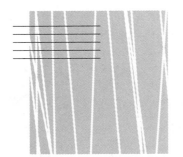

B. Describing the characteristics of places, objects, and time, using ～は～が

Topic		Comment		
Noun	Particle	Noun	Particle	Adjective
東京(とうきょう)	は	人	が	多(おお)い。

Tokyo has a lot of people.

山下： 今日(きょう)は風(かぜ)が強(つよ)いですね。
Today is windy, isn't it?
川口： そうですね。
Sure is.

日本の秋(あき)は木(こ)のはがきれいです。
Japan has pretty leaves in the autumn.

ハワイは気候(きこう)がよくていいね。
I like Hawaii because it has a nice climate.

ここは冬(ふゆ)が寒(さむ)くて大変(たいへん)だ。
We have cold winters here, and that's hard to take.

- In addition to describing a person's physical appearance (Volume 1, Chapter 10) and physical conditions (Volume 1, Chapter 11), ～は～が is also used to describe other characteristics or to express comments on things or concepts.

今年は雨(あめ)が少(すく)ない。	We have had little rain this year.
春(はる)ははながきれいだ。	Flowers are pretty in spring.
冬(ふゆ)は水がつめたい。	Water is cold in winter.
東京(とうきょう)はものが高い。	Things are expensive in Tokyo.
まどは南(みなみ)の方(ほう)がいい。	South (side) is good for a window.

- The particle は tells us what the rest of the sentence is going to be about. You can interpret ～は as *as for* ～ .

中華料理(ちゅうかりょうり)はラーメンがおいしい。	Noodles are among the best Chinese food.
田中さんは足がながい。	Tanaka-san has long legs.
川はミシシッピー川が一番(ばん)ひろい。	The Mississippi is the widest of the rivers.
この大学はけいざい学部(がくぶ)がゆうめいだ。	This university is famous for its School of Economics.

話してみましょう

A. Make a sentence using the verb て-form + いる with the following expressions. Then tell whether the sentence indicates an ongoing action or a resultant state.

Example

ごはんを食べる
ごはんを食べています。 Ongoing action

1. 雪(ゆき)がふる
2. そらがくもる
3. はながさく
4. 本を読む
5. 家に帰る
6. 木(こ)のはがあかくなる
7. 手紙(てがみ)を書く
8. 気温(きおん)が下(さ)がる。

B. Work as pairs. Describe what is going on in each of the following pictures and compare the similarities and differences among them.

Example

A: ３のえではなはさいていますが、２のえではさいていませんね。
B: そうですね。１のえでもはなはさいていませんよ。
３のえではなはさいていますが、１と２ではさいていません。

①

②

③

C. Describe what is going on in the following picture using verb て-form +いる.

Example

よく晴(は)れています。

D. Work as a class. Ask your classmates what kind of things they have been doing recently for fun or personal improvement. Work on a separate sheet of paper, headed なまえ and さいきんよくしていること.

Example

A: さいきん (recently)、どんなことをよくしていますか。
B: テニスをよくしています。

E. しつもんにこたえて下さい。

Example

ヨーロッパはどのまちが一番(ばん)好きですか。
<u>パリが好きです。</u>

1. 〜さんの大学は何がゆうめいですか。
2. 〜さんは何が上手ですか。
3. 冬(ふゆ)はどこがおもしろいですか。
4. 大学はどこが一番大きいですか。
5. 川はどの川が一番ながいですか。
6. 先生はどんな人がいいですか。
7. 日本語は何が一番むずかしいですか。

F. The following charts use stacked bars to indicate precipitation and dots to show the average temperatures of selected cities. Describe the climate in each city, using 〜は〜が. Find similarities among the different cities.

Example

東京(とうきょう)は八月が一番暑(あつ)いです。シンガポールは雨(あめ)が多(おお)いです。

東京(とうきょう)　カイロ　シンガポール　シドニー

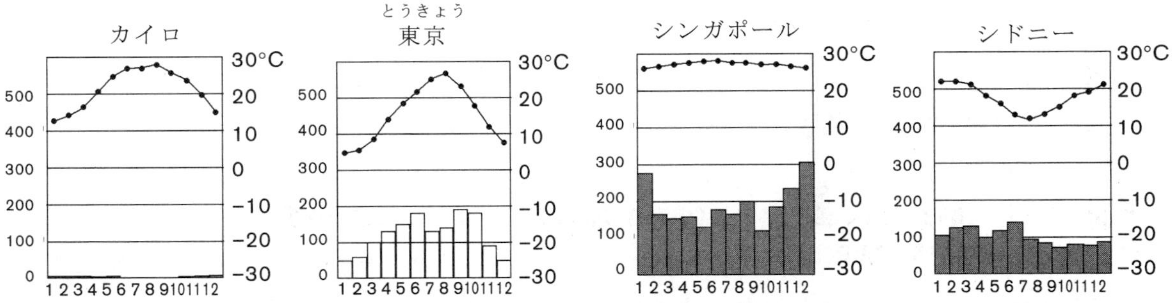

G. Work with a partner. Choose any town you would like. One person will ask the following questions about the town selected by the other and will take notes. Then write a short description about the town, using the 〜は〜が forms.

Example

A: 〜さんはどのまちが好きですか。

B: 私はメルボルンが好きです。

A: そうですか。メルボルンのどんなところがいいんですか。

B: メルボルンはこうえんがたくさんあって、とてもきれいです。

A: いいですね。気候(きこう)はどうですか。

B: そうですね。メルボルンは夏(なつ)もあまり暑(あつ)くありません。そして、冬(ふゆ)もあまり寒(さむ)くありません。でも、冬(ふゆ)は雨(あめ)が多(おお)いですね。

〜さんが好きなまちはメルボルンです。メルボルンはこうえんがたくさんあって、きれいです。気候(きこう)は夏(なつ)はあまり暑(あつ)くなくて、冬(ふゆ)も寒(さむ)くありません。でも、冬(ふゆ)は雨(あめ)が多(おお)いです。

1. 〜さんはどのまちが好きですか。
2. どうしてそのまちが好きなんですか。
3. そのまちの気候(きこう)はどうですか。
4. そのまちはどの季節(きせつ)がいいですか。どうしてですか。
5. そのまちは何がゆうめいですか。どこがおもしろいですか。

II. Expressing manner of action or outcome of changes, using the adverbial forms of adjectives and noun + に

A. Expressing manner, or how an action takes place

		い -adjective (adverbial)		
風(かぜ)	が	強(つよ)く	ふいています	よ。

The wind is blowing strong.

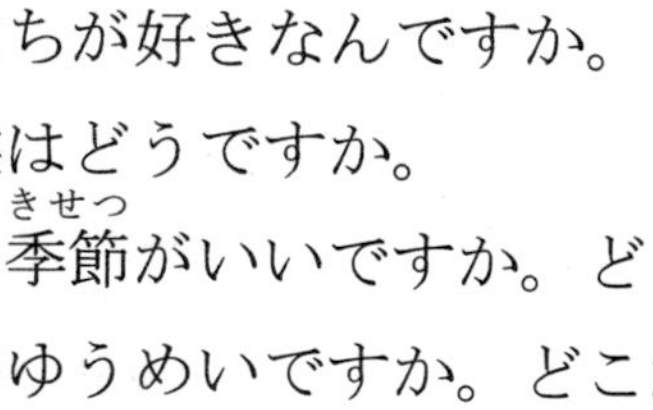

雨(あめ)がしずかにふっている。	It is raining quietly.
昨日(きのう)は風(かぜ)がやさしくふいていました。	The wind was blowing gently yesterday.

- The く -form of い -adjectives and the に -form of な -adjectives modify verbs. They are called adverbial forms.

い -adjective	Stem + く	おもしろ~~い~~	→	おもしろく
な -adjective	Stem + に	きれい~~な~~	→	きれいに

- Adverbial forms express the way certain actions take place.

しずかにあるく	to walk quietly
かんじを上手に書く	to write **kanji** skillfully (beautifully)
明(あか)るくわらう	to smile brightly (cheerfully)
はやくおきる	to get up early (or quickly)

B. Expressing the outcome of a change

B-1. Expressing a change of state, using the adverbial form of an adjective or noun に + する

な -adjective adverbial		
しずかに	して	下さい。

Please be quiet.

お母さん：	へやをきれいにして。
	Clean this room.
子供(こども)：	はい。
	Okay.
川田：	あたらしくくるまを買いました。
	I bought a car.
山下：	え、あたらしいくるまを買ったんですか。
	Really? You bought a new car?
川田：	いいえ。そうじゃありません。くるまをあたらしくしたんです。でも、ふるいくるまですよ。
	No, not really. I just bought it, but it's an older car.

B-2. Expressing outcomes, using the adverbial form or noun に + なる

		Noun	Particle			
私	は	先生	に	なりたい	ん	です。

I would like to be a teacher.

ぼく、ゆうめいになりたいんだ。	I want to be famous.
雪(ゆき)がひどくなりました。	It's started to snow hard.

- The adverbial form + なる means *to become* 〜. The verb なる can also be used with a noun +に [+ なる], as in 先生になる *(to become a teacher)*. Noun +に/the adverbial form + する means *to make something* 〜.

子供(こども)を先生にする	Parents learn from their children. (literally: [Parents] make their children into teachers.)
子供(こども)が先生になる	A child becomes a teacher.
しずかにする	to make something quiet
しずかになる	to become quiet
じゅぎょうをおもしろくする	(The teacher) makes the class interesting.
じゅぎょうがおもしろくなる	The class becomes interesting.

話してみましょう

A. しつもんにこたえて下さい。

Example

夏(なつ)は朝(あさ)何時ごろ明(あか)るくなりますか。

五時ごろ明(あか)るくなります。

1. 夏(なつ)は何時ごろ暗(くら)くなりますか。
2. 冬(ふゆ)は何時ごろ明(あか)るくなりますか。
3. 冬(ふゆ)は何時ごろ暗(くら)くなりますか。
4. 〜さんが住んでいるところは冬寒(ふゆさむ)くなりますか。何月ごろ寒(さむ)くなりますか。
5. 冬(ふゆ)は気温(きおん)が何度ぐらいになりますか。
6. 夏(なつ)は気温(きおん)が何度ぐらいになりますか。
7. 〜さんが住んでいるところはいつ 暖(あたた)かくなりますか。

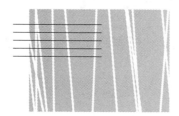

B. Work with a partner. You have met in your Japanese class when the weather was as described in 1-4 below. Greet each other and make small talk about the weather. Use both casual and formal speech.

Example

今日(きょう)は雨(あめ)が強(つよ)いです。

A: あ、こんにちは。

B: こんにちは。今日(きょう)は雨(あめ)が強(つよ)くふっていますね。／ふってるね。

A: ええ、いやですね。／ええ、いやね。(female)／うん、いやだね。(male) ひどい雨(あめ)で。

1. 今日(きょう)の風(かぜ)はつめたいです。
2. 今日(きょう)はやさしい風(かぜ)がふいていて、涼(すず)しいです。
3. 朝から、強(つよ)い風(かぜ)がふいていて、雪(ゆき)がふっています。
4. 今雪(ゆき)がふっていますが、風(かぜ)がありませんから、とてもしずかです。

C. Work with a partner. Your partner first draws a face without showing it to you, then gives you directions on how to draw an identical face. Compare the two faces when you are done. Use casual speech.

Example

A: かおを大きく、まるくかいて。
B draws a big round face.

A: そして、目を小さくかいて。はなはみじかくかいて。
B draws small eyes and a short nose.

D. A home remodeling expert is making suggestions on how to make a room more comfortable. Help him with his suggestions by completing the sentences, using the adverbial form of adjective + する or noun + にする.

Example

このスタンドは暗(くら)いですから、明(あか)るいのにしましょう。

1. おしいれがせまいから、____________________。
2. このまどは小さいですね。____________________。

3. かべ（wall）のいろがよくないから、＿＿＿＿＿＿＿＿＿。

4. このドアはちょっと大きいですね。＿＿＿＿＿＿＿＿＿。

5. このたたみはきたない (dirty) から、＿＿＿＿＿＿＿＿＿。

E. Discuss the results of the remodeling performed in Exercise D.

Example

スタンドを明(あか)るいのにしたので、へやが明(あか)るくなりました。

III. Making inferences based on direct observations, using the stem of verbs or adjectives + そうだ

		Adjective stem		
今日(きょう)	は	涼(すず)し	そうです	ね。

It looks cool today.

					Verb stem		
今日(きょう)	は	いい	お天気(てんき)	に	なり	そうです	ね。

It looks like the weather is going to be good today.

		Verb stem			
雨(あめ)	は	ふり	そうに	ありません	ね。

It doesn't look like it is going to rain.

- Conjugation of い-adjectives, な-adjectives, and verbs

Word	Affirmative stem	Affirmative	Negative stem	Negative
高い	高~~い~~＋そう	高そう	高くな~~い~~＋さ＋そう 高~~い~~＋そうじゃない	高くなさそう or 高そうじゃない
元気な	元気~~な~~＋そう	元気そう	元気じゃな~~い~~＋さ＋そう 元気＋そうじゃない	元気じゃなさそう or 元気そうじゃない
ふる	ふり~~ます~~＋そう	ふりそう	ふり~~ません~~＋そうにない	ふりそうに(も)ない

まもる：　あ、あのケーキ、おいしそう。食べてもいい。

That cakes looks delicious. Can I have some?

お姉さん：　だめよ。

No way.

今日(きょう)はあまり寒(さむ)そうじゃありませんね。

It doesn't look very cold today.

山田さん、元気がなさそうでしたよ。

Yamada-san didn't seem to have much pep.

キム：　おはよう。寒(さむ)いね。

Good morning. It's cold, isn't it?

田中：　うん、でもごごは暖(あたた)かくなりそうだね。

Yes, but it looks like it will become warm this afternoon.

キム：　そうね。もう雨(あめ)はふりそうにないわね。

I agree. It doesn't look like it's going to rain anymore.

- The verb/adjective stem + そう expresses an inference based on what the speaker has seen or felt. The degree of certainty in such statements is fairly low. In some cases, information is visual, but it can be auditory as well. It is similar to the expressions *to look (like)* or *to appear* in English. It cannot be used with adjectives of shape or color because these imply direct visual observations, not inferences.

- The affirmative form of the adjective いい with そう is よさそうだ .

天気(てんき)はよさそうだ。　The weather looks good.

- そう is a な -adjective and its prenominal form そうな can be used to describe nouns.

おいしそうなりょうり	delicious-looking cuisine
つめたそうな水	cold-looking water
よさそうなしごと	job that looks good

- Like other adverbial forms of adjectives, そうに can be used to describe manner.

おいしそうに食べる	to eat something to suggest enjoyment
元気そうにあるく	to walk energetically
かなしそうになく	to cry/weep sadly

今日はあまりさむそうじゃありませんね。

話してみましょう

A. Look at the drawings and express what appears to be taking place, using そうだ.

Example

このケーキ、おいしそうだね。(male)／おいしそうね。(female)

B. Work with a partner. Make a request using そうにする and ask your partner to act it out. If your partner is successful, he or she gets a point. Use casual speech.

Example

A: おいしそうに食べて。
Your partner pretends to eat something in a way that suggests that it tastes good.

C. Work with a partner. Choose one of the following adjectives, and act out its effect on you. Your partner should guess which adjective it is. Then he or she should ask you why you feel the way you do.

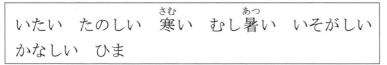

いたい	たのしい	寒(さむ)い	むし暑(あつ)い	いそがしい
かなしい	ひま			

Example

A acts out having a headache.
B: あたまがいたそうですね。
A: ええ／いいえ。
B: (If correct) どうしたんですか。
A: コンピュータのべんきょうをしているんです。

IV. Expressing uncertainty, using 〜でしょう, 〜かもしれない, and 〜かしら／かな

A. 〜でしょう／だろう, probably; I suppose

		Noun	
今日	は	くもり	でしょう。

It will probably be cloudy today.

			Adjective	
風（かぜ）	は	あまり	つめたくない	でしょう。

The wind probably isn't very cold.

			Noun	Particle	Verb	
明日（あした）	は	いい	天気（てんき）	に	なる	だろう。

The weather will probably turn nice tomorrow.

山田： 今晩（こんばん）雪（ゆき）がふるでしょうか。
Do you suppose that it will snow tonight?

川本： ええ、ふるでしょうね。
Yes, it will probably snow.

道子（みちこ）： 田中さん元気だった。
Was Tanaka-san okay?

トム: 会わなかったから、よくわからないけど、元気だろうね。
I didn't see him, so I'm not sure, but he's probably okay.

〜でしょう				
	い -adjective	な -adjective	Noun	Verb
Present affirmative	はやいでしょう	元気でしょう	学生でしょう	飲むでしょう
Present negative	はやくないでしょう	元気じゃないでしょう	学生じゃないでしょう	飲まないでしょう
Past affirmative	はやかったでしょう	元気だったでしょう	学生だったでしょう	飲んだでしょう
Past negative	はやくなかったでしょう	元気じゃなかったでしょう	学生じゃなかったでしょう	飲まなかったでしょう

- 〜でしょう indicates probability or conjecture. It can be used for both future and past events or actions. The probability expressed by 〜でしょう ranges from *probably* to *must be/must have been.*

  あしたは雨(あめ)がふるでしょう。 It will probably rain tomorrow.

- 〜でしょう is preceded by the plain form of verbs and adjectives. However, な-adjectives and nouns take the stem for the present affirmative form, as in the table above.

  いい天気でしょう。 It will probably be good weather.
  にぎやかでしょう。 It will probably be lively.

- 〜でしょうか (question form of 〜でしょう) is used to make questions more polite than those ending in 〜ですか.

すみませんが、田中先生はどこでしょうか。	Excuse me, but where might Professor Tanaka be?
すみませんが、田中先生はどこですか。	Excuse me, but where is Professor Tanaka?
今何時でしょうか。	Do you have the time? (more polite)
今何時ですか。	What time is it now?

- Also, 〜でしょう can be used with a rising intonation to ask for confirmation. This usage of 〜でしょう is rather casual and should be avoided with people of a higher social status.

  そとはむし暑(あつ)いでしょう。 It is humid outside, don't you think?
  あの人はアリスさんでしょう。 That's Alice over there, isn't it?

- The plain form of でしょう is だろう.

  あの水はつめたいだろう。 The water is probably cold.
  あの人は日本人だろう。 That person is probably Japanese.

- When 〜だろう is used in a question such as あの人は日本人だろうか, it can be interpreted as a self-directed question: *I wonder if that person is Japanese*. The polite speech version, あの人は日本人でしょうか, would be consistently interpreted as being a polite question.

- 〜でしょう is often used in weather forecasts.

  東京(とうきょう)はあしたはくもり時々(ときどき)雨(あめ)でしょう。よこはまは雨(あめ)でしょう。 It will be cloudy with occasional rain in Tokyo. It will be rainy in Yokohama.

B. 〜かもしれない, might

		Noun	
今晩(こんばん)	は	雨(あめ)	かもしれない。

It might be rainy tonight.

		Adjective	
晩(ばん)	は	むし暑(あつ)くない	かもしれない。

It might not be humid at night.

				Verb		
ごご	は	気温(きおん)	が	上(あ)がる	かもしれません	ね。

The air temperature might go up in the afternoon.

石田： 雨(あめ)がふりそうですね。
It looks like rain.

リー： そうですね。西(にし)のそらがくもっていますから、ふるかもしれませんね。
Yes, it does. The sky in the west is cloudy, so it might rain.

スミス： あの人は山田先生でしょうか。
Is that person (perhaps) Professor Yamada?

本田: さあ、どうでしょうね。Tシャツをきているから、学生かもしれませんよ。
Well, I'm not sure. He's wearing a t-shirt, so he may be a student.

〜かもしれない				
	い-adjective	な-adjective	Noun	Verb
Present affirmative	暑(あつ)いかもしれない	しずかかもしれない	学生かもしれない	いるかもしれない
Present negative	暑(あつ)くないかもしれない	しずかじゃないかもしれない	学生じゃないかもしれない	いないかもしれない
Past affirmative	暑(あつ)かったかもしれない	しずかだったかもしれない	学生だったかもしれない	いたかもしれない
Past negative	暑(あつ)くなかったかもしれない	しずかじゃなかったかもしれない	学生じゃなかったかもしれない	いなかったかもしれない

- 〜かもしれない also indicates probability or conjecture and can be used for both future and past events or actions. The probability expressed by かもしれない is about 50% or lower.
- The adjective and verb forms preceeding 〜かもしれない are the same as those for 〜でしょう.

C. 〜かな／かしら, I wonder 〜 (casual speech)

Noun	
台風(たいふう)	かな。／かしら。(female)

I wonder if it's a typhoon.

		Adjective	
そと	は	寒(さむ)い	かな。／かしら。(female)

I wonder if it's cold outside.

				Verb	
明日(あした)	は	気温(きおん)	が	下(さ)がる	かな。／かしら。(female)

I wonder if the temperature will go down tomorrow.

アリス：　今日(きょう)も雨(あめ)かしら。
I wonder if it will rain today, too.

けんいち：　ううん。今日(きょう)はふらないよ。
No, it won't.

道子(みちこ)：　これは石田さんのかな。リーさんのかな。
I wonder if this is Ishida-san's or Lee-san's.

かずお：　さあ、よく分からないけど。イニシャルがT.I. だから、石田さんのかもしれないね。
Well, I don't know, but it might be Ishida-san's because the initials are T. I.

石田：　アリスさんは来るかな。
I wonder if Alice is coming.

山下：　さあ、どうかしら。
Well, I wonder that, too.

～かな／かしら				
	い -adjective	な -adjective	Noun	Verb
Present affirmative	いいかな／かしら	ひまかな／かしら	学生かな／かしら	ふくかな／かしら
Present negative	よくないかな／かしら	ひまじゃないかな／かしら	学生じゃないかな／かしら	ふかないかな／かしら
Past affirmative	よかったかな／かしら	ひまだったかな／かしら	学生だったかな／かしら	ふいたかな／かしら
Past negative	よくなかったかな／かしら	ひまじゃなかったかな／かしら	学生じゃなかったかな／かしら	ふかなかったかな／かしら

- The expressions ～かな and ～かしら are used when the speaker is asking himself or herself about something. Since they express the speaker's monologue question, *I wonder* ～, they cannot be used for a third party, as in *he or she wonders* ～. Also, they indicate present tense and cannot be used to report events from the past, such as *I wondered* ～ or *he or she wondered* ～.
- The form of the adjective or verb that precedes ～かな and ～かしら is the same as that used with ～でしょう and ～かもしれない.
- The expression ～かな can be used by both males and females, but ～かしら is used only by females.
- The expressions ～かな and ～かしら are not used in straightforward questions to others, as is ～でしょうか, but they can be used to solicit a listener's answer indirectly. However, they should not be used with someone with a superior social status because they are used in fairly informal speech.

話してみましょう

A. Change the following questions to monologue questions using ～かな or ～かしら.

Example

今年の夏(なつ)は暑(あつ)いですか。

今年の夏(なつ)は暑(あつ)いかな。

1. 去年(きょねん)は暑(あつ)い日が多(おお)かったですか。
2. 今年の冬(ふゆ)は寒(さむ)いでしょうか。
3. 去年(きょねん)は雨(あめ)がたくさんふりましたか。
4. 去年(きょねん)の冬(ふゆ)は雪(ゆき)が少(すく)なかったでしょうか。
5. おととしの冬(ふゆ)はあまり寒(さむ)くありませんでしたか。
6. 今度の夏(なつ)は暑(あつ)くなりますか。

B. Work with a partner. The following chart shows the weather forecast for various cities. One person asks a question, using the words in 1-8 and ～でしょう. The other person answers the questions, using ～でしょう or ～かもしれません.

Example

東京(とうきょう)／いい天気(てんき)

A: 東京(とうきょう)はいい天気(てんき)でしょうか。

B: いいえ、あまりいい天気(てんき)じゃないでしょう。

東京(とうきょう)／雨(あめ)

A: 今日(きょう)東京(とうきょう)は雨(あめ)がふるでしょうか。

B: そうですね。東京(とうきょう)は雨(あめ)がふるかもしれませんね。

	東京(とうきょう)	アンカレッジ	ニューヨーク	シドニー	ロサンゼルス
天気(てんき)	くもり	雪(ゆき)	くもりのち雨(あめ)	晴(はれ)	くもり時々晴(ときどきはれ)
気温(きおん)	15°C	-20°C	5°C	33°C	25°C
雨(あめ)	50%	0%	80%	0%	30%
雪(ゆき)	0%	100%	15%	0%	0%

1. 東京(とうきょう)／むし暑(あつ)い
2. アンカレッジ／雪(ゆき)
3. ニューヨーク／寒(さむ)い
4. ニューヨーク／雨(あめ)

5. シドニー／いい天気(てんき)

6. ロサンゼルス／暖(あたた)かい

7. ロサンゼルス／雨(あめ)

8. シドニー／涼(すず)しい

C. Work as a class. Ask your classmates to guess what the weather in your area will be like during the next six months, using ～でしょうか and ～かもしれない.

Example

A: 今度の春(はる)は暖(あたた)かい日が多(おお)いでしょうか。

B: 去年(きょねん)は寒(さむ)かったから、今年は暖(あたた)かくなるかもしれませんね。

D. Work with a partner. You are a psychic and your partner, though skeptical, has come to see you. Convince your partner you are a legitimate psychic by answering the questions put to you and by making good guesses.

Example

A: 私のしゅみは何でしょう。

B: そうですね。本を読むのが好きでしょう。それからおんがくも好きでしょう。

A: そうですか。じゃあ、今週の週末(しゅうまつ)、私は何をするでしょう。

B: ～さんはともだちの家のパーティに行くでしょう。そこで、すてきな人に会うでしょう。

A: え、本当(ほんとう)ですか。

V. Expressing reasons, using the plain form + ので Skipped

Reason			Results
	Adjective (plain)		
ちょっと	寒(さむ)い	ので、	セーターをきています。

I am wearing a sweater because it's a bit cold.

今日(きょう)は雨(あめ)なので、出かけません。 — I'm not going out because it's raining today.

今日はなはさいたので、見に行きました。 — The flowers were blooming today, so I went to see them.

今日(きょう)はむし暑(あつ)くないので、気持(きも)ちがいいです。 — It feels good today because it's not muggy.

- The plain form of verbs or adjectives + ので expresses reason. This is similar to the plain form of verbs and adjectives + から, introduced in Chapters 6 and 11 in Volume 1, but ～ので is different from ～から in some important ways:
  1. When ので is combined with a noun and copula verb, or with な-adjectives, な is used in the plain present affirmative form, but when から is combined with these forms, it is preceded by だ. The ので construction is made with verbs and adjectives in the same way as is ～んです.

Type word	Case	ので	から
Noun + copula verb	Present affirmative Present negative Past affirmative Past negative	雨(あめ)なので 雨(あめ)じゃないので 雨(あめ)だったので 雨(あめ)じゃなかったので	雨(あめ)だから 雨(あめ)じゃないから 雨(あめ)だったから 雨(あめ)じゃなかったから
な-adjectives	Present affirmative Present negative Past affirmative Past negative	きれいなので きれいじゃないので きれいだったので きれいじゃなかったので	きれいだから きれいじゃないから きれいだったから きれいじゃなかったから
い-adjectives	Present affirmative Present negative Past affirmative Past negative	いいので よくないので よかったので よくなかったので	いいから よくないから よかったから よくなかったから
Verbs	Present affirmative Present negative Past affirmative Past negative	下(さ)がるので 下(さ)がらないので 下(さ)がったので 下(さ)がらなかったので	下(さ)がるから 下(さ)がらないから 下(さ)がったから 下(さ)がらなかったから

  2. Sentences with ので usually end with a statement and usually do not contain statements of volition or personal opinions, requests, suggestions, commands, or invitations issued by the speaker. Sentences with から can be used in cases where ので is not appropriate.

天気(てんき)がよくなったので、行って下さい。

天気(てんき)がよくなったから、行って下さい。

~~雪(ゆき)がふっているので、くるまで行きましょう。~~	雪(ゆき)がふっているから、くるまで行きましょう。
~~寒(さむ)いので、セーターをきたほうがいいよ。~~	寒(さむ)いから、セーターをきたほうがいいよ。

3. ので tends to be softer in tone than から when stating reasons. Therefore, ので is often used in polite speech.

話してみましょう

A. Connect the matching phrases in Columns A and B by using ので with the phrase in Column A.

Example

Column A: 暑(あつ)いです。　　Column B: およぎに行きます。

<u>暑(あつ)いので、およぎに行きます。</u>

Column A	Column B
明日(あした)の朝(あさ)、台風(たいふう)が来ます。	雨(あめ)がふるかもしれません。
とても風(かぜ)がつめたかったです。	あまりすみたくありません。
そらがくもっています。	セーターをきました。
雪(ゆき)がたくさんふりました。	むし暑(あつ)くなりませんでした。
そこは気候(きこう)がよくありません。	雪(ゆき)でまちがしろくなりました。
気温(きおん)があまり上(あ)がりませんでした。	ごごは雨(あめ)と風(かぜ)がひどくなるでしょう。

B. Work with a partner. One person should extend one of the invitations contained in selections 1–5 from Column A below. The other person should decline the invitation, using the corresponding phrase from Column B, with ので, and then offer an alternative activity.

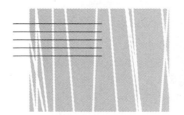

Example

Column A: およぎに行きます。 Column B: 寒(さむ)いです。

A: およぎに行きませんか。

B: ええ、でも、今日(きょう)はちょっと寒(さむ)いので、明日(あした)にしませんか。

A: ああ、いいですよ。じゃ、そうしましょう。

	Column A	Column B
1.	週末(しゅうまつ)にスキーに行きます。	暖(あたた)かくて、雪(ゆき)がないかもしれません。
2.	ピクニックに行きます。	天気予報(よほう)によるとごごは雨(あめ)だそうです。
3.	ごごゴルフをします。	今日(きょう)むし暑(あつ)くなりそうです。
4.	六月に日本に行きます。	六月の日本は雨(あめ)が多(おお)いです。
5.	今週の土曜日にパーティをします。	週末(しゅうまつ)に台風(たいふう)がくるかもしれません。

C. Work with the class. Ask your classmates which towns they like and dislike, and why, and write the answers on the chart your instructor will give you. Use ので to respond to questions.

Example

A: ～さんはどのまちが好きですか。

B: いつも暖(あたた)かいので、ホノルルが一番(ちばん)好きです。

A: そうですか。じゃあ、どのまちはあまり好きじゃありませんか。

B: そうですね。シカゴはあまり好きじゃありませんね。
冬寒(ふゆさむ)くて、風(かぜ)が強(つよ)いので。

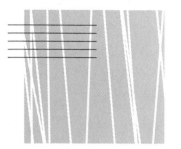

A: そうですか。

漢字

Component shapes of kanji 1: Introduction

Many **kanji** consist of more than one component. Certain components appear in many different **kanji.** Some of them are **kanji** by themselves while others are not. Since the number of these component shapes is much smaller than the total number of **kanji**—there are about 300 component shapes in all—they serve as organizers and aids for memorization.

The term "radical" (部首(ぶしゅ)) has traditionally been used to refer to components of characters. The concept of radicals was developed to classify and index a large number of **kanji.** In modern Japanese, slightly over 200 radicals are used to index **kanji.** A radical is assigned to every **kanji.** Although radicals are very useful in studying **kanji,** they are sometimes deceptive. For example, the radical of 家 is 宀, but the radical of 字 is 子.

In this book, we use the term "component shape" to refer to any shape that repeatedly appears as a part of different **kanji** (*e.g.,* 寸, 口, 又, 月, ル, etc.). Some component shapes are **kanji** by themselves, while some others appear only in other **kanji.** The approximately 300 component shapes include all shapes used as radicals.

Some of the component shapes indicate the meaning (or meaning category) of **kanji.** For example, if a **kanji** contains the component 日, it is likely that the meaning of the **kanji** is related to *day* or *sun.* Some other component shapes often indicate an **on**-reading of the **kanji. Kanji** that contain the component 青, for example, tend to have an **on**-reading of せい (*e.g.,* 静、精、清).

Component shapes appear in various places within **kanji,** but some shapes have a strong tendency to appear in fixed locations such as the left, right, top, or bottom of the character. The following is a list of major types of component shapes based on where they are found within the character.

Type*	Example		Example of Use
へん (left side)	亻	Meaning: person	休 体 住
つくり (right side)	冓	On-reading: /kou/	講 構 購
かんむり (top)	宀	Meaning: roof	家 寒
きゃく (bottom)	ル	Meaning: leg	兄 見 先 元
たれ (top to left)	疒	Meaning: sickness	病
かまえ (enclosure)	門	Meaning: gate	間 聞
くにがまえ (enclosure)	囗	Meaning: border	回 国
にょう (left to bottom)	辶	Meaning: walk, round	週

* These names are used to label radicals.

雨	rain ウ/あめ	天気は雨(あめ)のち晴(は)れです。
雪	snow セツ/ゆき	今年は雪(ゆき)がたくさんふる。
風	wind フウ/かぜ	きのうは風(かぜ)が強(つよ)かったですね。
晴	to clear, fine セイ/は（れる）	明日(あした)は晴(は)れるでしょう。
朝	morning チョウ/あさ	朝(あさ)は何時におきますか。毎朝(まいあさ)ジョギングをします。
昼	noon チュウ/ひる	昼(ひる)ごはんを食べましたか。
晩	evening バン	今晩(こんばん)、家で会いましょう。きのうの晩(ばん)は寒(さむ)かったです。
春	spring シュン/はる	春(はる)になりました。
夏	summer カ/なつ	日本の夏(なつ)はむし暑(あつ)いです。
秋	autumn シュウ/あき	秋(あき)は木(こ)のはがきれいです。

冬	winter	トウ/ふゆ	冬(ふゆ)は寒(さむ)くて、雪(ゆき)が多いです。
東	east	トウ/ひがし	東(ひがし)のそらが明(あか)るいです。東京(とうきょう)は人が多(おお)い。北東(ほくとう)
西	west	セイ/にし	西(にし)のそらが暗(くら)いから、雨(あめ)がふりますよ。南西(なんせい)
南	south	ナン/みなみ	南(みなみ)の方(ほう)は暖(あたた)かい。南東(なんとう)の風(かぜ)
北	north	ホク/きた	北(きた)の方(ほう)は寒(さむ)いです。北西(ほくせい)の風(かぜ)がふいています。
方	direction, person (polite)	ホウ/かた	東(ひがし)の方(ほう)が明(あか)るい。その方(かた)はどなたですか。
寒	cold (weather)	カン/さむい	今年(ことし)の冬(ふゆ)はとても寒(さむ)かったです。
暑	hot (weather)	ショ/あつ（い）	来週(らいしゅう)は暑(あつ)くなりそうです。
明	bright	メイ/あか（るい）	朝は五時ごろ明(あか)るくなります。　*明日(あした)(special reading)
暗	dark	アン/くら（い）	冬(ふゆ)ははやく暗(くら)くなりますね。

温	温	warm オン	この水の温度(おんど)は二十度です。 地球(ちきゅう)の温暖化(おんだんか) (global warming)
暖	暖	warm (weather) ダン/ あたた（かい）	今日(きょう)は暖(あたた)かいですね。でも明日(あした)は涼(すず)しくなるそうです。
涼	涼	cool (weather) リョウ/ すず（しい）	今日(きょう)は涼(すず)しくて、とても気持(きも)ちがいいです。
強	強	strong キョウ/ つよ（い）	明日(あした)は風(かぜ)が強(つよ)いです。
弱	弱	weak ジャク/ よわ（い）	体(からだ)が弱(よわ)い。 風(かぜ)が弱(よわ)くなりました。
季	季	season キ	どんな季節(きせつ)が好きですか。暖(あたた)かい季節(きせつ)がいいです。
節	節	season, time, paragraph セツ/ ふし	寒(さむ)い季節(きせつ)が来ました。 日本は季節(きせつ)が四つあります。
多	多	many, much タ/ おお（い）	中国は人が多(おお)いです。
少	少	a little, a few ショウ/すく（ない）すこ（し）	ここは人が少(すく)ないですね。 少(すこ)し下さい。
天	天	heaven テン	天気(てんき)がとてもいい。 東京(とうきょう)の天気(てんき)

あたらしい読みかた

木(こ)のは　明日(あした)　上(あ)がる　下(さ)がる

練習(れんしゅう)

1. 東京の天気は雨のち晴れです。午後には気温が二十五度まで上がるでしょう。
2. 今晩は風が強いですが、明日の朝は弱くなるでしょう。
3. 西の方が暗いですから、晴れないでしょう。
4. 夏は暑くて、冬は寒いです。
5. 北のまちの春はおそいです。
6. 昼ごはんの時は人が多いですが、そのあとは少なくなります。
7. 今の季節がとても好きです。
8. 今日は暖かかったけれど、明日は雨がふるそうだから、気温が下がって、涼しくなるかもしれないね。

上手な読み方

Getting used to vertical writing

Japanese text can be written either horizontally or vertically. In vertical writing, texts are read from top to bottom, right to left. Japanese newspaper articles are written vertically, including the weather forecast. Also, popular magazines and literary works are usually written vertically. Texts requiring scientific symbols, equations, formulas, and foreign words, such as science textbooks, language texts, and computer magazines, tend to be written horizontally.

新聞(しんぶん)の記事(きじ) (A newspaper article)

読む前(まえ)に

A. Mark the beginning and end of each of the short paragraphs in the newspaper article on the following page.

メルボルンに給水制限？

　メルボルンでは十三年ぶりに給水制限がしかれる可能性が大きいと見られている。
　一五〇年ぶりの低雨量を記録したメルボルン供給ダムの水量は、七二％と去年の同時期の九五％を大幅に下回り、関係者もこの状態を深刻に受け止めている様子。
　メルボルン水道局のベイリー氏は、市民に対し節水に協力してくれるよう積極的に呼びかけている。
　ちなみに、年間平均降雨量六三九ミリに対し、去年の降雨量はわずか三五九ミリだった。

B. Rewrite the following text vertically in two or more lines.

東京は今日(きょう)は晴れ時々曇(ときどきくも)り、午前(ごぜん)中は少し寒いですが、午後(ごご)には10度ぐらいになるでしょう。夜(よる)になって、雨が降(ふ)るでしょう。この雨は明日の午後(ごご)まで続(つづ)くでしょう。

C. The numbers on the following map represent various regions in Japan. Read the descriptions of each region below and write the number from the map that matches the description. Note that しま means *island*.

8 ＿＿ 山陰(さんいん)　本州(ほんしゅう)にあります。大阪(おおさか)の西で、四国(しこく)の北です。韓国(かんこく)に近いです。

1 ＿＿ 北海道(ほっかいどう)　日本で一番(ばん)北にあるしまです。

5 ＿＿ 関東(かんとう)　本州(ほんしゅう)にあります。東京(とうきょう)の近くです。

7 ＿＿ 近畿(きんき)　本州(ほんしゅう)にあります。東京(とうきょう)の南です。大阪(おおさか)やきょうとがあります。四国(しこく)に近いです。

10 ＿＿ 九州(きゅうしゅう)　四国(しこく)の南西にあるしまです。

4 ＿＿ 北陸(ほくりく)　本州(ほんしゅう)にあります。東京(とうきょう)の北西のほうです。

3	本州(ほんしゅう)	日本で一番(ばん)大きいしまです。
2	東北(とうほく)	本州(ほんしゅう)にあります。東京(とうきょう)の北のほうです。
6	東海(とうかい)	本州(ほんしゅう)にあります。東京(とうきょう)の少し南の方です。
9	四国(しこく)	日本にある四つのしまの中で一番(ばん)小さいしまです。
11	沖縄(おきなわ)	日本で一番(いちばん)南にあるしまです。

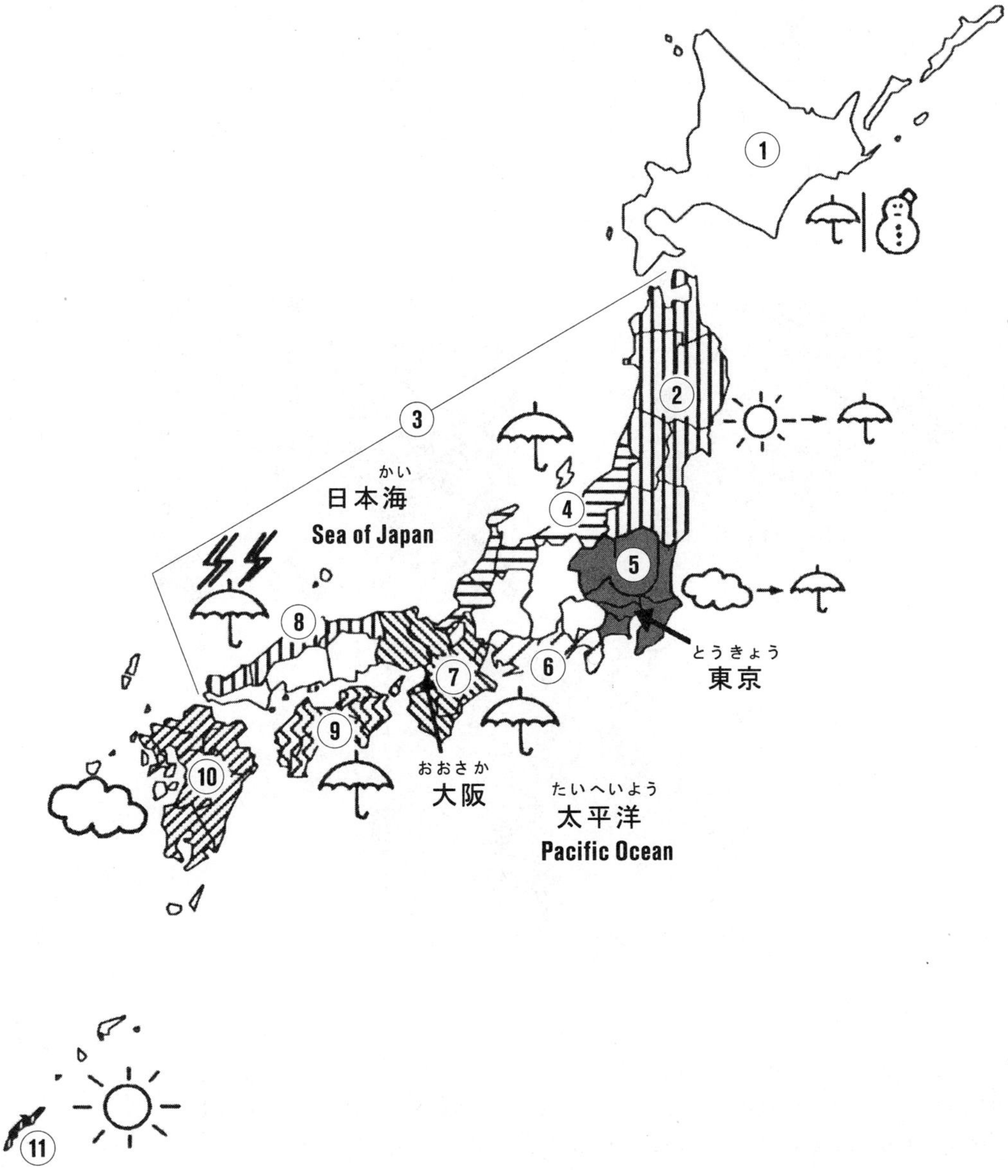

読んでみましょう

Read the following weather forecast and choose the weather map that corresponds to the forecast.

きょうの天気

前線を伴った低気圧が日本海から東北東に進み、全国的に天気はくずれる。本州の日本海側や四国、九州は朝から雨、関東、東北、北陸も午後から雨になる。山陰地方の海岸では所々で雷雨を伴い風も強まる。北海道は雪か雨、沖縄も晴れ後曇りで、昼過ぎから雨。

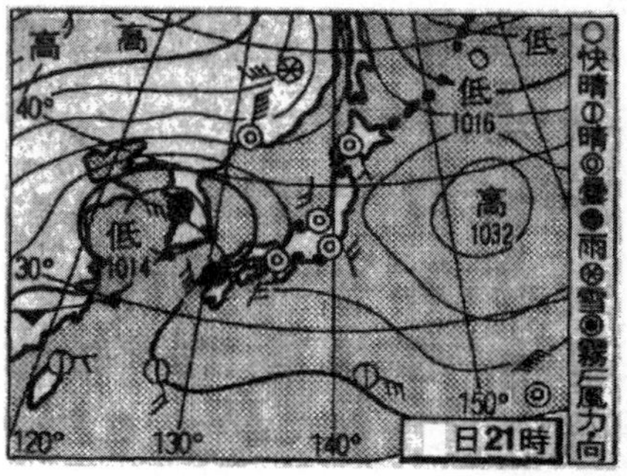

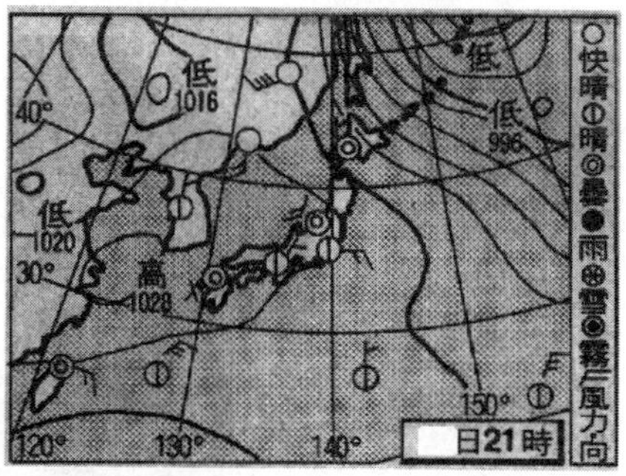

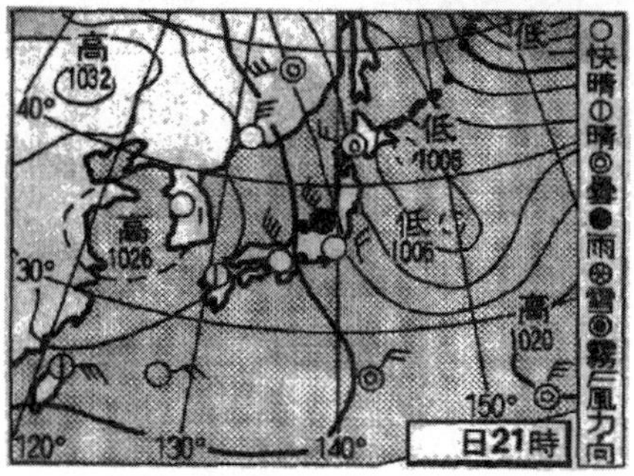

分かりましたか

A. The weather map on page 77 uses the weather symbols to show the weather projected for the various regions covered by the above forecast, but some of the weather symbols used on the map are not correct. Identify the mistakes and write the correct symbols.

B. 日本語でしつもんにこたえて下さい。

1. 四国(しこく)に住んでいる人は今日(きょう)かさをもって出かけたほうがいいですか。
2. 九州(きゅうしゅう)に住んでいる人は今日(きょう)どんなふくをきて出かけたほうがいいですか。
3. 北海道(ほっかいどう)に住んでいる人は今日(きょう)はかさをもって出かけたほうがいいですか。

読んだ後(あと)で

An out-of-town friend is planning to visit you for a week and has asked what the weather is like now. Compose an e-mail message to your friend giving details about the forecast for each of the next seven days. Information should include high and low temperatures, the chance of precipitation, etc.

上手な聞き方

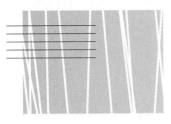

Understanding the organization of prepared speech

Unlike face-to-face conversations, news reports and weather forecasts are based on prepared text and hence do not have much redundant information. It is thus very important to understand the information the first time. Luckily, prepared speech usually has a set pattern. Being aware of the organization of speech helps you to identify when and to what to pay attention. For example, news reports usually start with *what* happens to *whom, where,* and *when*. Details come later.

天気予報(よほう)を聞く (Listening to weather forecasts)

聞く前に

What is the organization of a weather report? What kind of information is provided in what order?

STUDENT

聞いてみましょう

Listen to the following weather forecasts and complete the chart by writing in the weather and high and low temperatures of the city in the chart in English.

言葉(ことば)のリスト

最高気温(さいこう) — high temperature

さいてい気温 — low temperature

	天気予報(よほう)（Example）	天気予報(よほう)１	天気予報(よほう)２	天気予報(よほう)３
まち	きょうと	東京(とうきょう)	よこはま	きょうと
天気	雪			
気温	１度／-１度			

聞いた後(あと)で

しつもんに日本語でこたえて下さい。

1. 天気予報(よほう)１の季節はいつですか。
2. その季節の東京(とうきょう)とあなたの国とどちらの方が寒(さむ)いですか。
3. 天気予報(よほう)２の季節はいつですか。
4. その季節のよこはまとあなたの国とどちらの方があたたかいですか。
5. 天気予報(よほう)３の季節はいつですか。
6. あなたの国ではその季節に雨がたくさんふりますか。

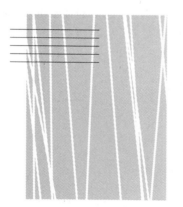

STUDENT

DICT-A-CONVERSATION

スミスさんは今から学校にいきます。家のそとで山田さんに会いました。

山田：________________________________

スミス：________________________________

山田：________________________________

スミス：________________________________

山田：________________________________

スミス：________________________________

山田：________________________________

聞き上手話し上手

Expressing agreement and solidarity using ね and も

Expressing agreement and emphasizing similarity are ways of showing support to your listener during a conversation. Doing so helps create a sense of sharing or solidarity, thus advancing the conversation. In Japanese, the particles ね and も are often used to show agreement. (See the discussion of the particle も in contrast with は in Volume 1, Chapter 6.) For example, the particle ね in Suzuki-san's speech below indicates that she is requesting a confirmation of her impression about the weather. The particle ね in Yamamoto-san's speech indicates that he agrees with Suzuki-san's assertion that it is humid today.

鈴木(すずき)：　今日(きょう)はむし暑いですね。
It's humid today, isn't it?

山本：　ええ、本当(ほんとう)に暑いですね。
It certainly is.

Similarly, the particle も in the following example emphasizes agreement between Suzuki-san and Yamamoto-san and indicates what they have in common.

鈴木(すずき)：　私はいぬが好きです。
I like dogs.

山本：　そうですか。ぼくもいぬが好きなんですよ。
Really? So do I.

Even if you disagree with a person, it is good to express one level of agreement before introducing disagreement. Starting a conversation with a disagreement often sounds rude or cold.

鈴木(すずき)： 今年は雪が多いですね。

It's snowed a lot this year.

山本： 本当(ほんとう)によくふりますね。でも、去年(きょねん)より少ないかもしれませんね。

It really has snowed a lot, hasn't it? But, there may be less snow than last year.

STUDENT

A. Listen to the people expressing opinions. After each person speaks, first, express your agreement using ね and も. Then express a point of disagreement, using ね and も to show your support at the same time.

B. Work with a partner. Your partner will express opinions about class, school, weather, a particular hobby, or parents. Agree with him or her using ね and も.

C. Work with a partner. Your partner will again express opinions about class, school, weather, a hobby or parents, but this time show your support for his or her opinion using ね and も, and then express your disagreement.

総合練習(そうごうれんしゅう)

明日のお天気

Work with a partner. Draw a map of your region and country. You are a TV meteorologist forecasting tomorrow's weather. As you make your forecast, draw appropriate weather symbols and temperatures on the map. Give your weather report to your class. Your classmates will choose the most creative and informative presentation.

ロールプレイ

A. You are talking to your roommate. You are planning to go out tonight, but the weather is getting worse. Ask your roommate what he or she knows about tonight's weather.

B. You meet your neighbor on your way to school. Yesterday was a cold rainy day, but the weather today is nice. Greet him or her and make small talk.

C. A typhoon is approaching your city. It is becoming windy, and it is raining harder. Talk with your friend about the weather.

D. Walk around the classroom. As soon as your instructor names a season, form a pair with one of your classmates, greet him or her as if you have bumped into one another on the street, and chat about the weather.

単語 (ESSENTIAL VOCABULARY)

Nouns

あめ （雨） rain; rainy
かぜ （風） wind
き （木） tree
きおん （気温） air temperature
きこう （気候） climate
きた （北） north
くも （雲） cloud
くもり （曇り） cloudy
このは （木の葉） tree leaves
そら （空） sky
たいふう （台風） typhoon
てんき （天気） weather
てんきよほう （天気予報） weather forecast
なんせい （南西） southwest
なんとう （南東） southeast
にし （西） west
のち （後） after
は （葉） leaf このは （木の葉） tree leaves
はな （花） flower
はれ （晴れ） sunny
ひがし （東） east
ほう （方） direction
ほくせい （北西） northwest
ほくとう （北東） northeast
マイナス minus
みなみ （南） south
ゆき （雪） snow, snowy

Pronouns

あなた you (The usage of あなた in this book is limited to the unspecific second person, such as one finds in surveys.)

う-verbs

あがる （上がる） (to) rise; (to) go up
くもる （曇る） (to) become cloudy
さがる （下がる） (to) fall; (to) go down
さく （咲く） (to) bloom
ふく （吹く） (to) blow
ふる （降る） (to) fall

る-verbs

はれる （晴れる） (to) become sunny

い-adjectives

おおい （多い） a lot; plentiful
すくない （少ない） a little; scarce
つよい （強い） strong
つめたい （冷たい） cold
むしあつい （蒸し暑い） humid
よわい （弱い） weak

な-adjectives

そう　look like, appear, seem

Suffixes

～ど　(～度)　degree

Passive Vocabulary

Nouns

おきなわ　(沖縄)　Okinawa (Island)
かし　(華氏)　Fahrenheit
かべ　(壁)　wall
かんとう　(関東)　Kanto Region
きじ　(記事)　article (newspapers and magazines)
きゅうしゅう　(九州)　Kyushu Island
きんき　(近畿)　Kinki Region
さいきん　(最近)　current; recently
さいこうきおん　(最高気温)　highest temperature
さいていきおん　(最低気温)　lowest temperature
さんいん　(山陰)　San'in Region
サングラス　sunglasses
さんよう　(山陽)　Sanyo Region
しこく　(四国)　Shikoku Island
しま　(島)　island
せっし　(摂氏)　Celsius
たいへいよう　(太平洋)　the Pacific Ocean
ちず　(地図)　map
つゆ　(梅雨)　rainy season
とうほく　(東北)　Tohoku Region
にほんかい　(日本海)　the Japan Sea
ほうがく　(方角)　compass direction
ほくりく　(北陸)　Hokuriku Region
ほっかいどう　(北海道)　Hokkaido Island
ほんしゅう　(本州)　Honshu Island

う-verbs

ちがう　(違う)　(to) be different
つかう　(使う)　(to) use
つづく　(続く)　(to) continue

い-adjectives

きたない(汚い)　dirty

For a list of supplementary vocabulary items that will facilitate communication, see the first page of Chapter 1 in your Workbook.

CHAPTER 2

第二課

The Kamakura Great Buddha is a popular travel destination.

旅行(りょこう)

Travel

Functions	Making and describing travel plans
New Vocabulary	Useful expressions related to travel; Travel; How long is your stay?; Conjunctions
Dialogue	今度の休み (This vacation)
Culture	Traveling in Japan
Language	I. Expressing intention and plans, using the volitional form of the verb + と思(おも)う, or the plain present form of the verb + つもり or 予定(よてい)
	II. Expressing direction, using the particle へ; Expressing time limits, using the particle までに
	III. Reporting speech, using と言(い)う
	IV. Expressing opinions about things, events, and actions, using the plain form + と思(おも)う
	V. Expressing chronological order, using 前(まえ) and 後(あと); Expressing occasion, using 時
Kanji	Component shapes of **kanji** 2: Side components
Reading	Using transition devices
Listening	Using transition devices, and the difference between そ-series and あ-series words
Communication	Introducing a new topic

新(あたら)しい言葉(ことば)

旅行(りょこう)の時につかうべんりな言葉(ことば) (Useful expressions related to travel)

計画(けいかく)をたてる　to make plans

予約(よやく)をする　to make a reservation

さがす　to look for

地図(ちず)をしらべる　to check a map

持(も)って行く　to bring

しつもんに答(こた)える　to answer a question

知(し)っている／知(し)らない　to know/not to know

家を出る　to leave home

わすれる　to forget

電車(でんしゃ)をつかう　to use a train

ホテルにつく　to arrive at a hotel

ホテルにとまる　to stay in a hotel

お金をはらう　to pay (money)

je t'adore ☺ mon ami — parce que tu es très, très chouette. Pas panique!

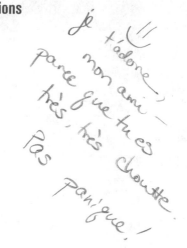

A. 旅行(りょこう)の前(まえ)と間にすることを書いて下さい。(Write down some of the things done before and during a trip.) Your instructor will supply a form for you to use.

B. Choose the appropriate words from the above list to complete the following sentences.

1. 旅行(りょこう)の計画(けいかく)を________________。ホテルの____________は今からします。
2. 日本のレストランではチップ (tip) は____________________。
3. 田中さんの住所は________________________が、行き方(かた)が分かりませんから、地図(ちず)で________________________。

4. 勉強(べんきょう)しなかったので、先生のしつもんに________________。

5. 晩の六時に東京(とうきょう)に____________________ので、その日は東京(とうきょう)駅(えき)の近くのホテルに________________________。

6. お金がないので、安(やす)いホテルを________________________。

7. 大きいスーツケースを____________________ので、えきまでタクシー (taxi) を________________________________。

8. 明日の朝、七時にここを________________________。
____________________________ないで下さいね。

9. 先生、すみません。しゅくだいを____________________。

旅行(りょこう) (Travel)

海外(かいがい) overseas	旅館(りょかん) Japanese-style inn
海外旅行(かいがいりょこう) overseas travel/travel to foreign countries	みんしゅく private guest house
かんこう sightseeing	くうこう airport
かんこう旅行(りょこう) sightseeing trip	パスポート passport
旅行会社(りょこうがいしゃ) travel agency	ガイドブック guidebook
ツアー tour	おみやげ souvenir
予約(よやく) reservation	クレジットカード credit card
計画(けいかく) plan	きっぷ ticket
場所(ばしょ) location	言葉(ことば) word, language
外国(がいこく) foreign country	スーツケース suitcase
みずうみ lake	べんりな convenient
店(みせ) store	カメラ camera

下の言葉(ことば)をおぼえていますか。(Do you remember these words?)

ホテル　うみ　家族　かばん　季節　山　国(くに)　車(くるま)　写真(しゃしん)
神社(じんじゃ)　おてら　電車(でんしゃ)　動物園(どうぶつえん)　博物館(はくぶつかん)　飛行機(ひこうき)　遊園地(ゆうえんち)
所　電車(でんしゃ)

C. Find a word that corresponds to the following descriptions. Some of them have more than one answer.

1. 外国(がいこく)にあそびに行くことです。
2. 飛行機(ひこうき)が出る所です。
3. おみやげが買える所です。
4. 旅行(りょこう)の時に読むものです。
5. 旅行(りょこう)の時にとまる所です。
6. 旅行(りょこう)の時に買うものです。
7. おもしろい所やきれいな所に行ったりすることです。
8. どうぶつは話せませんが、人は話せるものです。
9. レストランでよくつかうものですが、お金じゃありません。
10. 外国人(がいこくじん)がもっているものです。

D. しつもんに答(こた)えて下さい。

1. 旅行(りょこう)の時につかうべんりなものはどんなものですか。
2. 旅館(りょかん)やみんしゅくにとまったことがありますか。
3. きっぷはどこで買えますか。だれが安(やす)いきっぷやツアーについて知(し)っていますか。
4. 旅行(りょこう)の前(まえ) (before) に、何の予約(よやく)をしたほうがいいですか。

～泊(はく)～日(か) (How long is your stay? [How many overnights and days?])

～泊(はく)～日(か)	~ overnights, ~ days
一泊二日(いっぱくふつか)	one overnight, two days
二泊三日(にはくみっか)	two overnights, three days
三泊四日(さんぱくよっか)	three overnights, four days
四泊五日(よんはくいつか)	four overnights, five days
五泊六日(ごはくむいか)	five overnights, six days

E. Match the descriptions on the left with the appropriate number of days and nights on the right. Then work with a partner. One person should make a sentence similar to those in 1–5 below, and the other should say how many overnights and days are being referred to.

1. 月曜日に来て、金曜日に出ます。	一泊二日(いっぱくふつか)
2. 明日来てあさって帰ります。	二泊三日(にはくみっか)
3. おととい来ました。明日帰ります。	三泊四日(さんぱくよっか)
4. 月曜日の午後(ごご)から土曜日の朝までいます。	四泊五日(よんはくいつか)
5. 今日行って、あさって帰ります。	五泊六日(ごはくむいか)

Conjunctions

その後(あと)(で) after that	だけど but
その前(まえ)(に) before that	けれども however
その時(に) at that time	というのは it's because
その 間(あいだ) (に) during that time	(まず)はじめに first (of all)
それで then, so	つぎに next
ですから therefore, so	ところで by the way
だから so	また also

下の言葉(ことば)をおぼえていますか。(Do you remember these words?)

そして　それから　でも

F. Use the appropriate conjunctions to improve the flow between the following sentences.

Example

高男(たかお)くんは十五さいです。ビールは飲めません。

高男(たかお)くんは十五さいです。 だから / ですから ビールは飲めません。

1. 私はバレーボールをしました。山田さんはねていました。
2. 旅行(りょこう)の計画(けいかく)をたてます。安(やす)い旅館(りょかん)をさがします。旅館(りょかん)の予約(よやく)をします。 それで

3. 山田さんは病気です。今日は来られないそうです。
4. クレジットカードでお金をはらいました。お金がなくなったからです。
5. 夜ねます。はをみがきます。
6. ハワイにはおもしろいツアーがたくさんあります。いい店(みせ)もたくさんあります。
7. にぎやかなパーティですね。田中さんは来られません。

ダイアローグ

はじめに

しつもんに答(こた)えて下さい。

1. どんな所に旅行(りょこう)に行ったことがありますか。
2. 何日ぐらい行きましたか。
3. どんなことをしましたか。
4. 旅行(りょこう)の前(まえ)にどんなことをしますか。
5. 旅行(りょこう)に行く時、どんなものを持(も)って行ったらいいと思(おも)いますか。
6. 海外旅行(かいがいりょこう)はどこへ行きたいですか。どうしてですか。

今度の休み　(This vacation)

STUDENT

言葉(ことば)のリスト

まつり festival	本物(ほんもの) real thing	おなじ same
ひさしぶりに after a long time	じゅんび preparation	どうぞう statue

The following **manga** frames are scrambled, so they are not in the order described by the dialogue. Read the dialogue and unscramble the frames by writing the correct number in the box located in the upper right corner of each frame.

先生がリーさんとアリスさんに今度の休みについて聞いています。

先生：　今度の休みはどうしますか。

アリス：　北海道（ほっかいどう）に行くつもりです。石田（いしだ）さんがさっぽろに雪まつりを見に行くと言（い）っているので、一緒（いっしょ）に行こうと思（おも）っているんです。

リー：　北海道（ほっかいどう）？

アリス：　うん、さっぽろでは二月に雪まつりというゆうめいなおまつりがあるんだって。雪でたてものやどうぞうをつくるんだそうよ。

リー：　ああ、雪まつりか。それならぼくも聞いたことあるよ。雪でいろいろなものつくるんだよね。

アリス:　そうよ。本物（ほんもの）とおなじぐらい大きいたてものやどうぶつもあるそうよ。

先生：　でも、二月の北海道（ほっかいどう）はまだ寒いから、行く時にセーターやコートをもって行った方がいいですね。

アリス：　そうなんです。でも、私のコートふるいから、行く前（まえ）に買おうと思（おも）っているんです。

先生：　そうですか。ところで、リーくんの予定（よてい）は？

リー：　ぼくはたいわんへ帰るつもりです。

先生：　そうですか。いつ帰るんですか。

リー：　学期がおわった後、すぐ出る予定です。

アリス：そう。もうすぐね。じゃあ、今いそがしいわね。

リー：　そうなんだ。だから、今週の週末はおみやげとスーツケースを買いに行こうと思ってるんだ。あ、先生、ところで、しけんのことなんですが。

先生：　はい、何ですか。

リー：　十五日までに出すというお話でしたが、十四日でもいいでしょうか。

先生：　ええ、いいですよ。

分かりましたか

A. アリスさんとリーさんの休みの計画を下のひょう (chart) に書いて下さい。

	アリスさん	リーさん
行くところ		
行った時にすること		
行く前にすること		

B. 日本語でしつもんに答えて下さい。

1. アリスさんはどこへ行くと言いましたか。
2. アリスさんはだれとそこへ行くつもりですか。
3. 雪まつりでは何があるそうですか。
4. リーさんは休みに何をする予定ですか。
5. リーさんは休みの前に何をしようと思っていますか。

C. Identify to whom each of the speeches in the dialogue is directed. Pay attention to the level of formality used in various contexts.

D. Identify the transition conjunctions and use them to make your own sentences.

E. Identify the phrases that introduce a new topic.

日本の文化

Traveling in Japan. When you go on a trip, what kind of transportation do you usually use? What kind of accommodations do you prefer?

There are domestic airlines, a highway system, and several railroad systems in Japan, but the best way to travel through the country is probably by train. Various discount tickets and railway passes are available for travelers, but some of them must be purchased before you arrive in Japan. For example, JR, the largest railroad company, sells a pass that allows unlimited travel on its trains anywhere in Japan. The pass is available for travelers who stay in Japan for more than a week, but you must purchase it before arriving in Japan. JR trains include most local trains, the airport express, and the 新幹線 *(bullet train)*.

One of the pleasures of traveling by train is to enjoy 駅弁, station lunch boxes. They are sold in trains and stations all over Japan. They are cheap and convenient, and they usually contain some specialty of the area, making them popular with travelers. They cost from 500 to 1,000 yen. If you are traveling by local train or ordinary express, you can open the window and buy your 駅弁 without getting off the train.

There are all kinds of accommodations available in Japan. Western-style hotels（ホテル）are usually more expensive than others, though they are more likely to have staff who speak English. Also, they often have English newspapers, maps, and other services. The 旅館, or Japanese-style inns, tend to be less expensive. Although some 旅館 have Western-style rooms, many of them have only Japanese-style rooms. Also, Japanese-style breakfast and dinner are included in the price. Hotel personnel come to your room to spread

A Japanese inn（旅館）

or take away ふとん and serve meals, tea, and snacks. This may be one of the few occasions in Japan when tipping is accepted. (Tips are not necessary for most services such as restaurants and taxis.) Some 旅館(りょかん) have rooms with a bathroom, but many of them have communal baths and restrooms, which are segregated by sex. The 旅館(りょかん) also provide bathrobes, called ゆかた, to guests. It is perfectly acceptable to walk in and around a 旅館(りょかん) in ゆかた.

Private guest houses such as 民宿(みんしゅく) *(rooms let by private families)* and ペンション *(bed and breakfasts)* are usually less expensive than hotels or 旅館(りょかん), and are popular among young people and students. Both 民宿(みんしゅく) and ペンション serve breakfast and dinner in a separate dining area, but no special room service is provided, and the bathrooms and restrooms are communal. Youth hostels (ユースホステル) are the least expensive form of accommodation. The cost varies from 1,000 yen to 2,500 yen, and some serve breakfast in the morning. Youth hostels fill up quickly during vacation periods, so it is necessary to plan ahead.

LANGUAGE

I. Expressing intention and plans, using the volitional form of the verb + と思(おも)う, or the plain present form of the verb + つもり or 予定(よてい)

A. Expressing weak intentions with ～ようと思(おも)う (thinking of ～ ing)

				Verb (volitional)	Particle	
クレジットカード	で	お金	を	はらおう	と	思(おも)います。

I am thinking of paying with a credit card.

- Volitional form of verbs

Type verb	Dictionary form	Conjugation method	Example
Irregular	来る		こよう
	する		しよう
る -verbs (stem + よう)	見る	見＋よう	見よう
	食べる	食べ＋よう	食べよう
う -verbs (stem + /o/ + う)	書く	書＋こ＋う	書こう
	読む	読＋も＋う	読もう

旅館にとまろうと思(おも)います。	I'm thinking of staying in a Japanese-style inn.
山田さんは安(やす)いみんしゅくをさがそうと思(おも)っているそうだ。	I heard that Yamada-san is thinking of looking for a cheap private guest house.
そのことをわすれようと思(おも)う。	I think I'll just forget about it.

- The volitional form of the verb + と思(おも)う expresses a tentative intention.

  If the subject is the speaker, the use of 思(おも)っています indicates that the speaker has been thinking of doing something for some time, while the use of 思(おも)います merely indicates the speaker's current thinking.

  カメラを持(も)って行こうと思(おも)います。
  I am thinking of taking my camera with me.

  来年の夏休みは日本へともだちに会いに行こうと思(おも)っているので、アルバイトをしているんです。
  I've been thinking of going to Japan to meet my friend next summer vacation, so I am working part-time.

- If the subject is someone other than the speaker, 思(おも)っています expresses both the subject's current thinking as well as his or her thinking over some time.

  妹はガイドブックと地図(ちず)で場所(ばしょ)をしらべようと思(おも)っています。
  My younger sister is thinking of using her guidebook and a map to find a place.

  キムさんはクレジットカードでお金をはらおうと思(おも)っている。
  Kim-san is thinking of paying with a credit card.

- The volitional form alone indicates the speaker's willingness to do something. It is the plain form of ましょう, which means *let's* 〜 .

夏休みの計画(けいかく)をたてましょう。	Let's make plans for the summer. (polite)
夏休みの計画(けいかく)をたてよう。	Let's make plans for the summer. (casual)

- The volitional form is used before 〜かしら or 〜かな to express a monologue question about what the speaker should do.

明日行こうかしら。	I wonder if I should go tomorrow.
今日は何をしようかな。	I wonder what I should do today.

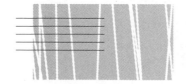

B. Expressing intention, using つもり (intend to ～)

		Verb (Plain form)	Noun	Copula
車(くるま)	を	買う	つもり	です

I intend to buy a car.

			Verb (plain present)	Noun	Particle	
あたらしい	車(くるま)	を	買う	つもり	は	ありません

I have no intention of buying a new car.

休みは家族でかんこう旅行(りょこう)に行くつもりです。 — I intend to go on a sightseeing trip with my family during vacation.
ツアーをつかうつもりです。 — I intend to use a tour.

- The word つもり expresses intentions of the speaker or someone close to the speaker. It expresses a stronger intention than does the volitional form of the verb + と思(おも)う.

私は日本へ行くつもりです。 — I intend to go to Japan.
母はアメリカに行くつもりです。 — My mother intends to go to America.

- The word つもり is a dependent noun and thus follows the plain present forms of verbs. It can also follow the demonstrative word その, as in そのつもり, which means *to intend to do so*.

先生に話すつもりです。 — I intend to speak to the teacher.
先生に話さないつもりです。 — I intend to not speak to the teacher.
母もそのつもりです。 — My mother also has that intention.

- Use the copula verb です／だ after つもり to indicate the presence of an intention or plan. Use ～つもりはありません／ない to indicate the lack of intention or plan.

ガイドブックを持(も)って行くつもりです。／ガイドブックを持(も)って行くつもりだ。
I intend to take a guidebook.

ガイドブックを持(も)って行くつもりはありません。／ガイドブックを持(も)って行くつもりはない。
I don't intend to take a guidebook.

C. Expressing intention using 予定(よてい) (plan to ～)

								Verb (plain present)	Noun	Copula
チョーさん	は	今年	の	冬	に	中国(ちゅうごく)	に	帰る	予定(よてい)	です。

Chong-san plans to go back to China this winter.

スミス：　今度の休みに何か予定(よてい)がありますか。
Do you have any plans for the vacation?

石田(いしだ)：　ええ、ともだちと上野(うえの)の美術館(びじゅつかん)に行く予定(よてい)です。スミスさんは？
Yes, I plan to go to the art museum in Ueno with my friend. How about you, Smith-san?

スミス：　とくに予定(よてい)はありませんが、どこかへ出かけようと思(おも)っています。
I don't have any particular plans, but I've been thinking of going out somewhere.

- Used without a modifier, 予定(よてい) is a noun meaning *plan*. It follows the plain present form of verbs when it is modified.

今日は予定(よてい)がありません。	I don't have any plans for today.
六時の飛行機(ひこうき)で出る予定(よてい)です。	I plan to leave here at six o'clock by plane.
ホテルにはとまらない予定(よてい)です。	I plan to not stay in a hotel.

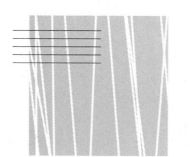

- Use the copula verb です／だ after 予定(よてい) to indicate the presence of a plan. Use ～つもり／予定(よてい)はありません／ない to indicate the lack of a plan. The adverb とくに *(particularly)* can be used with 予定(よてい) when there is no plan.

  バスでかんこうする予定(よてい)です。／バスでかんこうする予定(よてい)だ。
  I plan to sightsee by bus.
  バスでかんこうする予定(よてい)はありません／バスでかんこうする予定(よてい)はない。
  I don't plan to sightsee by bus.

- Any person can be the subject of a statement with 予定(よてい).

  私は日本へ行く予定(よてい)です。
  I plan to go to Japan.
  山本さんはアメリカに行く予定(よてい)です。
  Yamamoto-san plans to go to the United States.

話してみましょう

A. The following chart shows the summer plans of Alice and the other members of her family. A double circle (◎) indicates a definite plan, and a single circle (○) indicates an intention. A question mark (?) indicates a tentative plan. You are Alice. Describe each family member's plans and intentions using the volitional form of the verb + と思(おも)う and the plain present form of the verb + つもり or 予定(よてい).

お父さん	お母さん	パム（妹）	私（アリス）
○ 家をさがします	◎ 日本に来ます	◎ フランスに行きます。	○ 海外旅行(かいがいりょこう)をします
？家を買います。	？京都(きょうと)かんこうをします	○ フランス語を勉強します	◎ 日本語を勉強します
◎ 日本に来ます	○ きものを買います	？フランスでアルバイトをします	？安(やす)いツアーをさがします

Example

父は日本に来る予定(よてい)です。それから、家をさがすつもりです。父は家を買おうと思(おも)っているんです。

B. Work as a class. Ask your classmates about their plans for the weekend. Make a chart showing the plans of each of your classmates.

Example

A: 今週の週末(しゅうまつ)、何か予定(よてい)がありますか。／今週の週末(しゅうまつ)、何か予定(よてい)、あるの。

B: ええ、家でパーティをしようと思(おも)っています。／
ええ、家でパーティをしようと思(おも)ってるんだ。(male) ／
ええ、家でパーティをしようと思(おも)ってるの。(female)
or いいえ、とくに予定(よてい)はありません。／
いや、とくに予定(よてい)はないよ。

C. Work with a partner. Each should decide on plans for his or her next vacation. Ask your partner about his or her vacation plans, and take notes: 行くところ, ～泊～日, とまるところ, and すること. Use casual speech. Then report the plans to the class, using polite speech.

Example

A: 今度の休みの計画(けいかく)、たてた？

B: うん、たてたよ。家族でコロラドに旅行(りょこう)に行くつもりだよ。(male) ／
家族でコロラドに旅行(りょこう)に行くつもりよ。(female)

A: いいね。何日ぐらい行くの。

B: 三泊四日(さんぱくよっか)の予定(よてい)。

A: どこにとまる予定(よてい)なの。

B: 安(やす)いホテルにとまるつもりだよ。(male) ／安(やす)いホテルにとまるつもりよ。(female)

A: それで、コロラドでは、どんなことしようと思(おも)ってるの。

B: そうだね。山にのぼったり、キャンプしたりしようと思(おも)ってるんだ。(male) ／
そうね。山にのぼったり、キャンプしたりしようと思(おも)ってるの。(female)

A: それはたのしそうだね。(male) ／それはたのしそうね。(female)

Report:

私のパートナーは～さんです。～さんは三泊四日(さんぱくよっか)の予定(よてい)でコロラドに行く計画(けいかく)をたてました。～さんは安(やす)いホテルにとまるつもりです。そして、山にのぼったりキャンプをしたりしようと思っているそうです。

D. Work as a class. First, each person should decide on one social activity for the weekend and write the time and location on a schedule sheet. Prepare your schedules separately. The schedules should have a column for Saturday and one for Sunday, and a row for each hour of the day from 8 A.M. to midnight. Then each person should invite classmates to his or her activity. Anyone who decides to accept a classmate's invitation should add it to his or her schedule. If you decide not to accept an invitation due to a schedule conflict or lack of interest, politely refuse the invitation. Try to make your schedule as full as possible.

Example

B: 今週の土曜日はいそがしいですか。／今週の土曜日、いそがしい。

A: 朝はいそがしいですが、ごごはひまです。
朝はいそがしいけど、ごごはひまだよ。(male) ／
朝はいそがしいけど、ごごはひまよ。(female)

B: そうですか。テニスをしようと思(おも)っているんですが、どうですか。／そう。テニスしようと思(おも)ってるんだけど、どう。

A: 何時からですか。／何時から？

B: 一時から五時ごろまでです。／
一時から五時ごろまでだよ。(male) ／一時から五時ごろまでよ。(female)

A: そうですか。いいですよ。／そう。いいよ。
(Write テニス from 1:00 P.M. to 5:00 P.M. on Saturday.)
or すみません。三時からスミスさんの家に行く予定(よてい)なんです。／
ごめん。三時からスミスさんの家に行く予定(よてい)なんだ。(male) ／
ごめん。三時からスミスさんの家に行く予定(よてい)なの。(female)

II. Expressing direction, using the particle へ; Expressing time limits, using the particle までに

A. Expressing direction, using the particle へ

Noun	Particle				
本屋(ほんや)	へ	行って、	地図(ちず)	を	買います。

I'm going to go to the bookstore and buy a map.

暗くなるから、家へ帰ったほうがいいよ。
It'll be dark soon, so you'd better go home.

きっぷをわすれたから、後(あと)で家へ持(も)って行ってもいいですか。
I forgot my ticket, so can I bring it by your house later?

アリス： どこかへ出かけるの？
Are you going out somewhere?

道子(みちこ)： 天気がいいから、みずうみまであるいて行こうと思(おも)って。
I'm going to walk to the lake because the weather is so nice.

- The particle へ indicates a direction, while the particle に indicates a goal or final contact point. Native speakers use the particles に and へ interchangeably if either is acceptable, but へ is used only with verbs indicating transfer, such as 行く, 来る, and 帰る. Any noun used with へ must be a place noun, but the particle に can take other types of nouns as well, as in 山田さん<u>に</u>電話(でんわ)をする.
- Unlike へ, the particle まで can be combined with time expressions as well as place expressions. The use of place noun + まで means *as far as* ～ or *up to* ～. It does not indicate that the place is the destination, so the use of the particle まで in the following example implies that the speaker is going to Tokyo on his or her way to somewhere else. On the other hand, the use of the particle へ or に does not imply that the speaker is going somewhere else besides Tokyo.

今日は東京(とうきょう)まで行く。
I'm going as far as Tokyo today.

今日は東京(とうきょう)へ／に行く。
Today I'm going to Tokyo.

B. Expressing time limits, using the particle までに (by ～; by the time ～)

Noun	Particle					
明日	までに	ホテル	の	予約(よやく)	を	して下さい。

Please make hotel reservations by tomorrow.

明日の午後(ごご)までにはここを出て下さい。	Please leave here by noon tomorrow.
飛行機(ひこうき)は八時までにはくうこうにつくでしょう。	The plane will probably arrive at the airport by eight o'clock.
お金は来月の六日までにははらってね。	Please pay by the sixth of next month.

- The particle までに specifies a time limit within which an action or event must be completed.
- If までに is used, the action in the main clause must be completed. This is not true for the use of まで alone.

五時まで、ここにいます。	I'll stay here until five o'clock.
~~五時までに、ここにいます~~。	~~I'll stay here by five o'clock~~.
~~五時まで、ここに来て下さい~~。	~~Please come here until five o'clock.~~
五時までに、ここに来て下さい。	Please come here by five o'clock.

話してみましょう

A. The following chart shows a flight schedule from Narita Airport. You are an airline agent, and customers question you, as in sentences 1-5 below. Customers must be at the departure lounge thirty minutes before departure time. Tell them which gate to go to and the time by which they should be in the departure lounge.

Example

十二時半の飛行機(ひこうき)でホンコンに行く予定(よてい)なんですが。
十二時までに３８ばんゲートへ行って下さい。

FLIGHT	TO	TIME	STATUS	GATE
NW001	HONG KONG	12:30 P.M.	ON TIME	G38
ANA057	NEW YORK	12:45 P.M.	ON TIME	G25
TWA003	LOS ANGELES	12:55 P.M.	ON TIME	G48
KLM243	LONDON	1:03 P.M.	ON TIME	G10
JAL33	HONOLULU	1:10 P.M.	ON TIME	G22
QA046	SIDNEY	1:15 P.M.	ON TIME	G36

1. 一時十五分の飛行機(ひこうき)でシドニーに行く予定(よてい)なんですが。
2. 十二時五十五分の飛行機(ひこうき)でロサンゼルスに行く予定(よてい)なんですが。
3. 一時三分の飛行機(ひこうき)でロンドンに行く予定(よてい)なんですが。
4. 十二時四十五分の飛行機(ひこうき)でニューヨークに行く予定(よてい)なんですが。
5. 一時十分の飛行機(ひこうき)でホノルルに行く予定(よてい)なんですが。

B. Work with a partner. Using casual speech, ask each other questions 1–5 below and take notes on your partner's answers. Then report your and your partner's answers to the class, using polite speech.

Example

A: 今日は何時ごろまでに家に帰るつもりなの？

B: 六時までに帰るつもりだよ。(male)／六時までに帰るつもりよ。(female)

A: そう。～さんは、何時ごろまでに家に帰るつもり。

B: 五時ごろまでには帰ろうと思(おも)ってるの。

私は今日六時ごろまでに帰るつもりですが、～さんは五時ごろまでには帰ろうと思(おも)っているそうです。

1. 今日は何時ごろまでに学校を出ようと思(おも)いますか。
2. たいてい何時ごろまでに学校に来ますか。
3. 今度のしゅくだいはいつまでに出そうと思(おも)いますか。
4. 今度の休みにどこかへ行こうと思(おも)っていますか。
5. 外国(がいこく)へ行きたいと思(おも)いますか。どの国(くに)へ行こうと思(おも)いますか。

C. Work with a partner. One person is the tour guide and the other person a Japanese tourist. The guide is taking a group of Japanese tourists to various places in Melbourne and describes the following schedule as well as the place and time to get together before leaving for the next stop. The tourist takes notes.

Example

九時にホテルを出ますから、八時四十五分までに、ホテルのロビーに来て下さい。

十時にメルボルン動物園(どうぶつえん)につく予定(よてい)です。

時間	予定(よてい)
9:00	ホテル ⇨ メルボルン動物園(どうぶつえん)
9:30	メルボルン動物園(どうぶつえん)につく
12:00	動物園(どうぶつえん)のレストランで食事(しょくじ)
1:30	メルボルン動物園(どうぶつえん) ⇨ 国立美術館(こくりつびじゅつかん) (National Art Museum)
3:00	国立美術館(こくりつびじゅつかん) ⇨ オパール (Opal) 博物館(はくぶつかん)
5:00	オパール博物館(はくぶつかん) ⇨ ホテル
7:00	ホテル ⇨ レストラン
9:00	レストラン ⇨ ホテル

D. Work with a different partner. One person is the tour guide and the other person a Japanese tourist. The guide should decide where to take the tourist, then make a schedule similar to the one above. Describe the schedule as well as the place and time to get together before leaving for the next stop. Do not show the schedule to the tourist. The tourist should confirm the information and take notes.

Example

A: 九時にホテルを出ますから、八時四十五分までにホテルのロビーに来て下さい。

B: 八時半までにホテルのロビーに来て、九時にホテルを出るんですね。

A: ええ、九時にホテルを出ます。でも、ホテルのロビーには八時四十五分までに来て下さい。

III. Reporting speech, using と言(い)う

A. X を Y と言(い)う (call X Y)

(Looking at Japanese quotation marks, 「〜」)

Question				
Direct Object/Theme				
Noun	Particle/Particle	Question word	Particle	
これ	を／は	何	と	言(い)いますか。

What are these called?

Answer		
Noun	Particle	
かぎかっこ	と	言(い)います。

We call these **kagikakko.**

山田さんの名前(なまえ)はさとしと言(い)います。 Yamada-san's first name is Satoshi.

鈴木(すずき)さんはそのいぬをラッキーとよんでいる。 Suzuki-san calls the dog Lucky.

- The particle と indicates that the preceding clause is a quoted clause or phrase.
- The phrase 〜は日本語で何と言(い)いますか is an application of X を Y と言(い)う, where X is the topic of the sentence.

Taco は日本語でタコスと言(い)います。
Tacos are called **takosu** in Japanese.

日本人は tacos をタコスと言(い)います。
The Japanese call tacos **takosu.**

日本語ではこれをタコスと言(い)いますが、英語(えいご)では taco と言(い)います。
This is called **takosu** in Japanese, but it is called a *taco* in English.

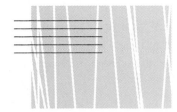

- Use とよぶ when you express a name that you have given, such as a dog's name.
- To ask how to pronounce unknown characters, use 読む instead of 言(い)う. (Smith-san is asking about the **kanji** compound 韓国.)

スミス：　このかんじは何と読みますか。
　　How do you read these **kanji**?

山田：　かんこくと読みます。
　　They are read **kankoku.**

- In colloquial speech, the particle と is often replaced by って. In a question, 何て is pronounced なんて.

アリスはこのねこをミッキーってよんでるのよ。
Alice calls this cat Mickey.

このかんじ、何(なん)て読むの。
How do you read this **kanji**?

B. X という Y (a Y called X)

Question					
Noun (specific)	**Particle**	**Verb**	**Noun (categorical)**		
山本さん	と	いう	人	を	知(し)っていますか。

Do you know a person called Yamamoto-san?

Answer
いいえ、知(し)りません。

No, I don't.

山水荘(さんすいそう)という旅館(りょかん)にとまりました。　I stayed in a Japanese-style inn called Sansuisoo.

びゅうプラザという所で、安(やす)いきっぷが買えますよ。　You can purchase a cheap ticket in the place called View Plaza.

山田っていう人が来たよ。　A person called Yamada has come.

コナっていう喫茶店(きっさてん)でまってるよ。　I'll be waiting for you at a coffee shop called Kona.

- In the expression X という Y, the noun Y indicates a general category such as person, place, school, name, etc., and the noun X indicates a specific instance of Y. In this usage, という is usually written in **hiragana** instead of **kanji.**

東京(とうきょう)大学という大学	A university called the University of Tokyo
スミソニアンという博物館(はくぶつかん)	A museum called the Smithsonian
ミラージュというホテル	A hotel called Mirage
ばらというはな	The species of flower called rose

C. X は Clause (Plain form) と言う, X says that ～／聞く, X asks if/whether ～／答(こた)える, X answers that ～

Question								
Topic (subject)		Clause						
					Verb (plain present)	Particle	Particle	
アリスさん	は	黒田(くろだ)さん	は	いつ	出かける	か	と	聞きました。

Alice-san asked when Kuroda-san would go out.

Answer					
Topic (subject)		Clause			
			Verb (plain present)	Particle	
スミスさん	は	明日	出かける	と	答(こた)えました。

Smith-san answered that he would go out tomorrow.

道子(みちこ)さんはあの人はだれかと聞きました。
Michiko-san asked who that person was.

石田(いしだ)さんはキムさんだと言(い)いました。
Ishida-san said that it was Kim-san.

キム： 田中さんにどこにとまったらいいかって聞いたの。
I asked Tanaka-san where we should stay.

サム： そう、で、田中さん何て答(こた)えたの？
I see. Then what did he say?

キム： みんしゅくが安(やす)くてべんりだって言(い)ってたよ。
He said that private guest houses are cheap and convenient.

- The use of 言(い)いました merely reports the fact that something was said, while 言(い)っていました tends to emphasize the content of what was said. The form 言(い)っています also focuses on content, but it implies that the listener did not hear or acknowledge the original statement, so it is being repeated. The form 言(い)います is used to quote words that are supposedly common knowledge, or to indicate a future action. The tenses of the quoted clause and the main clause do not have to agree.

  スミスさんはおみやげは買わないと言(い)いました。
  Smith-san said he will not buy a souvenir.

  スミスさんはおみやげは買わないと言(い)っていました。
  Smith-san was saying he would not buy a souvenir.

  スミスさんはおみやげは買わなかったと言(い)っています。
  Smith-san says he did not buy a souvenir.

  日本の六月は雨が多いと言(い)います。
  It is said (they say) that it rains a lot in June in Japan.

  明日スミスさんに電話(でんわ)をかけて、私が計画(けいかく)をたてると言(い)います。
  I'll call Smith-san tomorrow and tell him I'll make the plans.

- When the particle と is replaced by って in colloquial speech, the verb 言(い)う can be deleted if the subject of 言(い)う is not used.

  パスポートは来週の月曜日までにとれるって。
  I heard I can get my passport by next Monday. (literally: Someone said I can get my passport by next Monday.)

- To quote a question, use 聞く instead of 言(い)う in an indirect quote. To quote an answer, use either 答(こた)える or 言(い)う. The plain present affirmative form of the copula verb, だ, must be deleted before the question particle か.

  天気はいいかと聞きました。
  I asked whether the weather is good.

  天気はよかったかと聞きました。
  I asked whether the weather was good.

  天気はどうかと聞きました。
  I asked what the weather is like.

  ホテルがある所はべんりな場所(ばしょ)かと聞きました。
  I asked whether the hotel is located in a convenient location.

そのみんしゅくは安(やす)いと答(こた)えました。

I answered that **minshuku** are cheap.

そのみんしゅくは安(やす)かったと答(こた)えました。

I answered that **minshuku** were cheap.

そのみんしゅくはきれいだと答(こた)えました。

I answered that **minshuku** are clean.

D. Using direct quote と言(い)う (~ say " ~ ")

	Open quotation marker	Quoted clause	Close quotation marker	Particle	
スミスさんは	「	すみません。	」	と	言(い)いました。

Smith-san said, "I'm sorry."

アリス： 山田さんは鈴木(すずき)さんに何(なん)て言(い)ったの。
What did Yamada-san say to Suzuki-san?

道子(みちこ)： 「好きだ。」って言(い)ったのよ。
He said, "I love you."

アリス： それで、鈴木(すずき)さんは何(なん)て言(い)ったの。
Then what did Suzuki-san say?

道子(みちこ)： 「ごめんなさい。」って言(い)ったのよ。
She said, "I'm sorry." (This is a polite way of refusing his attentions.)

- In direct quotes, what was actually said is quoted without modification and placed inside quotation marks (「 」). In indirect quotes, the quoted clause must end with the plain form, and no quotation marks are used. Final sentences particles except for か (the question marker) are omitted from the indirect quote.

スミスさんは「カメラわすれたのよ。」と言(い)いました。

Smith-san said, "I forgot my camera."

スミスさんはカメラをわすれたと言(い)いました。

Smith-san said she forgot her camera.

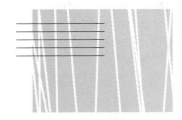

話してみましょう

A. Use the form ～という to ask whether someone knows about the following places and things. Use both casual and polite speech.

Example

山田さん

山田さんという人を知(し)っていますか。／山田さんって人知(し)ってる。

1. デニーズ
2. IBM
3. 東京(とうきょう)
4. ペプシ
5. うどん
6. ブラジル
7. ハイアット
8. グランドキャニオン

B. Work as a class. When you travel overseas, knowing some basic phrases in the language of the country comes in handy. Choose three expressions from the box and ask how they are said in other languages, such as German, French, or Spanish.

こんにちは　さようなら　はじめまして　すみません お元気ですか　ありがとう

Example

A: ～さんはフランス語が分かりますか。
B: ええ、分かりますよ。or
いいえ、分かりません。

A: フランス語で「こんにちは」は何と言(い)いますか。or
そうですか。しつれいしました。(Excuse me.)

B: 「Bonjour」と言(い)います。

C. You are thinking of going on a trip to Japan for two weeks and are gathering some information. Your friends volunteer the information in sentences 1–7 below. Confirm what they said with someone else using indirect quotes. Use both casual and polite speech.

Example

飛行機(ひこうき)はユナイテッドがべんりだよ

飛行機(ひこうき)はユナイテッドがべんりだと聞きましたが、本当(ほんとう)ですか。

1. 日本のえきにはエレベーター (elevator) がありません。
2. JR の安(やす)いきっぷは外国(がいこく)では買えません。
3. 成田空港(なりたくうこう)はあまりべんりじゃありません。
4. 東京(とうきょう)にはカプセルホテルという小さくて安(やす)いホテルがあります。
5. 東京(とうきょう)にはドルでお金がはらえる店(みせ)があります。
6. 京都(きょうと)の言葉(ことば)はむずかしいです。
7. 京都(きょうと)は春が一番(ばん)きれいです。

D. Work with a partner. The two of you should sit back-to-back and think of four questions about your travel experiences. Ask them to your partner, who restates them to you for affirmation. The partner should answer each question, and you restate the answer for affirmation. Use both casual and polite speech.

Example

A: 外国(がいこく)に行ったことがありますか。／外国(がいこく)に行ったことあるの？

B: 外国(がいこく)に行ったことがあるかと聞きましたね。
／外国(がいこく)に行ったことあるかって聞いたよね。

A: ええ、言(い)いました。／うん、言(い)ったよ。

B: ありますよ。／あるよ。

A: あると答(こた)えましたね。／あると答(こた)えたよね。

B: ええ、答(こた)えました。／うん、答(こた)えたよ。

IV. Expressing opinions about things, events, and actions, using the plain form + と思(おも)う

				い -adjective (plain present)	Particle	
この	ガイドブック	は	とても	いい	と	思(おも)います。

A. I think this guidebook is very good.

Question								
Question word						Verb (plain past)	Particle	
だれ	が	ホテル	の	予約(よやく)	を	した	と	思(おも)いますか。

B. Who do you think made the hotel reservation?

Answer				
		Verb (plain past)	Particle	
スミスさん	が	した	と	思(おも)います。

C. I think it was Smith-san.

トム： 外国(がいこく)に行くのはきらい？
You don't like going to foreign countries?

かずお：うん、あまり好きじゃないね。言葉(ことば)が分からないから大変(たいへん)だと思うんだ。
No, not really. I don't understand other languages, so I think it will be tough for me .

リー： この旅館(りょかん)をどう思いますか。
What do you think of this Japanese inn?

田中： ああ、ここにはとまったことがあります。いい旅館(りょかん)だったと思(おも)いますよ。
Well, I've stayed here before. I think it was a nice inn.

- The use of the plain form + と思(おも)います expresses the speaker's opinion about things or events, but not his /her desires or intentions. Use the volitional form of verbs + と思(おも)います to express intentions, and ～たいと思(おも)います to express desires.

山田さんはカメラを買うと思(おも)います。
I think Yamada-san is going to buy a camera.

私はそのカメラを買おうと思(おも)います。
I'm thinking of buying that camera.

私はそのカメラを / が買いたいと思(おも)います。
I think I'd like to buy that camera.

- Normally the subject of 思(おも)う is the speaker, but it is often omitted. The speaker can be specified for emphasis or if it is contextually unclear. When the subject of the main clause is someone other than the speaker, the form 思(おも)っている should be used instead of 思(おも)う.

私はそのツアーはいいと思(おも)います。
I think that tour is good.

でも、山下さんはちょっと高いと思(おも)っています。
But Yamashita-san thinks it's a bit too expensive.

- To form an information question, use a question word and end the sentence with か as in key sentence B. To ask for a general impression or opinion, use ～をどう思(おも)いますか *(what do you think of ～)*.

キム：　どんなおみやげがいいと思(おも)いますか。
　　What kind of souvenir do you think is appropriate?
川口：　そうですね。食べ物(もの)はどうですか。
　　Let's see. How about food?
アリス：　このみんしゅくどう思(おも)う？
　　What do you think of this guest house?
道子(みちこ)：　ちょっと高いけど場所(ばしょ)はべんりそうでいいと思(おも)うわ。
　　I think it's a bit expensive, but the location seems convenient, so it should be okay.

- The tense of the clause preceding と does not have to agree with that of 思(おも)う.

そのみずうみは水がきれいだと思(おも)います。
I think that lake has clean water.

十年前(まえ)はそのみずうみの水はきれいだったと思(おも)います。
I think the water in that lake was clean ten years ago.

そのみずうみは水がきれいだと思(おも)いました。
I thought that the lake had clean water.

十年前(まえ)はそのみずうみの水はきれいだったと思(おも)いました。
Ten years ago, I thought the water in that lake was clean.

話してみましょう

A. A friend of Michiko-san is thinking about applying to your school. Answer his or her questions, using the plain form + と思(おも)う.

Example

〜さんの大学は大きいですか。
いいえ、あまり大きくないと思(おも)います。

1. 〜さんの大学には外国人(がいこくじん)がたくさんいますか。
2. 〜さんの大学は日本文学が強いですか。
3. 大学がある町(まち)はどんな町(まち)ですか。
4. 気候(きこう)はどうですか。
5. その町(まち)には日本のレストランがありますか。
6. その町(まち)は日本人が多いですか。

B. Work with a partner. Your friend Kawaguchi-san and his family are planning a one-week vacation to visit you. They want to come to your town for a few days and visit some other places. Make recommendations about places to visit, places to stay, and things to do. Use casual speech.

Example

A: この町(まち)ではどのホテルがいいと思う？
B: ホリデーインがいいと思うよ。くうこうに近いからべんりだと思うよ。
A: あそう。じゃあ、そうする。

C. Form groups of four, and divide each group into two pairs. Columns A and B in the following chart contain items that are in opposition to one another in some way. One of the two pairs should become "advocates" for the items in Column A, and the other pair should advocate the advantages of the items in Column B. First, the two people in each pair should discuss the pros of their own item and the cons of those in the other column, then each pair should try to convince the other of the superiority of "their" items. Note that the phrase どんなところ in the example means *which point is*.

Example

A: 大きい町(まち)はどんなところがいいと思(おも)いますか。

B: 店(みせ)がたくさんあるから、べんりだと思(おも)います。

C: じゃあ、大きい町(まち)はどんなところがよくないと思(おも)いますか。

D: そうですね。ものが高いと思(おも)います。

A: 大きい町(まち)は店(みせ)がたくさんあるから、べんりだと思(おも)います。

C: でも、小さい町(まち)のほうがものが安(やす)いと思(おも)いますよ。

B: そうですね。でも . . .

A	B
大きい町(まち)	小さい町(まち)
女	男
日本の 車(くるま)	アメリカの 車(くるま)
先生	学生
日本りょうり	中華(ちゅうか)りょうり

V. Expressing chronological order, using 前(まえ) and 後(あと); Expressing occasion, using 時

A. Using 前(まえ)

A-1. Time expression (duration) + 前(まえ) （に）～ *(ago)*

Time	Suffix	Particle						
三年	前(まえ)	に	その人	に	会った	こと	が	あります。

I met that person three years ago.

A-2. Noun の 前(まえ) （に）*(before ～)*

Noun	Particle	Noun	Particle			
じゅぎょう	の	前(まえ)	に	話	が	あります。

I have something to talk about before class.

A-3. Verb (dictionary form) + 前(まえ) (に) *(before ～)*

	Verb (plain present affirm.)	Noun	Particle						
旅行(りょこう)に	行く	前(まえ)	に、	計画(けいかく)	を	たてた	方	が	いいですよ。

You should make plans before you go on a trip.

ここには三日前(みっかまえ)についた。　I arrived here three days ago.

しけんの前(まえ)はあまりねられない。　I cannot sleep well before an exam.

家を出る前(まえ)に、電話(でんわ)したよ。　I called before I left home.

- When 前(まえ) is used with time expressions, it means, ～ *ago* or *before*. The particle に expressing time is optional with ～前(まえ). Because it can be used as a topic, 前(まえ) can be combined with は as in 前(まえ)は or 前(まえ)には.
- The form should be noun + の + 前(まえ) or the dictionary form of the verb + 前(まえ). The use of the dictionary form in a subordinate clause with terms such as 前(まえ) indicates that the event in the subordinate clause was not completed before the performance of the event in the main clause. Since the event in the 前(まえ) clause cannot be completed until after the event in the main clause, the verb preceding 前(まえ) must be in the present form regardless of the tense used in the main clause.

出かける前(まえ)に、地図(ちず)で行き方(かた)をしらべるつもりです。
I intend to check out the route with a map before going out.

出かける前(まえ)に、地図(ちず)で行き方(かた)をしらべました。
I checked out the route with a map before going out.

- If the subject of the 前(まえ) clause is different from that of the main clause, it must be marked with the particle が.

母が来る前(まえ)に、私はへやをそうじしました。
I cleaned my room before my mother came.

- 前に can be used independently with no clause.

この映画(えいが)は前(まえ)に見たことがあります。
I have seen this movie before.

あのみずうみは前(まえ)はとてもきれいだった。
That lake was very clean before.

B. Using 後(ご／あと)

B-1. Time expression (duration) + 後(ご)（に）(after ～ , ～ later, ～ from now)

Time	Suffix	Particle			
三十分	後(ご)	に	えき	に	つきました。

I arrived at the station thirty minutes later.

B-2. Noun の 後(あと)（で）(after ～)

Noun	Particle	Noun	Particle	
旅行(りょこう)	の	後(あと)	で	ツアーでいっしょだった人に会いました。

I met someone from my tour after the trip.

B-3. Verb (plain past affirmative form) + 後(あと)（で）(after ～)

		Verb (plain past affirmative form)	Noun	Particle			
家	へ	帰った	後(あと)	で、	電話(でんわ)	を	かけます。

I'll call you after I go home.

ここには三日後(ご)についた。
I arrived three days after that.

食事(しょくじ)の後(あと)、映画(えいが)を見に行きました。
I went to a movie after we ate.

明日の三時のじゅぎょうがおわった後(あと)で、出ようと思っています。
I'm thinking of leaving here immediately after my 3 o'clock class tomorrow.

- The pronunciation of 後 is ご when it follows a time expression (二年後(にねんご) = *two years later*). The particle に expressing time is optional with ～後(ご).

- Use the plain past affirmative form of the verb, or noun +の, before 後(あと). The particle で is optional and ～後(あと) can appear in the forms ～後(あと)で,

〜後(あと)は、〜後(あと)では. Use of the plain past form in a subordinate clause indicates that the event in the subordinate clause was completed before the event in the main clause. Since completion of the event in the 後(あと) clause is necessary for the performance of the event in the main clause, the verb in the 後(あと) clause must be in the past tense regardless of the tense of the main clause.

ガイドブックを読んだ後(あと)で、旅行会社(りょこうがいしゃ)に電話(でんわ)をしました。
After I read the guidebook, I called up the travel agency.

さなえ： いつきっぷ買うつもり？
When do you intend to buy the tickets?

まもる： ホテルを予約(よやく)した後(あと)、買おうと思(おも)ってるの。
I think I'll buy the tickets after I've made the hotel reservation.

- If the subject of the 後(あと)で clause is different from that of the main clause, it must be marked with the particle が.

映画(えいが)は、山田さんが来た後(あと)で、はじまりました。
The movie started after Yamada-san arrived.

- 後(あと) can be used independently, with no clause.

後(あと)で地図(ちず)を見て下さい。
Please take a look at the map later.

C. Expressing occasion, using 時

C-1. Plain present form + 時 (uncompleted action)

				Verb (plain present affirmative form)	Noun			
母	は	本	を	読む	時、	めがね	を	かけます。

When my mother reads books, she wears her glasses.

		Verb (plain present affirmative form)	Noun			
買物(かいもの)	を	している	時、	ともだち	に	会いました。

I met a friend while I was shopping.

C-2. Plain past form + 時 (completed action)

				Verb (plain past affirmative form)	Noun		
これ	は	ハワイ	に	行った	時	に、	買いました。

I bought this when I went to Hawaii.

Type word	Tense	Modification rule	Example
Noun + copula verb	Affirmative	Noun + の ＋ 時	一人の時 (when I am alone)
	Negative	Noun + じゃない ＋ 時	一人じゃない時 (when I am not alone)
な -adjective	Affirmative	Stem + な ＋ 時	元気な時 (when I feel well)
	Negative	Stem + じゃない ＋ 時	元気じゃない時 (when I don't feel well)
い -adjective	Affirmative	Stem + い ＋ 時	たのしい時 (when it is fun)
	Negative	Stem + くない ＋ 時	たのしくない時 (when it isn't fun)
Verbs	Present affirmative	Dictionary form + 時	つかう時 (when I use it)
	Past affirmative	Plain past form + 時	つかった時 (when/right after I used it)
	Negative	Plain negative form + 時	つかわない時 (when I don't use it)

チョー：　日本ではだれかの家に行った時、何と言(い)いますか。

What do you say when you go to someone's house in Japan?

道子(みちこ)：　そうですね。げんかんの前(まえ)で「ごめん下さい」と言(い)って家の中に入る時、「おじゃまします」と言(い)います。

Let's see. We say **gomenkudasai** in front of the entrance. Then, when we go into the house, we say **ojamashimasu**.

ORAL
- Talk about experienced in overseas
- Which places in Japan you will visit
- What will you do before + after Japan
- Where you will stay in Japan

6 Grammar items

- The form of the adjectives, verbs, or nouns coming before 時 is the same used as when they modify nouns.
- The particle に expressing time is optional; 〜時 can appear in the forms 〜時に, 〜時は, or 〜時には.
- The use of 時 with nouns and adjectives was introduced in Chapter 10 of Volume 1. It is not necessary to use the past tense when pairing 時 with nouns, adjectives, or verbal expressions that express a state of being such as ある, いる, 〜ている, and 〜ない.

病気の時、病院に行きました。

I went to the hospital when I was sick.

病気じゃない時は、よくビールを飲みました。

I often drank beer when I was not sick.

ひまな時は、町(まち)のかんこうをしました。

I went sightseeing when I had free time.

ひまじゃない時は、あまりかんこうは出来ませんでした。
I couldn't do much sightseeing when I didn't have any free time.

いそがしい時、あまり出かけませんでした。
I didn't go out much when I was busy.

いそがしくない時、よく映画(えいが)を見ました。
I often watched movies when I wasn't busy.

- When 時 is combined with an action verb, the tense in the 時 clause indicates whether the action in this clause was completed at the time the action in the main clause took place. Thus, present tense indicates that the action in the 時 clause was not completed when the action in the main clause took place.

出かける時、電話(でんわ)して下さい。
Please call me when you leave home.

そのレストランに行く時、予約(よやく)をした方がいいでしょうか。
Should I make a reservation before I go to that restaurant?

子供(こども)がねている時は、しずかにして下さい。
Please hold it down when the child is sleeping.

- Use of the past tense in the 時 clause indicates that the event in this clause was or will have been completed at the time the event in the main clause took place.

そのさかなを食べた時、おなかがいたくなりました。
I got a stomachache when I ate that fish.

ホテルについた時、電話(でんわ)します。
I will call you when I have arrived at the hotel.

- The tense in the main clause indicates when the entire event took place.

日本に行く時、母に電話(でんわ)します。
I will call my mother before I go to Japan.

日本に行った時、母に電話(でんわ)します。
I will call my mother when I get to Japan.

日本に行く時、母に電話(でんわ)しました。
I called my mother when I went to Japan.

日本に行った時、母に電話(でんわ)しました。
I called my mother when I got to Japan.

- Use が to mark the subject of the 時 clause, if it is different from that of the main clause.

山田さんが来た時、鈴木(すずき)さんも来ました。
When Yamada-san got here, so did Suzuki-san.

話してみましょう

A. Describe the following travel plan, using 前(まえ)に and 後(あと)で.

10時	ホテルにつきます
	少し休みます
1時	美術館(びじゅつかん)に行きます
3時	おてらを見ます
4時	おみやげを買います
5時半	レストランで晩ごはんを食べます
7時	映画(えいが)を見ます
9時	おふろに入ります
10時半	父に電話(でんわ)します
12時	ねます

Example

美術館(びじゅつかん)に行く前(まえ)に、少し休みます。

ホテルについた後(あと)、少し休みます。

B. Choose the most appropriate main clause for each of the 時 clauses, and match the letters with the numbers.

Example

おなかがいたくなった時、薬(くすり)を飲みました。

1. おなかがいたくなった時
2. 家に帰る時
3. 旅行(りょこう)に行く時
4. 旅行(りょこう)に行った時
5. 映画(えいが)を見る時
6. 家に帰った時
7. 公園(こうえん)に行った時
8. 公園(こうえん)に行く時

A. いぬとあそびました。
B. ともだちがあそびに来ていました。
C. バスで帰りました。
D. めがねをかけました。
E. 薬(くすり)を飲みました。
F. おみやげを買いました。
G. ホテルの予約(よやく)をしました。
H. サンドイッチを持(も)って行きました。

C. Work as a class. Ask your classmates where and when they have traveled in the past, and when they think they might visit the same places again. Use polite speech.

Example

A: 〜さんはどんなところに旅行(りょこう)に行ったことがありますか。

B: 十年前(まえ)にグランドキャニオンへ行ったことがあります。

A: またグランドキャニオンへ行こうと思いますか。

B: ええ、十年後(ご)にはまた行きたいと思いますね。

D. Work with a partner. Discuss with each other what you will do before, during, and after a trip to a foreign country, using 〜時, 〜前(まえ), and 〜後(あと). Use casual speech. Then report to the class using polite speech.

Example

A: 海外旅行(かいがいりょこう)に行く前(まえ)に、何するの？

B: その国(くに)の言葉(ことば)ちょっと勉強すると思(おも)う。

A: 旅行(りょこう)に行く時、何持(も)って行く？

B: カメラ持(も)って行く。

A: じゃあ、旅行(りょこう)に行った時、何する。

B: たくさん写真(しゃしん)とると思う。

A: あ、そう。じゃあ、旅行(りょこう)から帰った後、何する？

B: りょうしんに電話すると思うよ。

海外旅行(かいがいりょこう)に行く前(まえ)にその国(くに)の言葉(ことば)を少し勉強します。そして、出かける時にはカメラを持(も)って行きます。旅行(りょこう)に行った時は、写真(しゃしん)をたくさんとって、旅行(りょこう)から帰った後では、りょうしんに電話をします。

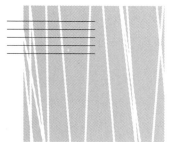

漢字

Component shapes of kanji 2: Side components

Common shapes appearing on the left side and the right side of **kanji** are listed here for some **kanji** you have learned so far. Examples in parentheses show the use of the component shape in a different location, or cases where a radical is used as a character by itself.

Name*		Meaning	Examples of use
さんずい	氵	water	泊 泳 海 湖 （川）
つちへん	土	land, soil	地 （土）
にんべん	亻	person	何 休 体 住 （人）
ひへん	日	day, sun	曜 時 晴 朝 （日 春 東）
きへん	木	tree	校 （木 本 東 来 末 親）
しょくへん	飠	eating	飲 館 （食）
ゆみへん	弓	bow	強 （弱 弟）
かねへん	釒	metal, gold	銀 （金）
おんなへん	女	female	姉 妹 （女）
かたへん	方	direction	族 旅 （方）
ぎょうにんべん	彳	way	行 後
ごんべん	言	say, language	読 話 語 （言）
のぎへん	禾	crop	私 秋
いとへん	糸	thread	約
たへん	田	rice field	町 （画 田）

Name*		Meaning	Examples of use
N/A	寺	**On**-reading: じ	時
N/A	月	Meaning: moon	朝 明 （前 育）
N/A	青	**On**-reading: せい	晴

* If the “component shape” is a traditional radical, the name of the radical is listed. Component shapes that are not radicals do not have particular names. We use the concept of component shapes strictly as a pedagogical tool, and there might be discrepancies between the explanations in this book and those in traditional **kanji** dictionaries.

Kanji	Meaning	Readings	Examples
予	previous	ヨ	行く予定(よてい)です。予約(よやく)をしました。天気(てんき)予報(よほう)
定	to fix, to decide, to establish	テイ/さだ（める）	今月は予定(よてい)がありません。
約	promise, approximately (prefix)	ヤク	ホテルを予約(よやく)する。
前	front, before	ゼン/まえ	家の前(まえ)。日本に行く前(まえ)。午前(ごぜん)２時
後	behind, after	ゴ/うし（ろ）あと	つくえの後(うし)ろにある。ホテルについた後(あと)。３年後(ご)
末	end of	マツ/すえ	週末(しゅうまつ)。月末(げつまつ)。年末(ねんまつ)
思	to think	ソウ/おも（う）	明日(あした)行こうと思(おも)います。日本に帰(かえ)ろうと思(おも)います。
言	to say, speech, word	ゲン/い（う）	病院に行くと言(い)いました。
知	to get to know, to know	チ/し（る）	日本語を知(し)っています。来月行くかも知(し)れません。
答	to answer, to respond	トウ/こた（える）	日本語で答(こた)えて下さい。

電 電 electricity デン

電気(でんき)をつける。電話(でんわ)をかける。電車(でんしゃ)にのる。

車 車 vehicle, wheel シャ/くるま

車(くるま)で行きます。自転車(じてんしゃ)。電車(でんしゃ)

写 写 to take a photograph, to copy シャ/うつ（す）

写真(しゃしん)をとります。

真 真 truth, reality シン

きれいな写真(しゃしん)ですね。旅行(りょこう)の写真(しゃしん)

映 映 to project エイ/うつ（す）

映画(えいが)を見る。映画館(えいがかん)に行く。

画 画 picture ガ、カク

日本の映画(えいが)。旅行(りょこう)の計画(けいかく)をたてる。

国 国 country コク、ゴク/くに

大きい国(くに)。中国(ちゅうごく)。韓国(かんこく)。

町 町 town チョウ/まち

小さい町(まち)の方が好きです。

銀 銀 silver ギン

後(あと)で銀行(ぎんこう)に行きます。

社 社 company シャ

コンピュータの会社(かいしゃ)。旅行会社(りょこうがいしゃ)

図 図

drawing, plan　ズ、ト

としょかん
図書館で本を読む。

館 館

large house, mansion　カン

りょかん　えいがかん　としょかん　はくぶつかん　びじゅつかん　たいくかん
旅館。映画館。図書館。博物館。美術館。体育館。

公 公

public　コウ/おおやけ

こうえん
公園であそぶ。

園 園

garden　エン/その

こうえん
きれいな公園。

店 店

store, shop　テン/みせ

きっさてん　みせ
しずかな喫茶店。小さい店

地 地

ground　チ、ジ

ちかてつ　ちず
地下鉄の地図。

京 京

capital　キョウ、ケイ

あした　きょうと
明日、京都に行きます。

計 計

to measure　ケイ/はか（る）

りょこう　けいかく　けいかく
旅行の計画はできましたか。高そうな計画ですね。

旅 旅

travel　リョ/たび

りょこう　りょかん
旅行をする。旅館にとまる。

安 安

inexpensive, peaceful, safe　アン/やす（い）

りょかん　やす　やす　かいがい
この旅館は安かったです。安い海外ツアーがあります。

あたらしい読み

ぎんこう　りょこう　あいだ　　あいだ　ことば　とけい
銀行　旅行　間　（その間に）言葉　時計

練習

下のぶんを読んで下さい。

1. 旅行に行く前にその旅館に電話をかけて予約をするつもりだ。
2. 今週の週末に映画を見に行く計画をたてた。
3. 今日は会社へ行く前に、銀行と図書館へ行きたいから、電車で行こうと思う。
4. 大川さんは写真をとるのが好きだと言っていました。
5. 夜おそかったので、その日は公園の近くにある安いホテルにとまった。
6. 私は中国から来ました。三年後に国に帰る予定です。
7. この町で一番（ばん）いい旅行会社を知っていますか。
8. 中国語で書かれた東京の地図をさがしているんですが、この店にあるでしょうか。
9. A:映画館の前にある喫茶（きっさ）店でコーヒーを飲みませんか。
   B:ああ、あの店ですか。いいですよ。

上手な読み方

Using transition devices

Transition devices such as conjunctions and clause connectors help clarify the relationships among sentences and paragraphs. Paying attention to these connectors will help you understand how the text is organized and provide clues for finding important information in the text. There are many expressions that use the そ -series of demonstrative expressions, such as そこ , その後 , その前 , その時 , and その人 . When they are used to refer to something that the speaker cannot physically see, they refer to something previously mentioned. In this sense, they are similar to *the* or *that* in English.

きのう
昨日レストランに行きました。そこはとても大きい。。。

きのう
昨日レストランに行きました。その後で、。。。

Complete the following sentences with appropriate transition devices from the box.

そして	それから	その後(あと)で	その前(まえ)に	それに	それで
つぎに	まず(はじめに)	というのは	ですから	でも	
ところが					

1. きのう公園へ行きました。＿＿＿＿＿山田さんのうちに行きました。＿＿＿＿山田さんはいませんでした。＿＿＿＿家へ帰りました。
2. 日本に行く時には、＿＿＿＿＿ガイドブックを買って読んだ方がいい。＿＿＿＿＿いい旅行会社をさがした方がいい。＿＿＿＿＿安い飛行機(ひこうき)のきっぷを買った方がいい。＿＿＿＿二か月ぐらい前に予約をとった方がいい。
3. きのうは学校に行けませんでした。＿＿＿＿＿ルームメートが病気になったので、いっしょに病院へ行ったのです。

ハワイ旅行 (Trip to Hawaii)

読む前に

1. ハワイに行ったことがありますか。
2. ハワイは何月がいいと思いますか。
3. ハワイではどんなことが出来ると思いますか。
4. ハワイではどんなおみやげが買えると思いますか。

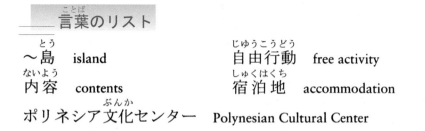

読んでみましょう

言葉(ことば)のリスト

～島(とう) island
自由行動(じゆうこうどう) free activity
内容(ないよう) contents
宿泊地(しゅくはくち) accommodation
ポリネシア文化(ぶんか)センター Polynesian Cultural Center

今年の冬は大阪(おおさか)からハワイに遊(あそ)びに行くつもりです。休みは十二月十九日から、一月八日までなので、その間に行こうと思います。五泊(はく)六日ぐらいで、オアフ島(とう)とマウイ島(とう)に行きたいと思っています。それから、ポリネシア文化(ぶんか)センターは面白(おもしろ)いそうですから、そこにも行きたいと思います。お金はあまりないので、安いツアーをさがしています。

分かりましたか。

この人に一番(ばん)いいツアーを下の旅行計画からさがして下さい。

■ 旅行代金　● おとな・こども同額

	ブーゲンビリアコース		
	５日コース	６日コース	７日コース
出発日	食事なし	食事なし	食事なし
	3110-0 MC	3105-0 MC	3115-0 MC
11/21, 22, 23, 25, 26, 27, 28, 29, 30	95,000	99,000	105,000
12/21	108,000	111,000	115,000
12/19, 20, 22, 23	114,000	116,000	120,000
1/5, 6, 7, 8, 9, 10, 12, 13, 14, 15, 16	139,000	143,000	149,000
2/1, 2, 3, 4, 5, 6, 7, 8, 9, 10, 11, 12	150,000	154,000	160,000
3/16, 17, 18, 19, 20, 22, 23, 24, 25	161,000	165,000	171,000
1/11, 2/15	178,000	182,000	188,000
3/15, 21	202,000	206,000	212,000

旅行日数			内容・宿泊地
5	6	7	
1	1	1	夜：大阪発→ホノルルへ（日付変更線通過） 午前：ホノルル着（レイグリーティングはありません。） 着後：バスにてワイキキヘトラベルBOXにて滞在中の説明愛（昼食は各自でお取り下さい。） 午後：ホノルル市内・近郊観光 ホテルチェックインは観光後になります。）　ワイキキ
2/3	2-4	2-5	終日：自由行動 （各種オプショナルツアーは観光後になります。）　ワイキキ
4	5	6	朝：バスにて空港へ 午前：ホノルル発→大阪へ（日付変更線通過）　機中
5	6	7	午後：大阪着

オプショナルツアー
OPTIONAL TOUR

マウイ島日帰り観光
コースNo. 3097-1
●約１１時間 ●毎日06:30前後発 ●昼食付き ●最小催行人員１名 ●大人28,000円、子供22,000円
＜主催：トラベルプラザ＞

カウアイ島島日帰り観光
コースNo. 3097-2
●約１１時間 ●毎日07:40前後発 ●昼食付き ●最小催行人員１名 ●大人28,000円、子供22,000円
＜主催：トラベルプラザ＞

ハワアイ島島日帰り観光
コースNo. 3097-3
●約１１時間 ●毎日07:40前後発 ●昼食付き ●最小催行人員１名 ●大人28,000円、子供22,000円
＜主催：トラベルプラザ＞

デラックス・ポリネシア文化センター
コースNo. 3098-1
●約９時間半 ●日曜日を抜く毎日13:50前後発 ●夕食付き ●最小催行人員１名 ●大人15,000円、子供13,000円
＜主催：トラベルプラザ＞

シーライフ・パーク・ツアー
●約４時間半 ●毎日09:40前後発●最小催行人員１名 ●大人5,000円、子供4,000円
＜主催：トラベルプラザ＞

読んだ後で

A. 下のしつもんに日本語で答えて下さい。そして、旅行計画をぶんしょう (paragraph) で書いて下さい。

1. 何日に大阪(おおさか)を出たらいいと思いますか。
2. 何日にホノルルを出たらいいでしょうか。
3. ポリネシア文化(ぶんか)センターにはいつ行けますか。
4. マウイ島(とう)へはいつ行ったらいいと思いますか。
5. お金はいくらぐらいかかる (cost) と思いますか。

B. 下の旅行計画を読んで下さい。Identify the transition devices in the text below. Point out the differences between this travel plan and the one you selected and described in Exercise A above.

一月一日の晩に大阪(おおさか)を出て、二日の朝、ホノルルに着(つ)く予定です。その後、ホテルに行きますが、ホテルへ行く時に、ホノルルの町をバスで観光(かんこう)します。昼ご飯(はん)はホテルに着(つ)いた時に食べて下さい。三日は朝十一時半にホノルルを出て、ポリネシア文化(ぶんか)センターに行く予定です。ポリネシア文化(ぶんか)センターでは、自由行動(じゆうこうどう)ですが、午後(ごご)八時から十時まで、ショーがありますから、七時半までにセンターの入口(いりぐち)にあつまって下さい。ショーが終わった後は、バスでホテルへ帰ります。三日目と四日目は自由行動(じゆうこうどう)です。六日の晩、ホノルルを出て、その日に大阪(おおさか)に着きます。

上手な聞き方

Using transition devices, and the difference between そ-series and あ-series words

As was the case with written material, conversation is also full of transition devices. These help the conversation proceed smoothly. In particular, the speaker often uses そ-words (for example, それ in comments like それはよかったですね) to refer to what is being said. Occasionally, the speaker chooses あ-series words instead of そ-series words. The difference between the two is that そ-series words are used when either the speaker or the listener is unfamiliar with what is being talked about, and あ-series words are used to refer to matters that both the speaker and the listener are familiar with and share information about. For example, その in the following dialogue indicates that 大木(おおき)さん does not know much about the 旅館. But あそこ implies that 木村(きむら)さん has stayed in, worked at, or checked out the 旅館 previously, and 木村(きむら)さん is expressing the fact that he shares knowledge about it with 山田さん.

山田：　高山(たかやま)旅館という旅館にとまったんですよ。

大木(おおき)：　その旅館はどこにあるんですか。

木村(きむら)：　高山(たかやま)にあるんですよ。あそこはとてもいい旅館ですね。

STUDENT

Listen to the following exchanges, circle the demonstrative word used in the conversation, and write what it refers to. Then explain why this particular demonstrative word was used and why the speaker chose そ or あ.

Example

それ／その／そこ／あれ／あの／あそこ　くろださん

男の人は黒田(くろだ)さんという人を知らないからです。

1. それ／その／そこ／あれ／あの／あそこ

   ____

2. それ／その／そこ／あれ／あの／あそこ ____________

   ____

3. それ／その／そこ／あれ／あの／あそこ

   ____

どのツアーにしましょうか。 (Which tour should I take?)

聞く前に

下のツアーのスケジュールを読んで、しつもんに答えて下さい。

1. 一番(ばん)安いツアーはどれですか。
2. 一番(ばん)時間がかかるツアーはどれですか。
3. スケジュールが大変(たいへん)なツアーはどれですか。
4. 夏休みに行くツアーはどれがいいですか。
5. 冬休みはどのツアーがいいですか。

STUDENT

聞いてみましょう

A. 三つのダイアローグを聞いて、女の人が行くツアーの名前（なまえ）を書いて下さい。それから、行くきかん (duration) も書いて下さい。

シドニーとゴールドコースト
６・７・８日間 199,000 円より

スケジュール（6・7・8日間）				
1			夕刻：大阪発→ブリスベンへ	機中泊
2			午前：（シドニー乗継ぎ）→ブリスベンへ 着後：ドリームワールドへ	ゴールドコースト泊
3	3・4		終日：自由行動	ゴールドコースト泊
4	5		午前：ブリスベン発→シドニーへ 着後：シドニー市内観光	シドニー泊
5	6	6・7	終日：自由行動	シドニー泊
6	7	8	午前：シドニー発→帰国の途へ 午後：大阪着	

サンフランシスコとロスアンゼルス
６日間　135,000 円より

スケジュール（６日間）		
1	夕刻：大阪発→サンフランシスコへ 午後：サンフランシスコ市内観光	サンフランシスコ泊
2	終日：自由行動	サンフランシスコ泊
3	午前：サンフランシスコ発→ロスアンゼルスへ 着後：ロスアンゼルス市内観光	ロスアンゼルス泊
4	終日：自由行動	ロスアンゼルス泊
5	午前：ロスアンゼルス発→帰国の途へ	機中泊
6	夕刻：大阪着	

ロンドンとローマとパリ
１０日間　178,000 円より

スケジュール（１０日間）		
1	夜：大阪発→ローマへ	機中泊
2	午前：ローマ発 着後：自由行動	ローマ泊
3	終日：自由行動	ローマ泊
4	午前：ローマ→パリへ 午後：パリ着→着後：自由行動	パリ泊
5・6	終日：自由行動	パリ泊
7	午前：パリ→ロンドンへ 着後：自由行動	ロンドン泊
8	終日：自由行動	ロンドン泊
9	午後：ロンドン発→帰国の途へ	機中泊
10	午後：（東京乗継ぎ）大阪着	

イタリアの休日
９日間　253,000 円より

スケジュール（９日間）		
1	午前：大阪発→夜：ローマ着	ローマ泊
2・3	終日：自由行動	ローマ泊
4	午前：自由行動 午後：ローマ→フィレンツェ	フィレンツェ泊
5	午前：フィレンツェ市内観光 午後：自由行動	フィレンツェ泊
6	午前：自由行動 午後：フィレンツェ→ミラノ	ミラノ泊
7	終日：自由行動	ミラノ泊
8	午前：ミラノ発→帰国の途へ	機中泊
9	午後：大阪着	

ニューヨーク
６日間　149,000 円より

スケジュール（６日間）		
1	夕刻：大阪発→ニューヨークへ 夜：ニューヨーク着→ホテルへ	ニューヨーク泊
2	終日：ニューヨーク市内観光	ニューヨーク泊
3・4	終日：自由行動	ニューヨーク泊
5	午後：ニューヨーク発→帰国の途へ	ニューヨークス泊
6	夕刻：大阪着	

ケアンズ
５・６日間　169,000 円より

スケジュール（５・６日間）			
1		午後：大阪→名古屋→ケアンズへ	機中泊
2		早朝：ケアンズ着 着後：ホテルへ	ケアンズ泊
3		終日：自由行動	ケアンズ泊
4	4	終日：自由行動	ケアンズ泊
	5	終日：自由行動	ケアンズ泊
5	6	午後：ケアンズ発→名古屋へ 夜：名古屋→大阪着	

B. もういちど会話を聞いてから、つぎのしつもんに答えて下さい。
(Listen to the dialogues again and answer the following questions.)

STUDENT

Dialogue 1

1. この女の人はいつツアーに行きますか。
2. どうしてそのツアーにしましたか。
3. この女の人と男の人のかんけい (relationship) は何ですか。

Dialogue 2

1. 女の人はいくらぐらいお金がありますか。
2. どうしてそのツアーにしましたか。
3. この女の人と男の人のかんけい (relationship) は何ですか。

Dialogue 3

1. 季節はいつですか。
2. 女の人はどうしてそのツアーにしましたか。
3. この女の人と男の人のかんけい (relationship) は何ですか。

聞いた後で

A. Work with a partner. One person is a student living in Japan and thinking about going on a trip during summer or winter vacation. The other person is a travel agent. The student should decide on a budget and the length of the trip and explain his or her preferences to the agent. The travel agent should make suggestions.

B. Work with a partner. Both of you work for a travel agency. Plan a trip to your country for Japanese college students during their summer or winter vacation.

STUDENT

DICT-A-CONVERSATION

Your friend Yamada-san approaches you to ask about your plans for spring break.

山田：________________________________

スミス：________________________________

山田：________________________________

スミス：________________________________

山田：________________________________

スミス：________________________________

山田：________________________________

聞き上手話し上手

Introducing a new topic

In Volume 1, you learned how to start a conversation by using phrases like あのう and あのう、すみません. Once you get the attention of the other person, you need to introduce a topic of conversation. An unfinished sentence ending with conjunctive particles such as けど or が is often used to introduce this topic. For example, the following phrases may be used as introductory remarks for asking questions about tours or making a request to change the date of a test.

いいツアーをさがしてるんですけど、
I am looking for a good tour so . . .

先生、来週の金曜日から家族で旅行に行く予定なんですが、
Sir, I am planning to go on a vacation with my family starting next Friday, so . . .

This function of けど and が is different from their original meaning *(but)* because what follows these particles is not in a negative relationship with the preceding statement.

After an introductory remark has been made to alert the other person about what is to come, then the speaker can introduce the main topic.

安くていいのをさがして下さい。
Could you please find a good inexpensive one?

テストを木曜日にしていただけませんか。
Could you hold the exam on Thursday?

The result may be the following "three step" conversation.

山田： あのう、すみません。
本田： はい、何ですか。
山田： 先生、来週の金曜日から家族で旅行に行く予定なんですが。。。
本田： ええ。
山田： テストを木曜日にしていただけませんか。
本田： いいですよ。じゃあ、木曜日の一時ごろ来て下さい。

Following these steps and allowing your listener to respond is considered much more polite in Japanese. Phrases such as 〜のことなんですけど／が、and 〜についてですけど／が、are commonly used to introduce conversational topics. For example,

今度の旅行のことなんですけど、 About our coming trip . . .
パーティについてですが、 It's about the party . . .

Once you get the attention of the listener, use these phrases to introduce a topic of conversation, and make comments after your listener responds to your introductory remark.

本田：　あのう、スミスさん、
スミス：はい。
本田：　今度の旅行のことなんですけど、
スミス：はい、何でしょうか。
本田：　すみません。母が来るので、私は行けないんですが。。。

If you wish to change a topic during a conversation, use ところで *(by the way)*, followed by the above expressions.

ところで、今度の旅行のことなんですけど、

A. Work with a partner. Think of a request, a question, or a conversational topic, then start a conversation and introduce your topic as shown in the examples above.

B. Work with a group of three or four. One person should introduce a topic and start a conversation. In the middle of the conversation, try to find an opportunity to change the topic without being rude. Then introduce your own topic.

総合練習

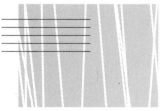

Work with a group of four. Safety is important when traveling. Discuss what one should do before and during a trip. Make a list of suggestions. Use casual speech.

Example

A: 旅行に行く前に何をしたらいいと思う。
B: トラベラーズチェックをつくったほうがいいよね。
C: そうだね。(male)／そうね。(female)
それに、ほけん (insurance) にも入ったほうがいいよね。
D: それから、旅行に行く時に、家族にホテルの電話(でんわ)ばんごうを言って行く。

ロールプレイ

A. You are in Tokyo. You are thinking of going to Hiroshima. Tell a travel agent where you want to go and what you want to see, and ask what is the best way to get there.

B. You want to make a hotel reservation in Kyoto. Call the hotel, tell the clerk you need to make a reservation, and find out if there is a room available. Ask the clerk to speak in easy Japanese rather than using the very polite forms. (Most hotel clerks speak very politely.) You need to specify the type of room (シングル、ダブル) you want and your arrival and departure dates.

C. You are in Tokyo and want to get a plane ticket to go to Hong Kong. Call a travel agent. Tell him or her when you want to go to Hong Kong and ask him or her to find the cheapest available ticket.

D. You are talking to a Japanese friend. Explain the most memorable trip you have had. Describe where you went, what you did, and what happened.

E. You are talking to a Japanese friend who is thinking of going to the United States this summer. Tell your friend what he or she should do before, during, and after going to the United States.

LAB

単語　(ESSENTIAL VOCABULARY)

Nouns

あと（後）　after
おみやげ（お土産）　souvenir
かいがい（海外）　overseas
かいがいりょこう（海外旅行）　overseas travel
がいこく（外国）　overseas; foreign country
ガイドブック　guidebook
カメラ　camera
かんこうりょこう（観光旅行）　sightseeing trip
きっぷ（切符）　ticket
くうこう（空港）　airport
クレジットカード　credit card
けいかく（計画）　plan
ことば（言葉）　language; words; expressions
しつもん（質問）　question
スーツケース　suitcase
ちず（地図）　map
ツアー　tour
つもり　intention
ばしょ（場所）　location
パスポート　passport
まえ（前）　before
みずうみ（湖）　lake
みせ（店）　store; shop
みんしゅく（民宿）　Japanese-style private guest house
よてい（予定）　schedule; plan
りょかん（旅館）　Japanese-style inn
りょこう（旅行）　travel; trip
りょこうがいしゃ（旅行会社）　travel agency

Verbal nouns

かんこう(観光) sightseeing; かんこうをする(観光をする) (to) go sightseeing; かんこうバス(観光バス) chartered bus for sightseeing

よやく(予約) reservation; よやくをする(予約をする) (to) make a reservation; きっぷをよやくする(切符を予約する) (to) reserve a ticket

う-verbs

いう(言う) (to) say

おもう(思う) (to) think; (to) feel

さがす(探す/捜す) (to) look for ～. Use 捜す to look for something that has been lost. Otherwise, use 探す.

つかう(使う) (to) use

つく(着く) (to) arrive

とまる(泊まる) (to) stay (as in a hotel)

はらう(払う) (to) pay

もっていく(持って行く) (to) take; (to) bring

る-verbs

こたえる(答える) (to) answer; しつもんにこたえる(質問に答える) (to) answer a question

しっている(知っている) (to) know. Use しらない(知らない) to express *do not know*. しる(知る) means *come to know* and is an う-verb.

しらべる(調べる) (to) check; (to) investigate; (to) explore

たてる(建てる/立てる) (to) build; (to) establish; (to) make. Use 建てる to build something. Otherwise, use 立てる.

でる(出る) (to) leave; うちをでる(家を出る) (to) leave home

わすれる (to) forget

な-adjectives

べんり(な)(便利な) convenient

Adverbs

とくに(特に) particularly, especially

Suffixes

～はく～か(～泊～日) ～ nights, ～ days

Conjunctions

けれども　however
そのあいだ(に)（その間）　during that time
そのあと(で)（その後で）　after that
そのとき(に)（その時に）　at that time
そのまえ(に)（その前に）　before that
それで　then; so
だから　so
だけど　but
つぎに　next
ですから　therefore; so
というのは　it's because
ところで　by the way
(まず)はじめに(まず始めに)　first (of all)
また　also

Expressions

～についてなんですが　it's about ～
～についてなんですけど　it's about ～
～のことなんですが　it's about ～
～のことなんですけど　it's about ～

Passive Vocabulary

Nouns

アロハシャツ　Hawaiian shirt
うそ　lie うそをつく　(to) tell a lie
えきべん（駅弁）　box lunch sold at train station
かぎかっこ　square bracket
がっき（学期）　academic period such as semester or quarter
こうどう（行動）　action, activity じゆうこうどう（自由行動）　free time, free activity
サーフィン　surfing
サーフボード　surfboard
じゆう（自由）　freedom
しゅうゆうけん（周遊券）　(travel) pass
シングル　single
タコス　taco
ダブル　double
トラブル　trouble, problems
トラベラーズチェック　traveler's check
ないよう（内容）　content
ばら　rose
はんにん（犯人）　criminal
ビーチ　beach
ペンション　Western-style private guest house
ほけん（保険）　insurance
ほんもの（本物）　real thing
まぐろ　tuna
まつり（祭り）　festival
ユースホステル　youth hostel
ゆかた　Japanese summer kimono
ゆきまつり（雪祭り）　The Snow Festival
ロビー　lobby

う-verbs

ころす（殺す） (to) murder
つく (to) tell (a lie); うそをつく (to) tell a lie

な-adjectives

おなじ（同じ） same

Suffixes

〜とう（〜島） 〜 island

Expressions

しつれいしました。(失礼しました。) Excuse me.

For a list of supplementary vocabulary items that will facilitate communication, see the first page of Chapter 2 in your Workbook.

CHAPTER 3

第三課

Instant cash machines make banking easier.

おねがいとやり方

Asking for Favors and Explaining How to Do Something

Functions Asking for favors and offering help and suggestions; Expressing how to do something

New Vocabulary Favors; How to do something; Machines and modern technology; Ingredients for cooking; Cooking

Dialogue コピーきの使い方 (How to use a copy machine)

Culture Vending machines and telephones

Language

I. Expressing degrees of politeness in requests, using the て-form of verbs + 下さる／くれる／いただける

II. Making a negative request, using ～ないで下さい; Expressing *without doing ~*, using the plain negative form of the verb + で

III. Expressing willingness, using verb stem + ましょうか／ましょう

IV. Expressing conditions and sequence, using the plain past form + ら

V. Trying something, using the て-form of verbs + みる; Expressing movement away from or toward the speaker through space and time, using the て-form of the verb + いく／くる

Kanji Component shapes of **kanji** 3: Top and bottom components

Reading Understanding the characteristics of written instructions

Listening Understanding transition devices used in instructions

Communication Making and declining requests or invitations

新(あたら)しい言葉(ことば)

おねがい (Favors)

たのむ　to ask (a favor)

やる　to do

貸(か)す　to lend

借(か)りる　to borrow

返(かえ)す　to return

待(ま)つ　to wait

つれて行く　to take (someone)

つれて来る　to bring (someone)

持(も)って行く　to take (something)

持(も)って来る　to bring (something)

ボタンをおす　to push a button

スイッチを入れる　to turn on a switch

電気をつける　to turn on the light

電気をけす　to turn off the light

れんしゅうをする　to practice

ノートを取(と)る　to take notes

作文(さくぶん)を書く　to write compositions

いみをおぼえる　to memorize meaning

かんじの読みを教(おし)える　to tell/teach the reading of a **kanji**

しごとを手伝(てつだ)う　to help with work

おくる　to send

下の言葉(ことば)をおぼえていますか。

うたう　けっこんする　～をおねがいする　出す　出る

食事(しょくじ)　ちゅうもんする　つつむ　乗る　入る　はく　着(き)る

洗濯(せんたく)　そうじ

A. 下線(かせん) (blanks) にてきとうな (appropriate) 言葉(ことば)をえらんで書いて下さい。

1. 寝(ね)る前に電気を＿＿＿＿＿＿＿＿＿＿＿＿＿＿＿＿＿＿。

2. 私はかんじを＿＿＿＿＿＿＿のがあまり好きじゃないんです。かんじの＿＿＿＿＿＿＿も＿＿＿＿＿＿＿もむずかしいから、大変(たいへん)です。

3. 先生は日本語を＿＿＿＿＿＿＿のが上手です。

4. テレビのスイッチを＿＿＿＿＿＿＿＿＿＿時は、このボタンを＿＿＿＿＿＿＿＿＿下さい。

5. 私は手紙(てがみ)を＿＿＿＿＿＿＿＿＿＿のはきらいだ。

6. 明日来る時、その本を＿＿＿＿＿＿＿＿＿＿下さい。

7. おとといは病気で学校に来られなかったので、山田さんにノートを＿＿＿＿＿＿。コピーをとった後、＿＿＿＿＿＿つもりです。

8. 暗くなったから、げんかんの電気を＿＿＿＿＿＿＿＿＿＿。

9. すみませんが、先週＿＿＿＿＿＿＿本を＿＿＿＿＿＿＿＿下さい。

10. 妹がけがをしたので、病院に＿＿＿＿＿＿＿＿＿＿＿＿＿。

11. 時々(ときどき)父のしごとを＿＿＿＿＿＿＿＿けど、将来(しょうらい)、そのしごとを＿＿＿＿＿＿＿＿＿か分かりません。

12. B: 先生にどんなおねがいをしたの？
A:「しゅくだいを明日まで、待(ま)って下さい。」と＿＿＿＿＿＿。

13. 日本では人の家に行く時は、おみやげを＿＿＿＿＿＿＿方がいいですよ。

14. 今からファックスを＿＿＿＿＿＿＿＿＿＿＿＿＿＿＿＿。

B. Work with a partner. Ask your partner if he or she has made any of the following requests, and if so, to whom. Circle the appropriate response in the table, and write the name of the requestee. Then make up requests, using the vocabulary labeled おねがい, and ask about these, too.

Example

A: 「ペンを貸(か)して下さい」とたのんだことがありますか。
Have you asked a favor by saying, "Please lend me a pen?"
B: はい、あります。
A: だれにたのみましたか。
B: 先生にたのみました。

たのんだことがある／ない		だれ
ペンを貸(か)す	ある／ない	先生
お金を返(かえ)す	ある／ない	
作文(さくぶん)を手伝(てつだ)う	ある／ない	
どこかにつれて行く	ある／ない	
友達(ともだち)をつれて来る	ある／ない	

やり方(かた) (How to do something)

飲み方(かた)	how to drink
作(つく)り方(かた)	how to make
食べ方(かた)	how to eat
使(つか)い方(かた)	how to use
取(と)り方(かた)	how to take
書き方(かた)	how to write
やり方(かた)	how to do

C. Explain how to form the Japanese phrase for *how to* ～ in English.

D. Work as a class. Ask your classmates the following questions and write down the names of the people who answer はい. Use casual speech.

Example

A: 天ぷらの作(つく)り方(かた)知ってる？
B: うん、知ってるよ。(male) ／うん、知ってるわよ。(female)
or
いや、知らないよ。(male) ／いや、知らないわよ。(female)

	名前(なまえ)
天ぷらの作(つく)り方(かた)	
おすしの食べ方(かた)	
コンピュータの使(つか)い方(かた)	
日本語の手紙(てがみ)の書き方(かた)	
ワインの飲み方(かた)	
エアロビクスのやり方(かた)	
ノートのとり方(かた)	

きかいとテクノロジー (Machines and modern technology)

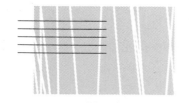

じどうはんばいき vending machine
コピーき copy machine
テレフォンカード telephone card
リモコン remote control
エアコン air conditioner
インターネット Internet; World Wide Web
電子(でんし)メール e-mail
ワープロ word processor
ファックス fax; fax machine

E. しつもんに日本語で答えて下さい。

1. 家の中にどんなきかいがありますか。
2. じどうはんばいきでどんなものが買えますか。
3. どんなリモコンの使い方を知っていますか。
4. テレフォンカードって何だと思いますか。
5. 「そうじき」と「せんたくき」のいみは何だと思いますか。
6. 大学のどこにコピーきがありますか。

料理の材料 (Ingredients for cooking)

鳥肉	chicken	パン	bread*
ぶた肉	pork	あぶら	oil
牛肉	beef	しお	salt
じゃがいも	potato	こしょう	pepper
たまねぎ	onion	さとう	sugar
バター	butter	しょうゆ	soy sauce

* パン comes from the Portuguese *pao,* meaning *bread,* and hence is written in **katakana.**

下の言葉をおぼえていますか。

野菜　肉　魚　くだもの　レタス　にんじん　トマト
バナナ　オレンジ　りんご　コーヒー　こうちゃ　コーラ
ワイン　ビール　おすし　おさしみ　てんぷら　うどん　そば
ラーメン　チャーハン　カレーライス　スパゲティ　サラダ
ピザ　ステーキ　ハンバーガー　スープ　おちゃ　ごはん
サンドイッチ　A ランチ　デザート　ケーキ　アイスクリーム
ミルク　ジュース　水

F. しつもんに日本語で答えて下さい。

1. 野菜はどれですか。肉はどれですか。くだものはどれですか。
2. 日本料理ではどんな材料をよく使いますか。中華料理ではどうですか。アメリカの料理はどうですか。

3. 体にいいものはどれですか。体によくないものはどれですか。
4. 日本人がよく食べるものはどれですか。
5. 下の料理(りょうり)の材料(ざいりょう)を言って下さい。知らない言葉(ことば)は先生に聞いて下さい。

   カレー　サラダ　ハンバーガー　ピザ　パン
   ケーキ　バーベキュー (barbecue)

料理(りょうり)の作(つく)り方(かた) (Cooking)

フライパン　frying pan
なべ　pot
(お)さら　plate
(お)はし　chopsticks
フォーク　fork
ナイフ　knife
洗(あら)う　to wash
まぜる　to mix
切(き)る　to cut
やく　to grill
にる　to boil; to stew
足(た)す　to add
ごはんをたく　to cook rice

G. 日本語でしつもんに答えて下さい。

1. 何をする時、フライパンを使いますか。何をする時、なべを使いますか。
2. 何を食べる時、おさらを使いますか。
3. 何を食べる時、おはしで食べますか。何を食べる時、ナイフとフォークで食べますか。

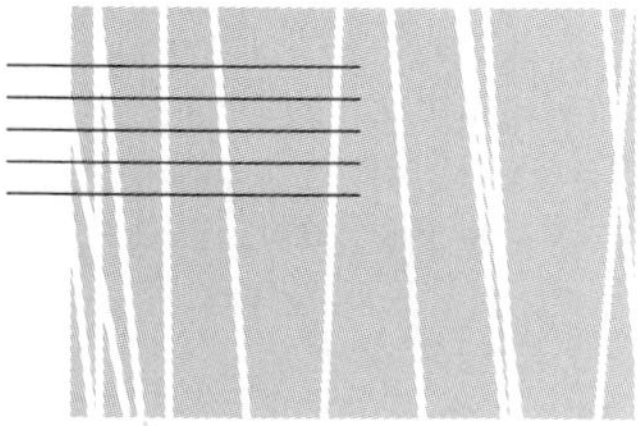

H. Complete the following recipes by using the appropriate form of the above expressions.

1. サラダを作(つく)る時は、野菜(やさい)をよく＿＿＿＿＿＿＿＿＿＿、ドレッシング (dressing) と＿＿＿＿＿＿＿＿＿＿下さい。
2. ステーキの肉(にく)はよく＿＿＿＿＿＿＿＿＿＿方が好きだ。
3. カレーライスを作る時は、牛肉(ぎゅうにく)とたまねぎとにんじんを大きく＿＿＿＿＿＿。そして、一時間ぐらい＿＿＿＿＿＿。その後、カレーこ (curry powder) を＿＿＿＿＿＿＿＿＿＿、＿＿＿＿＿＿＿＿＿＿。

ダイアローグ

はじめに

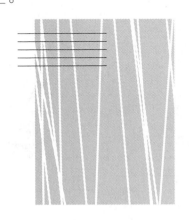

A. Do you know how to do the following things? If you don't, ask someone how to do them.

Send e-mail.
Use a fax machine.
Use a Japanese word processor.
Make a phone call to Japan.

B. Try to explain how to do the following:

Make a local phone call from a public phone 公衆電話(こうしゅうでんわ).
Make photocopies.

C. What kinds of expressions do you need to give instructions for Exercise B?

D. What kinds of transition words do you use to give instructions?

STUDENT コピーきの使(つか)い方(かた) (How to use a copy machine)

言葉(ことば)のリスト

おく	えらぶ	まいすう
to place	to select	number of sheets (of paper)

The following **manga** frames are scrambled, so they are not in the order described in the dialogue. Read the dialogue and unscramble the frames by writing the correct number in the box located in the upper right corner of each frame.

先生：　このコピー、ちょっと読めませんね。
アリス：　じゃあ、先生。私がきれいなコピーをとってきましょうか。
先生：　そうですか。それなら、十五まいとってきてくれますか。
アリス：　はい。

コピーきの前で

アリス：　あの、このコピーき、使(つか)ってもいいですか。
じむの人：あ、それ、こわれてるから、使(つか)わないで下さい。
コピーセンターのを使(つか)って下さい。

アリス：　あ、どうも。

コピーセンターの中で

アリス：　あ、石田さん、ちょっといい？

石田(いしだ)：　あ、いいよ。何？

アリス：　このコピーきの使(つか)い方(かた)がわからないんだけど。教(おし)えてくれない。

石田(いしだ)：　ああ、いいよ。じゃあ、一緒(いっしょ)にやってみよう。

アリス：　ええ。

石田(いしだ)：　まず、ここにかみをおいて、このボタンで、かみの大きさをえらぶんだ。

アリス：　ええ。

石田(いしだ)：　で、コピーのまいすうを入れたら、このみどりのボタンをおすんだよ。

アリス：　あ、そう。分かったわ。どうもありがとう。

石田(いしだ)：　いいや。

分かりましたか

A. コピーきの使(つか)い方(かた)を書いて下さい。

ステップ　1 ______________________________

ステップ　2 ______________________________

ステップ　3 ______________________________

ステップ　4 ______________________________

B. Underline any phrase that expresses a casual request. What expression precedes such a request?

C. Imagine that Alice is talking to Michiko instead of a professor at the beginning of the dialogue. Rewrite the dialogue as a conversation between Alice and Michiko. Use casual speech.

D. Imagine that Alice has received help from someone working at the copy center instead of Ishida-san. Rewrite the conversation between Alice and Ishida so it is a conversation between Alice and an employee at the copy center. Use a more polite style of speech.

日本の文化

- *Vending machines. What can you buy from vending machines in your country?*

There is a wide range of items sold at vending machines in Japan. These include soda, beer, cigarettes, magazines, rice, and hot noodles, to name a few. There is a large number of these machines operating 24 hours a day on street corners and in front of stores, and you can expect every one of them to be in good working order.

Another type of vending machine is the ticket machines found at train stations. The price of any ticket is dependent on the destination, and if you cannot read the name of your intended destination, buying a ticket will be difficult. (Some stations may use only **kanji** on the machines.)

Vending machines (left) and pay phones (right) that use telephone cards are common in Japan.

- *Telephones. How much does it cost to make a phone call using a public telephone? Is there a time limit?*

There are many public telephones available in and outside of stores and in telephone booths. Local calls cost ten yen for every three-minute increment. Because many calls require a considerable amount of change, it is more convenient to purchase a pre-paid telephone card (テレフォンカード) for either 500 yen or 1000 yen. You can purchase these cards at newsstands, station kiosks, bookstores, or souvenir shops. You can use a telephone card in almost any pay phone. After you pick up the handset, you simply insert the card. The phone displays how many yen are left on your card. When you hang up the phone, the card will be returned to you. You can make long distance calls with the same card.

Mobile phones have become extremely popular in recent years. You will find many people talking just about anywhere. The use of mobile phones is discouraged on trains and buses.

LANGUAGE

I. Expressing degrees of politeness in requests, using the て-form of verbs +下さる／くれる／いただける

		Verb (て-form) + Auxiliary verb			
電気	を	けして	下さいませんか／いただけませんか。	Formal ↑	先生 (superior)
			下さいますか／いただけますか。		
			くれませんか		
			くれますか		
			くれない		友達(ともだち)／家族
			くれる	↓ Casual	(equal/inferior)

学生: 先生、この言葉(ことば)のいみを教(おし)えていただけませんか。
Professor, could I ask you to tell me the meaning of this word?

先生： ああ、いいですよ。
Sure.

病院の人： 少しここで待(ま)っていただけますか。
Could you please wait here for a while?

病気の人： はい。
Okay.

山本： そのボタンをおしてくれませんか。
Could you push that button?

田中： はい、わかりました。
Okay, no problem.

アリス： 道子(みちこ)さん、しょうゆ、とってくれない。
Michiko, would you pass the soy sauce?

道子(みちこ)： ええ、いいわよ。はい、どうぞ。
Sure. Here it is.

ゆみ子： アリス、先週貸(か)したノート、終(お)わったら、返(かえ)してくれる？
Alice, if you're done with the notebook I lent you last week, would you give it back to me?

アリス： ええ。今日は持(も)って来(き)てないから、明日持(も)って来(き)てもいい？
Okay. Can I bring it tomorrow? I didn't bring it today.

- The requests in this section are phrased as questions. This is a less forceful way of making a request than using 下さい (the imperative form).
- Negative forms such as 下さいませんか and くれませんか are generally more polite than their affirmative counterparts such as 下さいますか and くれますか.

話してみましょう

A. The following is a list of things Koyama-san needs to ask and the people he will ask in each case. Make the requests, using the form most appropriate for the specific individuals being addressed.

たのみたい人	たのむこと
先生	ワープロの使(つか)い方(かた)を教(おし)える。かんじの読みを言う。クラスでゲームをする。
クラスメート	しゅくだいを見せる。ノートをとる。図書館で本を借(か)りてくる。
ルームメート	辞書(じしょ)を返(かえ)す。電気をつける。ステーキをやく。
お母さん	カレーの作(つく)り方(かた)を教(おし)える。お金をおくる。
お兄さん	しゅくだいを手伝(てつだ)う。車を貸(か)す。
妹	パンにバターをつける。たまねぎを切(き)る。

Example

先生　ワープロの使(つか)い方(かた)を教(おし)える。

ワープロの使(つか)い方(かた)を教(おし)えていただけませんか／下さいませんか。

B. Work with a partner. One person plays the role of A, and the other of B. In each case, B has a problem and asks A for help. A has the option of helping or refusing. If A decides not to help B, make sure to state the reason.

Example

B:　あのう、山田さん、おねがいがあるんですけど。

A:　何ですか。

B: 明日日本語のテストがあるんだけど、ぜんぜん分からないんですよ。教(おし)えてくれませんか。

A: ああ、いいですよ。

	A	B	Problem
1.	日本人の友達(ともだち)	日本語の学生	かんじがおぼえられない
2.	いしゃ	病気の人	あたまがいたい
3.	大学の先生	学生	大学院に行きたいけど，せいせき (grades) があまりよくない
4.	ルームメート	学生	病院に行きたいけど、車がない
5.	兄	弟	へやが暗い
6.	お母さん／お父さん	子供(こども)	コンピュータを買いたいけど、お金がない

C. Work as a class. Think of three favors you want to ask your classmates and write them on a piece of paper. Make the appropriate requests to your classmates and find someone who can help you. When you are asked a favor, respond truthfully. Use casual speech.

Example

A: ねえ、キムさん、おねがいがあるんだけど。
B: 何。
A: このかんじのいみ、教(おし)えてくれない。
B: あ、ごめん (sorry)、わからないよ。

D. Work with a partner. Think of three favors you want to ask your professor, who will be played by your partner. Make your requests politely and state the reasons for them.

Example

A: あのう、先生、おねがいしたいことがあるんですが。
B: 何ですか。
A: あのう、今度のスピーチコンテスト (speech contest) に出ようと思ってるんですが。
B: ええ。
A: 作文(さくぶん)を書いたので読んでいただけませんか。

II. Making a negative request, using ～ないで下さい; Expressing *without doing* ~, using the plain negative form of the verb + で

A. Making a negative request using the plain negative form of the verb + で下さい

		Verb (plain negative)		
図書館では	大きいこえで	話さない	で	下さい

Please do not speak loudly in the library.

家の中でゴルフのれんしゅうをしないで下さい。	Please do not practice golf inside the house.
電気をけさないで下さい。	Please don't turn off the light.
まだ、ごはんたかないで。今日はおそくなるから。	Do not the cook rice yet—I'll be late today.

- You can use 下さる／くれる／いただける to express varying degrees of politeness in the place of 下さい.

スイッチを入れないで下さい。		Please don't turn on the switch.
スイッチを入れないで	下さいませんか／いただけませんか。	Could I ask you not to turn on the switch?
	下さいますか／いだだますか。	Could you please not turn on the switch?
	くれませんか／くれますか。	Could you not turn on the switch?
	くれない／くれる。	Don't turn on the switch.

B. Expressing *without doing* ~, using the plain negative form of the verb + で

	Verb (plain negative)		
辞書(じしょ)を	使(つか)わない	で	本を読みました。

I read a book without using the dictionary.

野菜(やさい)を洗(あら)わないで切(き)った。	I cut the vegetables without washing them.
勉強(べんきょう)しないでクラスに行きました。	I went to class without studying.
れんしゅうをしないで上手になる人はいない。	No one gets good at anything without practice.

- The verb negative form + で下さい expresses a polite negative request. In casual speech, 下さい is dropped.

行かないで下さい。	Please don't go.
行かないで。	Don't go.

話してみましょう

A. Answer the following questions, using ～ないで下さい.

Example

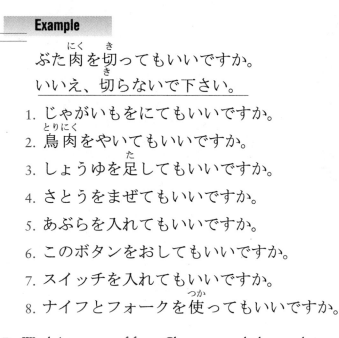

ぶた肉(にく)を切(き)ってもいいですか。
いいえ、切(き)らないで下さい。

1. じゃがいもをにてもいいですか。
2. 鳥肉(とりにく)をやいてもいいですか。
3. しょうゆを足(た)してもいいですか。
4. さとうをまぜてもいいですか。
5. あぶらを入れてもいいですか。
6. このボタンをおしてもいいですか。
7. スイッチを入れてもいいですか。
8. ナイフとフォークを使(つか)ってもいいですか。

B. Work in groups of four. Choose a workplace such as a 病院 or 図書館. Make as many rules as you can that are appropriate for the workplace you have selected. Tell the other members of the group your rules and see if they can identify what your workplace is.

Example

A: ここで走(はし)らないで下さい。たばこをすわないで下さい。
それから、大きいこえで話さないで下さい。
B: 図書館ですか。
A: いいえ。
C: 病院ですか。
A: はい、そうです。

C. Work with a partner. First, in the following chart check the はい column for things you do and the いいえ column for things you don't do. Then ask your partner whether or not he or she does them. Use both casual and polite speech.

Example

A: 電気をけして寝(ね)ますか。／電気けして寝(ね)る？

B: はい、けして寝(ね)ます。／うん、けして寝(ね)るよ。(male)／ええ、けして寝(ね)るわよ。(female)

or いいえ、けさないで寝(ね)ます。／いや、けさないで寝(ね)るよ。(male)／いえけさないで寝(ね)るわ。(female)

	私		パートナー	
	はい	いいえ	はい	いいえ
電気をけして寝(ね)る				
へやを暗くして寝(ね)る。				
夏はぼうしをかぶって出かける				
朝ごはんを食べて、学校に行く				
インターネットを使(つか)って勉強(べんきょう)する				
パンにバターをつけて食べる				
ステーキはよくやいて食べる				
コーヒーにさとうを入れて飲む				

D. Work with a partner. The following machines and technology make our lives easier. Tell your partner what the inventions help us do or save us from doing.

じどうはんばいき　コピーき　テレフォンカード

リモコン　エアコン　インターネット　電子(でんし)メール

Example

インターネット

新聞(しんぶん)を買(か)わないで、ニュースが読めます。

III. Expressing willingness, using verb stem + ましょうか／ましょう

A. Verb stem + ましょうか (*shall I* 〜)

	Verb
私が	行きましょうか。／行こうか。

Shall I go?

田中：　暑いね。
　　　　Hot, isn't it?
川口：　じゃあ、エアコンをつけましょうか。
　　　　Shall I turn on the air conditioner?

健一(けんいち)：　どうしたの。
　　　　What's wrong?
道子(みちこ)：　あたまがとてもいたいの。
　　　　I have a bad headache.
健一(けんいち)：　大変(たいへん)だね。薬、持(も)って来ようか。
　　　　That's too bad. Shall I bring medicine?

- In Chapter 8 of Volume 1, ましょうか *(shall we* 〜*)* and ましょう *(let's* 〜*)* are used to make suggestions. The same structure can also be used to express the speaker's willingness to do something for someone else.
- In casual speech, you can use the the plain forms of the volitional 〜ましょう, such as 行こう or 食べよう.

手伝(てつだ)いましょうか。	手伝(てつだ)おうか。	Shall I give you a hand?
ぼくが作(つく)りましょうか。	ぼくが作(つく)ろうか。	Shall I make (it)?
さあ、れんしゅうしましょう。	さあ、れんしゅうしよう。	Let's practice.
たのみましょう。	たのもう	Let's ask (him or her) for help.

B. The stem of verbs + ましょう (*I will* 〜)

	Verb
晩ごはんは　ぼくが	作(つく)りましょう。／作(つく)ろう

I will make (cook) the dinner.

まもる：　今日は何を食べようか。
　　　　What shall we have to eat today?

ゆみ：　ぶた肉があるから、やこうか。
There is some pork, so shall I grill it?

まもる：　じゃあ、ぼくがやくよ。
I'll do it.

アリス：　何か飲みたいですね。
I'd like to have something to drink.

リー：　じゃあ、じどうはんばいきで何か買って来ましょう。
Well, I'll bring something from the vending machine.

- To offer explicitly to help, rather than simply show willingness to do something, use the て-form of verb + あげましょう(か)／あげよう(か). The auxiliary verb あげる in あげましょう／あげよう indicates that the speaker is doing a favor for the listener. This form should not be used with a social superior, because expressing an offer of favor to a superior sounds arrogant in Japanese.

キム：　天ぷらの作り方が分からないんです。
I don't know how to make tempura.

川口：　じゃあ、作り方を教えてあげましょうか。
Well, shall I teach you how to make it?

アリス：　けしごむ、持ってないんだけど、だれか貸してくれない？
I don't have an eraser—can someone lend one to me?

石田：　じゃあ、ぼくのを貸してあげようか。
I can lend you mine.

アリス：　ありがとう。
Thank you.

話してみましょう

A. Offer a solution/help for each of the following situations using ましょう／ましょうか. Use formal speech.

Example

A: コーヒーが飲みたいですね。
B: じゃあ、私がコーヒーを入れましょう。／私がコーヒーを入れてあげましょうか。

1. しゅくだいがたくさんあって、終わりません。
2. いそがしくて、ごはんを作る時間がありません。

3. このかんじのいみが分からないんですが、辞書(じしょ)を持(も)って
いないんです。
4. このへやは寒(さむ)いですね。
5. かんじがおぼえられないんです。
6. ビールがなくなったんです。
7. ねつがあるから、学校に行けないんですが、今日はテストが
あるんです。

B. Work as a class. In the following chart mark the はい column for things you know how to do and the いいえ column if you don't know how to do what is listed. If you don't know how to do something, tell a classmate your problem. Your classmate will offer to help you if he or she has proficiency in the item in question. Write down the names of anyone who offers help. If someone else asks you for help with something you can do, offer assistance. Use the plain volitional forms or the て-form of the verb + あげよう(か).

Example

A: ごはんのたき方(かた)が分からないんだけど。
B: じゃあ、／私がたき方(かた)を教(おし)えてあげようか。／私がたいてあげようか。／私がたこうか。
A: そう、ありがとう。

わかる／できる	はい	いいえ	名前(なまえ)
ごはんをたく			
ファックスをおくる			
日本語のワープロを使(つか)う			
電子(でんし)メールをおくる			
インターネットを使(つか)う			
国際(こくさい) (international) 電話をかける			

C. Work in groups of four. Each group should plan a party and invite classmates. Decide what to buy, what to make, etc. Then decide on volunteers to do the various tasks. Write down who will do what.

Example

A: いつ、どこでしようか。
B: ぼくの家でしようよ。
C: いいね、土曜日の七時からはどう。
D: いいね、何を作ろうか。
A: 私がサラダを作ろうか。
B: じゃあ、ぼくはビールを買おう。

D. Work with a partner. Your partner is a guest at your house and you want him or her to feel at home. Try to suggest various things that might make the guest more comfortable.

Example

A: エアコンのスイッチを入れましょうか。
B: どうもありがとうございます。

IV. Expressing conditions and sequence, using the plain past form + ら

	Adjective (plain past)				
明日	暑かった	ら、	プール	に	行きましょう。

If it is hot tomorrow, let's go to the pool.

		Verb (plain past)				
来年日本	に	行った	ら、	ふじ山	が	見たいです。

If I go to Japan next year, I want to see Mt. Fuji.

もっとれんしゅうしたら、上手になります。
If you practice more, you will become good at it.

私が山田さんだったら、先生に話すでしょう。
If I were Yamada-san, I would talk to the teacher.

お金があったら、日本へ行きたいですね。
If I had money, I would like to go to Japan.

しおを足(た)したら、おいしくなるかもしれませんね。
Adding salt will probably make it taste better.

明日、天気がよかったら、いいですね。
It would be great if the weather were nice tomorrow.

家へ帰ったら、母が来ていました。
I got home, and there was my mother.

たまねぎを切(き)ったら、目がいたくなってきた。
My eyes started hurting when I cut up the onions.

- There are several types of conditional sentences in Japanese. The conditional たら is formed with the plain past form of verb/adjective + ら.

雨がふったら／ふらなかったら、	If it rains/does not rain
天気がよかったら、／よくなかったら、	If the weather is good/is not good
元気だったら／元気じゃなかったら、	If (a person) is healthy/is not healthy
学生だったら／学生じゃなかったら、	If (you are) a student/are not a student

- The condition expressed in the たら clause must be completed (or satisfied) before the action or event in the main clause can take place. Therefore, you can say 手紙(てがみ)を書いたら、ゆうびんきょくに持(も)っていって下さい *(After you write the letter, please take it to the post office)*, but you cannot say ~~手紙(てがみ)を書いたら、えんぴつで書きます~~ *(After I write a letter, I write it with a pencil)*. This is because the use of たら here implies that one act is completed before the other takes place.

- The たら clause can also express an actual sequence of events without introducing a condition. In this case, the event/action in the たら clause takes place before the event/action in the main clause.

家に帰ったら、電話します。	I'll call after I get home.
肉(にく)をやいたら、なべに入れます。	I'll put the meat in the pan after I grill it.

- Use of the past tense in the main clause indicates a situation that the speaker could not control. Thus, the main clause tends to express surprise or the realization that an unexpected event has transpired.

おさけを飲んだら、気分がわるくなった。	I didn't feel well after I drank the **sake.**
たばこをすったら、病気になった。	I got sick after I smoked the cigarette.
そとに出たら、雨がふってきた。	It started raining as soon as I went out.
アパートに行ったら、田中さんはいなかった。	When I went to his apartment, Tanaka-san was not there.

- If the main clause is in the present tense, it can be used to express an intention, request, or obligation of the speaker. However, it cannot express an event that has already transpired.

五月になったら、しごとをします。	I'll get a job in May.
フライパンのあぶらがあつくなったら、牛肉(ぎゅうにく)をやいて下さい。	When the oil in the frying pan gets hot, fry the beef.
食べたら、おさらを洗(あら)ってね。	Please do the dishes after you eat.
肉(にく)をなべに入れたら、じゃがいもと水を足(た)して、五分にます。	After putting the meat in the pot, add potatoes and water and boil five minutes.

話してみましょう

A. Complete the following sentences.

Example

日本に行ったら、<u>ふじ山にのぼりたいですね。</u>

1. 山田さんに会ったら、______________________________。
2. リモコンがあったら、______________________________。
3. 映画が終(お)わったら、______________________________。
4. 日本語が上手になったら、__________________________。
5. ____________________________、あそびに来てね。
6. __________________、作(つく)り方(かた)を教(おし)えてくれる？
7. _________________________、ワインを持(も)ってこようか。
8. ______________________、かんじがよくおぼえられるよ。

B. Work with a partner. Discuss how much the following items might cost in different countries. Use casual speech.

Example

A: アメリカではロードショーはいくらぐらいだと思う？
B: 九ドルぐらいだと思うけど、日本ではどう。
A: 日本だったら、二千円ぐらいだと思う。

	日本	アメリカ	オーストラリア
あたらしい映画			
はがきを送る (domestic)			
喫茶店のコーヒー (a cup of)			
ガソリン (gasoline) 1リットル*			
電話をかける (local)			

1ガロン (gallon) ≒　4リットル (liter)

C. Work with a partner. One person is a Japanese student and the other is an American student. The Japanese friend wants to know how to do a number of things. Role-play the following situations by having the Japanese friend ask for help and the American give instructions, using ～たら. Use polite speech.

Example

A: あのう、～さん。

B: 何ですか。

A: 手紙を出したいんですけど、英語の住所の書き方が分からないんです。教えてくれませんか。

B: ああ、いいですよ。まず、ふうとうの左の上のほうに、～さんの名前を書くんです。

A: ええ。

B: 名前を書いたら、つぎに住所を書くんです。

1. やすいひこうきのきっぷのかい方
2. チェックの書き方
3. 図書館での本の借り方
4. バスの乗り方

D. Work with a partner. Your partner will explain how to do something without saying specifically what the action is. Follow his or her directions and figure out what he or she is trying to explain. You can ask your partner what the next step is. Use casual speech.

Example

A: まずカードをきかいに入れるんだ。(male) ／まずカードをきかいに入れるの。(female)

B: 入れたら、すうじ (numbers) をおすの？

A: うん、そうだ。(male) ／ええ、そうよ。(female)

B: すうじをおしたら、何をするの？

A: お金を取(と)るんだよ。(male) ／お金を取(と)るのよ。(female)

V. Trying something, using the て-form of verbs + みる; Expressing movement away from or toward the speaker through space and time, using the て-form of the verb + いく／くる

A. Using the て-form of the verb +みる to express doing something in order to see how it is or what it is like

			Verb (て-form)	Auxiliary verb
きのう	おすし	を	食べて	みました。

I ate sushi yesterday (to see what it was like). = I tried sushi yesterday.

山田： このふく、着(き)てみてもいいですか。
May I try this dress on?

店の人： はい、どうぞ。
Yes, please.

石田： ヨーロッパに行ってみたいんだ。
I'd like to go to Europe (to see what it's like).

リー： ぼくも行ってみたいね。
I would like to go, too.

このワープロを使(つか)ってみたらどうですか。
How about trying this word processor?

もっとさとうを足(た)してみない？
Why don't we try adding in a bit more sugar?

- The て-form of the verb + みる is used to indicate that the speaker has done something on a trial basis (or experimentally) to see what the result would be. In this usage, みる is written in **hiragana**.

B. Using the て -form of the verb + いく when the direction is away from the current location or time of the speaker

B-1. The speaker does something and goes/leaves

		Verb て-form	Verb
朝ごはん	を	食べて	行きましょう。

Let's eat breakfast before we go. (literally: Let's eat breakfast and go/leave.)

B-2. The speaker does something in a direction away from where he or she started

								Verb て-form	Verb
私	は	田中さん	の	家	に	ケーキ	を	持(も)って	行きました。

I took some cake to Tanaka-san's house.

B-3. Continuation of a currently ongoing action (or situation) into the future

				Verb て-form	Auxiliary verb		
これから	も	日本語	を	勉強(べんきょう)して	いく	つもり	です。

I intend to continue the study of the Japanese language.

B-4. Process of change of an event or an action experienced by others

					Verb て-form	Auxiliary verb
その人	は	お金	を	少しずつ	返(かえ)して	いった。

He returned the money little by little.

ここでコーヒーを飲んで行きましょう。	Let's drink coffee here and go.
まだ時間があるから、テニスをやって行くよ。	I'll play tennis before I go because we still have some time.
これからはよるがながくなっていくよ。	Nights will start getting longer now.
少しずつあたらしい言葉(ことば)をおぼえていこうと思います。	I think I'll memorize the new words gradually.

- The verbs いく and くる do not necessarily correspond to the English *to come* and *to go*. For example, an English speaker might respond when called by saying *I'm coming*. In Japanese, however, the corresponding response would be すぐ行くよ. This is because the speaker is seen as the center of universe; いく is used when the speaker or someone or something else moves away from the speaker's current position, and くる when movement is toward the speaker. This is also true when いく is used as an auxiliary verb in the て-form of verb + いく. Therefore, the て-form of the verb + いく indicates an action or event that moves away from the speaker's current location in space or in time.

- In key sentence B-1, the speaker finishes eating and then goes out, so the meaning of the sentence is the same as 〜て *(and)*. In B-2, holding（持(も)つ）takes place in the direction away from where the speaker is. Thus, it expresses taking something to a location. The word いく in these usages tends to be regarded as a full verb rather than an auxiliary verb and retains the meaning *to go*.

- Key sentence B-3 illustrates a situation where the current location is temporal rather than spatial. The speaker can express his or her intention of continuing to study Japanese from now on.

- In key sentence B-4, the auxiliary verb いく indicates a change of state but does not express spatial or temporal movement. Rather, it indicates that the speaker views this process as something psychologically distant from himself or herself. Therefore, this use of 〜ていく describes an objective or impersonal situation and is often used for changes of process that do not involve the speaker or anyone close to the speaker. In B-3 and B-4, いく is considered an auxiliary verb because it no longer retains the meaning *to go*. For this reason, いく is often written in **hiragana** in these usages.

- In casual speech, the sound い in 〜ていく may be dropped.

ごはんを作(つく)っていきますよ。	ごはん作(つく)ってくよ。	I will cook a meal and go.
山田さんの所に持(も)っていって下さい。	山田さんの所に持(も)ってって。	Take (it) to Yamada-san.
晩ごはんを食べていったらどうですか。	晩ごはん食べてったらどう？	How about eating supper and going?

C. Using the て-form of the verb + くる when the direction is toward the current location or time of the speaker

C-1. Someone does something and comes toward the speaker

		Verb て-form	Verb
ビール	を	買って	来ました。

I bought beer before I came. (literally: I bought some beer and came.)

C-2. Someone does something and the action implies the direction toward the speaker

				Verb て-form	Verb
弟	を	ここ	まで	つれて	来ました。

I brought my little brother this far.

C-3. Continuation of an action or event that began in the past to the present day

			Verb て-form	Auxiliary verb
日本語	を	十年間	勉強(べんきょう)して	きました。

I have been studying Japanese for ten years now.

C-4. Beginning of a process experienced by the speaker or someone close to the speaker

		Verb て-form	Auxiliary verb
おゆ	が	わいて	きました。

The water has started to boil.

作文(さくぶん)を書いてきて下さい。

Please write a composition and bring it to class.

ジョン：　しゅくだいやってきた？
　　Did you bring your homework?

さなえ：　え、今日しゅくだいあったの？
　　What? Did we have an assignment for today?

あっ、雨がふってきたよ。	Oh, it has begun to rain.
日本語がおもしろくなってきました。	Japanese is getting interesting.
今までれんしゅうしてきたんだから、これからもやっていこうと思う。	I've practiced this much so far, so I think I'll keep it up.

- The て-form of the verb + くる is the exact opposite of the て-form of the verb + いく, both spatially and temporally. While the use of いく implies direction *away from* the current location of the speaker, くる indicates that the movement is *toward* the current location of the speaker. If the sentence were 今ビールを買ってきます, then it would mean that the person will go to the store, buy some beer, and come back. If the sentence were 明日ビールを買ってきます, the meaning would be that the person will buy the beer before coming to this location. In key sentence C-2, the speaker brings his or her brother to his or her current location. In these usages, the verb くる is the main verb, retaining its meaning, *to come*.

- Key sentence C-3 indicates an action or event that started in the past and has continued to the current time. In this usage, the auxiliary verb くる is usually in the past tense. Key sentence C-4 indicates the beginning of a process; it means *to begin to* 〜. In these usages, the verb くる no longer has the meaning of coming, but acts instead as an auxiliary verb. Therefore, it is often written in **hiragana**.

かんじがおもしろくなってきました。	**Kanji** have gotten interesting.
雪がふってきた。	It has just begun to snow.

- When the て-form of the verb + くる indicates a change of process, as in key sentences A-3 and A-4, the experiencer must be the speaker or someone close to the speaker. It therefore expresses the speaker's psychological involvement or subjectivity. In the following sentences, やせてきた indicates that *the speaker* began to lose weight. On the other hand, やせていった indicates *someone else's* process of losing weight and does not indicate the beginning of a process or a process involving the speaker or someone close to him or her.

やせてきた。	I have begun to lose weight.
鈴木さんはやせていった。	Suzuki-san has lost weight (over time).

話してみましょう。

A. Complete the following sentences using the て-form of the verb +みる.

Example

日本へ行ったことがないから、行ってみたいです。

1. ケーキを作(つく)ったことがないから、＿＿＿＿＿＿＿＿＿＿
2. おすしを食べたことがないから、＿＿＿＿＿＿＿＿＿＿
3. あたらしいコンピュータを買ったので、＿＿＿＿＿＿＿＿＿＿
4. 電子(でんし)メールを使ったことがないから、＿＿＿＿＿＿＿＿＿＿
5. おもしろそうな本なので、＿＿＿＿＿＿＿＿＿＿

B. Work as a class. Ask your classmates what they want to learn or try to do, and determine what the common interests are among your classmates. Write the information down in a table.

Example

A: どんなことをやってみたいと思いますか。
B: 日本に住んでみたいと思います。

C. The following diagram illustrates actions directed to certain people, places, or actions that have taken place before the subject moved toward a certain place. Express actions and directionality using 〜ていく／〜てくる.

Example

本を持(も)つ　　私は友達(ともだち)の家に本を持(も)って行きました。
歩(ある)く　　友達(ともだち)は私の家に歩(ある)いて来ました。

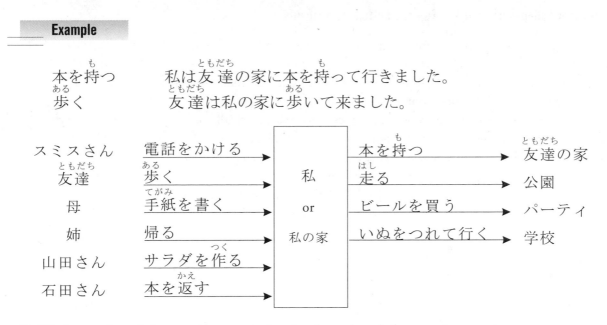

スミスさん	電話をかける →	私 or 私の家	本を持(も)つ →	友達(ともだち)の家
友達(ともだち)	歩(ある)く →		走(はし)る →	公園
母	手紙(てがみ)を書く →		ビールを買う →	パーティ
姉	帰る →		いぬをつれて行く →	学校
山田さん	サラダを作(つく)る →			
石田さん	本を返(かえ)す →			

D. Work as a class. Ask your classmates what they have done before coming to school, or what they have brought to school. Use casual speech.

Example

A: 今日は何をしてきたの？
B: 日本語のしゅくだいしてきたよ。(male) ／日本語のしゅくだいしてきたの。(female)
朝ごはんを食べてきたよ。(male) ／朝ごはんを食べてきたの。(female)

E. Work as a class. Ask your classmates what they want to accomplish in the future, what they have been doing to achieve the goal, and whether they think they will continue to do this. そのために means *for that purpose*.

A: 将来(しょうらい)何をしたいと思いますか。
B: 日本語の先生になりたいと思います。
A: そのために、どんなことをしてきましたか。
B: 日本語を勉強(べんきょう)してきました。
A: これからも日本語を勉強(べんきょう)していくつもりですか。
B: ええ、勉強(べんきょう)していくつもりです。

漢字

Component shapes of kanji 3: Top and bottom components

Some **kanji** have tops and bottoms. Common shapes for the tops and bottoms of **kanji** are listed below. As was mentioned in Chapter 2 of this volume, the term component shapes refers to shapes that repeatedly occur in different **kanji**. Most **kanji**, except very simple ones, contain more than one component shape. Radicals, on the other hand, are recursive shapes that have historically been used to categorize **kanji;** thus every **kanji** contains a single radical. Although many of the component shapes are used as radicals, not all of them are. Shapes that are not radicals do not have specific meanings or names.

In some cases, the traditional radicals of the **kanji** shown in the examples below are different from the component shapes being pictured.

Name		Meaning	Examples of use
くさかんむり	艹	grass; flower	薬 英 菜
うかんむり	宀	house	家 安 定 寝
ひとがしら	𠆢	person	今 会 金
あみがしら	罒	net	買
N/A	田	rice field	男 思
あめかんむり	⻗	rain	雨 雪
N/A	䒑	N/A	前
なべぶた	亠	lid	京

Name		Meaning	Examples of use
にんにょう	儿	leg	先 見 元 兄
こころ	心	heart	思
そうにょう	走	running	足 定 起 走

Kanji	Meaning	Reading	Examples
起	to get up, to wake up	キ/お（きる）	毎朝(まいあさ)六時に起(お)きます。
寝	to sleep, to lie down	シン/ね（る）	毎晩(まいばん)１２時ごろ寝(ね)ます。
使	to use	シ/つか（う）	リモコンの使(つか)い方(かた)が分かりますか。
作	to make	サク/つく（る）	カレーを作(つく)る。 作文(さくぶん) (composition)
教	to teach	キョウ/おし（える）	日本語を教(おし)える。 教室(きょうしつ)　教会(きょうかい)に行く
洗	to wash	セン/あら（う）	シャツを洗(あら)う。野菜(やさい)を洗(あら)ってくれる 洗濯(せんたく)する
切	to cut	セツ/き（る）	肉(にく)を切(き)る。トマトを小さく切(き)る。親切(しんせつ)な人
持	to have, to hold	ジ/も（つ）	車を持(も)っている。ビールを持(も)って行く
待	to wait	タイ/ま（つ）	ここで待(ま)ちましょう。待(ま)って下さい。
始	to begin	シ/はじ（まる）はじ（める）	映画は八時に始(はじ)まって、十時に終(お)わります。

終	to end	シュウ/お（わる）	日本語のクラスは一時に終(お)わります。
着	to arrive, to put on,	チャク/つ（く）き（る）	セーターを着(き)る。東京(とうきょう)に着(つ)く。
取	to take	シュ/と（る）	しおを取(と)って下さい。じゅぎょうを取(と)る。
貸	to lend	タイ/か（す）	お金を貸(か)す。本を貸(か)して下さい。
借	to borrow	シャク/か（りる）	お金を借(か)りる。辞書(じしょ)を借(か)りてもいいですか。
返	to return	ヘン/かえ（す）	借(か)りた本を返(かえ)す。
走	to run	ソウ/はし（る）	毎朝(まいあさ)5キロ走(はし)ります。走(はし)って帰(かえ)りました。
歩	to walk	ホ、ポ/ある（く）	大学に歩(ある)いて行きます。一緒(いっしょ)に歩(ある)きましょう。
乗	to ride	ジョウ/の（る）	車に乗(の)る。ひこうきに乗(の)らない。
友	friend	ユウ/とも	友達(ともだち)が二人日本から来ます。

Kanji		Meaning	Readings	Example
達	達	to reach, to arrive, to attain	タチ、ダチ タツ	こちらは私の友達(ともだち)の田中さんです。
肉	肉	meat	にく	牛肉(ぎゅうにく)を食べましょう。
魚	魚	fish	ギョ/さかな	魚(さかな)を食べましょう。
牛	牛	cow	ギュウ/うし	インドでは牛肉(ぎゅうにく)を食べない。
鳥	鳥	bird	チョウ/とり	鳥肉(とりにく)をやいて下さい。
野	野	field	ヤ/の	野菜(やさい)を作っています。野鳥(やちょう) (wild bird)
菜	菜	vegetables	サイ	野菜(やさい)も食べなければなりません。
料	料	material	リョウ	料理(りょうり)のし方を教(おし)える。
理	理	reason, logic	リ	日本料理(りょうり)を食べます。
材	材	material, timber	ザイ	天ぷらの材料(ざいりょう)は何ですか。

新(あたら)しい読み方(かた)

作(つく)り方(かた)　し方(かた)　親切(しんせつ)　足(た)す

練習(れんしゅう)

下のぶんを読んで下さい。

1. 私の友達は毎朝六時に起きて、三マイル走ります。夜は十一時に寝ます。
2. この魚料理の材料と作り方を教えてくれませんか。
3. 牛肉より鳥肉や野菜の方が好きです。
4. パーティは八時に始まりますから、もう少し待って下さい。
5. 図書館で借りた本は明日返します。
6. あのセーターを着ている人はだれですか。
7. 映画は十時に終わりますから、歩いて帰ります。
8. A: 車、貸してもらえない。
   B: ごめん。明日使うんだ。
9. 野菜を洗って、小さく切ったら、ここに持って来て。
10. 山田さんはひこうきに乗ったことがありません。
11. さとうさんはとても親切な人です。
12. もう少しバターを足した方がいいと思います。

上手な読み方

Understanding the characteristics of written instructions

Instructions appear in manuals and recipes, and written instructions are one of the easiest writing styles to understand.

Each step is usually separated, numbered, and often accompanied by illustrations. You can use visual cues and format to help you understand the text. Written instructions are also grammatically simple in Japanese. They are written in the present tense, and the text can be either in the plain or the formal form. Difficulties in understanding written instructions are usually due to area-specific vocabulary and the **kanji** associated with this vocabulary. It is important to brainstorm about the kinds of vocabulary that may be used.

A. Suppose you are to read a manual or recipe explaining the following. Identify what kinds of nouns and verbs you would need to know.

テレビのリモコン　ファミコン　電話（でんわ）　スパゲティ　ピザ

B. The following is a typical recipe in Japanese. Identify similarities and differences in format between recipes in Japanese and recipes in English.

ひき肉のパンあげ（１人分）

材料	食（しょく）パン	二まい
	牛のひき肉	50 g
	スライスチーズ	一まい
	しお、こしょう	少々（しょうしょう）

作り方
1 肉をしお、こしょうであじつけします。
2 食パンの間に{ をぬって、チーズをはさみます。
3 中温（ちゅうおん）の油（あぶら）で揚（あ）げた後、四つに切ります。

えびだんご (Shrimp dumplings)

読む前に

A. 日本とアメリカでは材料のはかり方 (measurement) がちがいます。下のしつもんに答えて下さい。

1. 100 グラム (gram) は何オンス (oz.) ですか。
2. 1 パイント (pt.) は何 cc ですか。
3. アメリカの１カップ (cup) は何パイント (pt.) ですか。何 cc ですか。
4. 日本の１カップ (cup) は 200 cc です。何パイント (pt.) ですか。
5. Tablespoon は日本語で「大（おお）さじ」と言います。Teaspoon は「小（こ）さじ」と言います。日本とアメリカでは大さじの大きさ (size) はおなじだと思いますか。小さじもおなじだと思いますか。

B. 写真を見て、えびだんごの作り方を言ってみてください。知らない言葉(ことば)があったら、先生に聞いて下さい。

Nouns: ______________________________

Verbs: ______________________________

①

②

③

④

⑤

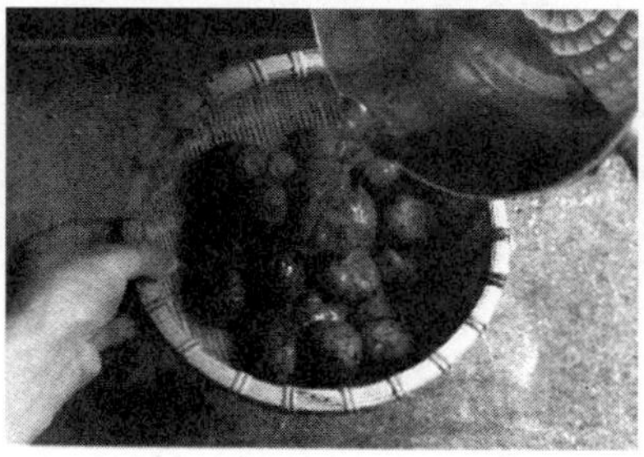

⑥

えびだんご

C. 下の材料を読んで、分からない言葉があったら、先生に聞いて下さい。A と B は何のことですか。

豆腐	1 ½ 丁 (450 g)
卵	1 つ
海老	300 g

Ⓐ	しお	小さじ 1/3
	みりん (sweet rice wine)	小さじ 4
	薄口しょうゆ (light soy sauce)	大さじ 1
	砂糖	小さじ 2

きくらげ (dried cloud ear mushroom)	2 つ
にんじん	½ 本

Ⓑ	だし (stock)	カップ 3
	みりん	大さじ 4½
	砂糖	大さじ 1
	しょうゆ	大さじ 2½

D. The following steps describe the recipe shown on the previous page, but they are out of order. Write the number of the picture for each step below.

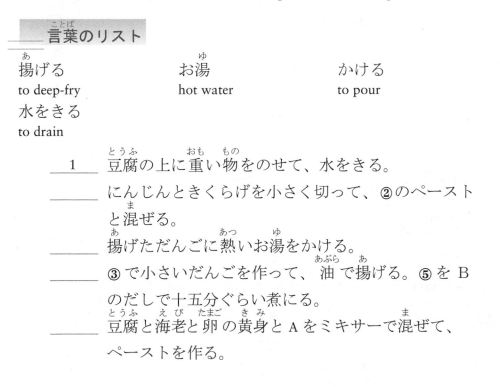

言葉のリスト

揚げる to deep-fry	お湯 hot water	かける to pour
水をきる to drain		

__1__ 豆腐の上に重い物をのせて、水をきる。

_____ にんじんときくらげを小さく切って、②のペーストと混ぜる。

_____ 揚げただんごに熱いお湯をかける。

_____ ③で小さいだんごを作って、油で揚げる。⑤を B のだしで十五分ぐらい煮にる。

_____ 豆腐と海老と卵の黄身と A をミキサーで混ぜて、ペーストを作る。

読んだ後で

A. しつもんに答えて下さい。

1. どんな料理が好きですか。
2. どんな料理を作ったことがありますか。
3. お母さんはどんな料理が上手ですか。お父さんはどうですか。
4. どんな料理を作ってみたいと思いますか。

B. 下のしつもんに答えて、好きな料理の作り方を日本語で書いて下さい。

1. どんな材料を使いますか。
2. フライパンやなべを使いますか。
3. ステップはいくつぐらいありますか。
4. まずはじめに何をしますか。
5. つぎに何をしますか。
6. その後、何をしますか。
7. 最後(さいご)に何をしますか。

上手な聞き方

Understanding transition devices used in instructions

When someone explains how to do something, he or she often uses expressions that indicate sequence, such as まず *(first)*, はじめに *(first, at the beginning)*, まずはじめに *(first of all)*, つぎに *(next)*, それから *(after that)*, そして *(and)*, and 最後(さいご)に *(lastly)*. It is important to pay attention to these devices because what follows them is the most important information in the instructions.

STUDENT

A. Listen to the following two dialogues, and identify the number of steps in each.

1. ファックスのおくり方____________________
2. 天ぷらの作り方____________________

STUDENT

B. Now listen to the conversations again. This time, try to write each step on a separate sheet of paper.

1. ファックスのおくり方
2. 天ぷらの作り方

三つのおねがい

聞く前に

There are many occasions when you ask for favors in your daily life. Write the types of requests you might make in Japanese in the following situations or relationships.

学校で　友達 ______________________________

　　　　先生 ______________________________

家で　　両親 ______________________________

　　　　兄 ______________________________

　　　　弟 ______________________________

　　　　近所の人 ______________________________

道で　　知らない人 ______________________________

　　　　友達 ______________________________

聞いてみましょう

STUDENT

Listen to the three dialogues on the audio CD. Complete the following figure by writing the name or title of the person who has made the request to the left of the box, the actual request inside the box, and the name or title of the person to whom the request was made to the right of the box. Then circle はい if the request was accepted, or いいえ if it was denied.

Example

A: 行ってきます。
B: あっ、まもる、今日はおばあちゃんが来るから、はやく帰ってきてよ。
A: ああ、わかったよ。

	Person making request	Request	Person asked		
	お母さん	家にはやく帰ってくる	こども or まもる	(はい)	いいえ
1.	______		______	はい	いいえ
2.	______		______	はい	いいえ
3.	______		______	はい	いいえ

聞いた後で

Based on the information you compiled in 聞いてみましょう, write a brief summary of each conversation.

STUDENT

DICT-A-CONVERSATION

Your friend Yamada-san approaches you to ask something.

山田：____

スミス：______________________________________

山田：____

スミス：______________________________________

山田：____

スミス：______________________________________

山田：____

聞き上手話し上手

Making and declining requests or invitations

A. There is a set structure for making requests. First, start the conversation with a conversation opener such as あのう or あのう、すみません. Then express the desire, problem, or other fact that will lead to the request, such as コピーをとったことがないんですけど. Finally, make the request itself: コピーのとり方を教えてくれませんか.

Example

山本：　あのう
スミス：　何ですか。
山本：　ビデオのとり方が分からないんですけど、このリモコンの使い方を教えていただけませんか。
スミス：　ええ、いいですよ。

B. Work with a partner. Practice making requests in the following situations.

1. You want to try on a pair of pants being displayed in the display case at a department store. Make a request to a store clerk.
2. You want to buy something to drink but don't have any money. Make a request to a close friend.
3. You want to use your friend's car for a date. Ask your friend for the use of the car.

C. If you need to decline a request or invitation, refuse beginning with an apology, such as すみません or ごめん, and follow with a reason. Avoid the use of ～たくありません *(don't want to do ～)*, since it is considered impolite in this situation. You can suggest an alternative (～てみたらどうですか). It is also a good strategy to indicate your willingness to do something with the person at another time (今度いっしょにごはんを食べましょう).

Example

まもる：明日ひまだったら、一緒(いっしょ)に映画、行かない。
道子(みちこ)：　あ、ごめん。明日はちょっとようじがあって。
まもる：あ、そう。
道子(みちこ)：　あさっては、大丈夫(だいじょうぶ)なんだけど、あさってはどう。
　（また、今度一緒(いっしょ)に映画行こうよ。）

1. Work with a partner. Your partner will invite you to one of the following events. Politely decline the invitation.

   誕生日(たんじょうび)パーティ　コンサート　映画　ディナー

2. Work with a partner. Your partner will ask you to teach him or her one of the following things. Politely turn down the request.

   how to play tennis　　how to use e-mail
   how to drive a car　　how to cook some dish

総合練習(そうごうれんしゅう)

クラスメートが出来ること

Work as a class. Each person should write on a piece of paper one thing he or she is good at and can teach others how to do. Your instructor will collect the papers and make a list of what everybody wrote. Choose two things you want to learn how to do. Then find someone who is good at them by making requests to your classmates. Once you find the person, ask him or her for instructions and write them down on the information sheet your instructor will give you. Use casual speech.

Example

A:　あの、～さん。
B:　何。
A:　ピザの作り方が分からないんだけど、教えてくれない？
B:　ごめん。ぼくもよく分からないんだ。or あ、いいよ。まず材料は...

ロールプレイ

A. You received a letter from a host family in Japan. You cannot read the letter because it contains a lot of **kanji.** (1) Ask a Japanese friend to read it for you. (2) Ask your teacher to read it with you.

B. You want to go to a nearby city (choose one) this weekend, but you don't have a car. Find out if your neighbor is planning to go there. Ask him or her to give you a ride.

C. Your professor has a rare book you want to read. Ask him or her to lend it to you.

D. Your next-door neighbor always plays loud music, and you cannot study or sleep. Ask your neighbor not to play loud music at night.

単語　(ESSENTIAL VOCABULARY)

Nouns

あぶら（油）　oil
いみ（意味）　meaning
インターネット　Internet
エアコン　air conditioner
おねがい（お願い）　favor; wish
きかい（機械）　machine
ぎゅうにく（牛肉）　beef
こしょう　pepper
コピーき（コピー機）　copy machine
ざいりょう（材料）　materials; ingredients
さくぶん（作文）　written composition
さとう（砂糖）　sugar
さら（皿）　plate
しお（塩）　salt
じどうはんばいき（自動販売機）　vending machine
じゃがいも　potato
しょうゆ（醤油）　soy sauce
スイッチ　switch
たまねぎ（玉ねぎ）　onion
テクノロジー　technology
テレフォンカード　pre-paid telephone card
でんき（電気）　electricity; electric lights
でんしメール（電子メール）　electronic mail; e-mail
とりにく（鳥肉）　chicken meat
ナイフ　knife
なべ（鍋）　pot
ノート　notes;　ノートをとる（ノートを取る）take notes
はし　chopsticks;　おはし　chopsticks
パソコン　personal computer
バター　butter
パン　bread
ファックス　fax; fax machine
フォーク　fork
ぶたにく（豚肉）　pork
フライパン　frying pan; skillet
ボタン　button
よみ（読み）　reading; pronunciation (of a character)
リモコン　remote control (リモートコントロール = リモコン)
ワープロ　word processor

Verbal nouns

れんしゅう（練習） practice れんしゅうをする（練習をする） (to) practice れんしゅうする（練習する） (to) practice

Irregular verbs

つれてくる（連れて来る） (to) bring (someone)
もってくる（持って来る） (to) bring (something)

う-verbs

あらう（洗う） (to) wash
おくる（送る） (to) send
おす（押す） (to) push
かえす（返す） (to) return something
かす（貸す） (to) lend
きる（切る） (to) cut
たく（炊く） (to) cook rice; ごはんをたく（ご飯を炊く） (to) cook rice
たす（足す） (to) add
たのむ（頼む） (to) ask (request)
つれていく（連れて行く） (to) take (someone)
てつだう（手伝う） (to) help; (to) assist
まつ（待つ） (to) wait for
やく（焼く） (to) bake; (to) fry
やる (to) do

る-verbs

おしえる（教える） (to) teach; (to) inform
おぼえる（覚える） (to) memorize; (to) remember
かりる（借りる） (to) borrow
つける（付ける） (to) turn on; (to) attach
にる（煮る） (to) boil; (to) stew
まぜる（混ぜる） (to) mix

Suffixes

～かた（～方） how to ～, way of ～

Conjunctions

さいごに（最後に） lastly, finally
まず first

Expressions

ごめん。（ご免。） I'm sorry. *(used in casual speech)*
ごめんなさい（ご免なさい。） I am sorry.

Passive Vocabulary

Nouns

あじつけ（味付け） flavoring
うすくちしょうゆ（薄口醤油） light soy sauce
えび（海老） shrimp
えびだんご（海老団子） shrimp dumpling
オンス ounce
ガソリン gasoline
カップ measuring cup
カレーこ（カレー粉） curry powder
きくらげ dried cloud ear mushroom
グラム gram
こくさい （国際） international
こくさいでんわ （国際電話） international call
コピーセンター copy center
しょくパン（食パン） sliced bread
すうじ（数字） number; numeral
スピーチコンテスト speech contest
スライスチーズ sliced cheese
せいせき （成績） grades (in school)
せんたくき（洗濯機） washing machine
そうじき（掃除機） vacuum cleaner
だし broth
だんご（団子） dumpling
ちゅうおん（中温） medium temperature (when cooking)
ドレッシング dressing
パイント pint
バーベキュー barbecue
ひきにく（挽肉） ground meat
まいすう（枚数） number of sheets (of paper, etc.)
みりん sweet rice wine for cooking
ゆ（湯） warm or hot water; おゆ（お湯） warm or hot water

う-verbs

えらぶ（選ぶ） (to) select
はさむ（挟む） (to) pinch
わく（沸く） (to) come to a boil

る-verbs

あげる（揚げる） (to) deep-fry
かける (to) pour
こわれる（壊れる） (to) break down, be broken

Expressions

しょうしょう（少々） a short time; a little bit (in cooking)
みずをきる（水を切る） (to) drain; (to) shake off water

For a list of supplementary vocabulary items that will facilitate communication, see the first page of Chapter 3 in your Workbook.

第四課

A neighborhood post office in Japan

きそく

Rules

Functions	Asking and giving permission; Expressing obligations and expectations; Expressing unacceptability
New Vocabulary	Postal and parcel delivery service; Banks; School; Things you should or should not do
Dialogue	郵便局(ゆうびんきょく)と銀行 (Post offices and banks)
Culture Notes	Postal service and delivery services; Banks
Language	I. Expressing unacceptable actions or situations, using the て-form + はいけない／だめ II. Expressing obligations and social expectations, using the negative stem + なければ／なくてはならない／いけない; Expressing a lack of obligation or social expectations, using the negative stem + なくてもいい III. Expressing the performance of two actions simultaneously, using the ます stem of verbs + ながら IV. Listing actions and states, using the plain form + し; Implying a reason, using the plain form + し V. Expressing conditions originated by others, using ～(の)なら
Kanji	Component shapes of **kanji** 4: Enclosing shapes
Reading	Bank accounts; Privacy
Listening	Living with host families
Communication	Changing the subject

新(あたら)しい言葉(ことば)

郵便(ゆうびん)と宅配(たくはい)サービス (Postal and parcel delivery service)

サービス	service	ふうとう	envelope
船便(ふなびん)	surface mail	ポスト	public mailbox
航空便(こうくうびん)	air mail	～キロ／ポンド	kilograms/pounds
宅急便(たっきゅうびん)	express parcel service	はやい	fast; early
小包(こづつみ)	small package	おそい	slow
切手(きって)	postage stamp	時間／お金が かかる	it takes time/money

下の言葉(ことば)をおぼえていますか。

郵便局(ゆうびんきょく)　手紙(てがみ)　葉書(はがき)　番号(ばんごう)　国　おもい　かるい
送(おく)る　出す　包(つつ)む　荷物(にもつ)

下の言葉(ことば)を読んで下さい。

何(なん)キロ　一(いち)キロ　二(に)キロ　三(さん)キロ　四(よん)キロ　五(ご)キロ　六(ろっ)キロ
七(なな)キロ　八(はち)キロ　九(きゅう) キロ　十(じゅっ) キロ　何(なん)ポンド　一(いち)ポンド
二(に)ポンド　三(さん)ポンド　四(よん)ポンド　五(ご)ポンド　六(ろく)ポンド
七(なな)ポンド　八(はち)ポンド　九(きゅう) ポンド　十(じゅっ) ポンド

A. 日本語で質問(しつもん)に答えて下さい。分からない言葉(ことば)があったら、先生に聞いて下さい。

1. 物(もの)を送(おく)る時、どの方法(ほうほう) (method) がはやいですか。どの方法(ほうほう) (method) がおそいですか。
2. 手紙(てがみ)を送(おく)る時、どれで送(おく)りますか。小包(こづつみ)はどうですか。
3. 何かをはやく送(おく)りたい時、どれをよく使いますか。
4. あなたの国では葉書(はがき)を出す時、お金がいくらかかりますか。
5. あなたの国では郵便局(ゆうびんきょく)で小包(こづつみ)を送(おく)る時、何日ぐらいかかりますか。
6. あなたの国では宅急便(たっきゅうびん)では何日ぐらいかかりますか。

7. あなたの国から日本に手紙(てがみ)を出す時、いくらぐらいかかりますか。何日ぐらいかかりますか。

8. あなたの国から日本に小包(こづつみ)を送(おく)る時、船便(ふなびん)で何日ぐらいかかりますか。航空便(こうくうびん)では何日ぐらいかかりますか。

9. あなたの国では航空便(こうくうびん)の小包(こづつみ)は何キロ／ポンドまでいいですか。

10.「郵便番号(ゆうびんばんごう)」の意味は何だと思いますか。

銀行 (Banks)

預金(よきん)(する) deposit (to deposit)

ふつう regular; normal

普通預金(ふつうよきん) regular savings account

口座(こうざ) account

はんこ personal stamp/seal

サイン signature

申込書(もうしこみしょ) application form

運転免許(うんてんめんきょ)(証(しょう)) driver's license

外国人登録証(がいこくじんとうろくしょう) alien registration card

口座(こうざ)をひらく to open an account

引(ひ)き出す to withdraw

貯金(ちょきん)する to save money

円をドルにかえる to exchange yen for dollars

サインがいる to need a signature

〜に記入(きにゅう)する to fill out 〜

〜証(しょう) means an *ID card*. 外国人登録証(がいこくじんとうろくしょう) consists of 外国(がいこく), 〜人, 登録(とうろく) *(registration)*, and 〜証(しょう). 運転免許(証)(うんてんめんきょしょう) consists of 運転(うんてん) *(driving)*, 免許(めんきょ) *(license)*, and 〜証(しょう).

下の言葉(ことば)をおぼえていますか。

あんない　借りる　貸す　返す

B. 下のことをする時、どんなものがいりますか。どんなことをしますか。

1. 口座(こうざ)をひらく ______________________________
2. お金を引(ひ)き出す ______________________________
3. 預金(よきん)する ______________________________
4. 円をドルにかえる ______________________________

C. クラスメートの中でパスポート、はんこ、外国人登録証(がいこくじんとうろくしょう)、運転免許証(うんてんめんきょしょう)を持っている人をさがして下さい。

1. パスポートを持っている人________________________
2. はんこを持っている人________________________
3. 外国人登録証(がいこくじんとうろくしょう)を持っている人________________________
4. 運転免許証(うんてんめんきょしょう)を持っている人 ________________________

学校 (School)

学期(がっき) semester; quarter

コース course

授業料(じゅぎょうりょう) tuition

学生証(しょう) student ID card

作文(さくぶん) composition

レポート report; paper

会話(かいわ) conversation

せいせき academic grade(s)

受(う)ける to take (a class/an exam)

忘(わす)れる to forget

おとす to drop

授業(じゅぎょう)におくれる to be late for class

セクションをかえる to change sections

かまいません (I) don't care; (it's okay)

下の言葉(ことば)をおぼえていますか。

小学校　中学校　高校　大学　大学院(いん)　大学生　一年生　二年生
三年生　四年生　大学院生　留学生(りゅうがくせい)　クラスメート
ルームメート　留学生(りゅうがくせい)センター　図書館　体育館　本部(ほんぶ)　本屋
ラボ　りょう　じむしつ　教室(きょうしつ)　けんきゅうしつ　せんこう
けいざい学　けいえい学　文学　アジアけんきゅう　工学(こうがく)
けいざい学部(がくぶ)　法学部(ほうがくぶ)　卒業(そつぎょう)　卒業式(そつぎょうしき)　休み　春休み　冬休み
夏休み　こくばん　けしゴム　えんぴつ　ペン　辞書(じしょ)　教科書(きょうかしょ)
クラス　つくえ　文房具(ぶんぼうぐ)　ボールペン　授業(じゅぎょう)　しけん　宿題(しゅくだい)
勉強(べんきょう)　休む　はらう　始まる　終わる　練習(れんしゅう)　ノートをとる

D. 下の言葉(ことば)の意味は何だと思いますか。

先学期(がっき)　今学期(がっき)　来学期(がっき)　秋学期(がっき)　春学期(がっき)　一学期(がっき)

E. 下線(かせん) (blanks) にてきとうな (appropriate) 言葉(ことば)を書いて下さい。

1. おさけを買う時は、________________を見せて下さい。
2. 私の学校では__________________は十五週間あります。
3. 宿題(しゅくだい)をぜんぜん出していないので、________________があまりよくなかった。だから、この________________は________________と思っている。
4. スミスさんは日本語で____________________を書くのがとても上手です。
5. 先生、まだ________________が終わりませんから、少し__________________かまいませんか。
6. 話すのが上手じゃないので、________________のしけんはきらいです。
7. 明日までに__________________をはらわないと、授業(じゅぎょう)が__________________ないそうです。
8. あのセクションは朝早いので、いつも授業に__________。だから、セクションを__________________と思う。

したほうがいいこと、しないほうがいいこと (Things you should or should not do)

おじぎをする to bow formally
握手(あくしゅ)をする to shake hands
かぎをかける to lock the door
ドアをしめる to close the door
ノックをする to knock on the door
くつをぬぐ to take off (one's) shoes
ペットをかう to keep/raise a pet
車を運転(うんてん)する to drive a car
大きいこえで話す to speak loudly

下の言葉(ことば)をおぼえていますか。

たばこをすう　ふとる　やせる　わらう　なく　おさけを飲む
よるおそくまで起きている　朝はやく起きる　けがをする
ゆびを切る　うんどうをする　シャワーをあびる　おふろに入る
予約(よやく)をする

F. Work as a class. Ask your classmates how often they do the following things, and complete the chart by checking the appropriate frequency word: いつも, よく, ときどき, あまり, or ぜんぜん. For example, check いつも if your classmates always do something, or check よく if they do it frequently.

	いつも	**よく**	**ときどき**	**あまり**	**ぜんぜん**
あいさつをする時、おじぎをする					
あいさつをする時、握手(あくしゅ)をする					
家にいる時、ドアにかぎをかける					
お手洗いを使った後、ドアをしめる					
お手洗いを使う時、ノックをする					
家の中に入る時、くつをぬぐ					
おさけを飲んだ時、車を運転(うんてん)する					
言葉(ことば)の授業(じゅぎょう)では大きいこえで話す					
よるおふろに入る					
たばこをすう					

ダイアローグ

はじめに

質問(しつもん)に日本語で答えて下さい。

1. あなたの国の銀行にはどんな口座(こうざ)がありますか。
2. 銀行の口座(こうざ)をひらく時、銀行に何を持って行かなければなりませんか。
3. 銀行の口座(こうざ)をひらく時、銀行はその人のどんなことを知らなければなりませんか。
4. あなたの国の郵便局(ゆうびんきょく)ではどんなサービスがありますか。
5. 外国(がいこく)に何か送(おく)る時、航空便(こうくうびん)ではどのくらいの大きさまで大丈夫(だいじょうぶ)ですか。
6. 外国(がいこく)に何か送(おく)る時、船便(ふなびん)ではどのくらいの大きさまで大丈夫(だいじょうぶ)ですか。何キロまで大丈夫(だいじょうぶ)ですか。

郵便局(ゆうびんきょく)と銀行 (Post offices and banks)

STUDENT

The following **manga** frames are scrambled, so they are not in the order described by the dialogue. Read the dialogue and unscramble the frames by writing the correct number in the box located in the upper right corner of each frame.

リーさんは普通預金(ふつうよきん)の口座(こうざ)をひらきたいと思っています。

リー：　ねえ、アリスさん、ちょっといい？

アリス：　あ、いいわよ。何？

リー：　銀行の口座(こうざ)をひらきたいんだけど、パスポートとお金を持ってけばいいの？

アリス：　ええ、そう。あ、でも、それに、外国人登録証(がいこくじんとうろくしょう)も持ってかなきゃね。

リー：　あ、そう。はんこはなくてもいいの？

アリス:　小さい銀行ならいるかもしれないけど、大きい銀行ならたいていサインが使えるし、いらないわよ。でも、日本でははんこはあったほうが便利(べんり)よ。

リーさんは銀行に行きました。

リー：　あのう、普通預金(ふつうよきん)の口座(こうざ)をひらきたいんですけど。

銀行の人A：　では、六番(ばん)の窓口(まどぐち)に行って下さい。

六番(ばん)の窓口(まどぐち)で

リー：　あのう、口座(こうざ)をひらきたいんですが。

銀行の人B：　普通預金(ふつうよきん)ですか。

リー：　はい。

銀行の人B：　外国(がいこく)の方ですね。

リー：　はい、そうです。

銀行の人B：　では、この申込書(もうしこみしょ)に記入(きにゅう)して下さい。あそこに記入(きにゅう)のし方のサンプルがありますから、見ながら書いて下さい。

リー：　はい、分かりました。

銀行の人B:　それから、パスポートと外国人登録証(がいこくじんとうろくしょう)をおねがいします。

リー：　あ、はい、これです。

銀行に行った後、リーさんは郵便局(ゆうびんきょく)へ行きました。

リー：　あのう、これ、航空便(こうくうびん)で送(おく)りたいんですけど。

郵便局(ゆうびんきょく)の人：　これは１．２キロですから、送(おく)れませんねえ。

リー：　え、だめなんですか。

郵便局(ゆうびんきょく)の人：　ええ、船便(ふなびん)なら５キロまで大丈夫(だいじょうぶ)ですけど、航空便(こうくうびん)は１キロをこえてはいけないんですよ。ですから、二つにして持って来て下さい。

リー：　分かりました。じゃ、また後で来ます。

分かりましたか

A. Complete the following paragraph based on the dialogue.

リーさんは ①＿＿＿＿＿＿＿＿ に銀行に行きました。行く前に、アリスさんにいるものについて聞きました。アリスさんは ②＿＿＿＿＿＿＿＿ と ③＿＿＿＿＿＿＿＿ と ④＿＿＿＿＿＿ はなければならないと言いましたが、⑤＿＿＿＿＿＿＿＿＿ は大きい銀行なら ⑥＿＿＿＿＿＿＿＿ てもいいそうです。リーさんは銀行に行った後で、郵便局(ゆうびんきょく)に ⑦＿＿＿＿＿＿＿ に行きました。航空便(こうくうびん)で送(おく)ろうと思いましたが、送(おく)れませんでした。郵便局(ゆうびんきょく)の人によると、航空便(こうくうびん)は ⑧＿＿＿＿＿＿＿＿＿ てはいけないそうです。船便(ふなびん)は ⑨＿＿＿＿＿＿＿＿＿＿ てもいいそうです。ですから、リーさんは小包(こづつみ)を ⑩＿＿＿＿＿＿。

B. Identify the phrases in the dialogue that Lee-san uses to start a conversation and those he uses to introduce the topic of a conversation.

C. Rewrite the conversation between Alice-san and Lee-san so that both of them are in your country; assume that Alice-san knows about the banking system in your country.

日本の文化

Postal service and delivery services. What kinds of services do post offices offer in your country? What other delivery services are commonly used in your country?

Japan has an efficient postal service. Regular postcards and letters usually reach their destinations within two days. Mail is delivered once a day except Sunday. However, you cannot leave outgoing mail in your mailbox (郵便受(ゆうびんう)け) for pickup. Instead, you must drop it in a public mailbox (郵便(ゆうびん)ポスト or ポスト). Mailboxes are red and have two slots: one for local mail (within a prefecture or city) and the other for out-of-prefecture mail and overseas mail. Stamps are sold at post offices and at stores (e.g., grocery stores) that display a sign outside. There are very few stamp vending machines. The current postage for a postcard is 50 yen, and for letters under 25 grams it is 80 yen.

There are other ways to send packages besides using the postal service. These are commonly called 宅配便(たくはいびん), or 宅急便(たっきゅうびん), and are

A private mailbox and a public mailbox

run by private companies. They offer pickup services as well as a large number of drop-off sites. Drop-off sites are usually at stores, and they are indicated by an easily noticeable banner. You can send a wide range of items through these services, including fresh seafood packed in dry ice. You can also send large pieces of luggage from a drop-off site to an airport or from an airport to your destination.

- *Banks. What kinds of services do banks offer in your country?*

Cash is the most prevalent method of personal financial transactions in Japan, although credit cards (クレジットカード) are accepted at hotels, restaurants, department stores, and supermarkets. Personal checks are not used, and banks do not have checking accounts for private use. Most business transactions, including payroll disbursement are made via bank transfer (振込[ふりこみ]). Other services offered by banks include automatic payment directly from an account for utility bills (自動引き落とし[じどうひきおとし]), foreign currency exchange (外国為替[がいこくかわせ]), travelers checks (トラベラーズチェック), and transfer of money (銀行振込[ぎんこうふりこみ]) from bank to bank. Bank transfers are used to make a variety of payments such as tuition and mail order charges. Bank transfers can be made at any bank, including ones where you have no account. You need to fill out an application form and give it to the teller along with the money to be transferred and a processing fee. Many banks have an automatic transfer machine (自動振込機[じどうふりこみき]). The processing fee is smaller for transactions between branches of the same bank.

An international student who wishes to open a regular savings account (普通預金口座[ふつうよきんこうざ]) at a bank is required to provide a valid passport (パスポート) and alien registration card (外国人[がいこくじん]

登録証). Foreigners must register at a municipal office within 30 days of arrival in Japan. In addition, some banks require a personal stamp or seal (印鑑 or はんこ), while other banks, especially those with foreign currency exchange service, let you open an account using your signature. Personal stamps usually have one's last name. Since personal stamps are so ingrained in Japanese society, it is probably a good idea to have an inexpensive one made at a local stamp shop (はんこや). You can use **katakana** or, if you prefer, you may come up with a **kanji** combination which approximates the sound of your last name.

Banks have special teller windows for regular savings accounts (left), and foreign customers can transact business using personal stamps with their names transcribed in katakana (see above).

LANGUAGE

I. Expressing unacceptable actions or situations, using the て-form + はいけない／だめ

		Verb (て-form)						
作文を	おそく	出して	は	いけません	が、	漢字の宿題は	いいです	よ。

You cannot turn in your composition late, but it's okay to be late with the **kanji** assignment.

Question				
	Copula (て-form)			
学生証	で	は	いけません	か。

Is a student identification card insufficient?

	Answer
ええ、	いけません。／だめです。

Yes, it won't be enough.

ノックをしないで、部屋(へや)に入ってはいけません。	You must not enter the room without knocking on the door.
レポートを忘(わす)れてはいけません。	You must not forget your paper.
せいせきがわるくてはいけません。	Your grades must not be poor.

学生： 先生、セクションをかえてはいけませんか。
Professor, is it okay if I change sections? (literally: Is it not acceptable if I change sections?)

先生： ええ、だめです。
No, that's not acceptable.

- ～てはいけない takes the て-form of verbs and adjectives.

	Dictionary form	～ては／ちゃ　いけない／だめ	Meaning
Copula verbs	学生だ	学生では／学生じゃ いけない／だめ	must not be a student
	子供(こども)だ	子供(こども)では／子供(こども)じゃ いけない／だめ	must not be a child
な-adjectives	きらいな	きらいでは／きらいじゃ いけない／だめ	must not dislike
	しずかな	しずかでは／しずかじゃ いけない／だめ	must not be quiet
い-adjectives	小さい	小さくては／小さくちゃ いけない／だめ	must not be small
	せまい	せまくては／せまくちゃ いけない／だめ	must not be cramped
Irregular verbs	来る	来ては／来ちゃ いけない／だめ	must not come
	する	しては／しちゃ いけない／だめ	must not do
う-verbs	送(おく)る	送(おく)っては／送(おく)っちゃ いけない／だめ	must not send
	飲む	飲んでは／飲んじゃ いけない／だめ	must not drink
る-verbs	いる	いては／いちゃ いけない／だめ	must not stay
	寝る	寝ては／寝ちゃ いけない／だめ	must not sleep

- The て-form + はいけない／だめ indicates that something is not allowed. This structure is commonly used to talk about rules. Use the て-form + もいい (Chapter 12 of Volume 1) to indicate permission.

- The colloquial format of ～てはいけない is ～ちゃいけない／じゃいけない。

このアパートではペットをかっ<u>ては</u>いけないよ。	このアパートではペットをかっ<u>ちゃ</u>いけないよ。

It is not acceptable to keep a pet in this apartment.

おそくまで起きてい<u>ては</u>だめです。	おそくまで起きてい<u>ちゃ</u>だめです。

It is not acceptable to stay up late.

- When answering questions with the て-form +はいけませんか／だめですか, use ええ、いけません／だめです to prohibit an action. Use いいえ、いいです to permit the action.

田中：	かぎをかけてはいけませんか。	Can't I lock the door?
先生：	ええ、（かけては）いけません。	No, you must not.
or	いいえ、（かけても）いいですよ。	Yes, you may.

話してみましょう

A. State what is or is not acceptable in each of the following places, using the expressions provided and ～てもいいです／～てはいけない .

Example

教室(きょうしつ)ではコーヒーを飲んでもいいですが、たばこをすってはいけません。

1. 教室(きょうしつ)
2. 病院
3. 図書館
4. 映画館
5. バー
6. レストラン

コーヒーを飲む	何か食べる	おそくまで起きている
たばこをすう	おさけを飲む	おくれて来る
大きいこえで話す	子供(こども)だ	食べ物(もの)を持って来る
いぬをつれて来る	明るい	しずかだ
寝る	せまい	二十一さいだ
ぼうしをかぶる	暗い	にぎやかだ

B. Work with the class. Circle いい if you are allowed to perform a given act in the place where you currently live, and circle いけない if you are not. Find a classmate who lives in the same kind of place by asking questions using ～てはいけない and ～てもいい. Use casual speech.

Example

A: ～さんの所では　たばこすってもいいの。
B: うん、いいよ。
　　いや、だめだよ。

よるおそくパーティをする	いい	いけない
たばこをすう	いい	いけない
ペットをかう	いい	いけない
料理をする	いい	いけない
おそくまで起きている	いい	いけない
大きいこえで話す	いい	いけない

C. Work with a partner. You are a doctor and your partner is your patient. For each of the physical conditions listed, create a dialogue between the doctor and the patient in which the doctor explains what the patient is allowed or not allowed to do.

Example

かぜ

A: 先生、今晩おふろに入ってもいいでしょうか。
B: いいえ。シャワーはあびてもいいですが、おふろに入ってはいけません。
A: あのう、今日はしけんがあるんですが、大学に行ってはいけませんか。
B: 行かない方がいいですね。
A: すみませんが、じゃあ、先生に出す手紙(てがみ)を書いていただけませんか。

1. 足のけが
2. かふん症(しょう)　(hay fever)
3. いかいよう　(stomach ulcer)
4. かろう　(stress, overworked)
5. 下痢(げり)　(diarrhea)

II. Expressing obligations and social expectations, using the negative stem + なければ／なくてはならない／いけない; Expressing a lack of obligation or social expectations, using the negative stem + なくてもいい

A. Using the negative stem + なければ／なくてはならない／いけない

A-1. Expressing obligation

	Verb (negative stem)		ならない／いけない
銀行の口座(こうざ)を	ひらか	なければ	なりません／いけません。

You/I must open a bank account.

	Verb (negative stem)		ならない／いけない
今学期(こんがっき)の授業料(じゅぎょうりょう)を	はらわ	なくては	なりません／いけません。

You must pay tuition for this semester.

明日ははやく起きなければならないんです。
I have to get up early tomorrow.

本田：　お金がかかるから、船便(ふなびん)で送(おく)ってもいいですか。
Since it's expensive, may I send it by surface mail?

ありさか：来週の月曜日までに着いていなければならないので、航空便(こうくうびん)で送(おく)って下さいませんか。
It has to arrive by next Monday, so could you send it air mail, please?

かおる：　どこ行くの？
Where are you going?

健一(けんいち)：　銀行。お金引(ひ)き出さなきゃなんないんだ。
The bank. I have to withdraw some money.

使った後はお手洗いのドアはしめなきゃだめよ。
You must close the bathroom door after use.

A-2. Expressing expectations of someone or something

	な-adjective negative stem		
子供(こども)は	元気じゃ	なければ	いけない／ならない。

Children should be healthy/energetic.

	い-adjective negative stem		
映画は	おもしろく	なくては	いけない／ならない。

Movies should be interesting (for me to like them).

航空便(こうくうびん)は１キロまでじゃなければならない。	Air mail must be no more than one kilogram.
せいせきがもっとよくなければならない。	Your grades have to improve.
パーティはにぎやかじゃなくちゃいけないよ。	Parties should be lively.
男の子は強くなきゃいけないよ。	Boys should be strong.

- なければ／なくては　ならない／いけない is derived from the negative ending 〜ない.

	Dictionary form	**Negative stem**	**Negative stem + なければ／なくては**
Copula verbs	学生だ	学生じゃ~~ない~~	学生じゃなければ／学生じゃなくては
な-adjectives	きれいだ	きれいじゃ~~ない~~	きれいじゃなければ／きれいじゃなくては
	しずかだ	しずかじゃ~~ない~~	しずかじゃなければ／しずかじゃなくては
い-adjectives	暗い	暗く~~ない~~	暗くなければ／暗くなくては
	やさしい	やさしく~~ない~~	やさしくなければ／やさしくなくては
Irregular verbs	来(く)る	来(こ)~~ない~~	来(こ)なければ／来(こ)なくては
	する	し~~ない~~	しなければ／しなくては
る-verbs	起きる	起き~~ない~~	起きなければ／起きなくては
	教える	教え~~ない~~	教えなければ／教えなくては
う-verbs	送(おく)る	送(おく)ら~~ない~~	送(おく)らなければ／送(おく)らなくては
	返す	返さ~~ない~~	返さなければ／返さなくては

- The combination of the verb negative stem + なければ／なくては with ならない／いけない indicates one must or has to do something. The combination of the adjective negative stem + なければ／なくては with ならない／いけない indicates one is expected to be a certain way.
- Although they are virtually interchangeable, いけません carries a stronger sense of obligation than なりません. When one talks about general obligations or necessities, なければなりません or なくてはなりません tends to be used. The use of なければいけません or なくてはいけません tends to indicate specific obligations or necessities.

ドルを円にかえなければなりません。 ドルを円にかえなくてはなりません。 ドルを円にかえなければいけません。 ドルを円にかえなくてはいけません。	I/You must exchange dollars for yen.

- The following contracted forms are used in casual conversational speech. Also, ならない／いけない can be omitted or replaced by だめ.

～なければ ——→ ～なきゃ
～なくては ——→ ～なくちゃ
ならない ——→ なんない

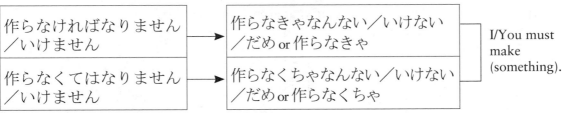

作らなければなりません／いけません	→	作らなきゃなんない／いけない／だめ or 作らなきゃ	I/You must make (something).
作らなくてはなりません／いけません	→	作らなくちゃなんない／いけない／だめ or 作らなくちゃ	

- Because the negative form of the verb ある is ない, なければ／なくてはならない／いけない alone means *something must exist* or *one must have something*.

ここに先生のサインがなければいけない。	You must have a teacher's signature here.
切手（きって）がなければいけませんよ。	You must have a postage stamp.

- To answer questions with なければ／なくてはなりませんか／いけませんか, use ええ、～なければ／なくてはいけません to express an obligation. Use いいえ、～なくてもいいです to express the lack of an obligation.

B. Expressing the acceptability of an action or state, using the negative stem + なくてもいい

Question		
今日	送（おく）らなくちゃ	いけませんか。

Do I have to send (it) today?

Answer			
	Verb negative stem		
いいえ、	送（おく）ら	なくても	いいですよ。

No, you don't have to send (it today).

ケイト：　くつをぬがなきゃいけないの？
Do I have to take off my shoes?

明(あきら)：　いや、ぬがなくてもいいよ。
No, you don't have to take them off.

学生：　外国人登録証(がいこくじんとうろくしょう)じゃなきゃいけませんか。
Do I have to have my alien registration card?

じむしつの人：　いや、外国人登録証(がいこくじんとうろくしょう)じゃなくてもいいですよ。学生証(しょう)でもいいです。
No, you don't need your alien registration card. Your student ID card will be fine.

おくさん：　このお金、貯金(ちょきん)しなくてもいいの？
Don't you have to save this money?

ご主人(しゅじん)：　ああ、いいんだ。
No, it's okay.

鈴木(すずき)：　おじぎはしなくてもいいんですか。
Don't I have to bow?

ブラウン：　ええ、いいですよ。でも、握手(あくしゅ)はしなくちゃいけませんよ。
No, you don't have to. (literally: Yes, not bowing is fine.) But you must shake hands.

- The negative stem + なくてもいい means that one does not have to do something or something does not have to be done in a certain way. This is the opposite of the negative stem + なければ／なくてはならない／いけない. The negative stem + なくてもいい is also derived from the negative ending 〜ない and is made according to the same rules described above for 〜なくては〜.
- The negative stem + なくてもいい by itself means something does not have to exist or one does not have to have something.

パスポートがなくてもいいですよ。　You don't have to have your passport.

- The negative stem + なくてもけっこうです and the negative stem + なくてもかまいません are used in polite speech, rather than the negative stem + なくてもいい. Store clerks, bank tellers, and post office clerks commonly use this more polite version.

学生証(しょう)はなくてもけっこうです。　You don't have to have your student ID.
かぎはかけなくてもかまいませんよ。　You don't have to lock the door.

話してみましょう

A. Answer the questions below using the following academic calendar. Use polite speech.

Example

課目(かもく)とうろく (course registration) はいつまでにしなければなりませんか。

八月三十日までにしなければなりません。／しなくてはなりません。／しなければいけません。／しなくてはいけません。

August 25-August 30	On-campus registration
September 1	Instruction begins
September 14	Last day to add a course or to change sections
September 21	Last day to pay tuition without penalty
October 30	Last day to drop a course
November 30	Last day to submit a graduation request
December 5	Instruction ends
December 8-14	Final examinations

1. セクションはいつまでにかえなければなりませんか。
2. 卒業(そつぎょう)する時はいつまでに申込書(もうしこみしょ)を出さなくてはいけませんか。
3. あたらしいコースをとりたい時は、いつまでにとらなければなりませんか。
4. 授業料(じゅぎょうりょう)はいつまでにはらわなくてはいけませんか。
5. コースをおとしたい時は、いつまでにおとさなければなりませんか。
6. きまつしけん (final examinations) はいつまでに受(う)けなければなりませんか。

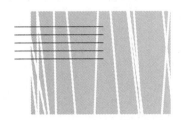

B. Respond to the following questions, requests, or invitations using ～なければ／なくてはならない／いけない and the appropriate phrase. Use casual or polite speech.

Example

映画見に行かない？／アルバイトをする
ありがとう、でも、アルバイトをしなくちゃなんないんだ。(male)／
アルバイトしなくちゃならないの。(female)

1. テニスしない？／病院に行く
2. 少し飲みませんか。／運転（うんてん）する
3. まだこの店にいるんですか。／おみやげを買う
4. もう帰りましょう。／銀行に行って、お金を引（ひ）き出す
5. 買い物に行きましょうか。／貯金（ちょきん）する
6. どうして電話をかけているんですか。／安い旅館をさがす

C. Work with a partner. Choose one of the occupations listed below and tell your partner what attributes are necessary for the job. Have him or her guess what it is. Take turns.

Example

A: きれいじゃなければいけません、そして、やせていなければなりません。
B: モデルですか。
A: はい、そうです。

モデル　小学校の先生　いしゃ　エンジニア　旅行会社（りょこうがいしゃ）の社員（しゃいん） (employee)　大学の先生　シェフ　スタイリスト　ミュージシャン　ダンサー　バスの運転手（うんてんしゅ） (driver)

D. A Japanese student is explaining Japanese customs and social obligations. Use なくては／なければ　ならない／いけない or なくてもいい to say whether or not they exist in your country also.

Example

日本では手紙（てがみ）を出す時、ポストに手紙（てがみ）を入れなければなりません。
アメリカではポストに入れなくてもいいです。

1. 日本では家の中に入る時、くつをぬがなければなりません。
2. 日本ではあいさつをする時、おじぎをしなければなりません。
3. 日本ではお手洗のドアはいつもしめなければなりません。
4. 日本ではアパートを借りる時、たくさんお金がなくてはいけません。
5. 日本では銀行の口座(こうざ)をひらく時、はんこがなくてはいけません。
6. 日本では車は左側(ひだりがわ)を走らなくてはなりません。
7. 日本では運転免許(うんてんめんきょ)を取る時、むずかしいしけんを受(う)けなければなりません。

III. Expressing the performance of two actions simultaneously, using the ます stem of verbs + ながら

	Verb ます stem			
テレビを	見	ながら、	勉強(べんきょう)しちゃ	だめですよ。

You shouldn't study while watching TV. / You shouldn't watch TV while you're studying.

電話をかけながら、車を運転(うんてん)していたので、こうつうじこにあった。
Because I was talking on the phone while driving I was involved in a car accident.

話しながらごはんを食べてはいけません。
You shouldn't talk while you are eating.

おんがくを聞きながら、勉強(べんきょう)するのが好きなんです。
I like to study while listening to music. / I like listening to music while I'm studying.

寝ながらたばこをすってはいけない。
You must not smoke in bed.

- The ます stem of the verb + ながら expresses an action that occurs simultaneously with another action, but which is subordinate to that action. The actions in the ながら clause and in the main clause must be performed by the same person.

	Dictionary form	ます stem	ます stem + ながら form
Irregular verb	する	し~~ます~~	しながら
る-verb	食べる	食べ~~ます~~	食べながら
う-verb	読む	読み~~ます~~	読みながら

来る is not normally used with ながら.

- When ながら is used to express simultaneous actions, the action expressed in the main clause is the main action, and that described in the ながら clause is the subordinate action. Thus, in the sentence コーヒーを飲みながら話しましょう *(Let's talk over a cup of coffee)*, the main action is talking, and the act of talking is done while the speaker is drinking coffee. The closest equivalent of ながら in English is *while* ～*ing*, but in English the main action can often be expressed in the while clause or in the main clause because both speaker and listener will have an unspoken agreement as to which action is dominant and which is subordinate. For example, コーヒーを飲みながら話しましょう can be translated as *Let's talk while drinking a cup of coffee.* (The dominant action is expressed in the main clause, and the subordinate action is expressed in the while clause.) On the other hand, 話しながら食べてはいけない should be translated as *You shouldn't talk while eating*. (The dominant action is eating, but it is expressed in the while clause.)

話してみましょう

A. Complete the following sentences by choosing an appropriate phrase from the box and using it with ～ながら.

Example

お金がなかったから、アルバイトをしながら学校に行きました。

コーヒーを飲む	アルバイトをする	私の目を見る	本を読む
なく	人に聞く	おじぎをする	大きいこえで話す
ノートをとる	地図を見る	あくしゅをする	たばこをすう
下を見る	電話で話す		

1. 友達と話す時は、よく喫茶店(きっさてん)で__________話します。
2. __________歩いていたら、お金を見つけた。(find)
3. 行ったことがなかったので、__________その店まで行った。
4. __________授業(じゅぎょう)を受(う)けた。
5. このケーキは__________作ったんですが、あまり上手に出来ませんでした。

6. ____________________車を運転(うんてん)していたら、こうつうじこにあった。

7. その人は____________________「よろしく」と言いました。

8. ____________________おさけを飲んでいたら、気分がわるくなった。

B. Work as a class. Ask your classmates what kinds of things they do while they are studying or eating dinner, using ～ながら. Find out the most common habits among your classmates.

Example

A: よく何かしながら、勉強(べんきょう)しますか。

B: ええ、します。

A: そうですか。どんなことをするんですか。

B: よくお菓子(かし)を食べながら、勉強(べんきょう)します。

C. Work with a partner. Think of three sets of actions you perform simultaneously. Act out each set to your partner and have him or her guess what it is.

Example

電話(でんわ)で話しながら、料理をする

A acts out a scene of cooking while talking on the phone.

B: 電話(でんわ)で話しながら、料理をするんですか。

A: はい、そうです。

IV. Listing actions and states, using the plain form + し; Implying a reason, using the plain form + し

A. Listing actions and states

	Adjective (plain)		Adjectives (plain)		
スミスさんは	やさしい	し、	きれいだ	し、	親切(しんせつ)です。

Smith-san is gentle, pretty, and kind as well.

				Verb (plain)				
山田さん	は	英語	も	話せる	し、	スペイン語	も	上手です。

Yamada-san can speak English and is also good at Spanish.

私は魚も食べないし、肉も食べません。 I don't eat fish, nor do I eat meat.

あの学生はよく授業(じゅぎょう)を休むし、いつもおくれて来るんです。 That student often misses class and is always late.

この銀行で普通預金(ふつうよきん)の口座(こうざ)をひらくなら、サインでもいいですし、はんこを使ってもいいですよ。 If you want to open a regular savings account in this bank, you can sign here or use your personal seal.

ありさかさんは頭もいいし、スポーツもよく出来るし、親切(しんせつ)だから、友達(ともだち)がたくさんいるんだ。 Arisaka-san is smart, good at sports, and kind, so she has a lot of friends.

- し is preceded by the plain form of adjectives, verbs, or copulas, which can be in the affirmative, negative, present tense, or past tense.

い-adjectives	いいし よくないし よかったし よくなかったし	**な-adjectives**	元気だし 元気じゃないし 元気だったし 元気じゃなかったし
Copula verbs	いい天気だし いい天気じゃないし いい天気だったし いい天気じゃなかったし	**Verbs**	するし しないし したし しなかったし

- し lists two or more mutually compatible states or facts. It can be used to list characteristics or factors that lead to a result or conclusion.
- The use of し is similar in some respects to the て-form, but し conveys more of a sense of making a list than does 〜て. The て-form can be used to connect states, and also to express a chronological sequence leading to a conclusion, while the use of し suggests states which are being listed in no particular order.

B. Implying a reason, using the plain form + し

	Plain, neg.		
今日は時間も	ない	し、	明日にしよう。

I don't have time today, so let's do it tomorrow.

宿題(しゅくだい)を忘(わす)れたし、時間もおそくなったし、今日は授業(じゅぎょう)に出ないつもりだ。
I forgot the assignment, and it's kind of late, so I'm not going to class today.

この学校はいい学校だけど、授業料(じゅぎょうりょう)が高いし、大変(たいへん)だ。
This is a good school, but the tuition is high, so it's very tough.

私はひろい所の方が好きだし、ペットもかいたいし、だからアパートより家の方がいいです。
I prefer a spacious place and want to have a pet, so a house would be better than an apartment.

トム： どうして宅急便(たっきゅうびん)で送らないの？その方がはやいよ。
Why don't you send it by air mail? It's faster.

キム： でも、今あまりお金がないし。
But I don't have much money, so . . .

- し can be used to imply a reason, instead of explicitly stating one. This is demonstrated in the key sentence above and the example sentences. This usage is more indirect than から or ので.

雨がふっているし、今日は家にいます。 It's raining, so I'll stay home today. (indirect)
雨がふっているから、今日は家にいます。 Since it's raining, I will stay home today. (direct)

- The particle も often appears with し to reinforce the meaning of し. It does not change the essential meaning.

雨<u>も</u>ふっている<u>し</u>、今日は家にいます。 It's raining, so I'll stay home today. (stronger)

話してみましょう

A. Combine the following sentences using 〜し.

Example

スミスさんはきれいです。それに、スミスさんは親切(しんせつ)です。
ですから、スミスさんはたくさん友達がいます。
スミスさんはきれいだし、親切(しんせつ)だし、たくさん友達がいます。

1. 昨日(きのう)はしけんを受(う)けました。作文(さくぶん)も書きました。ですから、とてもいそがしかったです。
2. 先生があまりよくありません。授業(じゅぎょう)もおもしろくありません。ですから、そのコースをおとすつもりです。
3. まどはしめました。かぎもかけました。ですから、もう出かけられます。
4. 今日はレポートを出しました。明日のじゅんびもしました。ですから、あそびに行こうと思います。
5. 部屋(へや)がきたなくなります。たたみをそうじするのは大変(たいへん)です。ですから、日本では家に入る時はくつをぬぎます。
6. あの店ではたばこをすってはいけません。ネクタイをしなければなりません。だから、行きません。
7. これはおもたいです。一番(ばん)大きいふうとうにも入りません。小包(こづつみ)にして宅急便(たっきゅうびん)で送(おく)ります。

B. Work with a partner. Below there are three choices each for apartments, tours, and restaurants. Select one choice from each group. Your partner will ask what you have chosen and why. Respond to him or her using 〜し.

Example

A: どうしてアパート A がいいんですか。
B: このアパートは安いし、あたらしいからです。

アパート A	アパート B	アパート C
えきから歩いて２０分	えきから歩いて１０分	えきから歩いて１５分
１ ＤＫ	２ ＬＤＫ	２ ＬＤＫ
30,000 円	78,000 円	50,000 円
築(ちく)二年	築(ちく)一年	築(ちく)十年

築(ちく)〜年 indicates how old the building is.

ツアー A	ツアー B	ツアー C
三泊四日	四泊五日	五泊六日
京都(きょうと)	京都(きょうと)と大阪(おおさか)	京都(きょうと)と奈良(なら) + おまつり
六万五千円	十万円	八万円

レストラン A	レストラン B	レストラン C
イタリア料理	メキシコ料理	スペイン料理
4,000 円から	2,000 円から	5,000 円から
バンドある	バンドなし	バンドある
バイキングなし	ランチある	日曜日バイキング

バイキング means *buffet style*.　なし = ない

C. Work with a partner. Create dialogues for the following situations. In each of the situations, one of the people in the pair is working at a given place, and the other is a visitor to that place. The visitor has done something inappropriate, and the "official" should explain what the action was and why it was inappropriate.

Example

図書館で／図書館の人と学生

A: あのう、ここでは物を食べないで下さい。

B: あ、いけないんですか。

A: ええ、本がきたなくなるし、つくえもきたなくなりますから。

B: あ、そうですか。すみません。

1. 病院で／いしゃとかんじゃ (patient)
2. 学校で／先生と学生
3. 郵便局(ゆうびんきょく)で／郵便局(ゆうびんきょく)の人ときゃく (customer)
4. うみで／お母さん (or お父さん) と子供

D. Work in groups of four. You have decided to establish a scholarship (奨学金(しょうがくきん)) that will send one student to a one-year intensive Japanese language program in Japan. Talk things over with your classmates and determine the qualifications and selection criteria, such as academic year, major, grades, Japanese proficiency, personality, and the purpose of studying abroad. Explain what type of person would best meet the various requirements, using 〜し (〜し). Use the chart your instructor will give you to list the requirements and the traits that are desired to meet them.

Example

A: どんな学生に奨学金(しょうがくきん)をあげたらいいでしょうか。

B: そうですね。大学院生の方がいいと思いますよ。大学院生の方がよく勉強(べんきょう)するし、これはとてもいい奨学金(しょうがくきん)ですからね。

C: そうですね。でも、大学院生じゃなくてもいいと思いますよ。大学生の中にもよく勉強(べんきょう)する人はいるし、大学院生にはいろいろな奨学金(しょうがくきん)があるし。

D: じゃあ、大学一年生でもいいですか。

V. Expressing conditions originated by others, using 〜（の）なら

Context: 小包(こづつみ)を送(おく)らなくてはいけないんです。

	Verb (plain)		
小包(こづつみ)を	送(おく)る	(の)なら、	宅急便(たっきゅうびん)の方が郵便(ゆうびん)よりいいですよ。

If you're going to send a small package, an express parcel service is better than the postal service.

キム：銀行の口座(こうざ)をひらきたいんです。
I would like to open a bank account.

先生：口座(こうざ)をひらく（の）なら、外国人登録証(がいこくじんとうろくしょう)とはんこがなくてはいけませんよ。
If you're going to open an account, you must have an alien registration card and a personal stamp.

リー：　あ、運転免許証(うんてんめんきょしょう)、忘(わす)れた。
Oh, I forgot my driver's license.

木村(きむら)：　免許証(めんきょしょう)がない（の）なら、車は借りられないよ。
If you don't have your license, we can't rent a car.

店の人：　このにんじん、安いですよ。
These carrots are cheap.

女の人：　安い（の）なら、買うわよ。
If they're cheap, I will buy (some).

山田：　ポストはどこにありますか。
Where's a mailbox?

大川：　ポストなら、あそこですよ。
If (you are talking about) a mailbox, there's one over there.

- Like ～でしょう, なら must be preceded by a clause ending with an adjective or verb in the plain form. The copula だ (for nouns and な-adjectives) is omitted from clauses followed by なら. Hence, one says さむい(の)なら (include い), but 病気(なの)なら (omit だ).

な-adjectives	上手だ	上手	(なの／なん)なら	if it is the case that *or* since you: are good at, are not good at, were good at, were not good at . . .
		上手じゃない 上手だった 上手じゃなかった	(の／ん)なら	
い-adjectives	寒い	寒い 寒くない 寒かった 寒くなかった	(の／ん)なら	if it is the case that *or* since it: is cold, is not cold, was cold, was not cold . . .
Copula verbs	病気だ	病気	(なの／なん)なら	if it is the case that *or* since you: are sick, are not sick, were sick, were not sick . . .
		病気じゃない 病気だった 病気じゃなかった	(の／ん)なら	
Verbs	来る	来る 来ない 来た 来なかった	(の／ん)なら	if it is the case that *or* since you: are coming, are not coming, came, did not come . . .

- なら is used when the speaker postulates something from a previous context as a condition. It is translated as *if it is the case that* 〜 or *since* 〜 . Insert the optional の or ん before なら to emphasize the sense of condition. This is translated as *if it is the case.*
- なら is different from たら in the following ways:
    1. なら uses something from a previous context as a condition. In this sense, the condition has usually originated from a source other than the speaker. The form たら, on the other hand, can be used without previous context, with a condition that has originated from the speaker. For example, when someone says 今週の土曜日、いそがしくなかったら、家に来ませんか *(if you are not busy this Saturday, would you like to come to my house?)*, he or she does not have have any information as to whether you are busy this Saturday. He or she has simply made the condition that you aren't busy as a stipulation for the invitation. But the speaker must have had a reason to assume you will not be busy this Saturday to say 今週の土曜日、いそがしくないなら、家に来ませんか *(Since you're not busy this Saturday, would you like to come to my house?)*. The reason would have been provided by a previous context which, in turn, usually originates from someone other than the speaker.
    2. The condition in the たら clause must be satisfied or completed before the event in the main clause can take place. For example, おさけを飲んだら、車を運転(うんてん)しない *(I don't drive if I have been drinking)* implies that the act of drinking must occur first for the speaker to decide not to drive. On the other hand, in the sentence おさけを飲むなら、車を運転(うんてん)してはいけない *(Since you are going to drink liquor, you should not drive)*, the speaker does not have to drink alcohol before deciding not to drive; the intention to drink alone is enough for him or her to avoid driving. In this sense, the condition expressed in the なら clause does not have to take place before the event in the main clause can take place.

話してみましょう

A. Make suggestions or requests, using なら and 〜た方がいいです, 〜たらどうですか, or 〜て下さい.

Example

口座(こうざ)をひらきたいんです。
口座(こうざ)をひらきたいのなら、この申込書(もうしこみしょ)に記入(きにゅう)して下さい。

1. セクションをかえたいんです。
2. 大きいふうとうがいります。
3. 普通預金(ふつうよきん)にお金がぜんぜんありません。
4. もっといいせいせきがとりたいんです。
5. ペットをかいたいんです。
6. はんこを作らなくてはいけません。
7. ドルを円にかえなければなりません。
8. 船便(ふなびん)は時間がかかります。

B. Work as a class. You are new to town and want to buy furniture, appliances, audio equipment, and food. Ask your classmates to suggest appropriate stores and to explain why they are appropriate. Find the best stores and say why they are the best. Use the chart your instructor will give you.

Example

A: つくえを買いたいんですが。
B: つくえなら、〜がいいですよ。たくさんあるし、安いですから。

C. Work with a partner. Find out from your partner (1) what things he or she was not allowed to do, and (2) what things he or she had to do as a child. Use casual speech.

Example

A: 子供(こども)の時どんなことをしなきゃなんなかったの。
B: 毎朝、新聞(しんぶん)を取りに行かなきゃいけなかったよ。
A: あ、そう。雨の日も。
B: いや、雨の日なら、行かなくてもよかったよ。

Example

A: 子供(こども)の時どんなことをしちゃいけなかったの。
B: 体が弱かったから、スポーツはしちゃいけなかったんだ。
A: あ、そう。何も。
B: いや、かるいうんどうをするのなら、よかったよ。

Component shapes of kanji 4: Enclosing shapes

Some **kanji** contain shapes that surround two, three, or four sides of the character.

Name たれ (left and top)		Meaning	Examples of use
やまいだれ	疒	sickness	病 (痛)
まだれ	广	N/A	度 店 (広)

Name にゅう (left and bottom)		Meaning	Examples of use
しんにゅう	辶	road	週 送 (近 遠 運 道)

Name かまえ (three or four sides)	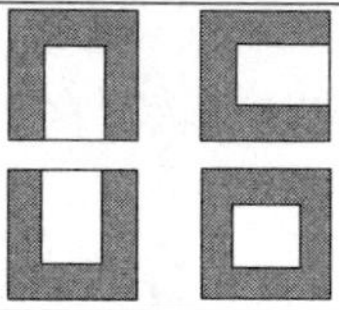	Meaning	Examples of use
まきがまえ、けいがまえ	冂	N/A	円
はこがまえ	匚	box	医
うけがまえ	凵	receiving box	画
もんがまえ	門	gate	問 間 聞 (開 閉)
くにがまえ	囗	enclosure	四 回 国 園 図

郵	郵	postal service ユウ	
		郵便局(ゆうびんきょく)で切手(きって)を買(か)います。	

Kanji	Meaning	Readings	Examples
便	mail, convenience	ベン、ビン	郵便(ゆうびん)ポストはどこにありますか。この辞書(じしょ)はとても便利(べんり)ですよ。
局	office, bureau	キョク	郵便局(ゆうびんきょく)
部	part, department	ブ、ヘ	きれいな部屋(へや)　部屋(へや)の番号(ばんごう)　文学部(ぶんがくぶ)
屋	shop	ヤ、オク	友達(ともだち)の部屋(へや)　薬屋(くすりや)　魚屋(さかなや)
番	number, order	バン	私は上から三番目(ばんめ)です。番号(ばんごう)を書いて下さい。
号	number, issue (magazine)	ゴウ	電話番号(でんわばんごう)は何ですか。
紙	paper	シ/かみ	友達(ともだち)に手紙(てがみ)を書きました。
物	thing (tangible) object	モツ、ブツ/もの	荷物(にもつ)を送(おく)る。食べ物(もの)を食べる。
包	to wrap, to cover	ホウ/つつ（む）	小包(こづつみ)を送る。紙(かみ)で包(つつ)んで下さい。
送	to send	ソウ/おく（る）	日本に荷物(にもつ)を送(おく)る。

Kanji	Meaning	Reading	Examples
両	both	リョウ	両親（りょうしん）の家　山田さんのご両親（りょうしん）
親	parent	シン/おや	両親（りょうしん）に会う。
供	attendant	トモ、ドモ	子供（こども）が三人います。子供（こども）の名前（なまえ）
名	name	メイ、ミョウ/な	ここに名前（なまえ）をペンで書いて下さい。有名（ゆうめい）な先生
英	England	エイ	英語（えいご）が話せます。
宿	inn	シュク/やど	日本語の宿題（しゅくだい）がたくさんあります。
題	topic, theme, title	ダイ	この宿題（しゅくだい）は来週出して下さい。
質	to inquire, quality	シツ	質問（しつもん）がありますか。
問	to question	モン/と（う）	質問（しつもん）して下さい。
漢	old China	カン	漢字（かんじ）を勉強（べんきょう）しています。

字	letter, orthography	ジ	漢字(かんじ)が好きです。
文	sentence, writing	ブン、モン、モ	日本語の文法(ぶんぽう)　文学部(ぶんがくぶ)の学生　作文(さくぶん)の宿題(しゅくだい)
法	law, method, doctrine	ホウ、ポウ	文法(ぶんぽう)の勉強(べんきょう)　法学部(ほうがくぶ)の先生
勉	to make efforts	ベン	一日三時間ぐらい勉強(べんきょう)します。
授	to grant, to instruct	ジュ/さず（ける）	今日(きょう)は授業(じゅぎょう)がありません。
業	occupation, industry, business	ギョウ、コウ	日本語の授業(じゅぎょう)は十時からです。
忘	to forget	ボウ/わす（れる）	すみません、宿題(しゅくだい)を忘(わす)れました。
受	to receive, to accept	ジュ/う（ける）	テストを受(う)ける。
卒	to finish	ソツ	大学を卒業(そつぎょう)する。

新(あたら)しい読み方

切手(きって)　荷物(にもつ)　口座(こうざ)　親切(しんせつ)　上(あ)げる　お菓子(かし)

練習(れんしゅう)

下の文を読んで下さい。

1. 友達の部屋の電話番号を忘れてしまいました。
2. 子供の時、英語の文法は好きでしたが、授業はきらいでした。
3. 両親は漢字はすぐ忘れるから、毎日勉強しなければならないと言います。
4. 昨日(きのう)の宿題の中のこの質問の答え、分かった？
5. この手紙、名前が書いてない。それに、切手もない。
6. 郵便局で小包は送れましたが、大きい物は送れませんでした。
7. 会話のしけんを受けなければなりません。
8. 今学期(き)に卒業する人は、このりょうを十四日までに出て下さい。

上手な読み方

銀行の口座(こうざ)　(Bank accounts)

読む前に

A. 質問に答えて下さい

1. 口座(こうざ)をひらく時、どんなことを知っていなければなりませんか。どんな物がいりますか。
2. お金を引(ひ)き出す時、どんなことを知っていなければなりませんか。どんな物がいりますか。何がなくてもいいですか。
3. 預金(よきん)する時、どんなことを知っていなければなりませんか。どんな物がいりますか。何がなくてもいいですか。

B. 下の言葉(ことば)の意味は何だと思いますか。日本語で言って下さい。

入金(にゅうきん)　口座(こうざ)番号　郵便番号　郵送(ゆうそう)　本人(ほんにん)
日付(ひづけ)（～年～月～日）　お電話　おところ

読んでみましょう

A. 下の申込書(もうしこみしょ)①、②、③を見て下さい。申込書(もうしこみしょ)①、②、③にはどんなことを書かなければなりませんか。どんな時に申込書(もうしこみしょ)①、②、③を使いますか。Although the forms are full of **kanji** and unknown words, you should be able to understand some **kanji** compounds and expressions. Make your best guess using these clues.

①

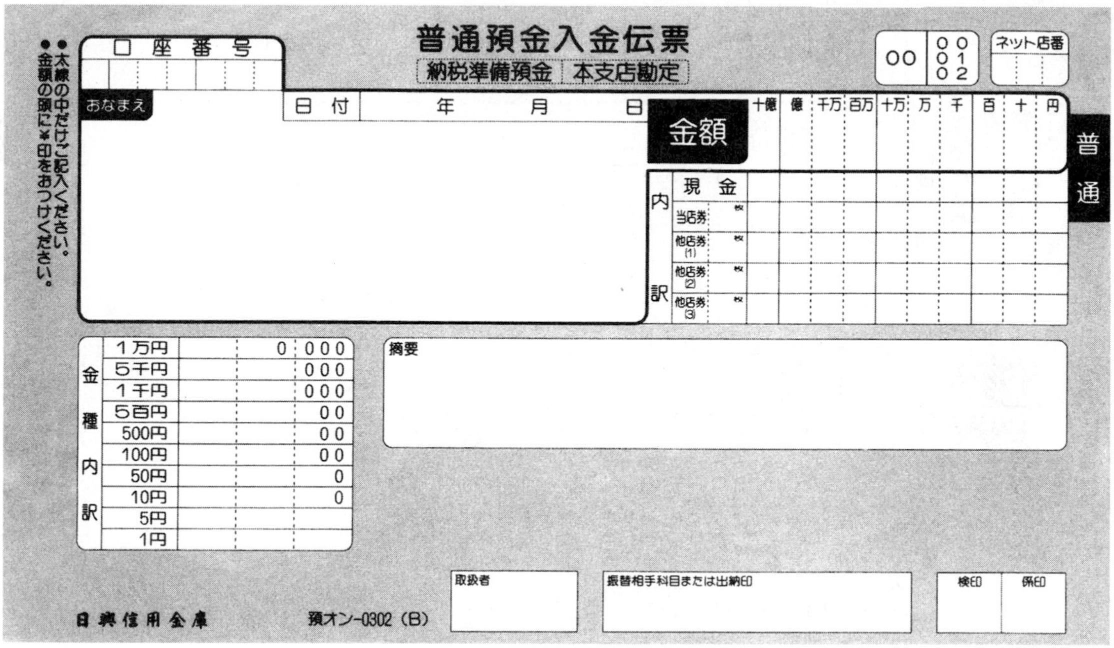

普通預金入金伝票

納税準備預金 本支店勘定

口座番号

00 | 00 01 02

ネット店番

●太線の中だけご記入ください。
●金額の頭に¥印をおつけください。

おなまえ

日付 年 月 日

金額

十億	億	千万	百万	十万	万	千	百	十	円

普通

内訳	
現金	
当店券	枚
他店券(1)	枚
他店券(2)	枚
他店券(3)	枚

金種内訳			
1万円		0	000
5千円			000
1千円			000
5百円			00
500円			00
100円			00
50円			0
10円			0
5円			
1円			

摘要

取扱者

振替相手科目または出納印

検印 係印

日興信用金庫 預オン−0302（B）

②

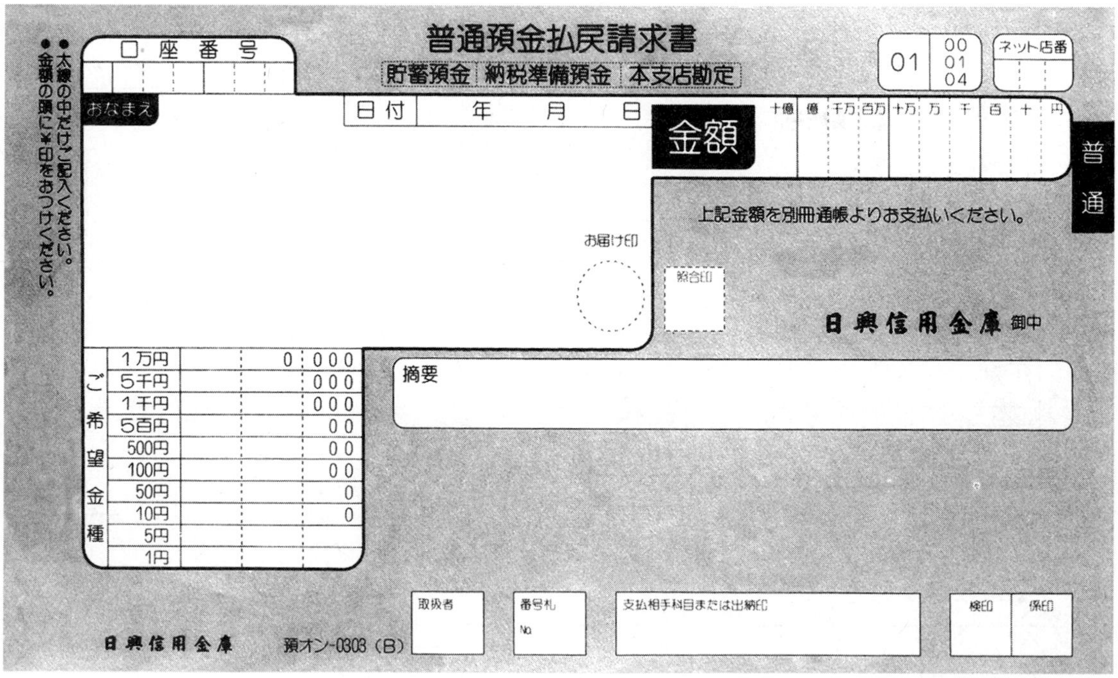

普通預金払戻請求書

貯蓄預金 納税準備預金 本支店勘定

口座番号

01 | 00 01 04

ネット店番

●太線の中だけご記入ください。
●金額の頭に¥印をおつけください。

おなまえ

日付 年 月 日

金額

十億	億	千万	百万	十万	万	千	百	十	円

普通

上記金額を別冊通帳よりお支払いください。

お届け印

照合印

日興信用金庫御中

ご希望金種			
1万円		0	000
5千円			000
1千円			000
5百円			00
500円			00
100円			00
50円			0
10円			0
5円			
1円			

摘要

取扱者

番号札 No.

支払相手科目または出納印

検印 係印

日興信用金庫 預オン−0303（B）

③

科目 00 | 02 | 00

本人確認書・CMIF登録票

改

年　月　日

●太線の中だけご記入ください。

フリガナ / おなまえ		お電話 ( )
おところ 〒 -		

氏名	カナ氏名 5 10 15 20 / 同名異人
住所	地区コード
	補助住所 5 10 15
	補足住所 5 10 15 20
TEL	—
コード	担当 / 業種 / 人格 / 性別
日付	会社設立/生年月日 元号 年 月 日
郵便番号	親 / 子
住所1	住所-1 5 10 15 20 25 30

●郵便番号、住所1は地区コード外住所の場合のみ必須入力

本人確認日	年 月 日	本人確認	1. 済　2. 未済
取引の種類	1. 口座開設　2. 保護預り　3. 貸金庫貸与 4. 大口現金取引（イ.他国との取引　ロ.外国通貨等の両替取引　ハ.その他）		
本人確認方法	1.確認書類等(　　　)　2.カード郵送　3.訪問　4.面識あり		
住所確認の参考情報		確認印	

店番	顧客番号	氏名	地区コード	処理日
住所 〒				

住所	電話番号	担当	業種	人格	性別	会社設立/生年月日	同名異人	新規取消

同名異人
0 通常新規
1 強制新規

人格
1 個人　3 金融法人　8 公金
2 一般法人　4 非課税法人　9 無記名

性別
1 男性
3 女性
5 個人以外

元号
1 明治
2 大正
3 昭和
4
0 平成

検印	オペレータ印	係印

日興信用金庫

願オン－0201（9207D）

B. Read the descriptions of the following three people and choose which of the forms on pages 221-222 each person will need.

私は日本に来て一週間になります。外国人登録(がいこくじんとうろく)もしましたし、銀行の口座(こうざ)がいるんです。今、ホストファミリーの家に住んでいます。(住所:東京都杉並区宮前(とうきょうとすぎなみくみやまえ) 3ー5リサ・ホーキンス)

私は普通預金(ふつうよきん)の口座(こうざ)を持っています。今、英語の家庭教師(かていきょうし)のアルバイトをしています。今日はお金を六万円もらったので、銀行に預金(よきん)するつもりです。(住所:神奈川県横浜市中区(かながわけんよこはましなかく)1ー22トム・ブラウン。口座番号(こうざばんごう):23985)

私は今日友達とコンサートに行く予定ですが、お金がないので、二万円ぐらい引(ひ)き出そうと思います。(住所:埼玉県川口市中島(さいたまけんかわぐちしなかじま)4ー5チョイ・スクミ。口座番号(こうざばんごう):7345)

読んだ後で

A. Complete the appropriate form from pages 221-222 for each of the three people in the above reading on your own, and compare your answers with those of your partner.

B. Work with a partner. Create a dialogue that could take place in the bank for each of the people pictured above, based on the information about them and the business they wish to transact.

プライバシー　(Privacy)

読む前に

Nowadays, you can do many things electronically, such as transferring money, managing your accounts, purchasing merchandise, etc. At the same time, our personal information may no longer be private (プライベート). Work with a partner and answer the following questions about privacy (プライバシー):

1. どんなことがプライベートなことだ思いますか。
2. どうしたらプライバシーをまもる (to protect)ことが出来ますか。

読んでみましょう

言葉(ことば)のリスト

考(かんが)える to think	大切(たいせつ)な important	知(し)り合(あ)い acquaintance
ぶつかる to bump into		

日本語には漢字やひらがなの言葉(ことば)でプライバシーを意味(いみ)する言葉(ことば)がない。プライバシーは英語から入って来た言葉(ことば)だ。昔(むかし)の日本人にはあまりプライバシーという考(かんが)え方がなかったし、今でもアメリカ人が考(かんが)えるプライバシーを大切(たいせつ)だと思わない日本人は多い。

____①____、日本人は友達や知り合いにとてもプライベートな質問をすることがある。子供がいないカップルに「いつ子供を作るんですか。」と聞いたり、近所の人が出かける時に「どこに行くんですか。」と聞いたりする。アメリカ人なら、こんな質問をされたら、“That's none of your business.” だと思うだろう。____②____、日本人の中にはこんな質問はしてもいいと思う人は多い。____③____、日本では電車の中や駅(えき)でだれかにぶつかったりぶつかりそうになった時、何も言わない**人**が多い。アメリカ人なら、たいてい “Excuse me” と言うだろう。

どうして日本ではプライバシーはあまり大切(たいせつ)じゃないのだろうか。日本人は一人一人よりグループを大切(たいせつ)にしてきたので、一人一人のプライバシーについてあまり考(かんが)えなかったのかも知れない。それに、日本はせまくて人が多いから、プライベートなスペースを持つことがむずかしいのかもしれない。

分かりましたか

A. List the main point and supporting statements of each paragraph in your words. You can write in Japanese or in English.

Paragraph 1 ______________________________

Paragraph 2 ______________________________

Support 1 ______________________________

Support 2 ______________________________

Paragraph 3 ______________________________

B. 質問に日本語で答えて下さい。

1. プライバシーという考(かんが)え方はいつから日本にあったと思いますか。
2. 日本とアメリカではプライバシーについてどんなちがい (difference) がありますか。
3. これを書いた人は、どうして日本人はプライバシーを大切(たいせつ)にしないと言っているのですか。

読んだ後で

A. Insert appropriate transition words in the numbered blanks by choosing among けれども , それから , その後 , and たとえば *(for example)*.

B. Identify the subject of the following sentences (second sentence in paragraph 2): 子供がいないカップルに「いつ子供を作るんですか。」と聞いたり、近所の人が出かける時に「どこに行くんですか。」と聞いたりする。

C. Underline the expressions that express the author's conjectures.

D. Underline the parts of the sentences that modify the nouns printed in boldface.

上手な聞き方

ホストファミリー (Living with host families)

聞く前に

A. Work with a partner. List the types of rules set for teenagers in high school or college in the United States. How are the rules different if a person lives with parents instead of in a dormitory?

B. Imagine that you are going to Japan to live with a host family. Japanese parents tend to be protective of their children, especially female children, even if they are in college. When a Japanese family accepts a host child, they assume responsibility for whatever happens to that person. Therefore, some foreign students who are used to being independent may feel rather restricted. Discuss with your partner the kinds of restrictions a host family might place on you.

聞いてみましょう

STUDENT

Listen to the conversations on the audio CD. In each conversation, two students are talking about their host families (families A, B, and C). Identify the rules each family has set and decide which host family you would prefer to live with. Use the chart your instructor will give you.

聞いた後で

A. Now state your choice of host families and reasons for it below. If you don't like any of the host families, explain what you think was wrong with them.

私は ______________________________

というのは、______________________________

____

____

____

STUDENT

B. Listen to this Japanese student who is studying in the United States. She is talking about her host family. Determine the differences and similarities between her host family and the Japanese host families described in 聞いてみましょう.

STUDENT

DICT-A-CONVERSATION

スミスさんは日本の学校で日本語の授業を受けています。

先生：______________________________

スミス：______________________________

先生：______________________________

スミス：______________________________

先生：______________________________

スミス：______________________________

先生：______________________________

聞き上手話し上手

Changing the subject

It is often necessary or desirable to change the subject during conversations, but it is not easy to initiate topic changes because they can be made in a very subtle manner. It is thus very important to pay attention to your listener's facial expressions and tone of voice, because these often indicate the listener's degree of interest in the topic.

A topic shift can be initiated by a summary or concluding statement. In the following conversation, for example, Yamashita's speech 病気の時は仕方(しかた)がありません *(When you are sick, it cannot be helped)* signals the end of the first topic—namely, Lee's illness. This allows Yamashita to begin a new topic.

リー：　昨日(きのう)はあたまがいたくて、学校を休んだんですよ。
山下：　そうですか。今日はもう大丈夫(だいじょう)ぶなんですか。
リー：　ええ、でも昨日(きのう)はテストもあったし、宿題も出さなくちゃいけなかったから、休みたくなかったんですけど。
山下：　でも、病気の時は仕方(しかた)がありませんね。
リー：　ええ。
山下：　で、明日のことなんですけど。

In the following example, はい、分かりました indicates Lee's understanding of Yamada's explanation and signals the conclusion of that topic.

山田： このボタンをおして、サイズをえらぶんです。
リー： ええ。
山田： そして、紙をここにおいて、スタートボタンをおすんです。
リー： はい、分かりました。それで、何まいコピーをとったらいいんですか。

Another strategy is to use a brief pause (which may be as long as five seconds), but a pause can also indicate lack of comprehension or communication difficulty.

Finally, the following expressions can be used to explicitly introduce a new topic.

～と言えば	speaking of
～そう言えばね	speaking of (what you have just mentioned)
ところで	by the way
あのう、話はかわりますが	Well, to change the subject . . .

Example

川口： 山田さん、昨日(きのう)来なかったよ。

友田： うん、病気だったんだって。

川口： そう言えば、山田さん、先週も休んだね。どこかわるいのかなあ。

友田： いや、どこもわるくないと思うけど。ところで、田中さんは昨日(きのう)来たの。

川口： うん、来たよ。すぐ帰ったけど。

友田： あのう話はかわるんだけど、明日のことなんだけどね。

STUDENT

A. Listen to these conversations between two people. Identify strategies used to change the topic. List four of them on a sheet of paper.

B. Work in groups of three. Two people should talk about something, such as the weather, their hobbies, daily life, etc. The other person should try to interrupt and change the subject.

総合練習(そうごうれんしゅう)

A. いろいろな国のマナー

Work as a class. This is a chance to learn about different customs and different cultures. First, classify the following list of activities into four categories (しなければならないこと, してもいいこと, しなくてもいいこと, してはいけないこと), based on your own culture. Then try to guess how the same set of activities might be classified in Japanese culture or any other culture. State the reasons for your judgment. Use the form your instructor will give you.

Example

A: アメリカではコーヒーを飲みながら、授業を受けてもいいと思いますか。
B: ええ、いいと思います。／いいえ、いけないと思います。
A: 日本ではどうですか。
B: 日本ではいけないだろうと思います。
A: どうしてですか。
B: 日本の学校のほうがアメリカよりフォーマルだし、先生がきびしい (strict) から。

1. 家の中でくつをぬぐ
2. 子供におさけやビールをうる (to sell)
3. 出かける時、たくさんお金を持っていく
4. あいさつをする時、握手(あくしゅ)をする
5. 旅行に行ったら、いろいろな人におみやげをたくさん買う

B. 家でのきそく
1. Work in groups of four. Write down the rules and expectations that your parents place upon you in the column under 私 in the chart your instructor will give you. Then ask the members of your group what they have written. Discuss which rules seem reasonable and which are too strict.
2. Work with the same group. Divide the group into two pairs. One pair becomes children and the other parents. The children should ask the parents to change any rule they think is too tough.
3. Work with the same group. Discuss whether the rules and expectations in Exercise 1 should be changed if they applied to high school students or if they were set by a host family. Report to the class what rules or expectations may or may not be changed.

ロールプレイ

A. You are invited to a party this weekend, but you don't want to go. Make up something you have to do and use it as an excuse. Then decline the invitation politely.

B. You are the manager of a dormitory. Explain the rules of that dormitory.

C. Your instructor gave you a 10-page composition to write. The title is 私の家族. You want to write about a different topic, and you would prefer a shorter assignment. Ask your instructor if you have to stick to the original topic and length.

単語 (ESSENTIAL VOCABULARY)

LAB

Nouns

うんてんめんきょしょう （運転免許証） driver's license
おじぎ bow
がいこくじん （外国人） foreigner
がいこくじんとうろくしょう （外国人登録証） alien registration card: がいこくじん（外国人）foreigner + とうろく（登録）registration + しょう（証）card
かいわ （会話） conversation
かぎ （鍵） key; lock
がくせいしょう （学生証） student identification がくせい（学生）+ しょう（証）card
がっき （学期） semester; quarter
きそく（規則） rule
きって （切手） postage stamp
こうくうびん （航空便） air mail
こうざ （口座） account (bank)
こえ （声） voice
コース course
こづつみ （小包） parcel post
サービス service
サイン signature; autograph
さくぶん （作文） written composition
じゅぎょうりょう（授業料） tuition; fee for instruction
せいせき （成績） grades
たくはいサービス （宅配サービス） parcel delivery service
たっきゅうびん （宅急便） express parcel delivery
はんこ （判子） personal stamp or seal
ふうとう （封筒） envelope
ふつう （普通） regular; normal
ふつうよきん （普通預金） regular savings account
ふなびん （船便） surface mail
ポスト public mailbox (for outgoing mail only)
もうしこみしょ （申込書） application form
ゆうびん （郵便） postal service
レポート report; (academic) paper

Verbal nouns

あくしゅ （握手） handshake; あくしゅをする （握手をする） (to) shake hands; あくしゅする （握手する） (to) shake hands
うんてん （運転） driving; うんてんをする （運転をする） (to) drive; うんてんする （運転する） (to) drive
きにゅう （記入） filling out; もうしこみしょの／にきにゅうをする （申込書の／に記入をする） (to) fill out an application; もうしこみしょにきにゅうする （申込書に記入する）+ (to) fill out an application
ちょきん （貯金） savings (money); ちょきんをする（貯金をする） (to) save money; ちょきんする （貯金する） (to) save money
ノック knock; ノックをする (to) knock (at a door); ノックする (to) knock (at a door)
よきん （預金） deposit; savings; よきんをする （預金をする）+ (to) deposit (money); (to) save (money at the bank); よきんする （預金する） (to) deposit (money); to save (money at the bank)

う-verbs

いる　（要る）　(to) need; おかねがいる（お金が要る） (to) need money
おとす　（落とす）　(to) drop; コースをおとす　（コースを落とす）　(to) drop a course
かう（飼う）　(to) keep a pet; いぬをかう（いぬを飼う）　(to) keep a dog
かかる　(to) take (time or money); おかねがかかる（お金がかかる）　it costs money
ぬぐ　（脱ぐ）　(to) take off; (to) remove; くつをぬぐ　（靴を脱ぐ）　(to) take off one's shoes
ひきだす（引き出す）　(to) withdraw (money from bank)
ひらく　（開く）　(to) open (an account; a book)

る-verbs

うける　（受ける）　(to) receive; じゅぎょうをうける　（授業を受ける）(to) attend a class
おくれる　（遅れる）　(to) be late; じゅぎょうにおくれる　（授業に遅れる） (to) be late for a class
かえる　（替える／変える）　(to) change; セクションをかえる　（セクションを替える）　(to) change a section
かける　(to) lock; かぎをかける　（鍵をかける）　(to) lock something up
しめる　（閉める）　(to) close something

い-adjectives

おそい　（遅い）　slow; late; おそくまでおきている（遅くまで起きている）　(to) stay up late
はやい　（早い）　early; はやくおきる（早く起きる）　(to) get up early

な-adjectives

だめ（な）　no good; useless

Suffixes

〜キロ　kilo (kilogram in this chapter; can also be kilometer)
〜ポンド　pound

Conjunctions

たとえば（例えば）　for example

Expressions

かまいません　(I) don't care
そういえば　（そう言えば）　speaking of that . . .
〜といえば　（そう言えば）　If you say 〜, it is . . .
はなしはかわりますが　（話はかわりますが）　(to) change the subject

Passive Vocabulary

Nouns

アパートだい　(アパート代)　rent
アラビアご　(アラビア語)　Arabic language
いんかん　(印鑑)　personal stamp or seal (same as はんこ, but いんかん is more formal)
エンジニア　engineer
がいこくかわせ　(外国為替)　foreign currency exchange
かもくとうろく　(科目登録)　course registration; かもく　(科目) course + とうろく　(登録) registration
かんじゃ　(患者)　patient
きゃく　(客)　customer; guest
キャッシュカード　cashing card for ATM
ぎんこうふりこみ　(銀行振込)　wire transfer of funds
けんこうほけん　(健康保険)　health insurance
サンプル　sample
シェフ　chef
じどうひきおとし　(自動引き落とし)　automatic deduction of bills (from bank account)
じどうひきだしき　(自動引き出し機)　ATM machine
じどうふりこみき　(自動振込機)　automatic money transfer machine
しゃいん　(社員)　employee
しょうがくきん　(奨学金)　scholarship
じょうけん　(条件)　condition; qualification
しりあい　(知り合い)　acquaintance
たくはいびん　(宅配便)　parcel delivery
ダンサー　dancer
ちがい　(違い)　difference
はんこや　(判子屋)　personal stamp shop
まどぐち　(窓口)　window (bank teller, municipal office, etc.)
マネージャー　manager
ミュージシャン　musician
もくてき　(目的)　purpose
モデル　model
ゆうびんうけ　(郵便受け)　mailbox (for incoming mail only)
ゆうびんばんごう　(郵便番号)　postal code
ワンルーム　one room (apartment)

な-adjectives

たいせつな　(大切な)　important

う-verbs

うる (売る)　(to) sell
ぶつかる　(to) bump into
まもる (守る)　(to) protect

る-verbs

かんがえる (考える)　(to) think

For a list of supplementary vocabulary items that will facilitate communication, see the first page of Chapter 4 in your Workbook.

CHAPTER 5

第五課

Japanese university graduation

私の将来(しょうらい)、じゅんび

My Future, Making Preparations

Functions	Expressing one's future plans; Talking about making preparations
New Vocabulary	Thinking about the future; Making preparations; Intransitive and transitive verbs
Dialogue	本田先生の研究室(けんきゅうしつ)で (At Professor Honda's office)
Culture	Changes in family structure; The Japanese economy and employment practices
Language	I. Using もう and まだ
	II. Expressing purpose and reason, using the plain form + ため; Expressing preparations, using the て-form of verbs + おく
	III. Using transitive and intransitive verbs; Expressing results of intentional actions, using the て-form of verbs + ある
	IV. Using the particle か (either ～ or ～); Making indirect questions, using ～か(どうか)
	V. Using question word + も + negative verb and question word + でも + affirmative verb or adjectives
Kanji	Types of **kanji** 5: Historical perspective
Reading	日本人と結婚(けっこん) (The Japanese and marriage)
Listening	将来(しょうらい)の計画 (Future plans)
Communication	Making confirmations and checking comprehension

新(あたら)しい言葉(ことば)

将来(しょうらい)のことを考(かんが)える (Thinking about the future)

考(かんが)える to think
同(おな)じ same
違(ちが)う to be different
やめる to quit
留学(りゅうがく)する to study abroad
研究(けんきゅう)する to do research
はたらく to work
しゅうしょくする to get a job
年をとる to become old
わかい young

売(う)る to sell
給料(きゅうりょう) salary
自分(じぶん) oneself
ぼうえき会社(がいしゃ) trading company
～屋(や) owner of ～ retail store
エンジニア engineer
べんごし lawyer
マネージャー manager
会計士(かいけいし) accountant
社長(しゃちょう) president of a company

次の言葉(ことば)をおぼえてますか。

先生　医者　つとめる　店　魚屋　本屋　旅行会社
結婚(けっこん)する　子供を作る　店を持つ　会社　外国(がいこく)　住む
かえる　家をたてる　貯金(ちょきん)する　アルバイト　大学院

A. 下の言葉(ことば)のいみは何だと思いますか。

花屋　飲み屋　くつ屋　食べ物屋　とうふ屋　電気屋
ペット屋　レコード屋　自転車屋(じてんしゃや)

B. 下の質問に答えて下さい。

1. 将来(しょうらい)何をしたいと考(かんが)えていますか。
2. ご両親はどんな仕事(しごと)をしていますか。
3. 将来(しょうらい)、お父さんやお母さんと同(おな)じ仕事(しごと)をしたいと思いますか。違(ちが)う仕事(しごと)をしたいと思いますか。
4. どんな仕事(しごと)が給料(きゅりょう)がいいと思いますか。どんな仕事(しごと)が給料(きゅりょう)が安いと思いますか。
5. わかい人に出来て、年をとった人に出来ないことはどんなことですか。

C. Match the phrases in Column A with the nouns in Column B.

Column A	Column B
1. 十二さいから三十さいぐらいまでの人	A. 会計士(かいけいし)
2. 六十さいぐらいの人	B. やめる
3. お金や税金(ぜいきん) (tax) のことをよく知っている人	C. 給料(きゅうりょう)
4. 私のこと	D. はたらく
5. 法学部(ほうがくぶ)を出た人	E. 年をとった人
6. きかいや電気についてよく知っている人	F. 自分(じぶん)
7. 違(ちが)わないこと	G. 社長(しゃちょう)
8. 大学の先生がすること	H. 研究(けんきゅう)する
9. 仕事(しごと)をすること	I. わかい人
10. 何かをしなくなること	J. べんごし
11. はたらいている人に会社が出すお金	K. エンジニア
12. 会社の中で一番給料(きゅうりょう)が高い人	L. 同(おな)じ

じゅんび (Making preparations)

式(しき) ceremony
結婚式(けっこんしき) wedding ceremony
卒業式(しき) graduation ceremony
同窓会(どうそうかい) reunion
会場(かいじょう) place of meeting
招待状(しょうたいじょう) invitation letter
招待(しょうたい)する to invite
じゅんびをする to prepare
そうだんする to consult

下の言葉(ことば)をおぼえていますか。

しらべる　予約する　電話をかける　計画をたてる　たのむ

D. 下の質問に答えて下さい。

1. どんな時に招待状(しょうたいじょう)を出しますか。
2. 何かそうだんしたいことがある時、だれにそうだんしますか。
3. ご両親にはどんなことをそうだんしますか。

4. 誕生日(たんじょうび)のパーティにだれを招待(しょうたい)しますか。誕生日のパーティの時どんなじゅんびをしますか。
5. 結婚式(けっこんしき)の前にはどんなじゅんびをしますか。
6. 同窓会(どうそうかい)をしたことがありますか。何の同窓会(どうそうかい)ですか。

じどうしとたどうし (Intransitive and transitive verbs)

The following table contains pairs of intransitive and transitive verbs. Blanks have been inserted for words you have already learned. Try to fill them in.

Intransitive verbs	Transitive verbs
人があつまる people get together	人をあつめる to gather people together
病気がなおる an illness heals	病気をなおす to cure an illness
仕事(しごと)が決(き)まる employment is decided	仕事(しごと)を決(き)める to decide on employment
仕事(しごと)がつづく a job continues	仕事(しごと)をつづける to continue a job
おゆがわく the water boils	おゆをわかす to bring the water to a boil
食べ物がのこる the food remains	食べ物をのこす to leave some food
* 漢字が間違(まちが)っている a **kanji** is wrong	漢字を間違(まちが)える to make a mistake in **kanji**
まどが開(あ)く a window opens	まどを________ to open a window
ドアが閉(し)まる a door closes	ドアを________ to close a door
さいふがおちる a wallet drops	さいふを________ to drop a wallet
電気がつく a light is on	電気を________ to turn on a light
電気がきえる a light goes off	電気を________ to turn off a light
電話がかかる the phone rings	電話を________ to make a phone call
仕事(しごと)がかわる a job changes	仕事(しごと)を________ to change a job
せいせきが________ grades go up	せいせきを上(あ)げる to raise one's grades
授業が________ a class ends	授業を終(お)える to finish a class
映画が________ a movie begins	映画を始める to begin a movie
子供が________ a child wakes up	子供を起こす to wake up a child
子供が車に________ the child gets in the car	子供を車に乗せる to put a child in a car

* 間違(まちが)う is commonly used in the form 間違(まちが)っている .

下の言葉(ことば)をおぼえていますか。

入れる　入る　出る　出す　帰る　返す　たつ　たてる

E. 下線(かせん) (blank) にてきとうな (appropriate) 言葉(ことば)を書いて下さい。

1. 風でまどが＿＿＿＿＿＿＿＿て、雨が家の中に入ってきた。
 だから、まどを＿＿＿＿＿＿＿＿下さい。
2. この漢字は違(ちが)うから、＿＿＿＿＿＿＿＿方がいいですね。
3. ケーキが少し＿＿＿＿＿＿＿＿から、食べませんか。
4. 学生が＿＿＿＿＿＿＿＿ら、映画を＿＿＿＿＿＿＿＿。
5. 子供はまだ寝ています。学校におくれるから、＿＿＿＿＿＿方がいいですね。
6. さいふをどこかで＿＿＿＿＿＿＿＿ので、今お金がありません。
7. 午後十時ですが、電気が＿＿＿＿＿＿＿＿から、今晩はどこかに出かけているんでしょう。
8. おゆが＿＿＿＿＿＿＿＿ら、こうちゃを入れます。
9. 仕事(しごと)が＿＿＿＿＿＿＿＿ので、家を新しい所に＿＿＿＿＿＿＿＿。
10. ほかにいい仕事(しごと)がないから、今の仕事(しごと)を＿＿＿＿＿＿＿＿つもりです。
11. せいせきを＿＿＿＿＿＿＿＿なら、もっと勉強したほうがいいですね。
12. 私の予定は＿＿＿＿＿＿＿＿から、あなたの予定を＿＿＿＿＿＿下さい。
13. 昨日(きのう)は朝まで電気が＿＿＿＿＿＿＿＿、寝ないで勉強していたんでしょう。
14. この部屋はちょっと暗いから、電気を＿＿＿＿＿＿＿＿下さい。
 それに、暑いから、まどを＿＿＿＿＿＿＿＿下さい。
15. 来る時にみち (road, way) を＿＿＿＿＿＿＿＿ので、おそくなりました。

F. Work with a partner. One person should select a verb pair and make a phrase, using either the transitive or intransitive verb from the pair. The partner should make a corresponding phrase with the other verb from the pair.

Example

A: まどを開(あ)けます。
B: まどが開(あ)きます。

ダイアローグ

はじめに

A. 下の質問に日本語で答えて下さい。

1. 何のために日本語を勉強していますか。
2. 将来(しょうらい)日本語が使える仕事(しごと)をしたいと思いますか。
3. 卒業したらどんな仕事(しごと)をしたいと思いますか。
4. そのために、今どんなことをしておかなければならないと思いますか。

B. 下のことをするためにはどんなじゅんびをしなければなりませんか。

1. 日本語のクラスのパーティをします。
2. 冬休みにクラスで日本に行きます。
3. 高校の同窓会(どうそうかい)をします。

STUDENT

本田先生の研究室(けんきゅうしつ)で (At Professor Honda's office)

言葉(ことば)のリスト

ゼミ	支社(ししゃ)	懇親会(こんしんかい)	がんばる
seminar	company branch office	get-together party	to do one's best

The following **manga** frames are scrambled, so they are not in the order described by the dialogue. Read the dialogue and unscramble the frames by writing the correct number in the box located in the upper right corner of each frame.

アリスさんは研究室(けんきゅうしつ)で先生と話しています。本田先生はアリスさんのゼミの先生です。

先生:　ありさかさんは日本に来てどのくらいになりますか。

アリス:　一年半になります。来年の八月にはアメリカに帰ります。

先生:　そうですか。もう一年半になるんですか。でもアメリカに帰ったら、どうするんですか。

アリス:　卒業までに後一学期(がっき)ありますから、大学にもどります。

先生:　その後はどうしますか。

アリス:　まだどうなるかよく分かりませんが、日本語が使える仕事(しごと)をさがすつもりです。出来たら、日本に支社(ししゃ)のあるアメリカの会社か日本の会社にしゅうしょくしたいと思います。

先生:　そうですか。ありさかさんなら大丈夫(だいじょうぶ)だと思いますから、がんばって下さい。

アリス:　どうも有難(ありがと)うございます。

アリスさんは本田先生の研究室(けんきゅうしつ)の外(そと)で石田(いしだ)さんに会いました。

石田(いしだ):　あ、アリスさん、ちょうどよかった。今度のゼミの懇親会(こんしんかい)のこと、本田先生に話した？

アリス:　あ、ごめん。さっきお会いしたんだけど、忘れてた。

石田(いしだ):　じゃ、まだ、話してないんだね。じゃ、いいよ。ぼくも後で先生に会うから、話しとくよ。

アリス:　有難う(ありがと)。それで、もうじゅんびは終わってるの？

石田(いしだ):　ほとんどね。会場(かいじょう)の予約はしてあるし、料理も注文(ちゅうもん)してあるから。

アリス:　あ、そう。招待状(しょうたいじょう)は？

石田(いしだ):　うん、先週出しといたから、そろそろ返事(へんじ)が来ると思うけど。

アリス:　すごいわね。石田(いしだ)さんは何でも出来て。私は出来ないわ。

石田(いしだ):　そんなことないよ。ぼくは、外国語は何も出来ないし。アリスさんは、一人で外国に来て、大学に行ってるんだから、アリスさんの方がずっとすごいと思うよ。

アリス:　そうかしら。

分かりましたか

A. Complete the following paragraph based on the dialogue.

アリスさんは①＿＿＿＿＿＿＿＿にアメリカに帰る予定です。そして、②＿＿＿＿＿＿＿＿ために、大学で一学期(がっき)勉強するつもりです。大学を卒業した後、日本で仕事(しごと)を③＿＿＿＿＿＿＿＿分かりませんが、日本語が使えるので、④＿＿＿＿＿＿＿＿か⑤＿＿＿＿＿＿＿＿につとめたいと思っています。

B. ゼミの懇親会(こんしんかい)について下の質問に日本語で答えて下さい。

1. 懇親会(こんしんかい)のために、どんなことがしてありますか。
2. まだ、何がしてありませんか。
3. 招待状(しょうたいじょう)の返事(へんじ) (reply) が来たら、何をしておかなければならないと思いますか。
4. アリスさんはどうして石田(いしだ)さんがすごいと思っているのですか。
5. 石田(いしだ)さんはどうしてアリスさんのほうがすごいといいましたか。

C. Underline the sentences or phrases where the speaker is confirming what has been said.

D. Change the conversation between Alice and Professor Honda so that Professor Honda is Ishida-san. Use casual speech.

E. Change the conversation between Alice and Ishida-san so that Ishida-san is Professor Tanaka. Use formal speech.

日本の文化(ぶんか)

Changes in family structure. What is the average age for marriage in your country? Do you want to get married in the future?

In Japan, the wife traditionally stays at home and takes care of the children, while the husband works outside of the home. It is also traditional for the eldest son to live with and take care of his parents. However, this traditional family structure is changing. The average family declined from 5.97 persons in 1955 to 2.84 in 1995. The number of single persons living alone also grew from 5.3% of the total number of households in 1960 to 24.8% in 1995, and the average number of children per family went down to 1.38 in 1998.

One reason for this is an increase in the number of senior citizens living alone. The number of elderly people has increased while the number of children has declined. Elderly people are also financially more stable than they were fifty years ago, thanks to post-war economic growth and a better social security system. If they are healthy, they often choose not to live with their children.

Another reason for the decline is that more people postpone marriage until their late twenties, and consequently have fewer children. Traditionally, marriage was considered to make a person a fully independent adult, but this idea is becoming less influential. Indeed, a growing number of young adults now view marriage as constraining.

In addition, the divorce rate increased from 7.4% in 1960 to 15.7% in 1995. However, the number of single-parent households with children (1%) and the number of children born out of wedlock (less than 1%) have remained constant for thirty years. Many Japanese believe that children must be raised in a two-parent household, so married couples will not divorce if they have children. This is one belief that the Japanese have maintained despite the occurrence of many social changes.

A traditional Japanese wedding

- *The Japanese economy and employment practices. What do you know about the Japanese economy or employment practices?*

Japan has suffered from a severe economic slowdown since Japan's "bubble economy" (バブル経済《けいざい》) burst in the late 1980s. This bubble economy was largely based on overpriced real estate. A small country with a large population, Japan placed a high value on real estate. During the 1980s, the price of real estate and stocks continued to surge. People started using real estate along with stocks for investment purposes to make a quick profit in a short period of time. This resulted in unreasonably high real estate prices, and this is why it was called the "bubble economy." During this period, banks made a number of loans based on overvalued real estate. When the price of real estate plunged (or when people finally came to their senses), an economic slump resulted. This was referred to as バブルがはじける *(the bubble bursts)*. Banks still have a large number of bad loans which cannot be recovered.

Due to the burst of the "bubble economy," many companies went through organizational restructuring (リストラ = *restructuring*), and Japan's employment system is now in transition. Although many people used to identify *lifetime employment* (終身雇用《しゅうしんこよう》) as the major characteristic of employment practices in Japan, this practice is becoming less prevalent than it was in the past. The lifelong employment system was somewhat blown out of proportion and treated by many as though it was the only or the prominent employment practice in Japan. In reality, employees of large corporations (大企業《だいきぎょう》) are the only people who ever enjoyed this "system." Workers at smaller businesses (中小企業《ちゅうしょうきぎょう》、零細企業《れいさいきぎょう》) did not have such luxuries. However, it is true that people tended to work for the same company for long periods of time.

Seniority (年功序列《ねんこうじょれつ》), traditionally the main factor in determining promotions in Japan, is being abandoned in some cases in favor of merit-based promotions. Thus it is more acceptable and economically viable for people to change jobs on their own initiative. People now have the chance to be hired at positions equivalent to the ones they gave up at their old companies, instead of at entry-level positions, as was once the case. Even though such changes are occurring, the pace of change remains slow.

LANGUAGE

I. Using もう and まだ

A. Using もう

A-1. もう～ affirmative, already; yet; now

		Adverb			Verb (affirmative)
子供	は	もう	車	に	乗せました。

I already put the kids into the car.

A-2. もう～ negative, not ～ anymore; not ～ any longer

Adverb	Verb (negative)
もう	行きません。

I don't go (there) anymore.

しゅうしょくはもう決(き)まりました。 I've already got a job.

お母さん： 明日のじゅんびはもうしたの？
Have you prepared for tomorrow yet?

子供： うん、もうしたよ。
Yeah, I already have.

この車はもうなおせないよ。 This car is beyond repair.

この仕事(しごと)は大変だから、もうやりたくありません。 This job is hard, so I no longer want to do it.

- The adverb もう indicates that a state which existed some time ago no longer exists. For example, 山田さんはもう出かけました *(Yamada-san has already left)* implies that Yamada-san was here some time ago, but he is not here now. Similarly, もう食べられません *(I can no longer eat)* implies that I was able to eat some time ago, but this state no longer exists. In English, もう corresponds to *already* or *now* in affirmative declarative sentences, to *yet* or *already* in affirmative interrogative sentences, and to *not anymore* or *not any longer* in negative sentences.

B. Using まだ

B-1. まだ～ affirmative, still

		Adverb			Verb (affirmative)
スミスさん	は	まだ	その仕事(しごと)	を	つづけています。

Smith-san is still doing that job. (literally: Smith-san is still continuing that job.)

B-2. まだ～ negative, not ～ yet; still not

Adverb			Verb (negative)
まだ	お金	を	あつめていません。

I have not collected the money yet.

学生１： もう授業始まった？
Has the class begun yet?

学生２： いや、まだ始まってないよ。
No, not yet.

田中： その本、もう売(う)ったんですか。
Have you sold that book yet?

山本： いいえ、まだ売(う)っていません。
No, I haven't sold it yet.

お母さん： あれ、ごはんがまだのこっているわよ。
Oh, there is still some food left.

子供： でも、もう食べたくないの。
But I don't want to eat any more.

先生： 宿題はもう終わりましたか。
Have you finished your homework yet? (literally: Is your homework done yet?)

学生： いいえ、今度の宿題は難(むずか)しいから、まだ色々(いろいろ)しらべています。
No, this homework is difficult, so I'm still checking various things.

- The adverb まだ indicates that a state which existed some time ago still remains. For example, 子供はまだ寝ています *(The child is still sleeping)* implies that the child was sleeping some time ago and this state still exists now. Also, 山田さんはまだ来ていません *(Yamada-san has not come here yet)* implies that Yamada-san was not here some time ago and is not here now. In English, まだ means *still* in affirmative sentences, and *yet* or *still* in negative sentences.

- When まだ is followed by an action verb + ていません, it expresses *have not done* 〜 *yet*. If まだ is used with the simple negative form of an action verb, it means *won't do* 〜 *for a while*.

まだ見ていません。　I have not seen it yet.
まだ見ません。　I won't see it for a while.

- まだです can be used to mean *not yet*.

山田：　映画はもう始まりましたか。
Have you seen this movie yet?
ブラウン：　いいえ、まだです。
No, not yet.

話してみましょう

A. The chart below contains the schedules for Miller-san, Hayashi-san, and Cheng-san for a day. The time now is 12 P.M. Answer the questions using もう or まだ.

Example

ミラーさんはもう学校に行きましたか。
いいえ、まだ行っていません。

	ミラー	はやし	チェン
6 A.M.		家に帰る	
7 A.M.		寝る	起きる
8 A.M.	起きる		朝ごはんを食べる
9 A.M.	朝ごはんを食べる		学校に行く
10 A.M.	学校に行く		
12 P.M.	– – – – – –	– – – – – –	– – – – – –
4 P.M.		起きる	家に帰る
5 P.M.		晩ごはんを食べる	勉強する
6 P.M.	家に帰る		
9 P.M.		仕事(しごと)に出かける	

1. ミラーさんはもう朝ごはんを食べましたか。
2. はやしさんはもう起きましたか。
3. ミラーさんはもう起きましたか。
4. チェンさんはもう学校に行きましたか。
5. はやしさんはもう家に帰りましたか。
6. チェンさんはもう家に帰りましたか。
7. はやしさんはまだねていますか。

B. Work with a partner. You are organizing a high school reunion party and you are checking what has or has not been done yet. The two worksheets below show preparations to be made by two people. Mark two or three of the tasks in Column A, and your partner will mark two or three from Column B. Do not show your worksheet to your partner. The tasks you marked are what you have already done. Ask each other what each has done and check the items your partner has completed. When you are done, check your answers with your partner.

Example

A: もう会場(かいじょう)の予約をしましたか。
B: ええ、もうしました。or いいえ、まだしていません。

Column A
____ 会場(かいじょう)の予約をする
____ 料理を注文(ちゅうもん)する
____ おさけを買う
____ 招待状(しょうたいじょう)を出す
____ 高校の先生に電話をかける

Column B
____ ゲームを考(かんが)える
____ バンド (music band) の予約をする
____ ポスター (poster) を作る
____ ステレオを借りてくる
____ スナック (snacks) を買う

C. Work with a partner. Using the phrases in the box, one person should fill out a schedule for Smith-san and the other a schedule for Kato-san. Use もう and まだ to ask each other about the other person's schedule and complete schedules for Kato-san and Smith-san using the form your instructor will provide.

起きる	朝ごはんを食べる	出かける	
仕事(しごと)を始める	仕事(しごと)を終える	会社を出る	
家に帰る	おふろに入る	ゴルフの練習(れんしゅう)をする	寝る

Example

A: 今、八時ですね。スミスさんはもう起きましたか。
B: いいえ、まだ寝ています。かとうさんはもう起きていますか。
A: ええ、起きています。

II. Expressing purpose and reason, using the plain form + ため; Expressing preparations, using the て-form verbs + おく

A. Expressing purpose and reason, using the plain form + ため

A-1. Expressing purpose, using the plain form + ため *(in order to ～; for ～)*

		Verb (plain present affirmative)	Noun	Particle	
医者(いしゃ)	に	なる	ため	に	この大学で勉強しています。

I am studying at this university in order to become a doctor.

せいせきを上げるために勉強する。	I study in order to raise my grades.
自分(じぶん)のためになる仕事(しごと)をしたい。	I want a job that will be good for me.
きらいな仕事(しごと)なら、何のためにその会社にしゅうしょくするんですか。	If you don't like the work, then why are you taking a job at that company?
将来(しょうらい)のために、わかい時は色々(いろいろ)なことをしてみた方がいい。	You should experience various things while you are young, for the sake of your future.

A-2. Expressing reason or cause, using the plain form + ため

		Adjective (plain past affirmative)	Noun	Particle	
結婚式(けっこんしき)のじゅんび	で	忙(いそが)しかった	ため	に	電話出来なかった。

Since I was busy with preparations for the wedding, I could not call (you).

仕事(しごと)をやめたために、生活(せいかつ)が大変(たいへん)になった。	Life got tough when I quit my job.
あの子供は、けががなおらないため、まだ入院している。	That child is still hopitalized because the injury has not healed.
しけんのために、今日はアルバイトに行けません。	I cannot go to my part-time job today because I have a test.

Category	Dictionary form	Example	Meaning
い -adjectives	いい	いいため	because it is good
		よくないため	because it isn't good
		よかったため	because it was good
		よくなかったため	because it wasn't good
Copula verbs	学生	学生のため	for the sake (because of) of the student
		学生じゃないため	because he/she isn't a student
		学生だったため	because he/she was a student
		学生じゃなかったため	because he/she wasn't a student
な -adjectives	元気な	元気なため	because he/she is healthy
		元気じゃないため	because he/she isn't healthy
		元気だったため	because he/she was healthy
		元気じゃなかったため	because he/she wasn't healthy
Verbs	する	するため	in order to do; because he/she does
		しないため	because he/she doesn't do something
		したため	because he/she did something
		しなかったため	because he/she didn't do something

- The plain form of the verb + ため expresses purpose *(for the purpose of 〜)* or reason or cause *(because)*. When the plain form of the verb + ため is used to indicate a purpose, the main clause will express an action or event controlled by the speaker. The word ため can also be preceded by noun + の or the plain present affirmative form of a verb; in these cases, it describes an action or event that can be controlled by the speaker. For example, this form can express the idea of someone standing up to open a door（ドアを開(あ)ける), an action that is controlled by the speaker. This expression cannot be used with ドアが開(あ)く, an action not controlled by the speaker. Therefore, the sentence should be ドアを開(あ)けるためにたった.

家族のために毎日はたらいています。 I work every day for the sake of my family.

留学(りゅうがく)するためにアルバイトをする。 I am working part-time in order to study abroad.

- The plain form of the verb + ため indicates a reason or cause in two cases: when ため is preceded by an adjective or by the past plain form of a verb or adjective, and when the main clause expresses an action or event that cannot be controlled by the speaker.

Past tense + ため *(because 〜)*:

マネージャーになったため、給料(きゅうりょう)が上がった。 My salary went up because I became a manager.

Adjective + ため *(because* ～*)*:

仕事(しごと)が大変(たいへん)なために、毎晩おそく帰る。	I go home late every day because I have a tough job.
博物館(はくぶつかん)へはここからは遠いため、車で行ったほうがいいでしょう。	You should probably go to the museum by car because it's a long way from here.

An uncontrollable event in the main clause *(because* ～*)*:

しゅうしょくが決(き)まらないために、毎晩寝られない。	I cannot sleep nights because I have not gotten a job.
仕事(しごと)のため、今日は家に帰れません。	I cannot go home today because of my job.
来週旅行に行くため、今週は忙(いそが)しい。	I am busy this week because I am going on a trip next week.

- The ます-stem of the verb + に is also used to express purpose (Chapter 9 of Volume 1), but this usage is limited to cases when the main verb is a motion verb, such as 行く, 来る, or 帰る. The word ため can be used with any verb. When ため is used with a motion verb, it is usually accompanied by a directional phrase, and ため expresses a rather important purpose. On the other hand, the ます-stem of verbs + に can be used without a directional phrase, and the purpose does not have to be important.

しけんの勉強をするために図書館にいます。	I am in the library to study for the exam.
しけんの勉強をするために図書館に行きました。	I went to the library to study for the exam.
しけんの勉強をしに行きました。	I went in order to study for the exam.
コーヒーを飲みに来ました。	I came to have some coffee.

- Grammatically, ため is a noun, so the form of any adjective or verb that precedes it is the same as in noun modifying clauses. Also, ため can be followed by the particle に (when it modifies a verbal phrase) or の when it modifies a noun. Use of the particle に is optional.

日本に留学(りゅうがく)するため（に）アルバイトをしているんです。	I'm working part-time in order to go to Japan to study.
これは新(あたら)しい車を買うための<u>の</u>お金です。	This is the money to buy a new car.

コーヒーをのみにきました。
らいしゅう test があるため、こんしゅうはいそがしい。

- When the plain form + ため expresses a reason or cause, it can be replaced by から or ので . But ため is more formal than から or ので , so it is rarely used in casual speech.

B. Expressing the making of preparations, using 〜ておく (do 〜 in advance)

			Verb (て-form)	Auxiliary verb
卒業(そつぎょう)する前に	大学院について	色々	しらべて	おきます。

I will check out various graduate schools before I graduate (from college).

今日、卒業式(しき)の会場(かいじょう)のじゅんびをしておかなければならない。
I have to set up the room for the graduation ceremony today.

学生が来るから、ドアを開(あ)けておいて下さい。
Please leave the door open. A student's coming.

もうすぐお父さんが帰ってくるから、おふろわかしといて。
Your father is coming back soon, so can you get the bath ready?

- The verb て-form + おく is used when someone has done or is doing something for a future purpose, or is leaving the current state as it is because of some future consideration. In key sentence B above, the act of checking graduate schools is done as a preparation or a precaution. In the second example sentence, the door is already open and the speaker wants to leave it open for a student to come in.
- The form 〜ておく／〜でおく is 〜とく／〜どく in casual speech.

食べ物をのこしておく	食べ物をのこしとく	to leave some food for someone
先生にそうだんしておく	先生にそうだんしとく	to consult with the teacher in advance
社長(しゃちょう)にたのんでおく	社長(しゃちょう)にたのんどく	to ask the president (a favor) in advance

- The verb おく conjugates as an う-verb.

話してみましょう

A. Match the phrases in Column A and Column B. Use ため in its sense of indicating a reason to make a new sentence expressing reason and result. Column A holds the reasons, and Column B the results.

Example

ドアが閉(し)まっています／中に入れません
ドアが閉(し)まっているため、中に入れません。

Column A	Column B
1. お金があつまりません	A. よく外国(がいこく)に行きます
2. 大きい会社は好きじゃありません	B. 間違(まちが)えることも多いですが、仕事(しごと)ははやいです
3. 人と同じなのはきらいです	C. お金がかかる研究(けんきゅう)は出来ません
4. 年をとりました	D. 私もべんごしになりました
5. まだわかいです	E. 違(ちが)う病院に行ってみようと思っています
6. ぼうえき会社につとめています	F. 足が弱くなりました
7. 父がべんごしでした	G. このふくを着ています
8. 病気がなおりません	H. この会社ではたらいています

B. Define each of the following objects, using the plain form + ための 〜 .

Example

はし／食べるためのものです。／食べるためのもの(だ)よ。

1. ファックス	3. えんぴつ	5. たんす	7. 車
2. CD	4. コンピュータ	6. かぎ	8. さいふ

C. Work as a class. Ask your classmates what they are studying and why, using 〜ために . Also, ask why they are studying Japanese. Use casual speech.

Example

A: せんこう、何？
B: けいえい学だよ。(male)／けいえい学よ。(female)
A: 何のためにけいえい学を勉強してるの。
B: ぼうえき会社にしゅうしょくするためだよ。(male)／ぼうえき会社にしゅうしょくするためよ。(female)
A: そう、じゃあ、日本語もぼうえき会社にしゅうしょくするために勉強してるの。
B: いや、自分(じぶん)の勉強のためだよ。(male)／自分(じぶん)の勉強のためよ。(female)

D. Answer the following questions, using the て-form of the verb + おく and the expressions in the box.

Example

結婚式(けっこんしき)の前に何をしておきますか。

友達に招待状(しょうたいじょう)をだしておきます。

友達に招待状を出す	お金をあつめる	車をなおす	おゆをわかす
新しい仕事をさがす	ドアを閉める	銀行とそうだんする	

1. よる出かける時、どうしますか。
2. おちゃを飲む前に、何をしますか。
3. 今の仕事をやめる前に、どうしますか。
4. クラスで先生の誕生日プレゼントを買う時、どうしますか。
5. ドライブに行く前に何をしますか。
6. 家を買う前に、何をしますか。

E. Use the て-form of the verb with おく to say as many things as possible you can do in advance to achieve the following goals.

Example

テストでいいせいせきをとります。
テストでいいせいせきをとるために、前の日によく勉強しておかなければなりません。

1. 大きい会社の社長になります。
2. 年をとる前に、仕事をやめます。
3. 日本に留学します。
4. いしゃになります。
5. 友達の結婚式に出ます。
6. 日本語でAをとります。

III. Using transitive and intransitive verbs; Expressing results of intentional actions, using the て-form of verbs + ある

A. Using transitive and intransitive verbs

Subject		Direct object			Transitive verb
お母さん	は	子供	を	八時に	起こします。

The mother wakes her child at eight o'clock.

Subject			Intransitive verb
子供	は	八時に	起きます。

The child wakes up at eight o'clock.

大川: ケーキがのこっていますよ。だれか食べませんか。
There's still some cake left. Would anybody like to eat it?

リー： あ、それはキムさんのケーキですから、のこしておいたんです。
Ah, that's Kim-san's cake, so I left it for him.

山田： この漢字は間違(まちが)ってますよ。
This **kanji** is wrong.

アリス： あ、本当(ほんとう)ですね。この漢字は難(むずか)しいから、よく間違(まちが)えるんです。
Oh, you're right. This **kanji** is so difficult I often get it wrong.

- Transitive verbs are verbs that express action performed directly on an object. This object, known as a direct object, is marked with the particle を in Japanese, as in 私はドアを開(あ)けた *(I opened the door)*. Intransitive verbs, however, do not take a direct object. Instead, they are used in situations where the object acts on its own. An example would be ドアが開(あ)いた (*The door opened* [on its own]). English has similar verb pairs, such as *to raise* and *to rise (Bob raised the flag* vs. *The flag rose)*. Native English speakers are often unaware of the differences between transitive and intransitive verbs, partly because the same verb can often be used in both transitive and intransitive constructions. The verb *to open* in the example above is one such verb. Japanese verbs, on the other hand, often come in transitive/intransitive pairs, such as 開(あ)ける／開(あ)く, and the same verb cannot be used for both functions in Japanese.

- Use an intransitive verb when the focus is on the event or action itself. Use a transitive verb when the focus is on the person who performs the action. Except for some verbs like 入る, which can take an animate subject as in 私はおふろに入る, many intransitive verbs take an inanimate subject and do not express an intentional action of the speaker. When they are used in the ～ている structure, they express a resultant state as introduced in Chapter 9 of Volume 1.

電気がついています。 The light is on.
まどがしまっています。 The window is closed.

B. Expressing the results of an intentional action, using the て-form of a verb + ある

	Particle	Verb (て-form)	Auxiliary verb		
晩ごはん	が／を	作って	あります	から、	後で食べて下さい。

I made dinner for you, so please eat it later. (literally: The dinner has been made for you, so please eat it later.)

トム： どうしてまどが開(あ)いているの。
Why is the window open?

かおり： 暑いから、開(あ)けてあるんです。
It's hot, so I left it open.

川口 来週から旅行ですね。もうじゅんびは終わりましたか。
The trip starts next week, doesn't it? Are you ready?
(literally: Have the preparations been finished?)

本田： ええ、ホテルの予約も取ってあるし、飛行機(ひこうき)の切符(きっぷ)も買ってあります。
Yes, I reserved a hotel room and bought a plane ticket.
(literally: Yes, the hotel reservation has been made, and a plane ticket has been purchased.)

そのことについては社長(しゃちょう)に少し話してあるから、そうだんしてみたらどうですか。
I've spoken to the president a little bit about it, so why don't you talk with him?

- The verb て-form + ある expresses a state that has resulted from an intentional action. It is usually used to express a situation where someone has done something for some purpose and the speaker wants to talk about the state resulting from that action. Therefore, 晩ごはんが作ってある in key sentence B indicates that dinner was cooked for a purpose and is ready.

- The verb in the ～てある construction can be transitive or intransitive, but it must express an intentional action.

雨がふりそうだから、まどが閉(し)めてあります。 Since it looks as if it will rain, the windows have been closed.

年はとっていますが、毎日よく歩いてあるから、ハイキングは大丈夫(だいじょうぶ)です。 Even though I'm getting old, I walk every day, so I should be fine on the hike.

- When the main verb is transitive, the direct object can be marked with either が or を. The particle を tends to be used if the speaker performed the action.

テレビがつけてあります。	テレビをつけてあります。
The television was turned on.	Someone turned on the television.

- Transitive verbs express intentional actions, so the て-form of the verb + ある is used to express a resulting state.

電気がつけてあります。	The light has been turned on.
まどが閉(し)めてあります。	The window has been closed.

- The difference between 電気がついています and 電気がつけてあります is that the former merely describes the fact that the light is on. On the other hand, 電気がつけてあります means that the light was deliberately turned on (and is still on) for some specific purpose.

話してみましょう

A. Make sentences using the following nouns and verbs.

Example

水／出る
水が出ます。

1. 水／出す	6. 時間／間違(まちが)える	11. 宿題／のこる
2. 仕事(しごと)／かわる	7. さいふ／おとす	12. 電話／かかる
3. 電気／つく	8. おゆ／わく	13. 病気／なおす
4. 車／乗せる	9. お金／あつまる	14. 卒業式(しき)の日／決まる
5. しあい／つづく	10. 電気／きえる	15. 授業／終える

B. Work in groups of four. Make cards for both transitive and intransitive verbs. One person should select a card and make a phrase using the verb written on it. The rest of the group will then try to make a phrase with the corresponding verb. The first person to correctly make a phrase wins.

Example

A: (The card has あく written on it.) まどが開(あ)きます。
B: まどを開(あ)けます。

C. Look at the picture of Ishida-san's room. Describe his room using intransitive verbs.

Example

電気がついています。

D. Ishida-san's parents are visiting him today, so he cleaned his room. Now describe his room in the following picture, using the て-form of the verb + ある.

Example

電気がけしてあります。

IV. Using the particle か (either ～ or ～); Making indirect questions, using ～か (どうか)

A. Using か (either ～ or ～)

Noun	Particle	Noun	Particle			
日本	か	アメリカ	で	仕事(しごと)を	さがす	つもりです。

I intend to look for a job either in Japan or in the United States.

将来(しょうらい)べんごしか会計士(かいけいし)になりたいです。

I want to become a lawyer or an accountant in the future.

このふくは結婚式(けっこんしき)か卒業式(しき)の時に着るつもりです。

I'm thinking of wearing these clothes for either a wedding or graduation.

この天気は明日かあさってまでつづくでしょう。

This weather will probably continue until tomorrow or the day after tomorrow.

B. Indirect questions

B-1. Indirect yes-no questions, whether or not ～; if ～

		Verb (plain form)	Particle		
この病気	は	なおる	か	どうか	聞いてみます。

I will ask if this illness will be cured.

かとう： 鈴木(すずき)さんは山本さんと同(おな)じ会社につとめているか（どうか）知っていますか。
Do you know whether Suzuki-san works for the same company as Yamamoto-san?

大木： いいえ、知りません。
No, I don't know.

さいふがおちたか（どうか）見て下さい。

Could you see whether my wallet is on the floor? (literally: Please see whether the wallet was dropped.)

B-2. Indirect information questions (when, what, where, etc.)

		Question word			Verb (plain form)	Particle	
山田さん	が	どんな	研究(けんきゅう)	を	している	か	分かりません。

I do not know what kind of research Yamada-san is doing.

だれをパーティーに招待(しょうたい)したか忘れました。 I forgot whom I invited to the party.

会場(かいじょう)はどこか教えてください。	Please tell me where the meeting hall is.
どのえを売(う)ったかおぼえていません。	I don't remember which picture I sold.

- A question embedded in another sentence is called an *indirect question*. There are two types of indirect questions, as shown in key sentences B-1 and B-2. In English, an embedded yes-no question is preceded by *whether (or not)* or *if*. In Japanese, it is expressed by using 〜か(どうか). The use of どうか in an indirect yes-no question is optional.

- 〜か（どうか）must be preceded by a sentence that ends with a plain form. The only exceptions are noun + the copula verb だ and な-adjectives. In these cases, だ is deleted. Thus, the formation of the construction is the same as for かもしれません and でしょう. (See Part V of the Language section in Chapter 2.)

Nouns + Copula		**な-adjectives**	
学生 学生じゃない 学生だった 学生じゃなかった	か（どうか）	好き 好きじゃない 好きだった 好きじゃなかった	か（どうか）
い-adjectives		**Verbs**	
いい よくない よかった よくなかった	か（どうか）	なおる なおらない なおった なおらなかった	か（どうか）

- Indirect questions can be followed by a variety of main verbs, such as 知っている, 見る, 聞く, 分かる, 考(かんが)える, 教える, 忘れる, and おぼえている.

話してみましょう

A. Answer the following questions, using the words in parentheses and the particle か.

Example

将来(しょうらい)、何になりたいですか。（医者(いしゃ)、べんごし）
医者(いしゃ)かべんごしになりたいです。

1. 何さいぐらいで結婚(けっこん)したいですか。(二十八さい、二十九さい)
2. 将来(しょうらい)どんな所ではたらきたいですか。(ぼうえき会社、旅行会社)
3. 将来(しょうらい)どんな所に住みたいですか。(ロンドン、ニューヨーク)
4. どんな所に家をたてたいと思いますか。(山の中、うみの近く)
5. 子供は何人ぐらいいたらいいと思いますか。(二人、三人)
6. 何さいぐらいで仕事(しごと)をやめたいですか。(五十五さい、六十さい)

B. Work with a partner. Imagine that a Japanese student who recently has come to town wants to do various things. Suggest the best places, people, etc., using the particle か. Use polite speech.

Example

日本のしょうゆがいるんです。

A: 日本のしょうゆはどこで買えますか。
B: そうですね。しょうゆならアジアマーケットかフード
コープで買えると思いますよ。

1. 会話のパートナーをさがしているんです。
2. 日本語のクラスが見たいんです。
3. 円をドルにかえたいんですが。
4. 安いコンピュータをさがしているんです。
5. 大学でどんなコースをとったらいいか分からないんです。
6. アパートをさがしているんです。

C. Answer the following questions about Japan. If you don't know the answer, respond using さあ、〜か(どうか)知りません／分かりません.

Example

日本では車は左側(ひだりがわ)を走りますか。
さあ、左側(ひだりがわ)を走るかどうか知りません／分かりません。

1. 日本で一番長(なが)い川は何という川ですか。
2. 日本で一番古(ふる)い建物(たてもの)は京都(きょうと)にありますか。
3. 京都(きょうと)はいつまで日本のしゅと (capital city) でしたか。
4. １５０年前に日本にアメリカ人が住んでいましたか。
5. 東京から京都(きょうと)まで車で何時間ぐらいかかりますか。
6. 日本で一番高い建物(たてもの)はどれですか。

D. Work with a partner. Ask each other what your lives might be like 10 years from now. If you have definite plans regarding your future, answer using ～と思う. If you are not sure, use ～か（どうか）分かりません. Write this information about each other in the chart your instructor will give you.

Example

A: ～さんは十年後に結婚(けっこん)してると思う？

B: うん、結婚(けっこん)してると思う。

A: 子供はいると思う？

B: さあ、子供がいるかどうか分からないなあ。(male) ／
さあ、子供がいるかどうか分からないわ。(female)

V. Using question word + も + negative verb and question word + でも + affirmative verb or adjectives

A. Question word + も + negative verb (not ～ any ～ ; no ～)

Question
昨日(きのう)だれか来ましたか。

Did anyone come yesterday?

	Question Word		Verb (negative)
いいえ、	だれ	も	来ませんでした。

No, no one came.

高田：昨日(きのう)はどこかへ行きましたか。
Did you go anywhere yesterday?

鈴木(すずき)：いいえ、どこへも行きませんでした。
No, I did not go anywhere.

リー：もう晩ごはんを食べましたか。
Have you eaten dinner yet?

山本：いいえ、まだ何も食べていません。
No, I haven't eaten anything yet.

リー：じゃあ、どこかへ食べに行きませんか。
Well then, would you like to go somewhere to eat?

社長(しゃちょう)は忙(いそが)しくて、自分(じぶん)のしたいことが何も出来ない。
The president is so busy he can't do any of the things he wants to do.

- The question word + も can be used only in sentences ending in a negative form. The addition of も to the question word causes the meaning of the phrase to become *(not)* ～*any*.

B. Question word + でも + affirmative verb, any; whatever/whenever/wherever, etc.

	Question word でも	Verb (affirmative)
木村（きむら）さんは	何でも	食べられます。

Kimura-san can eat anything.

川本：　だれを招待（しょうたい）しようか。
　　　　Whom shall we invite?
木村（きむら）：　だれでもいいよ。
　　　　Anybody you want to.

今日はだめですが、明日ならいつでもいいです。
Today is no good, but anytime tomorrow will be fine.

ジェフ：　どこに行きましょうか。
　　　　Where shall we go?
さなえ：　私はおいしい店ならどこでもいいです。
　　　　Anywhere will be fine as long as it serves good food.

- The question word + でも means *any* or *all*. It can be used only in sentences ending in an affirmative form.
- The following table summarizes phrases that can be created with a question word and the particles か, も, and でも.

Question word	+ か	+ も	+ でも
	Affirmative sentence	Negative sentence	Affirmative sentence
何	何か (something)	何も (nothing; not at all)	何でも (anything; whatever)
だれ	だれか (someone)	だれも (no one)	だれでも (anybody; whoever)
いつ	いつか (sometime)	*いつも (never)	いつでも (anytime)
どこ	どこか (somewhere)	どこも (nowhere)	どこでも (anywhere)

The phrase いつも can also be used in an affirmative sentence when it means *always*. For example, いつも朝ごはんを食べる means *I always eat breakfast.*

- The particles が and を are not used with the question word + も or でも. However, other particles, such as に and と, are inserted between the question word and 〜も or でも.

昨日（きのう）はだれにも会いませんでした。　I didn't meet anybody yesterday.

いぬはどこにもいません。　The dog isn't anywhere.

山田さんはだれとでも友達になります。　Yamada-san can be friends with anybody.

仕事（しごと）はいつからでも始められます。　I can start the work anytime.

話してみましょう

A. Answer the questions, using question word + も + negative or question word + でも + affirmative.

Example

どこかへ行きましたか。　*or*　どこに行きましょうか。
いいえ、どこへも行きませんでした。　どこでもいいですよ。

1. 朝何か飲みましたか。
2. だれかといっしょに住んでいますか。
3. どこかに日本語のワープロが使えるコンピュータがありますか。
4. 昨日(きのう)だれか来ましたか。
5. いつ買物に行きましょうか。
6. いくらお金を集めたらいいでしょうか。
7. どこで会いましょうか。
8. だれが社長(しゃちょう)になったらいいでしょうか。

B. Complete the following sentences using question word + も or でも.

Example

わかい時に勉強しておかないと、年をとって、勉強は何も出来ないよ。

1. 招待状(しょうたいじょう)を出しておかなかったから、パーティーには ________________来なかった。
2. 会場(かいじょう)の予約しておかなかったから、いい所が ________________ない。
3. 料理を注文(ちゅうもん)しておかなかったから、食べ物が ________________ない。
4. しゅうしょくのことでだれかにそうだんしたかったけど、忙(いそが)しくて、________________話せなかった。
5. 留学(りゅうがく)出来るのなら、________________行きます。
6. 社長(しゃちょう)になるためには、________________するつもりだ。
7. 給料(きゅうりょう)がいい所なら、________________はたらきます。
8. 明日会えるのなら、________________会いに行きます。

C. Kim-san and Lin-san have very different lifestyles and personalities. The following chart illustrates what each person does. Express how they are different, using question word + も〜 negative or question word + でも 〜 affirmative.

Example

リンさんは何でも食べられますが、キムさんは肉が食べられません。

	リン	キム
何が食べられるか	きらいな物はない	肉はだめ
どんな飲み物が飲めるか	ビールはだめ	きらいな物はない
どこで寝られるか	寝られない所はない	飛行機(ひこうき)の中では寝られない
だれと友達になれるか	みんな友達	友達がいない
どんなスポーツが出来るか	出来ないスポーツはない	スポーツはぜんぜん出来ない

D. Work as a class. Question your classmates, and discover who fits the descriptions on the grids that your instructor will provide. Find a person who fits in each category and write his or her name in the grid. The first person to complete a horizontal, vertical, or diagonal line (Bingo) is the winner.

Example

A: 朝何か食べましたか。
B: いいえ、何も食べませんでした。

漢字

Types of kanji 5: Historical perspective

In the introduction to **kanji** in Chapter 7 of Volume 1, we explained that some **kanji** were derived from pictures. As you have learned more **kanji**, you may have noticed that, although some **kanji** indeed retain pictographic features, many others do not. The ancient Chinese were aware that complex and abstract ideas were difficult to express with simple pictures, so they devised ways to create characters to represent those ideas. There are four major groups of characters, the first of which is *pictographs*.

The second type of character is called *logographs*. Examples are 一, 二, 三, 上, and 下. They all represent an idea rather than a concrete object. The **kanji** for the numbers 1, 2, and 3 require no explanation. The horizontal line found in 上 and 下 indicates the horizon, and the short line is the focus in the characters. The original forms resembled 丄 and 丅.

The third group is called *semantic compounds*. These consist of two or more components combined to form a new character. The meaning of the new character is derived by combining the meanings of the components. **Kanji** such as 明 (*bright*) and 森(もり) *(forest)* belong to this group. The character 明 is a combination of two pictographs, 日 *(sun)* and 月 *(moon)*, indicating the meaning *bright*, while 森(もり) (*forest*) consists of three 木 (*tree*), which represents many trees. Another example is 休(やす)む (*to rest*). This is a combination of 亻 *(person)* and 木 *(tree)*, and it expresses the idea of a person resting under a tree. In this way, the meanings of the different component shapes of a character combine to create a semantic compound.

The last and the largest group by far is called *phonetic compounds*. About 80 percent of all **kanji** belong to this group. They typically have one component shape indicating their semantic category and another indicating their pronunciation. In this case, "pronunciation" refers to the pronunciation of the character in Chinese at the time the character was adapted for use in Japan. Those pronunciations are still reflected in the Japanese *on*-reading. The semantic categories are represented by shapes such as 亻 *(person)*, 日 *(sun)*, and 訁 *(to say)*. When you become familiar with these shapes, you should be able to guess the general category in the meaning of a **kanji**. The sound component gives a clue as to the **on**-reading of **kanji**. For example, 冓 gives a **kanji** the **on**-reading こう. 講, 購, 構, 溝, and 媾 all have the **on**-reading こう, but they are not necessarily related in meaning. The component 青 gives a **kanji** the **on**-reading せい. The characters 精, 晴, 清, 静, and 請 all share the same **on**-reading. Although 青 by itself has the meaning of *blue*, these **kanji** are not necessarily related to the meaning of 青. That is, even if the phonetic component of a compound has a meaning, it is the pronunciation, not the meaning, of the component that is used to create the compound.

The historical background of **kanji** is another tool to organize your knowledge of **kanji**. Possessing this knowledge makes it possible, to some extent, to guess the meaning and/or the pronunciation of **kanji**.

Try the following:

1. Group **kanji** you know by looking for common component shapes.
2. Find some shared properties in their meanings and pronunciations.

Kanji		Meaning	Reading	Examples
研		to study, research	ケン	田中先生は日本語を研究(けんきゅう)しています。
究		to study	キュウ	難(むずか)しい研究(けんきゅう)。
練		to discipline, to polish	レン/ね（る）	毎日日本語の練習(れんしゅう)をしています。
習	習	to learn	シュウ/なら（う）	明日の宿題は漢字の練習(れんしゅう)です。
仕		work, to serve	シ/つか（える）	来年の仕事(しごと)の計画を立(た)てましょう。
事		thing, action, fact	ジ/こと、ごと	教える仕事(しごと)が好きです。おもしろい事(こと)がない。静(しず)かな店で食事(しょくじ)する。
医	医	medical	イ	医者(いしゃ)が少ない。山田医院(いいん)に行く。
者		person	シャ/もの	医者(いしゃ)になりたい。いい研究者(けんきゅうしゃ)
新		new	シン/あたら（しい）	新(あたら)しい車を買いました。新聞(しんぶん)を読むのが好きです。
古	古	old	コ/ふる（い）	この野菜(やさい)は少し古(ふる)いですね。これは古(ふる)い本です。

Kanji	Meaning	Readings	Example
長	long	チョウ/ なが（い）	昨日の宿題は長(なが)かった。社長(しゃちょう)は元気です。
短	short	タン/ みじか（い）	明日のテストはとても短(みじか)いですよ。
同	same	ドウ/ おな（じ）	友達と同(おな)じ会社に入りました。
違	to differ, different	イ/ちが（う）	いいえ、違(ちが)います。番号が違(ちが)っています。答えを間違(まちが)えた。
静	quiet	セイ/ しず（か）	図書館は静(しず)かですが、映画館は静(しず)かじゃありません。
難	difficult, obstacle	ナン/ むずか（しい）	この宿題の問題は難(むず)しかったです。
結	to connect, to tie	ケツ、ケッ/ むす（ぶ）	来年山田さんと結婚(けっこん)します。
婚	marriage	コン	結婚式(けっこんしき)はいつですか。
式	ceremony, form	シキ	結婚式(けっこんしき)は教会(きょうかい)でする予定です。卒業式(そつぎょうしき)に出る。
決	to decide	ケツ/き(まる) き(める)	大学を決(き)める。仕事(しごと)が決(き)まる。

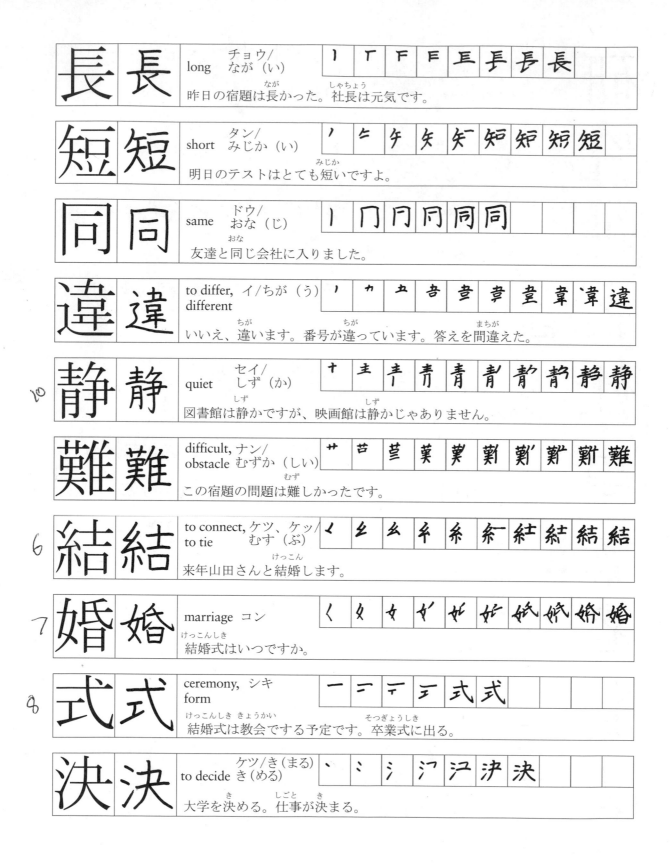

考 考 — to think — コウ/ かんが（える）

決(き)める前に、よく考(かんが)えた方がいいですよ。色々(いろいろ)な考(かんが)え方

忙 忙 — busy — ボウ/ いそが（しい）

とても忙(いそが)しかったです。あまり忙(いそが)しくありません。

色 色 — color — シキ/ いろ

緑色(みどりいろ)　黄色(きいろ)　茶色(ちゃいろ)　色々(いろいろ)な食べ物

々 々 — repetition marker

色々(いろいろ)な人に会う。時々(ときどき)行きます。

開 開 — to open — カイ/あ（く） ひら（く）、 あ（ける）

ドアを開(あ)ける。ドアが開(あ)く。口座(こうざ)を開(ひら)く。

閉 閉 — to close — ヘイ/し（める） し（まる）

ドアを閉(し)める。ドアが閉(し)まる

招 招 — to invite — ショウ/ まね（く）

友達を食事(しょくじ)に招待(しょうたい)する。

外 外 — outside, other — ガイ/ そと、ほか

外国人　まどの外(そと)に犬(いぬ)がいる。

留 留 — to stop, to fasten — リュウ、ル/ と（まる）

留学生(りゅうがくせい)　日本に留学(りゅうがく)する。

悪 悪 — bad — アク/ わる（い）

病気が悪(わる)くなった。社会(しゃかい)にはいい人も悪(わる)い人もいます。

新しい読み方

会計士(かいけいし)　会場(かいじょう)　新聞(しんぶん)

練習

下の文を読んでください。

1. 結婚式は六月に決めました。
2. 同じ漢字ですが、読み方が違います。
3. 安くても、悪い物はだめです。
4. 留学生は外国から来た学生です。
5. 新しい社長は仕事がよくできます。でも、話は長くて難しいです。
6. ミーティングは短いですから、色々な考えを言って下さい。
7. とても古い新聞を読みました。
8. 来週、食事に招待したいんですが。
9. ドアは開けたら、静かに閉めてください。
10. このごろ忙しくて、研究ができない。
11. 新しい漢字を練習してください。
12. 医者という仕事も大変だ。

上手な読み方

日本人と結婚　(The Japanese and marriage)

読む前に

A. In Japanese, genre rather than formality determines whether to use plain or polite forms in writing. For example, compositions, diaries, and newspaper articles are usually written in the plain form and letters and postcards are written in the polite form. Check the writing styles of the reading materials in the previous chapters as well as other authentic materials, and note which types are written in the plain form and which are written in the polite form.

B. 結婚について、下の質問に日本語で答えて下さい。

1. あなたの国では男の人は何さいぐらいで結婚しますか。女の人はどうですか。
2. 結婚した後、だれが家の外ではたらきますか。

3. 結婚した後、家事(かじ) (household work) や子供の世話(せわ) (care) はだれがしますか。
4. あなたは結婚したいと思いますか。したくありませんか。どうしてそう思いますか。

C. Work as a class. You are going to conduct a survey（アンケート）about what your classmates think about marriage.

1. First, look at the survey form your instructor will give you, the summary sheet below, and the expressions below. (The expressions in this activity also appear in the reading materials on page 270 of this chapter.) Identify the types of information that you need in order to complete the summary sheet. Then conduct the survey and complete the survey form by classifying the responses according to the gender of the interviewee.

平均(へいきん)	average	自由(じゆう)な	free; freedom
年齢(ねんれい)	age (formal expression)	家事(かじ)	household work
男性(だんせい)	formal word for 男の人	世話(せわ)	care
女性(じょせい)	formal word for 女の人	養(やしな)う	to support (financially)

Example

A: 何さいぐらいで結婚したいと思いますか。
B: 三十さいぐらいで結婚したいと思います。

2. Now complete the summary sheet based on the results of your survey.

	男性(だんせい)	女性(じょせい)
結婚したい平均年齢(へいきんねんれい)	_____さい	_____さい
家事(かじ)	ご主人(しゅじん)_____% おくさん_____% ご主人(しゅじん)とおくさん_____%	ご主人(しゅじん)_____% おくさん_____% ご主人(しゅじん)とおくさん_____%
子供の世話(せわ)	ご主人(しゅじん)_____% おくさん_____% ご主人(しゅじん)とおくさん_____%	ご主人(しゅじん)_____% おくさん_____% ご主人(しゅじん)とおくさん_____%
家族を養(やしな)う人	ご主人(しゅじん)_____% おくさん_____% ご主人(しゅじん)とおくさん_____%	ご主人(しゅじん)_____% おくさん_____% ご主人(しゅじん)とおくさん_____%
自由な生活	出来る_____% 出来ない_____%	

読んでみましょう

日本人の平均結婚年齢は毎年少しずつ上がっている。20 年前の平均結婚年齢は男性が 25.4 歳、女性が 24 歳だったが、今は男性が 28.5 歳，女性も 26.5 歳になっている。

これはどうしてだろうか。1994 年のアンケートでは男性の 55% が「結婚したら、やりたいことが出来なくなる。」と答えた。結婚したら家族のために働かなければならないから、好きな事が出来ないと言うのだ。①それに、二十年前より今の方が生活にお金がかかるので、わかい時に結婚したら大変だと考えているのだ。1996 年の朝日新聞のアンケートによると、「結婚した後、自分の給料で家族を養えるかどうか分からない」と答えた**男性**が多かった。

また、同じアンケートでは、多くの女性が「一人でも生活できるし、結婚したら自由な生活が出来ないから、あまり早く結婚したくない。」と答えていた。日本では働く女性が多くなってきているし、結婚した後仕事を続ける**人**も多くなってきている。けれども、②女性は結婚して子供が出来たら仕事をしないで、家事や子供の世話をしなければならないという**考え方**は強い。だから、③結婚するより、就職して好きなことをしたい、結婚したくなったらしようと考えるのかもしれない。

分かりましたか

A. Choose the sentence that best summarizes the above passage.

1. この文章 (text) は日本の男性と女性の平均結婚年令について書いてあります。
2. この文章 (text) はどうして日本人の女性が結婚しないか書いてあります。
3. この文章 (text) はどうして日本人が早く結婚したがらないか書いてあります。

B. Circle はい if the statement is consistent with the passage and いいえ if it isn't.

1. 日本人は男性(だんせい)も女性(じょせい)も早(はや)く結婚したいと思っている。　はい　いいえ
2. 女性(じょせい)は結婚したほうが､結婚する前より好きなことが出来る。　はい　いいえ
3. 働(はたら)く女性(じょせい)は多くなってきている。　はい　いいえ
4. 日本の男性(だんせい)は女性(じょせい)が結婚した後、働(はたら)いたほうがいいと思っている。　はい　いいえ
5. 日本では結婚した後、仕事をつづける女性(じょせい)が多い。　はい　いいえ
6. 日本の男性(だんせい)は結婚した後、自分が家族を養(やしな)わなければならないと思っている。　はい　いいえ

C. 下の質問に日本語で答えて下さい。

1. What does これ *(underlined)* refer to in the second paragraph of the reading text?
2. What are the subjects of underlined sentences ①, ②, and ③ in the reading passage?

D. Identify the portions of the sentences in the text that modify the nouns set in boldfaced type.

読んだ後で

A. Work with a partner. Using the following questions as a guide, discuss the results of your survey in Exercise C of 読む前に. Then write a short composition about your results.

1. クラスの人が考える平均(へいきん)結婚年令(ねんれい)と日本人の平均(へいきん)結婚年令(ねんれい)とどちらの方が高いですか。それはどうしてだと思いますか。
2. あなたのクラスでは結婚したら自由(じゆう)な生活が出来ないと思っている人は多いですか。どうしてそう思っているのでしょうか。
3. ご主人(しゅじん)の仕事とおくさんの仕事について、クラスメートの考え方は日本人の考え方は同じですか。違いますか。違うなら、どう違いますか。

上手な聞き方

将来（しょうらい）の計画　(Future plans)

聞く前に

Work with a partner. Look at the chart showing information about four female college students and discuss what kinds of careers and lifestyles they might have.

名前	山田ともみ	きくち たか子	さいとう やす子	高田 ゆり
年	18 さい	23 さい	19 さい	２１さい
専攻	文学	歴史（れきし）	美術（びじゅつ）	教育学（きょういくがく）
アルバイト	ウェイトレス	家庭教師（かていきょうし）	デパートの店員	じゅく (prep school) の先生
しゅみ	本を読む	旅行	テニス	おんがく

聞いてみましょう

Listen to three of the students from the above chart speak about their future plans and current lifestyles. They do not reveal their names in the conversation. Do the following:

1. Write the future plans of each, and what, if anything, each person has been doing to achieve her plan.

学生	**将来（しょうらい）の計画**	**しておくこと／してあること**
A		
B		
C		

2. Work with a partner. Try to identify the names of the women on the tape by comparing the conversation you have just heard with the descriptions in the chart in 聞く前に.

   A さんの名前 ______________________________

   B さんの名前 ______________________________

   C さんの名前 ______________________________

聞いた後で

A. 質問に答えて下さい。

1. A さんは、卒業したら、好きなことが出来ると思っていますか。
2. A さんは結婚したいと思っていますか。
3. A さんはしゅうしょくしたいと思っていますか。
4. B さんは来年何をするつもりですか。
5. B さんはどこでアルバイトをしていますか。
6. B さんは結婚したいと思っているでしょうか。
7. C さんは卒業したらすぐしゅうしょくするつもりですか。
8. C さんは英語が上手ですか。
9. C さんは英語の勉強をするために外国に行くのですか。

B. パートナーと下の質問について話して下さい。

1. A さん、B さん、C さんの中で、あなたはどの人に一番ちかいと思いますか。どうしてそう思いますか。
2. A さん、B さん、C さんの中で、あなたはどの人とはとても違うと思いますか。どうしてそう思いますか。
3. A さん、B さん、C さんはどんなせいかくだと思いますか。どの人と友達になりたいと思いますか。

STUDENT

Listen to the conversation between two people. One of the two people is one of the above students, A, B, or C. Use listening strategies such as listening for key words, your knowledge about the students, the speech style they use, etc. Try to guess which student is talking, where and with whom the conversation is taking place, and what the conversation is about. Then summarize the contents of the conversation.

学生の名前 ________________________________

学生が話している人 ________________________________

話している所 ________________________________

トピック ________________________________

ないよう (contents) ________________________________

____

C. Work with a partner. Each person should write a short description of his or her future plans on a piece of paper. Each person should include his or her age, interests, goals for the future, and what he or she is doing now or must to do to achieve these goals. The information should not include the name of the person. Then exchange descriptions and proofread each other's writing.

STUDENT

DICT-A-CONVERSATION

言葉(ことば)のリスト

日本史(し)　Japanese history

スミスさんはかとう先生の授業をとりたいと思っているので、先生に質問をしています。

先生：＿＿＿＿＿＿＿＿＿＿＿＿＿＿＿＿＿＿＿＿＿＿＿＿

スミス：＿＿＿＿＿＿＿＿＿＿＿＿＿＿＿＿＿＿＿＿＿＿＿

先生：＿＿＿＿＿＿＿＿＿＿＿＿＿＿＿＿＿＿＿＿＿＿＿＿

スミス：＿＿＿＿＿＿＿＿＿＿＿＿＿＿＿＿＿＿＿＿＿＿＿

先生：＿＿＿＿＿＿＿＿＿＿＿＿＿＿＿＿＿＿＿＿＿＿＿＿

スミス：＿＿＿＿＿＿＿＿＿＿＿＿＿＿＿＿＿＿＿＿＿＿＿

先生：＿＿＿＿＿＿＿＿＿＿＿＿＿＿＿＿＿＿＿＿＿＿＿＿

スミス：＿＿＿＿＿＿＿＿＿＿＿＿＿＿＿＿＿＿＿＿＿＿＿

聞き上手話し上手

Making confirmations and checking comprehension

Communication strategies, such as asking for repetition or paraphrasing, checking your conversation partner's comprehension, and confirming what has been said to you, are very important in sustaining conversation and preventing breakdowns in communication. Chapter 6 of Volume 1 discussed how to ask for repetitions and paraphrasing (あのう、すみません, もう一度言って下さい and ゆっくり言って下さい). You can also use もう一度おねがいします or ゆっくりおねがいします, both of which are more polite than 言って下さい.

This chapter focuses on making confirmations and checking comprehension. In order to check your conversation partner's comprehension, you can use わかりますか *(Are you following me?* or *Do you understand what I am saying?),* or わかりましたか *(Did you understand what I meant?).* If your conversation partner does not understand you, don't immediately give up or change the subject. Try your best to paraphrase what you want to say. Making this effort will give you more opportunities to try out a variety of structures and expressions. It helps you to increase your knowledge and retention as well as fluency.

Conversely, if you are not sure you have understood what your conversation partner said to you, confirm what has been said. This will help you get important information and prevent you from running into major misunderstandings.

There are several ways of confirming information in Japanese.

STUDENT

1. Repeat a word or expression with rising or falling intonation.

川田：　あのう、銀行はどこですか。／ねえ、銀行どこ？
　　　　Where is the bank?

山本：　そのケーキ屋(や)の後ろです。／
　　　　そのケーキ屋(や)の後ろだよ。(male)／そのケーキやの後ろよ。(female)
　　　　It's behind that cake shop.

川田：　ケーキ屋(や)の後ろですか。／ケーキ屋(や)の後ろ？
　　　　Behind the cake shop?

山本：　ええ。／うん。
　　　　Yes.

Another strategy is to use a brief pause (which may be as long as five seconds or so), but a pause can also indicate a lack of comprehension or communication difficulty.

2. Repeat a word or expression and add ですか with a rising intonation. In casual speech, simply repeat with a rising intonation.

川田：　電車は何時に出ますか。／電車は何時に出るの？
　　　　What time does the train leave?

山本：　朝六時半に出ますよ。／朝六時半に出るよ。
　　　　It leaves at 6:30 A.M.

川田：　六時半(に)ですか。／六時半(に)？
　　　　6:30 A.M?

山本：　ええ。／うん。
　　　　Yes.

A short rising intonation not only helps confirm information but also expresses surprise.

3. Repeat a word or expression and add ですね or ね (casual speech) with a short rising intonation. The intonation does not indicate any surprise. The use of ね, instead of か, indicates you are convinced or satisfied with the information given to you.

川田：　どこで事故(じこ)があったんですか。／どこで事故(じこ)があったの？
　　　　Where was the accident?

山本：　あの公園のそばにある高校の前で、ほら、喫茶店(きっさてん)があるところ。

It was in front of the high school near that park, you know, right where the coffee shop is.

川田：　ああ、分かりました。東高校の前ですね。／
ああ、分かった。東高校の前ね。

Oh, I see. In front of Higashi High School, right.

山本：　ええ、そうです。／
うん、そうだよ。(male)／ええ、そうよ。(female)

Yeah, that's it.

4. Repeat a sentence or verb phrase, using 〜んですね／〜んだわ／〜のね.

川田：　ビールとワインありますか。／ビールとワインある？

Do you have beer and wine?

山本：　ええ、買ってありますよ。／うん、買ってあるよ。

Yes, got them.

川田：　ビールもワインも買ってあるんですね。／
ビールもワインも買ってあるんだね。(male)／
ビールもワインも買ってあるのね。(female)

You've got beer and wine, right?

山本：　ええ。／うん。

Yes.

A. Complete the following conversations by providing confirming remarks.

1. A: あのう、すみません。お手洗はどこにありますか。
   B: お手洗は一階(かい)のエレベータのよこにあります。
   A: ______________________________

2. A: ねえ、今週日本の映画があるそうだけど、いつどこであるの？
   B: 金曜日の午後八時から、図書館の二階(かい)のラウンジであるそうよ。
   A: ______________________________

3. A: あの、来年の夏、日本で勉強したいと思うんですけど。
   B: じゃあ、三階(がい)にある留学生センターの事務室(じむしつ)に行ったら。
   A: ______________________________

4. A: ビールとワインは買ってあるから、ジュース買っといてくれる？
   B: ______________________________

B. Listen to the series of short statements. Confirm what has been said.

C. Listen to the series of three announcements about your Japanese class. Confirm what has been said, and write down the content of the announcements in Japanese.

D. Work with a partner. You are a reporter and your partner is a celebrity. Interview him or her, take notes, and confirm what you have written. Your partner will make sure you have understood what he or she said by checking your comprehension.

総合(そうごう)練習

そうだんしたいことがあります

Work in groups of four. You are consultants for people with problems. Read the following statements about various people's problems and discuss suggestions about what they should do to solve their problems.

Example

マクドナルドさん

私は十八さいで、スーパーではたらいていますが、仕事はおもしろくないし、給料(きゅうりょう)も悪いので、仕事をかえたいと思います。高校はきらいだったので、一年前にやめたんです。でも、卒業しておいたほうがよかったかもしれません。どうしたらいいですか。

A: 高校を卒業していないから、いい仕事がないんだと思います。仕事をやめて、高校に行ったほうがいいですね。
B: しけんをうけてみたら、どうでしょうか。
C: そうですね。そして、新しい仕事をさがす前に、大学も卒業しておいたほうがいいですね。

1. **ホンさん**

私は今大学二年生ですが、学生をつづけた方がいいかどうか分かりません。高校の時は何でもよく出来ましたが、大学に入ってから、いいせいせきがとれません。Dをたくさんとったんです。両親は大学を卒業した方が将来(しょうらい)のためにいいと言いますが、私には分かりません。

2. ジョンソンさん

日本人のガールフレンドがいるんですが、春に卒業して、日本に帰ったんです。ぼくはまだ学生ですが、将来（しょうらい）はその人と結婚したいと思っています。でも、彼女（かのじょ）(sweetheart) の両親は外国人はだめだと言うんです。どうして外国人はだめなのか、よく分かりません。今度の冬には日本へ行くつもりですが、その時彼女（かのじょ）の両親に会おうと思っています。今からどんなことをしておいたらいいでしょうか。

ロールプレイ

A. You broke your friend's computer. Tell him or her what you have done, apologize, and offer some compensation.

B. You are an organizer of a workshop. You want to make sure that everything is ready. You are talking to a Japanese assistant. Confirm with him or her that the following things are ready.

1. speaker's hotel reservation
2. conference site reservation
3. preparation for coffee and snacks
4. badges（バッジ）
5. helpers at the registration desk（うけつけ）

C. You lost your bag on a train in Japan. Important things such as your wallet, keys, and textbooks are in the bag. Go to the lost-and-found department, explain the situation, describe what is inside the bag, and ask for help. Also, leave your telephone number and ask to be called if the bag is found.

単語　(ESSENTIAL VOCABULARY)

LAB

Nouns

エンジニア　engineer
おゆ　（お湯）　hot water
かいけいし　（会計士）　accountant
かいじょう　（会場）　place of meeting
きゅうりょう　（給料）　salary, wage
さいふ　（財布）　wallet, purse
しき　（式）　ceremony; けっこんしき　（結婚式）　wedding ceremony; そつぎょうしき　（卒業式）　graduation ceremony
しゃちょう　（社長）　company president
じゅんび　（準備）　preparation
しょうたいじょう　（招待状）　invitation letter or card

しょうらい （将来） future
とし （年） age; year としをとる （年をとる） (to) grow old
どうそうかい （同窓会） reunion party
べんごし （弁護士） lawyer
ぼうえき （貿易） trading
ぼうえきがいしゃ （貿易会社） trading company
マネージャー manager

Verbal nouns

けんきゅう （研究） research; けんきゅうする （研究する） (to) do research; けんきゅうをする （研究する） to do research
しゅうしょく （就職） getting a job; 〜にしゅうしょくする （〜に就職する） (to) get a job at 〜
じゅんび （準備） preparation; じゅんびする （準備する） to prepare; じゅんびをする （準備をする） to prepare
しょうたい （招待） invitation; しょうたいする （招待する） to invite
そうだん （相談） consultation; そうだんする （相談する） to consult; to discuss; そうだんをする （相談をする） to consult; to discuss
りゅうがく （留学） study abroad; りゅうがくする （留学する） (to) study abroad; りゅうがくをする （留学をする） (to) study abroad

う-verbs

あく （開く） (for something) (to) open *(intr.)*
あつまる （集まる） (for something) (to) gather *(intr.)*
うる （売る） (to) sell
おこす （起こす） (to) wake up (someone) *(trans.)*
かかる (for a telephone) (to) ring
かわる （変わる／替わる） (for something) (to) change *(intr.)*
きまる （決まる） (for something) (to) be decided *(intr.)*
しまる （閉まる） (to) close (something) *(intr.)*
ちがう （違う） (to) be different *(intr.)*; A と B はちがう （A と B は違う） A and B are different A は B とちがう（A は B と違う） A is different from B
つく （付く） (for something) to turn on *(intr.)*
つづく （続く） (for something) to continue *(intr.)*
なおす （直す） to fix, to repair (something) *(trans.)*
なおる （直る） (for something) to heal, (to) be fixed *(intr.)*
のこす （残す） to leave (something) *(trans.)*
のこる （残る） (for something) (to) be left; to remain *(intr.)*
はたらく （働く） (to) work *(intr.)*
まちがう （間違う） (for someone) (to) be mistaken *(intr.)*
わかす （沸かす） to bring (something) (to) a boil *(trans.)*
わく （沸く） (for something) (to) boil *(intr.)*

る-verbs

あげる （上げる） (to) raise (something) *(intr.)*
あつめる （集める） (to) gather (something) *(tr.)*
おえる （終える） (to) end (something); (to) finish (something) *(trans.)*
おちる（落ちる）(for something) (to) fall *(intr.)*
かんがえる （考える） (to) think intellectually; (to) take (something) into consideration

きえる　（消える）　(for something) (to) go out; to go off *(intr.)*
きめる　（決める）(to) decide on (something) *(trans.)*
つづける　（続ける）(to) continue (something) *(trans.)*
のせる　（乗せる）(to) give a ride (to someone) *(trans.)*
はじめる　（始める）(to) begin (something) *(trans.)*
まちがえる　（間違える）(to) miss (something); (to) make a mistake *(trans.)*
やめる　（止める）(to) quit; (to) stop

い-adjectives

わかい　（若い）　young (わかい should be used for teenagers or someone older than teenage. It is not used for small children.)

な-adjectives

おなじ　（同じ）　same;　A と B はおなじ（A と B は同じ）A and B are the same;　A は B とおなじ（A は B と同じ）A is the same as B. There is no な used to modify nouns おなじひと（同じ人）.

Adverb

ゆっくり　slowly

Suffix

〜や　（〜屋）owner of 〜 retail store; さかなや　（魚屋）fish market owner; にくや　（肉屋）butcher;　はなや　（花屋）flower shop owner; ほんや　（本屋）bookstore owner

Expressions

ゆっくりおねがいします。（ゆっくりお願いします。）Slowly please.
としをとる　（年を取る）(to) become old

Passive Vocabulary

Nouns

アンケート　survey
うけつけ　（受付）receptionist desk; registration desk
かじ　（家事）household work
かのじょ　（彼女）girlfriend; sweetheart; she *(interpretation depends on the context)*
こんしんかい　（懇親会）get-together party
ししゃ　（支社）company branch office
じしん　（地震）　earthquake
じぶん　（自分）　oneself
じゆう　（自由）　freedom

しゅうしんこよう （終身雇用） lifetime employment
しゅと （首都） capital city
じょせい （女性） female (a formal word for おんなのひと [女の人])
ぜいきん （税金） tax
ゼミ seminar; ゼミ originally referred to a upper-level undergraduate seminar course in liberal arts. It also refers to the group of people who participate in the seminar, since they often have other actitives such as summer camp and parties (known as コンパ). ゼミ is often used with the professor's name (e.g., 田中ゼミ and 鈴木(すずき)ゼミ).
せわ （世話） care
だいきぎょう （大企業） large corporation
だんせい （男性） male (a formal word for おとこのひと [男の人])
ちゅうしょうきぎょう （中小企業） small business
どうそうかい （同窓会） reunion party (usually school reunion)
にほんし （日本史） Japanese history
ねんこうじょれつ （年功序列） seniority
ねんれい （年齢） age
バッジ badge
バブルけいざい （バブル経済） bubble economy
へいきん （平均） average
へんじ （返事） reply; response
リストラ restructuring
れいさいきぎょう （零細企業） small business

Verbal nouns

へんじ （返事） reply; response; へんじする （返事する） (to) reply; (to) respond; へんじをする （返事をする） (to) reply; (to) respond

う-verbs

がんばる （頑張る） (to) do one's best
やしなう （養う） (to) support (financially) *(trans.)*
もどる （戻る） (for someone/something) (to) return *(intr.)*

な-adjective

じゆうな （自由な） free

Expressions

バブルがはじける The bubble (economy) bursts.

For a list of supplementary vocabulary items that will facilitate communication, see the first page of Chapter 5 in your Workbook.

Japanese streets can be very crowded.

CHAPTER 6

第六課

道(みち)の聞き方と教え方

Asking for and Giving Directions

Functions	Asking for and giving directions
New Vocabulary	Words used when giving directions; Directions; Verbs and adjectives used in giving directions; Transportation and stations
Dialogue	ヒルトンホテルへの行き方 (Directions to the Hilton Hotel)
Culture	Streets and addresses in Japanese cities; The Japanese train system
Language	I. Expressing a route, using the particle を; Expressing a point of departure, using the particle を; Expressing scope or limit, using the particle で II. Expressing chronology, using the て-form of the verb +から; Expressing conditions leading to set consequences, using the plain form + と III. Expressing possibility, using the dictionary form of the verb + ことが出来る IV. Expressing limited degree, using だけ〜affirmative or しか〜negative V. Expressing presuppositions, using the plain form + はず
Kanji	Okurigana
Reading	Getting to Tokyo University
Listening	Asking for directions; Announcements at stations and in trains
Communication	How to ask for directions and how to give them

新しい言葉(ことば)

行き方を教える時に使う言葉(ことば) (Words used when giving directions)

駐車場(ちゅうしゃじょう) parking lot

ガソリンスタンド gas station

市役所(しやくしょ) city office

大使館(たいしかん) embassy

映画館(かん) movie theater

ターミナル terminal

バスてい bus stop

ビル building

川(かわ) river

このへん this area

～つ目 (一つ目の角(かど)) ～ the (first corner)

道(みち) road; street; way

道路(どうろ) road; street

横断歩道(おうだんほどう) pedestrian crosswalk

交差点(こうさてん) intersection

橋(はし) bridge

信号(しんごう) traffic signal

つきあたり T-roads

角(かど) corner

つぎ next

～メートル ～ meters

下の言葉(ことば)をおぼえていますか。

地図　学生会館　学校　喫茶店(きっさてん)　教会　公園　高校　交番(こうばん)
魚屋　神社(じんじゃ)　体育館(たいいくかん)　建物(たてもの)　地下　銀行　郵便局　アパート
(お)てら　図書館　博物館(はくぶつかん)　町　山　遊園地(ゆうえんち)　あんない
くうこう　案内所(あんないしょ)　みずうみ　店　駅(えき)　～番目

A. 下の言葉(ことば)を言って下さい。

何(なん)メートル　一(いち)メートル　二(に)メートル　三(さん)メートル　四(よん)メートル
五(ご)メートル　六(ろく)メートル　七(なな)メートル　八(はち)メートル　九(きゅう)メートル
十(じゅう)メートル

いくつ目(め)*　一(ひと)つ目(め)　二(ふた)つ目(め)　三(みっ)つ目(め)　四(よっ)つ目(め)　五(いつ)つ目(め)
六(むっ)つ目(め)　七(なな)つ目(め)　八(やっ)つ目(め)　九(ここの)つ目(め)

* ～つ目(め) is not used for large numbers. The larger the number, the less likely it is to be used. Use ～番目 (in Volume 1, Chapter 10) for large numbers.

B. 新しい言葉(ことば)を見て、下の質問に答えて下さい。

1. 建物(たてもの)はどれですか。
2. 道(みち)という漢字がある言葉(ことば)はどれですか。
3. 館という漢字がある言葉(ことば)はどれですか。
4. 車のためにあるものはどれですか。
5. 駅(えき)の近(ちか)くにある物はどれですか。

C. Supply the words that match the following descriptions.

1. 川をわたる所
2. 道(みち)にあって、もう行けなくなる所
3. 道(みち)をわたる所
4. 二つの道(みち)がかさなる (overlap) 所
5. 車にガソリンを入れる所
6. その国のビザ (visa) がいる時に行く所

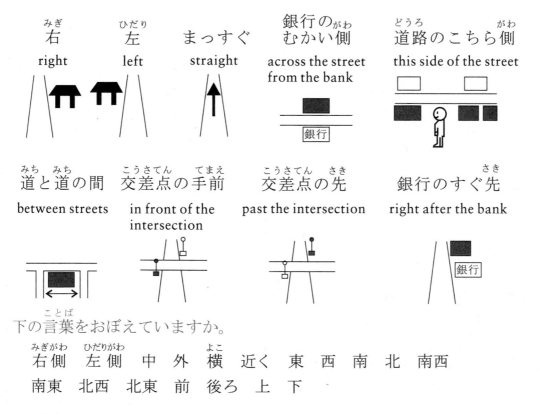

方向(ほうこう) (Directions)

右(みぎ)	左(ひだり)	まっすぐ	銀行のむかい側(がわ)	道路(どうろ)のこちら側(がわ)
right	left	straight	across the street from the bank	this side of the street

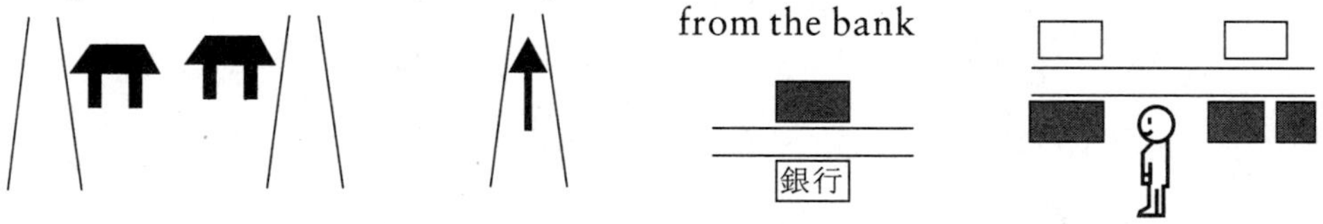

道(みち)と道(みち)の間	交差点(こうさてん)の手前(てまえ)	交差点(こうさてん)の先(さき)	銀行のすぐ先(さき)
between streets	in front of the intersection	past the intersection	right after the bank

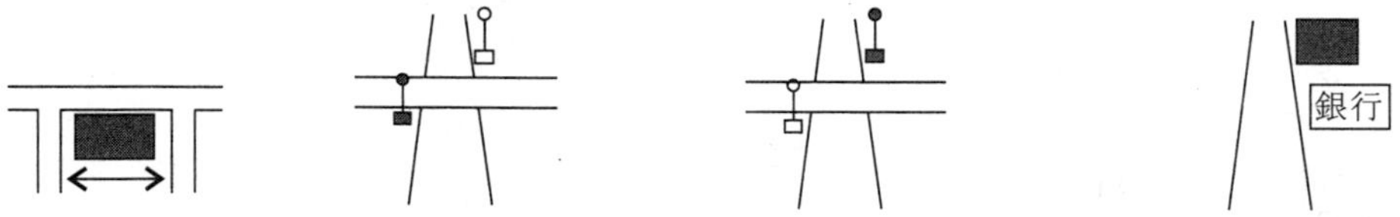

下の言葉(ことば)をおぼえていますか。

右側(みぎがわ)　左側(ひだりがわ)　中　外　横(よこ)　近く　東　西　南　北　南西

南東　北西　北東　前　後ろ　上　下

D. Look at the following map. Two people—A and B—are at the gas station walking toward the park. Complete the following sentences, using words indicating direction.

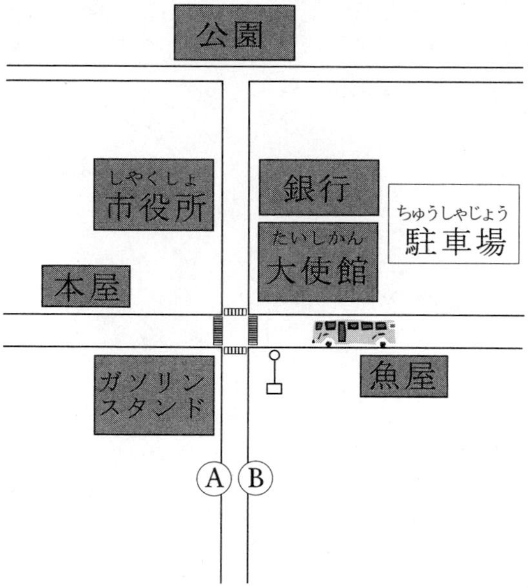

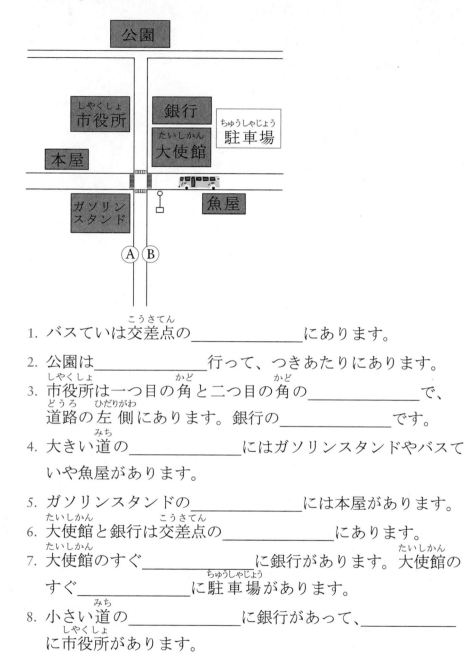

1. バスていは交差点(こうさてん)の______________にあります。
2. 公園は______________行って、つきあたりにあります。
3. 市役所(しやくしょ)は一つ目の角(かど)と二つ目の角(かど)の______________で、道路(どうろ)の左側(ひだりがわ)にあります。銀行の______________です。
4. 大きい道(みち)の______________にはガソリンスタンドやバスていや魚屋があります。
5. ガソリンスタンドの______________には本屋があります。
6. 大使館(たいしかん)と銀行は交差点(こうさてん)の______________にあります。
7. 大使館(たいしかん)のすぐ______________に銀行があります。大使館(たいしかん)のすぐ______________に駐車場(ちゅうしゃじょう)があります。
8. 小さい道(みち)の______________に銀行があって、____________に市役所(しやくしょ)があります。

E. Work with a partner. Imagine that you are in front of the building where you are studying. Tell each other what buildings and facilities are around your building, using the location and direction expressions above as well as other expressions you know. Verify the information you receive.

行き方を教えるためのどうしとけいようし (Verbs and adjectives used in giving directions)

～をわたる　to cross ～	～が見える　can see ～
～を通(とお)る　to go through/pass ～	～に近(ちか)い　close to ～
～が止(と)まる　(for something) to stop ～	～から遠(とお)い　far from ～
～を止(と)める　to stop something	
～をおりる　to get off ～	
～を右(みぎ)／左(ひだり)にまがる　to turn right/left at ～	
～で～から～に乗りかえる　to transfer from ～ to ～ at ～	

下の言葉(ことば)をおぼえていますか。

行く　来る　帰る　歩く　出る　乗る　乗せる
(時間が)かかる

F. Match the phrases in the box with the pictures.

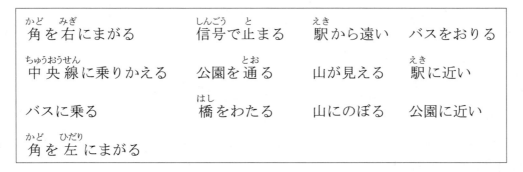

角(かど)を右(みぎ)にまがる	信号(しんごう)で止(と)まる	駅(えき)から遠い	バスをおりる
中央線(ちゅうおうせん)に乗りかえる	公園を通(とお)る	山が見える	駅(えき)に近い
バスに乗る	橋(はし)をわたる	山にのぼる	公園に近い
角(かど)を左(ひだり)にまがる			

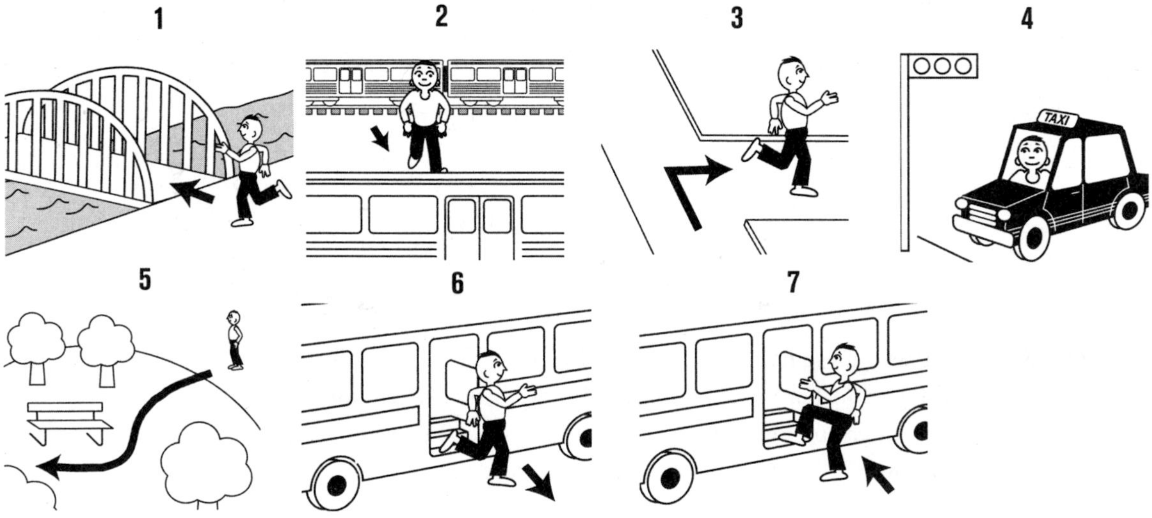

G. Draw the following directions on the street map at the bottom right.

1. 一つ目の角(かど)を右(みぎ)にまがる
2. 信号(しんごう)を右(みぎ)にまがって、左(ひだり)にある
3. 二つ目の交差点(こうさてん)を左(ひだり)にまがって、まっすぐ行く
4. まっすぐ行って、二つ目の角(かど)の手前(てまえ)
5. 50メートルぐらいまっすぐ行く
6. 一つ目の角(かど)を左(ひだり)にまがる
7. 公園を通(とお)って橋(はし)をわたる

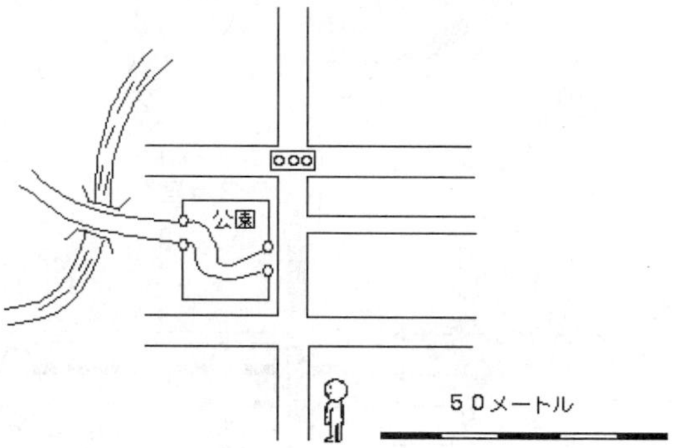

乗り物と駅(えき) (Transportation and stations)

地下鉄(ちかてつ) subway

タクシー taxi

各駅停車(かくえきていしゃ) local train

普通(ふつう)(列車(れっしゃ)) local train

急行(きゅうこう)(列車(れっしゃ)) express train

特急(とっきゅう)(列車(れっしゃ)) limited express train

〜せん（山の手線(やまのてせん)　京成線(けいせいせん)） 〜 line (Yamanote line, Keisei line)

〜行き（京都(きょうと)行き） bound for 〜 (bound for Kyoto)

〜番線(ばんせん) track number

下の言葉(ことば)をおぼえていますか。

電車　バス　飛行機(ひこうき)　自転車(じてんしゃ)

H. 下の質問に答えて下さい。

1. 一番近(ちか)くの町までバスでどのくらいかかりますか。タクシーでどのくらいかかりますか。
2. 町のバスはいくらぐらいかかりますか。
3. 一番近(ちか)くの空港(くうこう)から家までタクシーでどのくらいかかりますか。
4. どの町に地下鉄(ちかてつ)がありますか。
5. 地下鉄(ちかてつ)に乗ったことがありますか。どこで乗りましたか。

I. Look at the train map that connects Narita Airport and Ueno Station in Tokyo, and answer the questions below.

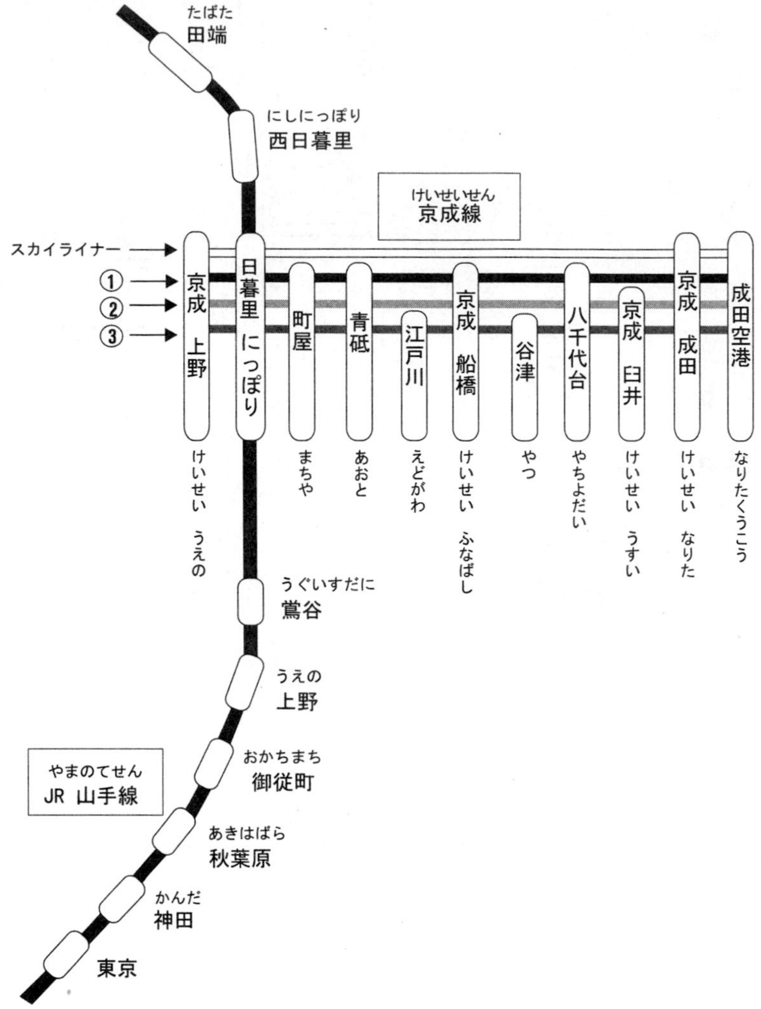

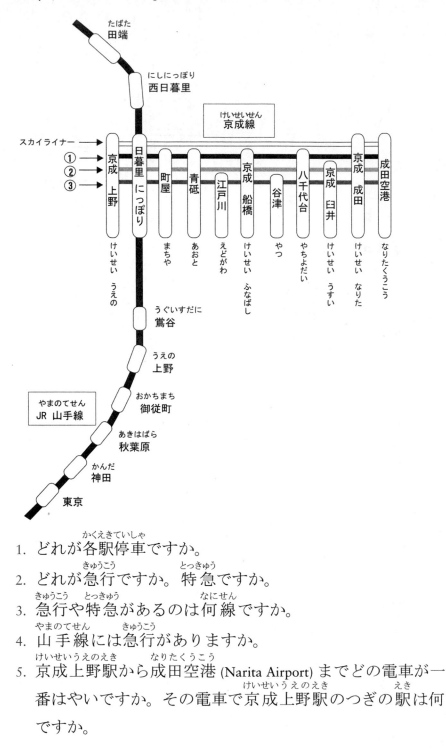

1. どれが各駅停車(かくえきていしゃ)ですか。
2. どれが急行(きゅうこう)ですか。特急(とっきゅう)ですか。
3. 急行(きゅうこう)や特急(とっきゅう)があるのは何線(なにせん)ですか。
4. 山手線(やまのてせん)には急行(きゅうこう)がありますか。
5. 京成上野駅(けいせいうえのえき)から成田空港(なりたくうこう) (Narita Airport) までどの電車が一番はやいですか。その電車で京成上野駅(けいせいうえのえき)のつぎの駅(えき)は何ですか。

J. 下のえ (picture) は東京駅のターミナルです。えを見て質問に答えて下さい。

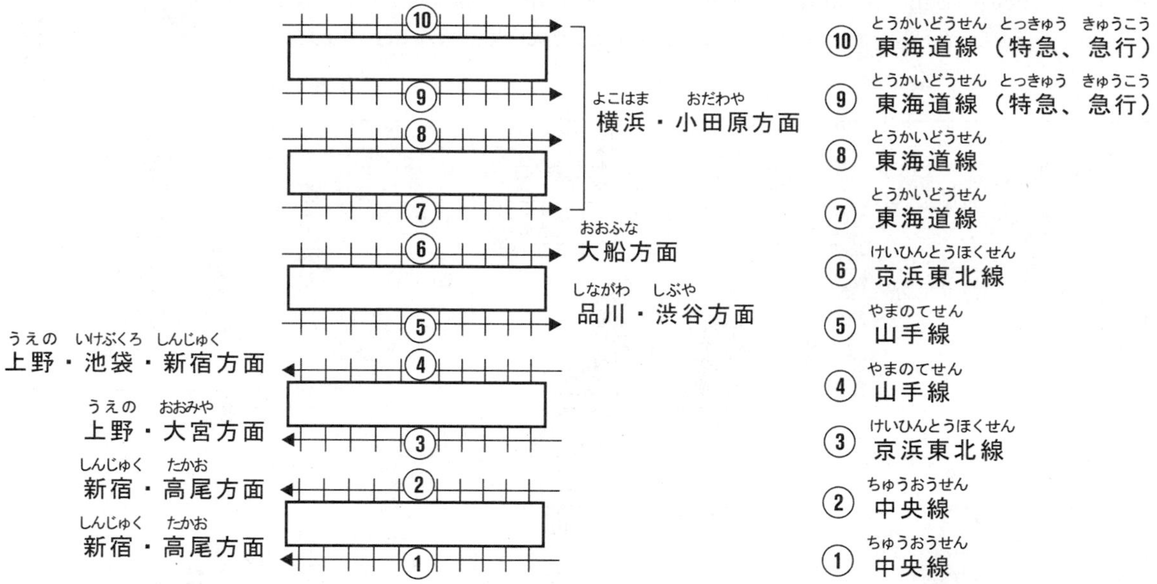

1. 横浜に行く時は何番線の電車に乗りますか。はやいのは何番線ですか。
2. 新宿に行きたい人は何線に乗りますか。
3. 池袋に行く人は何番線の電車に乗りますか。何線ですか。
4. 渋谷に行く人は何線に乗らなくてはいけませんか。何番線ですか。

ダイアローグ

はじめに

質問に答えて下さい。

1. 東京は電車のほうが車より便利です。あなたの町ではどうですか。
2. 電車でどこかへ行く時、どんな言葉を使いますか。
3. あなたの国では道を教える時、どんな建物や物の名前をよく使いますか。
4. 道を聞いている時、どんな言葉をよく聞かなければならないと思いますか。

STUDENT

ヒルトンホテルへの行き方 (Directions to the Hilton Hotel)

The following **manga** frames are scrambled, so they are not in the order described in the dialogue. Read the dialogue and unscramble the frames by writing the correct number in the box located in the upper right corner of each frame.

ブラウンさんはあさくさに住んでいます。明日ヒルトンホテルで道子（みちこ）さんと会う予定ですが、行き方がわからないので、電話で道子（みちこ）さんに行き方を聞いています。

ブラウン：　ここからヒルトンホテルまで、どう行ったらいいか分からないんだけど。

道子（みちこ）：　ああ、そう。じゃあ、新宿（しんじゅく）まで行き方分かる？

ブラウン：　ごめん。分からない。

道子（みちこ）：　じゃあ、いいわ。まず、地下鉄（ちかてつ）の銀座線（ぎんざせん）に乗って、神田（かんだ）まで行くの。

ブラウン：　銀座線で神田まで行って、それから？

道子：　神田で中央線に乗りかえて、三つ目が新宿だから、そこでおりるの。

ブラウン：　OK。中央線に乗って新宿でおりるのね。で、どの出口を出るの？

道子：　西口に出るのよ。出たら、すぐ目の前に地下道があるから、まっすぐ十分か十五分ぐらい歩いて行くの。

ブラウン：　西口を出てまっすぐ十分か十五分ぐらい行くのね。

道子：　ええ、そうよ。そうすると、高いビルがたくさんある所に出るわ。

ブラウン：　ああ、あの有名なビルがたくさんあるところ？

道子：　そうよ。ビルが見えてから、二つ目の角にハイアットホテルがあるわ。ハイアットの先には公園が見えるはずよ。

ブラウン：　ハイアットは道の右側、左側？

道子：　右側にあるわ。で、ハイアットの手前の角を右にまがるの。

ブラウン：　ハイアットの手前を右ね。

道子：　ええ、そうよ。右にまがってから、まっすぐ行って、つきあたりにヒルトンがあるわ。

ブラウン：　分かった。で、時間はどれくらいかかるの？

道子：　新宿の駅まで十五分から二十分ぐらい、ホテルまでは歩いて二十分ぐらいだから、四十分ぐらいかかると思うわ。

ブラウン：　ありがとう。じゃあ、明日一時にヒルトンのロビーでね。

道子：　じゃあ、明日ね。

つぎの日、ブラウンさんは神田駅にいます。

ブラウン：　あのう、すみません。中央線の新宿行きは何番線ですか。

男の人：　一番線ですよ。

ブラウン：　あ、どうも有難うございました。

ブラウンさんは新宿駅(しんじゅくえき)にいます。

ブラウン：　あのう、西口(にしぐち)はどちらでしょうか。
女の人：　あそこですよ。
ブラウン：　どうも。

ブラウンさんはホテルにつきました。

道子(みちこ)：　あ、ブラウンさん。ここよ。道(みち)、分かった。
ブラウン：　道子(みちこ)さん。ええ、すぐ分かった。
道子(みちこ)：　ああ、よかった。

分かりましたか

A. Circle the stations where Brown-san gets on or off trains; then follow her route on the map.

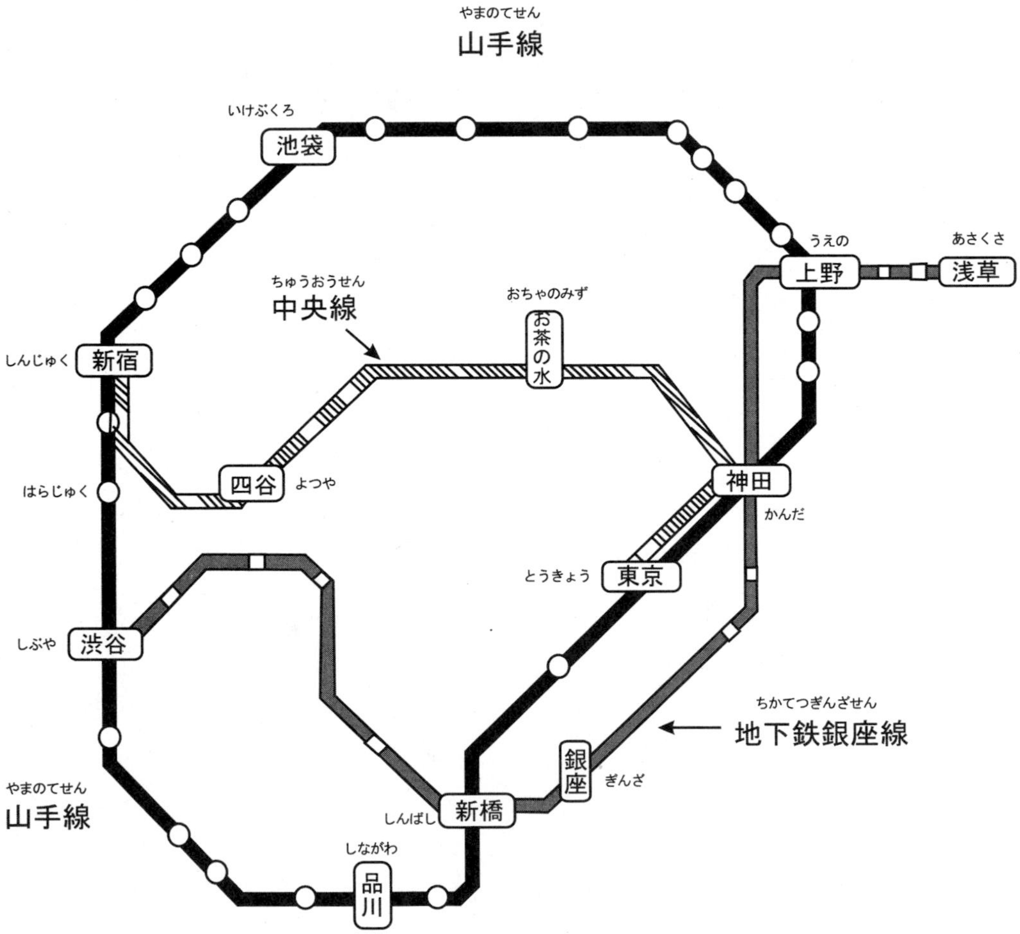

B. Follow Michiko-san's directions after Brown-san gets off the train at Shinjuku. The Hilton Hotel is building A, B, C, or D. Which is it?

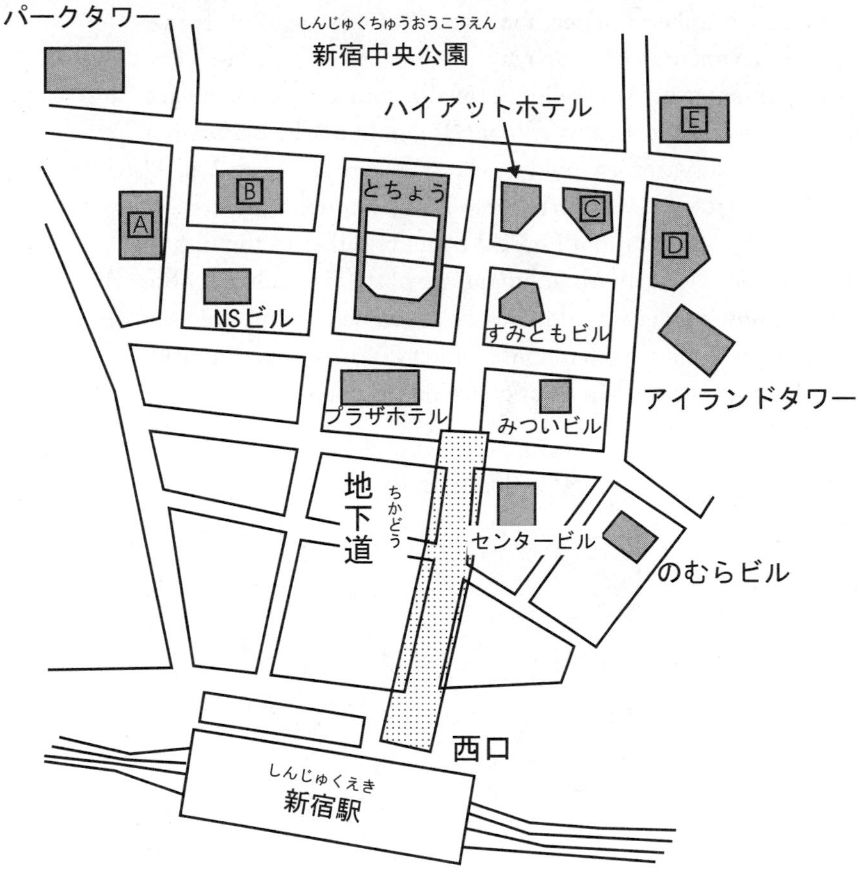

C. Identify the expressions in the dialogue where Brown-san confirms her understanding.

D. Suppose Brown-san is asking directions of her Japanese instructor. Rewrite the dialogue and make Michiko the **sensei.**

E. Explain how to go to パークタワー and the NS ビル from Shinjuku Station, using the map of Shinjuku in Exercise B.

日本の文化

Streets and addresses in Japanese cities. How are the streets organized in your town? Are the houses easy to locate? Which town or city is hard to get around in your country?

The Japanese address system is consistently different from that used in the United States. Because streets do not have names, it is impossible to specify a location with a number and a street name. In Japan, addresses are expressed in terms of a sub-area within a larger area. As shown in the map below, for example, 「神奈川県(かながわけん)山田市本町(しほんまち) 2ー 4ー 8」 indicates house number 8 in neighborhood 4 of sub-area 2 in Hon-machi district, Yamada-city, Kanagawa prefecture. (Yamada-city is fictitious.) Sub-areas are ordered, but the directions of the order are not consistent from one area to another. It would not be uncommon that residents of sub-area 1 would not know where sub-area 2 is. Also, house numbers are somewhat arbitrary. That is, house numbers 2 and 3 are likely to be adjacent, but house 2 could be either to the right or the left of house 3. Neighborhood maps are posted in each neighborhood to help non-residents find numbers. It can be difficult even for a Japanese person to find a given house address. When in doubt, ask local people or an officer at a local police box for assistance.

神奈川県(かながわけん)山田市(やまだし)

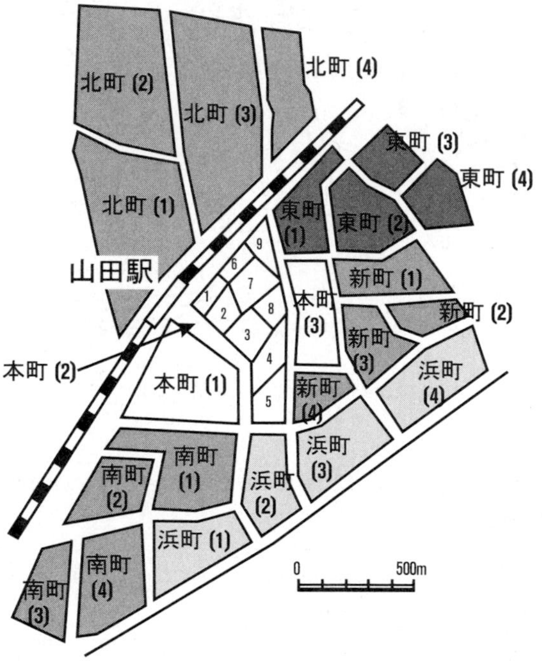

- *The Japanese train system. Do you take trains to commute to school? Which cities have good train systems in your country?*

The Japanese train system, including subways, is quite well developed and extremely reliable. If a train is scheduled to arrive at 12:58, it nearly always comes at 12:58. There are many different transportation companies, all of them now private. The largest one is JR, derived from Japan Railways and pronounced as ジェーアール. This is the former National Railway. Other private lines run in different directions and serve commuters in surrounding areas. Of the lines mentioned in this textbook, 山手線［やまのてせん］, 中央線［ちゅうおうせん］, and 新幹線［しんかんせん］ are JR lines, 京成線［けいせいせん］ is a private line, and 銀座線［ぎんざせん］ and 丸ノ内線［まるのうちせん］ are subway lines. The 山手線［やまのてせん］ is the loop for the Tokyo metro area and carries the largest number of passengers a day.

Japanese trains do not use tokens. Instead, they use tickets, which are punched, either automatically or manually, when the passenger enters the gate to the trains. It is important to retain the ticket throughout the ride because passengers give up their tickets at a checking machine when they leave the station. Fares increase with distance. Because you must purchase the ticket for your specific destination, you need to be able to figure out the fare by using a fare table or by asking others. The minimum fare is about 120 yen (current as of 1998). Many companies offer prepaid cards so frequent users do not have to purchase tickets each time they board. Commuters and students usually purchase passes（定期券［ていきけん］）that can be bought for one, three, or six months.

JR offers different types of discount tickets for travelers. One type is a pass to ride freely in a certain area for a fixed number of days (e.g., 5 days) called 周遊券［しゅうゆうけん］. If you are planning a trip to visit a series of different places, this type of ticket will save you money. JR also offers a 20% student discount（学生割引［わりびき］ or 学割［がくわり］）for tickets to travel more than 100 km one way. Travel agencies（旅行会社）and ビュープラザ (JR's own travel service found in major stations) are good sources of information for the types of discounts available.

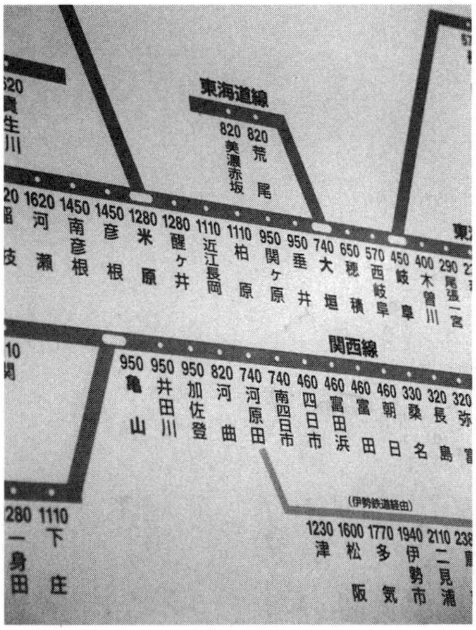

A fare display above a ticket machine.

LANGUAGE

I. Expressing a route, using the particle を; Expressing a point of departure, using the particle を; Expressing scope or limit, using the particle で

A. Expressing a route, using the particle を

	Noun (place)	Particle	
毎日	この道(みち)	を	通(とお)って、学校に行きます。

I take this road to school every day.

だい３コースをおよぎます。　(I) swim in lane 3.

毎日公園を走る。　I run (jog) in the park every day.

ゆみ:　ここから学校までは遠(とお)いから、歩きたくないわ。
I don't want to walk because the school is far away from here.

まもる:　そんなことないよ。あの駐車場(ちゅうしゃじょう)を通(とお)って行くと近(ちか)いよ。
It's not far. It's close if you go through that parking lot.

- The particle を indicates a location when movement occurs. It takes a verb of motion such as 行く, 来る, 帰る, 歩く, 通(とお)る, 走る, or およぐ.

B. Expressing a point of departure, using the particle を, (out of ～ ; from ～)

	Place/vehicle	Particle
バス	を	おりて、電車に乗りかえた。

I got off the bus and transferred to a train.

駅(えき)を出たら、すぐ右(みぎ)にまがります。　When you leave the station, you immediately turn right.

去年(きょねん)大学を卒業(そつぎょう)しました。　I graduated from college last year.

つぎの駅(えき)で地下鉄(ちかてつ)をおりる。　I get off the subway at the next station.

- The particle を here indicates a place or vehicle from which one gets off or leaves.

C. Expressing scope or limit, using the particle で

Counter expression	Particle	
十分	で	帰ります。

I will return in 10 minutes.

あと一週間で休みです。	Vacation starts in another week.
そのみかんは五つで三百円です。	Those oranges are 300 yen for five.
このシャツはセールだったから、五百円で買ったよ。	This shirt was on sale, so I bought it for 500 yen.

- When the particle で is preceded by an expression for quantity, time, or amount, it indicates an extent or limit.

話してみましょう

A. Complete the following sentences by supplying the particles を (*route*), を (*out of*; *from*), で (*location*), で (*limit*), に (*goal*), or から (*from*).

Example

市役所(しやくしょ)の前／通(とお)る
市役所(しやくしょ)の前を通(とお)る。

1. 交差点(こうさてん)／止(と)まる
2. 特急(とっきゅう)／乗る
3. 東京駅(えき)／電車／おりる
4. 四つ目の角(かど)／左(ひだり)／まがる
5. 公園／歩く
6. 橋(はし)／わたる
7. 三十分ぐらい／着く
8. 横断歩道(おうだんほどう)／わたる
9. 東京駅(えき)／山の手線(せん)／中央線(ちゅうおうせん)／乗りかえる
10. 川／遊(あそ)ぶ
11. 急行(きゅうこう)／各駅停車(かくえきていしゃ)／乗りかえる
12. バスていの前／通(とお)る

B. Work in groups of four. First, fill in the blanks with the appropriate particles. Then one person should choose an expression from the box and act it out. The other members try to guess which expression was chosen. Use casual speech.

横断歩道(おうだんほどう)＿＿わたる	橋(はし)＿＿わたる	右(みぎ)／左(ひだり)＿＿まがる
タクシー／バス／地下鉄(ちかてつ)＿＿乗る		タクシー／バス／地下鉄(ちかてつ)＿＿おりる
バス／電車／地下鉄(ちかてつ)＿＿乗りかえる		〜つ目の角(かど)＿＿右(みぎ)／左(ひだり)＿＿まがる
〜の前＿＿通(とお)る	信号(しんごう)＿＿車＿＿止(と)める	大きい道路(どうろ)＿＿歩く／行く

Example

A: 横断歩道(おうだんほどう)をわたるの？
B: いや、ちがうよ。
A: じゃ、橋(はし)をわたるの？
B: うん、そうだよ。(male)／ええ、そうよ。(female)

C. Work with a partner. Choose a place in your town that your partner knows. Explain how to get there from the building you are in. Use the expressions in Exercise B as well as other expressions when necessary, but do not use the name of the place you have in mind. Your partner may ask questions except for the name of the place. He or she should try to guess the place on the basis of your directions. Use polite speech.

Example

A: この建物(たてもの)を出て、横断歩道(おうだんほどう)をわたります。すぐ右(みぎ)にまがって、10メートルぐらい歩きます。その建物(たてもの)は右側(みぎがわ)にあります。
B: 大学の本屋ですか。
A: はい、そうです。

II. Expressing chronology, using the て-form of the verb + から; Expressing conditions leading to set consequences, using the plain form + と

A. Expressing chronology, using the て-form of the verb + から

	Verb (て-form)		
電話を	して	から	行きます。

I will go after I've made a phone call.

地図(ちず)で道(みち)をしらべてから、行った方がいいよ。 You should check the street on a map before you leave.

家に帰ってから、何をしたんですか。	What did you do after you got home?
あの駐車場(ちゅうしゃじょう)に車を止めてから、歩いて行きましょう。	Let's park the car at that lot and walk.

- The て-form of the verb + から means *after doing* 〜. It is similar to the plain past affirmative form of the verb 〜+後で. However, the main clause cannot express an event or action beyond the control of the subject (or the speaker) when the て-form of the verb + から is used.

~~道(みち)をわたってから、川(かわ)が見える。~~	You can see a river after you cross the road.
道(みち)をわたった後で、川(かわ)が見える。	You can see a river after you cross the road.

- The subject of clauses with the て-form of the verb +から must be marked by the particle が if it is different from the subject of the main clause.

信号(しんごう)が青(あお)になってから、道(みち)をわたった方がいいですよ。
You should cross the road after the signal turns green.

その交差点(こうさてん)で一度止(と)まってから、左(ひだり)にまがって下さい。
Stop at the intersection, and then turn left.

B. Expressing conditions leading to set consequences, using the plain form + と

	Verb (plain present)		
左(ひだり)に	まがる	と	公園がすぐ先(さき)に見えます。

If you turn to your left, you can see the park just ahead.

冬になると、このへんはとても寒くなります。	When the winter comes, it gets very cold around here.
このボタンをおすと、電気がつきます。	When you push this button, the light comes on.
駅(えき)を出ると、目の前に銀行が見えます。	When you leave the station, you can see a bank in front of you.

- The conditional と can be translated as *if*, *when*, or *whenever*. と is preceded by the plain non-past form of verbs, adjectives, and the copula verb.

Noun + copula	同じだと 同じじゃないと
い -adjectives	短いと 短くないと

な -adjectives	静かだと 静かじゃないと
Verbs	通(とお)ると 通(とお)らないと

- The interpretation of a sentence with と depends on the tense of the main clause. If the sentence ends in the present tense, と indicates a condition for which the event in the main clause is the natural or automatic consequence. Therefore, this usage tends to be for facts or statements of habit. *When* or *whenever* is the closest in meaning.

- A sequence of two events connected by と expresses an inevitable or habitual cause-and-effect relationship. On the other hand, a sentence with the たら conditional expresses a temporal, accidental cause-and-effect relationship. In this sense, と conveys a general statement of fact rather than any specific event. For example, the sentence 冬になると、スキーに行きます indicates that the speaker always goes skiing in winter. In contrast, 冬になったら、スキーに行きます means that the speaker plans to go skiing *this* winter.

- The other difference between と and たら is that the main clause in sentences containing the と conditional cannot express intention, desire, or a request, invitation, or command made by the speaker.

橋(はし)をわたると、左側(ひだりがわ)に学校が見えます。	You will see the school on your left immediately after you cross the bridge.
橋(はし)をわたったら、左側(ひだりがわ)に学校が見えます。	Upon crossing the bridge, the school can be seen on your left.
地下鉄(ちかてつ)をおりたら、電話して下さい。	Please call me when you get off the subway.
~~地下鉄(ちかてつ)をおりると、電話して下さい。~~	Please call me as a result of getting off the subway.
山田さんが来たら、行きましょう。	Let's go as soon as Yamada-san comes.
~~山田さんが来ると、行きましょう。~~	Let's go as a result of Yamada-san's arrival.

- When the main clause is in the past tense, it expresses an unexpected or surprising event resulting from the condition. In this case, と and たら are interchangeable.

家に帰ると、母が来ていた。	When I went home, my mother was there.
家に帰ったら、母が来ていた。	When I went home, my mother was there.

話してみましょう

A. Transform the following sentences without changing the meaning, using 〜てから.

Example

シャワーをあびた後、朝ごはんを食べます。
シャワーをあびてから、朝ごはんを食べます。

1. 市役所(しやくしょ)に行く前に、郵便局に行きます。
2. そのビルの前を通(とお)った後で、右(みぎ)にまがります。

3. ドライブに行く前に、ガソリンスタンドで車にガソリンを入れます。
4. 地下鉄(ちかてつ)に乗る前に、切符(きっぷ)を買って下さい。
5. 大使館(たいしかん)に着いた後、三時間待った。
6. 信号(しんごう)が青(あお)になったら、横断歩道(おうだんほどう)をわたります。
7. この川(かわ)の水を飲む前に、水をしらべたほうがいいです。
8. 山手線(やまのてせん)で東京駅まで行った後、成田(なりた)行きの急行(きゅうこう)に乗りかえます。

B. Look at the map below and describe what you have to do to go from place to place as specified below, using てから.

Example

駅(えき)から交番(こうばん)に行く
駅(えき)前の大通(おおどお)りに出てから、すぐ右(みぎ)にまがります。

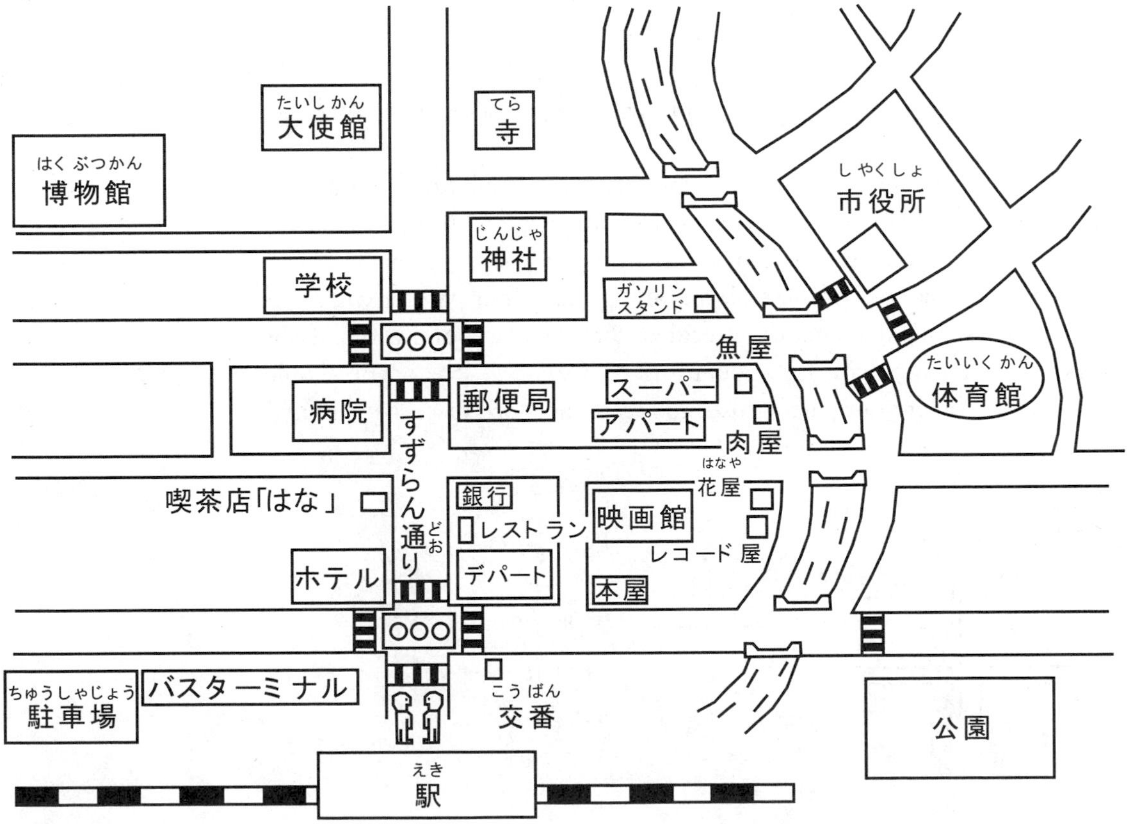

1. 駅(えき)からデパートに行く
2. 喫茶店(きっさてん)から郵便局に行く
3. 本屋から公園に行く
4. デパートから郵便局に行く
5. 公園からレストランに行く
6. ホテルから駐車場(ちゅうしゃじょう)に行く
7. 市役所(しやくしょ)から公園に行く
8. 神社(じんじゃ)から博物館(はくぶつかん)に行く

C. Look at the map in Exercise B. Describe what will be visible right after you perform the following activities.

Example

駅(えき)を出る

駅(えき)を出ると前に信号(しんごう)と横断歩道(おうだんほどう)が見える。

1. 駅(えき)を出て、右(みぎ)にまがります。
2. 駅(えき)を出て、横断歩道(おうだんほどう)をわたる。
3. 駅(えき)を出て、左(ひだり)にまがって、まっすぐ行く。
4. 駅(えき)を出て、すずらん通(どお)りを三つ目の角(かど)までまっすぐ行く。
5. 映画館の前の道(みち)を右(みぎ)にまっすぐ行く。
6. 公園の前の横断歩道(おうだんほどう)をわたって、まっすぐ行く。
7. デパートと本屋の間の道を通(とお)って、つきあたりまで行く。

D. Work with a partner. You are at the intersection at the bottom of the map below. You would like to know where the following are: bus stop, subway station, public phone, gas station, and parking lot. Ask your partner, who is a passerby, the locations of these objects and places. Your partner will have randomly assigned the numbers 1 through 5 to the places and will describe how to get to the location you ask about using 〜てから／〜と. You should then say which number your partner used to locate the place you asked about.

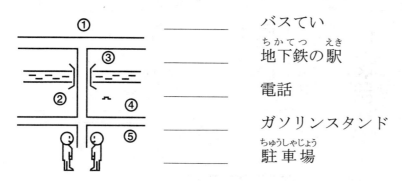

_______ バスてい

_______ 地下鉄(ちかてつ)の駅(えき)

_______ 電話

_______ ガソリンスタンド

_______ 駐車場(ちゅうしゃじょう)

Example

B has chosen location 1 for the public phone.

A:　このへんに電話がありますか。

B:　ええ、まっすぐ行くと、橋(はし)がありますから、橋(はし)をわたって下さい。わたると、目の前にあります。

A:　じゃあ、この地図だと一番の所ですか。

B:　ええ、そうです。

III. Expressing possibility, using the dictionary form of the verb + ことが出来る

	Verb (dictionary)	Noun	Particle	
山田さんの家まで電車を乗りかえないで	行く	こと	が	出来ますか。

Is it possible to get to Yamada-san's house without changing trains?

	Verb (dictionary)	Noun	Particle	
いいえ、	(行く	こと	は)	出来ません。

No, it isn't.

山田：　この道(みち)に入ることが出来ますか。
Can I pull into this street?

川口：　いいえ、ここは一方通行(いっぽうつうこう) (one-way street) だから、入れません。
No, you cannot because this is a one-way street.

東京駅(えき)で中央線(ちゅうおうせん)に乗りかえることが出来るよ。
You can transfer to the Chuo Line at Tokyo Station.

ここから田中さんの家までは近(ちか)いから、歩いて行くことが出来るよ。
Since Tanaka-san's house is near here, you can get there on foot.

- The dictionary form of the verb + ことが出来る means *can* or *be able to do* in English. It is similar to the potential form, indicating possibility or capability depending on the context, but it is usually a little more formal than the potential form and tends to be used to make objective statements about whether doing something is possible or not.

話してみましょう

A. Answer the questions using the dictionary form of the verb + ことが出来る.

Example

アメリカでは日本のテレビが見られますか。
ええ、大きい町なら見ることが出来ますよ。

1. 日本では二十さいでおさけが飲めますか。
2. アメリカ人ならだれでも大統領(だいとうりょう) (president) になれますか。
3. 十一さいならディズニーランドに安く入れますか。
4. 日本では十六さいになると、車の運転(うんてん)が出来ますか。
5. オーストラリアではスキーが出来ますか。
6. メキシコでは十ドルで車が借りられますか。

B. Work as a class. The following are traffic signs used in Japan. Find a person who knows what each sign means and write the meaning and the name of the person.

Example

A: あのう、このサインのいみ、何ですか。
B: ここでタクシーに乗ることが出来るんですよ。
A: ああ、そうですか。

1

2

3

4

5

6

7

8

9

C. Work with a partner. You are working for a travel bureau in Kyoto, and your partner is a tourist. Use the map your instructor will provide and the train and bus timetable on the following page to make recommendations about where your partner might go and how to get there.

Example

A: 今日一日京都(きょうと)かんこうをしたいんですが、どこへ行ったらいいでしょう？

B: そうですね。銀閣寺(ぎんかくじ)はどうですか。

A: 銀閣寺(ぎんかくじ)って何ですか。

B: とても有名(ゆうめい)な古いお寺(てら)ですよ。

A: 歩いて行くことが出来ますか。

B: いいえ、少し遠(とお)いですからね。でも、バスで行くことは出来ますよ。

A: バスだと何分ぐらいかかりますか。

B: 三十分ぐらいです。

JR奈良線(ならせん)

京都駅(きょうとえき) ¤ 宇治駅(うじえき)　(20分ぐらいかかる)

10分～20分に一本 (trains leave every 10 to 20 minutes)

市(し)バス (City bus)		かかる時間	Interval
5番	京都駅(きょうとえき) ¤ 銀閣寺(ぎんかくじ)	30分ぐらい	30分
206番	京都駅(きょうとえき) ¤ 東山通り(ひがしやまどお) to 知恩院(ちおんいん)、八坂神社(やさかじんじゃ)	20分ぐらい	5分～10分
100番	京都駅(きょうとえき) ¤ ぎおん、平安神宮(へいあんじんぐう)	20分ぐらい	20分
205番	京都駅(きょうとえき) ¤ 銀閣寺(ぎんかくじ)	40分ぐらい	5分
75番	京都駅(きょうとえき) ¤ 映画村(えいがむら)	60分ぐらい	30分

IV. Expressing limited degree, using だけ～ affirmative or しか～ negative

A. Using だけ～ affirmative (just, only)

Noun	Suffix	(Particle)	Verb (affirmative)
山田さん	だけ	(が)	来ました。

Only Yamada-san came.

道子(みちこ)：　まだ歩くの。
Do we still have to walk?

まもる：　もう少しだけ。あと百メートルだけ。
Just a little more. It's only a hundred meters.

特急(とっきゅう)は一番線(せん)にだけ来ます。
The limited express comes to Track 1 only.

昨日(きのう)はつかれていたので、宿題だけしてすぐ寝ました。
I was so tired yesterday, I just did my homework and went straight to bed.

- The word だけ must follow a noun or a quantity expression.
- When だけ is used with a noun, particles such as で and に may be placed either before or after it. Exceptions are particles が and を, which must be placed after だけ or not used at all.

図書館だけで勉強します。　or　図書館でだけ勉強します。
I study only at libraries.

大きい道(みち)だけにあります。　or　大きい道(みち)にだけあります。
It is on large streets only.

本だけを買いました。　or　本だけ買いました。
I bought only books.

山田さんだけが来ました。　or　山田さんだけ来ました。
Only Yamada-san came.

B. Using しか〜 negative (only)

Noun	Suffix	Verb (negative)
山田さん	しか	来ませんでした。

Only Yamada-san came. (literally: other than Yamada-san, no one else came)

ここは右(みぎ)にしかまがれません。　You can turn only to the right here.

山手線(やまのてせん)には各駅停車(かくえきていしゃ)しかないよ。　The Yamanote Line has only local trains.

ここから市役所(しやくしょ)までは歩いて五分しかかからない。　It takes only five minutes to walk to the city hall from here.

- Like だけ, しか also means *only*, but it must be used in sentences with negative endings. Also like だけ, しか is used with nouns and quantity expressions.

- When しか is used with a noun, the particle associated with it must precede it. The particles が and を are omitted, but other particles remain except for the に of location, which may be omitted.

山田さんしかいません。	Only Yamada-san is (here).
肉しか食べません。	I eat only meat.
ここ（に）しかありません。	It exists only here.
私は山田さんに大学でしか会いません。	I meet Yamada-san only on campus.

- しか implies *only* ～*and nothing else*, and sounds more emphatic than だけ. Therefore, しか is often used when the speaker finds less than expected.

一万円しかありません。	I have only 10,000 yen, and that is all. (I should have more.)
一万円だけあります。	I have only 10,000 yen.

話してみましょう

A. Answer the questions, using the expressions in parentheses and だけ or しか.

Example

昨日(きのう)たくさん人が来ていた？（高田さん）
いいえ、高田さんだけが来ていたよ。
いいえ、高田さんしか来ていなかったよ。

1. この電車、東京駅(えき)のほかに (other than) どこに止(と)まりますか？(なりた)
2. 新宿(しんじゅく)から横浜(よこはま)までいくつ乗りかえがありますか。（一つ）
3. どこで中央線(ちゅうおうせん)に乗りかえられますか。（東京駅(えき)）
4. えんぴつを貸してくれませんか。（一本）
5. 今週はずっと休みなの？（金曜日）
6. 昨日(きのう)たくさん電話があった？（田中さん）
7. このへんに魚屋はありませんか。（スーパー）

B. Look at the picture describing a transportation network between cities. Tell how you can get to different stations by using express, limited express, or regular trains. Note that 普通(ふつう) is used interchangeably with 各駅停車(かくえきていしゃ).

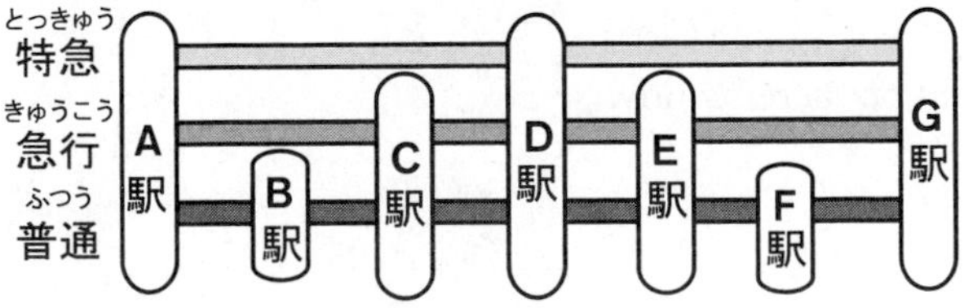

Example

A駅(えき)からB駅(えき)までは各駅停車(かくえきていしゃ)／普通(ふつう)でしか行けません。そして、A駅(えき)からC駅(えき)までは各駅停車(かくえきていしゃ)／普通(ふつう)と急行(きゅうこう)で行くことができます。

C. Work with a partner. Following the picture in Exercise B, draw a picture to show how different stations are connected through express, limited express, or regular trains, using the basic drawing provided by your instructor. Ask each other how to get to different stations by express, limited express, or regular train, and recreate your partner's drawing.

Example

A: A駅(えき)からB駅(えき)まで急行(きゅうこう)で行くことが出来ますか。

B: いいえ、各駅停車(かくえきていしゃ)でしか行くことは出来ません。

A: じゃあ、A駅(えき)からC駅(えき)まで急行(きゅうこう)で行くことが出来ますか。

B: はい、出来ます。

V. Expressing presuppositions, using the plain form + はず

		Verb (plain affirmative)	Dependent noun	
この電車は	新宿駅(しんじゅくえき)に	止(と)まる	はず	だ。

This train is supposed to/should stop at Shinjuku Station.

休みは昨日(きのう)じゃなかったはずです。
The day off was not supposed to have been yesterday.
あの人はまだ学生のはずです。
That person should still be a student.

川上： パーティはもう始まりましたか。
Has the party begun?
木村(きむら)： ええ、もう始まっているはずですよ。
Yes, it should have begun by now.
鈴木(すずき)： あのう、小包がとどいていないんですけど。
Excuse me, but my package has not arrived yet.
さとう： 先週送ったから、もうとどいているはずですけど。
Since I sent it last week, it should be there by now . . .

- はず indicates the speaker's judgment about the likelihood of an action or event happening, and can be translated as *I expect that* ～, *it is expected that* ～, *ought to* ～, or ～ *is supposed to* ～. The judgment is based on some objective information or knowledge. That is, the speaker thinks that the event or action ought to take place, if his or her interpretation of the information or knowledge is correct. In this sense, はず is very different from だろう, which expresses a subjective speculation.
- はず is grammatically a noun, but it never stands on its own. Therefore, the preceding verb and adjective forms must be identical to those in other instances where verbs and adjectives are used to modify nouns.

Copula verbs		**な -adjectives**	
急行(きゅうこう)の 急行(きゅうこう)じゃない 急行(きゅうこう)だった 急行(きゅうこう)じゃなかった	はずだ	元気な 元気じゃない 元気だった 元気じゃなかった	はずだ
い -adjectives		**Verbs**	
長い 長くない 長かった 長くなかった	はずだ	運転(うんてん)できる 運転(うんてん)できない 運転(うんてん)できた 運転(うんてん)できなかった	はずだ

- The subject of a sentence containing はず cannot be the speaker. Although it is possible to say *I'm supposed to do* ～ in English, はず cannot be used in this sense. Use ～なければならない／なくてはいけない instead.

私は明日東京に行かなければなりません。	I must go to Tokyo tomorrow.
田中さんは明日東京に行かなければなりません。	Tanaka-san must go to Tokyo tomorrow.
~~私は明日東京に行くはずです~~。	I am supposed to go to Tokyo tomorrow.
田中さんは明日東京に行くはずです。	Tanaka-san is supposed to go to Tokyo tomorrow.

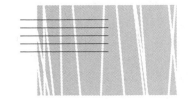

話してみましょう

A. Look at the following train and subway map. Answer the questions using はず.

Example

山手線(やまのてせん)で上野(うえの)に行けますか。
ええ、行けるはずです。

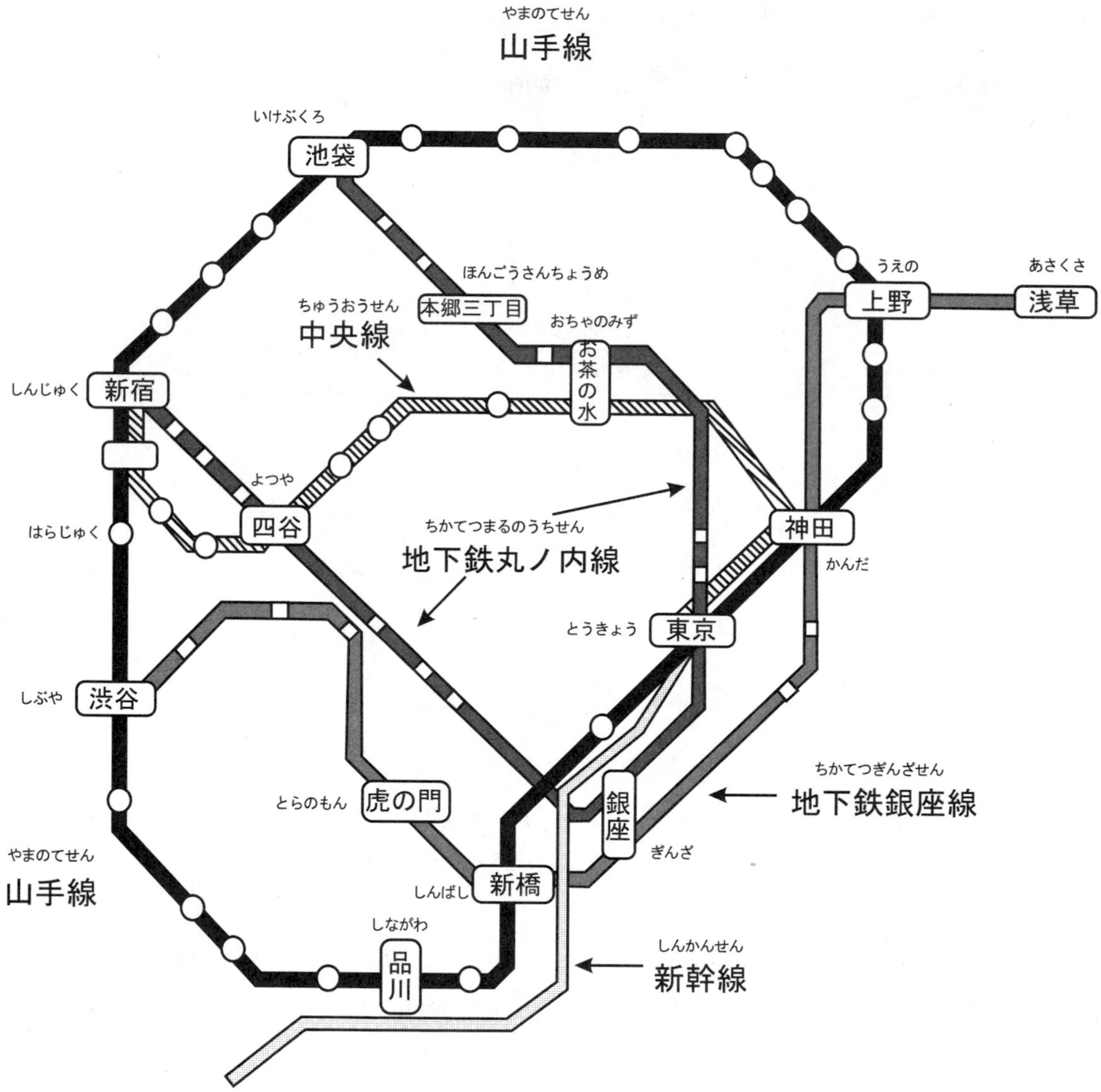

1. 山手線(やまのてせん)であさくさに行けますか。
2. 中央線(ちゅうおうせん)で神田(かんだ)のつぎの駅(えき)は何ですか。
3. まるのうちせんは銀座(ぎんざ)を通(とお)りますか。
4. 新宿(しんじゅく)でまるのうちせんに乗れますか。
5. 新宿(しんじゅく)で銀座線(ぎんざせん)に乗れますか。
6. 上野(うえの)で山手線(やまのてせん)から地下鉄(ちかてつ)に乗りかえられますか。
7. 上野(うえの)で山手線(やまのてせん)から中央線(ちゅうおうせん)に乗りかえられますか。

B. Based on the following information, make sentences that express an inference or judgment, using はず.

Example

天気予報(よほう)を見たら明日は晴れだと書いてありました。
<u>明日は晴れのはずです。</u>

1. 山田さんは昨日交通事故(きのうこうつうじこ)で入院しました。
2. スミスさんは日本に十年住んでいました。
3. キムさんは毎日午後九時に寝ます。
4. 京都(きょうと)は日本で一番古い町の一つです。
5. ビバリーヒルズには有名な人がたくさん住んでいます。
6. ハワイは一年中気候(きこう)がよくてきれいです。

C. Work as a class. Ask your classmates what time they leave school and how long it takes to get from school to their home. Then confirm the approximate time of arrival and complete the chart your instructor will give you.

Example

A: 今日は何時ごろ家に帰るの？
B: 五時ごろ帰るつもり。
A: 家までどのくらいかかるの？
B: 歩いて、十五分か二十分ぐらいかな。(male) ／
歩いて、十五分か二十分ぐらいかしら。(female)
A: じゃあ。五時二十分ごろには家に着くはずだね。(male)
／じゃあ。五時二十分ごろには家に着くはずね。(female)

漢字

送(おく)りがな

The word **okurigana** refers to the **hiragana** that follow adjectives and verbs written in **kanji**. For example, きい in 大きい and く in 行く are **okurigana**. Two main functions of **okurigana** are (1) to indicate inflectional endings of adjectives and verbs and (2) to minimize erroneous readings of **kanji**.

The following summarizes the conventions for the use of **okurigana** in modern Japanese.

A. **Okurigana** are used for inflectional endings of verbs and adjectives.

う-verbs:	行く　行かない　行きます　行ける . . .
	買う　買わない　買います　買って . . .
る-verbs:	見る　見ない　見ます
	食べる　食べない　食べます
	教える　教えない　教えます
い-adjectives:	古い　古くない　古かった
	強い　強くない　強かった
な-adjectives:	元気な　元気じゃない　元気だった

There are cases where the **okurigana** include more than just the final ending. These cases need to be learned individually.

大きい　大きくない　大きかった
新しい　新しくない　新しかった (All い-adjectives ending in ～しい follow this pattern.)
静かな　静かじゃない　静かだった

B. When two or more words are related in meaning and have similar pronunciations, such as intransitive/transitive verb pairs, the identical portion of the pronunciation is written in **kanji** and the rest in **okurigana**.

起(お)こす　起(お)きる　寝(ね)る　寝(ね)かす　上(あ)がる　上(あ)げる　始(はじ)まる　始(はじ)める
止(と)まる　止(と)める

C. When the same **kanji** is used in different words (which may or may not be related in meaning), **okurigana** are used to indicate the correct pronunciation.

着(つ)く	(九時に東京に着きました。)	着(き)る	(セーターを着ています。)
出(で)る	(家を出る)	出(だ)す	(手紙を出す)
後(あと)	(ごはんの後で)	後(うし)ろ	(銀行の後ろ)
三(さん)	(ペンが三本)	三(みっ)つ	(りんごを三つ)

Kanji	Meaning	Readings	Examples
右	right	ウ/みぎ	角(かど)を右(みぎ)にまがる。映画館の右側(みぎがわ)
左	left	サ/ひだり	駐車場(ちゅうしゃじょう)の先の角(かど)を左(ひだり)にまがってください。
側	side	ソク/がわ	薬屋(くすりや)の右側(みぎがわ)　道のこちら側(がわ)
横	side, width	オウ/よこ	いすの横(よこ)にねこがいる。横断歩道(おうだんほどう)をわたる。
近	near, close	キン/ちか(い)	動物園(どうぶつえん)は博物館(はくぶつかん)に近(ちか)い。
遠	far	エン/とお(い)	大学から遠(とお)い　遠(とお)い所から来る
向	to face, to turn	コウ/む(かい) む(く)	銀行の向(む)かい側(がわ)に郵便局があります。
急	to hurry, sudden	キュウ/いそ(ぐ)	特急(とっきゅう)はこの駅(えき)に止(と)まりません。でも、急行(きゅうこう)は止(と)まります。
赤	red	セキ、シャク/あか、あか(い)	信号(しんごう)が赤(あか)になる。赤(あか)い建物(たてもの)がある。
青	blue, green	セイ、ショウ/あお、あお(い)	信号(しんごう)が青(あお)になったら、わたる。青(あお)い自動車(じどうしゃ)

黄 黄

yellow オウ/き

黄色(きいろ)が好きです。黄色(きいろ)い自転車(じてんしゃ)　信号(しんごう)が黄色(きいろ)になったり、止(と)まります。

緑 緑

green リョク/みどり

緑(みどり)色のぼうしをかっぶている。

黒 黒

black コク/くろ（い）

大きい黒(くろ)い車　黒(くろ)いスーツ　黒(くろ)い橋(はし)があります。

白 白

white ハク/しろ（い）

白(しろ)いワインを飲む　すてきな白(しろ)い教会

駅 駅

station えき

市役所(しやくしょ)は駅(えき)に近(ちか)いですよ。

橋 橋

bridge キョウ/はし

橋(はし)をわたって、左側(ひだりがわ)です。

道 道

road, way ドウ/みち

道(みち)の向(む)こう側(がわ)にある。道路(どうろ)をわたる。

交 交

to be mixed, to cross, to associate with コウ

交差点(こうさてん)の近(ちか)くに交番(こうばん)がある。

差 差

difference サ/さ（す）

大きい交差点(こうさてん)

点 点

point, marks, dot テン

テストの点(てん)が悪かった。交差点(こうさてん)

Kanji	Meaning	Readings	Examples
遊	to play	ユウ/あそ（ぶ）	これから遊園地(ゆうえんち)に遊(あそ)びに行きませんか。
育	to bring up, to raise, to grow	イク/そだ（つ）、そだ（てる）	体育館(たいいくかん)の先を右(みぎ)にまがってください。専攻(せんこう)は教育(きょういく)です。
角	corner, angle	カク/かど	二つ目の角(かど)を右(みぎ)にまがる。
場	place, situation	ジョウ/ば	きれいな場所(ばしょ)　駐車場(ちゅうしゃじょう)の前
自	self, auto	ジ	自動車(じどうしゃ)　自転車(じてんしゃ)　自分(じぶん)
転	to turn	テン	自転車(じてんしゃ)に乗ることができます。自動車(じどうしゃ)の運転(うんてん)ができます。
動	to move, motion	ドウ/うご（く）	自動車(じどうしゃ)が動(うご)かない。動物園(どうぶつえん)に行く。
通	to go along, to pass through, to commute	ツウ/とお（る）とお（り）、かよ（う）	公園(こうえん)を通(とお)る。駅前(えきまえ)の大通(おおどお)り
運	to carry, to transport	ウン/はこ（ぶ）	車の運転(うんてん)ができる。体育館(たいいくかん)で運動(うんどう)する。
止	to stop	シ/と（まる）と（める）	信号(しんごう)で止(と)まる。車を止(と)める。

新しい読み方

新宿（しんじゅく）　大使館（たいしかん）　手前（てまえ）　先（さき）　西口（にしぐち）

練習

下の文を読んで下さい。

1. 明日は動物園に行ってから、遊園地で遊ぼうと思っています。
2. 道の右側にも左側にも店がたくさんあります。
3. この公園には緑が多いですね。駅からも遠くないし、便利（べんり）です。
4. 二つ目の角を右にまがると、橋があります。橋をわたると、左側に駅があります。
5. オーストラリアでは自動車は道の左側を走らなければなりません。
6. 広（ひろし）くんは自転車に乗れますが、まだうまく止まることが出来ません。
7. 赤い電車は特急で、青い電車は急行です。特急はこの駅には止まりません。
8. 交差点の近くに高くて黒いビルがあります。その向かい側にある白いレストランに七時に来て下さい。
9. （駅で）白線の後ろで電車を待って下さい。
10. A: 黒か青のペン、持ってない。
    B: ごめん、赤しかないわ。

上手な読み方

東京大学へ行く　(Getting to Tokyo University)

読む前に

A. 下の新幹線（しんかんせん）の時刻表（じこくひょう） (time schedule) を見て質問に答えて下さい。

1. 新大阪（しんおおさか）から東京まで一番はやい新幹線（しんかんせん）はどれですか。
2. 新大阪（しんおおさか）から京都（きょうと）と新横浜（しんよこはま）に行きたいのですが、どの新幹線（しんかんせん）に乗ることが出来ますか。
3. 一時ごろ東京に着きたいのですが、何時の新幹線（しんかんせん）に乗ったらいいでしょうか。

	ひかり 200	のぞみ 300	ひかり 126	こだま 404	ひかり 228	こだま 408	ひかり 032	ひかり 232	のぞみ 006	ひかり 034	ひかり 086	のぞみ 010
新大阪（しんおおさか）	6:00	6:12	6:43	9:00	9:57	10:00	10:17	10:39	10:54	11:17	11:26	11:54
京都（きょうと）	6:17	6:27	7:00	9:16	10:17	10:17	10:41	10:56	11:10	11:34	11:44	12:10
名古屋（なごや）	7:07	7:05	7:57	10:15	10:58	11:15	11:18	11:53	11:48	12:18	12:28	12:48
	|	|	|	○	|	○	|	|	|	|	|	|
	|	|	○	○	|	○	○	○	|	|	|	|
	|	|	|	○	|	○	|	|	|	|	|	|
新横浜（しんよこはま）	|	|	9:34	12:53	|	13:53	12:56	13:28	|	13:56	|	|
東京（とうきょう）	8:56	8:42	9:52	13:10	12:52	14:10	13:14	13:45	13:24	14:14	14:38	14:24

B. 310ページの地下鉄と電車のルートマップを見ながら、答えて下さい。新幹線（しんかんせん）で東京に来ました。つぎの所にはどう行ったら、いいですか。

1. 池袋（いけぶくろ）　2. 上野（うえの）　3. 新宿（しんじゅく）　4. 渋谷（しぶや）

読んでみましょう 1

パークさんは大阪（おおさか）大学の大学院で勉強している留学生です。あさって研究のために東京大学の大山（おおやま）先生に会いに行く予定です。大山先生は三時ごろ研究室（しつ）にいらっしゃるはずですから、パークさんは三時少し前には東京大学に着いていなければなりません。大山先生の助手（じょしゅ） (assistant) の下田（しもだ）さんが、東京駅から東大（とうだい）までの行き方をファックスで送ってきました。

分かりましたか

質問に日本語で答えて下さい。

1. パークさんは今どこに住んでいますか。
2. パークさんはいつ東京に行きますか。
3. パークさんは何時にどこに行かなければなりませんか。
4. だれからファックスが来ましたか。

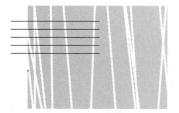

読んでみましょう２

九月十日

パークさんへ、

あさっての三時に大山先生が研究室でお待ちだそうです。東京駅から大学までの行き方を書いておきます。何か分からないことがあったら、私（下田（しもだ））に電話して下さい。番号は０３－１２３４－５６７８です。それではあさってお会いしましょう。

東京駅で地下鉄丸ノ内線（まるのうちせん）の池袋（いけぶくろ）行きに乗りかえます。そして、本郷三丁目（ほんごうちょうめ）という駅でおりて下さい。四つ目の駅です。電車をおりたら、本郷（ほんごう）通りの方に出る出口に行って下さい。本郷（ほんごう）通りはとても大きい道路（どうろ）です。

本郷（ほんごう）通りを左の方に行くと、大きい交差点があります。その交差点を通って、まっすぐ行くと、右側に赤い門（もん）(gate) が見えてきます。門（もん）の前に横断（おうだん）歩道がありますから、道路をわたって下さい。中に入ったら、すぐ左にまがります。大山先生の研究室（しつ）は門（もん）から二番目の建物（たてもの）で、三階の３０５号室です。本郷三丁目（ほんごうちょうめ）の駅から大学までは歩いて十分ぐらいかかります。

下田（しもだ）

分かりましたか

A. 310 ページのルートマップを見て、パークさんが乗る電車と駅に○をつけて下さい。おりる駅もさがして下さい。

B. The picture on the following page shows the subway station and Hongodori. Draw a line from the station to the approximate location of Professor Oyama's office.

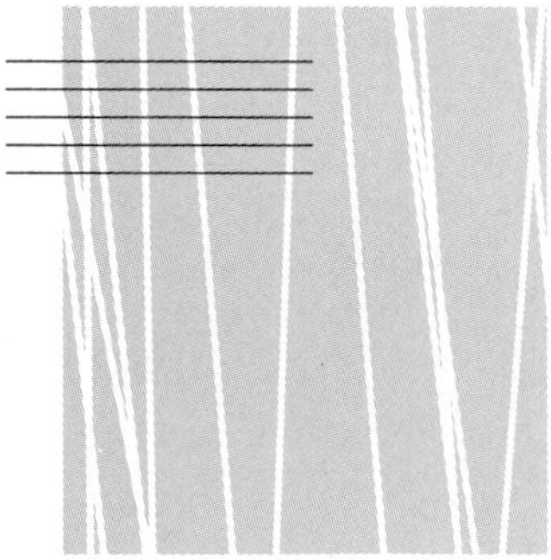

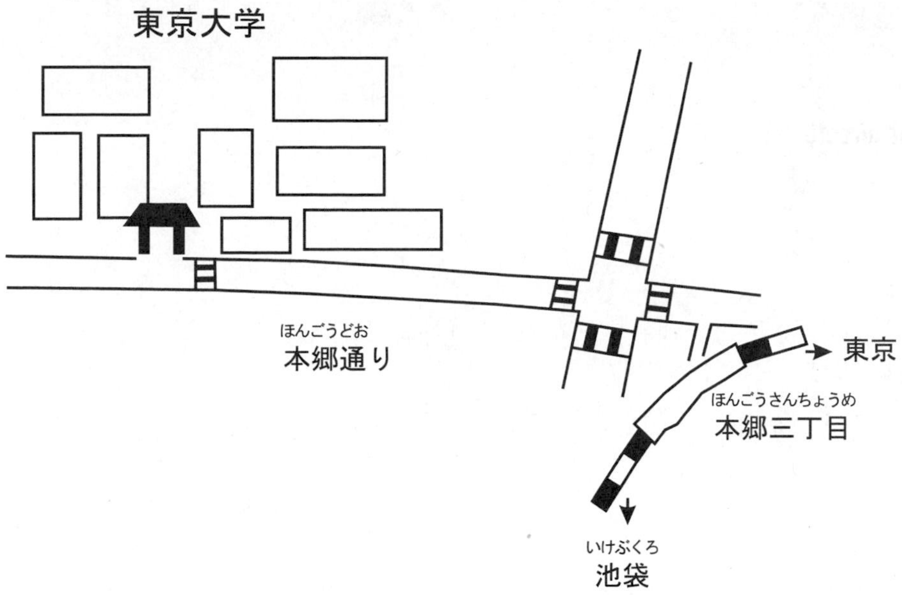

C. 地下鉄(ちかてつ)では一つの駅から次(つぎ)の駅まで三分ぐらいかかります。東京駅から東京大学まで何分ぐらいかかるか言って下さい。

D. 三時に大山先生の研究室に行くためには、パークさんは何時の新幹線(しんかんせん)に乗らなくてはいけませんか。317ページの新幹線(しんかんせん)の予定表(ひょう)を使って言って下さい。

読んだ後で

Park-san needs to send a fax to Shimoda-san to thank him for the directions and to confirm his visit. Complete the fax form your instructor will give you, being sure to include the following information.

1. Date.
2. Expression of thanks.
3. The time the train leaves Osaka.
4. Arrival time at Tokyo.
5. Estimated arrival time at Tokyo University.
6. What Park-san will do if he cannot get there on time.
7. Say that he is looking forward to meeting with them. (お会い出来るのをたのしみにしています。)

上手な聞き方

道(みち)を聞く (Asking for directions)

聞く前に

質問に答えて下さい。

1. どこかへの行き方を説明(せつめい)する時、どんな場所や目印(めじるし) (landmark) を使いますか。
2. どこかへの行き方を説明(せつめい)する時、どんな言葉(ことば)や文法を使いますか。

STUDENT

聞いてみましょう

下の地図を見て下さい。地図には建物(たてもの)がかいてありません。テープを聞きながら、建物(たてもの)の名前を地図に書いて下さい。

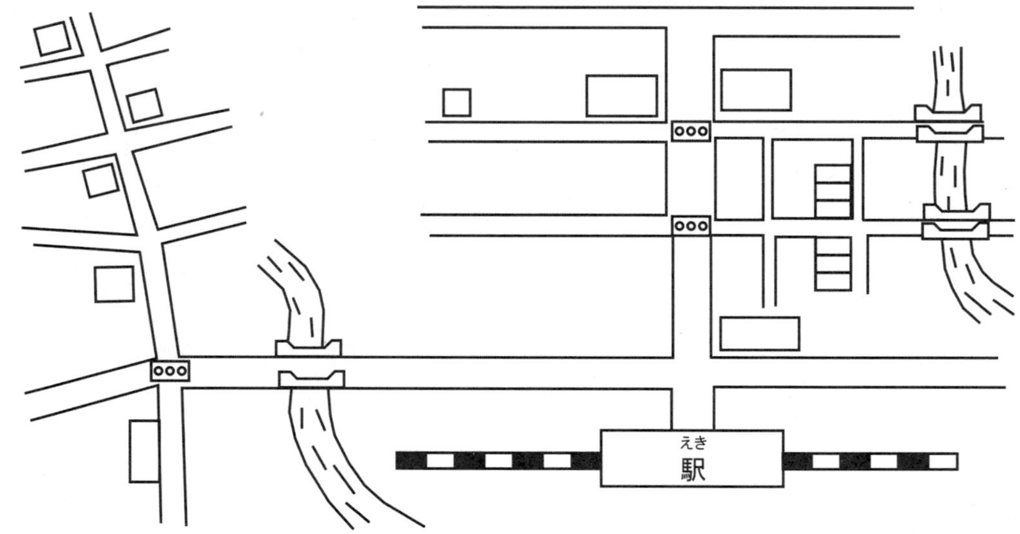

Example

A: あのう、このへんにそば屋がありますか。

B: 駅を出ると目の前に大きい道路(どうろ)があります。そば屋は道路(どうろ)をわたったところの右側の角にありますよ。

聞いた後で

Look at the map used for 聞いてみましょう. Write how to get from the station to the places you wrote names for.

駅と電車のアナウンス　(Announcements at stations and in trains)

聞く前に

A. Look at the photo of a platform in a train station. Tell what kind of signs you see in the picture. Also, guess why there is a white line（白線（はくせん））on the platform.

B. 下の質問に答えて下さい。

1. 駅でどんなアナウンスを聞いたことがありますか。
2. どんなアナウンスがあったらいいと思いますか。
3. 電車の中でどんなアナウンスを聞いたことがありますか。

聞いてみましょう

STUDENT

A. 日本の駅や電車の中でもいろいろなアナウンスがあります。次のアナウンスを聞いて何のためのアナウンスか考えて下さい。

Example

二番線（ばんせん）に電車がまいります。あぶないですから、白線（はくせん）の後ろにさがってお待ち下さい。

<u>二番線（ばんせん）に電車が来ます。</u>

1. ______________________________

2. ______________________________

3. ______________________________

4. ______________________________

B. もう一度アナウンスを聞いて、下の質問に答えて下さい。

1. どんな電車が来ますか。______________________

この電車はこの駅に止まりますか。______________

2. この電車はどこ行きですか。__________________

東京駅に行く人は何番線(ばんせん)の電車に乗りますか。

____

3. どんな電車ですか。__________________________

この電車はどこ行きですか。____________________

いつ出ますか。________________________________

4. この電車が止まる駅はどれですか。

Circle all that apply. 四谷(よつや) 信濃町(しなのまち) 千駄ケ谷(せんだがや) 代々木(よよぎ) 新宿(しんじゅく)

この電車が止まらない駅でおりたい人はどうしますか。

聞いた後で

Brown-san has not understood the announcements in 聞いてみましょう, so he asks you for help. Complete the following dialogues between Brown-san and you.

Example

ブラウン： あのう、今のアナウンスよく分からなかったんですが。

あなた： ああ、二番線(ばんせん)に電車が来るそうですよ。

ブラウン： ああ、そうですか。どうも有難(ありがと)うございます。

1. ブラウン： あのう、今のアナウンス、何て言ったんですか。
あなた： ____________________
ブラウン： あ、そうですか。どうも。

2. ブラウン： あのう、今のアナウンス、____________。
あなた： ____________________
ブラウン： あ、そうですか。その電車は東京に止まりますか。
あなた： ____________________

3. ブラウン： あのう、今のアナウンス、____________、この新幹線(しんかんせん)どこ行きですか。
あなた： ____________________
ブラウン： あ、そうですか。いつ出るんでしょうか。
あなた： ____________________

4. ブラウン: あのう、今のアナウンス、よく分からなかったんですけど、代々木(よよぎ)へはこの電車で行けますよね？
あなた： ____________________
ブラウン: あ、そうですか。あ、じゃあつぎの駅でおりなきゃいけないんですね。どうも有難(ありがと)うございます。

STUDENT

DICT-A-CONVERSATION

スミスさんはフランス大使館(たいしかん)をさがしています。交番でおまわりさん (police officer) に聞いています。

スミス： ____________________
おまわりさん： ____________________
____
スミス： ____________________
おまわりさん： ____________________
スミス： ____________________
おまわりさん： ____________________
スミス： ____________________
おまわりさん： ____________________

聞き上手話し上手

道の聞き方と教え方　(How to ask for directions and how to give them)

Japanese people do not use street names or terms like *north* and *south* when they give directions. Except for a few cities such as Kyoto, streets in Japanese cities run in various directions, so it is often difficult to orient oneself in terms of north, south, east, or west. Also, most streets do not have names. Japanese people thus use relative locational terms such as right and left, number of blocks, public facilities, large buildings, and other noticeable landmarks. Many people use trains and subways, where available. It is very common to give directions that start from a train station. When it is necessary to transfer to different lines or a different means of transportation, it is also necessary to explain where the transport being transferred to is going, where to get off, or where to transfer, as shown in the following example:

> 東京駅で三鷹(みたか)行きの中央線(ちゅうおうせん)に乗って、四つ目の駅が新宿(しんじゅく)ですから、そこでおりて下さい。新宿(しんじゅく)で中野(なかの)行きのバスに乗りかえて、二つ目でおりて下さい。(Take the Chuo Line Mitaka train at Tokyo Station and get off at Shinjuku Station, which is the fourth station from Tokyo Station. Then, at Shinjuku, transfer to the Nakano bus, and get off at the second stop.)

Common expressions used in asking for directions:

あのう、すみません。アメリカ大使館(たいしかん)に行きたいんですけど。
Excuse me, but I want to go to the American Embassy.

あのう、すみません、このへんにガソリンスタンドはありますか。
Excuse me, but is there a gas station around here?

あのう、すみません、郵便局はどこですか。
Excuse me, but where is the post office?

あのう、すみません、新宿(しんじゅく)まで行きたいんですが、どう行ったらいいでしょうか。
Excuse me. I want to go to Shinjuku. How can I get there?

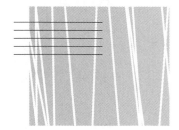

Use the following expressions to ask how long it takes to get to a specified place:

東京駅から新宿(しんじゅく)までバスで何分ぐらい／どのぐらいかかりますか。
How many minutes/how long does it take from Tokyo Station to Shinjuku by bus?

歩いてどのぐらいかかりますか。
How long does it take by foot?

大阪(おおさか)から東京まで新幹線(しんかんせん)で何時間ぐらい／どのぐらいかかりますか。
How many hours/how long does it take from Osaka to Tokyo by the Shinkansen Express?

To ask for specific buses, lines, tracks, or terminals, use:

新宿(しんじゅく)行きの電車は何線(なにせん)ですか。
Which tracks do the Shinjuku trains leave from?

中央線(ちゅうおうせん)の新宿(しんじゅく)行きは何番線(なんばんせん)ですか。
Which track is the Chuo Line train bound for Shinjuku?

新宿(しんじゅく)行きのバスはどれですか。
Which bus goes to Shinjuku?

新宿(しんじゅく)行きのバスはそのターミナルから出ますか。
Does the Shinjuku bus leave from that terminal?

Finally, it is very important to confirm your understanding using the confirmatory expressions introduced in Chapter 5 as well as the あいづち in Chapters 2 and 3 in Volume 1.

STUDENT

A. Listen to this series of six answers to questions. On a separate sheet of paper, make an appropriate question asking for directions for the answer.

B. Work with a partner. Ask your partner how to get from one place on the map on page 301 to some other place. (Decide where to start first.) Take notes on what your partner says, but don't look at the map. Make sure to confirm your understanding. Then look at the map and verify the locations.

C. Work with a partner. Ask your partner how to get from the station to various places on the map used with Exercise B. Take notes on what your partner says, but don't look at the map. Make sure to confirm your understanding, using あいづち and other confirmatory expressions. Then use your notes to trace a route on the map to verify what you have understood.

総合練習（そうごう）

A. 私の家

1. Work with a partner. Invite your partner for dinner and give him or her directions to your home. First, decide on a starting point. Draw a map and give directions as though you were in Japan, without using street names or expressions such as north, south, east, or west. Your partner should take notes while confirming the directions. Then he or she should also draw a map. Compare the two maps to verify how accurately you have given the directions.
2. Repeat the above activity, using another local place as a destination (parent's house, grandparent's house, friend's house, etc.).

B. 成田空港（なりたくうこう）で (At Narita Airport)

1. Brown-san and Jones-san have just arrived at Narita Airport. Jones-san calls up his Japanese friend. Listen to the conversation between Jones-san and the friend and identify the friend's name and why Jones called her.

   STUDENT

   名前：____

   理由（りゆう） (reason)：__________________________________

2. Listen to the conversation again and answer the following questions.
   1. ジョーンズさんはどこに行きますか。
   2. ジョーンズさんは何でそこに行くつもりですか。
   3. ジョーンズさんの友達によると京成線（けいせいせん）とJR線（せん）とどちらのほうが便利（べんり）ですか。どちらのほうがはやいですか。

3. Work with a partner. You and your partner have just arrived at Narita Airport. You are staying at the Plaza Hotel in Shinjuku (see the map on page 293). Look at the map and train information about the train services from Narita to downtown Tokyo on page 327. Discuss with your partner how you would go to Shinjuku. Use the map on page 310 for detailed information on the Tokyo metro area.

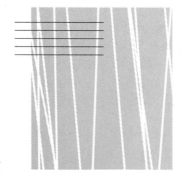

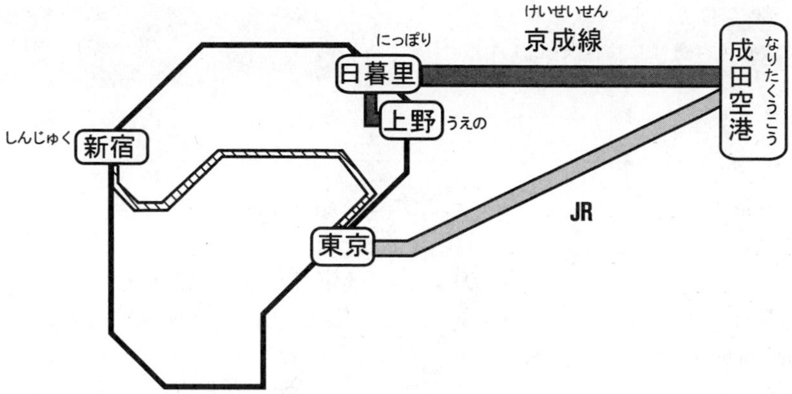

		かかる時間	りょうきん 料金 (fare)	座席 (seating)
けいせいせん 京成線				
スカイライナー	成田空港 → 上野	64 分	1920 円	していせき 指定席 (reserved)
特急とっきゅう	成田空港 → 上野	80 分	1000 円	じゆうせき 自由席 (non-reserved)
JR				
なりた 成田エクスプレス	成田空港 → 東京	58 分	2940 円	していせき 指定席 (reserved)
エアポート成田 (なりた)	成田空港 → 東京	90 分	1280 円	じゆうせき 自由席 (non-reserved)

ロールプレイ

A. You are looking for a mailbox. Ask a passerby where you can find one.

B. A Japanese student wants to go to the student union and a bookstore. Give him or her directions.

C. You want to go to the Statue of Liberty in New York. You are at Times Square. Ask someone for directions and how long it will take to get there.

D. You are new to town. Ask your friends about good restaurants, shops, etc. Ask how to get to each place and how long it takes.

E. You are in Tokyo Station. You want to go to Yokohama. Ask a passerby which train to take, whether you need to transfer, and how long it takes to get there. Use the diagram showing the Tokyo Station terminal on page 289.

LAB

単語 (ESSENTIAL VOCABULARY)

Nouns

えいがかん (映画館) movie theater
おうだんほどう (横断歩道) pedestrian crossing
かくえきていしゃ (各駅停車) local train (literally: train that stops at every station)
ガソリンスタンド gas station
かど (角) corner
かわ (川) river
きゅうこう (れっしゃ) (急行{列車}) express train
こうさてん (交差点) intersection
ＪＲ JR Line (pronounced as ジェーアール) It is the former national railway, now privatized.
しやくしょ (市役所) city hall
しんごう (信号) traffic signal
たいしかん (大使館) embassy
タクシー taxi
ターミナル terminal; バスターミナル bus depot
ちかてつ (地下鉄) subway
ちゅうしゃじょう (駐車場) parking lot
つぎ (次) next
つきあたり (突き当たり) T-road
どうろ (道路) road; street
とっきゅう (れっしゃ) (特急{列車}) limited express train
はし (橋) bridge
バスてい (バス停) bus stop
ビル building
ふつう(れっしゃ) (普通{列車}) local train
へん (辺) area; このへん (この辺) this area
みち (道) road; street; way

Location nouns

あいだ (間) between
こちらがわ (こちら側) this side
さき (先) beyond
てまえ (手前) just before
ひだり (左) left
みぎ (右) right
むかいがわ (向かい側) the other side; the opposite side

い-adjectives

ちかい(近い) close to; near; こうえんにちかい (公園に近い) close to the park
とおい(遠い) far from; こうえんからとおい (公園から遠い) far away from the park

う-verbs

とおる (通る) (to) go through; (to) pass
とまる (止まる) (for someone or something) (to) stop (*intr.*)
まがる (曲がる) (to) turn (*intr.*)
わたる (渡る) (to) cross (bridge, road, etc.)

る-verbs

おりる （降りる） (to) get off
とめる （止める） (to) stop (something) *(tran.)*
のりかえる （乗り換える） (to) transfer; (to) change transportation
みえる （見える） can see ～ (literally: something is visible)

Adverbs

まっすぐ straight
すぐ soon; shortly

Particles

で limit
を place in which movement occurs
を out of ～; from ～

Suffixes

～いき （～行き） bound for ～; とうきょういき （東京行き） bound for Tokyo; きょうといき （京都行き） bound for Kyoto
～がわ （～側） side; こちらがわ （こちら側） this side; むかいがわ （向い側） the other side; the opposite side; みぎがわ （右側） right side; ひだりがわ （左側） left side
～せん （～線）～ Line (train line) やまのてせん （山手線） the Yamanote Line, ちゅうおうせん （中央線） the Chuo Line
～つめ （～つ目） ordinal numbers; ひとつめ （一つ目） first
～ばんせん （～番線） track number; さんばんせん （三番線） Track 3
～メートル meter (distance measurement); １０メートル ten meters

Expressions

このへん （この辺） this area
～のをたのしみにしています （～のを楽しみにしています） (to) be looking forward to ～; おあいできるのをたのしみにしています(お会い出来るのを楽しみにしています) I am looking forward to seeing you soon.

Passive Vocabulary

Nouns

あさくさ　(浅草)　an old neighborhood in downtown Tokyo
がくわり　(学割)　student discout (shortened form of がくせいわりびき{学生割引})
ぎんざせん　(銀座線)　the oldest subway line in Japan
けいせいせん　(京成線)　a private line connecting Tokyo and Narita Airport
していせき　(指定席)　reserved seat
じゆうせき　(自由席)　non-reserved seat
しゅうゆうけん　(周遊券)　(travel) pass
ちかどう　(地下道)　under-path
ちゅうおうせん　(中央線)　JR Chuo Line
ていきけん　(定期券)　train/bus pass for commuters
とうきょうえき　(東京駅)　Tokyo Station
とちょう　(都庁)　Tokyo city office located in Shinjuku
にしぐち　(西口)　west exit of a station
ビザ　visa
まるのうちせん　(丸ノ内線)　a subway line connecting places inside the loop of the Yamanote line
やまのてせん(山手線) the JR's loop line in Tokyo

う-verb

かさなる　(重なる)　(to) overlap

Suffix

〜フィート　〜 foot; feet

For a list of supplementary vocabulary items that will facilitate communication, see the first page of Chapter 6 in your Workbook.

CHAPTER 7

第七課

Special gifts come in special envelopes.

贈(おく)り物

Gifts

Functions	Giving and receiving gifts; Expressing desire; Expressing opinions
New Vocabulary	Gifts; Gift-giving related vocabulary; Gift-giving occasions and purposes; Nouns derived from い-adjectives
Dialogue	アリスさんの誕生日(たんじょうび) (Alice's birthday)
Culture	Gift exchanges
Language	I. Using verbs of giving and receiving II. Expressing desire, using ほしい and the て-form of the verb + ほしい III. Expressing the fact something is easy or hard to do, using the stem of the verb + やすい／にくい IV. Expressing excessiveness, using the stem of the verb or adjective + すぎる V. Expressing an open hypothetical condition, using the ば conditional form
Kanji	Statistical facts about **kanji**; Learning tips
Reading	The etiquette of giving and receiving gifts
Listening	Christmas
Communication	Phrases used when giving or receiving gifts

新しい言葉(ことば)

贈(おく)り物 (Gifts)

プレゼント　present
お菓子(かし)　sweets
チョコレート　chocolate
クッキー　cookies
果物(くだもの)　fruit
(お) さけ　liquor; sake
お茶(ちゃ)　green tea
はちうえ　houseplant
カーネーション　carnation
バラ　rose
カード　card
腕時計(うでどけい)　wristwatch
ドレス　dress
スニーカー　sneakers

ゆびわ　ring
ボール　ball
コーヒーカップ　coffee mug
石(せっ)けん　soap
タオル　towel
CD(シーディー)　CD
人形(にんぎょう)　doll
おもちゃ　toy
ぬいぐるみ　stuffed animal
小説(しょうせつ)　novel
子〜　baby 〜
子犬(こいぬ)　puppy
子猫(こねこ)　kitten
しょうひんけん　gift certificate

下の言葉(ことば)をおぼえていますか。

あぶら　おみやげ　ガイドブック　切符(きっぷ)　切手　小包　おさら
招待状(しょうたいじょう)　せいせき　コンピュータ　パン　パソコン　ファックス
ふうとう　ノート　テレフォンカード　電子メール　地図
オレンジ　ジュース　車　ケーキ　かばん　けしゴム　紅茶(こうちゃ)
コート　コーヒー　コーラ　猫(ねこ)　犬(いぬ)　ネックレス　バナナ
スカート　パンツ　ハンドバッグ　ステレオ　ハンバーガー
ビール　ビデオ　ふく　帽子(ぼうし)　電話番号　とけい　テレビ　肉
手紙　デーパック　辞書(じしょ)　写真　ジャケット　シャツ　え
ボールペン　本　水　ミルク　めがね　レコード　ワイン
さいふ　ズボン　セーター　アクセサリー　なべ　花(はな)　葉書(はがき)
はこ　T-シャツ　えんぴつ　かさ　着物　くつ　くつした
ざっし　自転車　アイスクリーム　りんご　ベルト　スーツ

A. 下の場所でよく見る物を言って下さい。.

1. リビングルーム
2. ベッドルーム
3. お風呂(ふろ)
4. 台所(だいどころ) (kitchen)
5. げんかん
6. 子供の部屋
7. 体育館
8. 教室(きょうしつ)

B. List the words that fit in the following categories

1. 食べ物
2. 飲み物
3. ふく
4. アクセサリー
5. 動物(どうぶつ) (animals)
6. 植物(しょくぶつ) (plants)
7. 文房具(ぶんぼうぐ)
8. 読む物
9. 書く物
10. 聞く物
11. 買い物をする時に使う物
12. 料理をする時に使う物
13. 食べたり飲んだりする時に使う物
14. 勉強する時に使う物
15. 運動する時に使う物

贈(おく)り物をする時に使う言葉(ことば) (Gift-giving related vocabulary)

えらぶ to select
大切(たいせつ)な precious
つまらない uninteresting; unworthy
やくに立つ useful
世話(せわ)になる to be helped (by someone)
よろこぶ to be pleased
おめでとう（ございます） congratulations

下の言葉(ことば)をおぼえていますか。

新しい　古い　赤い　白い　黒い　青い　黄色い　緑
かわいい　おもしろい　好きな　大好きな　きらいな
きれいな　送る　包む　つける　返す　そうだんする

C. 質問に答えて下さい。

1. 何か大切(たいせつ)にしている物がありますか。どんな物を大切(たいせつ)にしていますか。
2. 日本語の勉強にはどんなものがやくに立(た)ちますか。
3. どんな人にお世話(せわ)になったことがありますか。

4. 日本ではお祝(いわ)いをする時、「おめでとうございます」とよく言います。あなたの国では何と言いますか。

5. 日本では贈(おく)り物をする時、よく「つまらないものですが」と言います。あなたの国では何と言いますか。

6. あなたがどんなことをすると、ご両親はよろこぶと思いますか。

D. 下線(かせん) (blank) にてきとうな (appropriate) 言葉(ことば)を書いて下さい。

1. 高校の時、その先生に色々＿＿＿＿＿＿＿＿＿＿＿＿＿＿。
2. この辞書(じしょ)はとても＿＿＿＿＿＿＿＿＿＿＿＿＿＿。
3. ミラーさんが結婚すると聞いたので、ミラーさんに＿＿＿＿＿＿＿＿＿＿＿＿と言った。
4. その男の子は誕生日(たんじょうび)ケーキを見て、とても＿＿＿＿＿＿＿＿。
5. この小説(しょうせつ)は＿＿＿＿＿＿＿＿＿＿けど、それはおもしろいですよ。
6. 母は私にとって一番＿＿＿＿＿＿＿＿＿＿人です。

何のための贈(おく)り物か　(Gift-giving occasions and purposes)

お中元(ちゅうげん)	mid-year gift exchange	(お) 見舞(みま)い	(present for) sympathy
おせいぼ	end-of-year gift exchange	お礼(れい)	thank-you (gift)
母の日(ひ)	Mother's Day	(お) 祝(いわ)い	congratulatory gift
父の日(ひ)	Father's Day	～祝(いわ)い	congratulatory gift for ～
クリスマス	Christmas	卒業祝(そつぎょういわ)い	graduation gift
バレンタインデー	Valentine's Day	結婚祝(けっこんいわ)い	wedding gift

下の言葉(ことば)をおぼえていますか。

誕生日(たんじょうび)　変(へん)な　卒業式(しき)　結婚式(しき)

E. Work as a class. Ask your classmates what kind of gifts they give in the following cases and determine the three most popular gifts for each situation.

Example

A: 母の日のプレゼントには何がいいと思いますか。
B: ケーキがいいと思います。

	一番	二番	三番
母の日			
父の日			
結婚祝い(けっこんいわ)			
病気の人のお見舞い(みま)			
お世話になった先生にするお礼(れい)			
バレンタインデー			
クリスマス			

F. 下線(かせん) (blank) にてきとうな (appropriate) 言葉(ことば)を書いて下さい。

1. 日本ではお世話(せわ)になった人に一年に二度贈り(おく)物をする季節があります。＿＿＿＿＿＿＿＿は七月にあります。＿＿＿＿＿＿＿＿は十二月にあります。
2. 十二月二十五日は＿＿＿＿＿＿＿＿です。二月十四日は＿＿＿＿＿＿＿＿です。
3. ＿＿＿＿＿＿＿＿は五月の二週目の日曜日ですが、＿＿＿＿＿＿＿＿はいつですか。
4. だれかがしゅうしょくした時にする贈り(おく)物を＿＿＿＿＿＿＿＿と言います。大学に入学した時にする贈り(おく)物を＿＿＿＿＿＿＿＿と言います。
5. 友達が入院したので、＿＿＿＿＿＿＿＿に果物(くだもの)を持って行きます。
6. 卒業祝い(いわ)をもらったので、＿＿＿＿＿＿＿＿のカードを書きました。

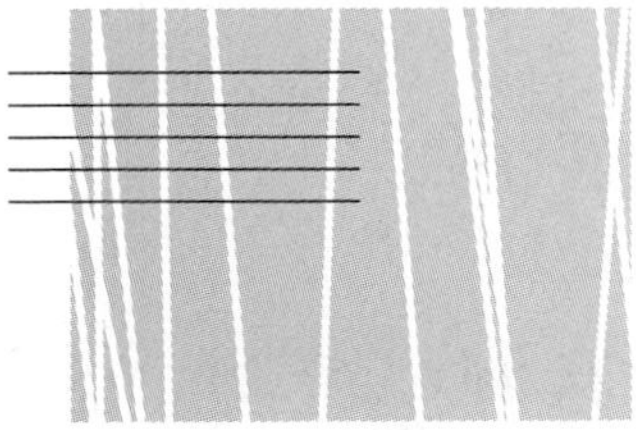

い-形容詞(けいようし)から出来た名詞(めいし) (Nouns derived from い-adjectives)

〜さ

大きさ　size

高さ　height

長さ　length

重(おも)さ　weight

G. 質問に答えて下さい。

1. 「さ」の前にはどんな言葉(ことば)がきますか。
2. 「さ」の前の言葉(ことば)はどんな形(かたち) (form) ですか。
3. 下の言葉の意味(いみ)は何だと思いますか。

　広(ひろ)さ　強さ　明るさ　早(はや)さ　暑さ　よさ　いたさ　かなしさ

　寒さ　白さ　やさしさ

H. Give the antonyms of the following words:

大きい　高い　長い　重い　広(ひろ)い　強い　明るい　はやい

暑い　暖かい　いい　白い　新しい

ダイアローグ

はじめに

質問に日本語で答えて下さい。

1. どんな時に友達に贈(おく)り物をしますか。
2. 女の人にはどんなプレゼントがいいと思いますか。男の人はどうですか。
3. 年を取った人にはどんなプレゼントがいいと思いますか。子供はどうですか。
4. 友達の誕生日(たんじょうび)プレゼントを買う時、いくらぐらいの物を買いますか。
5. 家族の誕生日(たんじょうび)プレゼントを買う時、お金をいくらぐらい使いますか。

アリスさんの誕生日(たんじょうび) (Alice's Birthday)

STUDENT

言葉(ことば)のリスト

予算(よさん)
budget

～でございます
polite form of です

店員(てんいん)
salesclerk

かしこまりました
certainly (polite language used by waiters, clerks, etc.)

The following **manga** frames are scrambled, so they are not in the order described by the dialogue. Read the dialogue and unscramble the frames by writing the correct number in the box located in the upper right corner of each frame.

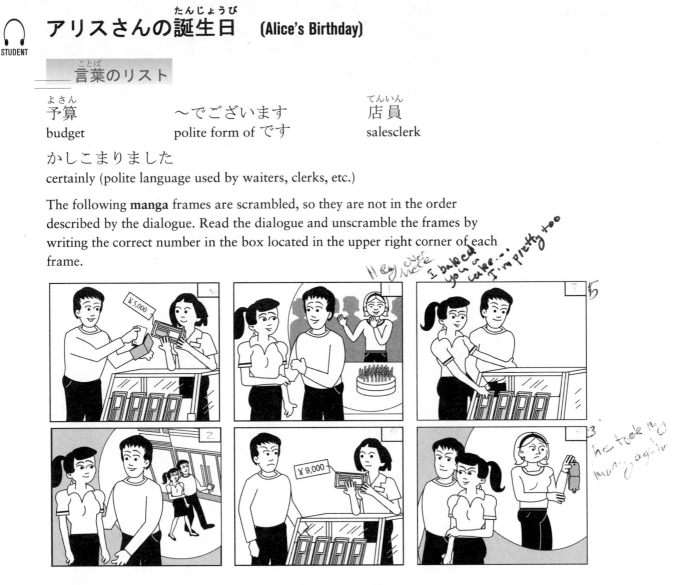

石田(いしだ)さんは道子さんとキャンパスで話をしています。

石田(いしだ)：　あのう、道子さん、もうすぐアリスの誕生日(たんじょうび)だよね。

道子：　ええ、そうよ。

石田(いしだ)：　何かあげようと思うんだけど、何を買えばいいかぜんぜん分からないんだ。

道子：　あ、そうか。

石田(いしだ)：　で、一緒(いっしょ)に買い物に行って何かえらんでほしいんだけど。

道子：　いいわよ。明日かあさってはどう？

石田(いしだ)：　有難(ありがと)う。ぼくはいつでもいいよ。

道子：　じゃあ、明日の午後(ごご)はどう？

石田(いしだ)：　いいよ。

石田(いしだ)さんと道子さんはデパートにいます。

道子：　予算(よさん)はいくらぐらい？

石田(いしだ)：　そうだね、五千円ぐらいかな。

道子:　じゃあ､おさいふはどう？アリスが今持っているのは古いし、新しいのをほしがってたわ。

石田(いしだ)：　どんなのがいいと思う？

道子:　使いやすいのがいいわね。この赤いのか茶色(ちゃいろ)いのはいいわね。

石田(いしだ)：　そうだね。あのう、すみません。

店員(てんいん)：　はい、いらっしゃいませ。

石田(いしだ)：　あのう、この赤いさいふいくらですか。

店員(てんいん)：　九千円でございます。

石田(いしだ)：　そうか、ちょっと高すぎるなあ。あのう、こっちの茶色(ちゃいろ)いのはいくらですか。

店員(てんいん)：　それは五千円です。

石田(いしだ)：　あ、じゃあ、これ下さい。

店員(てんいん)：　はい、かしこまりました。

分かりましたか

A. 質問に日本語で答えて下さい。

1. 石田(いしだ)さは道子さんに何についてそうだんしましたか。
2. 道子さんと石田(いしだ)さんはどこに行きましたか。何のためにそこへ行きましたか。
3. 道子さんは何を買ったらいいと言いましたか。どうしてそう言いましたか。
4. 石田(いしだ)さんは何を買いましたか。
5. 石田(いしだ)さんはどんなのを買いましたか。どうしてそれにしましたか。

B. Identify the phrases Ishida-san uses to start a conversation.

C. Suppose that Ishida-san were not a close friend of Michiko-san. Michiko-san and Ishida-san would then speak a little more politely than they do in the dialogue. Modify the conversation by using a more polite speech style.

D. Suppose Michiko-san wants to buy a Christmas present for Lee-san, but does not know what he likes. She asks Ishida-san to help her choose an appropriate present. Create a dialogue for this situation based on the dialogue above.

日本の文化

- *Gift exchanges. Do you have major gift-giving occasions in your country? Are there special customs observed when giving or exchanging gifts?*

While exchanging gifts is an intricate part of many cultures, each culture develops different social norms and expectations. In Japanese culture, the gift exchange is a highly ritualized social practice.

On a social level, there are two major gift-giving seasons. One, called お中元(ちゅうげん), is in July, and the other, お歳暮(せいぼ), is in December. People give gifts to those to whom they feel indebted, such as 上司(じょうし) (company bosses) and 恩師(おんし) (former teachers and mentoring professors). The following chart shows the ten most popular gifts for these seasons.

お中元(ちゅうげん) (in July)	お歳暮(せいぼ) (in December)
1. Gift certificates （しょうひんけん）	1. Gift certificates （しょうひんけん）
2. Beer （ビール）	2. Ham and sausages （ハムとソーセージ）
3. Non-alcoholic beverages （ジュース）	3. Salad oil （サラダオイル）
4. Gift certificates for beer （ビールけん）	4. Beer （ビール）
5. Detergent （洗剤(せんざい)）	5. Seaweed （のり）
6. Salad oil （サラダオイル）	6. Gift certificates for beer （ビールけん）
7. Dry noodles （かんめん）	7. Gift certificates for specific merchandise
8. Western-style sweets （洋菓子(ようがし)）	8. Japanese sake （日本酒(しゅ)）
9. Seaweed （のり）	9. Coffee （コーヒー）
10. Gift certificates for specific merchandise	10. Western-style sweets （洋菓子(ようがし)）

During the お中元(ちゅうげん) and お歳暮(せいぼ) seasons, department stores put gift packs on sale, distribute gift catalogs, and set up special sections to take orders and send out gifts. The customer fills out a form with his or her name and address and the recipient's name and address, and the department stores take care of the rest. Having gifts sent is quite accepted in Japan, but it is a nice gesture to deliver gifts personally to close acquaintances or friends.

Gifts in a department store

Other social events, such as weddings, funerals, or the birth of a new baby, also involve gifts. Money is common for such occasions, but it must be put in an envelope. There is a variety of special envelopes, specific to the different gift-giving occasions. Christmas in Japan is, by and large, a commercial event. Special Christmas presents are given to children by their parents, but there is no tradition of exchanging gifts among friends or relatives. At the New Year holiday, parents, relatives, and friends of the family give children pocket money called お年玉(としだま). On a personal level, the Japanese usually take a gift when they visit others' houses or when they come back from trips. It is a nice gesture to bring a small gift if you have been invited by a Japanese family for occasions such as dinner.

When sending a personal gift, the Japanese often write a short message or letter congratulating the recipient on his or her wedding, birthday, or employment. Usually the letter starts with a congratulatory message, such as お誕生日(たんじょうび)おめでとうございます *(Happy birthday)*, ご結婚おめでとうございます *(Congratulations on your marriage)*, or 就職(しゅうしょく)おめでとうございます *(Congratulations on your new job)*. This is followed by the writer's wish for the recipient's happiness and health, such as すばらしい一年であることをおいのりします *(I hope you will have a wonderful year)*, お二人のおしあわせをおいのりします *(I hope you are both very happy)*, or ご活躍(かつやく)をおいのりします *(Wishing for your success)*. You can add any news about yourself or a message about the gift you are sending.

Reciprocation is also an important aspect of gift giving. It is customary to reciprocate by spending about one half of the original amount when one receives a gift. This custom is called 半返し(はんがえし). In the case of お中元(ちゅうげん) or お歳暮(せいぼ), however, it is not necessary to give anything in return, though a thank-you letter or phone call is important.

LANGUAGE

I. Using verbs of giving and receiving

A. Using the verbs of giving 下さる and くれる

A-1. 下さる

Giver (superior)		Recipient	Particle	Noun	Particle	Verb
大川先生	は	私	に	シーディー CD	を	下さいました。

Professor Okawa gave me a CD.

A-2. くれる

Giver (equal or inferior)		Recipient	Particle	Noun	Particle	Verb
道子さん	は	妹	に	コーヒーカップ	を	くれました。

Michiko-san gave my younger sister a coffee cup.

先生は弟におもちゃを下さいました。 My professor gave my little brother a toy.
母は私にゆびわをくれました。 My mother gave me a ring.

近所の人：おいしそうなクッキーね。
These cookies look delicious.
子供：おばあちゃんがくれたの。
Grandmother gave them to me.
黒田 いい腕時計(うでとけい)ですね。
That's a nice wristwatch.
大川：社長が結婚祝(いわ)いに下さったんです。
The president (of my company) gave it to me as a wedding gift.

- Japanese has two sets of verbs for giving and one set of verbs for receiving. Usage is determined by the social relationships among giver, recipient, and speaker. The first group of verbs of giving—くれる and 下さる—is used when the recipient is the speaker or a member of the speaker's in-group (someone close to the speaker such as family members and close friends). The giver can be anyone except the speaker.

- The honorific verb 下さる should be used when the giver is a member of the speaker's out-group and is socially superior to the speaker. Otherwise, use くれる. くれる is normally used among family members. The social relationships involved are depicted by the following diagram:

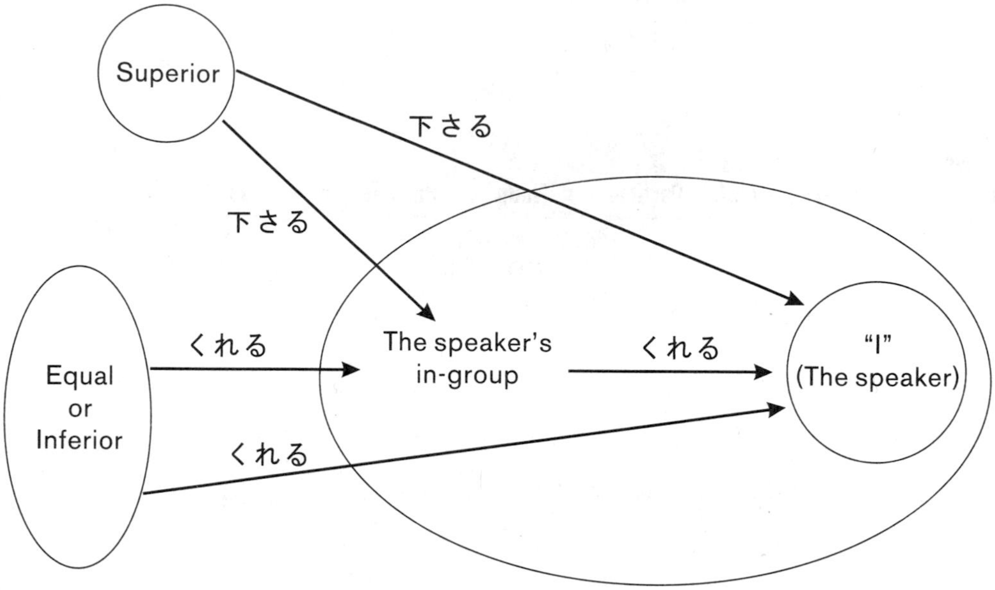

- The polite request ～を下さい is an extension of the use of 下さる.
- くれる is a る-verb and 下さる is a う-verb. The polite present form of 下さる is 下さいます, and not ~~下さります~~.

Plain negative form	下さらない	くれない
Polite affirmative form	下さいます	くれます
Plain affirmative (dictionary) form	下さる	くれる
Conditional form	下されば	くれれば
Volitional form	下さろう	くれよう
て-form	下さって	くれて

- Grammatically, the recipient is the indirect object, marked by the particle に.

B. Using verbs of giving さしあげる／あげる／やる

B-1. さしあげる

Giver		Recipient (superior)	Particle	Noun	Particle	Verb
私	は	田中先生	に	はちうえ	を	さし上(あ)げました。

I respectfully gave a houseplant to Professor Tanaka.

B-2. 上(あ)げる

Giver		Recipient (equal or inferior)	Particle	Noun	Particle	Verb
私	は	山田さん	に	子犬(こいぬ)	を	上(あ)げました。

I gave a puppy to Yamada-san.

B-3. やる

Giver		Recipient (very inferior)	Particle	Noun	Particle	Verb
私	は	花(はな)	に	水	を	やりました。

I watered a flower. (literally: I gave water to a flower.)

田中さんは鈴木(すずき)さんにチョコレートを上(あ)げました。
Tanaka-san gave Suzuki-san some chocolate.

けんじ：　ねえ、母の日にお母さんに何か上(あ)げるの。
Hey, are you going to give something to your mother on Mother's Day?

アリス：　そうね。私はいつもカーネーションを上(あ)げるんだけど。
Well, I always give her carnations.

スミス先生の誕生日(たんじょうび)におさけをさし上(あ)げました。
I gave Professor Smith some liquor for his birthday.

- The second group of verbs of giving— さし上(あ)げる, 上(あ)げる, and やる —is used when the the recipient *is not* the speaker or a member of the speaker's in-group. The giver can be anyone. The verbs さし上(あ)げる, 上(あ)げる, and やる are used when the giver is the speaker.
- If both the giver and the recipient are members of the speaker's in-group, 上(あ)げる or やる can be used more or less interchangeably with くれる. The use of くれる implies that the speaker feels closer to the recipient than to the giver, and thus presents the recipient's point of view, while the use of 上(あ)げる or やる implies that the speaker feels closer to the giver than to the recipient, or is at a neutral distance between them.

母が弟におかしをくれた。
My mother gave my brother some sweets. (The speaker identifies with his brother.

母が弟におかしを上(あ)げた。
My mother gave my brother some sweets. (The speaker is neutral or identifies with his mother.)

The diagram below shows these relationships.

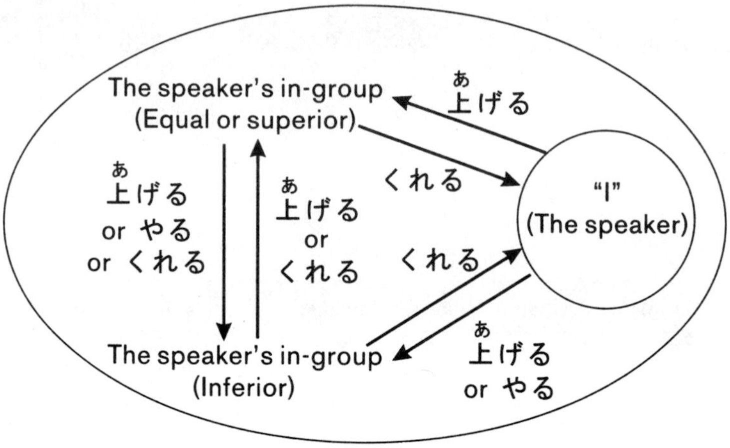

- The humble verb, さし上(あ)げる, is used if the recipient is socially superior to the speaker and is a member of the recipient's out-group. This might include professors, bosses, or older acquaintances. The verb やる is used if the recipient is socially inferior to the speaker. It includes mainly animals, plants, and younger family members. Otherwise, 上(あ)げる is used. The diagram below shows these relationships.

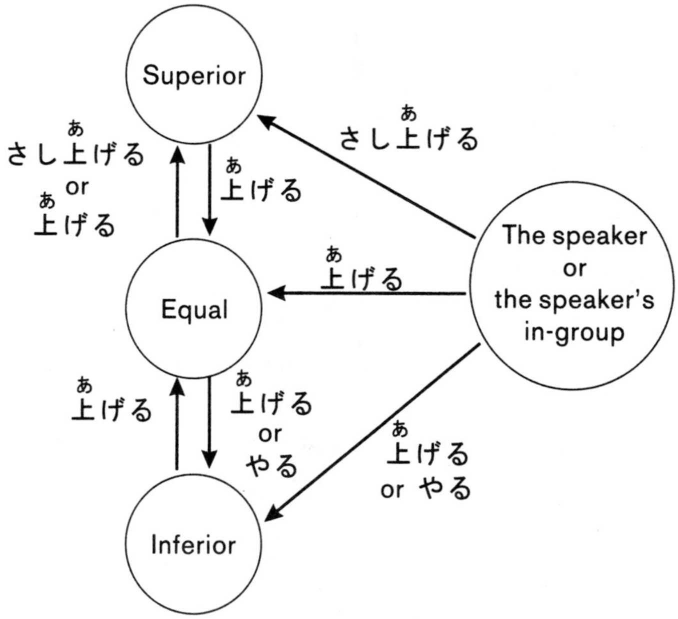

- さし上(あ)げる and 上(あ)げる are る-verbs, and やる is an う-verb. They conjugate as follows:

Plain negative form	さし上(あ)げない	上(あ)げない	やらない
Polite affirmative form	さし上(あ)げます	上(あ)げます	やります
Plain affirmative (dictionary) form	さし上(あ)げる	上(あ)げる	やる
Conditional form	さし上(あ)げれば	上(あ)げれば	やれば
Volitional form	さし上(あ)げよう	上(あ)げよう	やろう
て-form	さし上(あ)げて	上(あ)げて	やって

C. Using the verbs of receiving もらう and いただく

C-1. もらう

Recipient	Particle	Giver	Particle (Source)	Noun	Particle (Object)	Verb
田中さん	は	山本さん	に／から	バラの花(はな)	を	もらいました。

Tanaka-san received a rose from Yamamoto-san.

C-2. いただく

Recipient	Particle	Giver (superior)	Particle (Source)	Noun	Particle (Object)	Verb
私	は	先生	に／から	小説(しょうせつ)	を	いただきました。

I received a novel from my teacher.

妹は父に／からスニーカーをもらいました。
My younger sister received a pair of sneakers from our father.

父は父の日に兄に／からゴルフのボールをもらった。
My father received golf balls from my elder brother on Father's Day.

兄は先生に／からカードをいただいた。
My older brother received a card from the teacher.

- Both もらう and いただく mean *to receive*. They are used when the recipient is the subject of the sentence. It is important to remember that the giver cannot be the speaker, but the recipient can be anyone. The giver is marked by the particle に or から. The particle に indicates the source from which the gift originates. In cases where the giver is an institution such as 大学 rather than a human being, the particle から must be used; use of に implies that the speaker feels close to the giver.

アリスは大学から手紙をもらった。 ~~アリスは大学に手紙をもらった~~。
Alice received a letter from the university.

- The choice between もらう and いただく depends on the social relationships among the giver, recipient, and speaker. If the giver is socially superior to both speaker and recipient, use いただく. Otherwise, use もらう. Both もらう and いただく are う-verbs. They conjugate as follows:

Plain negative form	いただかない	もらわない
Polite affirmative form	いただきます	もらいます
Plain affirmative (dictionary) form	いただく	もらう
Conditional form	いただけば	もらえば
Volitional form	いただこう	もらおう
て-form	いただいて	もらって

- Before beginning to eat, Japanese people say いただきます *(I humbly receive)*. This expression comes from the verb いただく.

話してみましょう

A. The following chart illustrates gift exchanges among people. You are the speaker. Describe each exchange using 下さる or くれる.

Example

姉は私にゆびわをくれました。

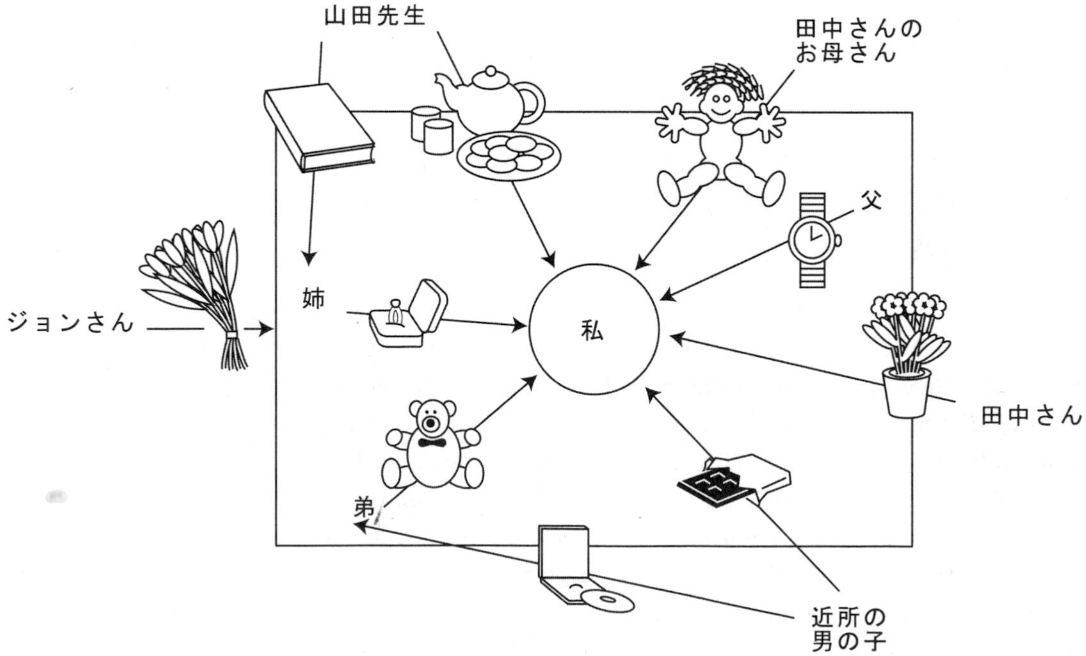

B. Express the same gift exchanges using the verbs of receiving いただく or もらう.

Example

私は姉にゆびわをもらいました。

C. The following chart illustrates gift exchanges among people. You are the speaker. Describe each exchange using さし上(あ)げる, あげる, or やる.

Example

私は田中さんにサッカーボールを上(あ)げました。

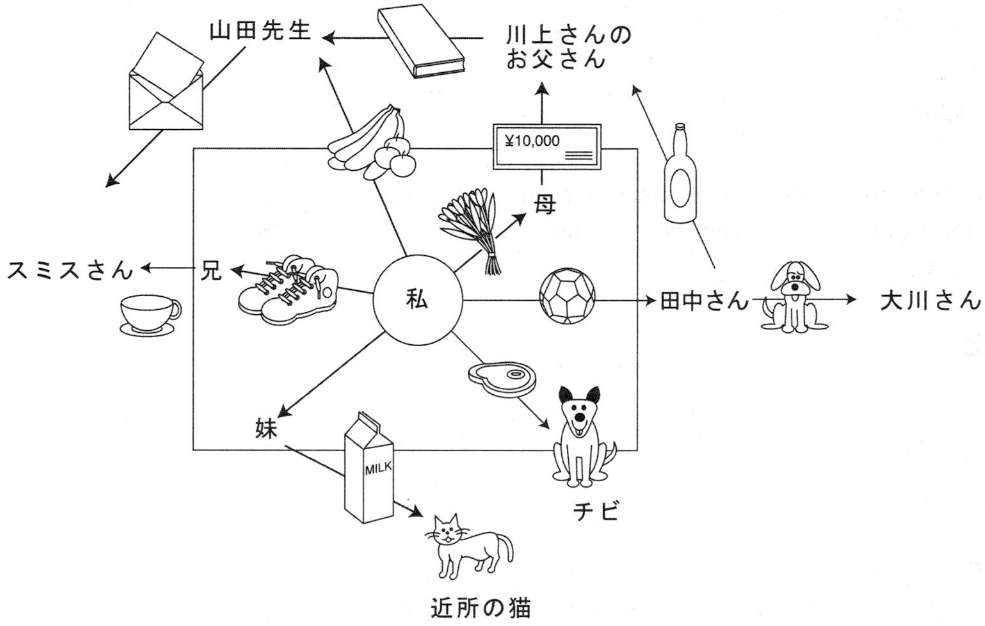

D. Express the same gift exchanges as in Exercise C using the verbs of receiving, and identify which exchanges cannot be expressed with a verb of receiving.

Example

私は田中さんにサッカーボールを上(あ)げました。
This cannot be expressed with もらう or いただく because the giver is 私.
田中さんは大川さんに子犬(こいぬ)を上(あ)げました。
大川さんは田中さんに子犬(こいぬ)をもらいました。

E. Work with a partner. The two of you want to jointly give a gift on the occasions shown in the table on page 348. Discuss what to give and why it will be an appropriate gift. Use casual speech.

Example

A: お見舞(みま)いに何あげたらいいと思う？

B: そうね。果物(くだもの)はどう？

A: でも、食べられなかったら、どうする？

B: そうだね。じゃあ、小説(しょうせつ)はどう？病院の生活(せいかつ)、つまらないし。(male) ／
そうね。じゃあ、小説(しょうせつ)はどう？病院の生活(せいかつ)、つまらないし。(female)

A: いいね。そうしよう。

Occasion	プレゼント	りゆう (Reason)
入院している友達の病気のお見舞(みま)い		
お世話(せわ)になった先生のお礼(れい)		
～先生のおせいぼ		

F. Work with a partner. Ask your partner what kind of gifts he or she has received and from whom, on the occasions noted in the table. Use verbs of receiving and casual speech.

Example

A: ～さん、去年(きょねん)の誕生日(たんじょうび)にどんなものをもらったの。

B: 父に腕時計(うでどけい)をもらったんだ。(male)／ 父に腕時計(うでどけい)をもらったの。(female)
そして、友達にコーヒーカップをもらったんだ。(male) ／
そして、友達にコーヒーカップをもらったの。(female)

	私がもらったもの		パートナーがもらったもの	
	だれに？	プレゼント	だれに？	プレゼント
誕生日(たんじょうび)				
クリスマス				
バレンタインデー				

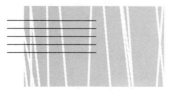

II. Expressing desire, using ほしい and the て-form of the verb + ほしい

A. Expressing desire for something with ほしい

Question			
	Noun (object)	Particle	い-adjective
クリスマスに	何	が	ほしいですか。

What do you want for Christmas?

Answer		
Noun (object)	Particle	い-adjective
子猫(こねこ)	が	ほしいです。

I want a kitten.

	Noun (object)	Particle	い-adjective (stem)	Auxiliary verb
田中さんは	ファックス	を	ほし	がっている。

Tanaka-san wants a fax machine.

きゃく： すみません、このバラの花(はな)がほしいんですが。
Excuse me, I'd like these roses.

店の人： はい、何本さし上(あ)げましょうか。
Yes, how many shall I give you?

山本さんは白いドレスがほしいと言っています。
Yamamoto-san says she wants a white dress.

鈴木(すずき)さんはお茶(ちゃ)がほしいんですよ。
Suzuki-san wants some green tea.

道子： このクッキーもらってもいい。
Can I have some of these cookies?

トム： ああ、いいよ。いくつほしいの。
Sure. How many do you want?

道子： ピーターもほしがってるから、五つ。
Peter wants some too, so five.

- ほしい indicates that the speaker wants something (a physical object). To express the speaker's wish to do something (an action), use ～たい (Volume 1, Chapter 11).

このチョコレートがほしい。 I want this chocolate.
このチョコレートが／を食べたい。 I want to eat this chocolate.

- ほしい is an い-adjective and takes が to mark its object.

	Polite form	Plain form	
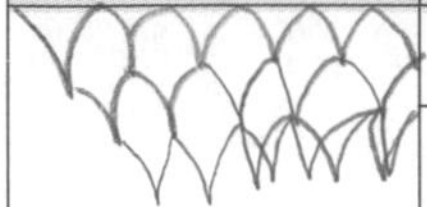 私は果物（くだもの）が	ほしいです。	ほしい。	I want some fruit.
	ほしくありません。 or ほしくないです。	ほしくない。	I don't want any fruit.
	ほしかったです。	ほしかった。	I wanted some fruit.
	ほしくありませんでした。 or ほしくなかったです。	ほしくなかった。	I didn't want any fruit.

- The subject of ほしい must be the speaker for statements; it can be either the speaker or the listener for questions. To express someone else's desire, ほしい must be followed by the suffix がる or by expressions such as 〜と言っています, 〜そうです, or 〜んです. The object of desire is marked by the particle を when the suffix がる is used. The word ほしがる is usually used in the progressive form, ほしがっている, which literally means *he or she is showing signs of wanting* 〜.

  The Japanese consider that no one but the person directly involved can know his or her emotional state, and that one can only guess about the feelings of others. Words such as ほしい and たい, which express emotive states, are thus reserved for the speaker. To indicate other people's emotions, use expressions that imply an understanding or guess on the part of the speaker, such as そうです *(I heard)*, 〜んです *(it is the case that 〜)*, and 〜がっている *(he or she is showing signs of 〜)*.

スミスさんは子犬（こいぬ）をほしがっています。	Smith-san wants a puppy.
スミスさんは子犬（こいぬ）がほしいと言っていました。	Smith-san was saying he wants a puppy.
スミスさんは子犬（こいぬ）がほしいそうです。	I heard Smith-san wants a puppy.
スミスさんは子犬（こいぬ）がほしいんです。	It is the case that Smith-san wants a puppy.

B. Expressing a desire to have someone do something, using the て-form of the verb + ほしい

	Verb て-form + ほしい	
石（せっ）けんを	取ってほしい	んですが。

I'd like you to get me some soap.

		Verb て-form + ほしい	
スミスさんが	山田さんに	来てほしい	と言っていました。

Smith-san was saying he wants Yamada-san to come.

リビングルームにおくはちうえをえらんでほしいんですが。

I'd like you to choose a houseplant for the living room.

山下先生はたけしくんにみどりちゃんをつれて行ってほしいと思っています。

Professor Yamashita thinks he'd like Takeshi to take Midori with him.

そのタオルは使ってほしくないんです。

I don't want you to use that towel.

- The て-form of the verb + ほしい is used to express the speaker's desire to have someone do something. Thus, it is often used as an indirect form of request. The person who actually performs the act is marked by the particle に but is usually omitted if understood from context. Similarly, 私 is usually omitted.
- The て-form of the verb + ほしい cannot be used to express the speaker's desire to have a socially superior person do something. Use the て-form of the verb + いただきたい (Chapter 8, Language Section 1, page 393).
- In order to express a desire to have someone not do something, use ～ほしくない, ～もらいたくない, or ～ないでほしい.

この石(せっ)けんは使ってほしくないんですけど。or この石(せっ)けんは使わないでほしいんですけど。

I do not want you to use this soap.

話してみましょう

A. Each of the following people wants certain gifts for certain occasions. Assume the identity of the people to tell others what you would like, using ほしい.

Example

Assume you are Smith-san.

私はお中元(ちゅうげん)にビールがほしいです。おせいぼにはタオルがほしいです。

Occasion	スミス	リー	ジョーンズ
お中元(ちゅうげん)	ビール	おさけ	果物(くだもの)
おせいぼ	タオル	しょうひんけん	石(せっ)けん
卒業祝(そつぎょういわ)い	自転車	コンピュータ	ドレス かスーツ

B. You heard that the following people want the items in the chart for various occasions. Tell what they want, using ほしがっている or ほしいそうです. Use casual speech.

Example

スミスさんは誕生日(たんじょうび)に子猫(こねこ)をほしがっているよ。
スミスさんは誕生日(たんじょうび)に子猫(こねこ)がほしいそうだよ。(male) ／
スミスさんは誕生日(たんじょうび)に子猫(こねこ)がほしいそうよ。(female)

Occasion	スミス	キム	モネ
誕生日(たんじょうび)	子猫(こねこ)	自転車	車
クリスマス	おさけ	コーヒーメーカー	ファックス
バレンタインデー	チョコレート	ゆびわ	バラの花(はな)

C. Work with a partner. Practice the following conversation by substituting the underlined expressions with the list of expressions in 1-5.

Example

母の日／料理を作る
A: 母の日に何をしてほしい？
B: そうね。料理を作ってほしいわね。
A: いいよ。

1. 父の日／車を洗う
2. バレンタインデー／フランス料理のレストランにつれて行く
3. クリスマス／おかしを作ってくる
4. お世話(せわ)になったお礼／小説(しょうせつ)を貸す
5. 母の日／花(はな)に水をやる

III. Expressing the fact something is easy or hard to do, using the stem of the verb + やすい／にくい

A. Expressing the fact it is easy to do something, using the stem of the verb + やすい

	Verb (stem)	Auxiliary adjective
この腕時計(うでどけい)は	見	やすいです。

This wristwatch is easy to read.

このくつは歩きやすいね。　These shoes are easy to walk in.

川口先生は話しやすい先生です。　Professor Kawaguchi is an easy teacher to talk with.

B. Expressing the fact something is hard to do, using the stem of the verb + にくい

	Verb (stem)	Auxiliary adjective
このコーヒーカップは	持ち	にくいです。

This coffee cup is hard to hold.

Suvekadesuka

この薬は飲みにくいですね。　This medicine is hard to take.

とうふははしで食べにくいと思います。　I think tofu is difficult to eat with chopsticks.

- やすい and にくい are い-adjectives that combine with verbs to indicate that an act is easy or hard to perform.

mochyasuimonogaiidesune

- Both やすい and にくい immediately follow the polite stem of the verb (e.g., 食べ in 食べます and 飲み in 飲みます).

t-shatsu wa doodesuka

話してみましょう

A. Tell what is easy or hard to do using the given verbs.

Example

食べる

<u>サンドイッチは食べやすいですが、とうふは食べにくいです。</u>

1. 食べる　3. 作る　5. 話す　7. 書く
2. 飲む　4. 使う　6. はく

B. Work with a partner. Choose one word from the box and explain how that object can be easy or hard to act on, but do not use the word itself. Your partner will try to guess what word you selected. Take turns. Work on as many words as you can in five minutes.

Example

A: これは食べやすいです。

B: サンドイッチですか。

A: ええ、そうです。

サンドイッチ　うどん　つめたい (cold) スープ　あついスープ
りょうのベッド　日本語の文法　先生の説明(せつめい)　日本の車
スニーカー　ハイヒールのくつ　着物　T- シャツ

C. Work with a partner. You want to buy gifts for the following occasions. Ask your partner for suggestions. He or she will make suggestions based on the ease or difficulty of doing something.

Example

A: 友達の結婚祝い(けっこんいわ)に何かあげようと思うんですが、何がいいと思いますか。
B: 使いやすい物がいいですね。
A: どんな物が使いやすいでしょうか。
B: しょうひんけんはどうですか。
A: ああ、そうですね。

1. 友達／結婚祝い(けっこんいわ)い
2. 先生／お中元(ちゅうげん)
3. ホストファミリー／おみやげ
4. 友達の子供／クリスマス
5. 先生／お見舞(みま)い
6. お父さん／父の日

IV. Expressing excessiveness, using the stem of the verb or adjective + すぎる

	い -adjective (stem)	Auxiliary verb
このセーターは	大き	すぎる。

This sweater is too big.

Verb-stem	Auxiliary verb	Noun	Particle	Adjective
飲み	すぎて、	気分	が	悪い。

I drank too much and now I feel sick.

この腕時計(うでどけい)はちょっと高すぎますね。 This wristwatch is a bit too expensive.
山本さんは話しすぎる。 Yamamoto-san talks too much.
ここは静かすぎて、いやだ。 I don't like it here because it is too quiet.

- When すぎる is added after the stem of a verb, い-adjective, or な-adjective, it implies that the action or state of that verb or adjective is excessive.

	Dictionary form	Stem + すぎる
な-adjectives	静か (quiet)	静かすぎる (too quiet)
い-adjectives	大きい (big) いい (good)	大きすぎる (too big) よすぎる (too good)
Irregular verbs	来る (to come) する (to do)	来(き)すぎる (to come too often) しすぎる (to do too much)
る-verbs	あげる (to give) 考える (to think)	あげすぎる (to give too much) 考えすぎる (to think too much)
う-verbs	もらう (to receive) やる (to give)	もらいすぎる (to receive too much) やりすぎる (to give too much)

Choto nagasugi desukedo moto mijikai no wa arimasen ka

- よすぎる is the correct form for いい when used with すぎる.
- すぎる is a る-verb and follows the conjugation pattern of る-verbs:

食べすぎない	do not eat too much	食べすぎれば	If I eat too much
食べすぎます	eat too much	食べすぎて	I eat too much, and
食べすぎる	eat too much		

Kibunga warui.

hai sukoshi ~~omashi~~ omachi kudasai

話してみましょう

A. Work with a partner. Use the example conversation below to make a conversation between a customer and a store clerk, using the words in 1–6 and the adjective stem + すぎる.

Example

ジャケット／大きい／小さい

A: そのジャケット、いかがですか。
B: ちょっと大きすぎるんですけど、もっと小さいのはありませんか。
A: はい、少々お待ち下さい。

1. パンツ／長い／短い
2. くつ／小さい／大きい
3. スカート／短い／長い
4. かばん／重(おも)い／軽(かる)い
5. スタンド／暗い／明るい
6. さいふ／高い／安い

B. Work with a partner. The two of you are shopping in a department store. You're looking at a number of items. Ask each other your opinions of their color, size, length, and price.

Example

A: このズボンどうですか。
B: 色と長さはいいんですけど、大きさがちょっと。
A: 大きすぎるんですか。
B: ええ、そうなんです。or いいえ、小さすぎるんです。
A: そうですか。ねだん (price) はどうですか。
B: ねだん (price) はいいです。

	色	大きさ	長さ	ねだん (price)
ズボン	茶色（ちゃいろ）	Petite S	28 inches (70 cm)	$80
スニーカー	白	Size 6 / 23.5 cm	-------	$35
コート	黒	LL	58 inches (145 cm)	$350
ベルト	赤	-------	33 inches (82.5 cm)	$20

C. Excessive behavior can cause problems. Describe what type of behavior could cause the following problems, using the verb stem +すぎる.

Example

足がいたくなる
歩きすぎると、足がいたくなりますよ。

1. あたまがいたくなる
2. おなかがいたくなる
3. のどがいたくなる
4. ねつが出る
5. 気分が悪くなる
6. 目がいたくなる

V. Expressing an open hypothetical condition, using the ば conditional form

A. Expressing an open hypothetical condition, using the ば conditional form

	ば-conditional clause			Main clause		
			Verb (conditional form)			
道子さんは花（はな）が好きだから、	はちうえ	を	上（あ）げれば	いい	と	思います。

Michiko likes flowers, so if you give her a houseplant, I think she will be pleased.

田中：　毎日運動しているけど、ぜんぜんやせないのです。
I am exercising every day, but I don't lose any weight at all.

川口：　寝る前に食べなければ、やせるよ。
If [and only if] you don't eat before you go to bed, you will lose weight.

そのおかしをくれれば、このチョコレートをあげるよ。
If [and only if] you give me that candy, I will give you these chocolates.

キム：　お手洗いはどこか知ってる？
Do you know where the restroom is?

まもる：　分からないけど。受付(うけつけ)で聞けば分かると思うよ。
I don't. But you should be able to find out if you ask at the reception desk.

- The ば conditional form is made as follows:

い-adjectives and the negative ending ない: Replace い with ければ				
おもしろい	⇒	おもしろ~~い~~　ければ	⇒	おもしろければ
いい	⇒	よ~~い~~　ければ	⇒	よければ (い becomes よ)
おいしくない	⇒	おいしくな~~い~~　ければ	⇒	おいしくなければ
な-adjectives and nouns: Replace だ with なら(ば) or であれば				
大切(たいせつ)だ	⇒	大切(たいせつ)~~だ~~　なら(ば)	⇒	大切(たいせつ)なら(ば)
学生だ	⇒	学生~~だ~~　なら(ば)	⇒	学生なら(ば)
Irregular verbs and る-verbs: Replace る with れば				
来(く)る	⇒	来(く)~~る~~　れば	⇒	来(く)れば
する	⇒	す~~る~~　れば	⇒	すれば
食べる	⇒	食べ~~る~~　れば	⇒	食べれば
見る	⇒	見~~る~~　れば	⇒	見れば
う-verbs: Replace /u/ with /e/ and add ば				
歩く	⇒	歩<u>け</u>　ば	⇒	歩けば
話す	⇒	話<u>せ</u>　ば	⇒	話せば

- The potential form of all verbs (e.g., 歩ける, *can walk*), is always a る-verb. Follow the pattern for る-verbs to make the conditional form of a potential (歩ける⇒歩ければ).

onaka gasuiteireba, sunakuo tsokurimasu

おなかがすいていれば, snack を つくります。

	Plain present affirmative form	ば conditional	
		Affirmative	Negative
Noun + copula	病気だ 子供だ	病気なら（ば） 子供なら（ば）	病気じゃなければ 子供じゃなければ
な-adjectives	元気だ 大切(たいせつ)だ	元気なら（ば） 大切(たいせつ)なら（ば）	元気じゃなければ 大切(たいせつ)じゃなければ
い-adjectives	早(はや)い いい	早(はや)ければ よければ	早(はや)くなければ よくなければ
Irregular verbs	来(く)る 勉強する	来(く)れば 勉強すれば	来(こ)なければ 勉強しなければ
る-verbs	あげる 着(き)る	あげれば 着(き)れば	あげなければ 着(き)なければ
う-verbs	話す もらう	話せば もらえば	話さなければ もらわなければ

- The ば conditional clause indicates a condition necessary for the event or action in the main clause to take place. In this sense, it can be translated as *if and only if*. The condition must be something that has not been realized.
- The negative form of the ばconditional is ～なければ, which is the same as the ～なければ found in～ なければならない. All negative forms use ～なければ, regardless of what part of speech they are.
- ～なら（ば）is used for the copula verb and な-adjectives. The ば in ～なら（ば）is optional.
- ～ばいい can express suggestions or the speaker's hope :

道子：　この店、今日閉まっている。
This store is closed today.
けんいち：　明日、また来ればいいよ。
It will be fine if we come tomorrow.

黒田：　山田さん、まだ来ませんね。
Yamada-san isn't here yet.
白川:　こまりましたね。三時までに来ればいいんですが。
We're in trouble. But it should be okay if he gets here by three o'clock.

川本：　天気が悪くなってきましたね。
The weather has gotten bad.

青木：　ええ。明日は出かけなけりゃならないから、晴れればいいんだけど、雨がふりそうね。
Yes. It would be nice if it cleared up, since I have to go out tomorrow, but it looks as though it will rain.

- The expressions ～ばいいのに／～ばいいんだけど／～ばいいんですが are often used when the speaker wishes something that can never happen in reality.

友子：　山田さん、今日は仕事で遅(おそ)くなるから、来られないって。
Yamada-san says he can't come today because he has to work late.

道子：　そう、ざんねんね！来られればいいのに。
That's too bad. I wish he could come.

あの人まだいるの？　はやく帰ればいいのに。
Is that person still here? I wish he'd go home soon.

白川：　スミスさんは交通事故(じこ)でけがをして、入院しているそうです。
I heard Smith-san had a traffic accident and was hospitalized.

横田：　ええ、そうなんですか。けがはひどいんですか。
Is that so? Is he badly injured?

白川：　さあ、分かりません。ひどくなければいいんですけどね。
I don't know. I hope it's not serious.

B. Expressing a hypothetical condition, using ～ば (verb conditional form) or ～ばよかった

B-1. ～ば (verb conditional form)

ば-conditional clause		Main clause
	Verb (conditional form)	
もっと日本語が	話せれば、	その会社にしゅうしょく出来たんですが。

If I could speak Japanese better, I could have gotten a job at that company.

B-2. ～ばよかった

	Verb (conditional form)	
昨日(きのう)	勉強すれば	よかった。

It would have been good if I had studied yesterday. (I wish I had studied yesterday.)

もっと足が長ければ、モデルになれるのに。 I could be a model, if my legs were longer.

山田さんが結婚していなければ、よかったんだけど。 I wish Yamada-san were not married.

早(はや)く寝ればよかった。 I wish I had gone to bed early.

電話をしておけばよかったんです。 I wish I had called first.

- The condition in the ば clause may express a counter-factual situation or a hypothetical condition. For example, in the key sentence B-1, the speaker did not get the job because he or she could not speak Japanese well enough. In sentence B-2, he or she wishes that he or she had studied yesterday, but he or she did not actually do so.
- ～ばよかった is used to express the speaker's regret about something that he or she wished he or she had done, or something that he or she wished had happened.
- The colloquial forms of the ばconstruction are shown below. There is no colloquial form for ～なら(ば). In the affirmative, ～れば becomes ～りゃ. For う-verbs, the /-eba/ becomes /-ya/. (The dash indicates a consonant sound, such as /m/ or /k/.) In the negative, なければ becomes なきゃ.

		Affirmative ば conditional	Negative ば conditional
な-adjectives	静かだ	静かなら(ば)⇒N/A	静かじゃなければ⇒静かじゃなきゃ
Copula verbs	学生だ	学生なら(ば)⇒N/A	学生じゃなければ⇒学生じゃなきゃ
い-adjectives	安い いい	安ければ⇒安けりゃ よければ⇒よけりゃ	安くなければ⇒安くなきゃ よくなければ⇒よくなきゃ
Irregular verbs	来(く)る する	来(く)れば⇒来(く)りゃ すれば⇒すりゃ	来(こ)なければ⇒来(こ)なきゃ しなければ⇒しなきゃ
る-verbs	食べる 見る	食べれば⇒食べりゃ 見れば⇒見りゃ	食べなければ⇒食べなきゃ 見なければ⇒見なきゃ
う-verbs	読む 書く	読めば⇒読みゃ 書けば⇒書きゃ	読まなければ⇒読まなきゃ 書かなければ⇒書かなきゃ

話してみましょう

A. Change each sentence in Column A using ば, and choose an appropriate result from Column B.

Example

天気がいい
天気がよければ、歩いて行きます。

Column A	Column B
天気がいい	大きい辞書(じしょ)を使った方がいいです。
寝られない	仕事がはやく終わります。
コンピュータを使う	安く本が買えるかもしれません。
けんこうじゃない	この仕事はつづきません。
私が運転する	この薬を飲むと寝られます。
学生です	十時ごろに着くと思います。
難しい単語(たんご)です	歩いて行きます。

B. Work with a partner. Think about what kinds of things you could do if you were in the following situations. Tell your partner what you would do.

Example

百万ドルあれば、新しい家が買えます。

百万ドルある	冬休みになる
日本に住んでいる	結婚する
大学を卒業する	

C. Work with a group of four. Choose one word from the list on page 362 and tell your group what would be possible or impossible if that item was or wasn't present. The rest of the group will try to guess what word you selected.

Example

A: これがあれば、おふろに入れます。これがなければ、人はしにます。

B: 水ですか。

A: はい、そうです。

水	風	火	山	月	雪	海（うみ）	お中元（ちゅうげん）	クリスマス	大学
勉強	誕生日（たんじょうび）	車	自転車	コンピュータ	テレビ	家			

D. Work with a partner. Use the cue sentence to create a dialogue that expresses your regret. Use the ～ばよかった form.

Example

友達の誕生日（たんじょうび）のプレゼントはセーターを買いましたが、小さすぎました。

A: どうしたんですか。

B: このセーター、買わなければよかったと思っているんです。

A: どうしてですか。

B: 友達の誕生日（たんじょうび）のプレゼントだったんですが、小さすぎたんです。

1. 腕時計（うでどけい）を買った後で、いい腕時計（うでどけい）をもらいました。
2. 安いコンピュータを買ったら、すぐこわれてしまいました。
3. ハイキングに行ったら、けがをしました。
4. 旅行に行った時、カメラを忘れました。
5. あまり花に水をやらなかったので、花がぜんぜんさきませんでした。
6. 一か月前に友達に本を貸しましたが、友達はまだ本を返して来ません。

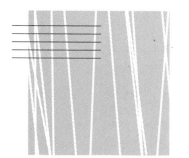

漢字

Statistical facts about kanji

You have learned about 280 **kanji** so far, and you may be wondering how many more you have to learn. Here are some statistical facts about the **kanji** used in Japan that should help you build an overall perspective.

1. There are about 50,000 characters listed in one comprehensive **kanji** dictionary, but most of these are not commonly used. The National Institute of Japanese Language Research conducted a study of the use of **kanji** in newspapers and magazines and found that the 200 most frequently used **kanji** accounted for about 50% of all **kanji** appearing in the text. The 500 most frequently used **kanji** accounted for over 80% of all **kanji**, and 1,000 **kanji** accounted for 90% of the total. The 2,000 most frequently used **kanji** accounted for about 99% of all **kanji**. Having learned 250 **kanji**, you should be able to recognize about one-half of the **kanji** appearing, for example, in a Japanese magazine. Once you learn 500, you will know 80% of the **kanji** you will encounter in most publications.
2. Japanese children learn about 150 to 200 **kanji** each year in elementary school. By the time they reach the sixth grade, they know about 1,000 **kanji**.
3. The most frequently used **kanji** are visually simpler (contain fewer strokes) than the less frequently used ones.
4. There are many **kanji** compounds, so it is important to build your vocabulary knowledge to improve your reading skills even if you know basic **kanji**.

Learning tips

As the number of **kanji** you have learned begins to grow, you will face the inevitable problem of retaining everything. To keep from forgetting characters, it is a good idea to create different groupings of **kanji**. One such grouping may be done according to meaning categories, while another grouping could be based on component parts. Different ways of organizing your knowledge of **kanji** should provide you with multiple ways of remembering them.

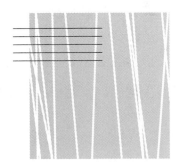

By component parts:

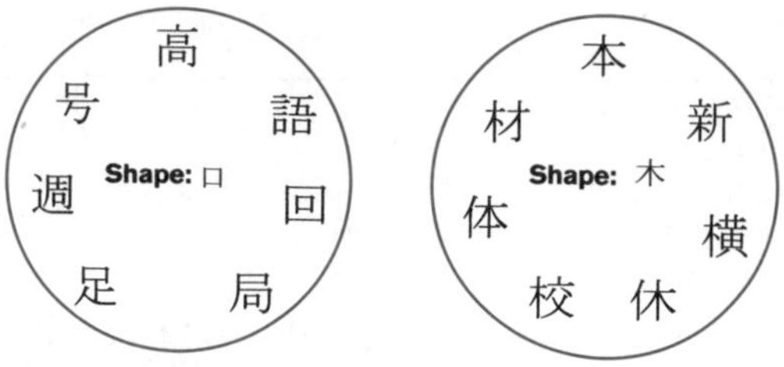

By semantic category:

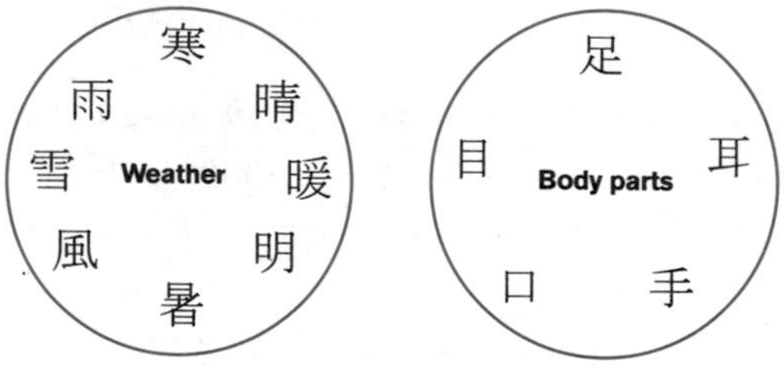

By part of speech:

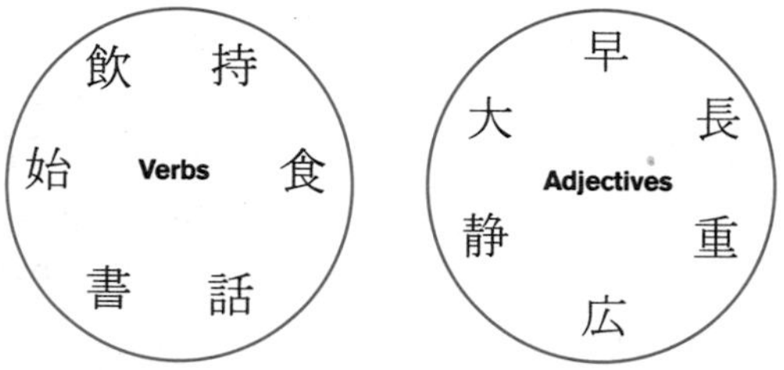

It is also a good idea to write **kanji** when you try to remember them. Writing in this case can also be done by moving your arm through the air. Research has shown that involving different parts of your body activates more regions in your brain, resulting in a higher degree of cognitive activity, which, in turn, leads to better retention.

Flashcards can be used to practice recognition, writing, and the grouping of **kanji**. You can make flashcards with the **kanji** on one side and the meaning, the **on**-reading (in **katakana**), and the **kun**-reading (in **hiragana**) on the other side. Then you can practice reading by looking at the **kanji** on the front of the card and practice writing by looking at the reading and meaning on the back. You can spread **kanji** on the floor and group them according to meanings, component shapes, and pronunciations.

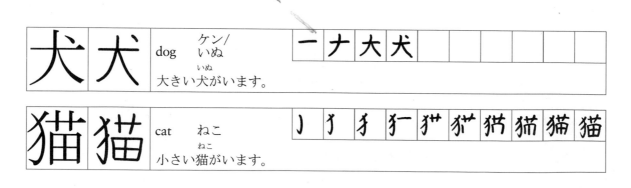

犬	犬	dog ケン/いぬ いぬ 大きい犬がいます。	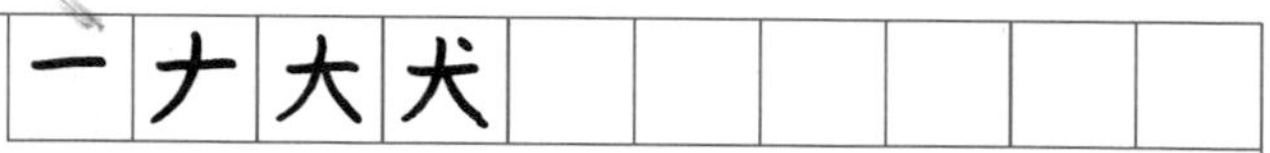
猫	猫	cat ねこ ねこ 小さい猫がいます。	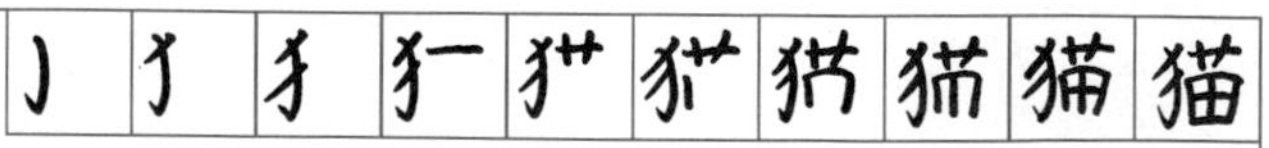

Kanji	Meaning	Readings	Examples
花	flower	カ/はな、ばな	きれいな花(はな)ですね。趣味(しゅみ)は生(い)け花(ばな)です。
葉	leaf	ヨウ/は	木(こ)の葉(は)が赤くなりました。この犬(いぬ)が言葉(ことば)が分かるんです。
石	stone, rock	セキ/いし	こちらは石田(いしだ)さんです。 大石(おおいし)さん来ませんね。
形	shape	ケイ、ギョウ かたち	フランス人形(にんぎょう) すてきな人形(にんぎょう)ですね。
服	Western clothes, dress	フク	きれいな服(ふく)を着る。 婦人服(ふじんふく)
有	to exist, to have	ユウ/あ（る）	田中先生は有名(ゆうめい)なお医者さんです。ここに本が有(あ)ります。有難(ありがと)う
音	sound	オン/おと	音楽(おんがく)はジャズが好きです。
楽	comfortable, enjoyable	ラク、ガク/たの（しい）	新しい音楽(おんがく)より古い音楽(おんがく)をよくききます。この仕事は楽しいです。
雑	rough	ザツ、ザッ	どんな雑誌(ざっし)が好きですか。
誌	record	シ	よく雑誌(ざっし)を読みます。

Kanji	Meaning	Readings	Example
意	mind, heart	イ	この漢字の意味(いみ)は何ですか。
味	taste	ミ/あじ	意味(いみ)を教えて下さい。
変	to change, strange	ヘン/か（わる）/か（える）	変(へん)な人がいます。 大変(たいへん)ですね。名前を変(か)えました。
辞	word, speech	ジ	いい辞書(じしょ)ですね。
早	early	ソウ/はや（い）	今朝(けさ)は早(はや)く起きました。
遅	late	チ/おそ（い）/おく（れる）	授業に遅(おく)れました。 遅(おそ)くなってすみません。
重	heavy	ジュウ/おも（い）	この荷物(にもつ)は重(おも)いので、郵便では送れません。
軽	light (weight, condition)	ケイ/かる（い）	もう少し軽(かる)ければ、航空便(こうくうびん)で送れます。軽(かる)いかぜですね。
広	wide, big (in area)	コウ/ひろ（い）	このアパートは広(ひろ)いですね。新聞に広告(こうこく)を出す。
狭	narrow, small (in area)	キョウ/せま（い）	狭(せま)い所ですが、どうぞお入り下さい。

Kanji	Meaning	Reading	Example
去	past, to leave	キョ/さる	去年(きょねん)の九月に日本へ行きました。
昨	last ~ (yesterday, last year)	サク	昨日(きのう)、病院に行った。(This is a special reading like 明日.)
立	to stand	リツ/た(つ) た(てる)	旅行の計画を立(た)てる。田中さんは立派(りっぱ)です。
派	group, party, school	ハ、パ	立派(りっぱ)な病院ですね。立派(りっぱ)になる。
誕	to be born	タン	誕生日(たんじょうび)はいつですか。
祝	to celebrate, celebration	ショク/いわ(う)	お祝(いわ)いに辞書(じしょ)をあげる。
礼	courtesy, thanks	レイ	お礼(れい)に本をさし上げます。失礼(しつれい)します。
茶	tea	チャ/サ	今年のお中元(ちゅうげん)はお茶(ちゃ)を送ります。喫茶店(きっさてん)に行きませんか。茶色(ちゃいろ)い服(ふく)

新しい読み方

人形(にんぎょう)　お中元(ちゅうげん)　大切(たいせつ)な　腕時計(うでどけい)　小説(しょうせつ)　葉書(はがき)

言葉(ことば)　昨日(きのう)　有名(ゆうめい)　有難(ありがと)うございます　上(あ)げる

練習

下の文を読んで下さい。

1. A: この言葉の意味を教えてほしいんですが。
   B: この辞書はとても使いやすいから、自分でしらべてみてください。
2. 石田さんが誕生日のお祝いに服をくれました。大石さんは人形をくれました。ですから、お礼に花をあげました。
3. この音楽を作った人はとても有名な人です。
4. A: 犬の写真がたくさんありますね。これは犬の雑誌ですか。
   B: いいえ、猫の写真もありますよ。
5. このアパートは広すぎるし、あのアパートは狭すぎるし、いいのがなくて大変です。
6. お中元においしいお茶をいただきました。
7. この猫の病気は軽いです。だから、早く病院につれて行けば、大丈夫(だいじょうぶ)ですよ。
8. 昨日の朝、寝すぎて授業に遅れた。
9. 去年の誕生日にもらったコートは重くて好きじゃなかったので、妹にやった。
10. 立派なケーキですが、ちょっと食べにくそうですね。

上手な読み方

贈(おく)り物のマナー (The etiquette of giving and receiving gifts)

読む前に

下の質問に答えて下さい。

1. あなたの国ではどんな時に贈(おく)り物をしますか。
2. 結婚祝いやしゅうしょく祝いにはどんな物を上げますか。上げてはいけない物はありますか。
3. 贈(おく)り物をする時、何と言いますか。
4. 贈(おく)り物をもらう時、何と言いますか。
5. 贈(おく)り物をもらった後で、よく何をしますか。

読んでみましょう

言葉（ことば）のリスト

目的（もくてき） purpose	〜によって depending on 〜	仲（なか） interpersonal relationships
お葬式（そうしき） funeral	宗教（しゅうきょう） religion	お返（かえ）し reciprocation
ねだん price	包丁（ほうちょう） kitchen knife	

日本では贈（おく）り物をあげる時には、いろいろなマナーがあります。まず、贈（おく）り物の目的（もくてき）によって、あげてもいい物とあげてはいけない物があります。例えば、結婚のお祝いに包丁（ほうちょう）をあげてはいけません。というのは、包丁（ほうちょう）は何かを切るものなので、結婚する二人の仲（なか）を切るという意味になるからです。

つぎに、贈（おく）り物をあげる相手（あいて）がどんな人かよく知っていなければなりません。例（たと）えば、お葬式（そうしき）に花をおくる時にはもらう人の宗教（しゅうきょう）によって、おくってもいい花とおくってはいけない花があります。それから、子供が多い人に何かあげる時は、たくさんある物がいいのです。

また、贈（おく）り物によってはいつあげるか決まっているものがあります。例えば、お中元は七月始めから八月十五日までに、お歳暮（せいぼ）は十二月十日ごろから十二月三十一日までにあげなければなりません。

最後に、よくお中元やお歳暮（せいぼ）はデパートから送りますが、果物（くだもの）や肉など悪くなりやすい食べ物をあげる時は、いつごろ着くか電話しておきます。また、使い方が分かりにくい物はどうやって使うか書いておいたほうがいいでしょう。

それから、贈（おく）り物をもらう時にも色々なマナーがあります。まず、贈（おく）り物をくれた人がよく知っている人じゃなければ、その人の前で贈（おく）り物を開けてはいけません。そして、贈（おく）り物をもらったらすぐ電話でお礼を言うか、お礼の手紙を書かなければなりません。最後に、お祝いをもらったら、お返しをしなければなりません。お返しのためには、たいていもらったものの半分ぐらいのねだんのものをあげます。

日本では色々な時に贈(おく)り物をしますが、マナーがとても難しいので、よく分からない時は日本人の友達にどうすればいいか聞いたほうがいいでしょう。

分かりましたか。

A. On a separate sheet of paper, write the things you have to be careful about when you give or receive gifts in Japan.

B. Circle はい if the statement is true and いいえ if it isn't.

1. はい　いいえ　結婚式にあげてはいけないものはない。
2. はい　いいえ　お葬式(そうしき)には花をおくってはいけない。
3. はい　いいえ　子供がいる人にはたくさんあるものを上げた方がいい。
4. はい　いいえ　あまり知らない人に、プレゼントをもらったら、その人の前でプレゼントを開けない方がいい。

C. 質問に答えて下さい。

1. 包丁(ほうちょう)にはどんな意味がありますか。
2. 食べ物をデパートから送る時、だれに電話をした方がいいのですか。
3. お返(かえ)しをする時、どんなものを上げますか。

D. The reading text beginning on page 369 can be divided into two major parts. Where is the division between them?

E. The first part identified in Exercise D consists of more than one paragraph, and several transition words are used to signal the organization of paragraphs or sentences. Underline the words and write an outline for this part.

読んだ後で

A. Work in groups of four. Discuss the similarities and differences in the etiquette of gift giving and receiving between your country and Japan.

B. When you receive a gift, it is a good idea to write a thank-you letter. As do other letters, a thank-you letter starts with a brief greeting phrase. This is followed by an expression of thanks and comments on the gift. Read the following letter, and identify (1) the initial greeting phrase, (2) the expression of thanks, (3) the gift that the writer has received and his or her comments about it, and (4) the final closing phrase.

> 寒くなってきましたが、お元気ですか。昨日はとてもかわいいクリスマスプレゼントをどうも有難うございました。私はぬいぐるみが大好きなので、とてもうれしかったです。大切にします。それでは、いいお年をおむかえ下さい。みなさんによろしく。
>
> 十二月二十日
>
> スーザン

C. Imagine that you recieved a new Japanese dictionary from your Japanese host family. Use the format of the letter in Exercise B to write a thank-you letter.

上手な聞き方

クリスマス (Christmas)

STUDENT

聞く前に

A. Listen to each short statement and write the name of the giver, receiver, and the gift.

Example

You hear: 父は私にお金をくれた。
Giver__父__ Receiver__私__ Gift__お金__

1. Giver ________ Receiver ________ Gift ________
2. Giver ________ Receiver ________ Gift ________
3. Giver ________ Receiver ________ Gift ________
4. Giver ________ Receiver ________ Gift ________
5. Giver ________ Receiver ________ Gift ________
6. Giver ________ Receiver ________ Gift ________
7. Giver ________ Receiver ________ Gift ________

B. Describe what people in your country do on Christmas Day.

STUDENT

聞いてみましょう

A. アリスさんと石田さんがクリスマスについて話をしています。会話をよく聞いて、クリスマスの何について話しているか考えて書いて下さい。

STUDENT

B. もう一度会話を聞いて、質問に答えて下さい。

1. 石田さんによると、日本ではクリスマスにはどんなことをしますか。
2. アリスさんの家族はクリスマスによくどんなことをしますか。
3. 石田さんとアリスさんは今年のクリスマスに何をしましたか。
4. アリスさんはだれから何をもらいましたか。
5. アリスさんはだれかに何かをあげましたか。石田さんはどうですか。

聞いた後で

A. Write a description of the most important holiday season for your family, explaining the activities that you and your family enjoy, the guests you often invite (if any), and what kinds of gifts you exchange.

B. Work with a partner. Ask your partner about the most important holiday season for his or her family. Ask him or her what his or her family does together, whether they invite friends and relatives (親戚 しんせき), whether they exchange any gifts with each other, and what kinds of gifts have been exchanged in the past.

STUDENT

DICT-A-CONVERSATION

Kimura-san is going to the United States to see her keypal (e-mail penpal). She will stay in her keypal's house. She is asking you (Smith) for some advice.

きむら
木村：______________________________

スミス：______________________________

きむら
木村：______________________________

スミス：______________________________

きむら
木村：______________________________

スミス：______________________________

きむら
木村：______________________________

贈(おく)り物をあげたりもらったりするときに使う言葉
(Phrases used when giving or receiving gifts)

When a Japanese person offers a gift, he or she often uses a set phrase. In formal situations, the most common phrase is これ、つまらないものですが、どうぞ. つまらない means *worthless* or *uninteresting* and the entire phrase means *This is a thing of little worth, but please (accept it)*. This expression is used even if the gift is a very valuable one. Some people choose to use other expressions, such as お好きだとよろしいのですが *(I hope this will be to your liking)*, お礼にと思いまして *(I thought I would make this a token of my appreciation)*, even in formal situations. In casual situations, a simple phrase like これ、～です。どうぞ is used.

Casual　　これ、おみやげ／お祝いです。どうぞ。
これ、ケーキです。みなさんでどうぞ。
これ、母が送ってきたんです。少しですが、どうぞ。

Very casual　　これ、おみやげ／お祝い。どうぞ。
これ、ケーキ。みんなで食べて。
これ、母が送ってきたの。少しだけど。

It is very common for the recipient of a gift to show hesitation when accepting it. This does not mean that he or she does not want the gift. Instead, hesitation indicates modesty on the part of the recipient. For example, in the following exchange, Tanaka-san says そんなしんぱいしないで下さい *(Don't go to so much trouble)* to show his hesitation.

スミス：　これ、ハワイからのおみやげです。どうぞ。
田中：　そんなしんぱいしないで下さい。
スミス：　いいえ、ほんの気持ちですから。
This is a token of my appreciation.
田中：　そうですか。じゃあ、すみません。

Other phrases used to express hesitation are:

Formal　　お気を使わせてしまいまして、もうしわけありません。
Oh, you shouldn't have gone to so much trouble for us.
That's really good of you.
そんなお気を使わないで下さい。
Please don't go to so much trouble.

Casual　　あまり気を使わないで下さい。
しんぱいしないで下さい。

Very casual　　そんな気、使わないで
そんなしんぱいしないで。

After the recipient shows hesitation, the giver can use phrases such as the following.

Formal ほんの気持ちですから。
本当につまらないものですから。
This really is a thing of little worth.

Casual ほんの気持ちですから。
たいしたものじゃありませんから。
ほんの少しですから。
It's not such a big deal.

Very casual 気持ちだから。
たいしたものじゃないし。

Then the recipient will usually accept the gift by saying そうですか、じゃあいただきます *(Is that so? Then, I will humbly receive it)*, すみませんね，ありがとう（ございます）*(Thank you so much for your trouble)*.

A. Act out the following gift exchanges.

1. A: あのう、これつまらないものですが、どうぞ。／これ、お礼にと思いまして。
   B: そんな、お気を使わないで下さい。
   A: いいえ、ほんの気持ちですから。
   B: そうですか。じゃあ、いただきます。
2. A: あのう、これ、クッキーです。みなさんでどうぞ。
   B: そんなしんぱいしないで下さい。
   A: いいえ、たいしたものじゃありませんから。
   B: すみませんね。ありがとうございます。

B. Act out the above conversations, using casual speech.

C. Work with a partner. Role-play various gift-giving situations with your partner.

Giver	Recipient	Occasion	Gift
友達	友達	誕生日	小説（しょうせつ）
学生	先生	お礼	ケーキ
近所の人	近所の人	旅行のおみやげ	おさけ
学生	ホストファミリー	はじめてホストファミリーの家に行く	人形

総合練習

そうごう

どんなプレゼントがいいですか

Work with a group of four. Discuss what kinds of gifts would be appropriate for each situation described below. Think of as many possibilities as you can.

Case 1 来年一年間日本に留学します。日本ではホストファミリーと住む予定です。ホストファミリーにはまだ会ったことがありませんが、四十五さいのお父さんと四十二さいのお母さんと中学生の女の子と十さいの男の子と七十さいのおばあさんがいます。ホストファミリーにどんなものを上げたらいいでしょうか。

Case 2 私は今日本の会社ではたらいています。今度の休みには二週間ぐらいアメリカに帰るつもりです。日本人は旅行に行くと、会社の人や近所の人におみやげをよく買うそうですね。でも、私は会社の人や近所の人におみやげを買ったことがないので、何を上げたらいいかよく分かりません。

Case 3 今までお世話になった先生が学校をやめるそうです。クラスで何か先生にお礼をしたいと思いますが、どんなものをさし上げたらいいでしょうか。

ロールプレイ

A. You are in Japan. You want to give an **oseibo** gift to your professor, but you don't know what is appropriate. Ask a friend for suggestions.

B. Your friend took care of you when you were sick, so you want to express your gratitude by doing something for him or her. Thank him or her and offer some help or a gift.

C. You invited a Japanese friend to your house to spend the winter vacation with your family. Your friend wants to bring a gift. Talk about your family and their favorite things and offer some suggestions.

D. You teach English to a Japanese child. Her mother has given you a rather expensive gift in addition to the tutoring fee. You feel a little uneasy about it but don't want to be rude to the mother. Ask your friend what you should do.

E. You are at a department store. You want to give a shirt to your Japanese friend on her birthday. But she is very petite, and you cannot find anything small enough to fit her. Ask a clerk for help.

単語 (ESSENTIAL VOCABULARY)

Nouns

うでどけい（腕時計） wristwatch
おいわい（お祝い） congratulatory gift
おかし（お菓子） sweets; candy
おくりもの（贈り物） gift
おせいぼ（お歳暮） end-of-year gift exchange
おちゃ（お茶） green tea; tea (in general)
おちゅうげん（お中元） mid-year gift exchange
おみまい（お見舞い） sympathy gift
おもちゃ toy
おれい（お礼） thank-you gift
カード card
カーネーション carnation
くだもの（果物） fruit
クッキー cookies
クリスマス Christmas
コーヒーカップ coffee cup; mug
(お)さけ（酒） liquor; alcoholic beverage; Japanese rice wine
CD audio CD (pronounced as シーディー)
しょうせつ（小説） novel
しょうひんけん（商品券） gift certificate
スニーカー sneakers; sport shoes
せっけん（石けん） soap
タオル towel
ちちのひ（父の日） Father's Day
チョコレート chocolate
ドレス dress
にんぎょう（人形） doll
ぬいぐるみ stuffed toy animal
はちうえ（鉢植え） houseplant
ははのひ（母の日） Mother's Day
バラ rose
バレンタインデー Valentine's Day
プレゼント present
ボール ball
ゆびわ ring

い-adjectives

つまらない uninteresting; boring
ほしい（欲しい） want

な-adjectives

たいせつな（大切な） important; precious

う-verbs

えらぶ（選ぶ） (to) choose
もらう (to) receive
やる (to) give (to socially inferior person)
よろこぶ（喜ぶ） (to) be pleased

る-verbs

あげる（上げる）(to) give (to a socially equal person)
くれる　(to) give (to a socially equal or inferior in-group person)
さしあげる（差し上げる）(to) give (to a socially superior out-group person)

Prefix

こ〜　（子〜）　baby 〜；こいぬ（子犬）puppy;　こねこ（子猫）kitten

Suffix

〜いわい（祝い）congratulatory gift for 〜；　けっこんいわい（結婚祝い）wedding gift; しゅうしょくいわい（就職祝い）gift for getting a new job;　そつぎょういわい（卒業祝い）graduation gift
〜さ　suffix to convert adjective to a noun for measurement 大きさ　高さ　長さ　重さ

Expressions

あまりきをつかわないで下さい。（あまり気を使わないで下さい。）Please don't put yourself out for me.
おきをつかわせてしまいまして。（お気を使わせてしまいまして。）I'm sorry to have caused you so much trouble.
おきをつかわないで下さい。（お気を使わないで下さい。）Please don't concern yourself on my behalf.
おすきだとよろしいのですが。（お好きだとよろしいのですが。）I hope you like it.
おれいにとおもいまして。（お礼にと思いまして。）I thought it would be a token of my appreciation.
おめでとうございます。congratulations
（そんな）しんぱいしないでください。（[そんな]心配しないで下さい。）Please do not worry about me.
せわになる（世話になる）(to) be cared for or helped by somebody
たいしたものじゃありませんから。（たいした物じゃありませんから。）It is of little value . . .
ほんのきもちですから。（ほんの気持ちですから。）Just a token of my appreciation.
ほんのすこしですから。（ほんの少しですから。）Just a little bit . . .
やくにたつ（役に立つ）useful

Passive Vocabulary

Nouns

アパートだい（アパート代） rent
おかえし（お返し） reciprocation
おそうしき（お葬式） funeral
おとしだま（お年玉） a small amount of money given to children on New Year's Day
おんし（恩師） former teacher and mentoring professor or advisor
かんめん（干麺） dried noodles
サラダオイル salad oil
しゅうきょう（宗教） religion
じょうし（上司） one's boss or superior in the workplace
しょくぶつ（植物） plants
せんざい（洗剤） detergent
ぜんぶ（全部） all
ソーセージ sausages
だいどころ（台所） kitchen
てんいん （店員） salesclerk
とうふ（豆腐） tofu
どうぶつ（動物） animal
なか（仲） interpersonal relationship
ねだん（値段） price
のり（海苔） seaweed
ハイヒール high-heeled shoes
ハム ham
はんがえし（半返し） custom of reciprocation by spending about one-half of the original amount when one receives a gift
ビールけん（ビール券） gift certificate for beer
ほうちょう（包丁） kitchen knife
もくてき（目的） objective; purpose
ようがし（洋菓子） Western-style sweets
よさん（予算） budget

い-adjectives

つめたい（冷たい） cold (thing)

Expressions

おふたりのおしあわせをおいのりします（お二人のお幸せをお祈りします） Wishing for your happiness as a couple
かしこまりました Certainly. (polite language used by waiters, clerks, etc.)
ごかつやくをおいのりします（ご活躍をお祈りします） Wishing for your success
ごけっこんおめでとうございます（ご結婚おめでとうございます） Congratulations on your marriage
すばらしいいちねんであることをおいのりします（素晴しい一年であることをお祈りします） I hope you will have a wonderful year
でございます (to) be (polite form of です)
〜によって depending on

For a list of supplementary vocabulary items that will facilitate communication, see the first page of Chapter 7 in your Workbook.

CHAPTER 8

第八課

Japanese students meet on campus with corporate recruiters.

しゅうしょくそうだん

就職相談

Talking about Employment

Functions	Expressing respect to social superiors; Making requests; Expressing opinions
New Vocabulary	Honorific and humble expressions; Polite expressions; Words used at work
Dialogue	リーさんの就職相談（しゅうしょくそうだん） (Lee-san talks about employment)
Culture	Getting a job in Japan; Employment of women; Hiring of non-Japanese
Language	I. Doing and asking favors, using the て-form of the verb + あげる／くれる／もらう
	II. Using honorific expressions to show respect
	III. Using humble expressions to show respect
	IV. Making or letting someone do something, using the causative form; Requesting permission to do something, using the causative form + て下さい
	V. Expressing completion, regret, and the realization that a mistake was made, using ～てしまう
Kanji	The structure of **kanji** compounds
Reading	Job-hunting
Listening	Job interviews
Communication	Responding to compliments and expressing politeness and modesty in formal situations

新しい言葉

そんけい語とけんじょう語 (Honorific and humble expressions)

Honorific expressions are used for actions performed by people with a higher social status than the speaker. You will learn more about these expressions in Language Section II. Humble expressions are used for actions performed by you or a member of your in-group when these actions affect or are related to a social superior. You will learn more about them in Language Section III. The following table shows the honorific and humble equivalents of many common verbs.

Meaning	Regular form	Honorific verbs	Humble verbs
to go	行く	いらっしゃる／おいでになる	まいる
to come	来る	いらっしゃる／おいでになる	まいる
to exist	いる	いらっしゃる／おいでになる	おる
to do	する	なさる	いたす
to see/look at	見る	ごらんになる	拝見(はいけん)する
to say	言う	おっしゃる	申(もう)す / 申(もう)し上げる
to know	知っている	ご存知(ぞんじ)だ	存(ぞん)じておる
to eat	食べる	めし上がる	いただく*
to drink	飲む	めし上がる	いただく*
to sleep	寝る	お休みになる	N/A
to meet	会う	N/A	お目にかかる
to inquire	聞く	N/A	うかがう
to visit	たずねる	N/A	うかがう
to think	思う	N/A	ぞんじる
to be (copula)	だ	でいらっしゃる	N/A

*いただく is also a humble expression for もらう, as introduced in Chapter 7.

下の言葉を覚(おぼ)えていますか

さし上げる

A. 下の文をそんけい語かけんじょう語を使って、書いて下さい。

1. 鈴木先生はおすしを食べました。石田先生はビールを飲みました。
2. 山田先生はこの映画をもう見ましたか。
3. 木村先生は来年オーストラリアに行きます。
4. 川上先生はゴルフをします。
5. 山下先生、先生は日本語の先生ですか。
6. 私は中山と言います。
7. 昨日、先生の家でビールを飲んで、おいしい料理を食べました。
8. 明日、大学で田中先生に会います。
9. 山田先生に聞いてみます。
10. 先週、先生のえを美術館(びじゅつかん)で見ました。

B. ペアかグループで下の練習をして下さい。

1. Work with a partner. Say an honorific verb, and let your partner respond with the corresponding regular verb. Use your book at first, but once you get used to this, try it with your book closed.
2. Work in groups of three. One person should say a regular verb, and the rest of the group should respond with the corresponding honorific verb. The first person to correctly name the honorific verb gets a point.
3. Work with a partner. You are a teacher and your partner is a student. Make a simple request or a question using the regular form of a verb. Your partner will respond using the corresponding humble form. When your partner gets used to it, try it with the book closed.

Example

A: ここに来て下さい。
B: はい、まいります。

4. Work in groups of three. One person plays the role of teacher and makes requests or asks questions. The other members of the group are students, and they should respond as quickly as possible with the corresponding humble form. The first person to respond correctly gets a point.

ていねい語 (Polite expressions)

Polite expressions are used in formal situations. The following table shows the polite equivalents to several regular words.

Meaning	Regular expression	ていねい語 (Polite expression)
to be	だ	でござる（ございます）
to exist	いる／ある	ござる（ございます）
good	いい	よろしい
Mr.; Mrs.; Ms.	〜さん（お客さん、山田さん）	〜様(さま)（お客様(きゃくさま)、山田様(さま)）
That way	そっち	そちら
That way over there	あっち	あちら
Polite prefixes for nouns or adjectives		お + word (Japanese origin)
sushi	すし	おすし
customer; visitor	客(きゃく)	お客(きゃく)
gentle	やさしい	おやさしい
beautiful/pretty	きれい	おきれい
		ご + word (Chinese origin)
sickness	病気	ご病気
kind	親切	ご親切
splendid	立派	ご立派

- そちら and あちら can be used as polite equivalents of その人 and あの人, respectively.
- Not all adjectives or nouns take polite prefixes. For example, the following words cannot be used with either お or ご:

  大きい　多い　黄色い　新しい　四角い　すてきな
  だめな　大丈夫(だいじょうぶ)な　大好きな　春　夏　秋　冬　研究室(しつ)

- Some words are always used with the particle お or ご:

  おたく　おなか　ごはん　ご主人(しゅじん) (your husband)　お茶

下の言葉を覚(おぼ)えていますか。What are their less polite equivalents?

こちら　どちら　この方　その方　あの方　お礼
お見舞(みま)い　お土産(みやげ)　おめでとうございます　おはようございます
有難うございます　お気を使わせてしまいまして
お気を使わないで下さい　お好きだとよろしいのですが

C. Change the verb in the following sentences into ていねい語.

Example

山田さんの家は立派ですね。
山田さんのおたくはご立派ですね。

1. 電話はかいだんの下にあります。
2. 婦人服売り場（ふじんふくう）は三かいです。
3. 先生の子供はとても元気です。
4. 今日は休みです。
5. 気分が悪いんです。
6. 駅の前に交番がある。
7. 小さくてもいいですか。
8. そっちは博物館（はくぶつかん）だ。

会社で使う言葉 (Words used at work)

上司（じょうし）	superior; boss	（申込）用紙（もうしこみ ようし）	(application) form
課長（かちょう）	section manager	履歴書（りれきしょ）	résumé
(お) 客（きゃく）	customer; guest	すいせんじょう	letter of reference
同僚（どうりょう）	colleague	大事（だいじ）な	important
プロジェクト	project	習（なら）う	to learn
会議（かいぎ）	meeting	出張（しゅっちょう）（する）	(to go on a) business trip
書類（しょるい）	documents	申（もう）し込（こ）む	to apply
専門（せんもん）	specialization	説明（せつめい）（する）	explanation (to explain)
面接（めんせつ）	interview	返事（へんじ）（する）	response (to respond)
広告（こうこく）	advertisement	経験（けいけん）	experience
受付（うけつけ）	reception desk		

下の言葉を覚（おぼ）えていますか

社長　相談（そうだん）（する）　研究（する）　えらぶ　働（はたら）く　海外（かいがい）
集（あつ）める　会計士（かいけいし）　決める　決まる　マネージャー　弁護士（べんごし）
給料　貿易（ぼうえき）会社　記入（きにゅう）する　計画　さがす　就職（しゅうしょく）する
じゅんびする　調（しら）べる

D. 下線（かせん） (blank) にてきとうな (appropriate) 言葉を書いて下さい。

1. 課長（かちょう）や社長のことです。________________
2. 一緒（いっしょ）に働いている人です。________________

3. 質問や招待(しょうたい)に答えることです。＿＿＿＿＿＿＿＿＿＿

4. 仕事のために行く旅行です。＿＿＿＿＿＿＿＿＿＿

5. 新聞やテレビでよく見る物です。＿＿＿＿＿＿＿＿＿＿

6. 先生が学生のためによく書く物です。＿＿＿＿＿＿＿＿＿＿

7. 家や会社に来る大事(だいじ)な人です。＿＿＿＿＿＿＿＿＿＿

8. その人に会って色々質問をすることです。＿＿＿＿＿＿＿＿＿＿

9. 何かに申(もう)し込(こ)む時に記入(きにゅう)する物です。＿＿＿＿＿＿＿＿＿＿

ダイアローグ

はじめに

下の質問に日本語で答えて下さい。

1. どんな仕事をしたことがありますか。
2. 仕事をさがす時、会社に何を送りますか。
3. 仕事をさがす時、だれかに相談(そうだん)しますか。どんなものを見たり読んだりしますか。
4. 将来(しょうらい)どんな仕事をしたいですか。

リーさんの就職相談(しゅうしょくそうだん) (Lee-san talks about employment)

STUDENT

The following **manga** frames are scrambled, so they are not in the order described in the dialogue. Read the dialogue and unscramble the frames by writing the correct order in the box located in the upper right corner of each frame.

リーさんと杉本(すぎもと)先生が話しています。

リー：　あのう、杉本(すぎもと)先生、就職(しゅうしょく)のことでちょっとご相談(そうだん)したいことがあるのですが。研究室(しつ)にうかがってもよろしいでしょうか。

杉本(すぎもと)先生：　ええ、いいですよ。今日はやってしまわなければならない仕事があるから、だめですが、明日なら大丈夫(だいじょうぶ)ですよ。

リー：　じゃあ、明日は何時ごろ研究室(しつ)にいらっしゃいますか。

杉本(すぎもと)先生：　一時ごろには来ていますが、来られますか。

リー：　ええ、大丈夫(だいじょうぶ)です。では、一時ごろまいります。

つぎの日、リーさんは杉本(すぎもと)先生の研究室(しつ)に来ました。

杉本(すぎもと)先生：　あ、どうぞ。

リー：　失礼(しつれい)します。

杉本(すぎもと)先生：　そこにすわって下さい。

リー：　はい。

杉本(すぎもと)先生：　相談(そうだん)したいことって何ですか。

リー：　はい。私は来年卒業なんですが、出来たら、日本で就職(しゅうしょく)したいと思っています。

杉本(すぎもと)先生：　そうですか。

リー:　それで、先生にすいせんじょうを書いていただけないかと思って。

杉本(すぎもと)先生:　いいですよ。でも、日本では、すいせんじょうはあまり使いませんよ。

リー：　えっ、そうなんですか。外国人もいらないんでしょうか。

杉本(すぎもと)先生：　ああ、そうですね。日本人はいらないけど、外国人と日本人では違うかもしれませんね。

リー：　じゃあ、もう一度調(しら)べてみます。

杉本(すぎもと)先生：　でも、ご両親はいいんですか。リーさんがたいわんに帰らなくても。

リー：　ええ、両親はいつも私の好きにさせてくれます。今度も日本で働(はたら)きたいなら、いいと言ってくれました。

杉本(すぎもと)先生：　そうですか。それはよかったですね。

分かりましたか

A. Lee-san is describing his discussion with Professor Sugimoto. Complete the following description using the appropriate expressions.

ぼくは来年__________んですが、出来たら、__________働(はたら)きたいと思っているんです。それで、杉本(すぎもと)先生に、__________を書いていただこうと思って、杉本先生の__________に行きました。杉本(すぎもと)先生によると日本では__________がいらないかもしれないそうです。

B. 質問に答えて下さい。

1. 杉本(すぎもと)先生はいつリーさんに会うのですか。どうして今日はだめなのですか。
2. リーさんはいつ就職(しゅうしょく)するつもりですか。
3. どこで就職(しゅうしょく)するつもりですか。
4. 杉本(すぎもと)先生は、仕事をさがす時、外国人と日本人は同じだと思っていましたか。
5. リーさんのご両親はリーさんの就職(しゅうしょく)についてどう思っていますか。

C. Identify the honorific and humble expressions used by Lee-san, and paraphrase them in regular polite speech.

日本の文化

Getting a job in Japan. How do college graduates look for a job in your country? What processes are involved in getting a job?

As in many other countries, Japanese college students start looking for permanent jobs once they become seniors in college. They request information about companies, attend information sessions organized by company personnel, and send applications. This is called 会社回(まわ)り, which means making the rounds of companies. Some companies give applicants written tests. All of them have interviews called 面接(めんせつ)試験(しけん) or 面接(めんせつ). The (mostly male) recruits (see below) typically cut their hair and wear navy or other dark suits for the occasion.

Two features that differentiate Japanese recruiting and job-hunting practices from those found elsewhere are that (1) everyone coming on to the job market in a given year does so at the same time, and (2) virtually no one has had significant work experience prior to graduation. The regular employment practice is to hire college graduates in April of every year, since the academic year ends in March. Japanese universities do not have co-op programs or other systems that enable their students to interact with the outside world. Also, virtually all college students maintain full-time student status throughout college. It is rare (and difficult) for a student to take, for example, a year off from college to take a job and then come back to finish school. This means that companies must rely on extensive on-the-job training for their new recruits. For this reason, companies generally look for graduates from the more famous schools, because they see these graduates as more promising "raw material" for development into full-fledged employees. This is, however, beginning to change, as Japanese companies venture further into the international world and have come to value diversity and individuality in the work force. Some companies now even mask the names of recruits' colleges during the recruiting process. Further, there is no longer the stigma that was once attached to changing jobs, so some people in the job market may have had work experience.

People working for Japanese companies are paid a monthly salary (サラリー). In addition, most companies pay a bonus (ボーナス) at the end of the year. The amount of the bonus is determined by the financial state of the company, but it is usually about two months' salary. Promotions traditionally have been made by seniority, but merit raises are becoming more common.

- *Employment of women. Do you think women are treated equally in terms of salary and types of work in your country?*

As in other countries, Japanese female workers face problems with inequalities in employment practices. Although the number of female workers and their net incomes have increased, the salary difference between male workers and female workers has remained larger than in other developed countries. (The average income of female workers is 60% of that of males.)

Promotions and pay raises for female workers can be seen only among those who graduated from four-year colleges—and the four-year college graduates amounted to only 5.2% of the entire female work force in 1992. This confirms the common belief that companies employ female workers for non-essential tasks, expecting them to get married and resign early. Since the Japanese economy began to slow down, job hunting has also grown difficult, especially for female graduates of four-year colleges. Female junior college graduates do better at finding jobs because they more closely fit the "traditional" image of women, who were not expected to stay in a company for a long time, especially after getting married or having a child. For this reason, promotion-track jobs have most commonly been offered to male graduates instead of female graduates.

Female workers have a better chance for advancement in professional sectors, where the traditional employment system has played a lesser role. Female workers claim majorities among pharmacists and teachers in primary and junior high schools, and the number of female lawyers, public accountants, doctors, and dentists is also steadily increasing.

In spite of the 男女雇用均等法(だんじょこようきんとうほう) (a law mandating employment equality between sexes), which was enacted in the late 1980s, gender inequality in Japan remains larger than in other developed countries. The recent change in the traditional employment system may provide an opportunity for female workers who have received little advantage under the traditional system.

- *Hiring of non-Japanese. Do you want to work for a Japanese company? Why or why not?*

The hiring of non-Japanese nationals for full-time positions is still rare, although the number of such cases is increasing. A few facts: (1) science majors do better in getting jobs than non-science majors, (2) people with graduate degrees do better than those without, and (3) a high level of proficiency in the Japanese language is required in most cases.

LANGUAGE

I. Doing and asking favors, using the て-form of the verb + あげる／くれる／もらう

A. Expressing appreciation for a favor done for you or a member of your in-group, using the て-form of the verb + くれる／下さる

A-1. Using て-form of the verb + 下さる

Giver		Recipient	Particle		Verb (て-form)	Auxiliary verb
先生	は	私	に	電話番号を	教えて	下さいました。

My teacher told me his telephone number (for my benefit).

A-2. Using て-form of the verb + くれる

Giver			Verb (て-form)	Auxiliary verb
母	は	私の部屋を	そうじして	くれました。

My mother cleaned my room (for me).

同僚(どうりょう)が妹を遊園地に連(つ)れて行ってくれました。

My co-worker took my younger sister to an amusement park.

道子：　あら、かわいい人形ね。どうしたの？

Oh, that's a cute doll. Where did you get it?

友子：　姉がむすめに買ってくれたのよ。

My sister bought it for my daughter.

先生がすいせんじょうを書いて下さいました。

My professor wrote a letter of reference for me.

入院していた時、上司(じょうし)がお見舞(みまい)に来て下さいました。

My boss was nice enough to visit me when I was hospitalized. (literally: When I was hospitalized, my boss visited me at the hospital.)

- In Japanese, an action that is done for the benefit of someone else can be expressed by using the て-form with the verbs of giving and receiving.
- Like くれる and 下さる (in Chapter 7, pages 341–342), the recipient of the て-form of the verb + くれる／下さる is the speaker or a member of the speaker's in-group. The giver can be anyone but the speaker. 下さる is used when the giver is an out-group person who is socially superior to the speaker.
- The in-group/out-group distinction can be applied in social contexts other than family. For example, the members of the speaker's company comprise

an in-group in contrast with those who do not belong to that company. In this case, use 下さる when a customer, who is regarded as a social superior to company members in a business context, does something for any member of the company, including the speaker's boss, or even the company president (who would be considered the speaker's superior in a strictly in-company relationship).

お客様(きゃくさま)が社長にお祝いを持って来て下さいました。
The customer kindly brought a congratulatory gift to the president.

- The て-form of the verb + 下さい (Volume 1, Chapter 8) and the て-form of the verb + くれる／下さる (Volume 2, Chapter 3) are derived from this structure.

- The recipient of a favor need not be overtly marked when it is obvious.

私が病気だったので、同僚(どうりょう)の山田さんが出張(しゅっちょう)に行ってくれた。
I was sick, so my collegue Yamada-san went on the business trip (for me).

B. Expressing willingness to help, using the て-form of the verb + あげる／やる

B-1. Using the て-form of the verb + あげる

Giver		Recipient	Particle		Verb (て-form)	Auxiliary verb
スミスさん	は	同僚(どうりょう)	に	書類(しょるい)を	持って行って	あげました。

Smith-san kindly brought the document to his colleague.

B-2. Using the て-form of the verb + やる

Giver			Verb (て-form)	Auxiliary verb
私	は	犬と	遊んで	やりました。

I played with the dog (for the benefit of the dog).

母は子猫をおふろに入れてやりました。
My mother gave a bath to the kitten (for the benefit of the kitten).

山田さんが忙しくて出来ないので、私がファックスで返事(へんじ)を出しておいてあげました。
Yamada-san was too busy, so I faxed a response.

道子：　五時までに駅に行かなきゃいけないんだけど、遅れそうなの。

I have to be at the station by five o'clock, but it looks like I'm going to be late.

まもる：　じゃあ、ぼくが車で送ってあげるよ。

Well, I can take you (to the station) by car.

- As is the case with あげる and やる (in Chapter 7, pages 343–345), the recipient of any action expressed by the て-form of the verb + あげる／やる is in the speaker's out-group. If both giver and recipient are in the speaker's in-group, it is okay to use the て-form of the verb + くれる／あげる／やる, but the use of くれる implies an identification with the recipient and use of あげる or やる indicates neutrality or an identification with the giver.
- The て-form of the verb + あげる／やる must be used if the giver is the speaker. Use あげる when the recipient is socially equal to the speaker and やる when he or she is socially inferior.
- Although it is theoretically possible to use さしあげる in this structure, in reality the て-form of the verb + さしあげる is rarely used. さしあげる explicitly indicates that the giver is doing a favor for a superior, and such explicit remarks are considered condescending. In such cases, use either a humble expression (Language Section III of this chapter) or the simple ます-form.

私は先生のかばんを持ってさし上げました。	I carried the professor's bag (for his benefit).
私は先生のかばんをお持ちしました。(humble form of 持つ)	I humbly carried the professor's bag.
私は先生のかばんを持ちました。	I carried the professor's bag.

C. Expressing that someone has benefited from someone else's action, using the て-form of the verb + もらう／いただく

C-1. Using the て-form of the verb + いただく

Recipient		Giver	Particle		Verb (て-form)	Auxiliary verb
私	は	上司（じょうし）	に	そのお客（きゃく）さんを	しょうかいして	いただきました。

I got my boss to introduce that customer to me.

C-2. Using the て-form of the verb + もらう

Recipient		Giver	Particle		Verb (て-form)	Auxiliary verb
弟	は	父	に	コンピュータを	買って	もらった。

My younger brother got my father to buy him a computer.

田中さんは同僚(どうりょう)にその書類(しょるい)を見せてもらいました。
Tanaka-san got his colleague to show him the document.

けんじくんは近所の人に遊(あそ)んでもらった。
Kenji got his neighbor to play with him.

弟は先生に本を貸していただいた。
My younger brother got the teacher to lend him the book.

- As is the case when もらう or いただく is used as the sentence's main verb, the recipient of the favor is the grammatical subject and the giver of the favor is the source in the て-form of the verb + もらう／いただく construction. The giver is marked by に or by から, but the use of から is limited to cases such as 送る where the main verb indicates a transfer of an object.

友達に／からしゃしんを送ってもらった。 I had my friend send pictures.
友達に本を読んでもらった。(The particle から cannot be used.) I had my friend read a book.

- Sentences with the て-form of the verb + もらう tend to imply that the recipient is asking or persuading the giver for a favor. This is especially true when the verb is used in the future tense.

私は父にコンピュータを買ってもらうつもりです。
I intend to get my father to buy me a computer.

課長(かちょう)は、大事(だいじ)な仕事だから鈴木(すずき)さんに出張(しゅっちょう)に行ってもらいたいと言っています。
The section manager says he wants to get Mr. Suzuki to go on this business trip because it is an important job.

- The request forms made with the て-form of the verb + いただける (Volume 2, Chapter 3) are derived from this structure. いただける is the potential form of いただく. The て-form of the verb + いただけませんか means *could I humbly receive the favor of your doing* ～. The potential form of もらう, もらえる, can be used instead of いただける to express a less formal request. The て-form of the verb + もらえませんか means *can I receive the favor of your doing* ～, and is interchangeable with the て-form of the verb + くれませんか (Volume 2, Chapter 3).

広告(こうこく)を出してもらえませんか。／広告(こうこく)を出してくれませんか。
Could you run an ad for me?
ねえ、その本取ってもらえる？／ねえ、その本取ってくれる？
Hey, could you hand me that book?

- Use the て-form of the verb + いただきたい to express a desire directed toward a superior. (いただきたい is a combination of いただく and たい.) The て-form of the verb + もらいたい (a combination of もらう and たい) also expresses a desire of the speaker, and can be used interchangeably with the て-form of the verb + ほしい (Chapter 7, page 351). The て-form of the verb + ほしい／もらいたい／いただきたい can be used for indirect requests, which are less forceful than 〜ていただけませんか／もらえませんか／くださいませんか／くれませんか。

この履歴書(りれきしょ)を読んでいただきたいんですが。
Could I ask you to read this resume for me?

山田：　明日の会議(かいぎ)に出てもらいたいんだけど。／
明日の会議(かいぎ)に出てほしいんだけど。
Can I get you to attend the meeting tomorrow? (literally: I want to get you to attend the meeting tomorrow.)
山本：　あ、ごめん。明日はもう予定があるんだ。
Oh, I'm sorry, but I already have plans for tomorrow.

- Use either the negative form of 〜ほしい or 〜たい(〜ほしくない, 〜もらいたくない, or 〜いただきたくない), or 〜ないでほしい, 〜ないでもらいたい, or 〜ないでいただきたい to express negative desires.

社長にはこのレポートをまだ読んでいただきたくないんです。／読まないでいただきたいんです。
I don't want the president to read this report yet. (polite)
このことはだれにも言ってもらいたくないんです。／言わないでもらいたいんです。
I don't want you to tell anybody about this.

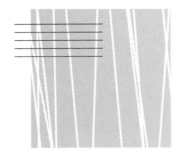

話してみましょう

A. The following chart illustrates favors done for the speaker or members of the speaker's in-group. You are the speaker. Describe each exchange using the て-form of the verb + 下さる／くれる.

Example

弟は（私に）申込用紙(もうしこみようし)を持って来てくれました。

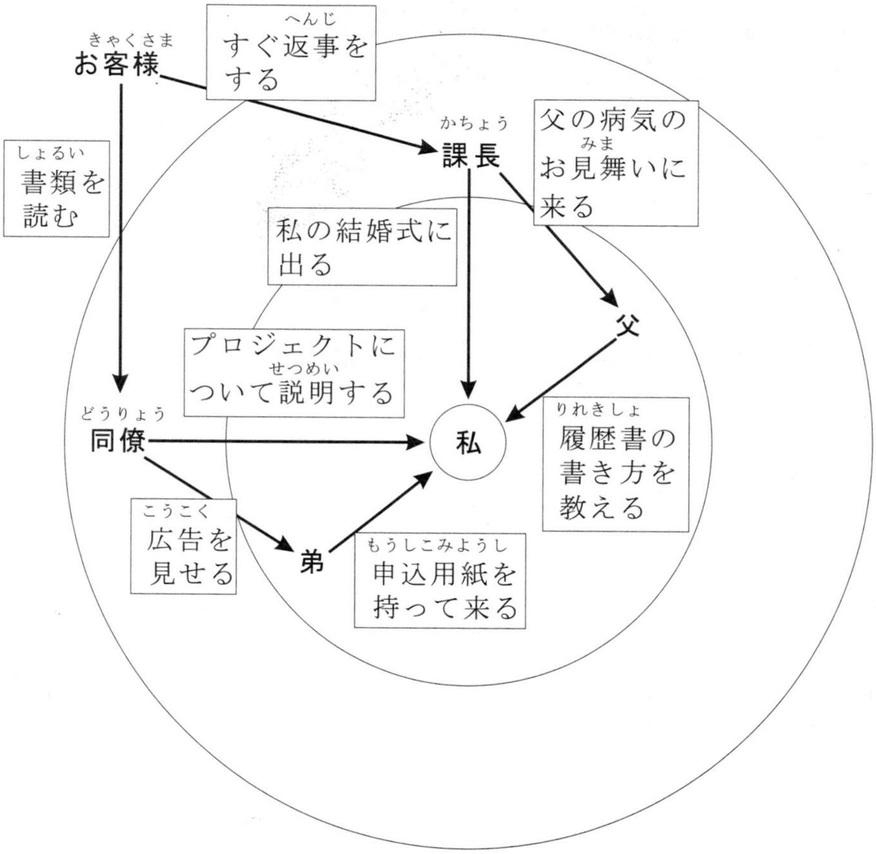

B. Express the same favors described in Exercise A, this time using the て-form of the verb + いただく／もらう.

Example

私は弟に申込用紙(もうしこみようし)を持って来てもらいました。

C. The following chart illustrates favors done by and for different people. Describe the exchanges using the て-form of the verb + あげる／やる.

Example

母は妹に服を買ってあげました。

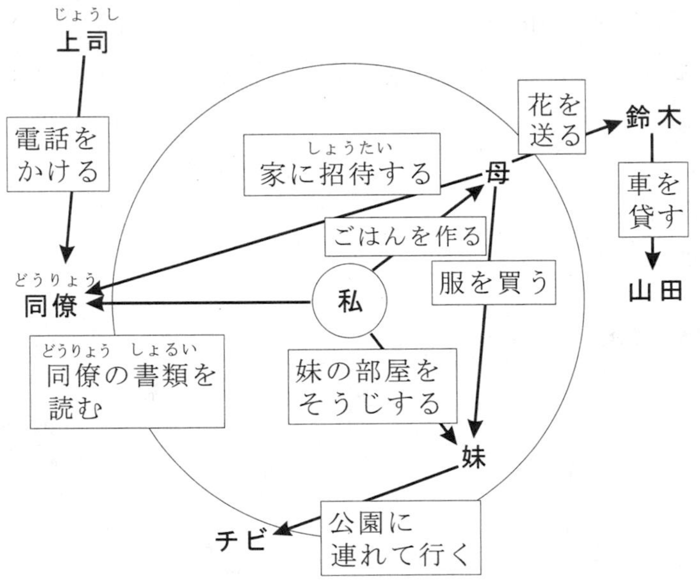

D. Express the same favors described in Exercise C, this time using the て-form of the verb + いただく／もらう. Note that not every exchange can be expressed with いただく or もらう.

Example

妹は母にふくを買ってもらいました。

E. Work as a class. Check four items in the column labeled 私 in the table your instuctor will give you that you would not mind doing for a classmate. Check four other items in the column labeled クラスメート as things you want to have someone do for you. Ask your classmates to do one of the favors you hope to receive, and write the name of the first person who agrees to do it for you. When you have found someone to do the first favor, proceed to the next, and so on. Your classmates will also ask you for favors. You are allowed to agree to do something for someone only if you have marked that item in the 私 column. Find a different person to do each favor for you. Give some reason for not doing a favor if you have not marked it in the 私 column. Use casual speech.

Example

A: あのう、１０ドル貸してくれない？。
B: 貸してあげたいけど、持ってないんだ。(male) ／
　 貸してあげたいけど、持ってないの。(female)
or
B: ええ、いいよ。貸してあげる。(male) ／
　 ええ、いいわよ。貸してあげる。(female)

F. Use the results from Exercise E to report to the class who helped you.

Example

〜さんに10ドル貸してもらいました。
〜さんにはノートを見せてもらいました。

II. Using honorific expressions to show respect

A. Using honorific verbs

Question	
	Verb (honorific)
山田先生はまだ	いらっしゃいますか。

Is Professor Yamada still here?

Answer				
	Verb (honorific)			
		Verb (stem)		
いいえ、もう	お	帰り	に	なりました。

No, he has already gone home.

ウエイター： 何をめし上がりますか。
What would you like to eat? (honorific)

客(きゃく) ： 天ぷらをおねがいします。
I'd like to have tempura.

それは先生がお書きになった本です。
That is the book the professor wrote.

山田： 課長(かちょう)は明日の会議(かいぎ)のことご存知(ぞんじ)ですか。
Section manager, do you know about the meeting tomorrow? (honorific)

鈴木課長(すずきかちょう)： ああ、知ってるよ。
Yes, I do.

今日、大川銀行の方がおいでになって、その書類(しょるい)を持っていらっしゃいました。
A representative from Okawa Bank came today and took the document. (honorific)

Verb types	Dictionary form		Honorific verbs
Verbal noun + する			お／ご + Verbal noun + なさる
	電話する (to call)	→	お電話なさる
	説明(せつめい)する (to explain)	→	ご説明(せつめい)なさる
る-verbs and う-verbs			お + Verb (stem) + に + なる
	帰る (to return)	→	お帰りになる
	待つ (to wait)		お待ちになる
	見せる (to show)	→	お見せになる

- In general, honorific verbs are formed by お + the stem of the verb + に + なる. The honorific form of verbal nouns is made by (お／ご)+ verbal noun + なさる. There are many irregular humble verbs shown in the table on page 380.

- So far, we have introduced two forms of speech—the polite (です and the ます form of the verb) and the plain (だ and dictionary form of verbs). These forms are used to express levels of formality and politeness toward one's listener. The polite forms are used in more formal situations, often when the listener is not close socially to the speaker, and the plain forms are used in casual situations, among friends. We come now to honorific and humble expressions, which introduce a new concept to the discussion, that of showing respect toward the topic of conversation or a socially superior listener. The topic of the conversation can be the person to whom you are speaking, or it can be a third person who is not even present. It is not uncommon in a Japanese conversational context for two friends talking about a teacher, for example, to use honorific and humble expressions while at the same time using plain form verb endings. In the following example, Kimura-san and Lee-san are friends and thus use plain verb forms in a casual conversational setting, but they still use the honorific お帰りになる to express the actions of Yamada-sensei.

木村(きむら)：　リーさん、山田先生、もうお帰りになった。
　Lee-san, has Yamada-sensei gone home?
リー：　うん、もうお帰りになったよ。
　Yes, he is already gone.

- Social superiority may be measured by age, social status, experience, or the benefactor-recipient relationship. For example, a recipient of a favor usually uses honorific expressions toward the giver. Furthermore, honorific expressions are often used in situations where the speaker knows little or nothing about the listener. It is very common to hear telephone operators, hotel clerks, and restaurant clerks using honorifics with their customers.

- なさる, いらっしゃる, and おっしゃる are う-verbs. Their polite forms are なさいます, いらっしゃいます, and おっしゃいます, respectively.
- When a verb is combined with an auxiliary verb such as 〜ている or 〜てくれる, you need to change only the auxiliary verb to its honorific form.

読んでいる → 読んでいらっしゃる
している → していらっしゃる
貸してくれる → 貸して下さる
起こしてくれる → 起こして下さる

- There are some exceptions to this rule for 〜ている, however:

行っている／来ている → おいでだ or いらっしゃっている
言っている → おっしゃっている
食べている／飲んでいる → めし上がっている／食べていらっしゃる／飲んでいらっしゃる
寝ている → お休みだ
着ている → おめしだ

- For some verbs, you can use お + verb stem + です instead of 〜ていらっしゃる.

書いている → お書きだ／書いていらっしゃる
待っている → お待ちだ／待っていらっしゃる

B. Making requests with honorifics

	お	Verb (stem)	下さい
ここで	お	待ち	下さい。

Please wait here.

そのペンをお使い下さい。 Please use that pen.

この履歴書(りれきしょ)をごらん下さい。 Please look at this résumé.

明日おいで下さいませんか。／明日おいでいただけませんか。 Could you please come here tomorrow?

こちらでお待ちいただけませんか。／こちらでお待ち下さいませんか。 Could you please wait here?

Verb types	Dictionary form		Honorific request
Verbal noun + する			お／ご + verbal noun + 下さい
	電話する (to call)	→	お電話下さい
	説明(せつめい)する (to explain)	→	ご説明(せつめい)下さい
る-verbs and う-verbs			お + verb (stem) + 下さい
	開ける (to open)	→	お開け下さい
	話す (to talk)	→	お話し下さい
	待つ (to wait)	→	お待ち下さい

- In general, honorific requests are formed by お + verb (stem) + 下さい. Honorific requests with verbal nouns are formed by お／ご + verbal noun + 下さい. Use 下さいませんか or いただけませんか to make the request even more polite.
- An honorific request using irregular honorific verbs ending with ～になる can be formed by replacing ～になる with 下さい.

Verb (dictionary form)	Honorific (dictionary form)	Honorific request
行く／来る／いる	おいでになる	おいで下さい
見る	ごらんになる	ごらん下さい
寝る	お休みになる	お休み下さい
着る	おめしになる	おめし下さい

- Honorific requests made from other irregular honorific verbs are formed by using the て-form of the verb + 下さい.

Verb (dictionary form)	Honorific (dictionary form)	Honorific request
行く／来る／いる	いらっしゃる	いらっしゃって下さい
する	なさる	なさって下さい
言う	おっしゃる	おっしゃって下さい
食べる／飲む	めし上がる	めし上がって下さい

- It is customary to use honorific requests when speaking to customers in locations such as restaurants, hotels, banks, and stores.

C. Using the honorific forms of adjectives

	Prefix	な-adjective	Noun	
社長のおくさまは	お	きれいな	方	だ。

The president's wife is a beautiful person.

課長(かちょう)はゴルフがお上手です。

The section manager is good at golf. (honorific)

社長はむすめさんが結婚なさったので、毎日おさびしそうです。

The president looks sad because his daughter got married. (honorific)

先生はとてもご立派な方です。

The professor is a very stately person. (honorific)

今日はご病気でいらっしゃれません。

(He/She) is ill and cannot come today. (honorific)

- Honorific adjectives are made by adding the prefix お to the adjective. Some な-adjectives such as 立派 take the prefix ご（ご立派）instead of お.
- Not all adjectives have honorific forms. For example, おもしろい, 大きい, and 有名な are some examples of adjectives without honorific forms.

話してみましょう

A. Change 私 to 先生 and rewrite the sentences using the appropriate honorific forms.

Example

私は明日から東京に行きます。
先生は明日から東京にいらっしゃいます。

1. 私は九時ごろ帰ります。
2. 私は申込用紙(もうしこみようし)に名前を書きました。
3. 私はそのプロジェクトについて調(しら)べました。
4. 私は会議(かいぎ)に出るつもりです。
5. 私は昨日十二時ごろ寝ました。
6. 私はここに来ています。
7. 私はワープロの使い方を習(なら)っています。
8. 私はとても元気です。
9. 私はテニスが上手です。

B. Work in groups of four. You are a company president. Write five sentences you can act out. The rest of the group will try to describe what you are doing, using honorific forms. Anyone who correctly describes your actions gets a point.

Example

A pretends to read a newspaper.

B: 社長は本を読んでいらっしゃいます。
A: いいえ、そうじゃないんです。
C: 社長は新聞を読んでいらっしゃいます。
A: はい、そうです。

C. Work with a partner. You are working in the locations cited in problems 1–6 below and need to make various requests to customers, as described. Your partner is a customer. Make a request, using the honorific request form.

Example

レストラン／ここで待ってほしい

A: お客様(きゃくさま)、こちらでお待ち下さいませんか。
B: はい。

1. レストラン／ここにすわってほしい
2. レストラン／ジャケットを着てほしい
3. 旅行会社／クレジットカードの番号を教えてほしい
4. 旅行会社／明日までにお金をはらってほしい
5. ホテル／この用紙(ようし)に名前を書いてほしい
6. ホテル／十一時までにロビーに来てほしい

D. Work with a partner. You are an editor of a school newspaper. Your partner is a famous Japanese person who has come to the campus to give a lecture. (Decide on the topic.) Interview the person politely so you can write an interesting article. Your instructor will give you a table containing the information you should obtain. Try to get more information about the person you are interviewing.

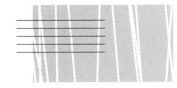

Example

学生:　始めまして、スミスともうします。よろしくおねがいします。お名前を教えていただけませんか。

先生：　始めまして。MIT の田中です。

学生：　田中さまのお仕事／ご専門(せんもん)は何ですか。

先生：　ロボットの研究です。

学生：　そうですか。いつこちらにおいでになりましたか。／いつこちらにいらっしゃいましたか。

先生：　おとといの晩着きました。

III. Using humble expressions to show respect

	Request from a superior
先生：	田中さんこの荷物(にもつ)ちょっと持ってくれませんか。

Tanaka-san, would you hold this bag for a minute?

		Verb (humble)		
		Prefix	Verb stem	する
田中：	はい、	お	持ち	します。

Yes, I will hold it (for you).

学生:　ちょっとお話ししたいことがあるのですが、研究室(しつ)にうかがってもよろしいでしょうか。
I have something I would like to talk with you about. May I come to your office?

先生：　ええ、いいですよ。
Yes, that would be fine.

先生：　ちょっと待ってくれますか。
Wait a little bit, okay?

学生：　はい、ここでお待ちします。
Yes, I'll wait here.

- In general, humble verbs are formed with お + verb stem + する. Humble equivalents of verbal nouns are formed by お／ご + verbal noun + する.

Verb types	Dictionary form		Humble verb
Verbal noun + する			お／ご + verbal noun + する
	電話する (to call)	→	お電話する
	説明(せつめい)する (to explain)	→	ご説明(せつめい)する
る-verbs and う-verbs			お + verb (stem) + する
	持つ (to hold)	→	お持ちする
	見せる (to show)	→	お見せする
	送る (to send)	→	お送りする

- There are many irregular humble verbs, shown in the table on page 380. Here are more examples of the special humble form:

連(つ)れて行く／連(つ)れて来る → お連(つ)れする
持って行く／持って来る → お持ちする

- Humble verbs are used to express respect for the subject of the conversation, who may or may not also be the listener. Honorifics are used to describe the actions of the person who is the object of respect, and humble verbs are used to describe the actions of the speaker, insofar as they affect the object of respect. Their intent is to show that the speaker considers himself or herself socially inferior to the person being discussed.
- Humble verbs are not used unless the speaker's actions are related to or in some way affect the social superior who is the subject of the conversation. For this reason, they are often used when the speaker does a favor for a social superior. Remember that the て-form of the verb + さし上げる can also be used in such situations (see Language Section I in this chapter).
- The following humble verbs are also used as polite forms. That is, they are used in formal situations and the action does not have to be related to the listener or a third party. The action must be the speaker's own.

まいる (to go)	山田：	どちらへいらっしゃるんですか。
	川口：	東京へまいります。
おる (to be/to have)	山田：	お子さんはいらっしゃいますか。
	川口：	ええ、一人おります。
申(もう)す (to say)	山田：	始めまして。山田と申(もう)します。
	川口：	始めまして。川口と申(もう)します。
いたす (to do)	山田：	いつも何時までお仕事なさいますか。
	川口：	十時までいたします。

話してみましょう

A. Your teacher has made the following requests or asked the following questions. Respond using humble verbs.

Example

いつ宿題を出すつもりですか。
明日お出しします。

1. 何時に研究室(しつ)に来るんですか。
2. 研究室(しつ)に来る前に電話をして下さい。
3. 研究室(しつ)に来る時に履歴書(りれきしょ)を持って来て下さい。
4. それから、私の本はもう読みましたか。
5. レポートはもう書きましたか。
6. 何時ごろまで待ってくれますか。
7. じゃあ、後でまた会いましょう。

B. Work in groups of four. Each person should think of five requests, assuming that he or she is the president of a company and that the others are employees. The president makes a request and the rest of the group must respond to the request using humble verbs. The first person to respond appropriately to the request scores a point.

Example

社長：　その本を取ってくれませんか。
A:　はい、お取りします。

C. Work with a partner. Imagine you are attending an orientation for new employees. You do not know anyone. You need to introduce yourself very politely using humble verbs.

Example

始めまして。私は〜と申(もう)します。〜からまいりました。
大学では〜を専攻(せんこう)いたしました。

D. Work with a partner. One person is a prospective employer and the other person is a student. The employer should interview the student. The student should respond with humble verbs and polite speech.

Example

A: 始めまして。山田です。

B: 始めまして。スミスと申します。どうぞよろしくおねがいします。

A: スミスさんの専門は何ですか。

B: 経営(けいえい)学です。／経営(けいえい)学でございます。

1. 専門(せんもん)は何ですか。
2. どうしてこの会社に就職(しゅうしょく)したいんですか。
3. 日本語で書いたものがあれば、何か見せてくれますか。
4. 出張(しゅっちょう)が多い仕事は大丈夫(だいじょうぶ)ですか。

IV. Making or letting someone do something, using the causative form; Requesting permission to do something, using the causative form + て下さい

A. Making or letting someone do something, using the causative form

A-1. The make-causative with intransitive verbs

Causer		Causee	Particle			Causative form (Intransitive verb)
社長	は	山田さん	を	京都(きょうと)	に	行かせた。

The president made Yamada-san go to Kyoto.

A-2. The let-causative with intransitive verbs

Causer		Causee	Particle			Causative form (Intransitive verb)
社長	は	山田さん	を／に	京都(きょうと)	に	行かせた。

The president let Yamada-san go to Kyoto.

A-3. The make-causative and let-causative with transitive verbs

Causer		Causee	Particle	Direct object		Causative form (Transitive verb)
社長	は	山田さん	に	その広告(こうこく)	を	出させた。

The president made/let Yamada-san submit that ad.

だれがこの子をなかしたの。

Who made this child cry?

父は妹をいすにすわらせた。

My father made/let my younger sister sit on the chair.

先生は学生に毎日漢字を十覚(おぼ)えさす。
The teacher makes the students memorize 10 **kanji** every day.
社長は社員(しゃいん)にコンピュータの使い方を習(なら)わせた。
The president made/let employees learn how to use computers.

Verb type	Dictionary form	Causative form
Irregular verbs	する (to do) 来る (to come)	させる or さす 来(こ)させる or 来(こ)さす
る-verbs		Replace る with させる or さす
	見る (to see) 食べる (to eat)	見~~る~~ + させる／さす → 見させる／見さす 食べ~~る~~ + させる／さす → 食べさせる／食べさす
う-verbs		Replace the negative ending ない with せる or す
	歩く (to walk) 話す (to talk) 飲む (to drink)	歩か~~ない~~ + せる／す → 歩かせる／歩かす 話さ~~ない~~ + せる／す → 話させる／話さす 飲ま~~ない~~ + せる／す → 飲ませる／飲ます

- There are two types of causative in English. One is the *make-causative,* used when someone (the causer) forces someone else (the causee) to do something. The other type is the *let-causative,* used when someone allows someone else to do something.

  Kate's mother made her go alone. (Kate did not want to go alone.)
  Kate's mother let her go alone. (Kate wanted to go alone.)

  Japanese also has two types of causative. These are distinguished by the particle marking the causee if the verb is an intransitive verb. The particle を can be used for both make-causative and let-causative constructions, as in key sentences A-1 and A-2, but the particle に is used only in let-causative constructions, as in A-2. Because the causee is always marked by に if the verb is transitive, it is not possible to tell the difference between make- and let-causitive constructions without context or additional words such as verbs of giving and receiving.

- The let-causative can be explicitly marked by combining the causative form with a verb of giving, which implies that the causer is doing the causee a favor by allowing him or her to do the action in question:

  課長(かちょう)は山田さんにその書類(しょるい)を書かせてあげた。
  The manager let Yamada-san write that document.
  父は私を／にイギリスに行かせてくれた。
  My father let me go to England.
  先生は私にその本を読ませて下さった。
  The professor let me read that book.

B. Requesting permission to do something, using the causative form + て下さい

			Causative て-form	
この	コンピュータ	を	使わせて	下さい。

Please let me use this computer.

写真をとらせて下さい。 Please let me take photographs.

電話をかけさせて。 Please let me make a phone call.

私に出張(しゅっちょう)に行かせていただけませんか。 Would you let me go on a business trip?

コピーを取らせてもらえませんか。 Would you let me make a copy?

- The て-form of causative verbs can be combined with a variety of endings, such as verbs of giving and receiving, to indicate requests. The general meaning of these varieties is *Please allow me to do* 〜 or *Please let me do* 〜.

英語を習(なら)わせてくれませんか。 Please let me learn English.

英語を習(なら)わせていただけませんか。 Please allow me to learn English.

英語を習(なら)わせてほしいんですが。 I'd like you to let me learn English.

話してみましょう

A. You are the project manager of a company and have assigned some work to your subordinates. The following chart shows these assignments. Your boss is now asking who will do each job. Answer him or her with sentences in the causative construction.

Example

Your boss: だれが書類(しょるい)を持って来るんだ。

You: 山田に持って来(こ)させます。

仕事	名前
書類(しょるい)を持って来る	山田
書類(しょるい)をしらべる	川口
用紙(ようし)を集(あつ)める	大木
銀行に行く	小山

仕事	名前
広告(こうこく)を出す	鈴木(すずき)
計画を立てる	さとう
コピーをとる	山本
社長に説明(せつめい)する	木村(きむら)

B. Work with the class. Ask your classmates what they would like to be allowed to do on a job. Use their answers to suggest a job for them. Use casual speech.

Example

A: 〜さんはどんな仕事がいいの。
B: そうだね。色々な所に行かせてくれる仕事がいいなあ。(male) ／そうね。色々な所に行かせてくれる仕事がいいわね。(female)
A: じゃあ、パイロットはどう？
B: ああ、おもしろそうだね。(male) ／ああ、おもしろそうね。(female)

C. Work with a partner. Tell your partner what you would, or would not, let your child do if you were the parent of a ten-year-old. Discuss as many things as you can.

Example

A: 〜さんに子供がいたら、何をさせてあげますか。
B: いろいろなスポーツをさせてやります。旅行もたくさん行かせます。
A: どんなことはさせませんか。
B: そうですね。変なふくは着させませんね。

D. Work with a new partner. Imagine you are ten years old and your partner is your parent. Ask your parent for permission to do something. Your partner will answer based on the information compiled in Exercise C. Decide how strict your parent is.

Example

A: ロックのコンサートに行かせてくれない。
B: ああ、いいよ。(male) ／ええ、いいわよ。(female) or
いや、だめだよ。(male) ／ううん、だめよ。(female)

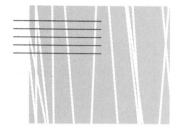

V. Expressing completion, regret, and the realization that a mistake was made, using ～てしまう

A. Expressing completion

	Verb て-form	Auxiliary verb
明日までに履歴書(りれきしょ)を	書いて	しまいます。

I will finish writing the resume by tomorrow.

そのことなら、もう返事(へんじ)してしまったよ。
I've already responded to the matter.

お母さん： 宿題は終わったの。
Is your homework finished?

子供： うん、もうしちゃったよ。
Yes, it's finished. (literally: I've finished it.)

- The て-form of the verb + しまう can have two interpretations. The first is an emphasis on the completion of an action. ごはんを食べてしまった indicates more clearly that the speaker has finished his or her meal than does ごはんを食べた.

B. Expressing regret and the realization that a mistake was made

	Verb て-form	Auxiliary verb
大事(だいじ)なレポートを	おとして	しまった。

I accidentally lost an important report.

田中： どうしたんですか、その足。
What's wrong with your foot?

ありさか： かいだんからおちちゃったんです。
I fell down the stairs.

課長(かちょう)は飛行機(ひこうき)が遅れてしまって、会議(かいぎ)においでになれなかったそうです。
I heard that the section manager could not come to the meeting because his plane arrived too late.

- The て-form of the verb + しまう can also indicate that something that should not have happened took place, or that someone did something that he or she should not have done. In this case, the て-form of the verb + しまう often conveys regret.

- Whether the て-form of the verb + しまう indicates completion or regret depends on the context.

  古くなったら、おいしくないから、今食べてしまった方がいいよ。(completion)
  It won't taste good if it gets old, so you should finish it now.
  すみません、田中さんのケーキを私が食べてしまったんです。(regret)
  I'm sorry, but I ate Tanaka-san's cake.

- 〜てしまう／でしまう becomes 〜ちゃう／じゃう in casual speech.

  友達が行ってしまった。　友達が行っちゃった。
  My friend is gone.
  その本はもう読んでしまったよ。　その本はもう読んじゃったよ。
  I finished reading the book.

- 〜てしまう conjugates as an う-verb.

Formal	Casual
食べてしまわない	食べちゃわない
食べてしまいます	食べちゃいます
食べてしまう	食べちゃう
食べてしまえば	食べちゃえば
食べてしまおう	食べちゃおう
食べてしまって	食べちゃって
食べてしまった	食べちゃった

話してみましょう

A. Make a sentence by choosing the appropriate main clause of the subordinate clause, then changing the appropriate verb in the main clause to the て-form + しまう.

Example

1. ケーキが少しのこっているから、／ A. 食べましょう。
<u>ケーキが少しのこっているから、食べてしまいましょう。</u>

1. ケーキが少しのこっているから、
2. 三時から面接(めんせつ)があるから、
3. 五時にお客(きゃく)さんがいらっしゃるから、
4. 申込用紙(もうしこみようし)はここにありますから、
5. 明日このプロジェクトのための会議(かいぎ)があるから、
6. 答えを早く知りたいと言っているから、
7. 大事(だいじ)な手紙なら、

A. 食べましょう。
B. この部屋をきれいにして下さい。
C. 今記入(きにゅう)したらどうですか。
D. 今返事(へんじ)をします。
E. 早く出したほうがいいですよ。
F. 五時までにこの書類(しょるい)のコピーを作ります。
G. 今履歴書(りれきしょ)を読みます。

B. Work with a partner. What kind of preparations should you finish before the following events? Make a dialogue using the phrases in 1–5 below with ～てしまう and ～てある. Use casual speech.

Example

パーティ／お母さんに話す／お父さんに言う

A: 今度のパーティのことなんだけど。
B: お母さんに話してあるの。
A: うん。もう話しちゃったよ。
B: あ、そう。じゃあ、お父さんにも言ってあるの？
A: それはまだ。明日言うつもり。

1. 会議(かいぎ)／書類(しょるい)を書く／コピーをとる
2. 旅行／切符(きっぷ)を買う／旅館の予約をする
3. 卒業式(しき)／ガウン (gown) を借りる／先生を呼(よ)ぶ
4. 母の日／プレゼントを買う／カードを書く
5. 同窓会(どうそうかい)／招待状(しょうたいじょう)を出す／料理を決める

C. You inadvertently did the things listed in 1–6 below, and need to apologize for your acts. Make an apology using the phrases in 1–6 and the て-form of the verb + しまう.

Example

マクレーさんの本をなくす (to lose)。
すみません。マクレーさんに借りた本をなくしてしまったんです。

1. 電話番号を間違えた。
2. 友達の音楽のテープがだめになった。
3. 事故(じこ)で、面接(めんせつ)に遅れた。
4. さいふを忘れた。
5. 友達のミルクを飲んだ。
6. 友達の手紙を読んだ。

D. Work with a partner. Create dialogues in which you must tell a person that you have done something unfortunate, then ask that person for help. Use the following situations and ～てしまう. Share your dialogues with the class by acting them out.

Example

<u>コンタクトレンズがおちた。</u>

A: あ、キムさん、どうしたの。

B: コンタクトレンズがおちちゃったんだ。(male) ／コンタクトレンズがおちちゃったの。(female)

A: 本当(ほんとう)。じゃあ、一緒(いっしょ)にさがそう。

1. 電車の中にかばんを忘れた。
2. さいふをおとした。
3. 道が分からなくなった。
4. 友達にけがをさせた。
5. 勉強しすぎて、あたまがいたくなった。

漢字

The structure of kanji compounds

As you have seen, two or more **kanji** are often combined to form a new word, known as a **kanji** compound. Different types of relationships can be found among the individual **kanji** in compounds, and a study of these relationships will help you better guess and learn the meanings of unknown compounds, thus increasing your vocabulary. Some of the common relationships between characters in compounds are described below.

1. The same **kanji** is repeated.

人々(ひとびと) (many people)　国々(くにぐに) (many countries) (See Chapter 5 for 々.)

2. Two **kanji** with similar meanings are put together.

教授 (teach + give = professor) 研究 (study + pursue = research)

3. Two **kanji** with opposite meanings are combined.

男女(だんじょ) (man and woman) 朝晩(あさばん) (morning and night) 兄弟 (older and younger brothers = siblings)

4. The first **kanji** is the subject of the second one, which is a verb/adjective.

新聞 (new + hear = newspaper) 音楽 (sound + joyful = music)

5. The first **kanji** modifies the second one.

大学 (big + school/study = university) 住所 (residing + place = address)

6. The first **kanji** is a verb and the second one is the subject/object/indirect object of the first.

有名 (exist/have + name = famous) 入学 (enter + school = entering school)

7. The first **kanji** is a prefix or the second **kanji** is a suffix.

毎朝 (every + morning = every morning) 肉屋 (butcher)

Try to classify the following **kanji** compounds into the above categories. Guess the meaning of each compound.

大小　新車　入国　毎日　通行　色々　飲食　白黒　朝食

乗車　急行　父母　家族　受験　生物

就	就	to sit, to engage in　シュウ 来年就職(しゅうしょく)します。	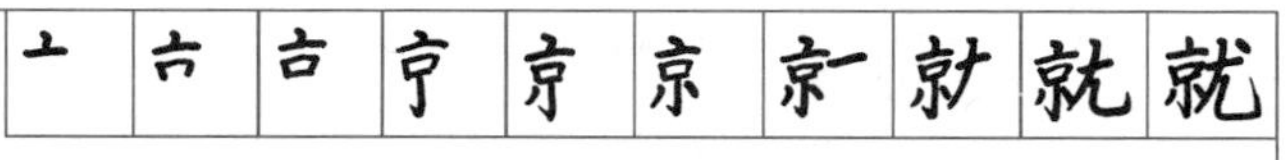
職	職	employment　ショク 日本で就職(しゅうしょく)が決まりました。	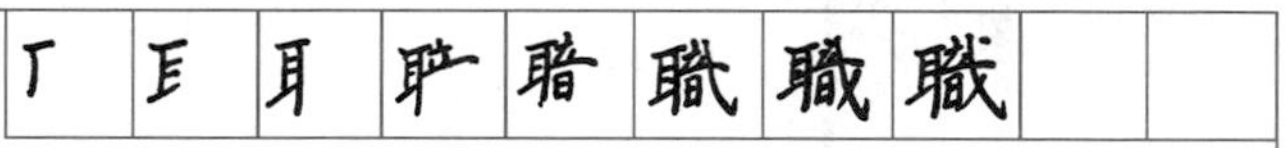
相	相	each other, mutual　ソウ/あい 先生に相談(そうだん)する。	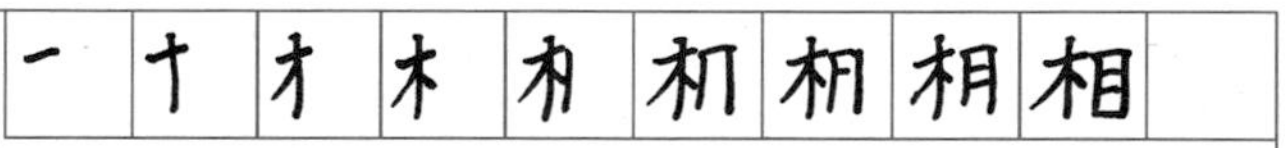
談	談	to talk　ダン いつでも相談(そうだん)して下さい。	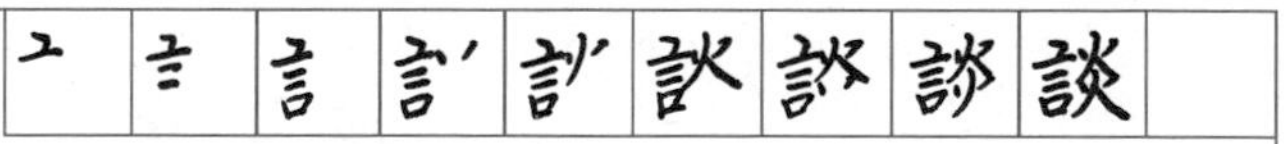

Kanji	Meaning	Readings	Examples
面	face, surface	メン/おもて	明日は仕事の面接(めんせつ)があります。面白(おもしろ)い本
接	to come into contact	セツ、セッ	面接(めんせつ)は九時からです。
試	to try	シ/ため(す)	来週、就職試験(しゅうしょくしけん)を受(う)ける。
験	to examine, effect	ケン	日本語の試験(しけん)は難しかったです。
経	to pass, reason, way	ケイ、キョウ/へ(る)	経験(けいけん)がある。経営学(けいえいがく)
専	exclusive	セン	専攻(せんこう)は経済学(けいざいがく)です。
攻	attack	コウ/せ(める)	私は音楽が専攻(せんこう)です。
門	gate	モン/かど	山田先生のご専門(せんもん)はコンピュータ工学(こうがく)です。
申	to say (humble)	シン/もう(す)	山田と申(もう)します。先生に申(もう)し上げました。申(もう)しわけありません。
込	to load, to include	こ(む)	ハワイツアーに申(もう)し込(こ)みました。申込用紙(もうしこみようし)

記	記	chronicle キ	ここに名前を記入（きにゅう）して下さい。
給	給	to supply キュウ	この仕事は給料（きゅうりょう）が安いんですよ。
働	働	to work ドウ はたら（く）	毎日八時間働（はたら）いています。
付	付	to attach, to turn on フ/つ（く） つ（ける）	受付（うけつけ） 電気を付（つ）ける。
客	客	guest キャク、カク	今日は大事（だいじ）なお客（きゃく）さんが来ます。
失	失	to lose, to miss シツ	失礼（しつれい）します。
説	説	opinion, to explain セツ/と（く）	先生が漢字の意味を説明（せつめい）して下さいました。
調	調	to investigate, to examine チョウ/しら（べる）	この漢字の意味が分からないので、辞書で調（しら）べてみます。
用	用	business, errand, to use ヨウ/もち（いる）	この申込用紙（もうしこみようし）に記入（きにゅう）して下さい。
覚	覚	to memorize, to remember カク/おぼ（える）	この漢字を覚（おぼ）えて下さい。

Kanji		Meaning	Readings	Example
集	集	to collect, to gather	シュウ/あつ（まる）あつ（める）	お金を集(あつ)めて人を助(たす)けます。
室	室	room	シツ	この教室(きょうしつ)は狭いですね。研究室(けんきゅうしつ)に来て下さい。
消	消	to turn off, to extinguish	ショウ/け（す）き（える）	電気を消(け)す。火が消(き)える。
呼	呼	to call, to invite	コ/よ（ぶ）	パーティに田中さんを呼(よ)びましょう。
助	助	to help, to assist	ジョ/たす（ける）、たす（かる）	すみません、ちょっと助(たす)けて下さい。助(たす)かりました。
連	連	group, to take along	レン/つ（れる）	東京に連(つ)れて行ってもらえる。

新しい読み方

習(なら)う　課長(かちょう)　返事(へんじ)　大事(だいじ)な　広告(こうこく)　面白(おもしろ)い

練習

下の文を読んで下さい。

1. 先生、就職のことでご相談したいんですが。
2. 昨日は日本語の面接試験があったから遅くなりました。
3. 私の専攻はコンピュータ工学(こうがく)です。先生のご専門は何ですか。
4. この仕事は給料がとても安いので、あまり働きたくありません。
5. 名前が覚えられません。
6. 去年、友達に京都(きょうと)に連れて行ってもらいました。

7. 受付で記入してもらった申込用紙を集めて下さいませんか。
8. お客さんに失礼なことを言ってはいけません。
9. 教室の電気を消して下さい。
10. 今度のパーティにはだれを呼んでありますか。
11. 山田さんに助けてもらいました。

上手な読み方

仕事さがし　(Job-hunting)

読む前に

下の質問に答えて下さい。

1. 求人広告（きゅうじんこうこく） (help wanted ads) にはどんなことが書いてあるか考えて下さい。
2. 求人広告（きゅうじんこうこく）にはどんな言葉が使ってありますか。それを英語では何といいますか。知らない言葉を先生に聞いて下さい。

読んでみましょう

A. 下はジャパントラベルという会社の求人広告（きゅうじんこうこく）です。知らない言葉がたくさんありますが、すいそくして (guess)、質問に答えて下さい。

ジャパントラベル

正社員・パート募集（ぼしゅう）

・マーケティングアナリスト

・ツアーガイド

経験者、バイリンガル優遇

詳細は山本まで

電話　(03) 3331-1234

ファックス (03) 3331-1235

1. ジャパントラベルは何の会社だと思いますか。
2. この会社は何が出来る人がほしいと思いますか。
3. この会社に就職したいと思う人は、だれに電話をしたらいいですか。

B. 下の二つの履歴書(りれきしょ)はジャポントラベルに来たものです。一人は日本人で、もう一人はアメリカ人です。二人の履歴書(りれきしょ)を見て、質問に答えて下さい。

1. 日本の履歴書(りれきしょ)にあって、アメリカの履歴書(りれきしょ)にないものがありますか。
2. アメリカの履歴書(りれきしょ)にあって、日本の履歴書(りれきしょ)にないものがありますか。
3. どんなことが日本の履歴書(りれきしょ)にもアメリカの履歴書(りれきしょ)にも書いてありますか。
4. この二人のどちらの方がジャパントラベルに就職出来ると思いますか。どうしてですか。

Jeff McGlone

Current Address	Permanent Address
1-1-1 Nakano	316 Hamilton Street
Nakano-ku, Tokyo	Lafayette, Indiana 47906
phone: (03) 1234-5678	phone: (765) 555-1234

Education

Bachelor of Arts in Japanese	
Purdue University	1995
Nanzan Exchange Program	1993
Westside Senior High School	1991

Work Experience

JET Japanese language program (worked as a JET assistant in Hiroshima)	1995–present

Certificates and Awards

Japanese Proficiency Test (Level 2)	1997

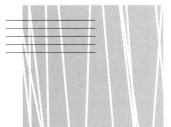

履歴書

平成 11 年 7 月 3 日現在

ふりがな	さとう　かずひろ
氏名	佐藤　和広　（印）
昭和 49 年 4 月 10 日生（満 25 歳）	※ 男・女 （男に丸）

写真をはる位置

写真をはる必要がある場合
1. 縦　36～40　mm
　横　24～30　mm
2. 本人単身胸から上
3. 裏面のりづけ

ふりがな　とうきょうと　おおたく　ちゅうおう	電話
現住所 〒143-0024 東京都 大田区 中央 4-5-6	(03) 1234-5678
ふりがな	電話
連絡先 〒　　（現住所以外に連絡を希望する場合のみ記入） 方	

年	月	学歴・職歴（各別にまとめて書く）
昭和55	4	大田区立 大森第三小学校 入学
〃 61	3	同校卒業
〃 61	4	大田区立 大森第二中学校入学
平成 1	3	同校卒業
〃 1	4	東京都立富士高等学校入学
〃 4	3	同校卒業
〃 4	4	日本大学 経済学部入学
〃 8	3	同校卒業
		職　歴
平成 8	4	JR 東日本株式会社 入社
		賞　罰
		なし

記入上の注意　①鉛筆以外の黒または青の筆記具で記入。　②数字はアラビア数字で、文字はくずさず正確に書く
③※印のところは、該当するものを○で囲む。

年	月	学歴・職歴（各別にまとめて書く）

年	月	免許・資格
平成4	8	普通自動車免許
〃 6	6	英語検定一級合格

志望の動機、特技、好きな学科など	通勤時間	
旅行・観光に関連した職種を希望	約　時間　分	
好きな学科　英語　　スポーツ　スキー・テニス	扶養家族数（配偶者を除く）　人	
趣味　旅行	配偶者　※　有・無	配偶者の扶養義務　※　有・無

本人希望記入欄（特に給料・職種・勤務時間・勤務地・その他についての希望などがあれば記入）
特になし

保護者（本人が未成年者の場合のみ記入） ふりがな		電話
氏　名	住　所〒	

古紙配合率100%の再生紙を使用しています。　　**日本法令**　労務12　10.7改

C. 下の履歴書（りれきしょ）はマグローンさんのを日本語で書いたものです。
これを見ながら、自分の履歴書（りれきしょ）を日本語で書いて下さい。

履歴書

平成 10 年 8 月 8 日現在

ふりがな 氏名　マグローン　ジェフ	男 女 印	写真
明治 大正 (昭和) 平成　48 年 3 月 3 日生 (満 26 才)	本籍　アメリカ合衆国 インディアナ州　都道府県	

ふりがな　とうきょうと　なかのく　なかの 現住所　東京都中野区中野 1 — 1 — 1　方	電話 市外局番 (03) 1234-5678 (方呼出)
ふりがな 連絡先（現住所以外に連絡を希望する場合のみ記入） 316 Hamilton Street, Lafayette, Indiana 47906　方	電話 0011 市外局番 (765) 555-1234 (方呼出)

年	月	職歴、学歴（格別にまとめて書く）
		学歴
昭和54	8	Hamilton Elementary School 入学
昭和60	6	同校卒業
昭和60	8	Hamilton Junior High School 入学
昭和62	6	同校卒業
昭和62	8	Westside Senior High School 入学
平成2	6	同校卒業
平成2	8	パデュー大学 入学
平成4	8	南山大学交換留学プログラム参加
平成5	6	同プログラム終了
平成7	6	パデュー大学 外国語学科　卒業
		職歴
平成7	8	JET日本語プログラム講師
		賞罰
		なし
		以上

平成 10 年 8 月 8 日現在

ふりがな 氏名　マグローン　ジェフ	とうきょうと　なかのく　なかの 現住所 (〒 156)　東京都中野区中野 1 — 1 — 1	電話 市外局番 (03) 1234-5678 (方呼出)

特技 日本語	健康状態 良好	特記事項
得意な学科 日本語	スポーツ ゴルフ	
趣味 映画	希望の動機 日本語が使える仕事につきたい	通勤時間　分 利用交通機関　JR　私鉄　バス　徒歩

年	月	免許・資格
昭和62	6	運転免許取得
平成9	1	日本語検定試験 2 級取得

本人希望欄　（給料・職種・勤務地・その他）

家族	氏名	性別・間柄	年令	扶養義務	
	マグローン　ジェームス	父	55	有 (無)	大学教員
	マグローン　ローラ	母	54	有 (無)	レストラン経営
				有 無	
				有 無	
				有 無	

連絡先（本人が未成年の場合は保護者） ふりがな 氏名　マグローン　ジェフ	住所 (〒 156)　東京都中野区中野 1 — 1 — 1　方	電話 市外局番 (03) 1234-5678 (方呼出)

上手な聞き方

面接試験　(Job interviews)

聞く前に

A. Work with a partner. Discuss and make up at least five questions in Japanese that a potential employer might ask an applicant.

B. Politely answer the questions you created in Exercise A as though you were applying for a job.

聞いてみましょう

STUDENT

Listen to the three interviews of the applicants by a representative of Japan Travel. Take notes about each applicant and complete the following table. Then rank the applicants.

	1	2	3
名前			
申し込んだ理由(りゆう) (reason)			
専攻(せんこう)			
英語			
コンピュータ			
外国に住む			

聞いた後で

Work in groups of four. Discuss your information and decide which person is the best candidate and why.

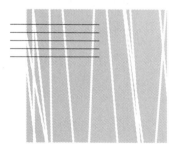

STUDENT

DICT-A-CONVERSATION

スミスさんは先生に就職について相談しています。

スミス：____

木村(きむら)：____

スミス：____

木村(きむら)：____

スミス：____

木村(きむら)：____

スミス：____

聞き上手話し上手

Responding to compliments and expressing politeness and modesty in formal situations

Compliments are often used to start a conversation. In the United States, compliments on clothing, hair styles, or other visual features such as "you have a nice ring," express friendliness. In Japan, however, it is rare to compliment visual features as a means of breaking the ice. Close friends may compliment clothing if it is related to the topic of the conversation. The Japanese people are more likely to compliment a person's skill or intelligence.

The Japanese usually respond to compliments with denials rather than saying "thank you," especially in formal situations. Saying "thank you" or otherwise accepting a compliment is not a normal practice, because it makes you sound arrogant or immodest. Stating something negative about yourself indicates that you are lowering your own social status and raising the listener's status, thereby showing respect and politeness. This type of denial is a common response to compliments directed to you personally, or to your family members. Instead of saying "thank you," you can use expressions such as the following:

いいえ、そうでもありません。／いいえ、そうでもございません。
No, that's not so.

いいえ、そんなことはありません。／いいえ、そんなことはございません。
No, that is not the case.

とんでもありません。／とんでもございません。
That's not at all the case.

まあまあです。
I am just so-so./ It's just so-so.

These expressions are often followed by some negative statement. For example, in the following conversation, いいえ、そんなことはありません is followed by the statement まだまだ勉強しなければならないことがたくさんあります *(I still have a lot to learn)*.

部長：　山田くんはわかいのによく仕事が出来るね。
　　　　Yamada-san, you're doing a good job for someone still so young.
山田：　いいえ、そんなことはありません。まだまだ勉強しなければならないことがたくさんあります。
　　　　No, that is not case. I still have a lot to learn.

When you say something in Japanese, you may be complimented immediately on your proficiency in Japanese, no matter how rudimentary it is. If you receive such compliments, you can respond by saying まだまだです.

青木：	日本語がお上手ですね。	Your Japanese is very good.
山田：	いいえ、まだまだです。	No, I still have a lot to learn.

Disparaging yourself to show politeness is also important in formal conversation. In America, a job candidate often emphasizes his or her qualifications. In Japan, explicitly stating what you can do can be misinterpreted as being impolite or arrogant. Therefore, a job candidate does not talk extensively about his or her qualifications during the interview unless specific questions are asked. Instead, he or she will emphasize his or her enthusiasm.

A. Write the appropriate response to the following compliments.

1. 日本語がお上手ですね。
2. よく仕事が出来るんですね。
3. ～さんのおたくはとても立派ですね。
4. いい車をお持ちですね。
5. テニスがお上手なんですね。

STUDENT

B. Listen to the following dialogues. Assume that you are Smith-san in the dialogue, and respond to the compliments.

Example

You hear:　A:　始めまして、スミスと申します。どうぞよろしくおねがいします。
　　　　　B:　山本です。こちらこそ。スミスさんは日本語がお上手ですね。
You write:　いいえ、まだまだです。

C. Work with a partner. Your partner praises you. Respond politely.

総合練習

新しい仕事

A. Work in groups of four. You are members of a company, and you need to hire someone, either for a full-time or a part-time position. Discuss the nature of your company and the position you wish to offer, and fill out the following chart. Then make up an ad and post it on the blackboard, along with a box or envelope to collect applications.

Example

A: どんな会社にしましょうか。
B: コンピュータの会社はどうですか。
C: 面白そうですね。
D: わたしは、旅行会社はどうかと思うんですが。
A: それもよさそうですね。どうしましょうか？

会社について	
名前	
どんな会社か	
仕事について	
フルタイムかパートか	
どんな仕事か	
どんな人がほしいか	
休み	
ボーナス (bonus)	
給料	

B. Using the forms provided by your instructor, each person in the class should now prepare a résumé and make a few copies of it. Each person is looking for a job, and should look at the ads on the blackboard, applying for two jobs by placing his or her résumé in the box provided by the companies. Participants are not allowed to apply for jobs they helped draft.

C. Go back to your original groups. Read the résumés, choose at least three candidates, and write a short message to invite them for an interview. Discuss in your group what questions need to be asked.

D. Interview the candidates. Take notes for each interview. After all interviews are done, go back to the group and negotiate on whom to offer the job. Report to your instructor whom you have selected and why.

ロールプレー

A. You are a secretary to the president of your company. He or she has several meetings today. Make a schedule and report to him or her using honorific forms.

B. You are talking with a consultant at an employment service center. Tell the person your educational background, other qualifications, and what kind of jobs you would like to do. Use polite expressions.

C. Your boss is assigned a project you are interested in, so you would like him or her to consider including you on the project team. Tell him or her why you should be chosen. Use humble forms.

LAB

単語 (ESSENTIAL VOCABULARY)

Nouns

うけつけ（受付） reception desk; registration desk
かいぎ（会議） meeting
かちょう（課長） section manager
きゃく（客） customer; guest
けいけん（経験） experience
こうこく（広告） advertisement
ごぞんじ （ご存知） to know (honorific)
じょうし 上司 boss
しょるい（書類） document
すいせんじょう（推薦状） letter of reference
せんもん（専門） field of speciality
どうりょう（同僚） colleague
プロジェクト project
めんせつ（面接） interview
ようし（用紙） form; もうしこみようし（申込用紙） application form
りれきしょ（履歴書） vita; résumé

Demonstrative nouns

あちら over there; that person over there (polite)
あっち over there
そちら that way; that person (polite)
そっち that way

Verbal nouns

しゅっちょう（出張） business trip; しゅっちょうをする（出張をする） (to) go on a business trip; しゅっちょうする（出張する） (to) go on a business trip
せつめい（説明） explanation; せつめいをする（説明をする） (to) explain; せつめいする（説明する） (to) explain
へんじ（返事） response; へんじをする（返事をする） (to) respond; へんじする（返事する） (to) respond

い-adjectives

よろしい　good (polite)

な-adjectives

だいじな（大事な）important

Irregular verb

はいけんする（拝見する）(to) look at (humble form)

う-verbs

いたす（致す）(to) do (humble)
いただく（頂く）(to) eat; (to) drink (humble)
いらっしゃる　(to) go; (to) come; (to) return; (to) be (honorific)
うかがう（伺う）(to) visit; (to) ask (humble)
おいでになる　(to) come in; (to) show up
おっしゃる　(to) say (honorific)
おめにかかる（お目にかかる）(to) meet (humble)
おやすみになる（お休みになる）(to) sleep (honorific)
おる　(to) exist; (to) be (humble)
ござる　(to) exist (polite verb for ある and いる)
ごらんになる（ご覧になる）(to) look at (honorific)
ぞんじておる（存じておる）(to) know (humble)
でござる　(to) be (polite verb for です)
なさる　(to) do (honorific)
ならう（習う）(to) learn
まいる（参る）(to) go; (to) come (honorific)
めしあがる（召し上がる）(to) eat; (to) drink (honorific)
もうしこむ（申し込む）to apply
もうす（申す）(to) say (humble)

る-verbs

おめにかける（お目にかける）(to) show (humble)
ぞんじる（存じる）(to) know (humble)
たずねる（訪ねる）(to) visit
もうしあげる（申し上げる）(to) say (humble)

Expressions

いいえ、そうでもありません。No, that's not so.
いいえ、そうでもございません。 No, that's not so.
いいえ、そんなことはありません。 No, it is not the case.
いいえ、そんなことはございません。 No, it is not the case.
とんでもありません。とんでもございません。That's not at all the case.
まあまあです。 It's just so-so.
まだまだです。I still have a lot to learn.

Passive Vocabulary

Nouns

かいしゃまわり（会社回り）college seniors going to different companies
けいけんしゃ（経験者）person with experience
じょうけん（条件）terms (of employment)
しょうさい（詳細）details
せいしゃいん（正社員）permanent staff member
バイリンガル bilingual
パート part-time worker
ぼしゅう（募集）recruitment
ボーナス bonus
ゆうぐう（優遇）preferred

な-Adjectives

いっしょうけんめい（一生懸命）with all one's might

For a list of supplementary vocabulary items that will facilitate communication, see the first page of Chapter 8 in your Workbook.

CHAPTER 9

第九課

Neighbors use signs to request behavior patterns from one another.

文句

もんく

Complaints

Functions	Expressing complaints requesting a change of behavior; Expressing the intention to change behavior
New Vocabulary	Relationships among people; Things you don't want others to do; Things you don't want to be forced to do; Expressing complaints and annoyance; Nouns derived from verbs
Dialogue	静かにするように言って下さい (Please tell him to hold down the noise)
Culture	Neighborhood relations
Language	I. Expressing problems and things that have taken place, using the passive form II. Expressing complaints, using the causative-passive form III. Expressing large and small quantities and frequencies, using a quantity expression + も IV. Expressing or requesting efforts to change behavior or to act a certain way, using the plain present form of the verb + ようにする; Describing what efforts are being made to attain a specific goal, using the plain present form of the verb + ように、〜 V. Using the plain form + のに to mean *despite* 〜; *although* 〜
Kanji	The importance of the sound components of **kanji**
Reading	Bullying
Listening	Annoying things
Communication	Expressing complaints or anger, and making apologies

新しい言葉

人と人とのかんけい　(Relationships among people)

知(し)り合(あ)い　acquaintance
近所(きんじょ)の人　neighbor
大家(おおや)（さん）　landlord; landlady
赤(あか)ちゃん　baby
親(おや)　parent
年上(としうえ)の子　older child
年下(としした)の子　younger child
ほめる　to compliment
なかがいい　to get along with someone
なかが悪い　to not get along with someone
心配(しんぱい)する　to worry

下の言葉を覚えていますか。

年を取る　家族　兄弟　両親　祖父(そふ)　祖母(そぼ)　父　母　兄　姉
弟　妹　主人(しゅじん)　つま　ご家族　ご兄弟　ご両親　おじいさん
おばあさん　お父さん　お母さん　お兄さん　お姉さん
弟さん　妹さん　ご主人(しゅじん)　おくさん

A. Which words fit the following descriptions?

1. お父さんやお母さん
2. 友達が病気の時に思うこと
3. 妹や弟
4. その人があまり好きじゃないこと
5. 私が少し知っている人
6. だれかがいいことをした時にすること
7. ０さいの子供
8. その人といい友達でいること
9. お姉さんやお兄さん
10. 家の近くに住んでいる人
11. アパートや家を貸す人

B. 質問に答えて下さい。

1. なかのいい人とはどんな話をしますか。知(し)り合(あ)いとはどんな話をしますか。近所(きんじょ)の人はどうですか。
2. アパートを借りるなら、どんな大家(おおや)さんがいいですか。
3. 子供は親にどんな心配(しんぱい)をさせてはいけないと思いますか。
4. どんな時に人をほめますか。
5. 年上(としうえ)の兄弟と年下(としした)の兄弟とどちらの方がいいと思いますか。
6. 赤(あか)ちゃんが好きですか。きらいですか。どうしてですか。
7. 日本人の知(し)り合(あ)いがいますか。

してほしくないこと　(Things you don't want others to do)

夜中(よなか)にさわぐ　to make noise until midnight
音(おと)を立てる　to make noise
ピアノをひく　to play the piano
こわす　to break
車をぶつける　to hit something with a car
汚(よご)す　to make something dirty
しかる　to scold
たたく　to hit
かべに落書(らくがき)をする　to write graffiti on the wall

足をふむ　to step on someone's foot
どろぼうが入る　(for) a thief to break in
お金をぬすむ　to steal money
うわさをする　to gossip
うそをつく　to tell a lie
人の悪口(わるくち)を言う　to speak ill of a person
からかう　to tease
いじめる　to bully
物を置(お)く　to place something

下の言葉を覚えていますか。

遅れる　遅い　さいふを落とす　しぬ　忘れる　動物をかう
かぎをかける　切る　たのむ　間違える　間違う　遠い
止める　止まる　やめる　お金を引き出す　雪がふる
終わる　きらい　けがをする　交通事故(こうつうじこ)にあう　たばこをすう
笑う　弱い　悪い

C. 下の文に適当(てきとう)な (appropriate) 言葉を書いて下さい。

1. 人の＿＿＿＿＿＿＿＿を言ったり、＿＿＿＿＿＿＿＿をついたりしてはいけない。
2. 先生は年上(としうえ)の子を＿＿＿＿＿＿＿＿。というのは、その子が年下(としした)の子を＿＿＿＿＿＿＿＿、泣(な)かせたからです。
3. ボブはマーサが好きだから、マーサを＿＿＿＿＿＿＿＿り＿＿＿＿＿＿＿＿りするんですよ。
4. 昨日の夜中(よなか)に＿＿＿＿＿＿＿＿が私の家に入って、お金を＿＿＿＿＿＿＿＿行きました。
5. 自分の車を前の車に＿＿＿＿＿＿＿＿、その車のテールランプ (tail lamp) を＿＿＿＿＿＿＿＿しまった。
6. 赤ちゃんが寝ているので、大きい＿＿＿＿＿＿＿＿を＿＿＿＿＿＿＿＿下さい。

D. 質問に答えて下さい。

1. 子供がよくすることはどんなことですか。
2. 大学生がよくすることはどんなことですか。
3. あなたが今までにやったことはどんなことですか。
4. やってみたいことはどんなことですか。
5. どんなことはやってはいけないと思いますか。

させられたくないこと　(Things you don't want to be forced to do)

日記(にっき)を付ける to keep a diary

むかえに行く to go to pick up someone

かたづける to organize; to clean up

犬の散歩(さんぽ)をする to walk a dog

ごみを捨(す)てる to take trash out; to discard trash

引(ひ)っ越(こ)す to move (residence)

下の言葉を覚えていますか。

勉強する　習う　休む　働く　説明する　洗濯(せんたく)をする
そうじをする

E. Work in groups of four. One person should act out one of the actions in the above list or the 下の言葉を覚えていますか list. The rest of the group should guess what is being done. The first person to guess correctly receives one point.

F. 質問に答えて下さい。

1. よくすることはどれですか。
2. 全然(ぜんぜん)しないことはどれですか。
3. よく人にどんなことをしてもらいますか。
4. よく人にどんなことをしてあげますか。

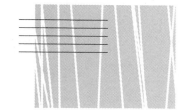

文句(もんく)を言う (Expressing complaints and annoyance)

迷惑(めいわく)な to be unpleasant; annoying

変(へん)な strange

いやな unpleasant

たまらない cannot stand; unbearable

汚(きたな)い dirty

うるさい noisy

あやまる to apologize

本当(ほんとう)だ true

(〜に) 気を付ける to watch out for

注意(ちゅうい)する to warn; to call attention to

おこる to get angry

下の言葉を覚えていますか。

困(こま)る　ごめん　ごめんなさい　やめる　むり　むりをする

気分が悪い　たのむ　相談する　ええっと／すみません。

それはちょっと　残念(ざんねん)　失礼(しつれい)ですが　大変　ひどい

G. 下の文に適当(てきとう)な (appropriate) 言葉を書いて下さい。

1. 道をわたる時は車に ______________________ 下さい。
2. その話はうそじゃなくて ______________________ です。
3. 悪いことをした時は、______________________ なければならない。
4. 友達が変なことを言ったので、______________________、文句(もんく)を言った。
5. となりの家のピアノのおとが ______________________ たまらない。
6. そのシャツは ______________________ から、洗いました。
7. 今の仕事は ______________________ から、やめたいと思う。

H. 質問に答えて下さい。

1. どんなことが迷惑(めいわく)だと思いますか。
2. どんなときに親に文句(もんく)を言いますか。
3. 何をするのがいやですか。
4. どんな時に人にあやまりますか。どんな時にはあやまりませんか。
5. どんな時に人に注意(ちゅうい)をしますか。
6. 汚(きたな)い物ってどんなものですか。

動詞(どうし)から出来た名詞(めいし) (Nouns derived from verbs)

ごみ出し／ゴミ出し　trash collection

いじめ　bullying

知り合(あ)い　acquaintance

引越(ひっこ)し　moving (residence)

Note: Verb stems are often used as nouns. They can also be combined with another word to form a compound noun.
ごみ may also be written in **katakana**, as ゴミ .

下の言葉を覚えていますか。

東京行き　お祝い　受付　乗り物　食べ物　飲み物
買い物　贈(おく)り物　晴れ　くもり　話　休み

I. List the verbs from which the above expressions are derived.

J. 下の言葉の意味は何だと思いますか。日本語で説明してください。

1. 違い
2. 手伝い
3. 残(のこ)り
4. 間違い
5. つかれ
6. 山のぼり
7. 遊び

K. Guess the meaning of the underlined nouns and the verbs from which they are derived.

1. 行きはよかったが、帰りは、行き止(ど)まりがあったので、大変だった。
2. 大学の時の一番いい思い出は友達との飲み会です。
3. 今度の休みは晴れだといいですね。
4. まだたくさん食べ物があるから、少し残(のこ)りを家に持って帰ってくれませんか。
5. 私の考えでは三階建(がいだ)ての家がいいと思います。
6. 昨日のさわぎで、全然寝られなかった。
7. 笑いはいい薬です。
8. 汚れはきれいに取ってください。
9. つとめに出られないと言った覚えはない。

ダイアローグ

はじめに

下の質問に日本語で答えて下さい。

1. あなたの住んでいる所では、何か問題がありますか。
2. となりの人がうるさい時、どうしますか。
3. 近所（きんじょ）の人の迷惑（めいわく）にならないようにどんなことに気を付けていますか。
4. どんな時に大家（おおや）さんと話をしますか。

STUDENT

静かにするように言って下さい
(Please tell him to hold down the noise)

The following **manga** frames are scrambled, so they are not in the order described in the dialogue. Read the dialogue and unscramble the frames by writing the correct order in the box located in the upper right corner of each frame.

リーさんはアルバイトの広告(こうこく)を見ています。そこに、アリスさんが来ました。

アリス：　リーさん、何、見てるの。
リー：　新しいアルバイトをさがしているんだ。
アリス：　え、どうして？前のアルバイトやめちゃったの？
リー：　いや、やめさせられちゃったんだよ。最近(さいきん)寝られなくて、何度も仕事に遅れちゃったから。
アリス：　寝られないって？どこか悪いの？
リー：　いや、そうじゃないんだ。となりの人がうるさくてね。
アリス：　となりの人？先月引(ひ)っ越(こ)してきた？
リー：　うん、毎晩(まいばん)遅くまで大きいおとでテレビを見たり音楽聞いたり。それに、よく友達が来て夜中(よなか)までさわぐんだから、たまらないよ。
アリス：　本当(ほんとう)。ひどいわね。文句(もんく)言ったの。
リー：　うん、もう五回も静かにするように言ったんだけど。
アリス：　そう、大家(おおや)さんに言って注意(ちゅうい)してもらうようにたのんでみたら。
リー：　うん、でも、あまり大家(おおや)さんには言いたくないんだけどね。

リーさんは大家(おおや)さんに電話をかけました。

リー：　もしもし、あの、さくらアパートに住んでいるリーなんですけれども。

大家（おおや）：　あ、リーさん、どうしたんですか。

リー：　あのう、ちょっと申し上げにくいことなんですが、おねがいしたいことがあるんです。

大家（おおや）：　何ですか？

リー：　すみませんが、となりの青木さんに少し静かにするように言っていただけないでしょうか。

大家（おおや）：　そんなにうるさいんですか。

リー：　ええ。よく夜中（よなか）に、テレビやステレオのおとを大きくしてさわぐので、寝られないんです。何度も静かにするようにたのんだんですが、聞いてくれないんです。

大家（おおや）：　そう、困（こま）りましたね。じゃあ、私の方から、言っておきますよ。

リー：　ご迷惑（めいわく）おかけして申しわけありませんが、よろしくおねがいします。

分かりましたか

A. 質問に答えて下さい。

1. リーさんはどうしてアルバイトをさがしているのですか。
2. リーさんはどうして寝られないのですか。
3. リーさんのとなりのアパートにはだれが住んでいますか。その人はどんな人だと思いますか。どうしてそう思いますか。
4. アリスんはリーさんにどうしたらいいと言いましたか。
5. 大家（おおや）さんはリーさんのためにどんなことをしてあげるつもりですか。

B. 下の文章（ぶんしょう） (paragraph) は青木さんが書いたものです。自分を青木さんだと思って、下線のところに適当な（てきとうな） (appropriate) 言葉を書いて下さい。

今日大家（おおや）さんから電話があって、________________ように言われた。となりの人が________________そうだ。ぼくはテレビやステレオのおとが________________とは思わなかったが、このアパートはかべがうすい (thin) のかもしれない。

C. Identify the phrases that express Lee-san's annoyance or complaints.

D. Rewrite the dialogue as it would be if Lee-san were talking to Tanaka-sensei instead of Alice-san.

日本の文化

Neighborhood relations. What types of problems exist in neighborhoods in your community?

Neighborhood relations are important in any country, but are probably more complicated in Japan due to the high population density. To comprehend the amount of living space available to the average Japanese person, first imagine the state of California, which has roughly the same area as Japan. Then remove 80% of that, since that much area in Japan is taken up by mountains and is not habitable. Finally, put one-half the entire U.S. population into the remaining 20% of California. This is the population density of Japan. A complicating factor is that the highly populated metro areas, which take up just 1% of the habitable land, house one-half of Japan's population. Therefore, 1 m^2 of living space in Tokyo costs several times more than it does in New York City. Many people live in high-rise apartment buildings rather than houses, but even so, the average living space per person is 30.9 m^2 in Japan, which is less than half of that in the United States (64.0 m^2). So you can see that many Japanese families live in very crowded areas.

One of the common problems in this situation is noise. There is not much distance between houses, and the walls between apartments are thin, so sound travels easily. Things that would not bother your neighbor in the United States can be a big nuisance in Japan. The sounds of someone pulling out a chair or taking a shower can be just as annoying as the sounds of children running in the room. It is therefore very important to prevent noise. For example, it is a good idea not to take a bath or shower, or do laundry, early in the morning or late at night if you live in an apartment. Also, placing stereo equipment and musical instruments away from the wall and on the carpet can prevent sounds from traveling to your neighbor. Department stores and do-it-yourself stores sell a variety of gadgets to reduce noise.

Another common problem is the collection of garbage and recycling. Garbage collection is very efficient but, at the same time, somewhat complicated in Japan. In Tokyo, for example, you first need to distinguish among combustible garbage (燃(も)えるごみ／可燃(かねん)ごみ), non-combustible (燃(も)えないごみ／不燃(ふねん)ごみ) garbage, recyclable waste (リサイクル), and large waste (粗大(そだい)ごみ) such as furniture and appliances. Combustible garbage is burned, and non-combustible garbage is broken into small pieces and taken to the dump site. Items in each category may differ slightly from place to place in Japan, depending on local laws. Garbage can be placed in trash buckets or special plastic bags approved by local authorities. Garbage placed in an unapproved container may not be collected.

A neighborhood trash pick-up schedule (left) and an approved trash bag (above)

Also, it is necessary to take garbage to the designated location on the day of collection. The collection days for each type of garbage are posted at every waste collection area. Waste must not be left overnight. Leaving uncollected garbage for a prolonged period of time in the collection area is a nuisance for people who live close to the area.

LANGUAGE

I. Expressing problems and things that have taken place, using the passive form

A. Direct passives

Subject	Agent				
Noun	Particle	Noun	Particle	Verb (passive)	
けんいちくん	は	先生	に	ほめられて、	とてもうれしそうだった。

Ken'ichi looked very happy because he was praised by the teacher.

この新聞はよく読まれています。	This newspaper is widely read.
その手紙は英語で書かれていた。	That letter was written in English.
その子は年上(としうえ)の男の子に文句(もんく)を言ったら、しかれてしまった。	When that child complained to the older boy, she was scolded by him.

Verb types	Meaning	Dictionary form	Passive form	
Irregular verbs	to come	来る		来(こ)られる
	to do	する		される
る-verbs			Add られる to the stem	
	to eat	食べる	食べ + られる	食べられる
	to see	見る	見 + られる	見られる
う-verbs			Add れる to the plain negative stem	
	to talk	話す	話さない	話される
	to get angry	おこる	おこらない	おこられる
	to place	置(お)く	置(お)かない	置(お)かれる

- When someone does something that affects another person, the situation can be expressed from two different points of view. One is the viewpoint of the performer of the action, and the other is the viewpoint of the person affected by the action. In English, the former is expressed in active sentences, such as "Tom kissed Mary," and the latter is expressed in passive sentences, such as "Mary was kissed by Tom." Similarly, in Japanese, an active sentence expresses the performer's point of view, and a passive sentence expresses the viewpoint of the receiving end of the action:

  その子はメアリーをからかった。 That child teased Mary.
  メアリーはその子にからかわれた。 Mary was teased by that child.

- A passive sentence takes the pattern "subject は／が agent に passive verb form." The particle に marks the agent (performer of the action), and the subject indicates the person who is affected by the action. (に can be replaced with から when the agent is considered a source from which something verbal is coming.)

  私は知(し)り合(あ)いに／から日本の大学について聞かれた。
  I was asked by an acquaintance about Japanese universities.

- The passive forms of る-verbs and 来る are the same as their potential forms. Sentence patterns, however, are very different in passive and potential sentences.

  田中さんは明日までにアンケートが集められると言いました。
  Tanaka-san said he can collect the survey by tomorrow.
  エイズの研究のために、毎年たくさんのお金が集められます。
  A lot of money is collected every year for AIDS research.

- （ら）れる conjugates as a る-verb.

negative form	いじめられない	からかわれない
polite form	いじめられます	からかわれます
dictionary form	いじめられる	からかわれる
conditional form	いじめられれば	からかわれれば
て-form	いじめられて	からかわれて

- There are two types of passive sentences in Japanese, the *direct* and *indirect* passive. The direct passive is similar to the English passive in that the action directly affects the direct object or indirect object of the active sentences. It can also be said that the direct passive sentence always has an active sentence counterpart.

山田さんは田中さんを起こした。　Yamada-san woke up Tanaka-san.

田中さんは山田さんに起こされた。　Tanaka-san was awakened by Yamada-san.

- The verb in direct passive sentences must be a transitive verb. The subject of the direct passive does not have to be animate. The agent in such sentences is often marked with によって instead of に.

この本は色々な人に読まれている。　This book has been read by many people.

アメリカはコロンブスによって発見（はっけん）された。　America was discovered by Columbus.

- The agent of the direct passive can be omitted if it is understood from the context, unknown, or of no particular interest.

このお寺は 1600 年にたてられました。　This building was built in 1600.

あの先生は日本でもよく知られている。　That professor is also well known in Japan.

B. Indirect passives

Agent			
Noun	**Particle**	**Verb (passive)**	**Auxiliary verb**
雨	に	ふられて	しまった。

I was rained on.

スミスさんに足をふまれた。
Smith-san stepped on my foot. (literally: [I had] my foot stepped on by Smith-san.)

なかの悪い男の子に日記（にっき）を読まれて、困（こま）っている。
I'm annoyed because a boy I don't get along with read my diary. (literally: [I had] my diary read by a boy I don't get along with, and I am annoyed.)

山本さんは十六さいの時に両親にしなれてから、ずっと一人だそうです。

I heard that Yamamoto-san has been alone since his parents died when he was sixteen years old. (literally: I hear that Yamamoto-san has been alone since he was died on by his parents when he was sixteen years old.)

お父さんにおこられちゃった。

I got scolded by my father. (literally: [I got] [angered at by] my father)

- The second type of passive is the *indirect passive* or *adversative passive*. In an indirect passive, someone does something or something happens, and the subject is adversely affected by it or troubled by the action or event. The subject has no direct involvement in the actual act or occurrence. For example, in the following sentence, the subject's TV was stolen by the burglar. In this case, the subject is not directly involved in the action although the TV was. However, the subject is adversely affected. The indirect passive sentence allows the subject to express his or her upset feeling caused by the event.

私はどろぼうにテレビをぬすまれた。

My TV was stolen by a thief. (literally: [I had] my TV stolen by a thief.)

となりの人に夜中(よなか)までさわがれて寝られない。

My next-door neighbor makes noise until late at night, so I cannot sleep. (literally: [I have] my next-door neighbor make noise until late and cannot sleep.)

- The action may be a natural occurrence or an accident, and the verbs in indirect passive sentences can be intransitive verbs.

私は赤(あか)ちゃんに泣(な)かれた。

The baby cried on me. (literally: I was cried by the baby.)

その子は年下(としした)の男の子に服を汚(よご)されて、おこっていた。

The child was angry because the younger boy made his clothes dirty. (literally: That child [had] the younger boy make his clothes dirty and he was angry.)

- Unlike the direct passive, the subject of an indirect passive is always animate. Also, the agent of indirect passive is usually specific and is rarely omitted.
- One crucial difference between the direct and indirect passive is that the indirect passive tends to have a negative connotation, but direct passives can have either a negative or a positive connotation.
- Many passive sentences in English are not necessarily expressed as passives in Japanese. For example, the verbs *to understand* and *to need* can be used in passive sentences such as *the message was understood* and *more efforts are needed*. But there is no passive form for わかる or いる *(to need)*. Similarly,

the mutually benefactive verbs such as *to marry* can appear in the passive form as in *I am married*, but the corresponding Japanese verb 結婚する rarely appears in a passive sentence in Japanese unless you want to indicate that one of the people involved in the action has been inconvenienced.

話してみましょう

A. Look at the following pictures and describe what has happened using passive constructions.

Example

①

②

③

④

⑤

Example

雨にふられました。／雨にふられてしまいました。／
雨にふられちゃったんです。

B. Work with the class. Use the passive construction to ask your classmates what they don't want others to do to them. Write their names and responses.

Example

A: 人にどんなことをされたら、いやですか。
B: そうですね。ごみ出しの日じゃないのに、ごみを捨(す)てられたら、いやですね。

名前	されたらいやなこと

C. Work with a partner. Use the list of things that annoy your classmates that you compiled in Exercise B to ask your partner whether he or she has had similar experiences. If so, use the passive construction to ask who did it. Use casual speech.

Example

A: だれかにいじめられたことある？

B: うん、あるよ。(male)／ええ、あるわよ。(female)

A: だれにいじめられたの。

B: 小学校の時、近所(きんじょ)の年上(としうえ)の子によくいじめられたんだ。(male)／
小学校の時、近所(きんじょ)の年上(としうえ)の子によくいじめられたの。(female)

D. Work as a class. Using the passive construction, ask your classmates about things and people with the following characteristics. Ask as many classmates as you can to find the most common answers.

Example

A: せかい (world) で一番よく知られているアメリカ人は
だれだと思いますか。

B: リンカーンだと思います。

せかいで一番～	クラスメートのこたえ
Well-known American	
Well-known Japanese	
Frequently read book	
Frequently eaten food	
Frequently drunk drink	
Frequently sung song	

II. Expressing complaints, using the causative-passive form

Subject (Causee)		Agent (Causer)		Action				
Noun	**Particle**	**Noun**	**Particle**	**Noun**	**Particle**	**Noun**	**Particle**	**Verb (causative-passive)**
私	は	母	に	犬	の	散歩(さんぽ)	に	行かされました。

I was made to take the dog for a walk by my mother.

私は毎日百メートル泳(およ)がされた。
I was made to swim one hundred meters every day.

家の子供にはいつも心配(しんぱい)させられる。
My child makes me worry all the time. (literally: I am made to worry by my child all the time.)

小学校の時、先生に日記(にっき)を付けさせられました。
My teacher made me keep a diary when I was in elementary school. (literally: I was made to keep a diary by my teacher in elementary school.)

トムは年上(としうえ)の子に泣(な)かされた。
An older child made Tom cry. (literally: Tom was made to cry by an older child.)

Verb types	Meaning	Dictionary form	Causative form	Causative-passive form
Irregular verbs	to come	来る	来(こ)させる	来(こ)させられる
	to do	する	させる	させられる
る-verbs	to eat	食べる	食べさせる	食べさせられる
	to discard	捨(す)てる	捨(す)てさせる	捨(す)てさせられる
う-verbs	to write	書く	書かせる or 書かす	書かせられる 書かされる
	to drink	飲む	飲ませる or 飲ます	飲ませられる 飲まされる

- A causative-passive sentence is a type of direct passive where the causee of the action is the subject and the causer is the agent of the action. Such sentences convey the viewpoint of the causee. In causative-passive sentences, the subject (the causee) is always forced to do something by the agent (the causer). Use the て + もらう／いただく if the subject is allowed to do something by the causer.

社長に日本に行かせられた。　I was made to go to Japan.
社長に日本に行かせていただいた。　I was allowed to go to Japan.

- The causer can be omitted if understood from the context.
  子供の時、毎日朝ご飯(はん)を食べさせられた。
  I was forced to eat breakfast every day when I was a child.
- う-verbs and the irregular verb 来る have two causative-passive forms, (さ)せられる and (さ)される, but る-verbs and the irregular verb する tend to have only (さ)せられる. However, when (さ)せられる and (さ)される are possible, the shorter causative passive sounds more direct and more colloquial.

話してみましょう

A. A mother is talking about what she is making her child do. You are the child and you don't like doing any of the things she has told you to do, but you are forced to do them anyway. Change the mother's statements to express your perspective, using the causative-passive construction.

Example

私は子供に毎朝ミルクを飲ますんです。
私は母に毎朝ミルクを飲まされるんです。

1. 私は子供に毎日運動をさせます。
2. 私は子供にごみを捨(す)てさせるんです。
3. 私は子供に時々近所(きんじょ)のスーパーに買い物に行かすんです。
4. 私は子供にそうじを手伝(てつだ)わすんです。
5. 私は子供に自分の部屋をかたづけさせるんです。
6. 私は子供に毎日日記(にっき)を付けさせるんです。
7. 私は子供にピアノを習(なら)わすんです。

B. Work with the class. Ask your classmates what kinds of things they were made to do by their parents when they were children. Use the form your instructor will give you to record their responses.

Example

A: 子供の時親(おや)にどんなことをさせられましたか。
B: おさらを洗わされました。

C. Your boss asked you to do the following things. You could not refuse his requests, so you have done them. Express your negative feelings about what you were asked to do using the causative passive.

Example

明日大阪(おおさか)に行ってくれないか。
大阪(おおさか)に行かされました。

1. コピーを 100 まいとっておいてくれないか。
2. くうこうまで知(し)り合(あ)いの子供をむかえに行ってもらいたいんだ。
3. 明日までにこのプロジェクトのレポートを出してほしいんだが。
4. ちょっとお茶を入れてもらえないか。
5. この荷物(にもつ)を持ってくれないか。
6. 今日は忙しいから、五時まで待ってくれないか。
7. このプロジェクトが終わらないから、手伝(てつだ)ってほしいんだ。
8. 今週の日曜日は会社に来てもらいたいんだ。

D. Work with a partner. Your instructor will give you a chart. First, write the things you would like your teacher, parents, roommate, and spouse to let you do (させてもらいたいこと) and the things you don't want them to make you do (させられたくないこと). Ask your partner what he or she would like these people to let him or her do and what he or she doesn't want to be made to do, and compare your responses to those of your partner.

Example

A: 先生にどんなことをさせていただきたいと思いますか。
B: そうですね。英語で話させていただきたいですね。
A: 私もそう思います。
B: じゃあ、先生にどんなことをさせられたくないですか。
A: そうですね、作文を書かされたくないですね。
B: そうですか。私は毎日テストを受けさせられたくないですね。

III. Expressing large and small quantities and frequencies, using a quantity expression + も

A. Expressing zero quantity or frequency, using 1 + counter ~ negative

	Frequency	Particle		Verb (negative)
山田さんは	一度	も	親(おや)にしかられたことが	ありません。

Yamada-san has never been scolded by his parents. (literally: Yamada-san has not been scolded by his parents even once.)

昨日のパーティには知(し)り合(あ)いは一人も来なかった。
Not even a single acquaintance came to the party yesterday.

おさけが一本もないよ。 There are no bottles of **sake** at all.
この部屋にはまどが一つもないですね。 There are no windows in this room.
私は車をぶつけたことは一度もありません。 I've never run into anything with my car.

- Expressions of quantity or frequency where the number one is followed by も and a negative ending indicate zero quantity or frequency and are usually translated as *not even one/once*.

B. Emphasizing a large quantity or high frequency, using number/question word + counter + も~ affirmative

B-1. Frequency/quantity (>1) + も~ affirmative

	Frequency	Particle	Verb (affirmative)
子供の時	四回	も	引(ひ)っ越(こ)した。

We moved FOUR TIMES when I was a child.

B-2. Question word + frequency/quantity counter + も~ affirmative

	Frequency	Particle		Verb (affirmative)
山田さんは昨日	何回	も	電話を	かけてきた。

Yamada-san called MANY TIMES yesterday.

トムはステーキを三まいも食べた。
Tom ate THREE steaks.

さとるには今まで何度もからかわれたから、おこってるんだ。
I've been teased by Satoru MANY TIMES in the past, so I am mad at him.

いいレポートを書くためには何さつも本を読まなければならない。
I must read MANY BOOKS in order to write a good report.

毎日下手なピアノを三時間もひくので、うるさくてたまらない。
He plays the piano up to THREE HOURS every day, and not very well, and I can't stand the noise.

- When も follows a quantity or frequency expression in an affirmative sentence, it indicates that the speaker feels the quantity or frequency is abnormally large. For example, the difference between 電話で二時間話した and 電話で二時間も話した is that, in the first sentence, the speaker does not think a two-hour telephone conversation is long, but in the second sentence, he or she does.

大木： 昨日何度も電話したんですが。
I tried to call you MANY TIMES yesterday.

道子： ああ、ごめんなさい。知り合いから電話がかかってきて、二時間ぐらい話していたんです。
Oh, I'm sorry. I got a phone call from an acquaintance and talked for about two hours.

大木： え、二時間も話してたんですか。
Really? You talked for TWO HOURS!

- If a quantity or frequency expression with も contains a question word instead of a number, it means *many*, *much*, or *a lot of* and is used to emphasize a large quantity or high frequency. The sentence must end with an affirmative verb form.

話してみましょう

A. The chart on page 450 shows how often Aoki-san and Chung-san did certain things last week. Answer the questions using a quantity or frequency expression and も.

Example

A: 青木さんは先週ご両親に電話をかけましたか。チョンさんはどうですか。
B: 青木さんは一度もかけませんでした。チョンさんは四回もかけました。

すること	青木	チョン
両親に電話をかける	0度	四回
テレビを見る	二十時間	0時間
本を読む	五さつ	0さつ
犬の散歩(さんぽ)に行く	0回	十回
ピアノをひく	0回	0回
アルバイトをする	十時間	三十時間
うそをつく	三度	一度
作文を書く	1ページ	10ページ
大家(おおや)さんに注意(ちゅうい)される	六回	0回

1. 青木さんはテレビを見ましたか。チョンさんはどうですか。
2. チョンさんは本を読みましたか。青木さんはどうですか。
3. チョンさんは犬の散歩(さんぽ)に行きましたか。青木さんはどうですか。
4. 青木さんはピアノをひきましたか。チョンさんはどうですか。
5. チョンさんはうそをつきましたか。青木さんはどうですか。
6. チョンさんは作文を書きましたか。青木さんはどうですか。
7. チョンさんはアルバイトをしましたか。青木さんはどうですか。
8. 青木さんは大家(おおや)さんに注意(ちゅうい)されましたか。チョンさんはどうですか。

B. Work with the class. Ask your classmates about things other people frequently do that annoy them.

Example

A: ～さんはいやなことをたくさんされたことがありますか。
B: ええ、あります。小学校の時、同じクラスにいた男の子に何度もからかわれたことがあります。

C. Work with the class. Ask your classmates whether they have done the things listed in the chart on page 451. If they have, ask them how frequently. Find out who in the class has performed each of the actions most frequently.

Example

A: 日本に行ったことがありますか。
B: いいえ、一度もありません。
or
B: はい、あります。
A: 何度ぐらい行ったことがありますか。
B: 三度ぐらいあります。
A: 三度も行ったんですか。いいですね。

	名前	～度／～回／～か月／～年 , etc.
日本に行く		
日本に住んでいる		
何かぬすまれる		
悪口(わるくち)を言われる		
変なうわさをされる		
先生にしかられる		

IV. Expressing or requesting efforts to change behavior or to act a certain way, using the plain present form of the verb +ようにする; Describing what efforts are being made to attain a specific goal, using the plain present form of the verb +ように、～

A. Expressing or requesting efforts to change behavior, using ～ようにする

A-1. Expressing behavior changes

Adverb	Adverb	Verb	Particle	Verb	
もっと	早く	来る	よう	に	します。

I will make an effort to come earlier.

A-2. Requesting a change of behavior

Noun	Verb	Particle	Verb	Auxiliary verb
夜遅く	さわがないよう	に	して	くれませんか。

Please try to not make noise late at night.

きたない部屋ね。少しはかたづけるようにしたらどう？
What a messy room! Why don't you straighten it up a little?

赤(あか)ちゃんが寝ているから、大きい声(こえ)を出さないようにして下さい。
The baby is sleeping, so please try not to speak loudly.

一日に一度は子供をほめるようにした方がいいですよ。
You should try to praise your child once a day.

- The plain present form of the verb + ようにする is used when behavior changes are expressed with a verb phrase; it means *to make an effort to do* 〜.

日記(にっき)を付けるようにします。　I will try to keep a diary.
うわさはしないようにします。　I will try not to gossip.

- The difference between a simple statement such as 早く来ます and the use of 〜ようにする, such as 早く来るようにします, is that the latter implies that the speaker will try to change his or her behavior for a prolonged period of time, but the former describes one occasion only.

- The plain present form of the verb + ようにします implies that the speaker intends to make an effort to act in a certain way. The plain present form of the verb + ようにしています indicates that the speaker is now making such efforts; it means *I make it a rule to* 〜.

一週間に一度部屋をかたづけるようにします。
I will make an effort to clean the room once a week.

一週間に一度部屋をかたづけるようにしています。
I make it a rule to clean the room once a week.

- 〜ようにして下さい, くれませんか, いただけませんか, etc. are less direct than 〜て下さい, くれませんか, いただけませんか, etc. and imply that the speaker wants the listener to make a prolonged effort to change his or her behavior. These expressions are often used for complaints about people's behavior.

B. Describing what efforts are being made to attain a specific goal, using 〜ように〜

	Verb (plain negative)		Particle	
赤(あか)ちゃんを	起こさない	よう	に	小さい声で 話して下さい。

Please speak quietly so as not to wake up the baby.

下のアパートに住んでいる人の迷惑(めいわく)にならないように、大きいおとを立てないようにしています。
I try not to make any noise so I won't bother the person who lives in the apartment below me.

しかられないように、早く帰ったほうがいいよ。
You should go home early so you won't be scolded.

また車をぶつけないように、注意(ちゅうい)して運転して下さい。
Please drive carefully so you don't hit something with your car again.

よく寝られるように、毎日一時間散歩(さんぽ)をしているの。
I take a walk for an hour every day so I can sleep well.

早く上手になるように毎日ピアノの練習をしています。
I practice the piano every day so I can improve quickly.

- In the ～ように、～ construction, the clause preceding ように describes the speaker's goal, and the main clause describes the efforts being made to attain that goal.
- ～ように言う indicates that the speaker has or will tell someone to make an effort to do something. It is an extension of the ～ように～ construction.

変なうわさをしたり人の悪口(わるくち)を言ったりしないように言った。
I told (them) not to gossip or speak ill of other people.

あの子がうそをついたんだから、あやまるよう言って下さい。
The child lied, so please tell him to apologize.

話してみましょう

A. Match the sentence halves in Column A and Column B and make a sentence using ～ように～.

Example

1. 日本語が上手になる／ g. 毎日日本人と話す
日本語が上手になるように、毎日日本人と話すようにしています。

A	B
1. 日本語が上手になる	a. 毎日千メートル泳(およ)ぐ
2. かぜをひかない	b. ごみ出しの日の朝、ごみを出す
3. やせられる	c. セーターとコートをきる
4. 近所(きんじょ)の人の迷惑(めいわく)にならない	d. 夜(よる)大きい声(こえ)で話さない
5. 赤(あか)ちゃんを起こさない	e. 宿題を早く出す
6. 晩御飯(ごはん)が食べられる	f. 今は何も食べない
7. 先生にほめられる	g. 毎日日本人と話す

B. Work with a partner. Imagine you are the manager of a dormitory. You are writing a set of rules to maintain order in dormitory life. Based on a discussion with your partner, write six regulations you want students to follow, using ～ように.

Example

A: りょうの学生にどんなことをするように言ったらいいでしょうか。
B: そうですね。十時までに、りょうに帰るように言ったらどうでしょうか。

You write: 十時までにりょうに帰るようにすること

C. Work with a partner. The two of you are neighbors, and you are having some problems with one another. Each of you should write five things the other has been doing that you find annoying; then ask the other to stop doing these things.

Example

A: あのう、すみませんが、
B: はい、何でしょうか。
A: 家の前に止めてある白い車、～さんのですか。
B: あ、そうですが。
A: 出られなくなるから、止めないようにしていただけませんか。
B: あ、すみません。

V. Using the plain form + のに to mean *despite* ～; *although* ～

Subordinate clause			Main clause
	Verb (plain present)	Conjunction	
赤(あか)ちゃんが	泣(な)いている	のに、	お母さんは何もしない。

Although the baby is crying, the mother is doing nothing.

今日はごみ出しの日じゃないのに、ごみが出ている。
Although today is not a trash collection day, people have put their trash out.

うそなのに、みんな本当(ほんとう)だと思っています。
Although it is a lie, everyone thinks it is true.

その子は大事なおもちゃをこわされたのに、全然(ぜんぜん)おこっていません。
The child is not at all mad, even though his precious toy was broken.

落書(らくが)きはしないように言ったのに、また落書(らくが)きをしている。
Even though I told him not to write graffiti, he is writing graffiti again.

- 〜のに is preceded by the same forms as 〜ので or 〜のです. な is used for the present affirmative tense of な-adjectives and the copula verb, and plain forms are used for all other adjectives, copula verbs, and verbs.

Category	Example	Meaning
い-adjectives	汚(きた)ない	dirty
	汚(きた)ないのに	Although it is dirty
	汚(きた)なくないのに	Although it is not dirty
	汚(きた)なかったのに	Although it was dirty
	汚(きた)なくなかったのに	Although it was not dirty
な-adjectives	いや	unpleasant
	いや<u>な</u>のに	Although it is unpleasant
	いやじゃないのに	Although it is not unpleasant
	いやだったのに	Although it was unpleasant
	いやじゃなかったのに	Although it was not unpleasant
Copula verb	うそ	lie
	うそ<u>な</u>のに	Although it is a lie
	うそじゃないのに	Although it is not a lie
	うそだったのに	Although it was a lie
	うそじゃなかったのに	Although it was not a lie
Verbs	ほめる	to praise
	ほめるのに	Although I praise
	ほめないのに	Although I don't praise
	ほめたのに	Although I praised
	ほめなかったのに	Although I didn't praise

- The conjunction のに *(although, despite)* indicates a strong contrast between two clauses. Its meaning is the exact opposite of 〜ので *(because)*. The のに construction is used to express a result that was not expected. In this sense, のに expresses the speaker's disbelief, surprise, regret, sorrow, frustration, or opposition to a situation that is the opposite of his or her expectations.

- As was also the case with 〜ので, the main clause can only express a statement or a question. For requests, commands, suggestions, offers, invitations, or other expressions indicating strong feelings, use 〜け(れ)ど or 〜が.

ちょっと重いですが、持ってくれませんか。	It's a little heavy, but could you hold it?
ちょっと重いけど、持ってくれませんか。	It's a little heavy, but could you hold it?
~~ちょっと重いのに、持ってくれませんか。~~	It's a little heavy, but could you hold it?

あまり時間はありませんが、先生に会いに行くつもりです。
I don't have a lot of time, but I intend to go see my teacher.

その人とはあまりなかはよくないけど、悪口(わるくち)は言いたくありません。
~~その人とはあまりなかはよくないのに、悪口(わるくち)は言いたくありません。~~
Although I don't get along with him very well, I don't want to speak ill of him.

- The 〜のに clause is translated as *should* or *should have* if the main clause is omitted. This usage is very common in conversation.

電話かければよかったのに。	You should have called.
いやならいやだと言えばいいのに。	He should say so if he doesn't like it.

話してみましょう

A. Make a sentence by adding のに to the cue sentence.

Example

日本に十年住んでいました。
<u>日本に十年住んでいたのに、日本語が話せません。</u>

1. ゴミ出しの日じゃありません。
2. そのうわさは本当(ほんとう)じゃありません。
3. 私は落書(らくが)きをしていません。
4. ピアノを習(なら)いたくありません。
5. どろぼうにお金をぬすまれました。
6. ようふくを汚(よご)されました。
7. 足をふまれました。
8. 引越(ひっこ)しをしました。

B. Work with a partner. Look at the following pictures and tell what is odd about them.

Example

A: この絵(え)、変ですね。
B: そうですね。天気がいいのに、かさをさしています。
(hold the umbrella open)

Example

①

②

③

④

⑤

⑥

⑦

⑧

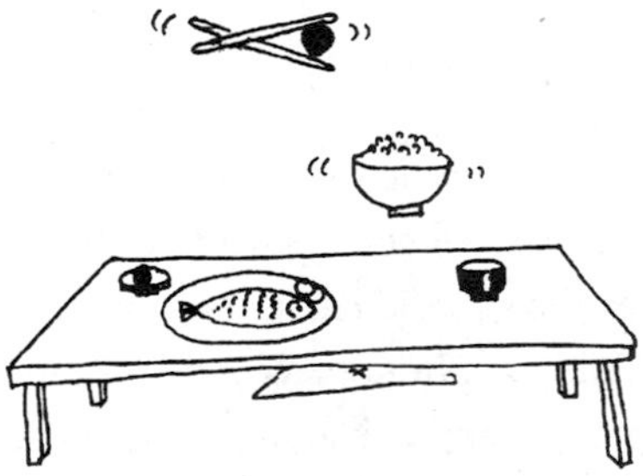

C. Work with a partner. One person should describe a problem, using sentences 1-5 below with のに, and the other person should then give advice.

Example

何度も文句(もんく)を言いましたが、となりの人は私の家の前に車を止めます。

A: どうしたんですか。

B: となりの人が家の前に車を止めるので、こまってるんですよ。

A: そうなんですか。となりの人と話はしたんですか。

B: ええ、何度も文句(もんく)を言ったのに、全然(ぜんぜん)だめなんです。

A: そうですか。じゃあ、家の前に自分の車を止めておいたらどうですか。

B: ああ、それはいいかもしれませんね。

1. 友達は、むかえに来るといいましたが、まだ来ていません。
2. となりの人に大きいおとを立てないようにたのみましたが、全然(ぜんぜん)静かにしてくれません。
3. ゴミ出しの日ですが、ゴミを出すのを忘れました。
4. どろぼうにかぎをこわされたんですが、大家(おおや)さんはかぎを直してくれません。
5. 山田さんの服を汚(よご)して、あやまりましたが、まだおこっています。

漢字

The importance of the sound components of kanji

Approximately 80% of the most frequently used 1,850 **kanji** belong to a type called *semantic-phonetic compounds* or *phonetic compounds* (形声文字(けいせいもじ)). This type of **kanji** consists of two distinctive components. The semantic component indicates the general category of the meaning of the **kanji** (e.g., water, tree, person, etc.), while the phonetic component indicates the **on**-reading of the **kanji**. The **on**-reading of a **kanji** is usually the one used when the **kanji** is a part of a multi-**kanji** word. Although the pronunciation of the phonetic components is not as consistent as the meaning of the semantic components, a certain level of regularity can be found. (Recent research has shown that sound is important—when native speakers read Japanese text, they tend to make substitution errors regarding **kanji** with the same pronunciation but different meanings.) Learners of Japanese know many words in the spoken form, but they may not know how to pronounce many of these when they are written in **kanji**. When you encounter a multi-**kanji** word, knowledge of the phonetic component should help you guess the **on**-reading of the **kanji**, which leads you to the pronunciation of the word.

Some common phonetic components are shown below. Circle the phonetic component of each **kanji**.

Sound (on-reading)	漢字
じ	寺　時　持
せん	先　洗
もん	門　問　悶
せい	青　晴　精　清
はん	反　飯　版　阪
き	己　記　紀　忌　起
ほう／ぼう	方　妨　防　坊
こう	講　構　購
せん	浅　銭　賎　践
せん	線　泉　腺

心	心	mind, heart　シン／こころ	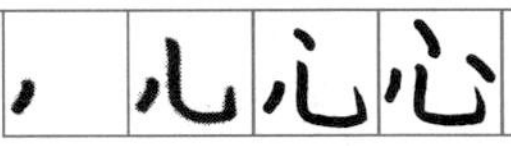
		母の病気のことが心配(しんぱい)です。	
配	配	to deliver　ハイ、パイ／くば（る）	
		試験のことは心配(しんぱい)しないほうがいいよ。	
迷	迷	to lose one's way, go astray　メイ／まよ（う）	
		ご迷惑(めいわく)をおかけしました。	
惑	惑	to go astray, be puzzled　ワク	
		ほかの人の迷惑(めいわく)になりますから静かにして下さい。	

Kanji	Meaning	Readings	Example
困	to be in trouble	コン/こま（る）	お金（かね）がなくて困（こま）っています。
句	clause, phrase, verse	ク	あまり文句（もんく）を言わないで下さい。
全	whole, entirely	ゼン/まった（く）	体（からだ）は全然（ぜんぜん）悪くありません。
然	so, yes	ゼン、ネン	病気が全然（ぜんぜん）よくならなくて、とても困（こま）っています。
当	to hit, to be equal, to win	トウ/あた（る）あて（る）	本当（ほんとう）にいい国を作るのは大変です。
注	to pour	チュウ/そそ（ぐ）	ラーメンを注文（ちゅうもん）して下さい。
置	to put, to place	チ/お（く）	その荷物（にもつ）はここに置（お）いて下さい。
拾	to pick up	シュウ/ひろ（う）	子供が捨（す）てられた猫を拾（ひろ）ってきた。
捨	to discard, to abandon	シャ/す（てる）	ゴミは金曜日に捨（す）てて下さい。
直	to mend, cure, correct	チョク/なお（す）	コンピュータを直（なお）せますか。

Kanji	Meaning	Readings	Example
残	to be left over, to leave	ザン/のこ（す）のこ（る）	まだ仕事が残(のこ)っています。残念(ざんねん)ですが、だめでした。
汚	dirty, to soil	オ/きたな（い）よご（す）	部屋(へや)が汚(きたな)いから、そうじしましょう。シャツを汚(よご)した。
笑	to laugh, to smile	ショウ/わら（う）	写真(しゃしん)をとりますから、笑(わら)って下さい。
泣	to cry, to weep	キョウ/な（く）	泣(な)かないで下さい。
散	to fall, to scatter	サン/ち（る）ち（らす）	散歩(さんぽ)が好きです。犬を散歩(さんぽ)させる。
泳	to swim	エイ/およ（ぐ）	プールで泳(およ)ぎました。趣味(しゅみ)は水泳(すいえい)です。
合	to be together, fit	ゴウ/あ（う）	今日は知り合(あ)いと食事に出かけます。
引	to pull	イン/ひ（く）	山田さんは昨日引(ひ)っ越(こ)しました。
落	to fall, to drop	ラク/お（ちる）お（とす）	昨日さいふを落(お)としてしまった。入学試験(にゅうがくしけん)に落(お)ちちゃった。
歌	song, to sing	カ/うた（う）	日本の歌(うた)を歌(うた)いましょう。

Kanji	Meaning	Readings	Example
声	voice	セイ/こえ	図書館では大きい声（こえ）で話さないで下さい。
荷	load, baggage	ニ	荷物（にもつ）を持ちましょうか。重い荷物（にもつ）
絵	drawing, picture	カイ/え	とてもきれいな絵（え）ですね。ゴッホの絵（え）です。
飯	meal, cooked rice	ハン/めし	朝御飯（あさごはん）を食べます。昼御飯（ひるごはん）をどこで食べますか。
売	to sell	バイ/う（る）	野菜（やさい）を売（う）る。売店（ばいてん）でコーラを買う。
夜	night	ヤ/よる	電車は夜（よる）十時に着きます。今夜（こんや）出かけます。

新しい読み方

悪口（わるくち）　近所（きんじょ）　日記（にっき）　文句（もんく）　夜中（よなか）　習（なら）う　大家（おおや）　親（おや）　年上（としうえ）　年下（としした）　音（おと）　知（し）り合（あ）い

練習

下の文を読んで下さい。

1. ここに置いてあった荷物を捨てられちゃったんです。
2. 近所の人が夜大きい声で話すので、迷惑です。
3. 御（ご）飯を食べてから､歌を歌いにカラオケに行きましょう。
4. 弟に日記を読まれて困っています。
5. 間違いが直せなくて心配しています。
6. この赤（あか）ちゃんはよく笑ったり泣いたりします。
7. この絵はいつまでも売れないで残っています。

8. 知り合いが近所に引っ越(こ)してきました。
9. カレーライスを注文したのに全然来ません。文句を言いましょうか。
10. 犬を散歩させていたら、服を汚してしまった。
11. 落書きをしないように注意しました。
12. この猫は拾われた時、とても汚かったです。

上手な読み方

いじめ (Bullying)

読む前に

A. 質問に答えて下さい。

1. 「いじめ」という言葉を聞いたことがありますか。
2. だれかにいじめられたことがありますか。どうしていじめられたのだと思いますか。
3. いじめられる人はどんな事をよくされるのですか。
4. どんな人がよくいじめられると思いますか。
5. いじめられている人はどうすればいじめられなくなると思いますか。

B. 下のグラフは 1990 年から 1995 年までの日本でのいじめのかず (number of reported incidents) をあらわしています (shows)。このグラフを見て、どんなことが分かるか話して下さい。

いじめのけんすう (reported number of bullying incidents)

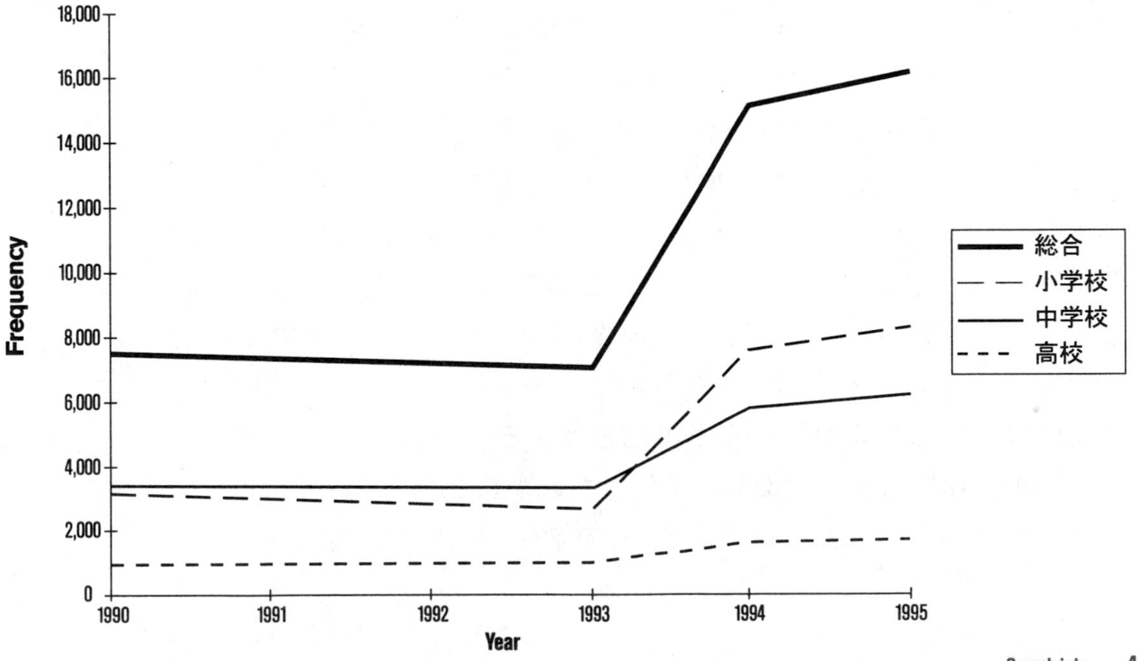

読んでみましょう

言葉のリスト

自殺(じさつ)	国際(こくさい)	行(おこ)なう	場合(ばあい)
suicide	international	conduct	the case

日本では、最近(さいきん)、いじめが問題になってきていて、いじめられたために、自殺(じさつ)をしたり、学校に行かなくなったりする子供も多い。いじめは日本だけの問題だと考える人が多いが、アメリカ、イギリス、ノルウェー、オーストラリアでも多くなってきていて、1996年の六月には「いじめ問題国際(こくさい)シンポジウム」が開かれた。このシンポジウムの前に、日本では、いじめについて、一万人の小学生、中学生、高校生にアンケートが行(おこ)なわれた。

そのアンケートによると、日本ではいじめをする学生はいじめられる学生のクラスメートであるケースが70%にもなることが分かった。また、いじめをした学生にどんな学生をいじめたかと聞くと、普通(ふつう)の友達をいじめた場合(ばあい)が一番多く、そのつぎに、仲(なか)がいい友達やあまりよく知らないクラスメートをいじめたケースが多かった。そして、「前から仲(なか)が悪かった」学生をいじめたと答えた学生は一番少なかった。つまり、いじめをした子供はそのクラスメートがきらいだから、いじめたのではない。

では、どうして子供達はきらいでもないクラスメートや仲(なか)がいい友達をいじめるのだろうか。この質問については、「いじめが面白いから、いじめてみたいから、いじめをするのだ。」という答えが多くみられた。いじめをした後、「面白かった」、「よかった」と思う子供は小学生で20%ぐらいだが、中学生では38%、高校生では41%ぐらいになる。これにたいして、いじめをした後、悪いことをしたと思う学生は、小学生の場合(ばあい)は、80%ぐらいいるが、中学生では70%、高校生になると、60%ぐらいにしかならない。

それでは、いじめられている子供はどうするのだろうか。いじめられた子供が小学生の場合(ばあい)、80%の子供がだれかに相談したり、いじめる子供にやめるように言ったりするが、中学生や高校生になると、

50%の学生がだれにも言わないし、３０%ぐらいの学生はいじめられても何もしない。そして、先生に相談する子供は小学生では30%ぐらいだが、中学生では20%、高校生になると、8%ぐらいしかいない。

　また、いじめを見ているクラスメートや友達もたいてい何もしないし、先生にも相談しない。これはどうしてだろうか。

　アンケートによると、小学生の場合(ばあい)、先生に言ったことがいじめている子供に分かるともっといじめられるという答えが多い。中学生や高校生では、先生は何も出来ないという答えが30%ぐらいで、いじめは自分達の問題だから先生には言わない方がいいという答えが30%ぐらいになる。

分かりましたか

A. Circle はい for statements that are true according to the above text, and いいえ for those that are not.

1. はい　いいえ　いじめの問題は日本だけの問題である。
2. はい　いいえ　日本ではクラスメートをいじめることが多い。
3. はい　いいえ　日本ではいじめをする学生はたいてい自分がきらいな学生をいじめる。
4. はい　いいえ　中学生の方が高校生よりいじめをした後、悪いことをしたと思っている。
5. はい　いいえ　高校生はいじめられた時、あまり先生に言わない。
6. はい　いいえ　いじめを見ている学生は、いじめられたくないから何もしない。
7. はい　いいえ　小学生は先生はいじめをやめさせることは出来ないと思っている。

B. 下の質問に答えて下さい。

1. どうして、「いじめ国際(こくさい)シンポジウム」が開かれたのですか。
2. 日本ではどうして「いじめは面白い」と思う子供が多いのだと思いますか。
3. 小学生と中学生と高校生ではいじめについてどんなことがにています (similar) か。どんなことが違いますか。
4. どうして年が上になると、いじめが悪いと思わなくなるのでしょうか。
5. いじめられている子供はどうしてほかの人に相談しないのですか。

読んだ後で

Work in pairs or groups of four. Discuss the following in your country, and report your findings to the class.

1. あなたの国でもいじめは大きい問題だと思いますか。
2. あなたの国ではどんな子供がどんな子供をいじめるケースが多いと思いますか。日本とはどんなことが同じですか。どんなことが違いますか。
3. いじめはどうすればなくなると思いますか。学校はいじめをやめさせるためにどんなことをしたらいいでしょうか。親はどうすればいいでしょうか。先生や友達はどうしたらいいと思いますか。

上手な聞き方

迷惑なこと (Annoying things)

聞く前に

A. Work with a partner. Discuss what kind of annoying things people in the situations described in 1-6 might experience.

1. 一人で住んでいる女の人
2. りょうに住んでいる学生
3. 外国人
4. アルバイトをしている学生
5. きびしい先生のコースを取っている学生
6. きびしい上司(じょうし)の下で働いている人

B. 質問に答えて下さい。

1. 今、だれにどんなことをされたら迷惑だと思いますか。
2. どんなことは人にしないようにしていますか。
3. いやなことがあった時、だれに相談しますか。
4. ご両親にはどんなことで相談しますか。友達にはどんなことを話しますか。

STUDENT

聞いてみましょう

つぎの会話を聞いて、だれについて話をしているのか書いて下さい。そして、どんな問題があるのか書いて下さい。

Example

You hear: 男の人： どうしたの。何かあったの？
女の人： 家のかべに車ぶつけられたの。
男の人： えっ？だれに。
女の人： ほら、あの、さくらアパートに住んでいる大学生。
男の人： ああ、あの、かみの長い。
女の人： そうよ。

You write: だれについて： さくらアパートに住んでいる大学生
問題： 女の人の家のかべに車をぶつけました。

ケース１ だれについて：＿＿＿＿＿＿＿＿＿＿＿＿

問題：＿＿＿＿＿＿＿＿＿＿＿＿＿＿＿＿

ケース２ だれについて：＿＿＿＿＿＿＿＿＿＿＿＿

問題：＿＿＿＿＿＿＿＿＿＿＿＿＿＿＿＿

ケース３ だれについて：＿＿＿＿＿＿＿＿＿＿＿＿

問題：＿＿＿＿＿＿＿＿＿＿＿＿＿＿＿＿

聞いた後で

A. Work with a partner. Write two possible solutions for each of the above three problems on a separate sheet of paper.

STUDENT

B. Listen to the follow-up conversations for each of the above three problems, and write the suggestions given to the person on a separate sheet of paper.

C. Work with the same partner you had in Exercise A. Compare the suggestions from Exercise B with your own suggestions, and explain which ones you think are the best solutions and why.

STUDENT

DICT-A-CONVERSATION

田中さんの家の前はゴミを出す所です。スミスさんは夜ゴミを捨てに来ています。

田中：______________________________

スミス：______________________________

田中：______________________________

スミス：______________________________

田中：______________________________

スミス：______________________________

田中：______________________________

聞き上手話し上手

文句を言う、おこる、あやまる
(Expressing complaints or anger, and making apologies)

Complaining about people or their actions is a sensitive topic. The Japanese people feel that complaints threaten the "face" of the person being complained about and make that person feel uneasy, which is not conducive to future harmonious relationships. Therefore, it is important to make complaints carefully, so as not to create an uneasy atmosphere. This is especially true if you are complaining about someone you know very well.

One way to make a complaint non-threatening is to talk around the actual complaint, stating the problem but not admitting to being actually bothered by it. This is often achieved by just mentioning a general topic, without any verbal phrase, as shown in the following example:

STUDENT

大木：　あのう、すみませんが、
　　　　Excuse me, but . . .
石川：　ええ、何でしょうか。
　　　　Yes, what is it?
大木：　あのう、ちょっとテレビのおとが . . .
　　　　Well, it's just the sound from your TV is . . .
石川：　あ、すみません、大きすぎましたか。
　　　　Oh, I'm sorry. Was it too loud?
大木：　ええ、おねがいします。
　　　　Yes, I'm sorry.

If the person does not realize what you are talking about, you can complain more explicitly.

STUDENT

大木：　あのう、ちょっとテレビのおとが . . .
Well, it's just the sound from your TV is . . .

石川：　え。テレビのおとがどうかしましたか。
What about the sound from my TV?

大木：　あのう、少し小さくしていただけませんか。もう十一時になりますので。
Could you turn it down just a little? It's already 11:00 P.M.

石川：　あ、そうなんですか。すみませんでした。気が付かなくて。これから気を付けます。
Oh, you're right. I'm sorry. I didn't realize—I'll watch it from now on.

大木：　おねがいします。
Oh, thank you.

In the above example, expressions like そうなんですか, 気が付かなくて, and これから気を付けます are useful expressions when apologizing. The phrase そうなんですか expresses B's acknowledgment of his mistake, 気が付かなくて expresses the absence of any ill will, and これから気を付けます indicates his intention to correct the mistake. Although what deserves apology differs from culture to culture, the Japanese apologize frequently. This is because apologies do not just mean the admittance of one's failure or guilt. Rather, apologies indicate that a person recognizes that his or her failure to meet the expectation of others is his or her responsibility. This in turn relieves the blame on others, and therefore shows thoughtfulness and kindness toward them. Also, apologies indicate admittance of one's weakness, and this is thought to deserve understanding and sympathy. The common expressions of apology are:

ごめん	Sorry; excuse me.	(casual)
ごめんなさい	Sorry; please forgive me.	↓
すみません	I'm sorry.	↓
申しわけありません	I'm sorry.	↓
申しわけございません	I'm sorry.	(polite and formal)

申しわけありません and すみません are also used to express gratitude, as when receiving a gift. It is customary to bow. The more deeply you feel sorrow, the more slowly and deeply you bow.

In general, the Japanese avoid showing anger in public. This is especially true of Japanese males, because losing one's temper is considered childish. When two people fall out over something, they make every effort to settle the dispute amicably through discussion, often by going out for drinks. However, expressions of anger are sometimes necessary, even toward strangers, to protect oneself from harassing phone calls, stalkers, etc. The following are common expressions used in such cases.:

やめて（下さい）／やめろ (male)	Cut it out.
何するのよ (female) ／何するんだよ (male)	What do you think you're doing?
いいかげんにしてよ (female) ／ いいかげんにしろよ (male)	Give me a break./Cut it out.
ほっといてよ (female) ／ほっといてくれよ (male)	Leave me alone.
ふざけないでよ (female) ／ふざけるなよ (male)	Don't be ridiculous.
じょうだんじゃないわよ (female) ／ じょうだんじゃないよ (male)	You've got to be kidding.

A. Work with a partner. Listen to the two versions of the conversation between Ishikawa-san and Ooki-san at the beginning of the Communication section; then practice the dialogue and act it out. Pay attention to the tone of voice.

B. Work with a partner. Your partner is your neighbor. Complain to him or her about trash, parking, noise, etc. Your partner apologizes. Listen to the model dialogue before starting.

C. Listen to the expressions of anger at the end of the Communication section, and repeat them. Pay particular attention to the intonation and the tone of voice.

D. Work with a partner. Your partner is a very persistent salesperson who comes to your house very often and makes frequent phone calls. Express your anger and tell him or her not to contact you again.

総合練習（そうごう）

学生生活（せいかつ）を楽しくしましょう (Let's make college life enjoyable)

Work with the class. Interview three classmates about things that make school life difficult, based on the categories in the chart your instructor will give you. Ask them how they cope with these problems.

Example

A: 〜さんはりょうに住んでいて、どんなことがいやですか。

B: そうですね。同じ部屋に住んでいる学生に部屋を汚されるので、困ります。

A: そうですか。それで、その学生に何か言いましたか。

B: ええ、一週間に一度そうじをするように言いました。

ロールプレイ

A. Your boss makes you do a lot of things that are not part of your job. Describe things you are forced to do and complain to your co-workers.

B. Your house has been burglarized. Call the police, describe the condition of your house, and tell the police what has been stolen.

C. Your classmate makes fun of you all the time. Tell your instructor about him or her, describe how he or she makes fun of you, and ask for help.

D. Your neighbor's son or daughter has been making a lot of noise. Complain to your neighbor.

E. You are a representative of a labor union, and you don't like the working conditions at your place of employment. Complain to the management.

LAB

単語 (ESSENTIAL VOCABULARY)

Nouns

あかちゃん（赤ちゃん） baby
いじめ (act of) bullying
うそ（嘘） lie; うそをつく（嘘をつく） (to) lie
うわさ（噂） rumor; うわさをする（噂をする） (to) gossip
おおや（大家） landlord; landlady
おと（音） sound
おや（親） parent
かべ（壁） wall
かんけい（関係） relationship
きもち（気持ち） feeling
きんじょ（近所） neighborhood
こ（子） child (こ is usually preceded by a modifier, as in としうえのこ[年上の子] older child, or いいこ [いい子] good child.)
ごみ／ゴミ trash; garbage (ごみ can be written either in **hiragana** or in **katakana**.)
ごみだし／ゴミだし（ごみ出し／ゴミ出し） putting out the trash
しりあい（知り合い） acquaintance
としうえ（年上） older
としした（年下） younger
どろぼう（泥棒） thief
なか（仲） relationship (among people); なかがいい（仲がいい） to have a good relationship; なかがわるい（仲が悪い） to have a bad relationship
にっき（日記） diary; にっきをつける（日記を付ける） (to) keep a diary
ひ（日） day
ピアノ piano
ひっこし（引越し） moving (one's residence)
ほんとう（本当） truth; ほんとうに（本当に） indeed; really
めいわく（迷惑） trouble; めいわくをかける（迷惑をかける） (to) give (someone) problems
よなか（夜中） late at night
もんく（文句） complaint もんくをいう（文句を言う） (to) complain
らくがき（落書き） graffiti; らくがきをする（落書きをする） (to) write graffiti
わるくち（悪口） insults; わるくちをいう（悪口を言う） (to) speak ill of

Verbal nouns

さんぽ（散歩） a walk; stroll; さんぽする（散歩する） (to) take a walk; さんぽをする（散歩をする） (to) take a walk
しんぱい（心配） worry; しんぱいする（心配する） (to) worry; しんぱいをする（心配をする） (to) worry
ちゅうい（注意） attention; warning; ちゅういする（注意する） (to) warn; (to) call attention to; ちゅういをする（注意をする） (to) warn; (to) call attention to

う-verbs

あやまる（謝る） (to) apologize
おく（置く） to place
おこる（怒る） to get angry
からかう (to) tease
こわす（壊す） (to) break; (to) destroy
さわぐ（騒ぐ） (to) make noise
しかる（叱る） (to) scold
なおす（直す） (to) fix; (to) correct
ぬすむ（盗む） (to) steal
ひく（弾く） (to) play (the piano/guitar, or other stringed instrument); ピアノをひく（ピアノを弾く） (to) play the piano
ひっこす（引っ越す） (to) move (residence)
ふむ（踏む） (to) step on
よごす（汚す） (to) make something dirty

る-verbs

いじめる (to) bully
かたづける（片付ける） (to) clean up; to organize
すてる（捨てる） (to) discard; (to) abandon
ごみをすてる（ごみを捨てる） (to) take the trash out
つける（付ける） (to) write (a diary); にっきをつける（日記を付ける） (to) write a diary
ぶつける (to) hit; (to) crash into
ほめる（誉める） (to) praise
むかえる（迎える） (to) meet or welcome; むかえにいく（迎えに行く） (to) go to pick up (someone)

な-adjectives

いや（な） unfavorable; unpleasant; hateful
めいわく（な）（迷惑｛な｝） troublesome; annoying
へん（な）（変｛な｝） strange

い-adjectives

うるさい noisy; shut up! (when used as a phrase by itself)
きたない（汚い） dirty
たまらない cannot stand; unbearable

Expressions

いいかげんにしてよ（いい加減にしてよ） Give me a break. (female speech)
いいかげんにしろよ（いい加減にしろよ） Give me a break. (male speech)
うそをつく（嘘をつく） (to) lie
おとをたてる（音を立てる） (to) make noise
きがつかなくて。（気が付かなくて） I did not realize it.
きをつける（気を付ける） (to) become careful, (to) pay attention
ごめいわくおかけしてもうしわけありません（ご迷惑おかけして申し訳ありません） I'm sorry to have caused you problems.
じょうだんじゃない（わ）よ（冗談じゃないよ） You've got to be kidding.
ふざけないでよ Don't be ridiculous. (female speech)
ふざけるなよ Don't be ridiculous. (male speech)
ほっといてくれよ Leave me alone. (male speech)
ほっといてよ Leave me alone. (female speech)
もうしわけありません（申し訳ありません） I'm sorry. (polite and formal)
もうしわけございません（申し訳ございません） I'm sorry. (very polite and formal)
やめろ Cut it out. (male speech)

Passive Vocabulary

Nouns

こくさい（国際） international
じさつ（自殺） suicide
せかい（世界） world
そだいごみ（粗大ごみ） large trash (e.g., tables, chairs, washing machines)
ばあい（場合） case 〜のばあい（〜の場合） in the case of 〜
リサイクル recycling

Verbal nouns

はっけん（発見） discovery; はっけんする（発見する） (to) discover

う-verbs

おこなう（行なう） (to) conduct
もえる（燃える） (to) burn; もえるごみ（燃えるゴミ） combustible garbage

い-adjective

うすい（薄い） thin

For a list of supplementary vocabulary items that will facilitate communication, see the first page of Chapter 9 in your Workbook.

CHAPTER 10

第十課

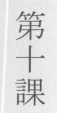

Pollution has made life difficult for many farmers.

環境と社会
(かんきょう　しゃかい)

The Environment and Society

Functions	Expressing one's opinions, agreement or disagreement, and conjectures
New Vocabulary	Disasters; Animals; Environmental issues; A livable society
Dialogue	この川で泳げるでしょうか。(Can I swim in this river?)
Culture	Earthquakes; Environmental concerns; Crimes
Language	I. Using the pronoun の and the noun こと
	II. Forming noun phrases with the nominalizers の or こと
	III. Expressing a change of state, using ～ようになる
	IV. Expressing opinions indirectly, using ～んじゃない（かと思う）
	V. Expressing conjecture based on indirect evidence, using ～らしい; Expressing conjecture based on direct evidence, using ～ようだ／みたいだ
Kanji	Using a **kanji** dictionary
Reading	Expressions used in writing; Global warming
Listening	Problems in my town
Communication	Expressing opinions, agreements, and disagreements

新しい言葉

災害(さいがい) (Disasters)

被害(ひがい)	damage	ハリケーン	hurricane
地震(じしん)	earthquake	こわい	frightening
火事(かじ)	fire	にげる	to escape
洪水(こうずい)	flood	焼(や)ける	(for something) to burn down

下の言葉を覚えていますか。

台風(たいふう)　気候　雨　雪　風　くも　くもり　晴れ　晴れる
ふる　気温が上がる　気温が下がる　天気　天気予報
暖かい　むし暑い　暑い　寒い　涼しい　焼(や)く

A. 下の文に適当(てきとう)な (appropriate) 言葉を書いて下さい。

1. 日本で多い______は______と台風(たいふう)です。
2. 日本には台風(たいふう)が来ますが、アメリカには______が来ます。
3. ______で家が焼(や)けてしまった。
4. たくさん雨がふって、______になってしまった。
5. ハリケーンはいつ来るか分かるので、______ことが出来るが、地震(じしん)はいつ起こるか分からないので、______ことは出来ないと思う。
6. 今度の火事(かじ)で大きい______が出た。家がたくさん______しまったし、にげられなかった人もいたそうだ。
7. 子供の時、地震(じしん)にあったことがありますが、とても______です。

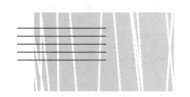

B. 下の質問に日本語で答えて下さい。

1. 今までに経験(けいけん)したことがある災害(さいがい)はどれですか。どんな被害(ひがい)がありましたか。
2. どの災害(さいがい)がこわいと思いますか。どうしてそう思いますか。
3. あなたの国ではどんな災害(さいがい)が多いですか。どこでよく起きますか。
4. 災害(さいがい)が起きた時、どんな所ににげたらいいと思いますか。

動物　(Animals)

鳥(とり)	bird	さる	monkey
くじら	whale	しか	deer
くま	bear	牛(うし)	cow
とら	tiger	ぶた	pig
ぞう	elephant	馬(うま)	horse

下の言葉を覚えていますか。

犬　猫　動物園

C. 下の質問に日本語で答えて下さい。

1. 動物園にいる動物はどれですか。
2. どの動物が泳げると思いますか。どの動物が泳げないと思いますか。
3. 肉を食べる動物はどれですか。肉を食べない動物はどれですか。
4. アメリカにいる動物はどれですか。アフリカにいる動物はどれですか。日本にいる動物はどれですか。オーストラリアにいる動物はどれですか。
5. どんな動物が好きですか。日本語の言葉を知らなかったら、先生か友達に聞いて下さい。

環境(かんきょう)問題　(Environmental issues)

地球(ちきゅう)	the earth	工場(こうじょう)	factory
世界(せかい)	world	公害(こうがい)	pollution
自然(しぜん)	nature	起(お)こす	to cause
空気(くうき)	air	起(お)きる	to take place
森(もり)	forest	汚(よご)れる	to become polluted

ころす to kill
なくなる (for something) to disappear
なくす to lose; to make (something) disappear
かずがふえる the number increases
音が聞こえる to be able to hear a noise
流す(ながす) to run, cause to flow (as water)

下の言葉を覚えていますか。

山 川 みずうみ 海(うみ) 空(そら) 木 木の葉 緑 花 さく 道 町
国 気分が悪い けんこうな せきが出る 汚い 汚す ごみ

D. 下の文に適当(てきとう)な (appropriate) 言葉を書いて下さい。

1. 「＿＿＿＿＿＿＿は青かった」と言った人はロシアの人でした。
2. 日本では結婚しない人が＿＿＿＿＿＿＿ので、子供の＿＿＿＿＿＿＿が少なくなっている。
3. 私の町にはコピーの機械(きかい)を作る＿＿＿＿＿＿＿があります。
4. 食器(しょっき)を洗う時に水を＿＿＿＿＿＿＿ながら、洗います。
5. となりの部屋から変な音が＿＿＿＿＿＿＿。
6. ＿＿＿＿＿＿＿で一番高い山はエベレスト山(ざん)です。
7. ＿＿＿＿＿＿＿には色々な鳥や動物が住んでいる。川や海には色々な魚が住んでいる。だから、＿＿＿＿＿＿＿は大切にしなければならないのだ。
8. 大きい町には車が多くて＿＿＿＿＿＿＿も汚れているし、工場(こうじょう)が起こす＿＿＿＿＿＿＿も問題になっているし、＿＿＿＿＿＿＿が悪くて住みたいと思わない。
9. 動物を＿＿＿＿＿＿＿り、いじめたりしてはいけない。
10. 洪水(こうずい)で家が＿＿＿＿＿＿＿。車もテレビもお金も全部＿＿＿＿＿＿＿。

E. 質問に答えて下さい。

1. 世界(せかい)でどの国の環境(かんきょう)が一番いいと思いまか。
2. 地球(ちきゅう)の環境(かんきょう)はどうなってきていると思いますか。
3. あなたの国ではどんな環境(かんきょう)問題がありますか。
4. 食べるために動物をころしてもいいと思いますか。
5. あなたの国では子供のかずはふえていますか。
6. どんなものがなくなったら、困りますか。

住みやすい社会(しゃかい) (A livable society)

景気(けいき)	economic conditions	関心(かんしん)を持つ	to have an interest in
はんざい	crime	守(まも)る	to protect
けいさつ	police	ふせぐ	to prevent
救急車(きゅうきゅうしゃ)	ambulance	必要(ひつよう)な	necessary
ニュース	news	安全(あんぜん)な	safe
最近(さいきん)	current; recent	不便(ふべん)な	inconvenient
お年より	senior citizen	むだな	wasteful

下の言葉を覚えていますか。

将来(しょうらい)　洗う　考える　しらべる　相談する　注意する　直す
残る　残す　止める　集める　こわす　さわぐ　心配する
ぬすむ　どろぼう　乗り物　車　自転車　飛行機(ひこうき)　交通事故(じこ)
大切な　大事な　やくに立つ　うるさい　迷惑な　わかい

F. Tell what words fit in the following descriptions:

1. テレビで見るもの
2. 何かがないと困ること
3. 便利(べんり)じゃないこと。
4. 必要(ひつよう)じゃないこと。
5. 親が子供にすること

6. 年を取っている人
7. 少し前のこと
8. 物をぬすんだり人を殺したりすること
9. 夜中に外を歩いていて心配しなくもいいこと
10. 病気の時、病院に連れて行ってくれるもの
11. これがいい時には買い物をする人が多くなる
12. 悪いことが起きないようにすること
13. どろぼうが入った時に呼ぶもの
14. 何かが大事だと思っていたり、おもしろいと思っていること

G. 下の質問に日本語で答えて下さい。

1. 最近(さいきん)どんなことに関心(かんしん)がありますか。
2. あなたの国のけいさつはいいですか。
3. どのニュースをよく聞きますか。
4. あなたの国は今景気(けいき)がいいですか。
5. 最近(さいきん)はんざいが多くなっていると思いますか。
6. どんなことをした時、むだなことをしたと思いますか。
7. きらいだけど必要(ひつよう)なものにはどんなもがあるでしょうか。
8. 飛行機(ひこうき)と車とどちらの方が安全(あんぜん)だと思いますか。

ダイアローグ

はじめに

質問に日本語で答えて下さい。

1. あなたの町ではどんな環境(かんきょう)問題がありますか。
2. あなたの国ではどんな社会(しゃかい)問題がありますか。
3. あなたの町の水はおいしく飲むことが出来ますか。
4. 川や海(うみ)の水が汚(よご)れないように、どんなことに気をつけなければなりませんか。

STUDENT

この川で泳げるでしょうか。 (Can I swim in this river?)

The following **manga** frames are scrambled, so they are not in the order described in the dialogue. Read the dialogue and unscramble the frames by writing the correct order in the box located in the upper right corner of each frame.

道子さんと石田さんは石田さんの家の近くの川まで散歩に来ました。

道子：　きれいな水ね。

石田：　うん、まあね。でも、二十年ぐらい前はこの川、汚くて泳げなかったんだよ。

道子：　そう、今は泳いでも大丈夫(だいじょうぶ)なの？

石田：　泳げるんじゃないかと思うけど、よく分からない。

道子：　そう。そう言えば、魚はあまりいないみたいね。でも、どうしてそんなに汚くなっちゃったの。

石田：　二十年ぐらい前にあそこに機械工場(きかいこうじょう)があったんだけどね。

道子：　ええ。

石田：　その工場(こうじょう)の排水(はいすい)で川が汚くなって、大変だったらしいんだ。

道子:　あ、そう。じゃあきれいになったのはいつごろから？

石田：　さあ、よく覚えていないなあ。

石田さんのお母さんが道子さんと石田さんの方に歩いてきます。

石田：　あ、母さん？

石田さんのお母さん：　あ、守（まもる）。あ、道子さんも一緒（いっしょ）なの？

道子：　こんにちは。

石田さんのお母さん：　こんにちは。

石田：　ねえ、今道子さんと話してたんだけど、この川、前はずいぶん汚かったよね。

石田さんのお母さん：　そうよ。工場（こうじょう）があったから。

道子：　でも、今はずいぶんきれいになっているようなんですが。

石田さんのお母さん：　それはね。十年ぐらい前に工場（こうじょう）がなくなったんですよ。それで、その後川をそうじしたんですよ。

道子：　ああ、そうだったんですか。

石田：　ねえ、この川泳げるの？

石田さんのお母さん:　まだだめらしいわよ。一度汚なくなると、きれいになるのには何年もかかるそうよ。

道子：　そうですね。公害（こうがい）をふせぐためには汚さないことが一番ですね。

石田さんのお母さん：　ええ、本当にそうね。

分かりましたか

A. 日本語で質問に答えて下さい。

1. 石田さんの家の近所の川はいつごろ汚なくなりましたか。
2. 川はどうして汚くなりましたか。
3. その川で泳いでもいいですか。いけませんか。それはどうしてですか。
4. その川はいつごろからきれいになりましたか。
5. 道子さんはどんなことが一番大切だと思っていますか。

B. Identify the phrases and sentences that express opinions.

C. Circle phrases that express agreement or disagreement.

D. Rewrite the conversation between Ishida-san and Michiko-san so that Michiko-san becomes Tanaka-sensei. Use polite speech.

日本の文化

- *Earthquakes. Do you have earthquakes in your country? What kinds of natural disasters are common in your country?*

The Great Kobe-Osaka Area Earthquake of 1995 (阪神大震災 はんしんだいしんさい) reconfirmed something the Japanese have long known: their country is prone to earthquakes (地震 じしん). More than 6,000 people were killed and 210,000 houses were completely or partially destroyed in this disaster. The cities appear to have recovered, but there are still many people whose lives have yet to be fully restored.

This massive earthquake gave the country a harsh lesson in the need for better preparedness for natural disasters and many local municipalities have been trying to play more active roles in this regard, but problems remain. A recent survey reports that the general public is still not adequately prepared for emergencies. Although most respondents reported that they had set aside a radio, flashlights, and medicine, fewer than 30% indicated that they have stockpiled emergency food and water. Nor had they run drills on how family members would communicate with one another during emergencies, checked emergency evacuation routes and procedures, begun to keep a bathtub filled with water, taken measures to prevent large furniture from falling, or taken any other proactive steps.

Cleaning up in the aftermath of the Great Kobe-Osaka Area Earthquake of 1995

- *Environmental concerns. What kinds of environmental issues are you interested in? Which issues concern you the most?*

The Japanese suffered from various forms of 公害 こうがい *(environmental pollution)* during the late 1960s and the 1970s when economic growth was the nation's top priority. The major types of environmental pollution are 大気汚染（たいきおせん） *(air pollution)*, 水質汚染（すいしつおせん） *(water pollution)*, 土壌汚染（どじょうおせん） *(soil pollution)*, 騒音（そうおん） *(noise)*, 振動（しんどう） *(vibration)*, 地盤沈下（じばんちんか） *(ground sinkage)*, and 悪臭（あくしゅう） *(foul odors)*. These are now on the decline in Japan, due to a number of regulations and new environmental laws.

Recently, people have started paying more attention to global environmental concerns. The international conference on global warming held in Kyoto in 1997 boosted public awareness nationally.

- *Crimes. What kinds of crimes are common in your country? Do you think the crime rate in your country is high?*

Japan is said by some to be safer than many other nations, and statistics support this claim. According to the National Police Agency, most crimes（はんざい）in Japan are non-violent. Some 88.2% of the criminal offenses reported in 1995 were theft, including pick-pocketing (37.7%), automobile theft (37.3%), and burglaries (13.2%). Another 3.2% of the crimes were fraud, and 0.3% were moral offenses. Only 0.7% were violent crimes such as robbery, arson, rape, kidnapping, and sexual assault.

The crime rate in Japan is on the rise, however, and people are concerned about recent trends. Some of the reasons for these concerns include the attack on the Tokyo subway system with sarin gas made by a religious cult in 1995, a general increase in the use of illegal drugs, and an increase in the number of violent crimes committed by teenagers.

(Number of reported crimes per 100,000 people)

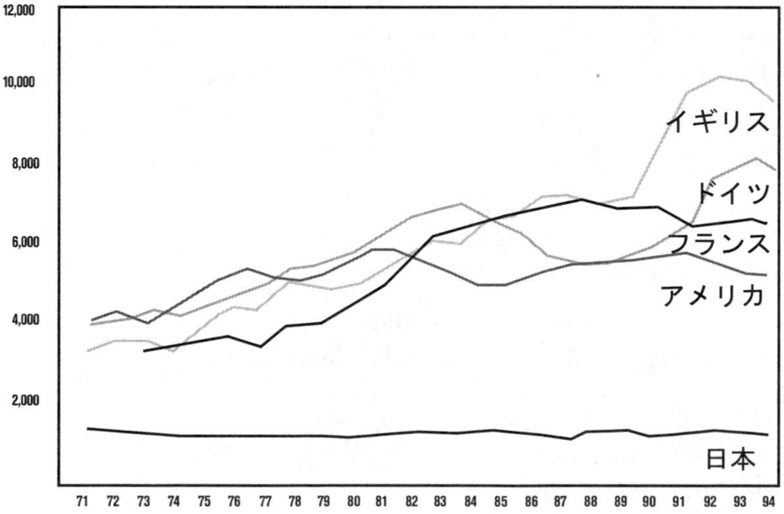

LANGUAGE

I. Using the pronoun の and the noun こと

A. Using の as an indefinite pronoun

Noun phrase			
Clause	**Pronoun**	**Particle**	
私が新聞で読んだ	の	は	フロリダの洪水(こうずい)のことです。

I read in the newspaper about the flood in Florida. (literally: What I read in the newspaper was about the flood in Florida.)

世界(せかい)で一番大切なのは私の子供だ。
The most important thing in the world is my child.

日本でよく話されているのは景気(けいき)の問題です。
One frequent topic of conversation in Japan is the economy.

私もあの店で安く売っていたのを買いました。
I also bought the one that was sold at a discount price at that store.

- The pronoun の can be modified by nouns, adjectives, and verbs. Use な for the present affirmative form of な-adjectives and for nouns + copula verbs. Otherwise, use the plain form.

	い-adjectives	な-adjectives	Noun + copula verb	Verbs
Root	いい (good)	必要(ひつよう)だ (necessary)	学生だ (to be a student)	読む (to read)
Present affirmative	いいの	必要(ひつよう)なの	学生なの	読むの
Present negative	よくないの	必要(ひつよう)じゃないの	学生じゃないの	読まないの
Past affirmative	よかったの	必要(ひつよう)だったの	学生だったの	読んだの
Past negative	よくなかったの	必要(ひつよう)じゃなかったの	学生じゃなかったの	読まなかったの

- The pronoun の is introduced as an indefinite pronoun in Chapter 4 of Volume 1 as in 大きいの *(large one)*. It occurs when the object it refers to is clear from the context.

このペンはちょっと小さいですね。もっと大きいのはありませんか。
This pen is a bit small. Is there a bigger one?

- This chapter introduces the pronoun の with a clause, as shown in the key sentences and examples. It is translated as *one*, *thing*, *what* (as in *what I want to do* 〜) in these cases.

- The pronoun の cannot stand alone. It has to be preceded by an adjective, a verb, a phrase, or a clause. It cannot be used with demonstrative expressions such as この, その, あの, or どの.

きれいなの clean one	きれいじゃないの the one that is not clean
聞こえるの the one I hear/what I hear	聞こえないの the one I can't hear/what I can't hear

- の can refer to either tangible or intangible things.

  田中さんが好きなのはしかです。
  What Tanaka-san likes is deer.

  田中さんが好きなのは山田さんのアイディアです。
  What Tanaka-san likes is Yamada-san's idea.

- Chapter 2 of Volume 1 introduced の when it is directly attached to a noun, as in 山田さんの *(Yamada-san's)*. Strictly speaking, this の is not an indefinite pronoun. It is instead a particle, connecting two nouns (see Chapter 2 of Volume 1). The noun following の is omitted in this usage because it can be inferred from the context.

  それは田中さんの鳥ですが、これは山田さんの<u>の</u>鳥です。
  That is Tanaka-san's bird but this is Yamada-san's.

B. Using こと as a noun

Noun phrase			
Clause	**Noun**	**Particle**	
先生がおっしゃった	こと	を	覚(おぼえ)ていますか。

Do you remember what the teacher said?

大事なことは忘れません。
I don't forget important things.

石田さんは牛(うし)やぶたのことをよく知っている。
Ishida-san knows a lot (of things) about cows and pigs.

自然(しぜん)を守(まも)るために今しなければならないことは何でしょうか。
What kinds of things should we do now to protect nature?

あの人が手紙に書いていたことは本当のことなんでしょうか。
Is what he wrote in the letter true?

- こと is introduced in Chapter 11 of Volume 1. It is a noun that refers to *intangible* things and can be translated as *thing* or *matter*. Just like any other noun, こと is used in noun modifying clauses.

私が言わなかったことを言っていた。	He was saying things that I did not say.
社長がご存知(ぞんじ)ないことは何もありません。	There is nothing that the president does not know.

- こと can be modified by nouns, adjectives, and verbs. To modify こと with a noun, use the particle の. Use な for the plain affirmative form to combine こと and a な-adjective. Otherwise, use the plain forms of adjectives and verbs.

Noun + の + こと:

世界(せかい)のこと	(Things) about the world
お年よりのこと	(Things) about elderly people

- The prenominal form of adjectives or verbs is used with こと as follows:

	い-adjectives	な-adjectives	Verbs
Dictionary form	いい (good)	不便(ふべん) (inconvenient)	起こす (to cause)
Present affirmative	いいこと	不便(ふべん)なこと	起こすこと
Present negative	よくないこと	不便(ふべん)じゃないこと	起こさないこと
Past affirmative	よかったこと	不便(ふべん)だったこと	起こしたこと
Past negative	よくなかったこと	不便(ふべん)じゃなかったこと	起こさなかったこと

- Unlike の, which cannot stand alone, こと can be used by itself and can also occur with demonstrative words.

ことは重大(じゅうだい)だ。	The matter is very important.
そのことはだれにも言わないで下さい。	Please do not tell anyone about that matter.

- Noun + の + こと is often translated as *about* 〜 when it is used with verbs such as 話す, 知っている, 言う, and 読む.

山田さんはそのニュースのことをよく知っていた。	Yamada-san knew a lot about the news.
中国であった洪水(こうずい)のことを話す。	I will talk about the flood that happened in China.

話してみましょう

A. Read the statements and use の to make a question that fits the answer.

Example

山田さんは昨日手紙を書きました。／手紙です。
<u>山田さんが昨日書いたのは何ですか。</u>

1. 昨日近所の動物園からくまがにげました。／くまです。
2. 雪で小学校は休みでした。／小学校です。
3. 洪水(こうずい)で田中さんの家が流(なが)されてしまいました。／田中さんの家です。
4. 近所の子供が火事(かじ)を見つけました。／近所の子供です。
5. あの工場(こうじょう)が汚い水を川に流(なが)しているんです。／あの工場(こうじょう)です。
6. 最近(さいきん)はんざいがふえています。／はんざいです。

B. Work with a partner. Ask each other about what you often speak to your friends about, what you write in your diaries, what you read in the newspapers, what you see on the Internet, and what you hear in school. Write your partner's responses in the chart your instructor will give you. Use casual speech.

Example

A: 友達によく話すことってどんなこと。
B: そうだね、好きな人のことかな。(male) ／
そうね、好きな人のことかしら。(female)

C. Work with the class. Ask your classmates which social and environmental problems they are most concerned or least concerned about. Ask them why. Record these concerns on the form your instructor will give you.

Example

A: 今どんな問題に関心(かんしん)がありますか。
B: そうですね。一番関心(かんしん)を持っているのは、地球(ちきゅう)が暖かくなってきていることです。
A: どうしてですか。
B: 最近(さいきん)新聞でよく読むからです。
A: そうですか。じゃあ、どんなことにはあまり関心(かんしん)がないんですか。

B: 公害(こうがい)の問題にはあまり関心(かんしん)がありませんね。

A: どうしてですか。

B: このへんでは公害(こうがい)があまりないからです。

D. Work with a partner. Discuss the results of the survey in Exercise C and make a report about your classmates' views of these problems.

Example

A: みんな地球(ちきゅう)が暖かくなってきていることには関心(かんしん)があるようですね。

B: ええ、でも、公害(こうがい)にはあまり関心(かんしん)がないみたいですね。

II. Forming noun phrases with the nominalizers の or こと

A. Using the nominalizer の

Topic		Noun phrase			
		Clause	Nominalizer	Particle	
私	は	火事(かじ)で自分の家が焼(や)ける	の	を	見た。

I saw my house burn in a fire.

けいさつが来るのを待つ。 I will wait for the police to come.

救急車(きゅうきゅうしゃ)が通るのが聞こえた。 I heard the ambulance passing by.

さるが木にのぼるのが見えます。 I can see the monkey climbing the tree.

お年よりが一人で生活(せいかつ)するのはよくないと思う。 I don't think it's a good thing for elderly people to live alone.

- Chapter 7 of Volume 1 introduced の in the structure ～は～のが好き／きらい／上手／下手だ, as in テニスをするのが好きだ. This type of の is called a nominalizer because it is used to make a clause into a noun phrase. This chapter introduces an expanded use of the nominalizer の. In English, there are several ways to make a clause into a grammatical noun: you can change a verb form into a gerund *(using e-mail)*, you can use the preposition *to (to use e-mail)*, and you can use *that* to form a clause *(that the earth is warming up)*. In Japanese, the nominalizer の is used to make a noun from a clause, and it does not have a particular meaning, unlike the pronoun の *(one* or *thing)*.

	English	Japanese
Noun	Monkeys are interesting.	さるは面白い。
Nominalized phrases or clauses	Making a pig a pet is interesting.	ぶたをペットにするのは面白い。
	I watch the bear eating the fish.	くまが魚を食べるのを見る。
	I don't like to come close to tigers.	とらの近くに行くのはいやだ。
	It's frightening that nature is disappearing.	自然(しぜん)がなくなっていくのがこわい。

- The nominalizer の can be combined with adjectives and verbs in the same way the pronoun の is combined. That is, use な for the present affirmative form of な-adjectives and nouns + copula verbs. Otherwise, use the plain form of adjectives and verbs before の.

- A nominalized clause is a noun phrase and thus can perform any role that normal noun phrases could perform, including being either subject or direct object. Because nominalized clauses are embedded, they must be marked by が if they serve as the subject of the sentence.

  ここからくじらが見えるのがうれしい。
  I'm glad we can see whales from here.

  ここからくじらが見えるのを知っていましたか。
  Did you know we can see whales from here?

- The nominalizer の is used to nominalize concrete actions or events and to express facts directly and immediately as perceived. For example, 食べるの refers to a specific case of someone eating rather than the general meaning of eating.

  この肉は大きすぎて、全部(ぜんぶ)食べるのは大変だ。
  This piece of meat is too big, so it's hard for anyone to eat all of it.

- The nominalizer の is used when the main verb or adjective expresses the speaker's subjective feelings and perceptions, as with words such as 好き, きらい, 面白い, かなしい, and かんじる *(to feel)*. It must be used when the main verb requires a concrete immediate action or expresses 待つ, 見る, 見える, or 聞く.

B. Using the nominalizer こと

Noun phrase				Noun phrase		
	Verb (plain affirmative)	Nominalizer	Particle	Adjective	Noun	
環境(かんきょう)を	守(まも)る	こと	は	大切な	こと	だ。

Protecting the environment is an important thing.

食べるために動物をころすことははんざいじゃないと思う。
I think it's not a crime to kill an animal to eat.

災害(さいがい)をふせぐことは必要(ひつよう)なことだ。
It's necessary to prevent disasters.

八月と九月にハリケーンが多いことはだれでも知っている。
Everyone knows there are a lot of hurricanes in August and September.

ジョン： 不景気(ふけいき)って何ですか。
What is meant by **fukeiki?**

恵子(けいこ)： 景気(けいき)が悪いことです。
It means that economic conditions are bad.

- The nominalizer こと also transforms clauses into noun phrases. In this case, the copula verb can be combined with こと, but だという or である must be used before こと for the present affirmative form of nouns.

	い-adjectives	な-adjectives	Noun + copula	Verbs
Dictionary form	いい (good)	必要(ひつよう)だ (necessary)	鳥だ (to be a bird)	読む (to read)
Present affirmative	いいこと	必要(ひつよう)なこと	鳥だということ／鳥であること	読むこと
Present negative	よくないこと	必要(ひつよう)じゃないこと	鳥じゃないこと	読まないこと
Past affirmative	よかったこと	必要(ひつよう)だったこと	鳥だったこと	読んだこと
Past negative	よくなかったこと	必要(ひつよう)じゃなかったこと	鳥じゃなかったこと	読まなかったこと

- Unlike の, こと nominalizes clauses referring to actions or events in more abstract, indirect, or general ways. A こと clause is thus used to express a formal and more distant feeling, pointing out conclusions reached after giving the matter some thought. For example, 食べること refers to the general fact of eating rather than any specific case of someone eating.

肉を食べることはよくないことだと思います。
I think it's not a good thing to eat meat.

- As a nominalizer, こと is often used with expressions such as 考える, which indicate a deductive or abstract thinking process.

交通事故(こうつうじこ)でしぬ人の方が飛行機事故(ひこうきじこ)でしぬ人より多いことを考えると、飛行機(ひこうき)の方が安全(あんぜん)だと思いませんか。
If you think about the fact that more people are killed in traffic accidents than in plane accidents, don't you think airplanes are safer?

- There are a number of idiomatic phrases in which こと cannot be replaced by の. You have learned some usages of こと to form a noun phrase. The following are some of the examples.

  Past experience (Verb/adjective plain past + ことがある):

  白いとらを見たことがある。　　I have seen a white tiger.

  Capability/possibility (Verb dictionary form + ことが出来る):

  馬(うま)に乗ることが出来る。　　I have the ability to ride horses.

- こと must be used to nominalize clauses attached to a verb. 〜って or 〜とは are used to introduce the term to be defined as the topic in such cases.

  水泳(すいえい)とは泳(およ)ぐことです。
  Suiei is/means to swim.

  公害(こうがい)とは工場(こうじょう)が空気(くうき)や水を汚すことです。
  Kougai is/means that factories pollute the air and water.

- In some sentences, the nominalizers の and こと can be interchangeable. In such cases, the use of の expresses more perceptive, concrete, subjective, or emotional feelings, and the use of こと has a more abstract, distant, or objective nuance.

  動物をかうのはいいことだ。　　(As my personal feeling) keeping an animal is good.

  動物をかうことはいいことだ。　　(As a general rule) keeping an animal is good.

話してみましょう

A. Circle の, こと, or both, depending on which is appropriate to the sentence.

Example

私は鳥をかう（(の)／こと）が好きです。

1. しゅみは馬(うま)に乗る(の／こと)です。
2. わかい人のはんざいがふえている(の／こと)を知っていますか。
3. お年よりが一人で生活(せいかつ)する(の／こと)はアメリカではよくある(の／こと)だが、日本ではまだ少ないらしい。
4. こうべの地震(じしん)では6300人がなくなった(の／こと)を考えると、日本の建物(たてもの)もあまり安全(あんぜん)じゃないと思う。
5. となりの人がピアノの練習をしている(の／こと)が聞こえる。

B. The window in your room faces a park, so you can see what people are doing there. The following picture illustrates a scene from your window. Describe what you see, using ～の.

Example

子供が泣いているのが見えます。

C. Work in groups of four. One person from each group selects a word from the following list and tells the others in the group which word he or she selected. The others try to define the word, using the nominalizer こと. The first person to correctly define the word is awarded a point, then allowed to choose a different word, so the game can begin again. Use casual speech.

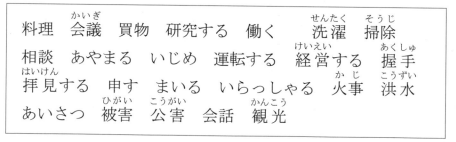

料理　会議（かいぎ）　買物　研究する　働く　洗濯（せんたく）　掃除（そうじ）
相談　あやまる　いじめ　運転する　経営（けいえい）する　握手（あくしゅ）
拝見（はいけん）する　申す　まいる　いらっしゃる　火事（かじ）　洪水（こうずい）
あいさつ　被害（ひがい）　公害（こうがい）　会話　観光（かんこう）

Example

A: 料理

B: 中国や日本の食べ物。

C: でも、とうふは中国の食べ物だけど、料理じゃないよ。

D: じゃあ、これはどう？
野菜や果物(くだもの)や肉や魚を使って、食べる物を作ること。

A: ああ、いいね。

D. Work with a partner. Devise three solutions for the following problems, using 〜こと.

Example

A: 地球(ちきゅう)が暖(あたた)かくならないように、今どんなことをしなければならないでしょうか。

B: そうですね。木をたくさん切らないことが大事(だいじ)だと思います。

	しなければならないこと
地球(ちきゅう)が暖(あたた)かくならないように	
ゴミがふえすぎないように	
子供のはんざいを少なくするために	
ハリケーンの被害(ひがい)をふせぐために	

III. Expressing a change of state, using 〜ようになる

		Verb (potential plain)	
公害(こうがい)問題が起きた後で、	自然(しぜん)を大切に	する	ようになった。

People have started to take better care of nature since the pollution problem has intensified.

日本語の新聞が読めるようになりたい。
I'd like to be able to read Japanese-language newspapers.

前はぶたをかっていたが、最近(さいきん)、牛(うし)や馬(うま)をかうようになりました。
I used to raise pigs, but lately I've started raising cattle and horses.

日本ではくじらを取りすぎて、くじらがあまり見られなくなった。
We harvested too many whales in Japan, and it's come to the point where we can no longer see many whales.

- Chapter 1 of this volume introduced the adverbial form adjective + なる *(become ～)*. The form ～ようになる is used when a change is expressed with a verb phrase; it means *to get to the state where ～*, or *to reach the stage of ～*. The verb preceding ～ようにする is in the plain present form. The negative form of ～ようになる is ～なくなる.

い-adjective	こわくなる	to become frightening
な-adjective	便利(べんり)になる	to become convenient
Noun + copula verb	ハリケーンになる	to become a hurricane
Verb (plain present affirmative form)	勉強するようになる	He gets to the stage where he is studying.
Verb (plain present negative form)	にげられなくなる	It has gotten to the stage where there is no escape.

- The form ～ようにする, treated in Chapter 9 of this volume, is related to ～ようになる because both constructions express a change of state or behavior. The use of する implies that someone is responsible for the action, regardless of whether this person is mentioned, but the use of なる implies that things have happened naturally. Therefore, even if the sentence describes an action that was carried out by a person, the focus is not on the act or the actor, but on the change of state. Whoever is responsible for the action is considered unimportant.

- The form ～ようになる is sometimes translated as *start to* ～ or *come to* ～, but it does not indicate a situation in which someone has started doing some physical task. Instead, it refers to the beginning of a new habit or ability after the change has taken place. In other words, ～ようになる tends to indicate the result of a gradual change.

- Verbs preceding the form ～ようになる tend to be in the potential form. When the potential form is used, the subject has come to the point where he or she is capable of doing something. On the other hand, use of the plain present affirmative form means that the subject has come to the point where he or she is habitually doing something.

  けががなおって、歩けるようになりました。
  My injury is healed, and I've come to the point where I can walk.

  けががなおって、歩くようになりました。
  My injury is healed, and I've come to the point where I walk regularly.

話してみましょう

A. Answer the following questions using ～ようになる.

Example

景気(けいき)がよくなると、どんなことが出来るようになりますか。
高いものが買えるようになります。

1. 景気(けいき)がよくなると、どんなことが出来るようになりますか。
2. 景気(けいき)が悪くなると、どんなことが出来なくなりますか。
3. 空気(くうき)が汚(よご)れると、どうなりますか。
4. 動物を大事にしないと、どんな悪いことが起きますか。
5. 木を切りすぎると、どんな悪いことが起きますか。

B. Work with the class. Ask your classmates which items listed in the table they are now able to do, and to what extent they can do them. Award three, two, one, or zero points depending how well they can perform the actions, and compute the average scores. Note that 大体(だいたい) means *for the most part*, まあまあ means *so-so*, and ～てん means ～*points*.

Example

A: 日本語で買い物が出来るようになりましたか。
B: ええ、大体(だいたい)出来るようになりました。
or ええ、まあまあ出来るようになりました。
or ええ、少し出来るようになりました。
or いいえ、まだ出来るようになっていません。

	大体(だいたい)（三てん）	まあまあ（二てん）	少し（一てん）	まだ～なっていない（０てん）
日本語で買い物をする				
日本語の新聞を読む				
日本語で電話で話す				
レストランで日本語で注文する				
日本語で手紙を書く				
日本語のテレビが分かる				

C. Work with a partner. Tell your partner some of the things you were able to do when you were growing up, using ～ようになる, and ask your partner at what age he or she was able to do them. Then report to the class. Use casual speech.

Example

A: 私は十さいの時に自転車に乗れるようになったんだけど。～さんはいつ自転車に乗れるようになったの。

B: 七さいの時に乗れるようになったよ。

or ざんねんだけど、まだ乗れないんだよ。(male) ／乗れないのよ。(female.)

IV. Expressing opinions indirectly, using ～んじゃない（かと思う）

	Verb (plain form)	
あの川は汚(よご)れているから、	泳げない	んじゃないかと思う。

That river is polluted, so I think you can't swim there.

あの工場(こうじょう)が公害(こうがい)を起こしているんじゃない？
I think that factory might be causing the pollution.

このぞうは病気なんじゃない？
I think this elephant might be sick.

あの火事(かじ)で田中さんの家も焼(や)けたんじゃないかと思って、心配していたんだ。
I thought Tanaka-san's house was one of those destroyed by the fire, so I was worried.

- ～じゃないかと思う expresses the speaker's opinion, but indicates some uncertainty. It is similar to ～だろうと思う, but it is less certain.

Certain ニュースは本当だと思う。
I think the news is true.

Less certain ニュースは本当だろうと思う。
I think the news is probably true.

Least certain ニュースは本当なんじゃないかと思う。
I think the news might be true.

- ～んじゃないか itself does not indicate a negative, but merely emphasizes the uncertainty. Use of the negative form before ～んじゃないか shows that the speaker's uncertainty is leaning toward the negative.

この森(もり)には大きい動物はいないんじゃないかと思う。
I don't think there are any big animals in these woods.

雨はふらないんじゃないかと思う。
I don't think it will rain.

- The forms ～んじゃないですか／でしょうか, ～じゃないかな (male) ／～じゃないかしら (female), and ～んじゃない？ can be used instead of ～じゃないかと思う to indicate that a statement is an opinion and not certain.

このへんも安全(あんぜん)になってきたんじゃない？
Don't you think it's becoming safe around here?

このへんも安全(あんぜん)になってきたんじゃないかな？ (male) ／
このへんも安全(あんぜん)になってきたんじゃないかしら？ (female)
I wonder if it's becoming safe around here.

子供のかずはふえているんじゃないですか。／
子供のかずはふえているんじゃないでしょうか。
I think the number of children might be increasing.

話してみましょう

A. Answer the questions using ～んじゃないかと思う.

Example

今日雪がふるでしょうか。
さあ、よく分かりませんが、ふるんじゃないかと思います。
さあ、よく分かりませんが、ふらないんじゃないかと思います。

1. 地震(じしん)が起(お)きた時、この建物(たてもの)は安全(あんぜん)だと思いますか。
2. 今ぞうのかずはふえていると思いますか。
3. さるは肉を食べるでしょうか。
4. ぶたはあたまがいいと思いますか。
5. くじらは魚だと思いますか。
6. 日本にもしかがいると思いますか。
7. 日本の社会(しゃかい)は大きい問題が少ないと思いますか。

B. Work with the class. In the 私 column of the chart below, write the names of the animals you think fit the descriptions. Then ask three classmates about what animals they think fit the descriptions, and complete the chart. Use the animal names in the following box.

さる　くま　くじら　とら　ぞう　しか　牛　ぶた　馬(うま) ペンギン　犬　パンダ

Example

A: 中国にいないのはどの動物だと思う？
B: そうだね。くじらじゃないかと思うけど。

	私	______さん	______さん	______さん
中国にいない動物				
オーストラリアにいない動物				
動物園では見られない動物				
かずがふえている動物				
かずが少なくなっている動物				

C. Work with a partner. Ask your partner whether he or she agrees with the statements in 1–4, and why.

Example

A: 災害(さいがい)の中でハリケーンが一番こわいと思う？。
B: ううん、ハリケーンより火事(かじ)の方がこわいんじゃない？
A: どうしてそう思うの？
B: そうだね。(male)／そうね。(female)
ハリケーンはいつ来るか分かるけど、火事(かじ)は分からないからね。

1. 災害(さいがい)の中でハリケーンが一番こわいです。
2. 食べるためなら、動物をころしてもいいです。
3. いじめははんざいだと思います。
4. 結婚しない人のかずはふえていると思います。

V. Expressing conjecture based on indirect evidence, using ～らしい; Expressing conjecture based on direct evidence, using ～ようだ／みたいだ

A. Expressing conjecture based on indirect evidence, using ～らしい *(I understand that ～; I hear that ～; the word is that ～)*

Clause						
					Verb (plain form)	Auxiliary adjective
昨日	東京	で	地震(じしん)	が	あった	らしい。

It seems that there was an earthquake in Tokyo yesterday.

台風(たいふう)の後、まだ電気が付かなくて、不便(ふべん)らしい。
I understand that it's inconvenient because the electricity has not been restored since the typhoon.

昨日火事(かじ)で焼(や)けた家にはお年よりが一人で住んでいたらしい。
The word is that that an elderly person lived by himself in the house that was destroyed by the fire yesterday.

動物園からにげたとらはころされたらしい。
I heard that the tiger that escaped from the zoo was killed.

被害(ひがい)はひどくなかったらしい。
The word is that the damage was not serious.

- The word ～らしい is used with nouns, adjectives, and verbs. The formation is the same as ～でしょう *(probably)* or かもしれない *(may)*. That is, use the noun or な-adjective stem + らしい for the plain present affirmative form. Otherwise, use the plain form + らしい.

	Noun	な-adjectives	い-adjectives	Verb
Dictionary form	ぞう (elephant)	安全(あんぜん) (safe)	こわい (frightening)	流(なが)す (to release)
Present affirmative	ぞうらしい	安全(あんぜん)らしい	こわいらしい	流(なが)すらしい
Present negative	ぞうじゃないらしい	安全(あんぜん)じゃないらしい	こわくないらしい	流(なが)さないらしい
Past affirmative	ぞうだったらしい	安全(あんぜん)だったらしい	こわかったらしい	流(なが)したらしい
Past negative	ぞうじゃなかったらしい	安全(あんぜん)じゃなかったらしい	こわくなかったらしい	流(なが)さなかったらしい

- The auxiliary adjective ～らしい is used to express conjecture made by the speaker on the basis of information obtained indirectly, such as through print or word of mouth. This expression can also be used with conjectures based on visual observations, but unlike the stem of verbs and adjectives + そうだ *(it looks like ～)*, which implies a guess based on what the speaker has seen, らしい implies that such conjectures have been based on more careful observation.

- When the speaker's conjecture is not strong, らしい is almost the same as the hearsay expression plain form + そうだ *(I heard ～)*.

ニュースによると、今年は大きい災害(さいがい)が多かったらしい。
According to the news, there were a lot of large-scale disasters this year.

ニュースによると、今年は大きい災害(さいがい)が多かったそうだ。
According to the news, there were a lot of large-scale disasters this year.

- A negative conjecture is expressed by ～ない／なかったらしい.

ハリケーンはこっちに来ないらしい。
The word is that the hurricane is not coming this way.

大きい台風(たいふう)じゃなかったらしい。
The word is that it was not a big typhoon.

B. Expressing conjecture based on direct evidence, using ～ようだ／みたいだ *(it appears that ～)*

Clause		
	Verb (plain form)	Auxiliary adjective
昨日東京で地震(じしん)が	あった	ようだ

It appears that there was an earthquake in Tokyo yesterday.

山本： 清水(しみず)先生は有名な先生のようだよ。
Apparently, Professor Shimizu is a famous professor.

高木： そうなの？あの先生、小さくてかわいくて、学生みたいだけど。
Really? She's so small and cute, she looks like a student.

このへんは冬になるとしかがよく出るようです。
Apparently, deer are often seen in this area in the winter.

私がしたことは時間のむだだったようだ。
It appears that what I did was a waste of time.

去年、日本は景気(けいき)がよくなかったけど、アメリカは景気(けいき)がよかったようだ。

Apparently, economic conditions weren't good in Japan last year, but they were okay in the United States.

- Both ～ようだ and ～みたいだ can be combined with nouns, adjectives, and verbs. The formation of ～みたいだ is the same as ～らしい. That is, nouns and な-adjectives are followed by な before ～みたいだ for the plain present affirmative form, but the plain form of adjectives and verbs is used for other forms. The combination of adjectives and verbs with ～ようだ is the same as that with 時. That is, nouns are followed by the particle の and な-adjectives are followed by な before ～ようだ for the plain present affirmative form, but the plain form of adjectives and verbs is used for other forms.

	Noun	**な-adjectives**	**い-adjectives**	**Verb**
Dict. form	火事(かじ) (fire)	むだ (wasteful)	いい (good)	出す (to submit)
Present affirmative	火事(かじ)<u>の</u>ようだ 火事(かじ)みたいだ	むだ<u>な</u>ようだ むだみたいだ	いいようだ いいみたいだ	出すようだ 出すみたいだ
Present negative	火事(かじ)じゃないようだ 火事(かじ)じゃないみたいだ	むだじゃないようだ むだじゃないみたいだ	よくないようだ よくないみたいだ	出さないようだ 出さないみたいだ
Past affirmative	火事(かじ)だったようだ 火事(かじ)だったみたいだ	むだだったようだ むだだったみたいだ	よかったようだ よかったみたいだ	出したようだ 出したみたいだ
Past negative	火事(かじ)じゃなかったようだ 火事(かじ)じゃなかったみたいだ	むだじゃなかったようだ むだじゃなかったみたいだ	よくなかったようだ よくなかったみたいだ	出さなかったようだ 出さなかったみたいだ

- The auxiliary adjective ～ようだ expresses a conjecture based on firsthand, reliable information (usually visual information) and the speaker's reasonable knowledge. Use of this form indicates that the speaker is virtually certain that an action or event will take place. Use of the verb/adjective stem + そうだ *(it looks like* ～*)*, however, indicates a guess based on the speaker's sensory input (what the speaker sees or feels), so the reliability will vary.

- The form ～ようだ is different from ～らしい in that ～らしい usually expresses a conjecture based on secondhand information obtained from reading or hearsay, while ～ようだ implies that the conjecture has come from firsthand information and the speaker's knowledge. Finally, it is different from ～でしょう／だろう, which expresses a conjecture that is not necessarily based on any information and often is a mere guess.
- The form ～みたいだ is a more colloquial version of ～ようだ. It does show, however, a lower degree of confidence regarding the conjecture than does ～ようだ.
- A negative conjecture is expressed by ～ないようだ／～ないみたいだ／なかったようだ／なかったみたいだ.

話してみましょう

A. You hear the following conversations. Express your conjectures, using ～らしい.

Example

A: 最近(さいきん)、公害(こうがい)の話はあまり聞かないね。

B: そうね。前より川や海の水もきれいになったし、空気(くうき)もきれいになったしね。

公害(こうがい)は少なくなったらしいです。

1. A: 昨日どろぼうに入られたんですって？
   B: ええ、家に帰ってきたら、テレビやステレオがなくなっていたんですよ。
2. A: 山田さんの家の近くで火事(かじ)があったそうですね。
   B: いいえ、火事(かじ)はあったけど家からはちょっと遠かったですよ。
3. A: 円が安(やす)くなっちゃったね。
   B: だから海外(かいがい)に遊びに行く人が少ないんだね。
4. A: 最近地震(さいきんじしん)が多いね。
   B: そうだね。一か月に一度は地震(じしん)があるね。
5. A: 救急車(きゅうきゅうしゃ)はまだ来ないんでしょうか。
   B: このへんは町から遠いから、二十分ぐらいはかかるでしょうね。

B. Work with a partner. Look at the following survey results and at the figures on crime rates and other information in the culture note in this chapter. Analyze the data and express your conjectures, using 〜ようだ. Use casual speech.

Example

A: 日本ははんざいが少なくて安全(あんぜん)なようだね。(male) ／
日本ははんざいが少なくて安全(あんぜん)なようね。(female)

B: そうだね、アメリカもはんざいは多くないようだね。(male) ／
そうね、アメリカもはんざいは多くないようね。(female)

1. 地球(ちきゅう)の環境(かんきょう)を守(まも)ることに関心(かんしん)がありますか？

	とてもある	少しある	ない
男	37.7%	51.9%	10.4%
女	34.8%	60.3%	4.9%
Total	36.4%	55.8%	7.8%

2. どんな環境(かんきょう)問題に関心(かんしん)がありますか？(1=一番関心(かんしん)がある)

1. オゾンそう (ozone layer) がなくなっていくこと
2. 地球(ちきゅう)が暖かくなること
3. 酸性雨(さんせいう) (acid rain)
4. 排気(はいき)ガス (car exhaust) で空気(くうき)が汚(よご)れること
5. 海(うみ)が汚くなること
6. 有害廃棄物(ゆうがいはいきぶつ) (hazardous waste)
7. 森(もり)がなくなっていくこと

3. 環境(かんきょう)を守(まも)るためにどんなことをしていますか？(1= 一番よくすること)

1. びん (bottle) やかん (cans) を外で捨てない
2. ゴミを外で捨てない
3. 新聞や雑誌をリサイクルする
4. ビールびんをリサイクルする
5. エアコンをむだに使わない
6. 車をふかさない (not rev the engine)
7. お風呂(ふろ)で水をむだに使わない
8. かみ (paper) をむだに使わない
9. 牛乳(ぎゅうにゅう)のパック (milk carton) をリサイクルする
10. 自転車を使ったり歩いたりする

C. Work in groups of three. You are a private investigator. A client has asked you to investigate three people who may be involved in the sale of stolen art pieces (びじゅつひん). Each one of you has investigated one person. Using the cards describing the suspects that your instructor will provide, think about what sort of person would be capable of dealing with such goods. Discuss each person's lifestyle and daily activities, make conjectures about the likelihood of that person dealing with art pieces (びじゅつひん), and decide who is the most likely suspect. Use casual speech.

Example

A: この人の家、狭いし、大きい物置く所はないようだね。(male)
／この人の家、狭いし、大きい物置く所はないようね。(female)

B: そうだね。でも時々絵をかいてるみたいだし、びじゅつひんのことはよく知ってるんじゃないかな。(male)
そうね。でも時々絵をかいてるみたいだし、びじゅつひんのことはよく知ってるんじゃないかしら。(female)

漢字

Using a kanji dictionary

As you begin reading more advanced materials, you will need to be able to use some sort of comprehensive **kanji** dictionary. There are several **kanji** dictionaries available for learners of Japanese, and most of them use variations of the traditional method to look up characters. (When you want to purchase one, you should compare them and consult with your instructor.)

Characters in a **kanji** dictionary are normally grouped according to traditional radicals (部首 ぶしゅ) and ordered according to residual stroke counts within each radical group. The residual stroke count is the number of strokes required to write a character exclusive of the radical. Radicals themselves are ordered from simplest to the more complex according to the number of strokes. Thus, in order to look up a character, you must first identify its traditional radical, then go to the correct section, and finally, you must count the residual strokes and sift through the pages until you find the character.

As was discussed in Chapter 1, identification of a traditional radical is sometimes difficult, yet it is the crucial first step in the use of a traditional **kanji** dictionary. To show how confusing it can get, the radical of 家 is 宀, but the radical of 字 is 子. For another example, the radical of 勝 *(to win)* is 力, and not 月. This difficulty comes from the fact that the traditional radical system was created more than 1,000 years ago for the purpose of classifying characters, and the most conspicuous component of the **kanji** was not necessarily assigned as the radical.

Most **kanji** dictionaries for learners of Japanese overcome this problem by rearranging radical groupings from traditional radicals to the most conspicuous components. In these dictionaries, you will find 家 and 字 in the same group, namely under 宀. 勝 is found in the 月 group instead of the 力 group. Once you become familiar with the idea of component shapes, it is fairly easy to identify the correct grouping in these dictionaries. The component shapes are ordered according to the number of strokes they contain, so you need to be able to count the number of strokes correctly. (宀 requires three strokes and 月 has four strokes.) Some dictionaries have tables on the back of the front cover such as the one shown here.

Simplified table of component shapes (or radicals)

2	亻	𠆢	亠	儿	匚	凵	冂
3	木	土	氵	女	弓	艹	宀	囗
4	彳	方	日	心	疋	疒		
5	禾	罒						
6	糸							
7	言							
8	門	⻗	金	食				

Once you identify the most conspicuous component shape and its stroke count, the second step is to count the residual strokes. Since there are no short cuts for this step, you must be able to count them correctly. Within each group, there might be several characters that share the same residual stroke count. Since they are not in any particular order, you will need to go through them one by one to find the character you are looking for.

Dictionaries also have a pronunciation index for **kanji** at the end, so if you know or can guess either the **kun-** or the **on-** reading of a character, you can look it up there, also. But remember that there are many **kanji** that share the same **on**-reading. Readings such as こう and せい, for example, are particularly common. Thus, if you have a choice between **on-** and **kun**-readings, it is better to use the **kun**-reading. The index will use romanization to indicate pronunciation. **On**-readings are usually written in uppercase letters and **kun**-readings are in lowercase letters.

練習

A. Practice counting the strokes of the following components.

a. 匚	d. 广	g. 口	j. 火	m. 田	p. 頁	s. 券	u. 然
b. 糸	e. 川	h. 月	k. 廴	n. 生	q. 己	t. 間	v. 聿
c. 日	f. 勹	i. 艹	l. メ	o. 付	r. 井		

B. Now use a **kanji** dictionary to look up the following **kanji** and the **kanji** appearing in this chapter.

1. 勝　3. 区　5. 囲　7. 細　9. 建　11. 順
2. 府　4. 包　6. 簡　8. 燃　10. 星

C. Using the same **kanji** dictionary, find the following characters by using their **kun**- and **on**-readings. See which is the fastest way to look them up.

1. 近 (on: KIN, kun: chikai)
2. 習 (on: SHUU, kun: narau)
3. 会 (on: KAI, kun: au)
4. 雪 (on: SETSU, kun: yuki)
5. 高 (on: KOU, kun: takai)
6. 兄 (on: KYOU, kun: ani)
7. 校 (on: KOU)
8. 究 (on: KYUU)
9. 静 (on: SEI, kun: shizuka)
10. 時 (on: JI, kun: toki)

環　環　link, ring, to surround　カン

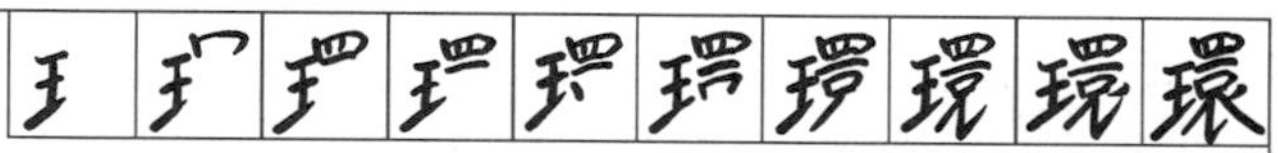

地球(ちきゅう)の環境(かんきょう)問題は大切な問題です。

境　境　border, boundary　キョウ、ケイ／さかい

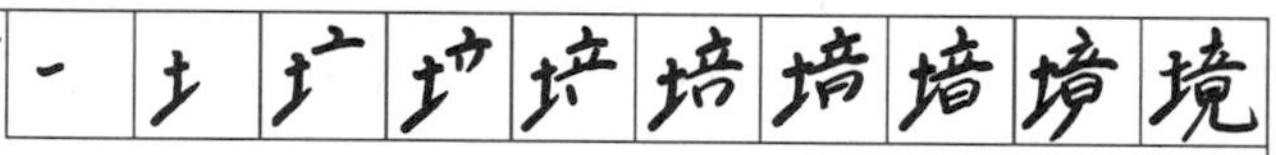

環境(かんきょう)を守(まも)ることは大変です。

世　世　world, age, reign　セ、セイ／よ

世界(せかい)の人々が困っている。世話(せわ)になる

界　界　world　カイ／

世界(せかい)で一番高い山　世界(せかい)が狭くなった。

空 sky, empty — クウ/そら

空(そら)が青くて空気(くうき)がきれいです。成田空港(なりたくうこう)

海 sea, ocean — カイ/うみ

海(うみ)をきれいにしましょう。日本海(にほんかい) (Sea of Japan) 海外旅行(かいがいりょこう)

森 forest — シン/もり

森(もり)の動物がいなくなった。森(もり)さん

球 sphere, globe — キュウ

地球(ちきゅう)はとてもきれいです。

機 loom — キ

私は機械(きかい)にとても弱いんです。コピー機(き)

械 machine — カイ

最近(さいきん)、コンピュータの機械(きかい)がとてもよくなりました。

飛 to fly — ヒ/と(ぶ)

飛行機(ひこうき)が飛(と)んでいる。

鉄 iron — テツ

地下鉄(ちかてつ)に乗る。

工 worker, construction — コウ、ク

工学部(こうがくぶ)の学生です。工場(こうじょう)の水で公害(こうがい)が起こりました。

災 misfortune — サイ

大きい災害(さいがい)

Kanji		Meaning	Reading	Example
害	害	harm, calamity	ガイ	台風(たいふう)の被害(ひがい)はあまりひどくなかった。公害(こうがい)問題
台	台	a stand	タイ、ダイ	大きい台風(たいふう)が来て、被害(ひがい)が出ました。
焼	焼	to burn, to bake	ショウ/や(く) や(ける)	火事(かじ)で家が焼(や)けた。牛肉を焼(や)く。焼(や)き鳥(とり)
流	流	stream, current, to flow	リュウ/なが(す)、なが(れる)	洪水(こうずい)で家が流(なが)されました。
守	守	to protect, to defend	シュ、ス/まも(る)	子供達のために環境(かんきょう)を守(まも)らなければなりません。
活	活	energy	カツ	景気(けいき)が悪いので、生活(せいかつ)が大変です。
必	必	without fail, by all means	ヒツ/かなら(ず)	海(うみ)をきれいにする必要(ひつよう)がある。必(かなら)ず来て下さい。
要	要	to require, to need, necessity	ヨウ	このプロジェクトには何か必要(ひつよう)ですか。
関	関	barrier	カン/せき	どんな環境(かんきょう)問題に関心(かんしん)がありますか。
不	不	dis-, in-, mal- ill- (negates what follows)	フ	駅から遠いので、少し不便(ふべん)です。

利	利	advantage, profit — リ	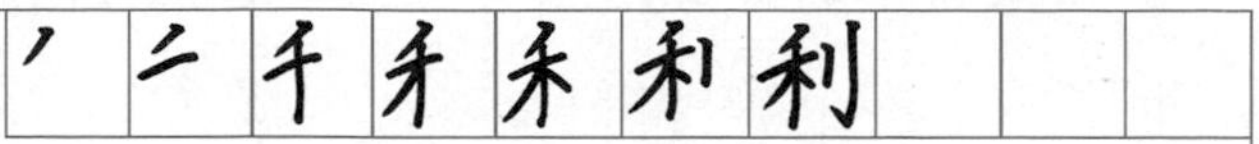
		この町はとても便利(べんり)ですね。便利(べんり)な辞書(じしょ)	
最	最	most- (prefix) — サイ/もっと（も）	
		最近(さいきん)、空気(くうき)が汚れてきた。	
景	景	view, scene — ケイ、ケ	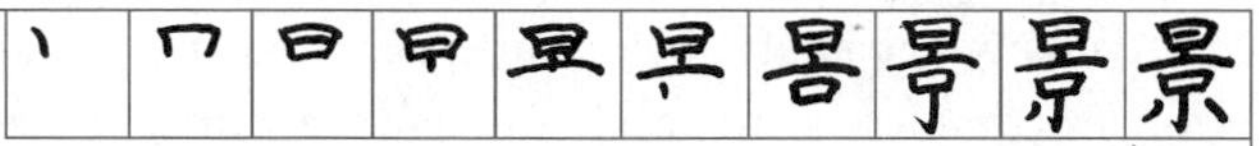
		景気(けいき)が悪いです。自然(しぜん)の景色(けしき)は本当にきれいですね。	
馬	馬	horse — バ/うま	
		昨日、馬(うま)に乗る練習をした。	
将	将	to be about to, soon — ショウ	
		将来(しょうらい)、先生になりたいです。	
次	次	next — ジ/つぎ	
		次(つぎ)の映画　次(つぎ)に何をしましょうか。	

新しい読み方

台風(たいふう)　社会(しゃかい)　火事(かじ)　安全(あんぜん)　最近(さいきん)　空気(くうき)　便利(べんり)　世話(せわ)になる
海外(かいがい)　練習(れんしゅう)　鳥(とり)　牛(うし)　自然(しぜん)

練習

下の文を読んで下さい。

1. 次の世界環境会議(かいぎ)は京都(きょうと)で開かれます。
2. 地球の自然を守らなければなりません。
3. 工場の機械がこわれて、汚い水が森に流されました。
4. ここは空も海も青くて、空気がとてもおいしいです。
5. 自然の災害より公害の問題に関心があります。
6. 火事で家が焼けてしまって、生活に必要なものが何もなくて、不便だ。

7. 将来日本の景気はよくなるでしょうか。
8. ピカソの「馬に乗った男の子」の絵を売りました。
9. 飛行機をおりてすぐ地下鉄に乗ると、便利です。

上手な読み方

Expressions used in writing

Written language is often very different from spoken language. It usually consists of longer complete sentences. For example, particles are less likely to be omitted in writing than in speech, and contractions are less frequently used in written language than in spoken language. Some expressions, though, are more frequently found in writing than in speech. For example, the stem of verbs such as 読み and 書き, and the adverbial form of い-adjectives, such as 多く and 少なく, are more often used in writing than are the て-form of verbs and adjectives such as 読んで, 書いて, 多くて, and 少なくて, to connect verbal phrases. Examples are データを調べ、レポートを書く *(I will check the data and write a report)*. Also, the plain form often appears in expository writing. In addition, the expression である is often used in expository writing instead of です.

Transform the following sentences into a more "written" style by using the plain form, the stem of verbs, である, and non-contracted forms.

Example

けんこうのためには、よく食べて、よく寝ることが一番です。
<u>けんこうのためには、よく食べ、よく寝ることが一番である。</u>

1. このへんは公害で空気が汚くて、水も汚れてるね。
2. 動物園からさるがにげたんだって。
3. この問題は私じゃなくて、マネージャーと話したらどうでしょうか。
4. 景気が悪いのに、こんな高い車を買っちゃっていいの？
5. 車がこわれてたから、むかえに行けなかったんですよ。

地球の温暖化(おんだんか)　(Global warming)

読む前に

A. 知っている漢字の意味を使って、下の言葉の意味は何か考えて下さい。

温暖化(おんだんか)　　全体(ぜんたい)

B. 下の文を読んで、下線（かせん） (underlined)の言葉の意味は何か考えて下さい。

1. 地球が暖かくなることを温暖化（おんだんか）といいます。
2. 小さい子供のおもちゃはプラスチックで出来たものが多い。
3. 赤ちゃんの食べ物を入れる入れ物もたいていプラスチックで出来ています。
4. 色々な国の人が集まってする会議を国際会議（こくさいかいぎ）と言います。
5. トースターやオーブンやドライヤーのことを電気製品（せいひん）と言います。
6. 人や動物は空気をすって二酸化炭素（にさんかたんそ）を出します。車も二酸化炭素（にさんかたんそ）を出します。
7. 地球は全体（ぜんたい）の 70 パーセントが海です。

C. 質問に答えて下さい。

1. 地球は毎年暖かくなってきていると言われますが、本当だと思いますか。
2. どうして地球は暖かくなってきているのだと思いますか。
3. 地球の気温が上がるとどうして困るのですか。
4. あなたの国ではこの問題について、どんなことをしていますか。
5. あなたは地球が暖かくならないようにどんなことをしていますか。

読んでみましょう

次の文章（ぶんしょう）は知らない言葉がたくさんありますが、心配しないで、がいよう (gist) をとるように読んで下さい。

言葉のリスト

温暖化（おんだんか）	海面水位（かいめんすいい）	二酸化炭素（にさんかたんそ）
warming	the water level of the sea	carbon dioxide

地球は今暖かくなってきているといわれている。何もしないでいると、2100年までには地球の気温は二度上がるそうである。そして、海面水位（かいめんすいい）は50cm ぐらい上がってしまうのだそうだ。このため、温暖化（おんだんか）をどうやって防（ふせ）ぐかが世界中で問題になっていて、1992年から毎年この問題について国際会議（こくさいかいぎ）が開かれている。1997年には日本でもその会議（かいぎ）が開かれた。

温暖化(おんだんか)を起こすものは色々あるが、そのうち64%は二酸化炭素(にさんかたんそ)である。1994年の調べでは、日本は世界で四番目に二酸化炭素(にさんかたんそ)を多く出していた。また、日本では、1992年から1994年までに、二酸化炭素(にさんかたんそ)が7%も増(ふ)えていた。

二酸化炭素(にさんかたんそ)が増(ふ)えたのは日本人の生活スタイルが変わってきたからのようだ。前より冷蔵庫(れいぞうこ)やテレビも大きくなり、オーブンやドライヤーなどの電気製品(せいひん)を使う人も多くなった。それに、スーパーやデパートでは野菜や果物(くだもの)や肉もプラスチックの入れ物に入れたり、プラスチックで包んだりするようになった。実際、私達の生活の中で出てくる二酸化炭素(にさんかたんそ)は全体(ぜんたい)の45%にもなるらしい。温暖化(おんだんか)を防(ふせ)ぐためには、国や工場や大会社が何かをするのではなく、一人一人が自分の生活を変えていかなければならない。便利だから、楽だからと言って、車や電気製品(せいひん)を使いすぎないように今からしていかなければ、この地球(ちきゅう)を守ることは出来ない。

分かりましたか

A. 下の質問に日本語で答えて下さい。

1. この作文を書いた人は何が言いたいのですか。
2. 2100年までにはどんなことが起きるかもしれませんか。それはどうしてですか。
3. 二酸化炭素(にさんかたんそ)はどうしてよくないのですか。
4. 日本では二酸化炭素(にさんかたんそ)がふえているようですが、それはどうしてですか。

B. Read the following statements about global warming and circle はい if the statement is true according to what you have read or いいえ if it isn't.

1. はい　いいえ　温暖化(おんだんか)を起こすのは二酸化炭素(にさんかたんそ)だけである。
2. はい　いいえ　電気を使うと二酸化炭素(にさんかたんそ)が多くなる。
3. はい　いいえ　日本で開かれた会議(かいぎ)には色々な国の人が来た。
4. はい　いいえ　日本では三年間で二酸化炭素(にさんかたんそ)が7パーセントふえた。
5. はい　いいえ　温暖化(おんだんか)を防(ふせ)ぐためには、公害を起こさないようにすることが一番大事だ。

読んだ後で

下のグラフは二酸化炭素(にさんかたんそ)をたくさん出している国のデータです。グラフを見て質問に答えて下さい。

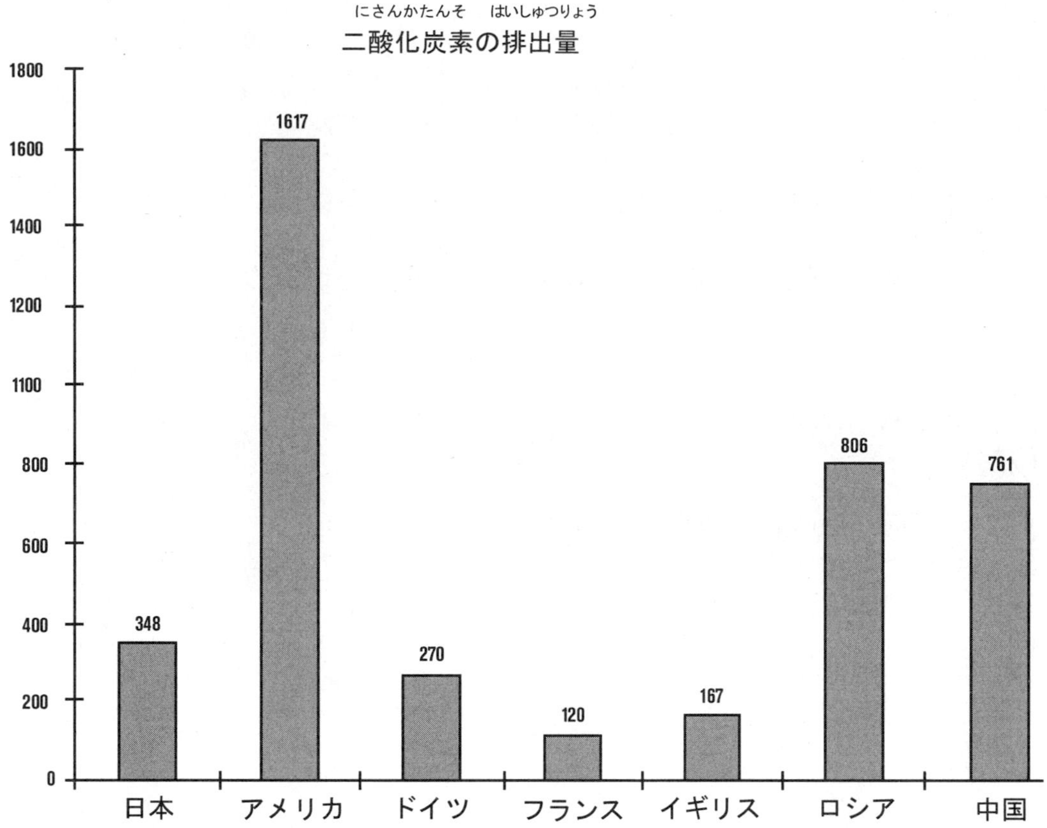

1. 二酸化炭素(にさんかたんそ)を世界で一番多く出している国はどの国ですか。
2. この国はどうして二酸化炭素(にさんかたんそ)を多く出しているのだと思いますか。
3. この国はどうすれば二酸化炭素(にさんかたんそ)を少なくすることが出来ると思いますか。
4. 二酸化炭素(にさんかたんそ)を世界で二番目に多く出している国はどの国ですか。
5. この国が二酸化炭素(にさんかたんそ)を出しているのはどうしてだと思いますか。
6. 二酸化炭素(にさんかたんそ)を出さないようするために何かしていますか。

上手な聞き方

私の町の問題　(Problems in my town)

聞く前に

A. 下の質問に日本語で答えて下さい。

1. ごみを少なくするために、どんなことをしていますか。どんなことをしたらいいと思いますか。
2. 火事になった時のために、何かしていますか。火事の時にはどうするのが大切ですか。
3. この町では地震やほかの災害がありますか。どんな災害がありますか。災害がある時、大きい被害(ひがい)が出ないようにどんなことをすればいいでしょうか。
4. 近所の工場が公害を起こしている時、町の人はどうしたらいいと思いますか。

B. Work with a partner. Write phrases that will help define the following words. Write as many as you can.

1. 火事	3. 地震(じしん)	5. ごみ
2. 洪水(こうずい)	4. はんざい	6. いじめ

STUDENT

聞いてみましょう

言葉のリスト

焼却場(しょうきゃくじょう)	さべつ
incineration facility	discrimination

次の会話を聞いて、何の問題について話しているか考えて下さい。次にどうしてその問題が起きたか考えて下さい。

Example

You hear:　私の町にはごみの焼却場(しょうきゃくじょう)があるんですが、最近となりの町のごみも捨てられているんです。でも、毎日ごみが焼かれるのではないので、焼却場(しょうきゃくじょう)においてあるごみがふえてとても困っています。

You write: 問題： 焼却場（しょうきゃくじょう）のごみがふえた。

どうして起きたか： となりの町からごみが来るようになった。

ケース１ 問題：＿＿＿＿＿＿＿＿＿＿＿＿＿＿＿＿＿＿＿＿

どうして起きたか：＿＿＿＿＿＿＿＿＿＿＿＿＿＿＿

ケース２ 問題：＿＿＿＿＿＿＿＿＿＿＿＿＿＿＿＿＿＿＿＿

どうして起きたか：＿＿＿＿＿＿＿＿＿＿＿＿＿＿＿

ケース３ 問題：＿＿＿＿＿＿＿＿＿＿＿＿＿＿＿＿＿＿＿＿

どうして起きたか：＿＿＿＿＿＿＿＿＿＿＿＿＿＿＿

聞いた後で

STUDENT

A. Listen to the two people discussing the above problems and write down their solutions to each of the problems.

B. Work with a partner. Write two possible solutions for each of the above problems.

C. Work with a partner. Compare the suggestions given in Exercise B and your own suggestions, and explain which ones you think are the best solutions and why.

STUDENT

DICT-A-CONVERSATION

スミスさんは台風（たいふう）が来ると聞きましたが、本当かどうかよく分からないので、田中さんに聞いています。

スミス：＿＿＿＿＿＿＿＿＿＿＿＿＿＿＿＿＿＿＿＿＿＿＿＿

田中：＿＿＿＿＿＿＿＿＿＿＿＿＿＿＿＿＿＿＿＿＿＿＿＿

スミス：＿＿＿＿＿＿＿＿＿＿＿＿＿＿＿＿＿＿＿＿＿＿＿＿

田中：＿＿＿＿＿＿＿＿＿＿＿＿＿＿＿＿＿＿＿＿＿＿＿＿

スミス：＿＿＿＿＿＿＿＿＿＿＿＿＿＿＿＿＿＿＿＿＿＿＿＿

田中：＿＿＿＿＿＿＿＿＿＿＿＿＿＿＿＿＿＿＿＿＿＿＿＿

スミス：＿＿＿＿＿＿＿＿＿＿＿＿＿＿＿＿＿＿＿＿＿＿＿＿

田中：＿＿＿＿＿＿＿＿＿＿＿＿＿＿＿＿＿＿＿＿＿＿＿＿

スミス：＿＿＿＿＿＿＿＿＿＿＿＿＿＿＿＿＿＿＿＿＿＿＿＿

聞き上手話し上手

意見(いけん)を言う、さんせいする、はんたいする。
(Expressing opinions, agreements, and disagreements)

It is common to end a sentence with 〜と思う when expressing thought. This expression makes the communication less domineering and allows the speaker to avoid sounding as though he or she is making blunt assertions. Another common topic is the use of 〜じゃないかと思う, which allows the speaker to express an opinion in an even more socially humble way. An even less direct way of expressing opinion is to use 〜じゃない as a question form, such as saying 〜じゃない in a rising intonation or using 〜じゃないかな(male) ／〜じゃないかしら(female), 〜じゃないですか, and 〜じゃないでしょうか.

All of the following sentences express the speaker's opinion that we must not waste things. The first two are direct and may be used in situations where the speaker is warning someone, speaking to himself or herself, or writing a rule. Sentences 3–10, though, are much more conversational. The Japanese use these strategies frequently to convey opinions or proposals without being confrontational, thereby showing politeness.

1. 電気をむだに使ってはいけない。
2. 電気をむだに使ってはいけません。
3. 電気をむだに使ってはいけないと思うけど。
4. 電気をむだに使ってはいけないんじゃないかと思うけど。
5. 電気をむだに使ってはいけないと思いますけど。／
   電気をむだに使ってはいけないと思うんですが。
6. 電気をむだに使ってはいけないじゃないかと思いますけど。
7. 電気をむだに使っちゃいけないんじゃない？
8. 電気をむだに使っちゃいけないんじゃないか(male)／
   電気をむだに使っちゃいけないんじゃないかしら？ (female)
9. 電気をむだに使ってはいけないんじゃないですか。
10. 電気をむだに使ってはいけないんじゃないでしょうか。

Expressions such as these are often accompanied by a sentence stating the reason.

> 電気をむだに使っちゃいけないんじゃない。環境に悪いし。
> We must not waste electricity. It's not good for the environment (if we do).
>
> 電気をむだに使ってはいけないんじゃないでしょうか。
> 環境に悪いですから。
> We must not waste electricity. It's not good for the environment (if we do).

In Chapter 1 of Volume 2, agreement was indicated by particles such as も and ね. (See page 81.) In addition, you can use よね to emphasize your agreement. Other expressions, such as そう思う, can also be used.

川口：　電気をむだに使ってはいけないと思います。環境に悪いですから。
We must not waste electricity. It's not good for the environment (if we do).

黒木:　そうですね。／そうだね。(male) ／そうね。(female)
That's right.

環境は守らなくてはいけませんね。／環境は守らなくちゃいけないよね。
We have to protect the environment, right?

私もそう思います。／ぼくもそう思う。(male)／
私もそう思う。(female)
I think so, too.

The speaker can directly express disagreement if the opinion has been expressed by a junior or someone with lower social status, and it is possible in such cases to use expressions such as だめ, よくない, 違う, and はんたいだ *(I am against it)*. However, such direct negative expressions cannot be used to a senior or someone of a higher social status. The Japanese usually voice their disagreement to equals or superiors diplomatically, by first voicing acceptance of what was said, and then by presenting a different opinion. An expression of agreement such as そうですね and the particle も are used to express acceptance, and this is followed by a connective such as 〜けど, 〜が, or でも.

部長：　会議(かいぎ)は明日にしよう。
Let's have a meeting tomorrow.

田中:　そうですね。明日もいいと思うんですが、できれば、水曜日の方がいいんじゃないでしょうか。来られる人が多いと思いますので。
Yes, tomorrow would be fine, but it might be better to have it on Wednesday. I think more people can come.

A. Read the following dialogues and act them out.

1. A: 子供のはんざいがふえているのは親がいけないからだと思う。
   B: そうかもしれないけど。でも親だけが悪いんじゃないかもしれないよ。最近のテレビや映画もひどいのが多いし。
   A: ああ、そういうこともあるね。

2. A: あの、川のそばの家、洪水(こうずい)で大きい被害(ひがい)が出たみたいですよ。

B: でも、よく洪水(こうずい)があるんだから、家をたてなきゃいいんじゃないですか。家をたてるのがいけないんですよ。

A: そうですね。もっと高いところにたてたほうがいいでしょうね。でも、お金がなくて引っ越(こ)せない人もいるんじゃないでしょうか。

B: ああ、そういうこともありますね。

3. A: 最近のアニマルライトアクティビスト (animal rights activist) をどう思いますか。

B: ちょっとやりすぎなんじゃないですか。動物を守るためには何をしてもいいっていうの、変ですよ。

A: そうですね。私もそう思います。

B: 何でもやってもいいことと悪いことがありますからね。

STUDENT

B. Listen to the following six statements. The first three statements are made by someone socially superior to you, and the next three by someone socially equal or inferior to you. Express your agreement or disagreement appropriately.

C. Work in pairs. Express your opinion about your university to your partner and to your instructor. Express agreement and disagreement with your partner's opinions.

D. Make suggestions to improve your Japanese class to your instructor.

E. Your instructor will express his or her opinions. Express your agreement or disagreement.

総合練習(そうごう)

災害(さいがい)の経験 (Experiences with natural disasters)

1. When you talk about either your personal experience or someone else's experience with accidents, natural disasters, etc., what sorts of details do you think are important to include?
2. If you are listening to people describing their experience with accidents, natural disasters, etc., what sorts of questions would you ask?
3. When listening to such stories, what kinds of expressions do you use to express your emotional support, interest, and understanding?

4. Work with a partner. Recall a personal experience with a natural disaster. (If you have never experienced one, relate the experience of a family member or friend.) Try to recall all the details so you can describe them to your partner. Ask each other questions. Then write about what you have heard and describe the story to the class.

Example

A: 〜さんは災害を経験したことがありますか。
B: ええ、あります。私は小学校三年生の時、日本に住んでいたんですが、その時、大きい地震がありました。
A: そうですか。日本のどこに住んでいたんですか。
B: 東京です。
A: そうですか。じゃあ、その時のことをもう少し話してくれませんか。
B: ええ、いいですよ。その日は日曜日で、私は家にいたんです。

ロールプレイ

A. A strong typhoon is coming. Ask your neighbor what you should do to prepare for it.

B. You heard about a severe earthquake in a town where some of your Japanese friends live. You tried to call your friends but the phone line seems to be jammed. You would like to know more about the situation. Tell another Japanese friend about it, and ask what you should do.

C. You suspect that the nearby factory is polluting your town and causing a health problem. Tell your neighbor about your suspicions and explain why you think this is indeed the case. Express your anger and concern.

D. You think that you are being discriminated against by your boss because of your race (or gender). Describe your situation to your friend and ask for suggestions.

E. Do you think that the current welfare system（生活保護（ほご））is working well? Why or why not? Explain your position.

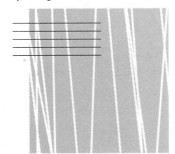

単語 (ESSENTIAL VOCABULARY)

LAB

Nouns

うし（牛） cow
うま（馬） horse
おとしより（お年より） senior citizen
かじ（火事） fire
かず（数） number
かんきょう（環境） environment
かんしん（関心） interest
〜にかんしんをもつ（〜に関心を持つ） to be interested in
きゅうきゅうしゃ（救急車） ambulance
くうき（空気） air
くじら（鯨） whale
くま（熊） bear
けいき（景気） economic conditions; business; けいきがいい（景気がいい） the economy is good
けいさつ（警察） police
こうがい（公害） industrial pollution
こうじょう（工場） factory
こうずい（洪水） flood
さいがい（災害） disaster
さいきん（最近） recent; current
さる（猿） monkey
しか（鹿） deer
じしん（地震） earthquake
しぜん（自然） nature
しゃかい（社会） society
せかい（世界） world
ぞう（象） elephant
ちきゅう（地球） the earth
どうぶつ（動物） animal
とら（虎） tiger
とり（鳥） bird
ニュース news
ハリケーン hurricane
はんざい（犯罪） crime
ひがい（被害） damage
ぶた（豚） pig
もり（森） forest

い-adjectives

こわい（怖い） fearful; frightened; こわさ（怖さ） fear; frightening thing

な-adjectives

あんぜん(な)（安全な） safe; secure
ひつよう(な)（必要な） necessary; essential
ふべん(な)（不便な） inconvenient
むだ(な)（無駄な） waste; fruitless; no good; useless

う-verbs

おこす（起こす） (to) cause something to happen
ころす（殺す） (to) kill; to murder
ながす（流す） (to) pour; to let something flow
なくす (to) lose; (to) make (something) disappear
なくなる (to) disappear
ふせぐ（防ぐ） (to) prevent
まもる（守る） (to) protect
よごす（汚す） (to) make something dirty *(transitive)*

る-verbs

おきる（起きる） (to) take place; to happen
きこえる（聞こえる） (to) be able to hear *(intransitive)*; きく（聞く） (to) listen
にげる（逃げる） (to) escape
ふえる（増える） (for something) (to) increase *(intransitive)*
やける（焼ける） (for something) (to) burn; やく（焼く） (to) burn; (to) grill; (to) broil
よごれる（汚れる） (for something) (to) become dirty *(intransitive)*

Expressions

はんたいだ（反対だ） I am against it.
わたしもそうおもいます。（私もそう思います。） I think so, too.

Passive Vocabulary

Nouns

あくしゅう（悪臭） foul smell
おんだんか（温暖化） warming
かいめん（海面） the surface of the sea
がか（画家） painter
かみ（紙） paper
かん（缶） can
ぎゅうにゅう（牛乳） cow's milk
じばんちんか（地盤沈下） ground sinkage
しょうきゃくじょう（焼却場） trash incineration facility
すいい（水位） water level
すいしつ（水質） water quality
そうおん（騒音） noise
どじょうおせん（土壌汚染） soil pollution
にさんかたんそ（二酸化炭素） carbon dioxide
はいきガス（排気ガス） exhaust gas
はいきぶつ（廃棄物） waste ゆうがいはいきぶつ（有害廃棄物） hazardous waste
パック carton; package
びじゅつひん（美術品） art piece
びん（瓶） bottle
リサイクル recycling
りょう（量） quantity

Verbal nouns

おせん（汚染） pollution おせんする（汚染する） to pollute すいしつおせん（水質汚染） water pollution

な-adjectives

じゅうだい（な）（重大な） important; critical

For a list of supplementary vocabulary items that will facilitate communication, see the first page of Chapter 10 in your Workbook.

APPENDIX A

English Translation of Dialogues

NOTE: IN THE DIALOGUE TRANSLATIONS, SOME IDIOMATIC EXPRESSIONS ARE GIVEN ENGLISH EQUIVALENTS RATHER THAN WORD-FOR-WORD TRANSLATIONS.

CHAPTER 1
It's cold.

Michiko-san has met Ishida-san in the classroom.

Michiko: Oh, good morning Ishida-san.
Ishida: Oh, Michiko-san. The wind sure is cold today.
Michiko: Yeah, it's a little cold today, for sure.
Ishida: It'll probably snow tonight.
Michiko: Yeah. It's cloudy now, so it will probably snow.
Ishida: But it's still only November.
Michiko: That's right. It looks like it's going to get cold early this year. That's too bad.
Ishida: I hate the cold.

The teacher comes in to the classroom.

Michiko: Oh, good morning, professor.
Professor: Oh, Ms. Suzuki and Mr. Ishida. Morning. Cold, isn't it?
Ishida: It's really cold. The temperature's gone down, and I bet it snows.
Professor: Well, the weather forecast said it's not supposed to snow.

Michiko-san has looked out the window. It is snowing.

Michiko: My goodness, it's snowing.
Ishida: So it is. It looks like today's going to be a cold one alright.

CHAPTER 2
This vacation

The professor is asking Alice-san and Lee-san about their plans for the upcoming vacation.

Professor: What do you plan on doing this vacation?
Alice: I intend to go to Hokkaido. Ishida-san says he's going to see the Snow Festival (Yuki matsuri) in Sapporo, so I thought I'd go along.
Lee: Hokkaido?
Alice: Yeah, they have a famous festival in February in Sapporo called the Snow Festival. I hear there's buildings and sculptures, all made out of snow.
Lee: Oh, the Snow Festival? Yeah, I think I've heard about that. They build a lot of things out of snow, right?
Alice: That's right. I hear they even have buildings and animals as large as the real thing.
Professor: But it's cold in Hokkaido in February. Be sure to take sweaters and a coat.
Alice: That's right. But my coat's kind of old, so I thought I'd buy one before I go.
Professor: Really? Well, Lee-san, what are your plans?
Lee: I'm going to go back to Taiwan for the first time in a while.
Professor: Really? When are you going?
Lee: I plan on leaving as soon as the semester is finished.
Alice: Well, that's real soon now. So I suppose you're pretty busy now, huh?
Lee: That's for sure. I want to get some presents and a suitcase this weekend. And by the way, Professor, about our test. . .
Professor: What about it?
Lee: You said to turn it in by the fifteenth, but would the fourteenth be okay?
Professor: Sure, that would be fine.

CHAPTER 3
How to use a copy machine

Professor: I can't read this copy.
Alice: Shall I make a better one?
Professor: OK. If you're going, then please make fifteen copies.
Alice: Yes (O.K.)

(In front of a copying machine)

Alice: Can I use this copy machine?
Business clerk: Oh, that one's broken, so please don't use it. Please use one of the machines in the Copy Center.
Alice: OK. Thank you.

(In the Copy Center)

Alice: Ishida-san, could you do me a favor?
Ishida: Sure, what is it?
Alice: I don't know how to use this copy machine. Could you show me?
Ishida: Sure. We'll do it together.
Alice: OK.
Ishida: First, you place the paper here, then select the size by pushing this button.
Alice: Yes. (O.K.)
Ishida: Then, enter the number of copies you want and push this green button.
Alice: Oh, I see. Thank you.

CHAPTER 4
At the bank and post office

Lee-san wants to open a regular savings account.

Lee: Alice, do you have a minute?
Alice: Sure. What do you need?
Lee: I want to open a bank account. Should I take my passport and money?
Alice: Yes. . . Oh, but you also have to take your alien registration card.
Lee: Oh, really. I don't need a personal stamp?
Alice: You may need one if it's a small bank, but you can use signature at large banks, so you don't need one for them. But it's helpful to have a personal stamp anyway.

Lee-san went to the bank.

Lee: Excuse me, I'd like to open a regular savings account.
Teller A: Please go to window #6.

At window #6

Lee: Excuse me, I'd like to open an account.
Teller B: A regular savings account?
Lee: Yes.
Teller B: You are a foreigner, aren't you?
Lee: Yes, I am.
Teller B: Then could you fill out this application form? There is a sample application over there you can use for reference.
Lee: I see.
Teller B: Also, could I have your passport and alien registration card?
Lee: Here they are.

After the bank, Lee-san went to a post office.

Lee: Excuse me, I'd like to send this by air mail.
Postal employee: This weighs 1.2 kilograms, so you can't send it.
Lee: Oh, I can't?
Postal employee: Yes, sea mail can be up to five kilograms, but air mail cannot exceed one kilogram. You'll have to break it up into two packages and come back.
Lee: I see. I'll come back later.

CHAPTER 5
At Professor Honda's office

Alice is talking with her teacher in his office. Prof. Honda is Alice's seminar teacher.

Professor: How long has it been since you came to Japan, Alice?
Alice: A year and a half. I'll be going back to the States in August of next year.
Professor: Really? A year and a half already? So what will you do when you go back to the States?
Alice: I still have one semester before I graduate, so I'll go back to school.
Professor: What will you do after that?
Alice: I am not sure yet, but I plan to look for a job where I can use Japanese. If possible, I would like to get a job at a Japanese company, or with an American company with a branch office in Japan.
Professor: Really. Well, you shouldn't have any problem with that, so keep working hard.
Alice: Thank you very much.

Alice meets Ishida-san outside Prof. Honda's office.

Ishida: Alice, good timing. Have you spoken with Prof. Honda about the party for the seminar?
Alice: Oops, sorry. I met him just now, but I forgot to say anything.
Ishida: So, you haven't spoken with him yet, right? No problem. I'll see him later, so I'll talk to him.
Alice: Thanks. Have the preparations been finished?
Ishida: Almost. A hall has been reserved, and the food has been ordered.
Alice: I see. How about the invitations?
Ishida: Done. I sent them last week, so responses should come back soon.
Alice: Wow. You can do everything, Ishida-san. I couldn't handle all that.
Ishida: That's not true. I can't speak any foreign languages. You've come to a foreign country by yourself, and you're going to a university. I think you're way better than me.
Alice: I wonder.

CHAPTER 6
Directions to the Hilton Hotel

Brown-san lives in Asakusa. She is planning to meet Michiko-san at Hilton Hotel, but does not know how to get there, so, she is asking Michiko-san for directions.

Brown: I don't know how to get to the Hilton Hotel from here. . .
Michiko: Really? Do you know how to get to Shinjuku?
Brown: Sorry. I don't.
Michiko: That's OK. First, you get on a Ginza Line subway and go to Kanda.
Brown: Go to Kanda on the Ginza Line, and then?
Michiko: Transfer to the Chuo Line at Kanda. Shinjuku is the third stop, so get off there.
Brown: OK. I get on the Chuo Line, go to Shinjuku. Then, which exit should I go out?
Michiko: You go out the West exit. When you go out, there's an underpath right in front of you. Walk straight for about ten or fifteen minutes.
Brown: Go out the West exit, and go straight for ten or fifteen minutes, right?
Michiko: Right. Then, you'll come out on a place with a lot of tall buildings.
Brown: Oh, this'll be that place that has so many famous buildings?
Michiko: That's right. From there, the Hyatt Hotel is on the second

corner. You should be able to see a park past the Hyatt.

Brown: Is the Hyatt on the right hand side or the left hand side of the street?

Michiko: The right. Then, you turn right at the corner before the Hyatt.

Brown: Go to the right before Hyatt, right?

Michiko: Yes. After you turn to the right, go straight, and the Hilton Hotel is at the end of the street.

Brown: I understand. How long does it take?

Michiko: Fifteen to twenty minutes to Shinjuku, and it takes about twenty minutes to the hotel on foot, so I imagine it will take you about forty minutes.

Brown: Thank you. Okay, I'll see you at one o'clock tomorrow at the Hilton lobby.

Michiko: See you tomorrow.

The nest day, Brown-san is at Kanda station.

Brown: Excuse me. What track does the Chuo Line Shinjuku train leave from?

Man: That's track one.

Brown: Thank you very much.

Brown-san is at Shinjuku Station.

Brown: Excuse me, but where is the west entrance?

Woman: Over there.

Brown: Thanks.

Brown has arrived at the hotel.

Michiko: Brown-san, here I am. Were you able to find the way?

Brown: Michiko-san. Sure, I found it with no problems.

Michiko: Good.

CHAPTER 7

Alice's Birthday

Ishida-san is talking to Michiko on campus.

Ishida: Say, Michiko, Alice's birthday is coming up shortly.

Michiko: Yes, it is.

Ishida: I'm thinking about giving her something, but I don't know what to buy at all.

Michiko: Really?

Ishida: So, I'd like for you to come shopping with me and help me select something.

Michiko: That's fine. How about tomorrow or the day after tomorrow?

Ishida: Thanks. Anytime's fine with me.

Michiko: Well then, how about tomorrow afternoon?

Ishida: Fine.

The next day, Ishida-san and Michiko are in a department store.

Michiko: How much do you want to spend? (literally, About how much is your budget?)

Ishida: Oh, about 5,000 yen.

Michiko: Then, how about a purse? The one she has now is old, she's been wanting a new one.

Ishida: What kind do you think I should buy?

Michiko: One that's easy to use. This red one or the brown one are both good.

Ishida: Yeah. Excuse me.

Sales clerk: Yes, how can I help you?

Ishida: How much is this red purse?

Sales clerk: It's 9,000 yen.

Ishida: Oh? That's a bit too expensive. Well, how much is this brown one?

Sales clerk: That one is 5,000 yen.

Ishida: OK, I'll take this one then.

Sales clerk: Certainly.

CHAPTER 8

Lee-san's consultation with the professor

Lee-san is talking with Professor Sugimoto.

Lee: Excuse me, Professor Sugimoto, but I would like to consult with you.

Prof. Sugimoto: Yes, that will be fine. I have something I have to finish up today, but tomorrow would be okay.

Lee: What time will you be in your office tomorrow?

Prof. Sugimoto: I will be in around 1 o'clock. Can you come then?

Lee: Yes, that's fine. I'll come around 1 o'clock, then.

The next day, Lee-san has come to the Professor Sugimoto's office.

Prof. Sugimoto: Come in.

Lee: Excuse me.

Prof. Sugimoto: Why don't you sit down there?

Lee: Okay.

Prof. Sugimoto: What is it you want to talk to me about?

Lee: Okay. I'm graduating next year and if I can, I would like to get a job in Japan.

Prof. Sugimoto: I see.

Lee: I was wondering if I could ask you to write a letter of reference.

Prof. Sugimoto: That's fine, but, we don't use letters of reference much in Japan.

Lee: Oh, really? Foreigners do not need them, either?

Prof. Sugimoto: Hum. . . Japanese people don't need them, but it's probably different for foreigners.

Lee: I'll check again, then.

Prof. Sugimoto: But, are your parents OK with this? You won't be going back to Taiwan.

Lee: Yes. My parents have always let me do what I want. So they said it would be fine for me to work in Japan.

Prof. Sugimoto: I see. That's good.

CHAPTER 9

Please tell him to hold down the noise

Lee-san is looking at an advertisement for part-time jobs. Alice-san has just come in.

Alice: Hi, Lee-san, what are you looking at?

Lee: I'm looking for a new part-time job.

Alice: Why? Did you quit yours?

Lee: No, I was fired. I haven't been able to sleep well lately, so I was late for the work many times.

Alice: You can't sleep? Is there anything wrong with you?
Lee: No, it's not that. They guy in the next-door apartment is too noisy.
Alice: The next-door apartment? The one who moved in last month?
Lee: Yes. He has the TV and music on loud late every night, and I can't sleep. And his friends sometimes come over and party all night. It's more than I can take.
Alice: Really? That's terrible. Have you complained?
Lee: Yes, I've asked him to be quiet five times already.
Alice: Then, you'd better get the landlord to warn him.
Lee: Yes, but I don't want to talk to the landlord.

Lee-san makes a phone call to the landlord.

Lee: Hello. This is Lee in the Sakura Apartment.
Landlord: Yes, Lee-san, what is it?
Lee: Well, I hate to ask you this, but I'd like a favor.
Landlord: What kind of favor?
Lee: I'm sorry to ask, but could you talk to Aoki-san next door and ask him to be a bit more quiet?
Landlord: Is he that noisy?
Lee: Yes. He plays the TV and his stereo really loud, and I can't sleep. I've asked him many times to quiet down, but he won't listen.
Landlord: I see, that is a problem. Okay, I'll talk to him.
Lee: I hate to bother you, but I would appreciate it.

CHAPTER 10
Can I swim in this river?

Michiko and Ishida-san have strolled to a river near Ishida's house.

Michiko: This water's clean isn't it?
Ishida: Yes, it is. But, twenty years ago nobody could swim in this river because the water was so dirty.
Michiko: Really? Is it OK to swim there know?
Ishida: I think you can, but I'm not sure.
Michiko: Really? Now that you mention it, there doesn't seem to be many fish. But, how did it get so dirty in the first place?
Ishida: There was a factory that made machines over there about twenty years ago.
Michiko: Yes.
Ishida: The waste water from the factory polluted the river, and it was pretty bad.
Michiko: I see. Well, when did it start getting cleaner?
Ishida: I don't really remember.

Ishida-san's mother walks toward Michiko and Ishida.

Ishida: Hi, Mother.
Ishida's mother: Oh, Mamoru. And Michiko's with you.
Michiko: Good afternoon.
Ishida's mother: Good afternoon.
Ishida: Hey, I was just talking with Michiko—this river was really dirty once, wasn't it?
Ishida's mother: Yes, it was. Because the factory was here.
Michiko: But, it looks like it's gotten much cleaner.
Ishida's mother: That's because the factory was closed about ten years ago. And then people cleaned up the river.
Michiko: Oh, really?
Ishida: Can people swim in this river?
Ishida's mother: I heard it's not good enough yet. I guess if takes years for a river to get clean once it's gotten dirty.
Michiko: The best way to prevent pollution is to not make it dirty in the first place, isn't it?
Ishida's mother: Yes, it sure is.

APPENDIX B

Adjective and Copula Verb Conjugation

			い-adjective	い-adjective	な-adjective	Copula Verb
Dictionary Form			おおきい (big)	いい (good)	しずかな (quiet)	日本人だ (to be a Japanese)
Plain	Present	Affirm	おおきい	いい	しずかだ	日本人だ
		Neg.	おおきくない	よくない	しずかじゃない	日本人じゃない
	Past	Affirm.	おおきかった	よかった	しずかだった	日本人だった
		Neg.	おおきくなかった	よくなかった	しずかじゃなかった	日本人じゃなかった
Polite	Present	Affirm.	おおきいです	いいです	しずかです	日本人です
		Neg.	おおきくありません／おおきくないです	よくありません／よくないです	しずかじゃありません／しずかじゃないです	日本人じゃありません／日本人じゃないです
	Past	Affirm.	おおきかったです	よかったです	しずかでした	日本人でした
		Neg.	おおきくありませんでした／おおきくなかったです	よくありませんでした／よくなかったです	しずかじゃありませんでした／しずかじゃなかったです	日本人じゃありませんでした／日本人じゃなかったです
Conditional			おおきければ	よければ	しずかなら	日本人なら
て-form			おおきくて	よくて	しずかで	日本人で
Prenominal			おおきい人	いい人	しずかな人	日本人の
Adverbial			おおきく	よく	しずかに	日本人に

APPENDIX C

Verb Conjugation

			Irregular Verb	Irregular Verb	る-Verb	う-Verb
Dictionary Form			くる (to come)	する (to do)	たべる (to eat)	いく (to go)
Plain	Present	Affirmative	くる	する	たべる	いく
		Negative	こない	しない	たべない	いかない
	Past	Affirmative	きた	した	たべた	いった
		Negative	こなかった	しなかった	たべなかった	いかなかった
Polite	Present	Affirmative	きます	します	たべます	いきます
		Negative	きません	しません	たべません	いきません
	Past	Affirmative	きました	しました	たべました	いきました
		Negative	きません でした	しません でした	たべません でしひた	いきません でした
Volitional	Plain		こよう	しよう	たべよう	いこう
	Polite		きましょう	しましょう	たべましょう	いきましょう
Potential	Plain		こられる	できる	たべられる	いける
	Polite		こられます	できます	たべられます	いけます
Passive	Plain		こられる	される	たべられる	いかれる
	Polite		こられます	されます	たべられます	いかれます
Causative	Plain		こさせる	させる	たべさせる	いかせる
	Polite		こさせます	させます	たべさせます	いかせます
Honorific	Plain		いらっしゃる	なさる	めしあがる	いらっしゃる
	Polite		いらっしゃいます	なさいます	めしあがります	いらっしゃいます
Humble	Plain		まいる	いたす	いただく	まいる
	Polite		まいります	いたします	いただきます	まいります
Conditional form			くれば	すれば	たべれば	いけば
て-form			きて	して	たべて	いって

う-Verb	う-Verb	う-Verb	う-Verb	う-Verb
およぐ (to swim)	かえる (to go home)	かく (to write)	のむ (to drink)	はなす (to talk)
およぐ	かえる	かく	のむ	はなす
およがない	かえらない	かかない	のまない	はなさない
およいだ	かえった	かいた	のんだ	はなした
およがなかった	かえらなかった	かかなかった	のまなかった	はなさなかった
およぎます	かえります	かきます	のみます	はなします
およぎません	かえりません	かきません	のみません	はなしません
およぎました	かえりました	かきました	のみました	はなしました
およぎません でした	かいりません でした	かきません でした	のみません でした	はなしません でした
およごう	かえろう	かこう	のもう	はなそう
およぎましょう	かえりましょう	かきましょう	のみましょう	はなしましょう
およげる	かえれる	かける	のめる	はなせる
およげます	かえれます	かけます	のめます	はなせます
およがれる	かえられる	かかれる	のまれる	はなされる
およがれます	かえられます	かかれます	のまれます	はなされます
およがせる	かえらせる	かかせる	のませる	はなさせる
およがせます	かえらせます	かかせます	のませます	はなさせます
おおよぎになる	おかえりになる	おかきになる	めしあがる	おはなしになる
おおよぎになります	おかえりになります	おかきになります	めしあがります	おはなしになります
N/A	N/A	おかきする	いただく	おはなしする
N/A	N/A	おかきします	いただきます	おはなしします
およげば	かえれば	かけば	のめば	はなせば
およいで	かえって	かいて	のんで	はなして

APPENDIX D

List of Particles

Particle	Meaning	Use	Text Reference
dake （だけ）	Only (affirmative)	山田さんだけ(が)来ました Only Yamada-san came. 山田さんにだけ話しました I told only Yamada-san.	305 (Vol. 2)
de （で）	1. Among ～	世界で一番高い山はヒマラヤです。 The Himalayas are the highest mountains in the world.	214 (Vol. 1)
	2. At, in, on (location of action)	図書館で勉強します。 I study at the library. 日本で日本語を勉強しました。 I studied Japanese in Japan.	141 (Vol. 1), 299 (Vol. 1)
	3. Means	バスで大学に行きます。 I go to the university by bus. 日本語で話して下さい。 Please speak in Japanese	167 (Vol. 1)
	4. Scope and limit	あと一週間で休みです。 Vacation starts in a week そのみかんは五つで３００円です。 Those oranges are 300 yen for five.	297 (Vol. 2)
e （へ）	Direction	来年日本へ行きます。 I will go to Japan next year.	101 (Vol. 2)
ga （が）	1. Subject marker The subject is marked by が in a noun-modifying clause. (378 (Vol. 1)) or in a subordinate clause with a conjuntion such as とき, のに, ので, or から.	だれが来ますか。 Who is coming. 山田さんと中山さんが来ます。 Yamada-san and Nakayama-san are coming. 私が先週買った本はこれです。 This is the book I bought last week.	115 (Vol. 1), 378 (Vol. 1), 116 (Vol. 2)
	2. Object with potential form When the verb is in the potential form, the direct object of the verb takes either が or を, except for できる, which takes only が.	にくが／を　食べられます。 I can eat meat. テニスが　できます。 I can play tennis.	401 (Vol. 1)

Particle	Meaning	Use	Text Reference
ka （か）	1. Question	ジョンさんはアメリカ人ですか。 Are you an American, John? 何時に寝ますか。 What time do you go to bed?	38 (Vol. 1)
	2. Indirect question	どこでその人に会ったかおぼえていません。 I don't remember where I met that person. その人に会ったかどうかおぼえていません。 I don't remember whether I met that person.	257 (Vol. 2)
kara （から）	From	日本語の授業は十時から十一時までです。 The Japanese class is from 10 o'clock to 11 o'clock.	167 (Vol. 1)
made （まで）	Until	きのう二時まで勉強しました。 I studied until two o'clock yesterday. madeni (までに)by (time limit)3-L2 明日までに宿題をします。 I will do the homework by tomorrow.	167 (Vol. 1)
madeni （までに）	By (time limit)	明日までに宿題をします。 I will do the homework by tomorrow.	101 (Vol. 2)
mo （も）	1. Also	山田さんも文学部の学生です。 Yamada-san is also a student in the school of liberal arts. ディズニーランドはフロリダにあります。 東京にもあります。 Disney Land is in Florida. It is also in Tokyo.	47 (Vol. 1), 182 (Vol. 1)
	2. Both ~ and ~ (lack of preference)	東京も京都もおもしろい所です。 Both Tokyo and Kyoto are interesting places.	214 (Vol. 1)
	3. As many as ~, not even one ~(emphasinzing quantity)	ジョンはステーキを三まいも食べられる。 John can eat as many as three steaks. 日本に一度も行ったことがありません。 I have not been to Japan even once. (I have never been to Japan.)	448 (Vol. 2)
	4. Any ~ (question word + でも), no ~ (question word + も)	私は何でも食べられます。 I can eat anything. 病気で今は何も食べられません。 Right now, I can't eat anything because I'm sick.	260 (Vol. 2)
ne （ね	Seeking agreement	おすしはおいしいですね。 Sushi is good, isn't it?	9 (Vol. 1), 9 (Vol. 2)

Particle	Meaning	Use	Text Reference
ni (に)	1. To (destination)	明日家に帰ります。 I am going back home tomorrow? 両親に手紙を書きました。 I wrote a letter to my parents.	141 (Vol. 1), 167 (Vol. 1)
	2. Extent of action	一週間に一度映画を見ます。 I watch a movie once a week.	177 (Vol. 1)
	3. At, in , on (location of existence)	いすの上に猫がいます。 There is a cat on the chair. 山田さんはどこにいますか。 Where is Yamada-san?	72 (Vol. 1), 118 (Vol. 1)
	4. Agent in a passive or causative sentence (An agent indicates the doer of an action.)	上司は山田さんに東京へ行かせた。 My boss made Yamada-san go to Tokyo. 私は先生にほめられました。 I was praised by my teacher.	405, 439, 445 (Vol. 2)
	5. By, from (source with receiving verb)	私は姉にゆびわをもらいました。 I received a ring from my sister. 田中さんは山田さんに花をもらいました。 Tanaka-san received a flower from Yamada-san. 弟は父にコンピュータを買ってもらった。 My brother got my father to buy us a computer. 私は先生に本を貸していただいた。 I had the teacher lend him the book.	341, 390–393 (Vol. 2)
	6. At, in, on (time)	何時に起きますか。 What time do you get up? 日本語の授業は水曜日にあります。 The Japanese class is held on Wednesday.	137 (Vol. 1)
	7. In order to do something (purpose)	本を読みに図書館に行きます。 I go to the library to read books.	293 (Vol. 1)
no (の)	1. It is that ~ (casual speech) (This is a contracted form of ～のです. It is often used by female speakers.)	どうして食べないの。 Why aren't you eating? おなかがいたいの。 Because my stomach hurts.	22 (Vol. 2)
	2. ~ing, that ~ (nominalizer)	私は本を読むのが好きです。 I like reading books. 日本語で映画を見るのはおもしろいです。 Watching movies in Japanese is interesting.	208 (Vol. 1), 488 (Vol. 2)
	3. Of, 's, in	山田さんは私の友達です。 Yamada-san is my friend. 山田さんはイリノイ大学の学生です。 Yamada-san is a student of University of Illinois. これは山田さんのペンです。あれは私の(ペン)です。 This is Yamada's pen. That is mine (my pen).	41 (Vol. 1)

Particle	Meaning	Use	Text Reference
no (の (cont.)	4. One (pronoun) (This の is classfied as a pronoun, not as a particle.)	私は黒いのが好きです。 I like the black one. 去年買ったのはあまりよくありませんでした。 The one I bought last year was not very good.	109 (Vol. 1), 484 (Vol. 2)
	5. Subject in noun-modifying clause (The particle の is often substituted for the subject marker が when the modifying clause is very short.)	私の／が見た映画はおもしろくありませんでした。 The movie I watched was not interesting.	378 (Vol. 1)
o (を)	1. Direct object	山田さんは水をたくさん飲みます。 Yamada-san drinks a lot of water. 七時にごはんを食べます。 I will eat a meal at seven.	141 (Vol. 1), 401 (Vol. 1)
	2. Out of~, from (point of detachment)	新宿で電車をおります。 I get off the train at Shinjuku. 朝七時に家を出ます。 I leave home at seven in the morning.	296 (Vol. 2)
	3. In, on, across, through (route)	私はこの道を通って、大学に行きます。 I take this road, and go to the university. 公園を通ります。 I go through the park.	296 (Vol. 2)
shika (しか)	Nothing/nobody/no~	ジョンは英語しか分かりません。 John understands only English. これは日本でしか食べられません。 You can eat this only in Japan.	305 (Vol. 2)
to (と)	1. And	ニューヨークとシカゴで仕事をしました。 I worked in New York and Chicago.	47 (Vol. 1)
	2. Quote	私は山田と申します。 I am "Yamada." 「タイタニック」という映画を見ました。 I saw a movie called "Titanic."	105 (Vol. 2)
	3. Together	昨日山田さんと図書館で勉強しました。 I studied in the library with Yamada-san yesterday.	167 (Vol. 1)
wa (は)	Topic and contrast marker	きのうは何も食べませんでした。 I did not eat anything yesterday. (topic) 東京は人が多い。 There are a lot of people in Tokyo. (topic) 新聞をよく読みますが、雑誌はあまり読みません。 I often read newspaper, but I don't read magazines very often. (contrast)	35 (Vol. 1), 115 (Vol. 1), 182 (Vol. 1)

Particle	Meaning	Use	Text Reference
wa（わ）	Female speech marker	今日はよく勉強したわ。 I studied a lot today. (female speaker) これ、おいしいわ。 This is good. (female speaker)	34 (Vol. 2)
ya（や）	And, so on~ (inexhaustive listing)	山田さんや田中さんがゴルフをしている。 Yamada-san and Tanaka-san and others are playing golf.	212 (Vol. 1)
yo（よ）	Giving information	これはおいしいですよ。 This tastes good, you know.	79 (Vol. 1), 9 (Vol. 2)
yori（より）	Than (comparison)	大阪の方が京都より大きいです。 Osaka is bigger than Kyoto.	214 (Vol. 1)

APPENDIX E

Kanji List

	Kanji	Volume	Chapter	Kun-reading	On-reading	Examples
1	山	1	7	やま	サン	山田さん、山下さん
2	日	1	7	ひ	ニチ、ニ	日本、 日曜日
3	田	1	7	た、だ	デン	田中さん、山田さん
4	人	1	7	ひと	ジン、 ニン	おとこの人、日本人
5	上	1	7	うえ	ジョウ	つくえの上
6	下	1	7	した	カ	つくえの下
7	中	1	7	なか	チュウ	はこの中
8	大	1	7	おお（きい）	ダイ	大きい人
9	小	1	7	ちい（さい）	ショウ	小さいくるま
10	本	1	7	もと	ホン、ボン	本、日本
11	学	1	7	まな（ぶ）	ガク	学生
12	生	1	7	なま	セイ	学生、先生
13	先	1	7	さき	セン	先生
14	私	1	7	わたし	シ	私の本
15	川	1	7	かわ	セン	川があります
1	一	1	8	ひと（つ）	イチ	一時
2	二	1	8	ふた（つ）	ニ	二時
3	三	1	8	みっ（つ）	サン	三時
4	四	1	8	よっ（つ）	シ、ヨン	四時
5	五	1	8	いつ（つ）	ゴ	五時
6	六	1	8	むっ（つ）	ロク	六時
7	七	1	8	なな（つ）	シチ	七時
8	八	1	8	やっ（つ）	ハチ	八時
9	九	1	8	ここの（つ）	キュウ　ク	九時
10	十	1	8	とお	ジュウ	十時
11	百	1	8		ヒャク	百円
12	千	1	8		セン	千円
13	万	1	8		マン	一万円
14	円	1	8		エン	五千円
1	月	1	9	つき	ゲツ、ガツ	一月、月曜日
2	火	1	9	ひ	カ	火曜日
3	水	1	9	みず	スイ	水曜日
4	木	1	9	き	モク	木曜日
5	金	1	9	かね	キン	金曜日
6	土	1	9	つち	ド	土曜日
7	曜	1	9		ヨウ	日曜日

	Kanji	Volume	Chapter	Kun-reading	On-reading	Examples
8	年	1	9	とし	ネン	一年
9	時	1	9	とき	ジ	三時間
10	間	1	9	あいだ	カン	八時間
11	週	1	9		シュウ	一週間
12	何	1	9	なに		何時
13	今	1	9	いま	コン	今、何時
14	分	1	9	わ（かる）	フン	五分
15	半	1	9		ハン	六時半
1	男	1	10	おとこ	ダン	男の子、男の人
2	女	1	10	おんな	ジョ	女の子、女の人
3	子	1	10	こ	シ	子ども
4	目	1	10	め	モク	目がいたい
5	耳	1	10	みみ	ジ	耳がわるい
6	口	1	10	くち	コウ	口が小さい
7	足	1	10	あし	ソク	足がながい
8	手	1	10	て	シュ	手が大きい
9	父	1	10	ちち　とう	フ	お父さん
10	母	1	10	はは　かあ	ボ	お母さん
11	兄	1	10	あに　にい	ケイ　キョウ	お兄さん
12	姉	1	10	あね　ねえ	シ	お姉さん
13	弟	1	10	おとうと	ダイ	私の弟
14	妹	1	10	いもうと	マイ	私の妹
15	家	1	10	いえ　うち	カ	私の家　家族
16	族	1	10		ゾク	家族
1	行	1	11	い（く）	コウ	銀行に行く
2	来	1	11	く（る）	ライ	学校に来る
3	帰	1	11	かえ（る）	キ	家に帰る
4	食	1	11	た（べる）	ショク	ごはんを食べる
5	飲	1	11	の（む）	イン	水を飲む
6	見	1	11	み（る）	ケン	テレビを見る
7	聞	1	11	き（く）	ブン	おんがくを聞く
8	読	1	11	よ（む）	ドク	本を読む
9	書	1	11	か（く）	ショ	てがみを書く
10	話	1	11	はな（す）	ワ	電話で話す
11	高	1	11	たか（い）	コウ	高校　高い
12	校	1	11		コウ	高校
13	出	1	11	で(る)、だ(す)	シュツ	てがみを出す
14	会	1	11	あ（う）	カイ	会社で会う
15	買	1	11	か（う）	バイ	車を買う
1	元	1	12	もと	ゲン	元気です
2	気	1	12		キ	元気な人、気分がわるい
3	入	1	12	はい（る）	ニュウ	大学に入る、入院する
4	薬	1	12	くすり	ヤク	薬をのむ
5	休	1	12	やす（む）	キュウ	休みの日、しごとを休みます

	Kanji	Volume	Chapter	Kun-reading	On-reading	Examples
6	体	1	12	からだ	タイ	体が大きい
7	病	1	12	やま（い）	ビョウ	病気　病院
8	院	1	12		イン	病院、入院する
9	住	1	12	す（む）	ジュウ	アパートに住む、住所
10	所	1	12	ところ	ショ	きれいな所、住所
11	語	1	12		ゴ	日本語
12	好	1	12	す（き）	コウ	好きな人
13	毎	1	12		マイ	毎日、毎年、毎
14	回	1	12	まわ（る）	カイ	三回飲む
15	度	1	12		ド	三度、今度
1	雨	2	1	あめ	ウ	雨のち晴れ
2	雪	2	1	ゆき	セツ	雪がふる
3	風	2	1	かぜ	フウ	風が強い
4	晴	2	1	は（れる）	セイ	明日は晴れる
5	朝	2	1	あさ	チョウ	朝ごはん
6	昼	2	1	ひる	チュウ	昼ごはんを食べる
7	晩	2	1		バン	今晩は
8	春	2	1	はる	シュン	春になる
9	夏	2	1	なつ	カ	夏は暑い
10	秋	2	1	あき	シュウ	秋は山がきれいだ
11	冬	2	1	ふゆ	トウ	冬は寒い
12	東	2	1	ひがし	トウ	東のそら、東京
13	西	2	1	にし	セイ、サイ	西のそらが暗い
14	南	2	1	みなみ	ナン	南の方は暖かい
15	北	2	1	きた	ホク	北は寒い
16	方	2	1	かた	ホウ	どちらの方が好きですか
17	寒	2	1	さむ（い）	カン	昨日は寒かった
18	暑	2	1	あつ（い）	ショ	来週は暑いでしょう
19	明	2	1	あか（るい）	メイ	五時ごろ明るくなります
20	暗	2	1	くら（い）	アン	はやく暗くなります
21	温	2	1		オン	温度は三十度です
22	暖	2	1	あたた（かい）	ダン	今日は暖かい
23	涼	2	1	すず（しい）	リョウ	涼しくて気持ちがいい
24	強	2	1	つよ（い）	キョウ	風が強い
25	弱	2	1	よわ（い）	ジャク	風が弱くなる
26	季	2	1		キ	季節
27	節	2	1	ふし	セツ	寒い季節
28	多	2	1	おお（い）	タ	人が多い
29	少	2	1	すく(ない)、すこ(し)	ショウ	家が少ない、少し暑い
30	天	2	1		テン	天気がいい
1	予	2	2		ヨ	予定　予約
2	定	2	2	さだ（める）	テイ	予定があります
3	約	2	2		ヤク	ホテルの予約
4	前	2	2	まえ	ゼン	日本に行く前　家の前

	Kanji	Volume	Chapter	Kun-reading	On-reading	Examples
5	後	2	2	うし（ろ）、あと	ゴ	いすの後ろ、日本に行った後
6	末	2	2	すえ	マツ	週末、月末
7	思	2	2	おも（う）	ソウ	日本に行こうと思います
8	言	2	2	い（う）	ゲン	私は山田と言います
9	知	2	2	し（る）	チ	その人を知っています
10	答	2	2	こた（える）	トウ	日本語で答える
11	電	2	2		デン	電話で話す
12	車	2	2	くるま	シャ	車で行く、電車
13	写	2	2	うつ（す）	シャ	写真をとる
14	真	2	2		シン	旅行の写真
15	映	2	2	うつ（す）	エイ	映画、映画館
16	画	2	2		ガ、カク	日本の映画、旅行の計画
17	国	2	2	くに	コク	中国、大きい国
18	町	2	2	まち	チョウ	小さい町
19	銀	2	2		ギン	銀行に行きました
20	社	2	2		シャ	会社、旅行会社
21	図	2	2		ズ　ト	図書館、地図
22	館	2	2		カン	旅館、図書館
23	公	2	2	おおやけ	コウ	公園
24	園	2	2		エン	公園であそぶ
25	店	2	2	みせ	テン	小さい店、喫茶店
26	地	2	2		チ、ジ	地下鉄、地図
27	京	2	2		キョウ、ケイ	京都、東京
28	計	2	2	はか（る）	ケイ	旅行の計画
29	旅	2	2	たび	リョ	旅行、旅館
30	安	2	2	やす（い）	アン	安いツアー
1	起	2	3	お（きる）	キ	六時に起きます
2	寝	2	3	ね（る）	シン	12時ごろ寝ます
3	使	2	3	つか（う）	シ	使い方を教えてください
4	作	2	3	つく（る）	サク	カレーを作る
5	教	2	3	おし（える）	キョウ	日本語を教える､教室、 教会
6	洗	2	3	あら（う）	セン	シャツを洗う
7	切	2	3	き（る）	セツ	肉を切る、親切
8	持	2	3	も（つ）	ジ	車を持っている
9	待	2	3	ま（つ）	タイ	待ってください
10	始	2	3	はじ（める）はじ（まる）	シ	八時に始まりました
11	終	2	3	お（わる）	シュウ	クラスは一時に終わります
12	着	2	3	つ（く）　き（る）	チャク	東京に着く、セーターを着る
13	取	2	3	と（る）	シュ	しおを取って下さい
14	貸	2	3	か（す）	タイ	お金を貸す
15	借	2	3	か（りる）	シャク	辞書を借りる

	Kanji	Volume	Chapter	Kun-reading	On-reading	Examples
16	返	2	3	かえ（す）	ヘン	借りた本を返す
17	走	2	3	はし（r）	ソウ	毎朝5キロ走ります
18	歩	2	3	ある（く）	ホ	歩いて行きます
19	乗	2	3	の（る）	ジョウ	車に乗る
20	友	2	3	とも	ユウ	友達が日本から来ます
21	達	2	3		タチ、ダチ、タツ	友達
22	肉	2	3		にく	牛肉を食べる
23	魚	2	3	さかな	ギョ	魚を食べましょう
24	牛	2	3	うし	ギュウ	牛肉を食べない
25	鳥	2	3	とり	チョウ	鳥肉を焼いてください
26	野	2	3	の	ヤ	野菜が大きくなった
27	菜	2	3		サイ	野菜はきらいでした
28	料	2	3		リョウ	料理のし方
29	理	2	3		リ	日本料理をたべますか
30	材	2	3		ザイ	天ぷらの材料
1	郵	2	4		ユウ	郵便局
2	便	2	4		ビン、ベン	郵便ポスト　便利
3	局	2	4		キョク	郵便局
4	部	2	4		へ、ブ	きれいな部屋　文学部
5	屋	2	4		オク、ヤ	部屋　薬屋　魚屋
6	番	2	4		バン	上から三番目　番号
7	号	2	4		ゴウ	電話番号
8	紙	2	4	かみ	シ	手紙を書く
9	物	2	4	もの	ブツ、モツ	荷物を送る、食べ物を食べる
10	包	2	4	つつ（む）	ホウ	小包を送る、紙で包む
11	送	2	4	おく（る）	ソウ	日本に荷物を送りました。
12	両	2	4		リョウ	両親の家　山田さんの両親
13	親	2	4	おや	シン	両親に会いたい
14	供	2	4		トモ、ドモ	子供の名前、子供が三人
15	名	2	4		メイ、ミョウ	名前を書いて下さい
16	英	2	4		エイ	英語が話せます
17	宿	2	4	やど	シュク	日本語の宿題
18	題	2	4		ダイ	宿題は来週出して下さい
19	質	2	4		シツ	質問がありますか.
20	問	2	4	と（う）	モン	質問して下さい。
21	漢	2	4		カン	漢字を勉強しています。
22	字	2	4		ジ	漢字をあまり知りません。
23	文	2	4		ブン、モン、モ	日本語の文法、文学部、作文
24	法	2	4		ホウ、ポウ	文法の勉強、法学部
25	勉	2	4		ベン	毎日勉強します
26	授	2	4	さず（ける）	ジュ	授業がありません。
27	業	2	4		ギョウ、ゴウ	日本語の授業は九時からです
28	忘	2	4	わす（れる）	ボウ	宿題を忘れました。
29	受	2	4	う（ける）	ジュ	テストを受ける。
30	卒	2	4		ソツ	大学を卒業する

	Kanji	Volume	Chapter	Kun-reading	On-reading	Examples
1	研	2	5		ケン	日本語の研究
2	究	2	5		キュウ	難しい研究
3	練	2	5	ね（る）	レン	練習する
4	習	2	5	なら（う）	シュウ	漢字の練習
5	仕	2	5	つか（える）	シ	仕事の計画
6	事	2	5	こと	ジ	仕事が好きです
7	医	2	5		イ	医者、医院
8	者	2	5	もの	シャ	研究者
9	新	2	5	あたら（しい）	シン	新しい車　新聞
10	古	2	5	ふる（い）	コ	古い本
11	長	2	5	なが（い）	チョウ	長いかみ　社長
12	短	2	5	みじか（い）	タン	短いテスト
13	同	2	5	おな（じ）	ドウ	同じ会社
14	違	2	5	ちが（う）	イ	番号が違う
15	静	2	5	しず（か）	セイ	静かなアパート
16	難	2	5	むずか（しい）	ナン	難しい問題
17	結	2	5	むす（ぶ）	ケツ	結婚します
18	婚	2	5		コン	結婚式
19	式	2	5		シキ	卒業式、結婚式
20	決	2	5	き（める）、き（まる）	ケッ	仕事が決まる
21	考	2	5	かんが（える）	コウ	よく考える
22	忙	2	5	いそが（しい）	ボウ	忙しかった
23	色	2	5	いろ	シキ	茶色、黄色、色々な食べ物
24	々	2	5	色々な人　時々		
25	開	2	5	あ(く)、あ(ける)、ひら(く)	カイ	ドアを開ける、ドアが開く
26	閉	2	5	し（める）、し（まる）	ヘイ	ドアを閉める、ドアが閉まる
27	招	2	5	まね（く）	ショウ	食事に招待する
28	外	2	5	そと	ガイ	外国人、外に犬がいる
29	留	2	5	と（まる）	リュウ　ル	留学生
30	悪	2	5	わる（い）	アク	病気が悪くなった
1	右	2	6	みぎ	ウ	映画館の右側
2	左	2	6	ひだり	サ	角を左にまがる
3	側	2	6	がわ	ソク	薬屋の右側
4	横	2	6	よこ	オウ	いすの横　横断歩道
5	近	2	6	ちか（い）	キン	家に近い
6	遠	2	6	とお（い）	エン	大学から遠い
7	向	2	6	む（く）、む（かい）	コウ	銀行の向かい側
8	急	2	6	いそ（ぐ）	キュウ	急行　特急
9	赤	2	6	あか（い）	セキ　シャク	信号が赤になる
10	青	2	6	あお（い）	セイ	青い目
11	黄	2	6	き	オウ	黄色が好きです

	Kanji	Volume	Chapter	Kun-reading	On-reading	Examples
12	緑	2	6	みどり	リョク	緑色のぼうし
13	黒	2	6	くろ（い）	コク	黒い車
14	白	2	6	しろ（い）	ハク	白ワイン、白い教会
15	駅	2	6		えき	駅に近い
16	橋	2	6	はし	キョウ	橋をわたって、左側
17	道	2	6	みち	ドウ	道の向こう側
18	交	2	6	まじ（わる）	コウ	交差点の近くに交番がある
19	差	2	6		サ	交差点
20	点	2	6		テン	テストの点が悪い
21	遊	2	6	あそ（ぶ）	ユウ	遊園地で遊ぶ
22	育	2	6	そだ（つ）、そだ（てる）	イク	体育館
23	角	2	6	かど	カク	二つ目の角
24	場	2	6	ば	ジョウ	きれいな場所、駐車場
25	自	2	6	みずか（ら）	ジ	自分、自転車
26	転	2	6		テン	自転車に乗る
27	動	2	6	うご（く）	ドウ	自動車　動物園
28	通	2	6	とお（る）	ツウ	公園を通る
29	運	2	6	はこ（ぶ）	ウン	車を運転する　運動する
30	止	2	6	と（まる）、と（める）	シ	信号で止まる
1	犬	2	7	いぬ	ケン	大きい犬
2	猫	2	7	ねこ		小さい猫
3	花	2	7	はな	カ	きれいな花、生け花
4	葉	2	7	は	ヨウ	木の葉、言葉
5	石	2	7	いし	セキ	石田さん、大石さん
6	形	2	7	かたち	ケイ、ギョウ	人形
7	服	2	7	ふく		きれいな服
8	有	2	7	あ（る）	ユウ	有名な医者
9	音	2	7	おと	オン	音楽
10	楽	2	7	たの（しい）	ガク　ラク	新しい音楽、楽しい人
11	雑	2	7		ザツ	雑誌を読みます
12	誌	2	7		シ	雑誌、スポーツ誌
13	意	2	7		イ	漢字の意味
14	味	2	7	あじ	ミ	言葉の意味
15	変	2	7	か（える）	ヘン	変な人、大変
16	辞	2	7		ジ	いい辞書
17	早	2	7	はや（い）	ソウ	早く起きました
18	遅	2	7	おそ（い）、おく（れる）	チ	授業に遅れる、遅い
19	重	2	7	おも（い）	ジュウ	荷物が思い
20	軽	2	7	かる（い）	ケイ	軽い荷物
21	広	2	7	ひろ（い）	コウ	広いアパート、新聞の広告
22	狭	2	7	せま（い）	キョウ	狭いところ
23	去	2	7	さ（る）	キョ	去年の九月

	Kanji	Volume	Chapter	Kun-reading	On-reading	Examples
24	昨	2	7	サク	昨日（きのう）	
25	立	2	7	た（つ）、 た（てる）	リツ	旅行の計画を立てる
26	派	2	7		ハ、パ	立派な病院
27	誕	2	7		タン	誕生日
28	祝	2	7	いわ（う）	シュク	お祝いに辞書をあげる
29	礼	2	7		レイ	失礼、お礼
30	茶	2	7		チャ、サ	お茶を飲む、喫茶店
1	就	2	8		シュウ	来年就職します
2	職	2	8		ショク	就職が決まる
3	相	2	8	あい	ソウ	先生に相談する
4	談	2	8		ダン	相談して下さい。
5	面	2	8		メン	仕事の面接
6	接	2	8		セツ	面接試験
7	試	2	8	ため（す）	シ	日本語の試験
8	験	2	8		ケン	就職試験
9	経	2	8	へ（る）	ケイ　キョウ	仕事の経験がある。
10	専	2	8		セン	専攻はアジア研究です。
11	攻	2	8	せ（める）	コウ	音楽が専攻です。
12	門	2	8	かど	モン	専門はコンピュータ工学です。
13	申	2	8	もう（す）	シ	山田と申します。
14	込	2	8	こ（む）		ツアーに申し込みました。
15	記	2	8		キ	名前を記入してください。
16	給	2	8		キュウ	給料が安いです。
17	働	2	8	はたら（く）	ドウ	毎日十時間働いています。
18	付	2	8	つ(く)つ(ける)	フ	会社の受付、電気を付ける
19	客	2	8		キャク	大事なお客さん
20	失	2	8		シツ	失礼します
21	説	2	8	と（く）	セツ	漢字の意味を説明する
22	調	2	8	しら（べる）	チョウ	辞書で調べる
23	用	2	8	もち（いる）	ヨウ	申込用紙に記入して下さい。
24	覚	2	8	おぼ（える）	カク	漢字を覚える
25	集	2	8	あつ（める） あつ（まる）	シュウ	お金を集める
26	室	2	8		シツ	研究室、狭い教室
27	消	2	8	き(える)、け(す)	ショウ	電気を消す、火が消える
28	呼	2	8	よ（ぶ）	コ	パーティに呼ぶ
29	助	2	8	たす（ける） たす（かる）	ジョ	助けて下さい
30	連	2	8	つ（れる）	レン	東京に連れていく
1	心	2	9	こころ	シン	病気のことが心配です
2	配	2	9	くば（る）	ハイ　パイ	試験のことを心配する
3	迷	2	9	まよ（う）	メイ	ほかの人の迷惑です
4	惑	2	9	ワク	ご迷惑をおかけしました	

	Kanji	Volume	Chapter	Kun-reading	On-reading	Examples
5	困	2	9	こま（る）	コン	お金がなくて困っています
6	句	2	9	ク	文句を言う	
7	全	2	9	まった（く）	ゼン	全然悪くない
8	然	2	9		ゼン、ネン	全然よくならない
9	当	2	9	あ（たる）、あ（てる）	トウ	本当です
10	注	2	9	そそ（ぐ）	チュウ	注文する
11	置	2	9	お（く）	チ	荷物を置く
12	拾	2	9	しろ（う）	シュウ	捨てられた猫を拾う
13	捨	2	9	す（てる）	シャ	ゴミを捨てないでください
14	直	2	9	なお（す）、なお（る）	チョク	コンピュータを直す
15	残	2	9	のこ（る）、のこ（す）	ザン	仕事が残る、残念
16	汚	2	9	きたな（い）よご（す）	オ	汚い部屋
17	笑	2	9	わら（う）	ショウ	笑って下さい
18	泣	2	9	な（く）	キュウ	泣かないで下さい
19	散	2	9	ち（る）、ち（らす）	サン	散歩が好きです
20	泳	2	9	およ（ぐ）	エイ	プールで泳ぐ、水泳
21	合	2	9	あ（う）	ゴウ	知り合いと出かける
22	引	2	9	ひ（く）	イン	引っ越し
23	落	2	9	お（ちる）、お（とす）	ラク	お金を落とす、試験に落ちる
24	歌	2	9	うた	カ	歌を歌いましょう
25	声	2	9	こえ	セイ	大きい声で話す
26	荷	2	9	ニ	思い荷物を持つ	
27	絵	2	9	え	カイ	モネの絵です
28	飯	2	9	めし	ハン	朝ご飯を食べる
29	売	2	9	う（る）	バイ	車を売る。
30	夜	2	9	よる	ヤ	夜十時に会いましょう
1	環	2	10		カン	地球の環境
2	境	2	10	さかい	キョウ　ケイ	環境を守る
3	世	2	10	よ	セ　セイ	世界の人々、世話になる
4	界	2	10		カイ	世界で一番高い山
5	空	2	10	そら	クウ	空が青い、成田空港
6	海	2	10	うみ	カイ	海をきれいにする、日本海
7	森	2	10	もり	シン	森の動物、大森さん
8	球	2	10		キュウ	地球は青かった
9	機	2	10		キ	機械に弱い
10	械	2	10		カイ	コンピュータの機械がいい
11	飛	2	10	と（ぶ）	ヒ	飛行機が飛ぶ
12	鉄	2	10		テツ	地下鉄は便利だ
13	工	2	10		コウ、ク	工学部の学生　工場
14	災	2	10	わざわ（い）	サイ	大きい災害

	Kanji	Volume	Chapter	Kun-reading	On-reading	Examples
15	害	2	10		ガイ	公害問題
16	台	2	10		ダイ、タイ	台風の被害
17	焼	2	10	や（く）、 や（ける）	ショウ	火事で家が焼けた
18	流	2	10	なが（す）、 なが（れる）	リュウ	家が流された
19	守	2	10	まも（る）	シュ	環境を守らなければならない
20	活	2	10		カツ	生活が大変だ
21	必	2	10	かなら（ず）	ヒツ	必ず来ます　必要
22	要	2	10		ヨウ	お金が必要です
23	関	2	10	せき	カン	環境問題に関心があります
24	不	2	10		フ	少し不便です
25	利	2	10		リ	便利な町です
26	最	2	10	もっと（も）	サイ	最近、空気が汚れてきた
27	景	2	10		ケイ、ケ	景気が悪い、景色
28	馬	2	10	うま	バ、マ	馬に乗る
29	将	2	10		ショウ	将来の計画
30	次	2	10	つぎ	ジ	次の問題

Japanese-English Glossary

This glossary contains all Japanese words that appear in the vocabulary lists at the end of each chapter. They are listed according to **gojuuon-jun** (Japanese alphabetical order). Each entry follows this format: word written in kana, word written in kanji, part of speech, English meaning, and chapter number where the word first appears. If the chapter number is followed by the letter P, the word is designated as passive vocabulary. If the chapter number is followed by the letter S, the word is in the Supplementary Vocabulary list in the corresponding Workbook chapter. Other abbreviations are identical to the labels used in the vocabulary lists in the chapters.

adv.	adverb	る*-v.*	る-verb	*n.*	noun	*pref.*	prefix
い*-adj.*	い-adjective	*ir. v.*	irregular verb	*loc. n.*	location noun	*suf.*	suffix
な*-adj.*	な-adjective	*conj.*	conjunction	*exp.*	expression	*part.*	particle
う*-v.*	う-verb	*interj.*	interjection	*demo.*	demonstrative	*pron.*	pronoun

CD *n.* audio CD, 7
JR *n.* JR Line, 6
OL *n.* female office worker (pronounced オーエル), 5S

あ

あいだ（間） *loc. n.* between, 6
あえる（和える） る*-v.* (to) mix, 3S
あかちゃん（赤ちゃん） *n.* baby, 9
あがる（上がる） う*-v.* (to) rise; (to)go up, 1
あく（開く） う*-v.* (for something) (to) open (*intr.*), 5
あくしゅ（握手） *vn.* handshaking, 4
あくしゅう（悪臭） *n.* foul smell, 10P
あくしゅする（握手する） *vn.* (to) shake hands, 4
あげる（揚げる） る*-v.* (to) deep-fry, 3P
あげる（上げる） る*-v.* (to) raise (something) (*tran.*), 5
あげる（上げる） る*-v.* (to) give (to a socially equal person), 7
あさくさ（浅草） *n.* old neighborhood in downtown Tokyo, 6P
あじつけ（味付け） *n.* flavoring, 3P
あたまにくる（頭に来る） *exp.* (to) get angry, 9S
あちら *demo.* that way over there; that person over there (polite), 8
あっち *demo.* that way over there; that person over there (casual), 8
あつまる（集まる） う*-v.* (to) get together; (to) gather, 5
あつめる（集める） る*-v.* (to) collect (something/someone) (*tran.*), 5
あと（後） *n.* after, 2
あなた *pron.* you (unspecific second person), 1
アパートだい（アパート代） *n.* rent, 4P, 7P
あぶら（油） *n.* oil, 3
あまりきをつかわないで下さい。（あまり気を使わないで下さい。） *exp.* Please don't put yourself out for me, 7
あめ（雨） *n.* rain; rainy, 1
あやまる（謝る） う*-v.* (to) apologize, 9
あらう（洗う） う*-v.* (to) wash, 3
あらし（嵐） *n.* storm, 1S
アラビアご（アラビア語） *n.* Arabic language, 4P
あられ *n.* hail, 1S
アルバム *n.* album, 7S
アロハシャツ *n.* Hawaiian shirt, 2P
アンケート *n.* survey, 5P
あんしょうばんごう（暗証番号） *n.* personal identification number (PIN), 4S
あんぜんな（安全な） な*-adj.* safe; secure, 10
あんない（案内） *n.* guidance, 2S
あんないしょ（案内所） *n.* information center, 2S
あんないする（案内する） *v.n.* (to) guide; (to) show, 2S

い

いいえ、そうでもありません。／いいえ、そうでもございません。 *exp.* No, it is not that good, 8
いいえ、そんなことはありません。／いいえ、そんなことはございません。 *exp.* No, that's not the case, 8
いいかげんにしてよ（いい加減にしてよ） *exp.* Give me a break. (female speech), 9
いいかげんにしろよ（いい加減にしろよ） *exp.* Give me a break. (male speech), 9
いう（言う） う*-v.* (to) say, 2
いか squid, 3S
〜いき（〜行き） *suf.* bound for 〜, 6
いじめ (act of) bullying, 9
いじめる） る*-v.* (to) bully, 9
いじわる mean behavior, 9S
いたす（致す） う*-v.* (to) do (humble), 8
いただく（頂く） う*-v.* (to)eat; (to) drink (humble), 8
いたまえ（板前） *n.* chef of Japanese cuisine, 5S
いためる（炒める） る*-v.* (to) stir-fry (cooking), 3S
いちご（苺） *n.* strawberry, 3S
いっしょうけんめい（一生懸命） *adv.* try something hard, 8P
いなびかり（稲光り） *n.* lightening, 1S
いびき *n.* snoring, 9S
いみ（意味） *n.* meaning, 3
いや *interj.* no (casual), Prelim.
いやな な*-adj.* unfavorable; unpleasant; hateful, 9
いやみ（嫌味） *n.* sarcastic remark, 9S
いらいらする *exp.* (to) get frustrated, 9S
いらっしゃる う*-v.* (to) go; (to) come; (to) return; (to) be (honorific), 8
いる（煎る） う*-v.* (to) roast, 3S
いる（要る） う*-v.* (to) need, 4
イルカ *n.* dolphin, 10S
〜いわい（祝い） *suf.* congratulatory gift for 〜, 7
いんかん（印鑑） *n.* personal stamp; seal, 4P
いんさつぶつ（印刷物） *n.* printed matter, 4S
インターネット *n.* Internet, 3

う

ううん *interj.* no (casual), Prelim.
うかがう（伺う） う*-v.* (to) visit; (to) ask (humble), 8
うけつけ（受付） *n.* receptionist desk; registration desk, 5P, 8
うける（受ける） る*-v.* (to) receive, 4
うさぎ *n.* rabbit, 10S
うし（牛） *n.* cow, 10
うすい（薄い） い*-adj.* thin, 9P
うすくちしょうゆ（薄口醤油） *n.* light soy sauce, 3P
ウスターソース *n.* Worcestershire sauce, 3S
うそ（嘘） *n.* lie, 2P, 9
うそをつく（嘘をつく） *exp.* (to) tell a lie, 2P, 9
うちをでる（家を出る） る*-v.* (to) leave home, 2
うでどけい（腕時計） *n.* wrist watch, 7
うま（馬） *n.* horse, 10
うらぎる（裏切る） う*-v.* (to) betray, 9S
うる（売る） う*-v.* (to) sell, 4P, 5
うるさい い*-adj.* noisy ; shut up!, 9
うわさ（噂） *n.* rumor, 9
うん *interj.* yes (casual), Prelim.
うんてん（運転） *n.n.* driving, 4
うんてんする（運転する） ***n.*vn.** (to) drive, 4
うんてんめんきょしょう（運転免許証） *n.* driver's license, 4

え

えいがかん（映画館） *n.* movie theater, 6
エアコン *n.* air conditioner, 3
えきべん（駅弁） *n.* box lunch sold at train station, 2P
エネルギー *n.* energy, 10S
えはがき（絵葉書） *n.* picture postcard, 2S
えび（海老） *n.* shrimp, 3P
えびだんご（海老団子） *n.* shirimp dumpling, 3P
えらぶ（選ぶ） う*-v.* (to) select, 3P, 7
エンジニア *n.* engineer, 4P, 5

お

おいでになる う*-v.* (to) come in; (to) show up (polite), 8
おいわい（お祝い） *n.* congratulatory gift, 7
おうだんほどう（横断歩道） *n.* pedestrian crossing, 6
おうぼ（応募） v*n.* application, 8S
おうぼする（応募する） v*n.* to apply, 8S
おえる（終える） る*-v.* (to) end (something) ; (to) finish (something) (*tran.*), 5
おおあめ（大雨） *n.* heavy rain, 1S
おおい（多い） い*-adj.* a lot; plentiful, 1
おおきさ（大きさ） *n.* size, 4S
おおごえ（大声） *n.* shouting; loud voice, 9S
おおどおり（大通り） *n.* wide street; major street, 6S
オーブン *n.* oven, 3S
おおや（大家） *n.* landlord; landlady, 9
おおゆき（大雪） *n.* heavy snow, 1S
おかえし（お返し） *n.* reciprocation, 7P
おかし（お菓子） *n.* candy; confection, 7
おきる（起きる） る*-v.* to take place; to happen, 10

おきをつかわせてしまいまして。（お気を使わせてしまいまして。） *exp.* I'm sorry to have caused you so much trouble, 7
おきをつかわないで下さい。（お気を使わないで下さい。） *exp.* Please do not concern me, 7
おく（奥） *loc. n.* inner part of a house or a room, 6S
おく（置く）う *-v.,* (to) place, 9
おくりもの（贈り物） *n.* gift, 7
おくる（送る）う *-v.* (to) send, 3
おくれる（遅れる）る *-v.* (to) be late, 4
おこす（起こす）う *-v.* (to) wake up (someone) (*tran.*), 5
おこす（起こす）う *-v.* to cause something to happen, 10
おこなう（行なう）う *-v.* (to) conduct, 9P
おこる（怒る）う -v., (to) get angry
おしうり（押し売り） *n.* coercive touter, 9S
おしえる（教える）る *-v.* (to) teach; (to) inform, 3
おじぎ *n.* bow, 4
おす（押す）う *-v.* (to) push, 3
おすきだとよろしいのですが。（お好きだとよろしいのですが。） *exp.* I hope you like it, 7
おせいぼ（お歳暮） *n.* end-of-year gift exchange, 7
おせっかい（お節介） *n.* officiousness; meddling, 9S
おせっかいな（お節介な）な *-adj.* officious; meddlesome, 9S
おせん（汚染） v*n.* pollution, 10P
おそい（遅い）い *-adj.* slow; late, 4
おそうしき（お葬式） *n.* funeral, 7P
オゾンそう（オゾン層） *n.* ozone layer, 10S
おたま *n.* ladle, 3S
おちゃ（お茶） *n.* green tea; tea, 7
おちゅうげん（お中元） *n.* mid-year gift exchange, 7
おっしゃる う *-v.* (to) say (honorific), 8
おと（音） *n.* sound, 9
おとしだま（お年玉） *n.* money given to children on New Year's Days, 7P
おとしより（お年より） *n.* senior citizen, 10
おとす（落とす）う *-v.* (to) drop, 4
おどす（脅す）う *-v.* (to) threaten, 9S, 10S
おとをたてる（音を立てる） *exp.* (to) make noise, 9
おなくなりになる（お亡くなりになる）う *-v.* (to) die, 8S
おなじ（同じ）な *adj.* same, 2P, 5
おなら fart, 9S
おねがい（お願い） *n.* favor; wish, 3
おひゃくしょう（お百姓） *n.* farmer, 5S
おふたりのおしあわせをおいのりします（お二人のお幸せをお祈りします） *exp.* Wishing for your happiness, 7P
おぼえる（覚える）る *-v.* (to) memorize; (to) remember, 3
おみまい（お見舞い） *n.* gift for sympathy, 7
おみやげ（お土産） *n.* souvenir, 2
おめしになる（お召しになる）う *-v.* (to) put on/wear, 8S
おめでとうございます。） *exp.* congratulations, 7
おめにかかる（お目にかかる）う *-v.* (to) meet (humble), 8
おめにかける（お目にかける）る *-v.* (to) show (humble), 8
おもう（思う）う *-v.* (to) think; (to) feel, 2
おもさ（重さ） *n.* weight, 4S
おもちゃ *n.* toy, 7
おや（親） *n.* parent, 9
おやすみになる（お休みになる）う *-v.* (to) sleep (honorific), 8
おゆ（お湯） *n.* hot water, 3P, 5
おりる（降りる）る *-v.* (to) get off, 6
おる う *-v.* (to) exist; (to) be (humble), 8
おれい（お礼） *n.* thank-you gift, 7
おれいにとおもいまして。（お礼にと思いまして。） *exp.* I though it would make a token of appreciation, 7
おんし（恩師） *n.* former teacher and major professor, 7P
オンス *n.* ounce, 3P
おんせん（温泉） *n.* hot spring, 2S
おんだんか（温暖化） *n.* warming, 10P
おんど（温度） *n.* temperature, 1S

か

か（蚊） *n.* mosquito, 10S
カード *n.* card, 7
カーネーション *n.* carnation, 7
かいがい（海外） *n.* overseas, 2
かいがいりょこう（海外旅行） *n.* overseas travel, 2
かいぎ（会議） *n.* meeting, 8
かいけいし（会計士） *n.* accountant, 5
がいこく（外国） *n.* overseas; foreign country, 2
がいこくかわせ（外国為替） *n.* foreign currency exchange, 4P
がいこくじん（外国人） *n.* foreigner, 4
がいこくじんとうろくしょう（外国人登録証） *n.* Alien registration, 4
かいしゃいん（会社員） *n.* businessman; company man, 5S
かいしゃせつめいかい（会社説明会） *n.* information session organized by company for new recruits, 8S

かいしゃまわり（会社回り）*n.* college seniors going to different companies, 8P
かいじょう（会場）*n.* place of meeting, 5
かいそく（快速）*n.* express train (no additional cost), 6S
ガイド *n.* guide, 2S
ガイドブック *n.* guidebook, 2
かいめん（海面）*n.* the surface of the sea, 10P
かいわ（会話）*n.* conversation, 4
かう（飼う）う*-v.* (to) keep (a pet), 4
かえす（返す）う*-v.* (to) return something, 3
かえる（替える／変える）る*-v.* (to) change, 4
かえる（蛙）*n.* frog, 10S
がか（画家）*n.* painter, 10P
かがくやくひん（科学薬品）*n.* chemical substance, 10S
かかる う*-v.* (to) take (time or money), 4
かかる う*-v.* (for a telephone) (to) ring, 5
かぎ（鍵）*n.* key; lock, 4
かぎかっこ square bracket, 2P
かきとめ（書留）*n.* registered mail, 4S
かきまぜる（かきまぜる）る*-v.* (to) mix thoroughly, 3S
かくえきていしゃ（各駅停車）*n.* local train, 6
がくせいしょう（学生証）*n.* student identification, 4
がくわり（学割）*n.* student discount, 6P
かける る*-v.* (to) pour, 3P
かける る*-v.* (to) lock, 4
かける る*-v.* (to) take time (*tran.*), 5S
かさなる（重なる）う*-v.* (to) overlap, 6P
かし（華氏）*n.* Fahrenheit, 1P
かじ（家事）*n.* household work, 5P
かじ（火事）*n.* fire, 10
かしこまりました。*exp.* Certainly. (Polite language used by waiters, clerks, etc..), 7P
かしゅ（歌手）*n.* singer, 5S
かす（貸す）う*-v.* (to) lend, 3
かず（数）*n.* number, 10
かぜ（風）*n.* wind, 1
ガソリン *n.* gasoline, , Prelim. S, 3P
ガソリンスタンド *n.* gas station, 6
〜かた（〜方）*suf.* how to 〜; way of 〜, 3
かたづける（片付ける）る*-v.* (to) clean up; to organize, 9
かちょう（課長）*n.* section chief, 8
がっき（学期）*n.* semester; quarter, 2P, 4
カップ *n.* measuring cup, 3P
かど（角）*n.* corner, 6
かねづつみ（金包み）*n.* money wrapped in paper as a gift, 7S
かのじょ（彼女）*n.* girl friend; sweet heart; she, 5P
かびん（花瓶）*n.* vase, 7S
かふんしょう（花粉症）*n.* hay fever, , Prelim. S
かべ（壁）*n.* wall, 1P, 9
かみ（紙）*n.* paper, 10P
かみなり（雷）*n.* thunder, 1S
カメラ *n.* camera, 2
かもくとうろく（課目登録）*n.* course registration, 3P, 4P
からかう う*-v.* (to) tease, 9
かりる（借りる）る*-v.* (to) borrow, 3
カレーこ（カレー粉）*n.* curry powder, 3P
かろう（過労）*n.* stress; excessive fatigue, , Prelim. S
かわ（川）*n.* river, 6
〜がわ（〜側）*suf.* side, 6
かわかす（乾かす）う*-v.* (to) dry (something) (*tran.*), 5S
かわく（乾く）う*-v.* (for something/someone) (to) dry (*intr.*), 5S
かわる（変わる／替わる）う*-v.* (for something) (to) change (*intr.*), 5
かん（缶）*n.* can, 10P
かんがえる（考える）る*-v.* (to) think intellectually; (to) take (something) into consideration, 4P, 5
カンガルー *n.* kangaroo, 10S
かんきょう（環境）*n.* environment, 10
かんけい（関係）*n.* relationship, 9
かんこう（観光）*vn.* sightseeing, 2
かんこうきゃく（観光客）*n.* tourist, 2S
かんこうち（観光地）*n.* sightseeing spot, 2S
かんこうバス（観光バス）*n.* chartered bus for sightseeing, 2
かんこうりょこう（観光旅行）*n.* sightseeing trip, 2
かんこうをする（観光をする）*vn.* to go sightseeing, 2
かんじゃ（患者）*n.* patient, 4P
かんしん（関心）*n.* interest, 10
かんづめ（缶詰）*n.* canned food, 7S
かんとう（関東）*n.* Kanto Region, 1P
がんばる（頑張る）う*-v.* (to) do one's best, 5P
かんぶつ（乾物）*n.* dried food, 7S
かんべんしてほしい（勘弁してほしい）*exp.* (to) want something to be stopped, 9S
かんめん（干麺）*n.* dried noodles, 7P

き

き（木）*n.* tree, 1
きあつ（気圧）*n.* air pressure, 1S
きえる（消える）る*-v.* (for something) (to) go out; (to) go off (*intr.*), 5
きおん（気温）*n.* air temperature, 1

きかい（機械）*n.* machine, 3
きがつかなくて。（気が付かなくて）*exp.* I did not realize it, 9
きくらげ dried cloud ear mushroom, 3P
きこう（気候）*n.* climate, 1
きこえる（聞こえる）る*-v.* to be able to hear (*intr.*), 10
きじ（記事）*n.* article (newspapers and magazines), 1P
きそく（規則）*n.* rule, 4
きた（北）*n.* north, 1
きたぐち（北口）*n.* north entrance, 6S
きたない（汚い）い*-adj.* dirty, 1P, 9
きって（切手）*n.* postal stamp, 4
きつね（狐）*n.* fox, 10S
きっぷ（切符）*n.* ticket, 2
きっぷをよやくする（切符を予約する）*vn.* (to) reserve a ticket, 2
きにゅうする（記入する）*vn.* (to) fill out an application, 4
きびしい（厳しい）い*-adj.* strict, 4P
きぼう（希望）*n.* hope, 8S
きまる（決まる）う*-v.* (for something) (to) be decided (*intr.*), 5
きめる（決める）る*-v.* (to) decide on (something) (*tran.*), 5
きもち（気持ち）*n.* feeling, 9
きゃく（客）*n.* customer; guest, , Prelim. S, 4P, 8
キャッシュカード *n.* cash card for ATM, 4P
きゅうか（休暇）*n.* vacation, 8S
きゅうきゅうしゃ（救急車）*n.* ambulance, 10
きゅうこう(れっしゃ) *n.*（急行(列車)）*n.* express train, 6
きゅうしゅう（九州）*n.* Kyushu Island, 1P
ぎゅうにく（牛肉）*n.* beef, 3
ぎゅうにゅう *n.* milk, 10P
きゅうり（胡瓜）*n.* cucumber, 3S
きゅうりょう（給料）*n.* salary; wage, 5
きょうし（教師）*n.* teacher; instructor, 5S
きょうじゅ（教授）*n.* professor, 5S
きらす（切らす）う*-v.* (to) run out of (something) (*tran.*), 5S
きり（霧）*n.* fog, 1S
キリン *n.* giraffe, 10S
きる（切る）う*-v.* (to) cut, 3
きれる（切れる）る*-v.* (for something) (to) be cut (*intr.*), 5S
〜キロ *suf.* kilo (kilogram or kilometer), 4
きをつける（気をつける）*exp.* (to) pay attention; (to) watch out, 9
きんき（近畿）*n.* Kinki Region, 1P
ぎんこういん（銀行員）*n.* bank employee, 5S
ぎんこうふりこみ（銀行振込）*n.* wire transfer of funds, 4P
ぎんざせん（銀座線）*n.* the oldest subway line in Japan, 6P
きんじょ（近所）*n.* neighborhood, 9
きんむ（勤務）*vn.* work; duty, 8S
きんむする（勤務する）*vn.* to work, 8S

く

くうき（空気）*n.* air, 10
くうこう（空港）*n.* airport, 2
くじら（鯨）*n.* whale, 10
くだもの（果物）*n.* fruit, 7
くちべに（口紅）*n.* lipstick, 7S
クッキー *n.* cookies, 7
くま（熊）*n.* bear, 10
くも（雲）*n.* cloud, 1
くもり（曇り）*n.* cloudy, 1
くもる（曇る）う*-v.* (to) become cloudy, 1
くやくしょ（区役所）*n.* Ward office, 6S
グラム *n.* gram, 3P
グリーンしゃ（グリーン車）*n.* first class car of a train, 6S
クリスマス *n.* Christmas, 7
クルーズ *n.* cruise, 2S
クレジットカード *n.* credit card, 2
くれる る*-v.* (to) give (to a socially equal or inferior in-group person), 7
くわえる（加える）る*-v.* (to) add, 3S

け

けいかく（計画）*n.* plan, 2
けいき（景気）*n.* economic conditions; business, 10
けいけん（経験）*n.* experience, 8
けいけんしゃ（経験者）*n.* person with experience, 8P
けいさつ（警察）*n.* police, 10
けいさつかん（警察官）*n.* police officer, 5S
げいじゅつか（芸術家）*n.* artist, 5S
けいせいせん（京成線）*n.* a private line connecting Tokyo and Narita Airport, 6P
けしき（景色）*n.* scenery, 2S
けしきがいい（景色がいい）*n.* nice scenery, 2S
けしょうひん（化粧品）*n.* cosmetics, 7S
けむり（煙）*n.* smoke, 10S
けれども *conj.* however, 2
けんきゅう（研究）*vn.* research 5
けんきゅういん（研究員）*n.* researcher, 5S
けんきゅうする（研究する）*vn.* (to) do research, 5

げんきんかきとめ（現金書留）*n.* registered mail for cash, 4S
けんこうほけん（健康保険）*n.* health insurance, 4P
けんしゅう（研修）*n.* training, 8S
げんせいりん（原生林）*n.* old-growth forest, 10S
けんちくか（建築家）*n.* architect, 5S

こ

こ（子）*n.* child　こ is usually preceded by a modifier, 9
こ〜（子〜 *pref.* baby 〜 こいぬ(子犬) puppy　こねこ(子猫) kitten, 7
コアラ koala, 10S
こういん（工員）*n.* factory worker, 5S
こうえん（講演）*n.* lecture, 8P
こうがい（公害）*n.* industrial pollution, 10
こうくうびん（航空便）*n.* airmail, 4
こうこく（広告）*n.* advertisement, 8
こうざ（口座）*n.* account (bank), 4
こうさてん（交差点）*n.* intersection, 6
こうじょう（工場）*n.* factory, 10
こうすい（香水）*n.* perfume, 7S
こうずい（洪水）*n.* flood, 1S, 10
こうすいりょう（降水量）*n.* amount of precipitation, 1S
こうどう（行動）*n.* action; activity, 2P
ごうとう（強盗）*n.* robbery, 10S
こうぼ（公募）*n.* open search, 8S
こうむいん（公務員）*n.* public office employee, 5S
こえ（声）*n.* voice, 4
コース *n.* course, 4
コーヒーカップ *n.* coffee cup; mug, 7
コーヒーメーカー coffee maker, 7S
コーンスターチ *n.* corn starch, 3S
ごかつやくをおいのりします（ご活躍をお祈りします）*exp.* Wishing for your success, 7P
こぎって（小切手）*n.* check (not for personal use), 4S
ごきぶり cockroach, 10S
こくさい（国際）*n.* international, 3P, 9P
こくさいでんわ（国際電話）*n.* international call, 3P
ごけっこんおめでとうございます（ご結婚おめでとうございます）*exp.* Congratulations on your marriage, 7P
こさめ（小雨）*n.* light rain, 1S
ござる う*-v.* (to) exist (polite verb for ある and いる), 8
こしょう（胡椒）*n.* pepper, 3
ごぞんじ（ご存じ）*n.* (to) know (honorific), 8
こたえる（答える）る*-v.* (to) answer, 2
こちらがわ（こちら側）*loc. n.* this side, 6
こづつみ（小包）*n.* postal parcel, 4
ことば（言葉）*n.* language; words; expressions, 2
このは（木の葉）*n.* tree leaves, 1
このへん（この辺）*exp.* this area, 6
コピーき（コピー機）*n.* copying machine, 3
コピーセンター *n.* copy center, 3P
ごみ／ゴミ *n.* trash; garbage (ごみ is written either in hiragana or in katakana.), 9
ごみだし／ゴミだし（ごみ出し／ゴミ出し）*n.* putting out the trash, 9
こむぎこ（小麦粉）*n.* flour, 3S
ごめいわくおかけしてもうしわけありません（ご迷惑おかけして申しわけありません）*exp.* I'm sorry to cause you problems, 9
ごめん。（ご免。）*exp.* I am sorry. (used in casual speech), 3
ごめんなさい（ご免なさい。）*exp.* I am sorry, 3
こようせいど（雇用制度）*n.* employment system, 8S
ごらんになる（ご覧になる）う*-v.* (to) look at (honorific), 8
ゴリラ *n.* gorilla, 10S
ころす（殺す）う*-v.* to kill; to murder, 2P, 10
こわい（怖い）い*-adj.* fearful; frightened, 10
こわす（壊す）う*-v.* (to) break (something) (*tran.*), 5S, 9
こわれる（壊れる）る*-v.* (for something) (to) break (*intr.*), 3P, 5S
コンサルタント *n.* consultant, 5S
こんしんかい（懇親会）*n.* get-together party, 5P

さ

〜さ *suf.* suffix to convert adjective to a noun for measurement, 7
サービス *n.* service, 4
サーフィン *n.* surfing, 2P
サーフボード *n.* surf board, 2P
さいがい（災害）*n.* disaster, 10
さいきん（最近）*n.* recent; current, 1P, 10
さいこうきおん（最高気温）*n.* highest temperature, 1P
さいごに（最後に（*conj.* lastly; at last, 3
さいていきおん（最低気温）*n.* lowest temperature, 1P
さいふ（財布）*n.* wallet; purse, 5
ざいりょう（材料）*n.* material; ingredient, 3
サイン signature; autograph, 4
さがす（探す／捜す）う*-v.* (to) look for〜, 2
さがる（下がる）う *v.* (to) fall; (to) go down, 1
さき（先）*loc. n.* ahead; beyond, 6
さぎ（詐欺）*n.* swindle; con game, 10S

く）う -v. (to) bloom, 1
ん（作文）*n.* composition, 3
さ（酒）*n.* liquor; alcoholic beverage; Japanese rice wine, 7
さげる（下げる）る-*v.* (to) lower (something) (*tran.*), 5S
さしあげる（差し上げる）る-*v.* (to) give (to a socially superior out-group person), 7
さつじん（殺人）*n.* murder, 10S
さとう（砂糖）*n.* sugar, 3
さます（冷ます）う-*v.* (to) let (something) cool, 3S
さやえんどう（さやえんどう）*n.* snow pea, 3S
さら（皿）*n.* plate, 3
サラダオイル *n.* vegetable oil (lit. salad oil), 3S, 7P
サラリーマン *n.* white collar worker, 5S
さる（猿）*n.* monkey, 10
ざる *n.* strainer, 3S
さわぐ（騒ぐ）う-*v.* (to) make noise, 9
さんいん（山陰）*n.* San'in Region, 1P
ざんぎょう（残業）*n.* over time, 8S
さんぎょうはいきぶつ（産業廃棄物）*n.* industrial waste, 10S
サングラス *n.* sun glasses, 1P, 7S
さんせいう（酸性雨）*n.* acid rain, 10S
サンプル *n.* sample, 4P
さんぽ（散歩）*vn.* a walk; stroll, 9
さんぽする（散歩する）*vn.* (to) take a walk, 9
さんぽをする（散歩をする）*vn.* (to) take a walk, 9
さんよう（山陽）*n.* Sanyo Region, 1P

し

シェフ *n.* chef, 4P
しお（塩）*n.* salt, 3
しか（鹿）*n.* deer, 10
しかる（叱る）う-*v.* (to) scold, 9
しき（式）*n.* ceremony, 5
しこく（四国）*n.* Shikoku Island, 1P
じさつ（自殺）*n.* suicide, 9P
ししゃ（支社）*n.* company branch, 5P, 8S
じしん（地震）*n.* earthquake, 5P, 10
しぜん（自然）*n.* nature, 10
しちめんちょう（七面鳥）*n.* turkey, 10S
しっている（知っている）る-*v.* (to) know, 2
しつど（湿度）*n.* humidity, 1S
しつもん（質問）*n.* question, 2
しつれいしました。（失礼しました。）*exp.* Excuse me, 2P
しつれいな（失礼）な-*adj.* rude, 9S
していせき（指定席）*n.* reserved seat, 6P
じどうはんばいき（自動販売機）*n.* vending machine, 3
じどうひきおとし（自動引き落とし）*n.* automatic deduction of bills, 4P
じどうひきだしき（自動引き出し機）*n.* ATM machine, 4P
じどうふりこみき（自動振込機）*n.* automatic money transfer machine, 4P
しばかり（芝刈り）*n.* lawn mowing, 9S
じばんちんか（地盤沈下）*n.* ground sinkage, 10P
じぶん（自分）*n.* oneself, 5P
しぼう（志望）*n.* wish, 8S
しま（島）*n.* island, 1P
しまる（閉まる）う-*v.* (for something) (to) close (*intr.*), 5
じむいん（事務員）*n.* business clerk, 5S
しめる（閉める）る-*v.* (to) close something, 4
しゃいん（社員）*n.* employee, 4P
しゃいんけんしゅう（社員研修）*n.* training for company employees, 8S
しゃかい（社会）*n.* society, 10
じゃがいも *n.* potato, 3
しやくしょ（市役所）*n.* City Hall, 6
しゃたく（社宅）*n.* company apartment, 8S
しゃちょう（社長）*n.* company president, 5
ジャム *n.* jam, 3S
しゃもじ *n.* rice spatula, 3S
シャワーつき（シャワー付き）*n.* equipped with shower, 2S
じゆう（自由）*n.* freedom, 2P, 5P
しゅうきょう（宗教）*n.* religion, 7P
じゆうこうどう（自由行動）*n.* free time; free activity, 2P
しゅうしょく（就職）*vn.* getting a job, 5
しゅうしょくかつどう（就職活動）*n.* job hunt, 8S
しゅうしょくぐち（就職口）*n.* employment possibility, 8S
しゅうしょくさき（就職先）*n.* company or organization to be employed at, 8S
しゅうしょくする（就職する）*vn.* (to) get a job at 〜, 5
しゅうしんこよう（終身雇用）*n.* life-time employment, 5P
じゆうせき（自由席）*n.* non-reserved seat, 6P
じゅうだいな（重大な）な-*adj.* important; critical, 10P
じゆうな（自由な）な-*adj.* free, 5P
しゅうゆうけん（周遊券）*n.* ticket which allows a passenger to travel freely in a certain area, 2P, 6P

じゅぎょうりょう（授業料）*n.* tuition; fee for instruction, 4
しゅっちょう（出張）*vn.* business trip, 8
しゅっちょうする（出張する）*vn.* to go on a business trip, 8
しゅと（首都）*n.* capital city, 5P
じゅんび（準備）*vn.* preparation, 2S, 5
じゅんびする（準備する）*vn.* (to) prepare, 2S, 5
しょうエネ（省エネ）*n.* energy conservation; energy efficiency, 10S
しょうかく（昇格）*n.* promotion, 8S
しょうがくきん（奨学金）*n.* scholarship, 4P
しょうきゃくじょう（焼却場）*n.* trash incineration facility, 10P
じょうけん（条件）*n.* condition; qualification, 4P, 8P
しょうさい（詳細）*n.* details, 8P
じょうし（上司）*n.* one's boss/superior in work place, 7P, 8
じょうしゃぐち（乗車口）*n.* entrance to get on train/bus, 6S
しょうしょう（少々）*exp.* a little bit (cooking), 3P
しょうせつ（小説）*n.* novel, 7
しょうたい（招待）*vn.* invitation , 5
しょうたいじょう（招待状）*n.* invitation letter or card, 5
しょうたいする（招待する）*vn.* (to) invite, 5
じょうだんじゃない(わ)よ（冗談じゃないよ）*exp.* You've got to be kidding, 9
しょうひんけん（商品券）*n.* gift certificate, 7
しょうぼうし（消防士）*n.* firefighter, 5S
しょうゆ（しょう油）*n.* soy sauce, 3
しょうよ（賞与）*n.* semiannual bonus, 8S
しょうらい（将来）*n.* future, 5
しょくちゅうどく（食中毒）*n.* food poisoning, Prelim.
しょくパン（食パン）*n.* sliced bread, 3P
しょくぶつ（植物）*n.* plants, 7P
じょせい（女性）*n.* female (a formal word for おんなのひと（女の人）) *n*, 5P
しょっき（食器）*n.* tableware, 7S
しょるい（書類）*n.* document, 8
しらべる（調べる）る*-v.* (to) check; (to) investigate; (to)explore, 2
しりあい（知り合い）*n.* acquaintance, 4P, 9
しる（知る）う*-v.* (to) come to know, 2
シングル single, 2P
しんごう（信号）*n.* traffic signal, 6
しんじょうしょ（身上書）*n.* personal information form, 8S
しんにゅうしゃいん（新入社員）*n.* new recruits, 8S
しんぱい（心配）*vn.* worry, 9
しんぱいする（心配する）*vn.* (to) worry, 9
しんりん（森林）*n.* forest, 10S

す

す（酢）*n.* vinegar, 3S
すいい（水位）*n.* water level, 10P
すいしつ（水質）*n.* water quality, 10P
すいせんじょう（推薦状）*n.* letter of reference, 8
スイッチ switch, 3
すいはんき（炊飯器）*n.* rice cooker, 3S
すうじ（数字）*n.* number, 3P
スーツケース *n.* suitcase, 2
すぐ（*adv.* soon; shortly, 6
すくない（少ない）い*-adj.* a little; scarce, 1
スタイリスト *n.* stylist, 4P
スチュワーデス flight attendant, 5S
すてる（捨てる）る*-v.* (to) discard; (to) abandon, 9
スニーカー *n.* sneakers; sport shoes, 7
スパイス *n.* spice, 3S
すばらしいいちねんであることをおいのりします（素晴しい一年であることをお祈りします）*exp.* I hope you will have a wonderful year, 7P
スピーチコンテスト *n.* speech contest, 3P
スライスチーズ *n.* sliced cheese, 3P

せ

せいかつほご（生活保護）*n.* welfare, 10S
ぜいきん（税金）*n.* tax, 5P
せいじか（政治家）*n.* politician, 5S
せいしゃいん（正社員）*n.* permanent staff, 8P
せいせき（成績）*n.* grades, 4, 3P
せいりけん（整理券）*n.* ticket indicating where a passenger gets on a bus, 6S
せかい（世界）*n.* world, 9P, 10
せっけん（石鹸）*n.* soap, 7
せっし（摂氏）*n.* Celsius, 1P
せっとう（窃盗）*n.* theft, 10S
せつめい（説明）*vn.* explanation, 8
せつめいかい（説明会）*n.* information session, 8S
せつめいする（説明する）*vn.* to explain, 8
ゼミ *n.* seminar, 5P
せわ（世話）*n.* care, 5P
せわになる（世話になる）*exp.* (to) be cared by somebody, 7
〜せん（〜線）*suf.* 〜 Line (train line), 6
せんざい（洗剤）*n.* detergent, 7P
せんたくき（洗濯機）*n.* washing machine, 3P

ぜんぶ（全部） *n.* all, 7P
せんもん（専門） *n.* field of specialty, 8

そ

そう な*-adj.* look like; appear; seem, 1
ぞう（象） *n.* elephant, 10
そういえば *exp.* speaking of that, 4
そうおん（騒音） *n.* noise, 10P
そうじき（掃除機） *n.* vacuum cleaner, 3P
そうだん（相談） *vn.* consultation, 5
そうだんする（相談する） *vn.* (to) consult;(to) discuss, 5
そくたつ（速達） *n.* express mail, special delivery, 4S
ソース sauce, 3S
ソーセージ sausages, 7P
そだいごみ（粗大ごみ） *n.* large trash, 9P
そちら *demo.* that way; that person (polite), 8
そっち *demo.* that way; that person (casual), 8
そのあいだ(に)（その間(に)（*conj.* during that time, 2
そのあと(で)（その後(で)（*conj.* after that, 2
そのとき(に)（その時(に)（*conj.* at that time, 2
そのまえ(に)（その前(に)（*conj.* before that, 2
そら（空） *n.* sky, 1
それで（*conj.* then; so, 2
ぞんじておる（存じておる） う*-v.* (to) know (humble), 8
ぞんじる（存じる） る*-v.* (to) know (humble), 8
そんなしんぱいしないでください。（そんな心配しないで下さい。） *exp.* Please do not worry about me, 7

た

たいきおせん（大気汚染） *n.* air pollution, 10S
だいきぎょう（大企業） *n.* large corporation, 5P
たいぐう（待遇） *n.* terms of employment such as salary, raise, vacation, insurance, etc, 8S
たいしかん（大使館） *n.* embassy, 6
たいしたものじゃありませんから。（たいした物じゃありませんから。） *exp.* It is of little value, 7
だいじな（大事な） な*-adj.* important, 8
たいせつな（大切な） な*-adj.* important; precious, 4P, 7
だいどころ（台所） *n.* kitchen, 7P
たいふう（台風） *n.* typhoon, 1
たいへいよう（太平洋） *n.* the Pacific Ocean, 1P
たいへいようがわ（太平洋側） *n.* Pacific ocean side (east side) of Japan, 1S
たおす（倒す） う*-v.* (to) knock down (something) (*tran.*), 5S
タオル *n.* towel, 7
たおれる（倒れる ） る*-v.* (for something) (to) fall (*intr.*), 5S
だから（*conj.* so, 2
たく（炊く） う*-v.* (to) cook rice, 3
タクシー taxi, 6
タクシーのりば（タクシー乗り場） *n.* taxi stand, 6S
たくはいサービス（宅配サービス） *n.* parcel delivery service, 4
たくはいびん（宅配便） *n.* parcel delivery service, 4P
だけど *conj.* but, 2
たこ *n.* octopus, 3S
タコス *n.* taco, 2P
だし *n.* broth, 3P
たす（足す） う*-v.* (to) add, 3
たずねる（訪ねる） る*-v.* (to) visit, 8
たっきゅうびん（宅急便） *n.* parcel delivery, 4
たつまき（竜巻） *n.* tornado, 1S, 10S
たてる（建てる／立てる)） る*-v.* (to) to build; (to) establish; (to) make, 2
たとえば（例えば） *conj.* for example, 4
たぬき raccoon, 10S
たのむ（頼む） う*-v.* (to) ask (request), 3
ダブル double, 2P
たまねぎ（玉ねぎ） *n.* onion, 3
たまらない い*-adj.* cannot stand; unbearable, 9
ターミナル *n.* terminal, 6
だめな な*-adj.* no good; useless, 4
だんご（団子） *n.* (edible) ball, 3P
ダンサー *n.* dancer, 4P
だんせい（男性） *n.* male (a formal word for おとこのひと（男の人)） *n,* 5P

ち

チェック *n.* personal check, 4S
ちかい（近い） い*-adj.* close to; near, 6
ちがい（違い） *n.* difference, 4P
ちがう（違う） う*-v.* (to) be different (*intr.*), 1P, 5
ちかてつ（地下鉄） *n.* subway, 6
ちかどう（地下道） *n.* under-path, 6P
ちきゅう（地球） *n.* the earth, 10
チケット ticket, 7S
ちず（地図） *n.* map, 1P, 2
ちちのひ（父の日） *n.* Father's day, 7
ちゃわん（茶碗） *n.* bowl, 3S
ちゅうい（注意） *vn.* attention; warning, 9
ちゅういする（注意する） *vn.* (to) warn; (to) call attention to, 9
ちゅうおうせん（中央線） *n.* JR Chuo-line, 6P

ちゅうおん（中温） *n.* medium temperature (cooking), 3P
ちゅうじえん（中耳炎） *n.* ear infection, Prelim. S
ちゅうしゃじょう（駐車場） *n.* parking lot; parking garage, 6
ちゅうしょうきぎょう（中小企業） *n.* small business, 5P
ちゅうしょく（昼食） *n.* lunch, 2S
ちゅうしょくつき（昼食付き） *n.* lunch included, 2S
ちゅうせいぶ（中西部） *n.* Midwest region (USA), 1S
ちょうしょく（朝食） *n.* breakfast, 2S
ちょうりし（調理師） *n.* chef; cook, 5S
ちょきん（貯金） vn. savings (money), 4
ちょきんする（貯金する） vn. (to) save money, 4
チョコレート *n.* chocolate, 7
チンパンジー *n.* chimpanzee, 10S

つ

ツアー *n.* tour, 2
つうきん（通勤） *n.* commuting, 8S
つかう（使う） う-*v.* (to) use, 1P, 2
〜つき（〜付き） *suf.* 〜included; equipped with 〜, 2S
つぎ（次） *n.* next, 6
つきあたり（突き当たり） *n.* dead end, 6
つぎに（次に） *conj.* next, 2, 3
つきまとう う-*v.* (to) follow a person about, 9S
つく（着く） う-*v.* (to) arrive, 2
つく う-*v.* (to) tell (a lie), 2P
つく（付く） う-*v.* (for something) (to) turn on (*intr.*), 5
つける（付ける） る-*v.* (to) attach; (to) turn on; (to) apply (medicine), 3
つける（付ける） る-*v.* (to) write (a diary), 9
つづく（続く） う-*v.* (for something) (to) continue (*intr.*), 1P, 5
つづける（続ける） る-*v.* (to) continue (something) (*tran.*), 5
つつみがみ（包み紙） *n.* wrapping paper, 7S
つなみ（津波） *n.* tsunami; tidal wave, 1S, 10S
つまらない い-*adj.* uninteresting; boring, 7
〜つめ（〜つ目） *suf.* ordinal numbers, 6
つめたい（冷たい） い-*adj.* cold, 1
つもり intention, 2
つゆ（梅雨） *n.* rainy season, 1P
つよい（強い） い-*adj.* strong, 1
つれていく（連れて行く） う-*v.* (to) take (someone), 3
つれてくる（連れて来る） *ir.* v. (to) bring (someone), 3

て

で *part.* limit, 6
ていきけん（定期券） *n.* train/bus path for commuters, 6P
テクノロジー *n.* technology, 3
でござる う-*v.* (to) be (polite verb for です), 7P, 8
ですから *conj.* so; therefore, 2
てつだう（手伝う） う-*v.* (to) help; (to) assist, 3
てまえ（手前） *loc. n.* this side; just before, 6
でる（出る） る-*v.* (to) come out; (to) leave, 2
テレビゲーム *n.* TV game, 7S
テレフォンカード *n.* pre-paid telephone card, 3
てんいん（店員） *n.* store clerk, prelim. S 7
てんき（天気） *n.* weather, 1
でんき（電気） *n.* light; electricity, 3
てんきず（天気図） *n.* weather map, 1S
てんきよほう（天気予報） *n.* weather forecast, 1
でんしメール（電子メール） *n.* electric mail, 3
でんしレンジ（電子レンジ） *n.* microwave oven, 3S

と

〜ど（〜度） count, degree, 1
というのは *conj.* it's because, 2
〜といえば *exp.* If you say 〜; it is..., 4
〜とう（〜島） *suf.* 〜island, 2P
どうき（同期） *n.* people who join in the same year, 8S
とうきょうえき（東京駅） *n.* Tokyo Station, 6P
どうそうかい（同窓会） *n.* reunion party, 5
とうふ（豆腐） *n.* tofu, 7P
どうぶつ（動物） *n.* animal, 7P, 10
とうほく（東北） *n.* Tohoku Region, 1P
どうりょう（同僚） *n.* colleague, 8
どうろ（道路） *n.* road; street, 6
とおい（遠い） い-*adj.* far from, 6
とおす（通す） う-*v.* (to) put (something) through (*tran.*), 5S
〜とおもいます（〜と思います） *exp.* I think that 〜, prelim. S
とおる（通る） う-*v.* (for something/someone) (to) go through (*intr.*), 5S, 6
とかす（解かす） う-*v.* (to) thaw, 3S
とかす（溶かす） う-*v.* (to) melt (something) (*tran.*), 5S
どくしんりょう（独身寮） *n.* dormitory for singles, 8S
とくに（特に） *adv.* particularly; especially, 2
とける（溶ける） る-*v.* (for something) (to) melt (*intr.*), 5S
ところで *conj.* by the way, 2
とし（年） *n.* age; year, prelim. S, 5
としうえ（年上） *n.* older person, 9
とした（年下） *n.* younger, 9
どしゃぶり downpour of rain, 1S

どじょうおせん（土壌汚染） *n.* soil pollution, 10P
としょけん（図書券） *n.* gift certificate for books, 7S
としをとる（年を取る） *exp.* (to) become old, 5
とちょう（都庁） *n.* Tokyo city office located in Shinjuku, 6P
とっきゅう（れっしゃ） *n.*（特急(列車)） *n.* limited express train, 6
とまる（泊まる） う*-v.* (to) stay, 2
とまる（止まる） う*-v.* (for someone/something) (to) stop, 6
とめる（止める） る*-v.* (to) stop (something), 6
とら（虎） *n.* tiger, 10
トラブル *n.* trouble, 2P
トラベラーズチェック traveler's check, 2P
とり（鳥） *n.* bird, 10
とりにく（鳥肉） *n.* chicken meat, 3
ドレス dress, 7
ドレッシング *n.* dressing, 3P
どろぼう（泥棒） *n.* thief, 9
とんでもありません。（とんでもございません。） *exp.* It is not at all the case, 8

な

ナイフ *n.* knife, 3
ないよう（内容） *n.* content, 2P, 8S
なおす（直す） う*-v.* (to) fix; (to) repair (something) (*tran.*), 5
なおす（直す） う*-v.* (to) fix; (to) correct, 9
なおる（直る） う*-v.* (for something)(to) heal; to be fixed (*intr.*), 5
なか（仲） *n.* relationship among people, 7P, 9
ながさ（長さ） *n.* length, 4S
ながす（流す） う*-v.* (to) let (something) flow (*tran.*), 5S
ながす（流す） う*-v.* to pour; to let something flow, 10
ながでんわ（長電話） *n.* talking on the phone for a long time, 9S
なかまはずれ（仲間外れ） *n.* someone which is kept out of a group, 9S
ながれる（流れる） る*-v.* (for something) (to) flow (*intr.*), 5S
なくす う*-v.* (to) lose; (to) make something disappear, 10
なくなる う*-v.* to disappear, 10
なぐる（殴る） う*-v.* (to) hit someone, 9S
なさる う*-v.* (to) do (honorific), 8
なべ（鍋） *n.* pot, 3
なやむ（悩む） う*-v.* (to) be troubled, 9S
ならう（習う） う*-v.* (to) learn, 8
ならぶ（並ぶ） う*-v.* (for something/someone) (to) line up (*intr.*), 5S
ならべる（並べる） る*-v.* (to) line (something) up (*tran.*), 5S
なんせい（南西） *n.* southwest, 1
なんせいぶ（南西部） *n.* Southwest region, 1S
なんとう（南東） *n.* southeast, 1
なんぶ（南部） *n.* South region, 1S

に

にげる（逃げる） る*-v.* (to) escape, 10
にさんかたんそ（二酸化炭素） *n.* carbon dioxide, 10P
にし（西） *n.* west, 1
にじ（虹） *n.* rainbow, 1S
にしかいがん（西海岸） *n.* West coast region, 1S
にしぐち（西口） *n.* west exit of a station, 6P
〜についてなんですが *exp.* it's about 〜, 2
〜についてなんですけど *exp.* it's about 〜, 2
にっき（日記） *n.* diary, 9
にほんかい（日本海） *n.* the Japan Sea, 1P
にほんかいがわ（日本海側） *n.* Sea of Japan side (west side) of Japan, 1S
にほんし（日本史） *n.* Japanese history, 5P
にほんしゅ（日本酒） *n.* Japanese sake, 7S
にもつ（荷物） *n.* luggage, 2S
ニュース *n.* news, 10
〜によって *exp.* depending on, 7P
にる（煮る） る*-v.* (to) boil; (to) stew, 3
にわかあめ（にわか雨） *n.* shower, 1S
にわとり（鶏） *n.* chicken, 10S
にんぎょう（人形） *n.* doll, 7

ぬ

ぬいぐるみ stuffed animal toy, 7
ぬぐ（脱ぐ） う*-v.* (to) take off; remove, 4
ぬすむ（盗む） う*-v.* (to) steal, 9

ね

ねかす（寝かす） う*-v.* (to) put (someone) in bed (*tran.*), 5S
ねぎ scallion, 3S
ねだん（値段） *n.* price, 7P
ねったいうりん（熱帯雨林） *n.* tropical rain forest, 10S
ねったいりん（熱帯林） *n.* tropical forest, 10S
ねまき（寝巻） *n.* pajamas, 7S
ねんこうじょれつ（年功序列） *n.* seniority, 5P
ねんれい（年令） *n.* age, 5P

の

の *part.* explantion and emotional emphasis by female and children (casual), Prelim.
〜のあんないをする（〜の案内をする） *vn.* (to) guide〜; (to) show 〜, 2S
ノート *n.* notebook, 3
のこす（残す） う*-v.* (to) leave(something) (*tran.*), 5
〜のことなんですが *exp.* it's about 〜, 2
〜のことなんですけど *exp.* it's about 〜, 2
のこる（残る） う*-v.* (for something) (to) be left; to remain(*intr.*), 5
のし label to be attached to a gift indicating the purpose and the sender, 7S
のせる（乗せる） る*-v.* (to) give a ride (to someone) (*tran.*), 5
のち（後） *n.* after, 1
ノック vn. knock, 4
ノックする vn. (to) knock (the door), 4
のり（海苔） *n.* seaweed, 7P
のりかえる（乗り換える） る*-v.* (to) transfer; to change transportation, 6
のりもの（乗り物） *n.* transportation, 2S
〜のをたのしみにしています（〜のを楽しみにしています） *exp.* to be looking forward to 〜, 6

は

は（葉） *n.* leaf, 1
ばあい（場合） *n.* case, 9P
はいきガス（排気ガス） *n.* exhaust gas, 10P
はいきぶつ（廃棄物） *n.* waste, 10P
はいけんする（拝見する)smi. v. (to) look at (humble form), 8
ばいしゅん（売春） *n.* prostitution, 10S
はいすい（排水） *n.* waste water, 10S
ハイヒール high heel shoes, 7P
はいゆう（俳優） *n.* actor; actress, 5S
バイリンガル bilingual, 8P
パイロット *n.* pilot, 5S
パイント *n.* pint, 3P
〜はく〜か（〜泊〜日） *suf.* 〜nights 〜days, 2
バザー bazaar, Prelim. S
はさむ（挟む） う*-v.* (to) pinch, 3P
はし（箸） *n.* chopsticks, 3
はし（橋） *n.* bridge, 6
はじめる（始める） る*-v.* (to) begin (something) (*tran.*), 5
ばしょ（場所） *n.* location, 2
バスてい（バス停） *n.* bus stop, 6
パスポート *n.* passport, 2
パソコン personal computer, 3
バター butter, 3
はたらく（働く） う*-v.* (to) work (*intr.*), 5
はち（蜂） *n.* bee, 10S
はちうえ（鉢植え） *n.* potted plants, 7
パック *n.* carton; package, 10P
はっけん（発見） *vn.* discovery, 9P
はっけんする（発見する） *vn.* discover, 9P
バッジ *n.* badge, 5P
はと（鳩） *n.* pigeon, 10S
パート *n.* part time worker, 8P
はな（花） *n.* flower, 1
はなしはかわりますが（話はかわりますが） *exp.* to change the subject, 4
ははのひ（母の日） *n.* Mother's day, 7
バブルがはじける *exp.* The bubble (economy) bursts, 5P
バブルけいざい（バブル経済） *n.* Bubble economy, 5P
バーベキュー *n.* barbecue, 3P
ハム ham, 7P
はやい（早い／速い） い*-adj.* early; fast, 4
バラ／ばら *n.* rose, 2P, 7
はらう（払う） う*-v.* (to) pay, 2
はらがたつ（腹が立つ） *exp.* (to) get angry, 9S
ハリケーン *n.* hurricane, 10
はれ（晴） *n.* sunny, 1
はれる（晴れる） る*-v.* (to) become sunny, 1
バレンタインデー *n.* St. Valentine's Day, 7
パン *n.* bread, 3
はんがえし（半返し） *n.* custom of reciprocation by spending about one half of the original amount when one receives a gift, 7P
ハンカチ *n.* handkerchief, 7S
はんこ（判子） *n.* personal stamp; seal, 4
パンこ（パン粉） *n.* bread crumbs, 3S
はんこや（判子屋） *n.* personal stamp shop, 4P
はんざい（犯罪） *n.* crime, 10
〜ばんせん（〜番線） *suf.* track number, 6
パンダ panda, 10S
はんたいだ（反対だ） *exp.* I am against it, 10
はんにん（犯人） *n.* criminal, 2P
パンやきき（パン焼き機） *n.* bread maker, 7S

ひ

ひ（日） *n.* day, 9
ピアノ *n.* piano, 9
ビーチ *n.* beach, 2P
ビールけん（ビール券） *n.* gift certificate for beer, 7P

ひえる（冷える）る-*v.* (for something) (to) cool (*intr.*), 5S
ひがい（被害）*n.* damage, 10
ひがえり（日帰り）*n.* day trip, 2S
ひがし（東）*n.* east, 1
ひがしかいがん（東海岸）*n.* East coast region, 1S
ひがしぐち（東口）*n.* east entrance, 6S
ひきだす（引き出す）う-*v.* (to) withdraw (money from bank), 4
ひきにく（ひき肉）*n.* ground meat, 3P
ひく（弾く）う-*v.* (to) play (the piano/guitar, etc.), 9
ひこう（非行）*n.* misconduct; delinquency, 10S
ビザ visa, 2S, 6P
びじゅつひん（美術品）*n.* art piece, 10P
ひじょうじ（非常時）*n.* emergency, 10S
ひだり（左）*loc. n.* left , 6
ひっきしけん（筆記試験）*n.* paper and pencil test, 8S
ひっこし（引っ越し）*n.* moving (one's residence), 9
ひっこす（引っ越す）う-*v.* (to) move residence, 9
ひつじゅひん（必需品）*n.* essential items, 10S
ひつような（必要な）な-*adj.* necessary; essential, 10
ひでり（日照り）*n.* drought, 1S
ひとじち（人質）*n.* hostage, 10S
ひやす（冷やす）う-*v.* (to) cool; chill (something) (*tran.*), 5S
ひょう *n.* hail, 1S
びようし（美容師）*n.* beautician, 5S
ひらく（開く）う-*v.* (to) open (an account; a book), 4
ビル *n.* building, 6
びん（瓶）*n.* bottle, 10P

ふ

ファックス *n.* fax; fax machine, 3
〜フィート *suf.* 〜foot; feet, 6P
ふうせん（風船）*n.* balloon, 7S
ふうとう（封筒）*n.* envelope, 4
ふえる（増える）る-*v.* (for something) to increase (*intr.*), 10
フォーク *n.* fork, 3
ぶか（部下）*n.* subordinate, 8S
ふく（吹く）う-*v.* (to) blow, 1
ふざけないでよ *exp.* Don't be ridiculous. (female speech), 9
ふざけるなよ *exp.* Don't be ridiculous. (male speech), 9
ふせぐ（防ぐ）う-*v.* to prevent, 10
ぶた（豚）*n.* pig, 10
ぶたにく（豚肉）*n.* pork, 3
ぶちょう（部長）*n.* general manager, 8S
ふつう（普通）*n.* regular; normal, 4
ふつう(れっしゃ)（普通(列車)）*n.* local train, 6
ふつうよきん（普通預金）*n.* regular saving account, 4
ぶつかる う-*v.* (to) bump into, 4P
ぶつける る-*v.* (to) hit; (to) crash into, 9
ぶどう（葡萄）*n.* grape, 3S
ふなびん（船便）*n.* surface mail; sea mail, 4
ふね（船）*n.* ship, 2S
ふぶき（吹雪）*n.* snowstorm, 1S
ふべんな（不便な）な-*adj.* inconvenient, 10
ふまん（不満）*n.* dissatisfaction, 9S
ふむ（踏む）う-*v.* (to) step on, 9
フライパン *n.* frying pan; skillet, 3
ふる（降る）う-*v.* (to) fall, 1
ブレスレット *n.* bracelet, 7S
プレゼント *n.* present, 7
プロジェクト *n.* project, 8

へ

へいきん（平均）*n.* average, 5P
へび（蛇）*n.* snake, 10S
ヘルニア *n.* hernia, Prelim. S
へん（辺）*n.* area, 6
ペンギン *n.* penguin, 10S
べんごし（弁護士）*n.* lawyer, 5
へんじ（返事）*vn.* reply; response, 5P, 8
へんじする（返事する）*vn.* to reply; to respond, 5P, 8
ペンション western-style private guest house, 2P
べんりな（便利な）な-*adj.* convenient, 2
へん(な)（変{な}）な-*adj.* strange, 9

ほ

ほう（方）*n.* direction, 1
ぼうえき（貿易）*n.* trading, 5
ぼうえきがいしゃ（貿易会社）*n.* trading company, 5
ほうがく（方角）*n.* direction, 1P
ぼうさい（防災）*n.* disaster prevention, 10S
ぼうそう（暴走）*vn.* reckless driving, 9S
ぼうそうする（暴走する）*vn.* (to) drive vehicle recklessly, 9S
ほうちょう（包丁）*n.* kitchen knife, 7P
ボウル *n.* mixing bowl, 3S
ほうれんそう（ほうれん草）*n.* spinach, 3S
ボール ball, 7
ほくせい（北西）*n.* northwest, 1
ほくとう（北東）*n.* northeast, 1
ほくりく（北陸）*n.* Hokuriku Region, 1P
ほけん（保険）*n.* insurance, 2P
ほしい（欲しい）い-*adj.* want, 7
ぼしゅう（募集）*n.* recruitment, 8P

ポスト *n.* public mailbox (for outgoing mail only), 4
ボタン *n.* button, 3
ほっかいどう（北海道） *n.* Hokkaido (northernmost main island of Japan), 1P
ほっといてくれよ *exp.* Leave me alone. (male speech), 9
ほっといてよ *exp.* Leave me alone. (female speech), 9
ほどう（歩道） *n.* side walk, 6S
ほどうきょう（歩道橋） *n.* pedestrian bridge, 6S
ボーナス bonus, 8P
ほめる（誉める） る-*v.* (to) praise, 9
ほんしゃ（本社） *n.* headquarter, 8S
ほんしゅう（本州） *n.* Honshuu Island, 1P
～ポンド *suf.* pound, 4
ほんとう（本当） *n.* truth, 9
ほんのきもちですから。（ほんの気持ちですから。） *exp.* Just a token of my appreciation, 7
ほんのすこしですから。（ほんの少しですから。） *exp.* Just a little bit, 7
ほんもの（本物） *n.* real thing, 2P

ま

まあまあです。 *exp.* so-so, 8
まいすう（枚数） *n.* number of sheets, 3P
マイナス *n.* minus, 1
まいる（参る） う-*v.* (to) go; (to) come (honorific), 8
まえ（前） *loc. n.* in front of; in the front; before, 2
まがる（曲がる） う-*v.* (to) turn, 6
まぐろ tuna, 2P, 3S
まず *conj.* first, 3
まず(はじめに)（まず(始めに)（*conj.* first (of all), 2, 3
まぜる（混ぜる） る-*v.* (to) mix, 3
また *conj.* also, 2
まだまだです。 *exp.* I still have a lot to learn, 8
まちがう（間違う） う-*v.* (for someone) (to) be mistaken (*intr.*), 5
まちがえる（間違える） る-*v.* (to) miss (something); (to) make a mistake (*tran.*), 5
まつ（待つ） う-*v.* (to) wait for, 3
まっすぐ（*adv.* straight, 6
まつり（祭り） *n.* festival, 2P
まどぐち（窓口） *n.* window (bank teller, municipal office, etc.), 4P
まとわりつく う-*v.* (to) cling around, 9S
まないた（まな板） *n.* cutting board, 3S
マネージャー *n.* manager, 4P, 5
まめ beans, 3S
まもる（守る） う-*v.* (to) protect, 4P, 10
まやく（麻薬） *n.* drugs, 10S
まるのうちせん（丸ノ内線） *n.* a subway line connecting places inside the loop of the Yamanote line, 6P
まわす（回す） う-*v.* (to) turn (something) (*tran.*), 5S
まわる（回る） う-*v.* (for something/someone) (to) turn (*intr.*), 5S
まんなか（まん中） *loc. n.* in the right middle of; in the center of, 6S

み

みかん mandarin orange, 3S
みえる（見える） る-*v.* can see ～ (lit. something is visible), 6
みぎ（右） *loc. n.* right, 6
ミキサー *n.* mixer, 3S
みずうみ（湖） *n.* lake, 2
みずをきる（水を切る） *exp.* (to) drain; (to) shake off water, 3P
みせ（店） *n.* store; shop, 2
みそ（味噌） *n.* soy bean paste, 3S
みぞれ *n.* sleet, 1S
みち（道） *n.* road; street; way, 6
みちなり（道なり） *n.* following a street, 6S
みちにそって（道に沿って） *exp.* along a street, 6S
みなみ（南） *n.* south, 1
ミュージシャン *n.* musician, 4P
みりん sweet rice wine for cooking, 3P
みんしゅく（民宿） *n.* Japanese-style private guest house, 2

む

むかいがわ（向かい側） *loc. n.* the other side; the opposite side, 6
むかえる（迎える） る-*v.* (to) welcome, 9
むこう（向こう） *loc. n.* beyond, 6S
むし（虫） *n.* insect, 10S
むし（無視） *vn.* act of ignoring, 9S
むしあつい（蒸し暑い） い-*adj.* humid, 1
むしする（無視する） *vn.* (to) ignore, 9S
むす（蒸す） う-*v.* (to) steam, 3S
むだな（無駄な） な-*adj.* waste; fruitless; no good; useless, 10

め

めいさんひん（名産品） *n.* local favorite food, 7S
めいわく（迷惑） *n.* trouble, 9
めいわくな（迷惑な） な-*adj.* troublesome; annoying, 9
～メートル *suf.* meter, 6

めしあがる（召し上がる）う-*v.* (to) eat; (to) drink (honorific), 8
めんせつ（面接）*n.* interview, 8

も

もうしあげる（申し上げる）る-*v.* (to) say (humble), 8
もうしこみしょ（申込書）*n.* application form, 4
もうしこみようし（申込用紙）*n.* application form, 8
もうしこむ（申し込む）う-*v.* (to) apply, 8
もうしわけありません（申し訳ありません）*exp.* I'm sorry (polite and formal), 9
もうしわけございません（申し訳ございません）*exp.* I'm sorry (very polite and formal), 9
もうす（申す）う-*v.* (to) say (humble), 8
もえる（燃える）う-*v.* (to) burn, 9P
もくてき（目的）*n.* objective; purpose, 4P, 7P
もっていく（持って行く）う-*v.* (to) take; (to) bring, 2, 3
もってくる（持って来る）*smi. v.* (to) bring (something), 3
モデル *n.* model, 4P, 5S
もどす（戻す）う-*v.* (to) return (something) (*tran.*), 5S
もどる（戻る）う-*v.* (for someone/something) (to) return (*intr.*), 5P
もらう う-*v.* (to) receive, 7
もり（森）*n.* forest, 10
もんく（文句）*n.* complaint, 9

や

〜や（〜屋）*suf.* owner of 〜 retail store, 5
やく（焼く）う-*v.* (to) bake; (to) fry, 3
やくにたつ（役に立つ）*exp.* useful, 7
やける（焼ける）る-*v.* (for something) to burn, 10
やしなう（養う）う-*v.* (to) support (financially) (*tran.*), 5P
やど（宿）*n.* accommodations, 2S
やまのてせん（山の手線）*n.* the JR's loop line in Tokyo, 6P
やむ（止む）う-*v.* (for something/someone) (to) stop (*intr.*), 5S
やめる（止める）る-*v.* (to) quit; (to) stop, 5
やめろ *exp.* Cut it out. (male speech), 9
やる う-*v.* (to) do, 3
やる う-*v.* (to) give (to socially inferior person), 7

ゆ

ゆ（湯）*n.*., warm or hot water, 3P
ゆうかい（誘拐）*n.* abduction, 10S
ゆうぐう（優遇）*n.* favorable treatment, 8P
ゆうしょく（夕食）*n.* dinner, 2S
ユースホステル *n.* youth hostel, 2P
ゆうだち（夕立ち）*n.* evening shower, 1S
ゆうびん（郵便）*n.* postal service, 4
ゆうびんうけ（郵便受け）*n.* mailbox (for incoming mail only), 4P
ゆうびんちょきん（郵便貯金）*n.* postal savings account, 4S
ゆうびんこづつみ（郵便小包）*n.* postal parcel, 4S
ゆうびんばんごう（郵便番号）*n.* post code, 4P
ゆかた Japanese summer kimono, 2P
ゆき（雪）*n.* snow; snowy, 1
ゆきまつり（雪祭り）*n.* the snow festival in Sapporo, 2P
ゆっくり *adv.* slowly, 5
ゆっくりおねがいします。（ゆっくりお願いします。）*exp.* Slowly please, 5
ゆびわ（指輪）*n.* ring, 7

よ

ようがし（洋菓子）*n.* Western-style sweets, 7P
ようし（用紙）*n.* form, 8
ようしゅ（洋酒）*n.* Western alcoholic beverages (whisky, brandy, etc.), 7S
よきん（預金）*vn.* deposit; saving, 4
よきんする（預金する）*vn.* (to) deposit (money); to save (money at the bank), 4
よきんつうちょう（預金通帳）*n.* record book for an account, 4S
よけいなおせっかいだ（余計なお節介だ）*exp.* That's none of your business; Mind your own business, 9S
よごす（汚す）う-*v.* (to) make (something)dirty (*tran.*), 5S, 10
よごれる（汚れる）る-*v.* (for something) (to) get dirty (*intr.*), 5S, 10
よさん（予算）*n.* budget, 7P
よてい（予定）*n.* schedule; plan, 2
よなか（夜中）*n.* midnight, 9
よみ（読み）*n.* reading; pronunciation, 3
よやく（予約）*vn.* reservation, 2
よやくする（予約する）*vn.* (to) make a reservation, 2
よる（寄る）う-*v.* (to) drop by, 6S
よろこぶ（喜ぶ）う-*v.* (to) be pleased, 7
よろしい い-*adj.* good (polite), 8
よわい（弱い）い-*adj.* weak, 1

ら

ライオン *n.* lion, 10S
らくがき（落書き）*n.* graffiti, 9
らくだ *n.* camel, 10S

り

リサイクル *n.* recycling, 9P, 10
りす *n.* squirrel, 10S
リストラ *n.* restructuring, 5P
リモコン *n.* remote control (リモートコントロール = リモコン), 3
りゅうがく（留学）*vn.* study abroad, 5
りゅうがくする（留学する）*vn.* (to) study abroad, 5
りょう（量）*n.* quantity, 10P
りょうがえ（両替）*n.* currency exchange, 4S
りょうし（漁師）*n.* fisherman, 5S
りようし（理容師）*n.* barber, 5S
りょかん（旅館）*n.* Japanese style inn, 2
りょこう（旅行）*n.* trip; traveling, 2
りょこうがいしゃ（旅行会社）*n.* travel agency, 2
りれきしょ（履歴書）*n.* vita; résumé, 8

れ

れいさいきぎょう（零細企業）*n.* small business, 5P
レポート *n.* report; (academic) paper, 4
れんしゅう（練習）*vn.* practice, 3
れんしゅうする（練習する）*vn.* to practice, 3

ろ

ろうどうじょうけん（労働条件）*n.* work condition, 8S
ロビー *n.* lobby, 2P

わ

わ *part.* (female speech marker), Prelim.
ワープロ *n.* word processor, 3
ワイングラス wine glass, 7S
わかい（若い）い*-adj.* young, 5
わかす（沸かす）う*-v.* (to) bring (something) to boil (*tran.*), 3S, 5
わく（沸く）う*-v.* (for something) (to) boil (*intr.*), 3P, 5
わすれる（忘れる）る*-v.* (to) forget, 2
わたしもそうおもいます。（私もそう思います。）*exp.* I think so, too, 10
わたる（渡る）う*-v.* (to) cross (bridge, road), 6
わに）*n.* alligator; crocodile, 10S
わる（割る）う*-v.* (to) break, 9S
わるくち（悪口）*n.* abuse, 9
ワンルーム *n.* one-room (apartment), 4P

を

を *part.* (Place in which movement occurs), 6
を *part.* out of 〜; from 〜, 6

English-Japanese Glossary

A

a little すくない（少ない）い-*adj.*, 1
a little bit (cooking) しょうしょう（少々）*exp.*, 3P
a lot おおい（多い）い-*adj.*, 1
(to) abandon すてる（捨てる）る-*v.*, 9
abduction ゆうかい（誘拐）*n.*, 10S
academic period such as semester or quarter がっき（学期）*n.*, 2
accommodations やど（宿）*n.*, 2S
account (bank) こうざ（口座）*n.*, 4
accountant かいけいし（会計士）*n.*, 5
acid rain さんせいう（酸性雨）*n.*, 10S
acquaintance しりあい（知り合い）*n.*, 4P, 9
act of ignoring むし（無視）*vn.*, 9S
action こうどう（行動）*n.*, 2P
activity こうどう（行動）*n.*, 2P
actor はいゆう（俳優）*n.*, 5S
actress はいゆう（俳優）*n.*, 5S
(to) add くわえる（加える）る-*v.*, 3S
(to) add たす（足す）う-*v.*, 3
advertisement こうこく（広告）*n.*, 8
after あと（後）*n.*, 2
after のち（後）*n.*, 1
after that そのあと(で) その後(で)）*conj.*, 2
age ねんれい（年令）*n.*, 5P
age とし（年）*n.*, Prelim. S
air くうき（空気）*n.*, 10
air conditioner エアコン *n.*, 3
air pollution たいきおせん（大気汚染）*n.*, 10S
air pressure きあつ（気圧）*n.*, 1S
air temperature きおん（気温）*n.*, 1
air mail こうくうびん（航空便）*n.*, 4
airport くうこう（空港）*n.*, 2
album アルバム *n.*, 7S
alcoholic beverage さけ（酒）*n.*, 7
alien registration がいこくじんとうろくしょう（外国人登録証）*n.*, 4
all ぜんぶ（全部）*n.*, 7P
alligator わに *n.*, 10S
along a street みちにそって（道に沿って）*exp.*, 6S
also また *conj.*, 2
ambulance きゅうきゅうしゃ（救急車）*n.*, 10
amount of precipitation こうすいりょう（降水量）*n.*, 1S
animal どうぶつ（動物）*n.*, 7P, 10
an old neighborhood in downtown Tokyo あさくさ（浅草）*n.*, 6P
annoying めいわくな（迷惑な）な-*adj.*, 9
(to) answer こたえる（答える）る-*v.*, 2
(to) apologize あやまる（謝る）う-*v.*, 9
appear そう な-*adj.*, 1
application おうぼ（応募）*vn.*, 8S
application form もうしこみしょ（申込書）*n.*, 4
application form もうしこみようし（申込用紙）*n.*, 8
(to) apply おうぼする（応募する）*vn.*, 8S
(to) apply もうしこむ（申し込む）う-*v.*, 8
Arabic language アラビアご（アラビア語）*n.*, 4P
architect けんちくか（建築家）*n.*, 5S
area へん（辺）*n.*, 6
(to) arrive つく（着く）う-*v.*, 2
art piece びじゅつひん（美術品）*n.*, 10P
article (newspapers and magazines) きじ（記事）*n.*, 1P
artist げいじゅつか（芸術家）*n.*, 5S
(to) ask (humble) うかがう（伺う）う-*v.*, 8
(to) ask (request) たのむ（頼む）う-*v.*, 3
(to) assist てつだう（手伝う）う-*v.*, 3
at that time そのとき(に) その時(に)）*conj.*, 2
ATM machine じどうひきだしき（自動引き出し機）*n.*, 4P
(to) attach つける（付ける）る-*v.*, 3
attention ちゅうい（注意）*vn.*, 9
audio CD CD *n.*, 7
autograph サイン *n.*, 4
automatic deduction of bills じどうひきおとし（自動引き落とし）*n.*, 4P
automatic money transfer machine. じどうふりこみき（自動振込機）*n.*, 4P

average へいきん（平均） *n.*, 5P

B

baby あかちゃん（赤ちゃん） *n.*, 9
baby ～ こ～（子～） pref., 7
badge バッジ *n.*, 5P
(to) bake やく（焼く） う*-v.*, 3
ball ボール *n.*, 7
balloon ふうせん（風船） *n.*, 7S
bank employee ぎんこういん（銀行員） *n.*, 5S
barbecue バーベキュー *n.*, 3P
barber りようし（理容師） *n.*, 5S
bazaar バザー *n.*, Prelim. S
(to) be (honorific) いらっしゃる） う*-v.*, 8
(to) be (humble) おる う*-v.*, 8
(to) be (polite verb for です) でござる う*-v.*, 7P, 8
(to) be able to hear *(intr.)* きこえる（聞こえる） る*-v.*, 10
(to) be cared for or helped by somebody せわになる（世話になる） *exp.*, 7
(to) become careful きをつける（気を付ける） *exp.*, 9
(to) be cut *(intr.)* きれる（切れる） る*-v.*, 5S
(to) be decided *(intr.)* きまる（決まる） う*-v.*, 5
(to) be different *(intr.)* ちがう（違う） う*-v.*, 1P, 5
(to) be fixed *(intr.)* なおる（直る） う*-v.*, 5
(to) be late おくれる（遅れる） る*-v.*, 4
(to) be left *(intr.)* のこる（残る） う*-v.*, 5
(to) be looking forward to ～ ～のをたのしみにしています（～のを楽しみにしています） *exp.*, 6
(to) be mistaken *(intr.)* まちがう（間違う） う*-v.*, 5
(to) be pleased よろこぶ（喜ぶ） う*-v.*, 7
(to) be troubled なやむ（悩む） う*-v.*, 9S
beach ビーチ *n.*, 2P
beans まめ *n.*, 3S
bear くま（熊） *n.*, 10
beautician びようし（美容師） *n.*, 5S
(to) become cloudy くもる（曇る） う*-v.*, 1
(to) become old としをとる（年を取る） *exp.*, 5
(to) become sunny はれる（晴れる） る*-v.*, 1
bee はち（蜂） *n.*, 10S
beef ぎゅうにく（牛肉） *n.*, 3
before まえ（前） *loc. n.*, 2
before that そのまえ(に) その前(に)） *conj.*, 2
(to) begin (something) *(tran.)* はじめる（始める） る*-v.*, 5
(to) betray うらぎる（裏切る） う*-v.*, 9S
between あいだ（間） *loc. n.*, 6
beyond さき（先） *loc. n.*, 6
beyond むこう（向こう） *loc. n.*, 6S
bilingual バイリンガル *n.*, 8P
bird とり（鳥） *n.*, 10
(to) bloom さく（咲く） う*-v.*, 1
(to) blow ふく（吹く） う*-v.*, 1
(to) boil *(intr.)* わく（沸く） う*-v.*, 3P, 5
bonus ボーナス *n.*, 8P
boring つまらない い*-adj.*, 7
(to) borrow かりる（借りる） る*-v.*, 3
boss じょうし（上司） *n.*, 7P, 8
bottle びん（瓶） *n.*, 10P
bound for ～ ～いき（～行き） *suf.*, 6
bow おじぎ *n.*, 4
bowl ちゃわん（茶碗） *n.*, 3S
box lunch sold at train station えきべん（駅弁） *n.*, 2P
bracelet ブレスレット *n.*, 7S
bread パン *n.*, 3
bread crumbs パンこ（パン粉） *n.*, 3S
bread maker パンやきき（パン焼き機） *n.*, 7S
(to) break わる（割る） う*-v.*, 9S
(to) break *(intr.)* こわれる（壊れる） る*-v.*, 3P, 5S
(to) break (something) *(tran.)* こわす（壊す） う*-v.*, 5S, 9
breakfast ちょうしょく（朝食） *n.*, 2S
bridge はし（橋） *n.*, 6
(to) bring もっていく（持って行く） う*-v.*, 2
(to) bring (someone) つれてくる（連れて来る） *ir. v.*, 3
(to) bring (something) もってくる（持って来る） *ir. v.*, 3
(to) bring (something) to boil *(tran.)* わかす（沸かす） う*-v.*, 3S, 5
(to) build たてる（建てる／立てる）る*-v.*, 2
broth だし *n.*, 3P
The bubble (economy) bursts. バブルがはじける *exp.*, 5P
Bubble economy バブルけいざい（バブル経済） *n.*, 5P
budget よさん（予算） *n.*, 7P
bug むし（虫） *n.*, 10S
building ビル *n.*, 6
(to) bully いじめる る*-v.*, 9
(act of) bullying いじめ *n.*, 9
(to) bump into ぶつかる う*-v.*, 4P
(to) burn やける（焼ける） る*-v.*, 10
(to) burn もえる（燃える） う*-v.*, 9P
bus stop バスてい（バス停） *n.*, 6
business clerk じむいん（事務員） *n.*, 5S
business trip しゅっちょう（出張） *vn.*, 8
businessman かいしゃいん（会社員） *n.*, 5S
but だけど *conj.*, 2
butter バター *n.*, 3
button ボタン *n.*, 3
by the way ところで *conj.*, 2

(to) call attention to ちゅういする（注意する） *vn.*, 9

C

camera カメラ *n.*, 2
camel らくだ *n.*, 10S
can かん（缶） *n.*, 10P
can see 〜 (lit. something is visible) みえる（見える） る-*v.*, 6
candy おかし（お菓子） *n.*, 7
canned food かんづめ（缶詰） *n.*, 7S
cannot stand たまらない い-*adj.*, 9
capital city しゅと（首都） *n.*, 5P
carbon dioxide にさんかたんそ（二酸化炭素） *n.*, 10P
card カード *n.*, 7
care せわ（世話） *n.*, 5P
carnation カーネーション *n.*, 7
carton パック *n.*, 10P
case ばあい（場合） *n.*, 9P
cashing card for ATM キャッシュカード *n.*, 4P
(to) cause something to happen おこす（起こす） う-*v.*, 10
Celsius せっし（摂氏） *n.*, 1P
ceremony しき（式） *n.*, 5
Certainly. (Polite language used by waiters/clerks) かしこまりました。 *exp.*, 7P
(to) change かえる（替える／変える） る-*v.*, 4
(to) change *(intr.)* かわる（変わる／替わる） う-*v.*, 5
(to) change the subject はなしはかわりますが（話はかわりますが） *exp.*, 4
(to) change transportation のりかえる（乗り換える） る-*v.*, 6
chartered bus for sightseeing かんこうバス（観光バス） *n.*, 2
(to) check しらべる（調べる） る-*v.*, 2
check (not for personal use) こぎって（小切手） *n.*, 4S
chef シェフ *n.*, 4P
chef ちょうりし（調理師） *n.*, 5S
chef of Japanese cuisine いたまえ（板前） *n.*, 5S
chemical substance かがくやくひん（科学薬品） *n.*, 10S
chicken にわとり（鶏） *n.*, 10S
chicken meat とりにく（鳥肉） *n.*, 3
child こ is usually preceded by a modifier. こ（子） *n.*, 9
(to) chill (something) *(tran.)* ひやす（冷やす） う-*v.*, 5S
chimpanzee チンパンジー *n.*, 10S
chocolate チョコレート *n.*, 7
chopsticks はし（箸） *n.*, 3
Christmas クリスマス *n.*, 7
City Hall しやくしょ（市役所） *n.*, 6
(to) clean up かたづける（片付ける） る-*v.*, 9
climate きこう（気候） *n.*, 1
(to) cling around まとわりつく う-*v.*, 9S
(to) close *(intr.)* しまる（閉まる） う-*v.*, 5
(to) close something しめる（閉める） る-*v.*, 4
close to ちかい（近い） い-*adj.*, 6
cloud くも（雲） *n.*, 1
cloudy くもり（曇り） *n.*, 1
cockroach ごきぶり *n.*, 10S
coercive touter おしうり（押し売り） *n.*, 9S
coffee cup コーヒーカップ *n.*, 7
coffee maker コーヒーメーカー *n.*, 7S
cold つめたい（冷たい） い-*adj.*, 1
colleague どうりょう（同僚） *n.*, 8
college seniors going to different companies かいしゃまわり（会社回り） *n.*, 8P
(to) come (honorific) まいる（参る） う-*v.*, 8
(to) come (honorific) いらっしゃる う-*v.*, 8
(to) come (polite) おいでになる う-*v.*, 8
come to know しる（知る） う-*v.*, 2
(to) come to a boil わく（沸く）う-*v.*, 3
commuting つうきん（通勤） *n.*, 8S
company apartment しゃたく（社宅） *n.*, 8S
company branch office ししゃ（支社） *n.*, 5P, 8S
company man かいしゃいん（会社員） *n.*, 5S
company or organization to be employed at しゅうしょくさき（就職先） *n.*, 8S
company president しゃちょう（社長） *n.*, 5
compass direction ほうがく（方角） *n.*, 1P
complaint もんく（文句） *n.*, 9
con game さぎ（詐欺） *n.*, 10S
condition じょうけん（条件） *n.*, 4P
(to) conduct おこなう（行なう） う-*v.*, 9P
confection おかし（お菓子） *n.*, 7
congratulations おめでとうございます。 *exp.*, 7
Congratulations on your marriage ごけっこんおめでとうございます（ご結婚おめでとうございます） *exp.*, 7P
congratulatory gift おいわい（お祝い） *n.*, 7
congratulatory gift for 〜 〜いわい（祝い） *suf.*, 7
(to) consult そうだんする（相談する） *vn.*, 5
consultant コンサルタント *n.*, 5S
consultation そうだん（相談） *vn.*, 5
content ないよう（内容） *n.*, 2P, 8S
(to) continue *(intr.)* つづく（続く） う-*v.*, 1P, 5
(to) continue *(tran.)* つづける（続ける） る-*v.*, 5
convenient べんりな（便利な） な-*adj.*, 2
conversation かいわ（会話） *n.*, 4
cook ちょうりし（調理師） *n.*, 5S
(to) cook rice たく（炊く） う-*v.*, 3

cookies クッキー *n.*, 7
(to) cool *(intr.)* ひえる（冷える）る-*v.*, 5S
(to) cool *(tran.)* ひやす（冷やす）う-*v.*, 5S
copy center コピーセンター *n.*, 3P
copying machine コピーき（コピー機）*n.*, 3
corn starch コーンスターチ *n.*, 3S
corner かど（角）*n.*, 6
(to) correct *(tran.)* なおす（直す）う-*v.*, 9
cosmetics けしょうひん（化粧品）*n.*, 7S
course コース *n.*, 4
course registration かもくとうろく（課目登録）*n.*, 3P, 4P
cow うし（牛）*n.*, 10
cow's milk ぎゅうにゅう（牛乳）*n.*, 10P
(to) crash into ぶつける る-*v.*, 9
credit card クレジットカード）*n.*, 2
crime はんざい（犯罪）*n.*, 10
criminal はんにん（犯人）*n.*, 2P
critical じゅうだいな（重大な）な-*adj.*, 10P
crocodile わに *n.*, 10S
(to) cross (bridge/road わたる（渡る）う-*v.*, 6
cruise クルーズ *n.*, 2S
cucumber きゅうり（胡瓜）*n.*, 3S
currency exchange りょうがえ（両替）*n.*, 4S
current さいきん（最近）*n.*, 1P, 10
curry powder カレーこ（カレー粉）*n.*, 3P
custom of reciprocation by spending about one-half of the original amount when one receives a gift はんがえし（半返し）*n.*, 7P
customer きゃく（客）*n.*, Prelim. S, 4P, 8
(to) cut きる（切る）う-*v.*, 3
Cut it out. (male speech) やめろ）*exp.*, 9
cutting board まないた（まな板）*n.*, 3S

D

damage ひがい（被害）*n.*, 10
dancer ダンサー *n.*, 4P
day ひ（日）*n.*, 9
day trip ひがえり（日帰り）*n.*, 2S
(to) decide on (something) *(tran.)* きめる（決める）る-*v.*, 5
(to) deep-fry あげる（揚げる）る-*v.*, 3P
deer しか（鹿）*n.*, 10
degree ～ど（～度）count., 1
delinquency ひこう（非行）*n.*, 10S
depending on ～によって *exp.*, 7P
deposit よきん（預金）*vn.*, 4
(to) deposit (money) よきんする（預金する）*vn.*, 4
(to) destroy こわす（壊す）う-*v.*, 9
details しょうさい（詳細）*n.*, 8P
detergent せんざい（洗剤）*n.*, 7P
diary にっき（日記）*n.*, 9
(to) die おなくなりになる（お亡くなりになる）う-*v.*, 8S
difference ちがい（違い）*n.*, 4P
dinner ゆうしょく（夕食）*n.*, 2S
direction ほう（方）*n.*, 1
dirty きたない（汚い）い-*adj.*, 1, 9
(to) disappear なくなる う-*v.*, 10
disaster さいがい（災害）*n.*, 10
disaster prevention ぼうさい（防災）*n.*, 10S
(to) discard すてる（捨てる）る-*v.*, 9
(to) discover はっけんする（発見する）*vn.*, 9P
discovery はっけん（発見）*vn.*, 9P
(to) discuss そうだんする（相談する）*vn.*, 5
dissatisfaction ふまん（不満）*n.*, 9S
(to) do やる う-*v.*, 3
(to) do (honorific) なさる う-*v.*, 8
(to) do (humble) いたす（致す）う-*v.*, 8
(to) do one's best がんばる（頑張る）う-*v.*, 5P
(to) do research けんきゅうする（研究する）*vn.*, 5
document しょるい（書類）*n.*, 8
doll にんぎょう（人形）*n.*, 7
dolphin イルカ *n.*, 10S
Don't be ridiculous. (female speech) ふざけないでよ *exp.*, 9
Don't be ridiculous. (male speech) ふざけるなよ *exp.*, 9
dormitory for singles どくしんりょう（独身寮）*n.*, 8S
double ダブル *n.*, 2P
downpour of rain どしゃぶり *n.*, 1S
(to) drain みずをきる（水を切る）*exp.*, 3P
dress ドレス *n.*, 7
dressing ドレッシング *n.*, 3P
dried cloud ear mushroom きくらげ）*n.*, 3P
dried food かんぶつ（乾物）*n.*, 7S
dried noodles かんめん（干麺）*n.*, 7P
(to) drink (honorific) めしあがる（召し上がる）う-*v.*, 8
(to) drink (humble) いただく（頂く）う-*v.*, 8
(to) drive うんてんする（運転する）*vn.*, 4
(to) drive vehicle recklessly ぼうそうする（暴走する）*vn.*, 9S
driver's license うんてんめんきょしょう（運転免許証）*n.*, 4
driving うんてん（運転）*vn.*, 4
(to) drop おとす（落とす）う-*v.*, 4
(to) drop by よる（寄る）う-*v.*, 6S
drought ひでり（日照り）*n.*, 1S
drugs まやく（麻薬）*n.*, 10S
(to) dry *(intr.)* かわく（乾く）う-*v.*, 5S

(to) dry (something) *(tran.)* かわかす（乾かす）う*-v.*, 5S
dumpling だんご(団子)*n.*, 3
during that time そのあいだ(に)（その間(に)）*conj.*, 2
duty きんむ（勤務）*vn.*, 8S

E

early はやい（早い）い*-adj.*, 4
the earth ちきゅう（地球）*n.*, 10
earthquake じしん（地震）*n.*, 5P, 10
east ひがし（東）*n.*, 1
East coast region ひがしかいがん（東海岸）*n.*, 1S
east entrance ひがしぐち（東口）*n.*, 6S
(to) eat (honorific) めしあがる（召し上がる）う*-v.*, 8
(to) eat (humble) いただく（頂く）う*-v.*, 8
ear infection ちゅうじえん（中耳炎）*n.*, prelim. S
economic conditions けいき（景気）*n.*, 10
electric mail でんしメール（電子メール）*n.*, 3
electricity でんき（電気）*n.*, 3
electric lights でんき（電気）*n.*, 3
elephant ぞう（象）*n.*, 10
e-mail でんしメール（電子メール）*n.*, 3
embassy たいしかん（大使館）*n.*, 6
emergency ひじょうじ（非常時）*n.*, 10S
employee しゃいん（社員）*n.*, 4P
employment possibility しゅうしょくぐち（就職口）*n.*, 8S
employment system こようせいど（雇用制度）*n.*, 8S
(to) end (something) *(tran.)* おえる（終える）る*-v.*, 5
end-of-year gift exchange おせいぼ（お歳暮）*n.*, 7
energy エネルギー *n.*, 10S
energy conservation しょうエネ（省エネ）*n.*, 10S
energy efficiency しょうエネ（省エネ）*n.*, 10S
engineer エンジニア *n.*, 4P, 5
entrance to get on train/bus じょうしゃぐち（乗車口）*n.*, 6S
envelope ふうとう（封筒）*n.*, 4
environment かんきょう（環境）*n.*, 10
equipped with ～ ～つき（～付き）*suf.*, 2S
equipped with shower シャワーつき（シャワー付き）*n.*, 2S
(to) escape にげる（逃げる）る*-v.*, 10
especially とくに（特に *adv.*, 2
essential ひつような（必要な）な*-adj.*, 10
essential items ひつじゅひん（必需品）*n.*, 10S
(to) establish たてる（建てる／立てる)）る*-v.*, 2
evening shower ゆうだち（夕立ち）*n.*, 1S
excessive fatigue かろう（過労）*n.*, Prelim. S
Excuse me. しつれいしました。（失礼しました。）*exp.*, 2P
exhaust gas はいきガス（排気ガス）*n.*, 10P
(to) exist (polite verb for ある and いる) ござる う*-v.*, 8
(to) exist(humble) おる う*-v.*, 8
experience けいけん（経験）*n.*, 8
(to) explain せつめいする（説明する）*vn.*, 8
explanation せつめい（説明）*vn.*, 8
explantion and emotional emphasis by female and children (casual) の *part.*, Prelim.
(to) explore しらべる（調べる）る*-v.*, 2
express mail, special delivery そくたつ（速達）*n.*, 4S
express parcel delivery たっきゅうびん（宅急便）*n.*, 4, 4P
express train きゅうこう(れっしゃ)（急行{列車}）*n.*, 6
express train (no additional cost) かいそく（快速）*n.*, 6S
expressions ことば（言葉）*n.*, 2

F

factory こうじょう（工場）*n.*, 10
factory worker こういん（工員）*n.*, 5S
Fahrenheit かし（華氏）*n.*, 1P
(to) fall ふる（降る）う*-v.*, 1
(to) fall さがる（下がる）う*-v.*, 1
(to) fall *(intr.)* たおれる（倒れる）る*-v.*, 5S
far from とおい（遠い）い*-adj.*, 6
farmer おひゃくしょう（お百姓）*n.*, 5S
fart おなら *n.*, 9S
fast はやい（速い）い*-adj.*, 4
Father's day ちちのひ（父の日）*n.*, 7
favor おねがい（お願い）*n.*, 3
favorable treatment ゆうぐう（優遇）*n.*, 8P
fax ファックス *n.*, 3
fear こわさ（怖さ）い*-adj.*, 10
fearful こわい（怖い）い*-adj.*, 10
fee for instruction じゅぎょうりょう（授業料）*n.*, 4
(to) feel おもう（思う）う*-v.*, 2
feeling きもち（気持ち）*n.*, 9
female (a formal word for おんなのひと（女の人）じょせい（女性）*n.*, 5P
female office worker (pronounced オーエル)ＯＬ *n.*, 5S
female speech marker わ *part.*, Prelim.
festival まつり（祭り）*n.*, 2P
field of specialty せんもん（専門）*n.*, 8
(to) fill out an application きにゅうする（記入する）*vn.*, 4
filling out きにゅう（記入)*vn.*, 4
finally さいごに conf., 3

(to) finish (something) *(tran.)* おえる（終える）る*-v.*, 5
fire かじ（火事）*n.*, 10
firefighter しょうぼうし（消防士）*n.*, 5S
first まず *conj.*, 3
first (of all) まず(はじめに) まず(始めに)) *conj.*, 2, 3
first class car of a train グリーンしゃ（グリーン車）*n.*, 6S
fisherman りょうし（漁師）*n.*, 5S
(to) fix *(tran.)* なおす（直す）う*-v.*, 5, 9
flavoring あじつけ（味付け）*n.*, 3P
flight attendant スチュワーデス *n.*, 5S
flood こうずい（洪水）*n.*, 1S, 10
flour こむぎこ（小麦粉）*n.*, 3S
(to) flow *(intr.)* ながれる（流れる）る*-v.*, 5S
flower はな（花）*n.*, 1
fog きり（霧）*n.*, 1S
(to) follow a person about つきまとう う*-v.*, 9S
following a street みちなり（道なり）*n.*, 6S
food poisoning しょくちゅうどく（食中毒）*n.*, Prelim. S
〜foot/feet 〜フィート *suf.*, 6P
for example たとえば（例えば）*conj.*, 4
foreign country がいこく（外国）*n.*, 2
foreign currency exchange がいこくかわせ（外国為替）*n.*, 4P
foreigner がいこくじん（外国人）*n.*, 4
forest しんりん（森林）*n.*, 10S
forest もり（森）*n.*, 10
(to) forget わすれる（忘れる）る*-v.*, 2
fork フォーク *n.*, 3
form ようし（用紙）*n.*, 8
former teacher and major professor or advisor おんし（恩師）*n.*, 7P
foul smell あくしゅう（悪臭）*n.*, 10P
fox きつね（狐）*n.*, 10S
free じゆうな（自由な）な*-adj.*, 5P
free activity じゆうこうどう（自由行動）*n.*, 2P
free time じゆうこうどう（自由行動）*n.*, 2P
freedom じゆう（自由）*n.*, 2P, 5P
frightened こわい（怖い）い*-adj.*, 10
frightening thing こわさ（怖さ）い*-adj.*, 10
frog かえる（蛙）*n.*, 10S
from 〜 を *part.*, 6
fruit くだもの（果物）*n.*, 7
fruitless むだな（無駄な）な*-adj.*, 10
(to) fry やく（焼く）う*-v.*, 3
frying pan フライパン *n.*, 3
funeral おそうしき（お葬式）*n.*, 7P
future しょうらい（将来）*n.*, 5

G

garbage ごみ is written either in hiragana or in katakana.) ごみ／ゴミ *n.*, 9
gas station ガソリンスタンド *n.*, 6
gasoline ガソリン *n.*, Prelim. S, 3P
(to) gather あつまる（集まる）う*-v.*, 5
general manager ぶちょう（部長）*n.*, 8S
(to) get a job at 〜 しゅうしょくする（就職する）*vn.*, 5
(to) get angry あたまにくる（頭に来る）*exp.*, 9S
(to) get angry はらがたつ（腹が立つ）*exp.*, 9S
(to) get angry おこる(怒る)る*-v.*,
(to) get frustrated いらいらする *exp.*, 9S
(to) get off おりる（降りる）る*-v.*, 6
get-together party こんしんかい（懇親会）*n.*, 5P
getting a job しゅうしょく（就職）*vn.*, 5
gift おくりもの（贈り物）*n.*, 7
gift certificate しょうひんけん（商品券）*n.*, 7
gift certificate for beer ビールけん（ビール券）*n.*, 7P
gift certificate for books としょけん（図書券）*n.*, 7S
gift for sympathy おみまい（お見舞い）*n.*, 7
giraffe キリン *n.*, 10S
girlfriend かのじょ（彼女）*n.*, 5P
(to) give (to a socially equal or inferior in-group person) くれる る*-v.*, 7
(to) give (to a socially equal person) あげる（上げる）る*-v.*, 7
(to) give (to a socially superior out-group person) さしあげる（差し上げる）る*-v.*, 7
(to) give (to socially inferior person) やる う*-v.*, 7
(to) give a ride (to someone) *(tran.)* のせる（乗せる）る*-v.*, 5
Give me a break. (female speech) いいかげんにしてよ（いい加減にしてよ）*exp.*, 9
Give me a break. (male speech) いいかげんにしろよ（いい加減にしろよ）*exp.*, 9
(to) go (honorific) まいる（参る）う*-v.*, 8
(to) go (honorific) いらっしゃる う*-v.*, 8
(to) go down さがる（下がる）う*-v.*, 1
(to) go off *(intr.)* きえる（消える）る*-v.*, 5
(to) go on a business trip しゅっちょうする（出張する）*vn.*, 8
(to) go out きえる（消える）る*-v.*, 5
(to) go sightseeing かんこうをする（観光をする）*vn.*, 2
(to) go through *(intr.)* とおる（通る）う*-v.*, 5S, 6
(to) go to pick up (someone) むかえにいく（迎えに行く）*exp.*, 9
(to) go up あがる（上がる）う*-v.*, 1

good (polite) よろしい い-*adj.*, 8
(to) grill やく（焼く）う-*v.*, 10
gorilla ゴリラ *n.*, 10S
grades せいせき（成績）*n.*, 4
graffiti らくがき（落書き）*n.*, 9
gram グラム *n.*, 3P
grape ぶどう（葡萄）*n.*, 3S
green tea おちゃ（お茶）*n.*, 7
ground meat ひきにく（ひき肉）*n.*, 3P
ground sinkage じばんちんか（地盤沈下）*n.*, 10P
guest きゃく（客）*n.*, Prelim. S, 4P, 8
guidance あんない（案内）*vn.*, 2S
(to) guide あんないする（案内する）*vn.*, 2S
guide ガイド *n.*, 2S
(to) guide〜 〜のあんないをする（〜の案内をする）*vn.*, 2S
guidebook ガイドブック *n.*, 2

H

hail あられ; ひょう *n.*, 1S
ham ハム *n.*, 7P
handkerchief ハンカチ *n.*, 7S
handshake あくしゅ（握手）*vn.*, 4
(to) happen おきる（起きる）る-*v.*, 10
hateful いやな な-*adj.*, 9
Hawaiian shirt アロハシャツ *n.*, 2P
hay fever かふんしょう（花粉症）*n.*, Prelim. S
headquarter ほんしゃ（本社）*n.*, 8S
(to) heal *(intr.)* なおる（直る）う-*v.*, 5
health insurance けんこうほけん（健康保険）*n.*, 4P
heavy rain おおあめ（大雨）*n.*, 1S
heavy snow おおゆき（大雪）*n.*, 1S
(to) help てつだう（手伝う）う-*v.*, 3
hernia ヘルニア *n.*, prelim. S
high-heel shoes ハイヒール *n.*, 7P
highest temperature さいこうきおん（最高気温）*n.*, 1P
(to) hit ぶつける る-*v.*, 9
(to) hit someone なぐる（殴る）う-*v.*, 9S
Hokkaido (northernmost main island of Japan) ほっかいどう（北海道）*n.*, 1P
Hokuriku Region ほくりく（北陸）*n.*, 1P
Honshuu Island ほんしゅう（本州）*n.*, 1P
hope きぼう（希望）*n.*, 8S
horse うま（馬）*n.*, 10
hostage ひとじち（人質）*n.*, 10S
hot spring おんせん（温泉）*n.*, 2S
hot water おゆ（お湯）*n.*, 5
hot water ゆ（湯）*n.*, 3P
household work かじ（家事）*n.*, 5P
houseplant はちうえ（鉢植え）*n.*, 7
how to〜 〜かた（〜方）*suf.*, 3
however けれども *conj.*, 2
humid むしあつい（蒸し暑い）い-*adj.*, 1
humidity しつど（湿度）*n.*, 1S
hurricane ハリケーン *n.*, 10

I

I am against it. はんたいだ（反対だ）*exp.*, 10
I am sorry. ごめんなさい（ご免なさい。）*exp.*, 3
I'm sorry. (used in casual speech) ごめん。（ご免。）*exp.*, 3
I did not realize it. きがつかなくて。（気が付かなくて）*exp.*, 9
I hope you like it. おすきだとよろしいのですが。（お好きだとよろしいのですが。）*exp.*, 7
I hope you will have a wonderful year. すばらしいいちねんであることをおいのりします（素晴しい一年であることをお祈りします）*exp.*, 7P
I still have a lot to learn. まだまだです。*exp.*, 8
I think so, too. わたしもそうおもいます。（私もそう思います。）*exp.*, 10
I think that〜 〜とおもいます（〜と思います）*exp.*, Prelim. S
I though it would be a token of appreciation. おれいにとおもいまして。（お礼にと思いまして。）*exp.*, 7
I'm sorry . (polite and formal) もうしわけありません（申し訳ありません）*exp.*, 9
I'm sorry . (very polite and formal) もうしわけございません（申し訳ございません）*exp.*, 9
I'm sorry to cause you problems. ごめいわくおかけしてもうしわけありません（ご迷惑おかけして申しわけありません）*exp.*, 9
I'm sorry to have caused you so much trouble. おきをつかわせてしまいまして。（お気を使わせてしまいまして。）*exp.*, 7
If you say〜 〜といえば *exp.*, 4
(to) ignore むしする（無視する）*vn.*, 9S
important だいじな（大事な）な-*adj.*, 8
important じゅうだいな（重大な）な-*adj.*, 10P
important たいせつな（大切な）な-*adj.*, 7, 4P
in the center of まんなか（まん中）*loc. n.*, 6S
in the right middle of まんなか（まん中）*loc. n.*, 6S
〜included 〜つき（〜付き）*suf.*, 2S
inconvenient ふべんな（不便な）な-*adj.*, 10
(to) increase *(intr.)* ふえる（増える）る-*v.*, 10
industrial pollution こうがい（公害）*n.*, 10
industrial waste さんぎょうはいきぶつ（産業廃棄物）*n.*, 10S

(to) inform おしえる（教える）る-*v.*, 3
information center あんないしょ（案内所）*n.*, 2S
information session せつめいかい（説明会）*n.*, 8S
information session organized by company for new recruits かいしゃせつめいかい（会社説明会）*n.*, 8S
ingredients ざいりょう（材料）*n.*, 3
inner part of a house or a room おく（奥）*loc. n.*, 6S
insect むし（虫）*n.*, 10S
instructor きょうし（教師）*n.*, 5S
insults わるくち（悪口）*n.*, 9
insurance ほけん（保険）*n.*, 2P
intention つもり *n.*, 2
interest かんしん（関心）*n.*, 10
international こくさい（国際）*n.*, 3P, 9P
international call こくさいでんわ（国際電話）*n.*, 3P
Internet インターネット *n.*, 3
interpersonal relationships なか（仲）*n.*, 7P
intersection こうさてん（交差点）*n.*, 6
interview めんせつ（面接）*n.*, 8
(to) investigate しらべる（調べる）る-*v.*, 2
invitation しょうたい（招待）*vn.*, 5
invitation letter or card しょうたいじょう（招待状）*n.*, 5
(to) invite しょうたいする（招待する）*vn.*, 5
〜island 〜とう（〜島）*suf.*, 2P
island しま（島）*n.*, 1P
It is of little value... たいしたものじゃありませんから。（たいした物じゃありませんから。）*exp.*, 7
it is.... 〜といえば *exp.*, 4
it's about 〜 〜についてなんですが *exp.*, 2
it's about 〜 〜についてなんですけど *exp.*, 2
it's about 〜 〜のことなんですが *exp.*, 2
it's about 〜 〜のことなんですけど *exp.*, 2
it's because というのは *conj.*, 2

J

jam ジャム *n.*, 3S
the Japan Sea にほんかい（日本海）*n.*, 1P
Japanese history にほんし（日本史）*n.*, 5P
Japanese rice wine さけ（酒）*n.*, 7
Japanese sake にほんしゅ（日本酒）*n.*, 7S
Japanese-style inn りょかん（旅館）*n.*, 2
Japanese summer kimono ゆかた *n.*, 2P
Japanese-style private guest house みんしゅく（民宿）*n.*, 2
job hunt しゅうしょくかつどう（就職活動）*n.*, 8S
JR Chuo-line ちゅうおうせん（中央線）*n.*, 6P
JR Line ＪＲ *n.*, 6
the JR's loop line in Tokyo やまのてせん（山の手線）*n.*, 6P
Just a little bit... ほんのすこしですから。（ほんの少しですから。）*exp.*, 7
Just a token of my appreciation. ほんのきもちですから。（ほんの気持ちですから。）*exp.*, 7
just before てまえ（手前）*loc. n.*, 6

K

kangaroo カンガルー *n.*, 10S
Kanto Region かんとう（関東）*n.*, 1P
(to) keep (a pet) かう（飼う）う-*v.*, 4
key かぎ（鍵）*n.*, 4
(to) kill ころす（殺す）う-*v.*, 2P, 10
kilo (kilogram or kilometer) 〜キロ *suf.*, 4
Kinki Region きんき（近畿）*n.*, 1P
kitchen だいどころ（台所）*n.*, 7P
kitchen knife ほうちょう（包丁）*n.*, 7P
knife ナイフ *n.*, 3
(to) knock (at a door) ノックする *vn.*, 4
knock ノック *vn.*, 4
(to) knock down *(tran.)* たおす（倒す）う-*v.*, 5S
(to) know しっている（知っている）る-*v.*, 2
(to) know (honorific) ごぞんじ（ご存じ）*n.*, 8
(to) know (humble) ぞんじる（存じる）る-*v.*, 8
(to) know (humble) ぞんじておる（存じておる）う-*v.*, 8
koala コアラ *n.*, 10S
Kyushu Island きゅうしゅう（九州）*n.*, 1P

L

label to be attached to a gift indicating the purpose and the sender のし *n.*, 7S
ladle おたま *n.*, 3S
lake みずうみ（湖）*n.*, 2
landlady おおや（大家）*n.*, 9
landlord おおや（大家）*n.*, 9
language ことば（言葉）*n.*, 2
large corporation だいきぎょう（大企業）*n.*, 5P
large trash そだいごみ（粗大ごみ）*n.*, 9P
lastly さいごに（最後に）*conj.*, 3
late おそい（遅い）い-*adj.*, 4
late at night よなか（夜中）*n.*, 9
lawn mowing しばかり（芝刈り）*n.*, 9S
lawyer べんごし（弁護士）*n.*, 5
leaf は（葉）*n.*, 1
(to) learn ならう（習う）う-*v.*, 8
(to) leave でる（出る）る-*v.*, 2
(to) leave home うちをでる（家を出る）る-*v.*, 2

Leave me alone. (female speech) ほっといてよ *exp.*, 9
Leave me alone. (male speech) ほっといてくれよ *exp.*, 9
(to) leave(something) *(tran.)* のこす（残す） う*-v.*, 5
lecture こうえん（講演） *n.*, 8P
left ひだり（左） *loc. n.*, 6
(to) lend かす（貸す） う*-v.*, 3
length ながさ（長さ） *n.*, 4S
(to) let (something) cool さます（冷ます） う*-v.*, 3S
(to) let (something) flow *(tran.)* ながす（流す） う*-v.*, 5S
(to) let something flow ながす（流す） う*-v.*, 10
letter of reference すいせんじょう（推薦状） *n.*, 8
lie うそ（嘘） *n.*, 2P, 9
lifetime employment しゅうしんこよう（終身雇用） *n.*, 5P
light rain こさめ（小雨） *n.*, 1S
light soy sauce うすくちしょうゆ（薄口醤油） *n.*, 3P
lightening いなびかり（稲光り） *n.*, 1S
limit で *part.*, 6
limited express train とっきゅう（れっしゃ）（特急(列車)） *n.*, 6
(to) line (something) up *(tran.)* ならべる（並べる） る*-v.*, 5S
〜 Line (train line) 〜せん（〜線） *suf.*, 6
(to) line up *(intr.)* ならぶ（並ぶ） う*-v.*, 5S
lion ライオン *n.*, 10S
lipstick くちべに（口紅） *n.*, 7S
liquor さけ（酒） *n.*, 7
(to) listen きく（聞く）う*-v.*, 10
lobby ロビー *n.*, 2P
local favorite food めいさんひん（名産品） *n.*, 7S
local train かくえきていしゃ（各駅停車） *n.*, 6
local train ふつう(れっしゃ) 普通(列車)) *n.*, 6
location ばしょ（場所） *n.*, 2
(to) lock かける る*-v.*, 4
lock かぎ（鍵） *n.*, 4
(to) look at (honorific) ごらんになる（ご覧になる） う*-v.*, 8
(to) look at (humble form) はいけんする（拝見する *ir. v.*, 8
(to) look for〜 さがす（探す／捜す） う*-v.*, 2
look like そう な*-adj.*, 1
(to) lose なくす う*-v.*, 10
loud voice おおごえ（大声） *n.*, 9S
(to) lower (something) *(tran.)* さげる（下げる） る*-v.*, 5S
lowest temperature さいていきおん（最低気温） *n.*, 1P
luggage にもつ（荷物） *n.*, 2S
lunch ちゅうしょく（昼食） *n.*, 2S
lunch included ちゅうしょくつき（昼食付き） *n.*, 2S

M

machine きかい（機械） *n.*, 3
mailbox (for incoming mail only) ゆうびんうけ（郵便受け） *n.*, 4P
major street おおどおり（大通り） *n.*, 6S
(to) make たてる（建てる／立てる)） る*-v.*, 2
(to) make noise おとをたてる（音を立てる） *exp.*, 9
(to) make something dirty *(tran.)* よごす（汚す） う*-v.*, 5S, 9
(to) make something disappear なくす う*-v.*, 10
(to) make a mistake *(tran.)* まちがえる（間違える） る*-v.*, 5
(to) make a reservation よやくする（予約する） *vn.*, 2
(to) make noise さわぐ（騒ぐ） う*-v.*, 9
male (a formal word for おとこのひと（男の人)) だんせい（男性） *n.*, 5P
manager マネージャー *n.*, 4P, 5
mandarin orange みかん *n.*, 3S
map ちず（地図） *n.*, 1P, 2
materials ざいりょう（材料） *n.*, 3
mean behavior いじわる *n.*, 9S
meaning いみ（意味） *n.*, 3
measuring cup カップ *n.*, 3P
meddlesome おせっかいな（お節介な） な*-adj.*, 9S
meddling おせっかい（お節介） *n.*, 9S
medium temperature (cooking) ちゅうおん（中温） *n.*, 3P
(to) meet (humble) おめにかかる（お目にかかる） う*-v.*, 8
meeting かいぎ（会議） *n.*, 8
(to) meet or welcome むかえる（迎える）る*-v.*, 9
(to) melt *(intr.)* とける（溶ける） る*-v.*, 5S
(to) melt *(tran.)* とかす（溶かす） う*-v.*, 5S
(to) memorize おぼえる（覚える） る*-v.*, 3
meter 〜メートル *suf.*, 6
microwave oven でんしレンジ（電子レンジ） *n.*, 3S
mid-year gift exchange おちゅうげん（お中元） *n.*, 7
Midwest region (USA) ちゅうせいぶ（中西部） *n.*, 1S
Mind your own business. よけいなおせっかいだ（余計なお節介だ） *exp.*, 9S
minus マイナス *n.*, 1
misconduct ひこう（非行） *n.*, 10S
(to) miss (something) まちがえる（間違える） る*-v.*, 5
(to) mix あえる（和える） る*-v.*, 3S
(to) mix まぜる（混ぜる） る*-v.*, 3
(to) mix thoroughly かきまぜる（かきまぜる） る-*v.*, 3S
mixer ミキサー *n.*, 3S
mixing bowl ボウル *n.*, 3S
model モデル *n.*, 4P, 5S

money wrapped in paper as a gift かねづつみ（金包み） *n.*, 7S
monkey さる（猿） *n.*, 10
mosquito か（蚊） *n.*, 10S
Mother's day ははのひ（母の日） *n.*, 7
(to) move (residence) ひっこす（引っ越す） う-*v.*, 9
movie theater えいがかん（映画館） *n.*, 6
moving (one's residence) ひっこし（引っ越し） *n.*, 9
mug コーヒーカップ *n.*, 7
(to) murder ころす（殺す） う-*v.*, 2P, 10
murder さつじん（殺人） *n.*, 10S
musician ミュージシャン *n.*, 4P

N

nature しぜん（自然） *n.*, 10
near ちかい（近い） い-*adj.*, 6
necessary ひつような（必要な） な-*adj.*, 10
(to) need いる（要る） う-*v.*, 4
neighborhood きんじょ（近所） *n.*, 9
new recruits しんにゅうしゃいん（新入社員） *n.*, 8S
news ニュース *n.*, 10
next つぎ（次） *n.*, 6
next つぎに（次に） *conj.*, 2, 3
nice scenery けしきがいい（景色がいい） *n.*, 2S
〜nights, 〜days 〜はく〜か（〜泊〜日） *suf.*, 2
no good だめな な-*adj.*, 4
no good むだな（無駄な） な-*adj.*, 10
no (casual) いや *interj.*, P
no (casual) ううん *interj.*, P
No, that's not so. いいえ、そうでもありません。 *exp.*, 8
No, that's not so. いいえ、そうでもございません。 *exp.*, 8
No, it is not the case. いいえ、そんなことはありません。 *exp.*, 8
No, it is not the case. いいえ、そんなことはございません。 *exp.*, 8
noise そうおん（騒音） *n.*, 10P
noisy うるさい い-*adj.*, 9
non-reserved seat じゆうせき（自由席） *n.*, 6P
normal ふつう（普通） *n.*, 4
north きた（北） *n.*, 1
north entrance きたぐち（北口） *n.*, 6S
northeast ほくとう（北東） *n.*, 1
northwest ほくせい（北西） *n.*, 1
notes ノート *n.*, 3
novel しょうせつ（小説） *n.*, 7
number すうじ（数字） *n.*, 3P
number かず（数） *n.*, 10
number of sheets まいすう（枚数） *n.*, 3P

O

objective もくてき（目的） *n.*, 4P, 7P
octopus たこ *n.*, 3S
officious おせっかいな（お節介な） な-*adj.*, 9S
officiousness おせっかい（お節介） *n.*, 9S
oil あぶら（油） *n.*, 3
old-growth forest げんせいりん（原生林） *n.*, 10S
older person としうえ（年上） *n.*, 9
the oldest subway line in Japan ぎんざせん（銀座線） *n.*, 6P
one's boss or superior in work place じょうし（上司） *n.*, 7P, 8
one room (apartment) ワンルーム *n.*, 4P
oneself じぶん（自分） *n.*, 5P
onion たまねぎ（玉ねぎ） *n.*, 3
(to) open (an account/a book) ひらく（開く） う-*v.*, 4
(to) open *(intr.)* あく（開く） う-*v.*, 5
open search こうぼ（公募） *n.*, 8S
the opposite side むかいがわ（向かい側） *loc. n.*, 6
ordinal numbers 〜つめ（〜つ目） *suf.*, 6
(to) organize かたづける（片付ける） る-*v.*, 9
the other side むかいがわ（向かい側） *loc. n.*, 6
ounce オンス *n.*, 3P
out of 〜 を *part.*, 6
oven オーブン *n.*, 3S
over time ざんぎょう（残業） *n.*, 8S
(to) overlap かさなる（重なる） う-*v.*, 6P
overseas かいがい（海外） *n.*, 2
overseas がいこく（外国） *n.*, 2
overseas travel かいがいりょこう（海外旅行） *n.*, 2
over there あちら *demo.*, 8
over there あっち *demo.*, 8
owner of 〜 retail store 〜や（〜屋） *suf.*, 5
ozone layer オゾンそう（オゾン層） *n.*, 10S

P

the Pacific Ocean たいへいよう（太平洋） *n.*, 1P
Pacific ocean side (east side) of Japan たいへいようがわ（太平洋側） *n.*, 1S
package パック *n.*, 10P
painter がか（画家） *n.*, 10P
pajamas ねまき（寝巻） *n.*, 7S
panda パンダ *n.*, 10S
(academic) paper レポート *n.*, 4
paper かみ（紙） *n.*, 10P
paper and pencil test ひっきしけん（筆記試験） *n.*, 8S
parcel delivery service たくはいサービス（宅配サービス） *n.*, 4

parcel post こづつみ（小包） *n.*, 4
parent おや（親） *n.*, 9
parking garage ちゅうしゃじょう（駐車場） *n.*, 6
parking lot ちゅうしゃじょう（駐車場） *n.*, 6
part-time worker パート *n.*, 8P
particularly とくに（特に *adv.*, 2
(to) pass とおる（通る）う-*v.*, 6
passport パスポート *n.*, 2
patient かんじゃ（患者） *n.*, 4P
(to) pay はらう（払う） う-*v.*, 2
(to) pay attention きをつける（気をつける） *exp.*, 9
pedestrian bridge ほどうきょう（歩道橋） *n.*, 6S
pedestrian crossing おうだんほどう（横断歩道） *n.*, 6
penguin ペンギン *n.*, 10S
people who join in the same year どうき（同期） *n.*, 8S
pepper こしょう（胡椒） *n.*, 3
perfume こうすい（香水） *n.*, 7S
permanent staff member せいしゃいん（正社員） *n.*, 8P
person with experience けいけんしゃ（経験者） *n.*, 8P
personal check チェック *n.*, 4S
personal computer パソコン *n.*, 3
personal identification number (PIN) あんしょうばんごう（暗証番号） *n.*, 4S
personal information form しんじょうしょ（身上書） *n.*, 8S
personal stamp はんこ（判子） *n.*, 4P
personal stamp いんかん（印鑑） *n.*, 4P
personal stamp shop はんこや（判子屋） *n.*, 4P
piano ピアノ *n.*, 9
picture postcard えはがき（絵葉書） *n.*, 2S
pig ぶた（豚） *n.*, 10
pigeon はと（鳩） *n.*, 10S
pilot パイロット *n.*, 5S
(to) pinch はさむ（挟む） う-*v.*, 3P
pint パイント *n.*, 3P
(to) place おく（置く）う-v., 9
Place in which movement occurs を *part.*, 6
place of meeting かいじょう（会場） *n.*, 5
plan けいかく（計画） *n.*, 2
plan よてい（予定） *n.*, 2
plants しょくぶつ（植物） *n.*, 7P
plate さら（皿） *n.*, 3
(to) play (musical instrument) ひく（弾く） う-*v.*, 9
Please do not concern yourself on my behalf. おきをつかわないで下さい。（お気を使わないで下さい。） *exp.*, 7
Please do not worry about me. そんなしんぱいしないでください。（そんな心配しないで下さい。） *exp.*, 7
Please don't put yourself out for me. あまりきをつかわないで下さい。（あまり気を使わないで下さい。） *exp.*, 7
plentiful おおい（多い） い-*adj.*, 1
police けいさつ（警察） *n.*, 10
police officer けいさつかん（警察官） *n.*, 5S
politician せいじか（政治家） *n.*, 5S
(to) pollute おせんする る-v., 10
pollution おせん（汚染） *vn.*, 10P
pork ぶたにく（豚肉） *n.*, 3
postage stamp きって（切手） *n.*, 4
post code ゆうびんばんごう（郵便番号） *n.*, 4P
postal parcel ゆうびんこづつみ（郵便小包） *n.*, 4S
postal savings account ゆうびんちょきん（郵便貯金） *n.*, 4S
postal service ゆうびん（郵便） *n.*, 4
pot なべ（鍋） *n.*, 3
potato じゃがいも *n.*, 3
pound ～ポンド *suf.*, 4
(to) pour かける る-*v.*, 3P
(to) pour ながす（流す） う-*v.*, 10
(to) practice れんしゅうする（練習する） *vn.*, 3
practice れんしゅう（練習） *vn.*, 3
(to) praise ほめる（誉める） る-*v.*, 9
pre-paid telephone card テレフォンカード *n.*, 3
precious たいせつな（大切な） な-*adj.*, 7
preparation じゅんび（準備） *vn.*, 2S, 5
(to) prepare じゅんびする（準備する） *vn.*, 2S, 5
present プレゼント *n.*, 7
(to) prevent ふせぐ（防ぐ） う-*v.*, 10
price ねだん（値段） *n.*, 7P
printed matter いんさつぶつ（印刷物） *n.*, 4S
a private line connecting Tokyo and Narita Airport けいせいせん(京成線)n., 6P
problems トラブル n., 2P
professor きょうじゅ（教授） *n.*, 5S
project プロジェクト *n.*, 8
promotion しょうかく（昇格） *n.*, 8S
pronunciation (of a character) よみ（読み） *n.*, 3
prostitution ばいしゅん（売春） *n.*, 10S
(to) protect まもる（守る） う-*v.*, 4P, 10
public mailbox (for outgoing mail only) ポスト） *n.*, 4
public office employee こうむいん（公務員） *n.*, 5S
purpose もくてき（目的） *n.*, 4P, 7P
purse さいふ（財布） *n.*, 5
(to) push おす（押す） う-*v.*, 3
(to) put (someone) in bed *(tran.)* ねかす（寝かす） う-*v.*, 5S
(to) put (something) through *(tran.)* とおす（通す） う-*v.*, 5S

(to) put on (polite) おめしになる（お召しになる）う-*v.*, 8S
putting out the trash ごみだし n.,9

Q

qualification じょうけん（条件）*n.*, 4P, 8P
quantity りょう（量）*n.*, 10P
quarter がっき（学期）*n.*, 2P, 4
question しつもん（質問）*n.*, 2
(to) quit やめる（止める）る-*v.*, 5

R

rabbit うさぎ *n.*, 10S
raccoon たぬき *n.*, 10S
rain あめ（雨）*n.*, 1
rainbow にじ（虹）*n.*, 1S
rainy あめ（雨）*n.*, 1
rainy season つゆ（梅雨）*n.*, 1P
(to) raise *(tran.)* あげる（上げる）る-*v.*, 5
reading よみ（読み）*n.*, 3
real thing ほんもの（本物）*n.*, 2P
(to) receive うける（受ける）る-*v.*, 4
(to) receive もらう う-*v.*, 7
recently さいきん（最近）*n.*, 1P, 10
reception desk うけつけ（受付）*n.*, 5P, 8
reciprocation おかえし（お返し）*n.*, 7P
reckless driving ぼうそう（暴走）*vn.*, 9S
record book for an account よきんつうちょう（預金通帳）*n.*, 4S
recruitment ぼしゅう（募集）*n.*, 8P
recycling リサイクル *n.*, 9P, 10
registered mail かきとめ（書留）*n.*, 4S
registered mail for cash げんきんかきとめ（現金書留）*n.*, 4S
registration desk うけつけ（受付）*n.*, 5P, 8
regular ふつう（普通）*n.*, 4
regular saving account ふつうよきん（普通預金）*n.*, 4
relationship (among people) なか（仲）*n.*, 7P, 9
relationship かんけい(関係) *n.*, 9
religion しゅうきょう（宗教）*n.*, 7P
(to) remember おぼえる（覚える）る-*v.*, 3
remote contro lリモコン(リモートコントロール = リモコン) *n.*, 3
(to) remove (clothes/shoes) ぬぐ（脱ぐ）う-*v.*, 4
rent アパートだい（アパート代）*n.*, 4P, 7P
(to) repair *(tran.)* なおす（直す）う-*v.*, 5, 9
(to) reply へんじする（返事する）*vn.*, 5P, 8
reply へんじ（返事）*vn.*, 5P, 8
report レポート *n.*, 4
research けんきゅう（研究）*vn.*, 5
researcher けんきゅういん（研究員）*n.*, 5S
reservation よやく（予約）*vn.*, 2
(to) reserve a ticket きっぷをよやくする（切符を予約する）*vn.*, 2
reserved seat していせき（指定席）*n.*, 6P
(to) respond へんじする（返事する）*vn.*, 5P, 8
response へんじ（返事）*vn.*, 5P, 8
restructuring リストラ *n.*, 5P
resume りれきしょ（履歴書）*n.*, 8
(to) return (honorific) いらっしゃる う-*v.*, 8
(for someone/something to) return *(intr.)* もどる（戻る）う-*v.*, 5P
(to) return something かえす（返す）う-*v.*, 3
(to) return (something) *(tran.)* もどす（戻す）う-*v.*, 5S
reunion party どうそうかい（同窓会）*n.*, 5
rice cooker すいはんき（炊飯器）*n.*, 3S
rice spachelar しゃもじ *n.*, 3S
right みぎ（右）*loc. n.*, 6
(for a telephone) (to) ring かかる う-*v.*, 5
ring ゆびわ（指輪）*n.*, 7
(for a telephone to) ring かかる う-v., 5
(to) rise あがる（上がる）う-*v.*, 1
river かわ（川）*n.*, 6
road どうろ（道路）*n.*, 6
road みち（道）*n.*, 6
(to) roast いる（煎る）う-*v.*, 3S
robbery ごうとう（強盗）*n.*, 10S
rose バラ／ばら *n.*, 2P, 7
rude しつれいな（失礼）な-*adj.*, 9S
rule きそく（規則）*n.*, 4
rumor うわさ（噂）*n.*, 9
(to) run out of (something) *(tran.)* きらす（切らす）う-*v.*, 5S

S

safe あんぜんな（安全な）な-*adj.*, 10
salad oil サラダオイル n., 7P
salary きゅうりょう（給料）*n.*, 5
salesclerk てんいん(店員)n., Prelim. S, 7
salt しお（塩）*n.*, 3
same おなじ（同じ）な-*adj.*, 2P, 5
sample サンプル *n.*, 4P
San'in Region さんいん（山陰）*n.*, 1P
Sanyo Region さんよう（山陽）*n.*, 1P
sarcastic remark いやみ（嫌味）*n.*, 9S
sauce ソース *n.*, 3S
sausages ソーセージ *n.*, 7P
(to) save (money at the bank) よきんする（預金する）*vn.*, 4
(to) save money ちょきんする（貯金する）*vn.*, 4

saving よきん（預金）*vn.*, 4
savings (money) ちょきん（貯金）*vn.*, 4
(to) say いう（言う）う-*v.*, 2
(to) say (humble) もうす（申す）う-*v.*, 8
(to) say (honorific) おっしゃる う-*v.*, 8
(to) say (humble) もうしあげる（申し上げる）る-*v.*, 8
scallion ねぎ *n.*, 3S
scarce すくない（少ない）い-*adj.*, 1
scenery けしき（景色）*n.*, 2S
schedule よてい（予定）*n.*, 2
scholarship しょうがくきん（奨学金）*n.*, 4P
(to) scold しかる（叱る）う-*v.*, 9
Sea of Japan side (west side) of Japan にほんかいがわ（日本海側）*n.*, 1S
seal はんこ（判子）*n.*, 4
seal いんかん（印鑑）*n.*, 4P
seaweed のり（海苔）*n.*, 7P
section chief かちょう（課長）*n.*, 8
secure あんぜんな（安全な）な-*adj.*, 10
seem そう な-*adj.*, 1
(to) select えらぶ（選ぶ）う-*v.*, 3P, 7
(to) sell うる（売る）う-*v.*, 4P, 5
semester がっき（学期）*n.*, 2P, 4
semiannual bonus しょうよ（賞与）*n.*, 8S
seminar ゼミ *n.*, 5P
(to) send おくる（送る）う-*v.*, 3
senior citizen おとしより（お年より）*n.*, 10
seniority ねんこうじょれつ（年功序列）*n.*, 5P
service サービス *n.*, 4
(to) shake hands あくしゅする（握手する）*vn.*, 4
(to) shake off water みずをきる（水を切る）*exp.*, 3P
she かのじょ（彼女）*n.*, 5P
Shikoku Island しこく（四国）*n.*, 1P
ship ふね（船）*n.*, 2S
shop みせ（店）*n.*, 2
shortly すぐ *adv.*, 6
shouting おおごえ（大声）*n.*, 9S
(to) show (humble) おめにかける（お目にかける）る-*v.*, 8
(to) show around あんないする（案内する）*vn.*, 2S
(to) show ～ ～のあんないをする（～の案内をする）*vn.*, 2S
(to) show up (polite) おいでになる う-*v.*, 8
shower にわかあめ（にわか雨）*n.*, 1S
shrimp えび（海老）*n.*, 3P
shirimp dumpling えびだんご（海老団子）*n.*, 3P
shut up! うるさい い-*adj.*, 9
side ～がわ（～側）*suf.*, 6
side walk ほどう（歩道）*n.*, 6S
sightseeing かんこう（観光）*vn.*, 2
sightseeing spot かんこうち（観光地）*n.*, 2S
sightseeing trip かんこうりょこう（観光旅行）*n.*, 2
signature サイン *n.*, 4
singer かしゅ（歌手）*n.*, 5S
single シングル *n.*, 2P
size おおきさ（大きさ）*n.*, 4S
skillet フライパン *n.*, 3
sky そら（空）*n.*, 1
(to) sleep (honorific) おやすみになる（お休みになる）う-*v.*, 8
sleet みぞれ *n.*, 1S
sliced bread しょくパン（食パン）*n.*, 3P
sliced cheese スライスチーズ *n.*, 3P
slow おそい（遅い）い-*adj.*, 4
slowly ゆっくり *adv.*, 5
Slowly please. ゆっくりおねがいします。（ゆっくりお願いします。）*exp.*, 5
a small amount of money given to children on New Year's Day おとしだま（お年玉）*n.*, 7P
small business ちゅうしょうきぎょう（中小企業）*n.*, 5P
small business れいさいきぎょう（零細企業）*n.*, 5P
smoke けむり（煙）*n.*, 10S
snake へび（蛇）*n.*, 10S
sneakers スニーカー *n.*, 7
snoring いびき *n.*, 9S
snow ゆき（雪）*n.*, 1
The Snow Festival ゆきまつり（雪祭り）*n.*, 2P
snow pea さやえんどう（さやえんどう）*n.*, 3S
snowstorm ふぶき（吹雪）*n.*, 1S
snowy ゆき（雪）*n.*, 1
so だから *conj.*, 2
so ですから *conj.*, 2
so それで *conj.*, 2
so-so. まあまあです。*exp.*, 8
soap せっけん（石鹸）*n.*, 7
society しゃかい（社会）*n.*, 10
soil pollution どじょうおせん（土壌汚染）*n.*, 10P
someone which is kept out of a group なかまはずれ（仲間外れ）*n.*, 9S
soon すぐ *adv.*, 6
sound おと（音）*n.*, 9
south みなみ（南）*n.*, 1
South region なんぶ（南部）*n.*, 1S
southeast なんとう（南東）*n.*, 1
southwest なんせい（南西）*n.*, 1
Southwest region なんせいぶ（南西部）*n.*, 1S
souvenir おみやげ（お土産）*n.*, 2
soy bean paste みそ（味噌）*n.*, 3S

soy sauce しょうゆ（しょう油）*n.*, 3
(to) speak ill of わるくち（悪口）*n.*, 9
speaking of that. .そういえば *exp.*, 4
speech contest スピーチコンテスト *n.*, 3P
spice スパイス *n.*, 3S
spinach ほうれんそう（ほうれん草）*n.*, 3S
sport shoes スニーカー *n.*, 7
square bracket かぎかっこ *n.*, 2P
squid いか *n.*, 3S
squirrel りす *n.*, 10S
(to) stay とまる（泊まる）う*-v.*, 2
(to) steal ぬすむ（盗む）う*-v.*, 9
(to) steam むす（蒸す）う*-v.*, 3S
(to) step on ふむ（踏む）う*-v.*, 9
(to) stew にる（煮る）る*-v.*, 3
(to) stir-fry (cooking) いためる（炒める）る*-v.*, 3S
(to) stop やめる（止める）る*-v.*, 5
(to) stop *(intr.)* とまる（止まる）う*-v.*, 6
(to) stop *(intr.)* やむ（止む）う*-v.*, 5S
(to) stop (something) とめる（止める）る*-v.*, 6
store みせ（店）*n.*, 2
store clerk てんいん（店員）*n.*, Prelim. S
storm あらし（嵐）*n.*, 1S
straight まっすぐ *adv.*, 6
strainer ざる *n.*, 3S
strange へん(な)(変{な})な*-adj.*, 9
strawberry いちご（苺）*n.*, 3S
street どうろ（道路）*n.*, 6
street みち（道）*n.*, 6
stress かろう（過労）*n.*, Prelim. S
stroll さんぽ（散歩）*vn.*, 9
strong つよい（強い）い*-adj.*, 1
student discount がくわり（学割）*n.*, 6P
student identification がくせいしょう（学生証）*n.*, 4
(to) study abroad りゅうがくする（留学する）*vn.*, 5
study abroad りゅうがく（留学）*vn.*, 5
stuffed toy animal ぬいぐるみ *n.*, 7
subordinate ぶか（部下）*n.*, 8S
subway ちかてつ（地下鉄）*n.*, 6
a subway line connecting places inside the loop of the Yamanote line まるのうちせん（丸ノ内線）*n.*, 6P
suffix to convert adjective to a noun for measurement 〜さ *suf.*, 7
sugar さとう（砂糖）*n.*, 3
suicide じさつ（自殺）*n.*, 9P
suitcase スーツケース *n.*, 2
sunglasses サングラス *n.*, 1P, 7S
sunny はれ（晴れ）*n.*, 1
(to) support (financially) *(tran.)* やしなう（養う）う*-v.*, 5P
surfboard サーフボード *n.*, 2P
surface mail ふなびん（船便）*n.*, 4
the surface of the sea かいめん（海面）*n.*, 10P
surfing サーフィン *n.*, 2P
survey アンケート *n.*, 5P
sweetheart かのじょ（彼女）*n.*, 5P
sweet rice wine for cooking みりん *n.*, 3P
sweets おかし（お菓子）*n.*, 7
swindle さぎ（詐欺）*n.*, 10S
switch スイッチ *n.*, 3
sympathy gift おみまい（お見舞い）*n.*, 7

T

tableware しょっき（食器）*n.*, 7S
taco タコス *n.*, 2P
(to) take もっていく（持って行く）う*-v.*, 2, 3
(to) take (time or money) かかる う*-v.*, 4
(to) take (someone) つれていく（連れて行く）う*-v.*, 3
(to) take (something) into consideration かんがえる（考える）る*-v.*, 4P, 5
(to) take a walk さんぽする（散歩する）*vn.*, 9
(to) take a walk さんぽをする（散歩をする）*vn.*, 9
(to) take off (clothe/shoes) ぬぐ（脱ぐ）う*-v.*, 4
(to) take place おきる（起きる）る*-v.*, 10
(to) take time *(tran.)* かける る*-v.*, 5S
talking on the phone for a long time ながでんわ（長電話）*n.*, 9S
tax ぜいきん（税金）*n.*, 5P
taxi タクシー *n.*, 6
taxi stand タクシーのりば（タクシー乗り場）*n.*, 6S
tea おちゃ（お茶）*n.*, 7
(to) teach おしえる（教える）る*-v.*, 3
teacher きょうし（教師）*n.*, 5S
(to) tease からかう う*-v.*, 9
technology テクノロジー *n.*, 3
(to) tell (a lie) つく う*-v.*, 2P
(to) tell a lie うそをつく（嘘をつく）*exp.*, 2P, 9
temperature おんど（温度）*n.*, 1S
terminal ターミナル *n.*, 6
terms of employment such as salary, raise, vacation, insurance, etc. たいぐう（待遇）*n.*, 8S
thank-you gift おれい（お礼）*n.*, 7
that person (polite) そちら *demo.*, 8
that person over there (polite) あちら *demo.*, 8
that way (casual) そっち *demo.*, 8
that way (polite) そちら *demo.*, 8
That's none of your business. よけいなおせっかいだ（余計なお節介だ）*exp.*, 9S
That's not at all the case とんでもありません。／とんでもございません。*exp.*, 8

(to) thaw とかす（解かす） う-*v.*, 3S
theft せっとう（窃盗） *n.*, 10S
then それで *conj.*, 2
therefore ですから *conj.*, 2
thief どろぼう（泥棒） *n.*, 9
thin うすい（薄い） い-*adj.*, 9P
(to) think おもう（思う） う-*v.*, 2, 4P
(to) think intellectually かんがえる（考える） る-*v.*, 4P, 5
this area このへん（この辺） *exp.*, 6
this side こちらがわ（こちら側） *loc. n.*, 6
this side てまえ（手前） *loc. n.*, 6
(to) threaten おどす（脅す） う-*v.*, 9S, 10S
thunder かみなり（雷） *n.*, 1S
ticket きっぷ（切符） *n.*, 2
ticket チケット *n.*, 7S
ticket indicating where a passenger gets on a bus せいりけん（整理券） *n.*, 6S
tidal wave つなみ（津波） *n.*, 1S, 10S
tiger とら（虎） *n.*, 10
(to) build たてる（建てる／立てる)） る-*v.*, 2
to remain *(intr.)* のこる（残る） う-*v.*, 5
tofu とうふ（豆腐） *n.*, 7P
Tohoku Region とうほく（東北） *n.*, 1P
Tokyo city office located in Shinjuku とちょう（都庁） *n.*, 6P
Tokyo Station とうきょうえき（東京駅） *n.*, 6P
tornado たつまき（竜巻） *n.*, 1S, 10S
tour ツアー *n.*, 2
tourist かんこうきゃく（観光客） *n.*, 2S
towel タオル *n.*, 7
toy おもちゃ *n.*, 7
track number ～ばんせん（～番線） *suf.*, 6
trading ぼうえき（貿易） *n.*, 5
trading company ぼうえきがいしゃ（貿易会社） *n.*, 5
traffic signal しんごう（信号） *n.*, 6
train ticket that allows a passenger to travel freely in a certain area しゅうゆうけん（周遊券） *n.*, 2P, 6P
train/bus path for commuters ていきけん（定期券） *n.*, 6P
training けんしゅう（研修） *n.*, 8S
training for company employees しゃいんけんしゅう（社員研修） *n.*, 8S
(to) transfe rのりかえる（乗り換える） る-*v.*, 6
transportation のりもの（乗り物） *n.*, 2S
trash ごみ／ゴミ *n.*, 9
trash incineration facility しょうきゃくじょう（焼却場） *n.*, 10P
travel りょこう（旅行） *n.*, 2
travel agency りょこうがいしゃ（旅行会社） *n.*, 2
traveler's check トラベラーズチェック *n.*, 2P
(travel) pass しゅうゆうけん（周遊券） *n.*, 2P
tree き（木） *n.*, 1
tree leaves このは（木の葉） *n.*, 1
trip りょこう（旅行） *n.*, 2
T-road つきあたり（突き当たり） *n.*, 6
tropical forest ねったいりん（熱帯林） *n.*, 10S
tropical rain forest ねったいうりん（熱帯雨林） *n.*, 10S
trouble トラブル *n.*, 2P
trouble めいわく（迷惑） *n.*, 9
troublesome めいわくな（迷惑な） な-*adj.*, 9
truth ほんとう（本当） *n.*, 9
tsunami つなみ（津波） *n.*, 1S, 10S
tuition じゅぎょうりょう（授業料） *n.*, 4
tuna まぐろ *n.*, 2P, 3S
turkey しちめんちょう（七面鳥） *n.*, 10S
(to) turn まがる（曲がる） う-*v.*, 6
(to) turn *(intr.)* まわる（回る） う-*v.*, 5S
(to) turn (something) *(tran.)* まわす（回す） う-*v.*, 5S
(to) turn on つける（付ける） る-*v.*, 3
(to) turn on *(intr.)* つく（付く） う-*v.*, 5
TV game テレビゲーム *n.*, 7S
typhoon たいふう（台風） *n.*, 1

U

unbearable たまらない い-*adj.*, 9
under-path ちかどう（地下道） *n.*, 6P
unfavorable いやな な-*adj.*, 9
uninteresting つまらない い-*adj.*, 7
unpleasant いやな な-*adj.*, 9
(to) use つかう（使う） う-*v.*, 1P, 2
useful やくにたつ（役に立つ） *exp.*, 7
useless だめな な-*adj.*, 4
useless むだな（無駄な） な-*adj.*, 10

V

vacation きゅうか（休暇） *n.*, 8S
vacuum cleaner そうじき（掃除機） *n.*, 3P
Valentine's Day バレンタインデー *n.*, 7
vase かびん（花瓶） *n.*, 7S
vending machine じどうはんばいき（自動販売機） *n.*, 3
vinegar す（酢） *n.*, 3S
visa ビザ *n.*, 2S, 6P
(to) visit たずねる（訪ねる） る-*v.*, 8
(to) visit (humble) うかがう（伺う） う-*v.*, 8
vita りれきしょ（履歴書） *n.*, 8
voice こえ（声） *n.*, 4

W

wage きゅうりょう（給料） *n.*, 5
(to) wait for まつ（待つ） う-*v.*, 3
(to) wake up (someone) *(tran.)* おこす（起こす） う-*v.*, 5
walk さんぽ（散歩） *vn.*, 9
wall かべ（壁） *n.*, 1P, 9
wallet さいふ（財布） *n.*, 5
want ほしい（欲しい） い-*adj.*, 7
(to) want something to be stopped かんべんしてほしい（勘弁してほしい） *exp.*, 9S
Ward office くやくしょ（区役所） *n.*, 6S
warm or hot water ゆ（湯） *n.*, 3P
warming おんだんか（温暖化） *n.*, 10P
(to) warn ちゅういする（注意する） *vn.*, 9
warning ちゅうい（注意） *vn.*, 9
(to) wash あらう（洗う） う-*v.*, 3
washing machine せんたくき（洗濯機） *n.*, 3P
waste はいきぶつ（廃棄物） *n.*, 10P
waste むだな（無駄な） な-*adj.*, 10
waste water はいすい（排水） *n.*, 10S
water level すいい（水位） *n.*, 10P
water pollution すいしつおせん（水説汚染） *n.*, 10
water quality すいしつ（水質） *n.*, 10P
way みち（道） *n.*, 6
way of ～ ～かた（～方） *suf.*, 3
weak よわい（弱い） い-*adj.*, 1
(to) wear (polite) おめしになる（お召しになる） う-*v.*, 8S
weather てんき（天気） *n.*, 1
weather forecast てんきよほう（天気予報） *n.*, 1
weather map てんきず（天気図） *n.*, 1S
weight おもさ（重さ） *n.*, 4S
(to) welcome むかえる（迎える） る-*v.*, 9
welfare せいかつほご（生活保護） *n.*, 10S
west にし（西） *n.*, 1
West coast region にしかいがん（西海岸） *n.*, 1S
west exit of a station にしぐち（西口） *n.*, 6P
Western alcoholic beverages (whisky, brandy, etc.) ようしゅ（洋酒） *n.*, 7S
Western-style private guest house. ペンション *n.*, 2P
Western-style sweets ようがし（洋菓子） *n.*, 7P
whale くじら（鯨） *n.*, 10
white collar worker サラリーマン *n.*, 5S
wide street おおどおり（大通り） *n.*, 6S
wind かぜ（風） *n.*, 1
window (bank teller, municipal office, etc.) まどぐち（窓口） *n.*, 4P
wine glass ワイングラス *n.*, 7S
wire transfer of funds ぎんこうふりこみ（銀行振込） *n.*, 4P
wish おねがい（お願い） *n.*, 3
wish しぼう（志望） *n.*, 8S
Wishing for your happiness as a couple おふたりのおしあわせをおいのりします（お二人のお幸せをお祈りします） *exp.*, 7P
Wishing for your success ごかつやくをおいのりします（ご活躍をお祈りします） *exp.*, 7P
with all one's might いっしょうけんめい（一生懸命） *adv.*, 8, 8P
(to) withdraw (money from bank) ひきだす（引き出す） う-*v.*, 4
Worcestershire sauce ウスターソース *n.*, 3S
word processor ワープロ *n.*, 3
words ことば（言葉） *n.*, 2
(to) work きんむする（勤務する） *vn.*, 8S
work きんむ（勤務） *vn.*, 8S
(to) work *(intr.)* はたらく（働く） う-*v.*, 5
work condition ろうどうじょうけん（労働条件） *n.*, 8S
world せかい（世界） *n.*, 9P, 10
(to) worry しんぱいする（心配する） *vn.*, 9
worry しんぱい（心配） *vn.*, 9
wrapping paper つつみがみ（包み紙） *n.*, 7S
wristwatch うでどけい（腕時計） *n.*, 7
(to) write (a diary) つける（付ける） る-*v.*, 9
written composition さくぶん（作文） *n.*, 3

Y

yes (casual) うん *interj.*, *Prelim.*
you (unspecific second person) あなた *pron.*, 1
You've got to be kidding. じょうだんじゃない(わ)よ（冗談じゃないよ） *exp.*, 9
young わかい（若い） い-*adj.*, 5
younger person としした（年下） *n.*, 9
youth hostel ユースホステル *n.*, 2P

Index

adjective (adjective stem), 58
adjective (adverbial form), 54
adjective (conditional form), 356
adjective (honorific), 396
adjective (negative stem), 199
adjective (plain form)
+ **darou,** 61
+ **deshou,** 61
+ **hazu,** 308
+ **ka douka,** 257
+ **kamoshirenai,** 61
+ **kana,** 61
+ **kashira,** 61
+ **keredo,** 454
+ **mitaida,** 499
+ **njanai (kato omou),** 496
+ **nda** (casual speech), 22
+ **(no) nara,** 212
+ **node,** 67
+ **noni,** 454
+ **rashii,** 499
+ **shi,** 207
+ **toki,** 115
+ **to omou,** 94, 112
+ **youda,** 499
adjective (plain form, casual speech), 12
adjective (plain past form) + **tara,** 160
adjective (plain present form) + **to,** 298
adjective (**sou**), 58
adjective (stem)
+ **souda** (direct observation), 58
+ **sugiru,** 354
adjective (te-form) + **ikenai/dame,** 195
adverbial form (adjective and noun), 54
adversative passive, 439
agemashou, 157
ageru, 341, 157
ageyou, 157
agreement , 81, 516
anger, 468
announcements at stations and in trains, 321
annoying things, 466
apologies, 468
aru (casual speech), 9
asking favor, 389
asking for directions, 320, 324
~ato, 115
~ba (condition), 356
~ba ii, 356
~ba yokatta, 356
bank accounts, 220
benefit from someone else's action, 389
bullying, 463
casual speech
iru, 9
iya, 5
ne, 9
no, 22
plain form of verb, 16
rising intonation, 2
un, 5
uun, 5
yo, 9
~chau/jau, 409
~nakya, conditional, 356
~nda, 22
~rya, conditional, 356
~teru, 31
~toku/doku, 247
causative form (verb), 405
causative form (verb) + **kudasai,** 405
causative-passive form (verb), 445
cause (**tame**), 247
~chaikenai, 195
change of state, 493
changing the subject, 227
characteristics of places, objects, and time (**~wa ~ga**), 48
characteristics of written instruction, 174
~chau/jau (casual speech, **shimau**), 409
checking comprehension, 274
Christmas, 371
chronological order, 115
chronology, 298
classified ads, 417
common problems in a work place, 438
complaints, 468
complaints with causative-passive, 445
completion, 409
compliments, 423
condition for natural consequences, 298
conditional form (adjective), 356
conditional form (verb), 356
conditions and sequence, 160
conditions originated by others, 212
confirmations, 274
conjecture based on indirect evidence, 499
copula (plain form, casual speech), 12
crimes, 482
~dake ~ affirmative, 305
daredemo, 260
daremo, 260
~darou, 61
de (scope and limit), 296
degrees of politeness in requests, 151
deleting particles (casual speech), 12, 16, 20
deleting verbal endings (casual speech), 2
demo ~ affirmative, 260
desire, 349
~deshou, 61

dictionary form (verb)
+ **kotoga dekiru,** 303
+ **mae,** 115
direct passive, 439
direction, 101
disagreements, 516
doing favor, 389
dokodesu, 260
dokomo, 260
e (direction), 101
earthquakes, 482
easy to do something, 352
economy , 241
effort to change behavior, 451
efforts made to attain a specific goal, 451
employment practice, 241
environmental concerns, 482
events with passive form, 439
excessiveness, 354
family structure, 241
~**ga** (but), 454
ga (**toki**-clause), 115
getting a job in Japan, 387
gift exchanges, 339, 368, 373
giving, 341
global warming, 510
~**go,** 115
hard to do something, 352
~**hazu,** 308
honorific (adjective), 396
~**hoshii,** 349
host family, 226
humble (verb), 402
hypothetical condition, 356
ikenai/dame, 195
~**iku** (movement away from speaker), 164
implying reason (~shi), 207
indirect passive, 439
indirect question, 257
inference based on direct observation, 58
intention, 94
intransitive verb, 252
introducing a new topic, 134
inviting (casual speech), 28
iru (casual speech), 9
~**itadakeru,** 151
itadaku, 341
itsudemo, 260
itsumo, 260
iu (reporting speech), 105
iya (casual speech), 5
~**jaikenai,** 195
Japan's climate, 47
job interviews, 422
ka (either ~, or), 257
~**ka douka,** 257
~**kamoshirenai,** 61
~**kana,** 61
kara (passive), 439
kara (source of favor), 389
kara (source), 341
~**kashira,** 61
~**keredo,** 454
kiku (reporting speech), 105
kotaeru (reporting speech), 105
koto (nominalizer), 488
koto (noun), 484
~**kotoga dekiru,** 303
~**kudasaimasenka,** 151
kudasaru, 341
kureru, 341
kuru (movement toward speaker), 164
lack of obligation, 199
large quantities and high frequencies, 448
let-causative, 405
letting someone do something, 405
limited degree, 305
listing actions and states, 207
look like ~, 58
mada ~ affirmative, 243
mada ~ negative, 243
made (time limit), 101
madeni (time limit), 101
~**mae,** 115
make-causative, 405
making someone do something, 405
manner of action, 54
marriage, 268
~**mashou,** 157
~**mashouka,** 157
metric system, 293
miru (trial), 164
mo (quantity expression), 448
mo ~negative, 260
modesty in formal situations, 423
morau, 341
mou ~ negative, 243
mou ~affirmative, 243
movement away from or toward speaker, 164
must/have to, 199
na-adjective (**sou**), 58
+ **nagara,** 205
+ **nai** (casual speech), 28
+ **naide** (without doing ~), 154
+ **naidekudasai,** 154
+ **nakereba ikenai,** 199
+ **nakereba naranai,** 199
+ **nakucha,** 199
+ **nakutemo ii,** 199
+ **nakutemo kamawanai,** 199
+ **nakutemo kekkou,** 199
+ **nakutewa ikenai,** 199
+ **nakutewa naranai,** 199
+ **nakya,** 199
+ **nakya** (conditional form in casual speech), 356
nandemo, 260
nanimo, 260
~**nannai,** 199
nante (quote), 105
~(**no**)**nara,** 212
~**nda** (casual speech), 22
ne (casual speech), 9
negative request, 154
negative stem (verb and adjective), 199
neighborhood relations, 438
ni (adverbial form of noun), 54
ni (causative), 405
ni (causative-passive), 445
ni (goal), 101
ni (passive), 439
ni (source of favor), 389
ni (source), 341
~**ni** naru, 54
~**ni** suru, 54
~**ni** yotte (passive), 439
~nikui, 352
~**njanai(kato omou),** 496
no (casual speech), 22
no (nominalizer), 488
no (pronoun), 484
~**node,** 67
~**noni,** 454
not have to, 199
noun phrase with **no** or **koto,** 488
~number/question word + counter + **mo** (quantity expression), 448
o (causative), 405

o (point of detachment), 296
o (route), 296
o + verb (stem) + suru (humble), 402
o + verb (stem)+ kudasai (honorific request), 396
o + verbal noun + nasaru (honorific), 396
o/go + verb (stem) + ninaru (honorific), 396
o/go + verbal noun + kudasai (honorific request), 396
o/go + verbal noun + suru (humble), 402
o/go adjective (honorific), 396
obligation, 199
omitting particles, 12, 20
omitting verbal endings, 2
on-going action, 48
one + counter + **mo** + negative, 448
only, 305
open condition, 356
opinions, 516
opinions about things, events, and actions, 112
opinions expressed indirectly, 496
outcome of a change, 54
~o~toiu, 105
parcel delivery services, 193
particles
  (**de**), 296
  (**ka**) either, or, 257
  (**kara**) passive, 439
  (**kara**) source, 341
  (**kara**) source of favor, 389
  (**mo**) quantity expression, 448
  (**ni**) causative, 405
  (**ni**) passive, 439
  (**ni**) source, 341
  (**ni**) source of favor, 389
  (**o**), 296
  (**o**) causative, 405
passive form (verb), 439
permission to do something, 405
plain form, 61, 67, 112, 115
plain form (adjective and copula, casual speech), 12
plain form (verb and adjective), 212
  + **darou**, 61
  + **deshou**, 61
  + **hazu**, 308
  + **ka douka**, 257
  + **kamoshirenai**, 61
  + **kana**, 61
  + **kashira**, 61
  + **keredo**, 454
  + **mitaida**, 499
  + **nda** (casual speech), 22
  + **njanai (kato omou)**, 496
  + **node**, 67
  + **noni**, 454
  + **rashii**, 499
  + **shi**, 207
  + **toki**, 115
  + **to omou**, 94, 112
  + **youda**, 499
plain form (verb), 94
plain form (verb) + tame, 247
plain form (verb) casual speech, 16
plain negative form (verb)
  + **naide** (without doing ~), 154
  + **naidekudasai**, 154
plain past affirmative form (verb) + **ato**, 115
plain past form, 115
plain past form (verb and adjective) + **tara**, 160
plain present form (verb and adjective) + **to**, 298
plain present form (verb)
  + **kotoga dekiru**, 303
  + **mae**, 115
  + **to**, 298
  + **tsumori**, 94
  + **yotei**, 94
  + **youninaru**, 493
  + **youni shite kuremasenka**, 451
  + **youni suru**, 451
plan, 94
point of detachment (o), 296
politeness, 423
politeness in requests, 151
possibility, 303
postal service, 193
preparation, 247
prepared speech, 79
presupposition, 308
problems with passive form, 439
public telephones, 150
purpose, 247
~question word + counter + **mo**, 448
question word + **demo** ~affirmative, 260
question word + **mo** ~negative, 260
quotation, 105
~rashii, 499
realization of making a mistake, 409
reason (**tame**), 247
receiving, 341
regret, 409
repeated action, 48
reporting speech, 105
request, 26, 180, 396
respect
respect with honorific expressions, 396
respect with humble expressions, 402
result of intentional action, 252
résumé, 417
rising intonation (casual speech), 2
route, 296
~rya (conditional form in casual speech), 356
~sasete kudasai, 405
sashiageru, 341
scope and limit (de), 296
~shi, 207
~shika ~ negative, 305
signaling devices, 178
social expectation, 199
solidarity, 81
~souda (direct observation), 58
~souna, 58
~souni, 58
stem (verb) + **yasui/nikui,** 352
stem (verb and adjective)
  + **souda** (direct observation), 58
  + **sugiru,** 354
streets, 293
~sugiru, 354
~tai, 94
~tame, 247
~tara, 160, 212
~te (casual speech), 26
~te ageru, 389
~te aru, 252
~te hoshii, 349
~te iru, 48, 243
~te itadaku, 389
~te kara, 298
~te kudasaru, 151

~te kureru, 151, 389
~te morau, 389
~te oku, 247
~te shimau, 409
~te yaru, 389
te-form
+ **ikenai/dame**, 195
te-form (verb), 48
+ **ageru/kureru/morau**, 389
+ **ageru/yaru**, 389
+ **aru**, 252
+ **hoshii/hoshigaru**, 349
te-form (verb)
+ **iku/kuru**, 164
+ **kara**, 298
+ **miru**, 164
+ **morau/itadaku**, 389
+ **oku**, 247
+ **shimau**, 409
~teru (casual speech), 31
time limit , 101
~to, 298
to (quote), 105
~to omou, 94, 112
~to iu, 105
~toki, 115
~toku/doku (casual speech), 247
topic (**wa**), 48
towns and streets, 293
transition device, 127, 130
transitive verb, 252
transportation, 293
traveling, 93
trial, 164
~tsumori, 94
~tte (quote), 105
turning down a request or an invitation, 180
two simultaneous actions, 205
un (casual speech), 5
unacceptable actions or situations, 195
uncertainty, 496, 61
uun (casual speech), 5
vending machines, 150
vertical writing, 75
verb (causative form)+ **kudasai**, 405
verb (causative-passive form), 445
verb (conditional form), 356
verb (dictionary form)
+ **kotoga dekiru**, 303
+ **mae**, 115
verb (intransitive), 252
verb (negative stem), 199
verb (passive form), 439
verb (plain form)
+ **darou**, 61
+ **deshou**, 61
+ **hazu**, 308
+ **ka douka**, 257
+ **kamoshirenai**, 61
+ **kana**, 61
+ **kashira**, 61
+ **keredo**, 454
+ **mitaida**, 499
+ **nda** (casual speech), 22
+ **njanai (kato omou)**, 496
+ **node**, 67
+ **noni**, 454
+ (no) **nara**, 212
+ **rashii**, 499
+ **shi**, 207
+ **tame**, 247
+ **toki**, 115
+ **youda**, 499
verb (plain past affirmative form) + **ato**, 115
verb (plain past form), 160
verb (plain present form)
+ **kotoga dekiru**, 303
+ **mae**, 115
+ **to**, 298
+ **tsumori**, 94
+ **yotei**, 94
+ **youni**, 451
+ **youninaru**, 493
+ **younisuru**, 451
verb (plain present negative form)
+ **naide** (without doing ~), 154
+ **naidekudasai**, 154
verb (stem), 205
honorific, 396
humble, 402
+ **nagara**, 205
+ **souda** (direct observation), 58
+ **sugiru**, 354
+ **yasui/nikui**, 352
verb (**te**-form), 164
+ **ageru/kureru/morau**, 389
+ **aru**, 252
+ **hoshii/hoshigaru**, 349
+ **ikenai/dame**, 195
+ **kara**, 298
+ **morau/itadaku**, 389
+ **oku**, 247
+ **shimau**, 409
verb (transitive), 252
verb (verb stem), 58
verb (volitional form), 94
verbal noun (honorific request, **o ~ kudasai**), 396
verbal noun (honorific, **o ~ nasaru**), 396
verbal noun (humble), 402
verbs (honorific), 396
verbs of giving, 341
verbs of giving and receiving, 341
volitional form (verb), 94, 157
wa (casual speech), 12, 34
wa (topic), 48
~wa ~ga (characteristics of palaces, objects, and time), 48
~wa ~ga (desire), 349
willingness, 157
willingness to help, 389
without doing ~, 154
yaru, 341
~ yasui, 352
yo (casual speech), 9
yomu (quote), 105
yosasouda, 58
~yotei, 94
~youni ~, 451
~youninaru, 493
~younisuru, 451
zero quantity or frequency, 448